COLLINGWOOD
AND THE REFORM OF
METAPHYSICS

COLLINGWOOD
AND THE REFORM OF
METAPHYSICS
A STUDY IN
THE PHILOSOPHY OF
MIND

Lionel Rubinoff

UNIVERSITY OF TORONTO PRESS

© University of Toronto Press 1970

Printed in Canada by
Reprinted in 2018

University of Toronto Press, Toronto and Buffalo

ISBN 8020-5213-4
ISBN 978-0-8020-7692-2_2 (paper)

TO MY MOTHER AND FATHER

Preface

The aim of this study is to reconstruct Collingwood's philosophy into a system, using as the central theme the relation between philosophy and history. The majority of the criteria employed, while derived from Collingwood's philosophy itself, have escaped the notice of his critics. As a result, his thought has been consistently misunderstood and misrepresented. Under the influence of Collingwood's editor, T. M. Knox, there has developed what I have chosen to call the 'radical conversion hypothesis': the thesis that sometime between 1936 and 1939 Collingwood underwent a radical conversion from 'idealism' to 'historicism.' According to this view the bulk of his later philosophy, and in particular his alleged 'reform of metaphysics,' is founded on the premise (derived from Croce) that philosophy has been liquidated by being absorbed into history; a doctrine which is assumed to infect the whole of *The Autobiography* and *An Essay on Metaphysics* written in 1938 and 1939 respectively. The result, according to Knox and his followers, is a thoroughgoing scepticism.

Against this view I shall argue the following claims: that there is no radical conversion; that on the contrary there is a strong continuity between the early and later writings; that the structure of Collingwood's system and the clue to the rapprochement between philosophy and history which he actually offered, are to be found first in *Speculum Mentis*, published in 1924, and later in *An Essay on Philosophical Method*, published in 1933; and finally, that the remainder of Collingwood's writings after 1933 come very close to fulfilling the requirements of the idea of philosophy as a scale of forms which is expounded in the earlier works. I am claiming, in other words, that the actual development of Collingwood's system is itself an example of his own theory of philosophy as expounded in *Speculum Mentis*, and that the reform of metaphysics is therefore fully consistent with the plan of *Speculum Mentis*. If these claims can be consistently maintained then the main reason for the charge that Collingwood underwent a radical conversion to historicism, leaving his thought marred by a thorough-going discontinuity, seems to me to have been eliminated, and Collingwood's own claim to have produced a dialectically coherent system has been vindicated.

Along the way I have received help and encouragement from many different sources. But I want especially to thank Professor W. H. Dray whose patience and criticisms, first as a teacher, and later as a friend and colleague, helped bring my ideas from relative confusion to a much greater measure of clarity. I would also like to express my gratitude to Professor Alan Donagan with whom I have had a strong, but respectful, disagreement concerning the interpretation of Collingwood's thought. The willingness of both men to help a fellow scholar through a project with whose conclusions they are in basic disagreement is a testament to the real spirit of scholarship and philosophy which seeks to transcend personal preference and dogma for the sake of a higher truth. My colleague, Professor H. S. Harris, came to my rescue on many occasions when I needed someone to reassure me that my enterprise was not in vain. I am especially grateful for having had the opportunity of availing myself of his sizeable knowledge of Italian philosophy, as well as for his interesting views on the possible influence of the latter on Collingwood's thought. Others to whom I am indebted for their help from time to time are Professors Emil Fackenheim, H. Lewis, R. J. Butler, and Mr. Jerry Rusk who, in addition to commenting on an earlier stage of the manuscript, provided me with many valuable bibliographical references. I am also indebted to my late colleague, Guenter Seiburth, whose incisive comments during many long hours of conversation concerning the merits of Collingwood's thought gave me a much better perspective on what I was attempting to do.

A special debt of gratitude is due to one of my former teachers Professor Martyn Estall of Queen's University and to Miss Francess Halpenny, at that time Managing Editor of the University of Toronto Press, who together first prompted me to submit the manuscript for consideration. Miss Prudence Tracy, who was assigned the editorial supervision of the manuscript, has been of immense help in seeing it through to final publication.

Earlier versions of some portions of this book have appeared in the following journal articles: "Historicism and the A Priori of History," *Dialogue: Canadian Philosophical Review* III, 1 (June 1964), 81–8;

"Collingwood and the Radical Conversion Hypothesis," *Dialogue: Canadian Philosophical Review*, v, 1 (June 1966), and "Collingwood's Theory of the Relation between Philosophy and History," *Journal of the History of Philosophy*, vi, 4 (October 1968). Materials have also been drawn from my previously published edition of Collingwood's papers in the philosophy of religion, *Faith and Reason*, Chicago, Quadrangle Books, 1967, and from my introduction and commentary to F. H. Bradley's *The Presuppositions of Critical History*, Toronto, J. M. Dent/Chicago: Quadrangle Books, 1968. I am grateful to the editors and publishers for permission to draw freely upon these works.

Finally I wish to thank both the Canada Council and York University for generous grants which covered the expenses incurred while preparing the manuscript. This volume has been published with the help of grants from the Publications Fund of the University of Toronto Press and from the Humanities Research Council using funds provided by the Canada Council.

L. R.
Toronto, April 1970

Contents

PREFACE
page v

ABBREVIATIONS AND BIBLIOGRAPHICAL CONVENTIONS
page xiii

I PHILOSOPHY AND HISTORY
THE NEED FOR A RAPPROCHEMENT
page 3

1 The Priority of History in Twentieth-Century Thought	3
2 History and the Science of Human Nature	5
3 Philosophy and the Rapprochement between Theory and Practice	7
4 History and the Problem of Historicism	9
5 Collingwood and his Critics	14
6 The Idea of Philosophy as a Scale of Forms: A New Interpretation of Collingwood's Thought	26
7 The Aim and Plan of this Book	31

II THE RELATION BETWEEN PHILOSOPHY AND HISTORY IN COLLINGWOOD'S EARLY WRITINGS: 1916–1922
page 35

1 The Interdependence of Philosophy and History	35
2 The Simultaneity of Philosophy and History	38
3 The Relation between History and Science	43
4 Collingwood's Classification of the Sciences	45
5 Idealism and the Doctrine of Universal Judgment	47

III SPECULUM MENTIS: PHILOSOPHY AND THE TRANSCENDENTAL STRUCTURE OF EXPERIENCE
page 50

1. Transition from *Religion and Philosophy* to *Speculum Mentis* — 50
2. Philosophy and the Phenomenology of Experience — 55
3. The Ontological Structure of Consciousness and Experience — 66
4. Towards a Re-interpretation of Collingwood's Thought — 72

IV HISTORY AS IMPLICIT PHILOSOPHY
page 76

1. The Phenomenology of Experience — 76
2. History as the Assertion of Concrete Fact: The Categorical Singular Judgment — 105
3. The Negation of History — 117

V PHILOSOPHY AS A SCALE OF FORMS: DOGMATIC PHILOSOPHY
page 123

1. The General Characteristics of Dogmatic Philosophy — 124
2. Dogmatic Philosophy of History as a Scale of Forms — 132

VI PHILOSOPHY AS ABSOLUTE KNOWLEDGE
page 150

1. The Transcendental Principles of Phenomenology — 152
2. The Theory of the Concrete Universal — 154
3. The Logic of the Overlap of Classes — 160
4. The Doctrine of Dialectical Necessity — 176

VII PHILOSOPHY AS CATEGORICAL THINKING
page 184

1. The Distinction between Categorical and Hypothetical Thinking — 184
2. The History of the Conception of Philosophy as Categorical Thinking — 187
3. Philosophy and the Ontological Argument — 194
4. Categorical Thinking and Metaphysics — 204
5. Categorical Thinking and the Rapprochement between Faith and Reason — 208

6 Categorical Thinking and the Understanding of the
   Historical Past   209
7 Categorical Thinking and the Analysis of the
   Presuppositions of Experience   210

VIII PHILOSOPHY AS HISTORY
page 213

1 Categorical Thinking and the Problem of Universals   213
2 The Logic of Belief   218
3 The Theory of Metaphysics as a Science of
   Presuppositions   221
4 Metaphysics as the Science of Absolute
   Presuppositions   232
5 The Alleged Historicism of the Science of Absolute
   Presuppositions   238
6 The Essay as a Response to Logical Positivism   241
7 Metaphysics as a Dialectical History of Errors   248
8 The Theory of Error and the Conditions of Historicity 264
9 Truth and Historicity: The Presuppositions of
   Metaphysics   270
10 Metaphysics as Transcendental Analytics   286

IX HISTORY AND THE SCIENCE OF HUMAN NATURE
page 289

1 From Facts to Thoughts   289
2 The Standpoint of the *Idea of History*   292
3 History as Self-Knowledge of Mind   299
4 Historicity and Historical Relativism   306

X PHILOSOPHY AS SELF-KNOWLEDGE:
THE RAPPROCHEMENT BETWEEN PHILOSOPHY AND HISTORY
page 311

1 Philosophy as Immanence-Transcendence   311
2 The Theory of the Mind as Pure Act   315
3 The Pure Act as the Transcendental Ground of
   Historicity   322
4 Summary and Recapitulation   331
5 The Drama of Absolute Mind   334

APPENDICES

page 337

I	Positivism, Historicism, and the Idea of a Science of Human Nature	338
II	Technical Terms employed in this Study	364
III	The Categories and Habits of Mind: The Disciplines and Separate Standpoints derived from Categories	367
IV	Types of Philosophy	368
V	The Principles of Dogmatic Philosophy	369
VI	The Transhistorical Principles of Absolute Philosophy	370
VII	The Scale of the Forms of Experience and their Corresponding Moments of Philosophic Reflection	371
VIII	Correlation of Collingwood's Main Writings with the Three Levels of Philosophic Activity	373

NOTES

page 374

BIBLIOGRAPHY

page 394

INDEX

page 407

Abbreviations
AND BIBLIOGRAPHICAL CONVENTIONS

The titles of Collingwood's works are abbreviated as follows:

BOOKS
- RP   *Religion and Philosophy* (1916)
- SM   *Speculum Mentis* (1924)
- OPA   *Outlines of a Philosophy of Art* (1925)
- EPM   *An Essay on Philosophical Method* (1933)
- RB/ES *Roman Britain and the English Settlements* (1937)
- PA   *The Principles of Art* (1938)
- A   *An Autobiography* (1939)
- EM   *An Essay on Metaphysics* (1940)
- FML   *The First Mate's Log* (1940)
- NL   *The New Leviathan* (1942)
- IN   *The Idea of Nature* (1945)
- IH   *The Idea of History* (1946)

ARTICLES
- D   "The Devil" (1916)
- CPH   "Croce's Philosophy of History" (1921)
- RUP   "Ruskin's Philosophy" (1922)
- PE   "What is the Problem of Evil" (1922)
- HS   "Are History and Science Different Kinds of Knowledge" (1922)
- ST   "Sensation and Thought" (1923)
- CNI   "Can the New Idealism Dispense with Mysticism" (1923)
- NAPH "The Nature and Aims of a Philosophy of History" (1925)

EPS	"Economics as a Philosophical Science" (1925)
PPA	"Plato's Philosophy of Art" (1925)
SPT	"Some Perplexities about Time: with an Attempted Solution" (1926)
PAE	"The Place of Art in Education" (1926)
RSP	"Religion, Science, and Philosophy" (1926)
RFCI	"Reason is Faith Cultivating Itself" (1927)
THC	"Oswald Spengler and the Theory of Historical Cycles" (1927)
AE	"Aesthetic" (1927)
FR	"Faith and Reason" (1928)
LHK	"The Limits of Historical Knowledge" (1928)
PA	"Political Action" (1928)
PP	"A Philosophy of Progress" (1929)
PH	"The Philosophy of History" (1930)
FN	"Fascism and Nazism" (1940)
PNP	"The Present Need of a Philosophy" (1942)

UNPUBLISHED MANUSCRIPTS

CRC	Correspondence between Gilbert Ryle and R. G. Collingwood (May–June 1935)

OTHER WORKS CITED

MP	*Modern Philosophy*, Guido de Ruggiero, translated by R. G. Collingwood and A. H. Hannay (1921)
PBA	*Proceedings of the British Academy*, xxix (1943)

All references to the above texts are to page numbers. The vast majority of references to Collingwood's own works have been placed in the main text rather than in the notes. With few exceptions, page references to all other works will be found in the notes.

With reference to the latter, except in a few cases I have chosen to cite only the title and page number in the text itself. But full bibliographical references for such citations will be found in the bibliography.

Translations of passages from works in languages other than English are my own where the original work is cited in the notes. Where an English translation of the work also exists reference is usually also given to the corresponding passage in it.

*"For now we recognize the nature of our disease.
What is wrong with us
is precisely the detachment of those forms of experience
— art, religion, and the rest — from one another;
and our cure can only be their reunion in a
complete and undivided life.
Our task is to seek for that life,
to build up the conception of an activity which is at once
art, and religion, and science, and the rest."*
(R. G. Collingwood, SM, 36)

*"It is the character of that philosophy that
I wish to make clear to you:
its historical and dialectical, as opposed to a
mathematical and logical, character;
its scorn of scholastic distinctions;
its breadth and imaginativeness;
above all, its intensely synthetic nature —
its refusal to separate any one aspect of life from any other,
and its resolute envisagement of the spirit as a
single and indivisible whole."*
(Collingwood on Ruskin's philosophy, RUP, 43)

ROBIN GEORGE COLLINGWOOD was born at Cartnel Fell near Coniston, North Lancashire, on 22 February 1889. His father, W. G. Collingwood (1854–1932), was a close friend of and private secretary to John Ruskin (d. 1900). The elder Collingwood was also a painter, amateur archaeologist of Roman Britain, and author of many books. Until he was 13 years old, at which time he entered Rugby, R. G. Collingwood was educated at home by his father. As a measure of gratitude the son dedicated the most important of his early works, *Speculum Mentis* (1924), to his father, describing him as his "first and best teacher of Art, Religion, Science, History and Philosophy."

In 1908 the young Collingwood went up to Oxford from which he was graduated in 1912 with a first in *Literae Humaniores*. The same year he was elected by the fellows of Pembroke college to be a fellow and tutor in philosophy. From 1927–35 he served as university lecturer in Philosophy and Roman History and in 1935 he was appointed Waynflete professor of Metaphysical Philosophy from which he resigned in 1941 because of ill health. He died at Coniston on 9 January 1943 at the age of 53. In addition to having established a well-earned reputation as one of the major philosophers of the twentieth century, R. G. Collingwood was generally regarded as one of the leading historians and archaeologists of Roman Britain.

∽ I ∽

Philosophy and History:
The Need for a
RAPPROCHEMENT

1 THE PRIORITY OF HISTORY IN TWENTIETH-CENTURY THOUGHT

In 1938, a few years before his death, Collingwood characterized his life work as "in the main an attempt to bring about a *rapprochement* between philosophy and history" (A, 77). Indeed, his deep concern with history is evident from the very outset of his career. In 1919, for example, in his address to the Ruskin Centenary Conference, he argued that the main virtue of Ruskin's thought lay in its specifically historical character. In this essay, Collingwood characterized what he called "the historical habit of thought" (RUP, 12) as "the philosophy of the future" (RUP, 14); it "aims at freedom and variety," and "its natural inclination is always towards tolerance" (RUP, 12). And in 1920 he expressed a similar conviction when he wrote, together with A. H. Hannay, in the preface to their translation of de Ruggiero's *Filosophia contemporanea*, that Italian philosophy is to be recommended to English readers because of its "penetrating study and exposition of history" (MP, 6).

It was Collingwood's belief, lasting throughout his entire career, that historiography and philosophy of history had priority over other philosophical interests because history itself, the study of human affairs, had become the central preoccupation of the present age. The priority of historiography and philosophy of history in twentieth-century thought had, for Collingwood, a practical as well as a theoretical basis. Collingwood charged, in the *Autobiography*, that the first world war (including the Treaty of Versailles which concluded it) was a "war of unprecedented ferocity closed in a peace-settlement of unprecedented folly" (A, 89), an unprecedented triumph for natural science on the one hand and an unprecedented disgrace to the human intellect on the other hand (A, 90).

The contrast between success in controlling situations which were part of the physical world and failure to control situations in which human beings are elements, left an indelible mark on Collingwood's memory.

By 1937 the situation had become desperate. The dangers of any failure to control human situations were more serious than they had ever been before. Not only would such failure result in more and more widespread destruction as natural science added triumph after triumph, but the consequences would tend more and more to the destruction of whatever was good and reasonable in the civilized world. At such a time the academic bickerings of the philosophical sects struck Collingwood as an amusement for the foolish. There was really only one question for the serious philosopher to face: "what can we do to be saved from these present distresses?" (SM, 35)

Collingwood's answer was that such a calamity could be avoided only through a proper understanding of the human mind. An attempt in this direction had been undertaken by both behaviouristic psychology and the positivistically conceived social sciences. But Collingwood regarded both of these enterprises as thoroughly misguided. Behaviourism and positivism treat human nature as though it were a mere species of nature proper, whereas a genuine science of mind must apprehend its object under the category of freedom. It was Collingwood's lifelong belief that the right way of investigating mind is by the methods of history. History is what the science of human nature professes to be. (IH, 209, 318–20; NL, 61–2) And it is only through history, therefore, that we can grasp the fact that human activity is free (IH, 315, 319–20).

The problem is rendered all the more urgent when it is recognized that the historical thought which apprehends the fact of freedom is itself a necessary condition of the existence of that freedom. Historical self-knowledge, in other words, is a form of historical self-making; the historical process "is a process in which man creates for himself this or that kind of human nature by recreating in his own thought the past to which he is heir" (IH, 226). Historical knowledge is to be regarded, therefore, not simply as a luxury, or mere amusement of a mind at leisure from more pressing occupations, but as a prime duty, "whose discharge is essential to the maintenance, not only of any particular form or type of reason, but of reason itself" (IH, 227–8). History, he wrote in *The New Leviathan* (1942), is the proper object of study for any man who has taken part in in the progress of human thought down to the present time; for it is in the world of history rather than in the world of nature that man finds the central problems he has to solve (NL, 129). Indeed, he wrote elsewhere, "history occupies in the world of to-day a position analogous to that occupied by physics in the time of Locke" (IH, 209); and just as the chief business of seventeenth-century philosophy was to reckon with seventeenth-century natural science, so, Collingwood contended, the chief business of twentieth-century philosophy is to reckon with twentieth-century history (A, 78–9).

As the seventeenth century needed a reasoned conviction that nature is intelligible and the problems of science in principle soluble, so the twentieth needs a reasoned conviction that human progress is possible and that the problems of moral and political life are in principle soluble. In both cases the need is one which only philosophy can supply. What is needed to-day is a philosophical reconsideration of the whole idea of progress or development, and especially its two main forms, 'evolution' in the world of nature and 'history' in the world of human affairs. What would correspond to the Renaissance conception of nature as a single intelligible system would be a philosophy showing that the human will is of a piece with nature in being genuinely creative; a *vera causa*, though singular in being consciously creative; that social and political institutions are creations of the human will, conserved by the same power which created them, and essentially plastic to its hand; and that therefore whatever evils they contain are in principle remediable. In short, the help which philosophy might give to our 'dissatisfied, anxious, apprehensive generation' would lie in a reasoned statement of the principle that there can be no evils in any human institution which human will cannot cure. (PNP, 264–5)

2 HISTORY AND THE SCIENCE OF HUMAN NATURE

The most significant feature of history, according to Collingwood, is the success with which it provides a basis for the unification of the various and diverse forms of human experience. On at least two occasions he cites with approval Hume's famous remark "that all the sciences have a relation, greater or less, to human nature ... since they lie under the cognizance of man, and are judged of by their powers and faculties" (*Treatise*, xix; cited by Collingwood in IH, 82, 83, 207), and he gives every indication of further agreeing with Hume that "in pretending therefore to explain the principles of human nature, we in effect propose a compleat system of the sciences, built on a foundation almost entirely new, and the only one upon which they can stand with any security" (*Treatise*, xx; IH, 83, 207). Until recently, however, the attempt at a science of human nature failed because its method was distorted by the analogy of the natural sciences (IH, 208). This attempt at a naturalistically conceived science of human nature was part of the general programme of positivism, which, according to Collingwood, is founded on a philosophical error – the error of dogmatically assuming that all of the sciences are species of a common genus, and then proceeding to define the genus according to the differentia of only one of its species, the species of natural science. It was Collingwood's contention that the proposal of positivism, to investigate human nature by the methods of the natural sciences, has been successfully challenged by the counter claim that the right way of investigating mind is by the methods called historical.[1]

In the *Idea of History* Collingwood insists that human nature is the concern of the philosophical and historical sciences only in so far as it is regarded as rational, that is to say, as an expression of mind. Other aspects of man, his body, his emotions, and anything that generally derives from his co-called animal nature (including the irrational), are more properly the concern of the natural sciences (IH, 216, 302–3). In the *New Leviathan*, however, Collingwood seems to have transcended the mind-body dualism altogether and is now prepared to bring even the body under the sciences of mind. The concept of the historicity of embodied mind, which lies at the centre of the *New Leviathan*, is the culminating moment of Collingwood's philosophical achievements.

There is another source of Collingwood's tendency to characterize the sciences of mind as historical; namely, his lifelong rejection of the classical theory of metaphysics which defines reality as a permanent and eternal substance existing independently of its phenomenal appearances. He was therefore committed to repudiate all theories which presuppose the conception of mind or human nature as a fixed and unchanging substance: whether such theories take the form of the empirical study of attributes or the a priori study of essences. Neither reality in general nor mind in particular can be so defined. Reality is a "dialectical" process of change, and the *being* of mind, if it is to be found at all, is to be found only in its acts, as art, religion, science, history, morality, philosophy, and so on.[2] Since such a study must necessarily be historical, it follows that Hume's proposal for the unity of science depends upon the possibility of establishing and maintaining an autonomous and self-justifying science of history whose methods are free from the domination of the natural sciences.

Thus, according to Collingwood, the task of twentieth-century philosophy is clear. It is to construct a critique of historical reason which will accomplish for the historical sciences what Kant's first critique has accomplished for the natural sciences: a critique which would answer the question, "How or under what conditions is historical knowledge possible?" (A, 110, IH, 282) It is with respect to this task that Collingwood urged the wise philosopher to "concentrate with all his might on the problems of history, at whatever cost, and so do his share in laying the foundations of the future" (A, 88).

3 PHILOSOPHY AND THE RAPPROCHEMENT BETWEEN THEORY AND PRACTICE

Collingwood's programme for the unity of science derives, then, from a profound need to lay the foundations for a new rapprochement between theory and practice. For Collingwood the main value of philosophy lies in its practical effects: a view which he identified with "the classical tradition in philosophy." "The philosophers of the classical tradition," he wrote, "were men who used their trained faculties of thinking in order to think about facts, and primarily of facts of practical importance in relation to the lives of their fellow-men" (FML, 176). His interest in this rapprochement was a consequence of his steadily developing opposition to the principle of philosophical realism that *knowing makes no difference to the object known*. The opposite of this dogma seemed to Collingwood not only a truth, but a truth which, for the sake of one's integrity and efficacy as a practical agent, ought to be familiar to every human being: namely, that in our capacity as moral, political, or economic agents we live not only in a world of hard facts to which thoughts make no difference but in a world which is *essentially* one of thoughts. Which means, in other words, that a change in the moral, political, and economic theories generally accepted by society will result in a change in the very structure of that society itself, while a change in one's own personal theories will result in a change in one's relation to that society. In either case, the end result will be a change in the way we act.

Collingwood argued that the violation of the rapprochement between theory and practice implied by the principles of philosophical realism was one of the consequences of the disruption of the unity of the sciences which derived from the Renaissance concept of specialization. The motto of the Renaissance, regarding the relation of the sciences, was the principle that the secret of the well-being of each standpoint lay in mutual separation (SM, 34). Each science in its search for freedom demanded a complete separation from every other form of life; art for art's sake, truth for truth's sake, religion for religion's sake, and so on. The result of this trend of thought was that each science, in so far as it was cut off from the others, tended more and more to lead its followers into a desert where the world of human life was lost until finally the very motive for going on seemed to disappear altogether. Each tended to become a specialized activity pursued by specialists for the applause of specialists, useless to the rest of mankind and unsatisfying even to the specialist when he turned upon himself and asked why he was doing it.[3]

This is the state of affairs which Collingwood believed his own generation to have reached: a state in which scholars, scientists, artists, and even philosophers "work only for themselves and their own kind in a vicious circle of academicism," with the result that they have lost contact not only with each other but with the public as well. "The producers and the consumers of spiritual wealth," he wrote, "are out of touch"[4] (SM, 20). Thus has the Renaissance search for abstract freedom come home to roost, in the form of a complete disruption of life. Today, wrote Collingwood, "we can be as artistic, we can be as philosophical, we can be as religious as we please, but we cannot ever be men at all; we are wrecks and fragments of men, and we do not know where to take hold of life and how to begin looking for that happiness which we know we do not possess" (SM, 35).

Against the radical pluralism of Renaissance thought Collingwood contended that the various forms of human activity were identical, that the theoretical moment of any experience had practical effects on that experience itself, and, in view of the unity of experience, on every other form of experience as well. He describes in his *Autobiography* how he set out to reconsider all the familiar topics and problems of morals, politics, and economics (A, 148). There were, he held, no merely moral actions, no merely political actions, and no merely economic actions. Every action was moral, political, and economic (A, 149). He even argued, with equal conviction, that scientific, historical, or philosophical thinking depends quite as much on moral qualities as on intellectual ones and that moral difficulties are to be overcome not by moral force alone but by clear thinking (A, 150).

At the same time Collingwood realized that while the various forms of human activity could not be separated, neither is their identity a night in which all cows are black, a blind abstract identity which is indifferent to differences. "All such identities," he wrote, "are barren abstractions" (SM, 246). On the contrary, he argued, the basis of the unity of the forms of experience is a concrete dialectical identity to which difference is essential and organic. "To assert the identity without the difference," he charged, "or the difference without the identity is to turn one's back on reality and amuse oneself with paradoxes" (SM, 246). It was to the task of establishing the basis for such an identity that Collingwood devoted a great deal of his philosophical career and it was with the faith that this task could be accomplished that he proposed his remedy for the disease of his age.

For we now recognize the nature of our disease. What is wrong with us is precisely the detachment of those forms of experience – art, religion, and the rest – from one another; and our cure can only be their reunion in a complete and undivided life. Our task is to seek for that life, to build up the conception of an activity which is at once art, and religion, and science, and the rest. (SM, 36)

4 HISTORY AND THE PROBLEM OF HISTORICISM

Collingwood's emphasis on, and lifelong concern with, history has created the impression among most of his critics that as his thought developed he came closer and closer to accepting a doctrine – hereafter referred to as 'radical historicism' – which he had originally repudiated: the doctrine, advanced by Croce, that philosophy is not only superseded but annihilated by history, and that philosophy, therefore, is nothing more than the methodological moment of history. Since Collingwood's relation to Croce as well as to other leading historicist thinkers is one of the main issues of this book, it would be advisable at this point to explain in some detail just what the doctrine of radical historicism asserts.

The core of this doctrine is well summed up in a famous declaration by the nineteenth-century philosopher York Von Wartenburg. Writing to Dilthey, Von Wartenburg declared with respect to the nature of philosophy, that "there is no genuine philosophizing which is not historical. The distinction between systematic philosophy and history of philosophy is in principle false."[5] In Croce's philosophy this doctrine is given further support. "It is a curious fate," writes Croce, "that history should for a long time have been considered and treated as the most humble form of knowledge, while philosophy was considered the highest, and that now it not only is superior to philosophy but annihilates it."[6] Thus Croce defines historicism as "the affirmation that life and reality are history and history alone."[7]

> Every judgement is an historical judgement ... Whatever it is that is being judged, is always an historical fact ... Historical judgement is embodied even in the merest perception of the judging mind ... historical judgement is not a variety of knowledge, but is knowledge itself; it is the form which completely fills and exhausts the field of knowing, leaving no room for anything else ... Philosophy ceased to enjoy an autonomous existence because its claim to autonomy was founded upon its metaphysical character ... that which has taken its place is history.[8]

It follows from these statements that philosophy and history can no longer be regarded as either separate or distinct forms of experience. Their relation is one not simply of mutual interaction but of complete or immediate identity.

> The a priori synthesis which is the concreteness of the individual judgement and of definition is at the same time the concreteness of philosophy and of history. It is the formula of thought which by constituting itself qualifies intuition and constitutes history. History neither precedes philosophy nor philosophy history. They are both born in one act.[9]

A parte subjecti, then, radical historicism may be properly defined as "the tendency to interpret the whole of reality, including what up to the romantic period had been conceived as absolute and unchanging human values including philosophy itself, in historical, that is to say, relative terms."[10] *A parte objecti* it is "that standpoint which regards 'being in time' as the fundamental form of being, and all other forms of being as derived from it ... which regards time as more important than space ... which regards man as *animal historicum* ... and which assumes that we cannot understand man's activities or his creations, like art, philosophy, religion, science, etc., except in their dependence on the flux of history."[11]

Such definitions must be carefully distinguished, however, from a variety of other more popular ones which tend to provide misleading descriptions of historicism. Sir Karl Popper, for example, defines historicism as "an approach to the social sciences which assumes that *historical prediction* is their principal aim, and which assumes that this aim is attainable by discovering the 'rhythms' or the 'patterns', the 'laws' or the 'trends' that underlie the evolution of history,"[12] and on the basis of which we may therefore "prophesy the course of historical events."[13] An equally misleading definition is given by Arnold Hauser, who defines historicism as "the doctrine that uncovers and stresses the unique and unrepeatable character of all historical events, but none the less asserts that everything historical is the manifestation of some superhuman and timeless principle." In this view, according to Hauser, "the individuals who build this world of time are just the servants of a world architect who is 'cunning' enough to play upon their impulses and interests ... to give them a sense of freedom and creativity, whereas all the time they are only carrying out menial tasks for him."[14] These definitions represent the two most common misunderstandings of historicism. In Popper's definition it is clear that historicism is confused with historical positivism, while Hauser's definition (intended, no doubt, as a description of Hegel's philosophy of history) is really about some kind of supernaturalism. But historicism, of whatever variety, is neither positivism nor supernaturalism; for historicism is committed to the very opposite of any view which sees history as the mere temporal expression of either natural or supernatural laws transcending the events of history themselves.

If radical historicism, then, as represented by Croce and as defined above, is in fact the doctrine which Collingwood himself eventually embraced, then his alleged rapprochement must certainly be judged a failure. For radical historicism gives to history precisely the same dogmatic status as positivism gives to science and is therefore open to the same criticisms. More importantly, radical historicism is a complete repudiation of Collingwood's lifelong campaign against all forms of abstract identity. Collingwood's own attitude to radical historicism (at least during the period 1916 to 1936) can be easily reconstructed from various passages in *Religion and Philosophy* (1916), "Croce's Philosophy of History" (1921), *Speculum Mentis* (1924), and "Human Nature and Human History" (1936). *Religion and Philosophy*, for example, is directed as much against the implications of radical historicism as against those of positivism and extreme empiricism.

In the first place Collingwood explicitly rejects the principle that to understand a thing we need only know its history and origin (RP, 5). This, together with his avowed commitment to the existence of transhistorical truths (such as the knowledge of God), is already a sufficient repudiation of radical historicism. "The attainment of any real truth," he writes, "is an event, doubtless in time, and capable of being catalogued in the chronologies of abstract history; but the truth itself is not historically circumscribed" (RP, 167). Elsewhere, in the course of an important discussion of the concept of identity, he rejects all forms of abstract identity, such as pure "immanent pantheism," a doctrine which carries the same implications as radical historicism (RP, 149 ff.). Against this he considers another kind of identity which permits of identity in difference (RP, 150). Further evidence of Collingwood's rejection of historicism can be found in "Croce's Philosophy of History," which is an uncompromising rejection of Croce's desertion of philosophy for history (CPH, 20–2), and *Speculum Mentis* which characterizes all views which define the whole of knowledge in terms of only one of its species as cases of vicious dogmatism. And since, according to the argument of *Speculum Mentis*, historicism, scientism (i.e., positivism), realism, aestheticism, and theism all rest on the same set of presuppositions, the arguments against each are essentially the same.[15] By accusing the later Collingwood of historicism, then, the critics are declaring that after 1936 (the period during which Collingwood is supposed to have undergone his radical conversion), he had come to adopt the very views which prior to 1936 he had explicitly repudiated.

It is my purpose in this book to take issue with any interpretation that charges Collingwood with having undergone a radical conversion to historicism (a view which will be hereafter referred to as 'the radical conversion hypothesis'). It must be confessed, however, that the radical conversion hypothesis finds some support in the *apparent* change in emphasis which characterizes the development of Collingwood's thought from 1916 until 1941. Before developing in some detail my own interpretation of the growth of Collingwood's thought it would be advisable, therefore, not only to take an objective look at the 'facts' themselves, but also to consider the major interpretations which have so far been placed upon those 'facts.'

Let us begin with a brief description and catalogue of the facts as revealed by a comprehensive but superficial reading of the texts. In *Religion and Philosophy*, published in 1916, Collingwood argued that history and philosophy were "the same thing." By this he meant simply that they have the same object, that they mutually presuppose each other, and that they are equally valid forms of knowledge. Precisely the same view is attributed to the relation between history and science in "Are History and Science Different Kinds of Knowledge?" (1922) In *Speculum Mentis* (1924) philosophy and history are still identified, but the identity is now characterized as "dialectical," with philosophy assuming ontological priority. *Speculum Mentis* is specifically described as "a New Treatise of Human Nature *philosophically* conceived" (SM, 9) (italics mine), the aim of which is to enable us better to answer the question, "What shall we do to be saved from our present distress?" (SM, 35)

The doctrine of the priority of philosophy over history, characteristic of the writings following *Speculum Mentis*, was asserted as part of a wider doctrine concerning the autonomy of philosophy in general. In "Economics as a Philosophical Science" (1925), for example, he distinguished clearly betwen philosophical studies of economic wealth and human conduct, and empirical studies of the same subject matters (EPS, 163). And in "The Nature and Aims of a Philosophy of History" (1925) he specifically argues (as he does later in the *Idea of History*) that whereas the historian's thought is always of an object *other* than his own thinking, the philosopher's thought is knowledge of himself (NAPH, 165). If this view is applied specifically to the categorial relation between philosophy and history it follows that the philosophical act of thinking (and hence philosophy of history) is distinct from the actual act of historical thinking: a distinction which is explicitly affirmed in the introductory remarks to the *Idea of History* where history is described as "thought of the first degree" and philosophy as "thought of the second degree" (IH, 1–3).

The most definitive expression of the autonomy of philosophy is given in *An Essay on Philosophical Method* (1933). The latter explores various aspects of the identity between philosophy and history; but in each case the identity is represented as "dialectical," and philosophy enjoys a clear-cut priority both in the order of knowledge and in the order of being. History, for example, is explicitly identified with philosophy in the sense that philosophy is conceived of as a system which itself develops in history. But, while the content of the system is progressively realized in history, the form or idea of it is transhistorical. Philosophy is also identified with history when both are defined as "categorical" judgments as opposed to the "hypothetical" judgments of natural science (EPM,136); philosophy is categorical universal while history is categorical singular. But again, the priority of philosophy is assured when (as in *Speculum Mentis*) the various forms of experience – art, religion, science, history, and philosophy – are placed on an overlapping scale of forms with philosophy at the summit: philosophy is not only implicit in all the other forms of experience but *is the act through which the implicit unity of the particular forms is rendered explicit.*

Beginning with the *Idea of History*, however, there appears to be a change of emphasis. It is true that the Introduction, written in 1936, continues to emphasize the priority of philosophy and its distinctness from history proper. But the main body of this work, written between 1936 and 1939, places more and more emphasis on history as the science of mind par excellence, and, according to his critics, it was precisely during this period that Collingwood is supposed to have changed his mind concerning the relation betwen history and philosophy. But the most telling evidence in support of Collingwood's change of attitude derives from the *Autobiography* (1939) and *An Essay on Metaphysics* (1940). In both works Collingwood argues for an identity between metaphysics and history based on a denial of the distinction between the purely historical question, What was so-and-so's answer to a particular question? and the purely philosophical question, Was he right? This newly conceived identity of the philosophical and the historical question is extended in the *Autobiography* to all branches of philosophy (A, 67). And it is this apparent historicization of the whole of philosophy which suggests that philosophy has now been liquidated by being absorbed into history.

The *Principles of Art*, which appeared in 1938, does not at first sight appear to have any relevance to the question of Collingwood's conversion to historicism. But the *New Leviathan* (1942), Collingwood's last work, seems to favour the radical conversion hypothesis. Not only does the *New Leviathan* present history as the supreme object of study (NL, 129), but it presents itself explicitly as an historical account of man as mind (NL, 61–2), as a Treatise on Human Nature *historically* conceived, with the purpose of "deciding how to deal with the present attack on Civilization" (NL, 62). And this, as we noted above, is precisely the problem which in 1924 was regarded as the fundamental one of philosophy.

It is clear then that throughout his entire career Collingwood repudiated any merely abstract separation of philosophy and history. Yet given this starting point at least two separate moves are possible. The first is the attempt to explicate the identity of philosophy and history in terms of the concept of a "dialectical *rapprochement.*" This means regarding history and philosophy as *distinct* but not *separate* forms on an overlapping scale: in the sense that the latter renders explicit what is implicit in the former. But the second possibility leads in the direction of radical historicism for which philosophy is totally subsumed under the category of history. It was Collingwood's own view that he had taken the first step while most of his critics have argued that he took the second. Let us then compare Collingwood's own interpretation of his thought with those of his critics.

5 COLLINGWOOD AND HIS CRITICS

A *Collingwood's own interpretation*

In his *Autobiography,* written in 1938, Collingwood provides a brief but lucid account of the development of his own philosophy. A highly significant feature of this account is the fact that at no time does he make any mention of a radical shift from one point of view to another. He argues, for example, that his original criticisms of the realist doctrine of "eternal problems," which led eventually to a denial of the abstract separation of philosophical from historical questions, occurred to him for the first time during the first world war. His speculations at this time involved a complete rejection of the realist dogma which postulated "propositional logic" as the organon of philosophy. Against the dogma of realism Collingwood proposed a dialectical logic of inquiry, which on some occasions he called "the logic of question and answer," and which was related, as I hope to show, to the wider doctrine of *An Essay on Philosophical Method* called the "logic of the overlap of classes."[16]

Collingwood claims to have worked out the basis of the new logic of question and answer in an unpublished book called "Truth and Contradiction" (A, 42). This was written in 1917 but, according to Collingwood, the manuscript was subsequently destroyed (A, 99n1). But any doubts as to whether at least on Collingwood's own account, "Truth and Contradiction" really did contain an exposition of the logic of question and answer may be dispelled by the following textual considerations. The logic of question and answer is mentioned for the first time on page 37 of the *Autobiography*. There follows from page 37 to 42 a description of it. On page 42 Collingwood writes: "All this, during my spare time in 1917 I wrote out at considerable length ... in a book called *Truth and Contradiction*." Assuming that the "All this" refers to the contents of pages 37–42, are we not justified in asserting that the subject of this book was in fact the logic of question and answer? Moreover, if it can be shown (as I will attempt to in this book) that the description of the logic of question and answer given on pages 37–42 of the *Autobiography* matches the description of what, in both *An Essay on Metaphysics* and various parts of the *Autobiography*, Collingwood calls the method of metaphysical analysis (the general aim of which, as I also hope to show, is to apply the method of question and answer to the arrangement of knowledge into an overlapping scale of forms) then it is surely plausible to conclude that "Truth and Contradiction" was an earlier version of what later became *An Essay on Metaphysics* – a claim which will be made the more plausible in chapter VIII when we consider the published version of Collingwood's Ruskin Centenary address, delivered in 1919.

The foundation of the logic of question and answer, as Collingwood describes it in the *Autobiography*, is an explicit denial of the distinction between philosophy and history as the realists understood it. He therefore argues that the rapprochement between philosophy and history, which is the main theme of *An Essay on Metaphysics*, was actually a product of his wartime speculations (A, 60 ff.). Collingwood stated his conclusions on this matter as follows:

> It became clear to me that metaphysics (as its very name might show, though people still use the word as if it had been "paraphysics") is no futile attempt at knowing what lies beyond the limits of experience, but is primarily at any given time an attempt to discover what the people of that time believe about the world's general nature; such beliefs being the presuppositions of all their "physics," that is, their inquiries into its detail. Secondarily, it is the attempt to discover the corresponding presuppositions of other peoples and other times, and to follow the historical process by which one set of presuppositions has turned into another. (A, 65–6)

He then adds, as we have seen, that there is no recognized branch of philosophy to which the idea of rapprochement did not apply. For every branch of philosophy, the problems, as well as the solutions proposed for them, have their own history (A, 67).

As Collingwood states them, these conclusions can be variously interpreted. But to assume that the historicization of philosophy to which they refer is a radically historicist one seems to me to be premature. Of course, if such an interpretation is placed upon them there is no doubt that the *Autobiography* is inconsistent with the earlier texts, for the alleged radical historicism of the *Autobiography* was most certainly not a characteristic of Collingwood's thought prior to 1936. In other words, if the *Autobiography* does espouse the doctrine of radical historicism then it cannot be taken seriously as an authentic history of Collingwood's thought.

If, on the other hand, the doctrines of the *Autobiography* are themselves in need of interpretation according to criteria supplied by the rest of Collingwood's writings, in particular the early ones, then Collingwood's claim to have worked out the doctrine of the identity of philosophy and history between the publication of *Religion and Philosophy* (in which some kind of identity is openly advocated) and *Speculum Mentis* can be made to stand up. But, if Collingwood is right, if the rapprochement of the *Autobiography* (and hence of *An Essay on Metaphysics*) is the same as the rapprochement of the earlier period, and if this doctrine has never been explicitly repudiated, then in view of what Collingwood actually said in *Speculum Mentis* and *An Essay on Philosophical Method*, as well as in parts of the *Idea of History*, it could not possibly be a radically historicist one.

This view is made the more plausible by the fact that in the *Autobiography* Collingwood writes, concerning the doctrines of *Speculum Mentis*, that while "much of it now fails to satisfy me ..." there is nevertheless "not a great deal that needs to be retracted" (A, 56n). One would not expect such a statement from a philosopher who had knowingly abandoned the "idealism" of *Speculum Mentis* for the "historicism" of the *Autobiography* and *An Essay on Metaphysics* – and it is hard to believe that such a radical change in outlook could occur unknowingly. If the rapprochement of the *Autobiography* and *An Essay on Metaphysics* was really a radically historicist one, while the rapprochement of *Speculum Mentis* and *An Essay on Philosophical Method* is a complete denial of this (which it clearly is), then either Collingwood did not understand the obvious implications of his own philosophy or else he was deliberately misleading us.

B *Knox's Interpretation: From Idealism to Historicism*

Collingwood's own assessment of the development of his thought has been challenged by the first editor of Collingwood's posthumous publications, T. M. Knox (IH, v-xxiv; PBA, 469-74). Knox's chief reason for questioning Collingwood's account is that the doctrine of the *Autobiography* and *An Essay on Metaphysics* which Collingwood traces to his earliest writings, are, as far as Knox is concerned, clearly incompatible with the doctrines which are in fact expounded in those early writings. In particular, Knox argues, these later doctrines, which according to Collingwood had been arrived at before he wrote *An Essay on Philosophical Method*, could not possibly have appeared until some time between 1936 and 1938. Knox claims, for example, to have documentary evidence that in 1936 Collingwood still believed in the possibility of a purely philosophical science of pure being (IH, x–xi). Indeed it is Knox's contention that the whole of Collingwood's early thought evolves around a commitment to a science of pure being. But, he argues, the philosophy which emerged between 1936 and 1938 was a complete repudiation of this notion together with the distinction between philosophy and history which it presupposes. Knox therefore concludes that the *Autobiography* is not a true account of the development of Collingwood's thought because it does not take into account the radical change in doctrine from *An Essay on Philosophical Method* to *An Essay on Metaphysics*.

But while the change which occurred between 1936 and 1938 was radical it was not, according to Knox, an unheralded revolution. In fact, "the philosophy which 'emerged' after 1936 was not an entirely new growth but had its roots in the author's past" (IH, xi). In particular, the philosophy of 1939 marks a triumph in Collingwood's thought of certain sceptical and dogmatic tendencies which were characteristic of his earlier thought. These sceptical and dogmatic tendencies had suffered a temporary defeat between 1932 and 1936, and Knox cites *An Essay on Philosophical Method* as the precise point at which Collingwood worked his way beyond the historical scepticism implied in *Speculum Mentis* (PBA, 470; IH, xi).

These conclusions imply that Collingwood's thought developed through three distinct periods; an early period of scepticism characterized by *Speculum Mentis*, a middle period characterized by the rapprochement between philosophy and history in *An Essay on Philosophical Method*, and a later period characterized by the radical historicism of the *Autobiography* and *An Essay on Metaphysics*. This is precisely the basis upon which Knox proceeds to organize and arrange Collingwood's philosophical writings:

They may perhaps be divided into three groups, although some development of thought may be traceable within the works of each group. The first consists of what he came to regard as juvenilia, *Religion and Philosophy* (1916) and *Speculum Mentis* (1924). The second begins with the *Essay on Philosophical Method* (1933) and continues with the *Idea of Nature* (which dates, except for its Conclusion, from 1934) and much (1936) of the *Idea of History*. The last comprises the *Autobiography* (1939), the *Essay on Metaphysics* (1940), and the *New Leviathan* (1942). The *Principles of Art* (1938) is akin in part to the second group, in part to the third. (IH, vii)

The collapse of philosophy into history begins, according to Knox, with Collingwood's attempt to define history as the true science of mind (PBA, 470). This attempt began in earnest around 1935. From this point onwards Collingwood's writings contain an impressive argument for the recognition of history as productive of results no less entitled to be called knowledge than those of natural science. But he was not content merely to disprove the positivistic programme for the absorption of philosophy into natural science; he went further and took up a position equally intransigent, claiming for history precisely what his opponents claimed for science (IH, xiii). "Philosophical scepticism," Knox writes, "in one form or another was the price he paid for the endeavour to compress philosophy into history" (IH, xi). For Knox the tragic denouement is summed up in Collingwood's own declaration (which Knox cites from an unpublished manuscript written in 1939) that "philosophy as a separate discipline is liquidated by being converted into history" (IH, x).

Thus Knox assigns to Collingwood's later philosophy a doctrine which had been expressly repudiated on several occasions between 1916 and 1936. To the question, Why did Collingwood change his views so radically? Knox gives no satisfactory answer. His reference to Collingwood's illness, for example, is of no philosophical relevance.[17] Nor is the question answered by simply pointing out that Collingwood's growing interest in and enthusiasm for history "tended to make him 'turn traitor' to his philosophical vocation" (IH, xix–xx). To say that the later philosophy marks a triumph of sceptical and dogmatic tendencies which are characteristic of *Speculum Mentis* does not explain why those views should have triumphed. What are these sceptical and dogmatic tendencies? Knox does not say. If he is referring to the conclusions of *Speculum Mentis* which allege a commitment to the historicity and relativity of philosophical thought, he is betraying a failure to appreciate the significance of this doctrine. For, as we shall see later on, the historicity of philosophy in *Speculum Mentis* is asserted only in the context of its transhistoricity which is explicitly acknowledged as a necessary presupposition of the possibility of the former. As for the claim that "philosophy as a separate discipline is liquidated by being converted into history," this too can be reconciled with the doctrine of rapprochement when it is recognized that even in *Speculum Mentis* and *An Essay on Philosophical Method* Collingwood denied that philosophy and history were separate. If what is "liquidated" is simply philosophy's claim to abstract separateness then the statement is virtually nothing more than a reaffirmation of the central thesis of *Speculum Mentis* which quite clearly has "liquidated" (*aufgehauben*) the separateness of philosophy by showing how it is "dialectically" convertible into history. In other words, when viewed from the standpoint of dialectical philosophy, such a statement ceases to have the radical implications attributed to it by Knox. I would therefore contend that had Knox taken a more serious view of the rapprochement philosophy of *Speculum Mentis* (which he dismisses as juvenilia) he might well have seen that the doctrines of the later period could in fact be reconciled with the position of *An Essay on Philosophical Method*. And his reason for distrusting the *Autobiography* would accordingly have to be reconsidered.

c *Donagan's Interpretation: Beyond Idealism and Historicism*

A more recent interpretation of Collingwood's philosophy is *The Later Philosophy of R. G. Collingwood* by Alan Donagan.[18] Donagan begins by accepting Knox's thesis that, so far as the relationship between philosophy and history is concerned, there is an important difference between the early and the later philosophy. "Knox's demonstration," writes Donagan, "that between 1936 and 1938 Collingwood radically changed his mind about the relation of philosophy to history must be the foundation of any interpretation of his later works."[19] Donagan does not, however, accept Knox's explanation of Collingwood's change of mind, nor does he accept Knox's division of the later philosophy into two distinct groups, "historicist" and "non-historicist." Knox's explanation of the eventual triumph in Collingwood's thought of sceptical and dogmatic tendencies which he had temporarily defeated between 1932 and 1936 must be supplemented, according to Donagan, by identifying Collingwood's reasons for allowing them to triumph.[20] Donagan argues that these reasons are to be found primarily in the *Principles of Art* and the *New Leviathan* rather than in the *Autobiography* and *An Essay on Metaphysics*, and his explanation of Collingwood's alleged conversion may therefore be distinguished from Knox's on the following points.

Donagan begins by pointing out that in *An Essay on Philosophical Method* Collingwood distinguished between the "categorical singular" judgments of history and the "categorical universal" judgments of philosophy. Both are distinguished from the hypothetical universal judgments of theoretical science. In 1937, however, while writing the *Principles of Art*, Collingwood found it necessary to redefine the nature of thought, as distinct from imagination. The result, according to Donagan, was a notion of thinking as "essentially analytic and abstract": a doctrine which, Donagan maintains, is further elaborated in the *New Leviathan* where Collingwood argues that all forms of thinking, from the highest to the lowest, are conceptual, and that all concepts are abstract. But this concept of thinking is plainly inconsistent with the central thesis of *An Essay on Philosophical Method*, which is, that there is at least one kind of thinking, namely, the philosophy of being or metaphysics, which is a non-abstract form of thinking and whose subject matter is no mere hypothesis but *die Sache selbst*. It was therefore clear to Collingwood that a non-abstract or concrete concept of being was impossible. If there is to be a concept of being at all it must be abstract, and presumably its subject matter must likewise be a mere abstraction or hypothesis and not a concrete existing entity.

But, as Donagan himself points out, the conclusion that a non-abstract concept of being is impossible does not yet lead to the conclusion that philosophy as a separate discipline is liquidated by being converted into history. Metaphysics may take forms other than a chimerical non-abstract concept of being; and even if metaphysics in all its forms turns out to be impossible it has not yet been shown that philosophy as a separate discipline must be metaphysical.[21] The full rationale of Collingwood's conversion, then, still remains a mystery.

In order further to dispel this mystery Donagan makes the following claims. In the first place, the re-definition of metaphysics as a form of history was a consequence of the fact that Collingwood was deeply committed to saving metaphysics from total eclipse. He knew that, if there was to be such a thing as metaphysics at all, it would have to be a form of abstract thinking about an equally abstract subject-matter. Under what conditions, then, is metaphysics (conceived as a form of abstract thinking) possible?

Collingwood's answer to this question may be found in *An Essay on Metaphysics*. This work shows that Collingwood had studied A. J. Ayer's *Language, Truth and Logic* and that he had come to endorse Ayer's view that the propositions of traditional metaphysics are unverifiable. In order to vindicate the usefulness of traditional metaphysics Collingwood argued that the affirmations which Ayer took to be unverifiable propositions were not propositions at all, but absolute presuppositions which are neither true nor false. This pointed to a further claim that metaphysics is not a futile inquiry into which absolute presuppositions are true, but an inquiry into which absolute presuppositions have been held, by whom, and why: and prima facie, these questions are historical. Collingwood's "reform of metaphysics" therefore means, according to Donagan, that metaphysics becomes a branch of history and metaphysical statements are nothing more than empirical statements about what beliefs have been held on various occasions about the nature of reality.

Thus does Donagan explain the rationale of Collingwood's historicist interpretation of the relation between philosophy and history in *An*

Essay on Metaphysics.[22] Donagan goes on, however, to argue that the historicist outlook was finally abandoned in the *New Leviathan*, which, no less than the *Essay on Philosophical Method,* exemplifies philosophy as a form of thought distinct from history.[23] If, as Donagan contends, the *New Leviathan* neither endorses nor exemplifies the doctrine of the relation of philosophy to history which, according to Knox, is the chief characteristic of the third group, then the *New Leviathan* could not possibly belong to that group. Donagan therefore suggests that in the *New Leviathan* Collingwood's thought took a new turn which involved a departure from not only the historicism which characterized his thought from 1936 until roughly 1939 but also from the idealism of his early thought.

D *Other Versions of the Radical Conversion Hypothesis*

Except for his somewhat unorthodox interpretation of the *New Leviathan*, then, Donagan is clearly an exponent of what I have called "the radical conversion hypothesis." Indeed it would seem that nearly everyone who has written about Collingwood tends to subscribe to this view. F. H. Heinemann gives a typical verdict when he writes that Collingwood "made philosophy dependent on history." Heinemann notes that according to Collingwood "Metaphysics is an historical science," and "Cosmology is a super-history." Such statements, he complains, "reveal the degree to which philosophy has become unilaterally dependent on history."[24]

Even sympathetic critics such as E. E. Harris and Nathan Rotenstreich have come to regard the *Essay on Metaphysics* as a radical departure from the achievements of *An Essay on Philosophical Method*. Harris, for example, argues that *An Essay on Metaphysics* "obfuscates the philosophical insights of the earlier period." He then goes on to accuse Collingwood of philosophical amnesia, declaring that he has not "so much rejected as forgotten what he had written in earlier works."[25] Rotenstreich on the other hand, has a somewhat more elaborate explanation for Collingwood's conversion. He claims that the identity of philosophy and history which characterizes the later writings was an attempt to overcome the immanent historicism in the realm of history proper. This Collingwood sought to accomplish by making history more philosophical. And although, according to Rotenstreich, he was relatively successful in this regard, he could not avoid, as a result of having levelled philosophy down to the sphere of history, an historicist invasion into the realm of philosophy itself.[26] Finally, at the other end of the scale hostile critics like Leo Strauss are prepared to dismiss the whole of Collingwood's thought on the grounds that it is thoroughly corrupted by historicist thinking.[27]

An even further indication of the extent to which the radical conversion hypothesis tends to have been accepted can be gathered from the comments of the many able reviewers of Donagan's book. Thus, for example, Dorothy Emmet writes: "as Mr. Donagan shows, Collingwood's views did change substantially, especially as between the constructive metaphysics of the *Essay on Philosophical Method* and the historical relativism of the *Essay on Metaphysics*."[28] Similar views have been expressed by C. K. Grant:

> Donagan ... rightly concentrates on the remarkable change in Collingwood's views regarding the nature of metaphysics. In the *Essay on Philosophical Method* metaphysics was said to be the study of Being: the 'reform' of this subject in *Metaphysics* was in a sceptical and historicist direction, for it was there represented as an historical investigation of the absolute presuppositions of past science, these presuppositions being themselves neither true nor false.[29]

H. B. Acton:

> In his earlier writings ... he was by no means unsympathetic towards Idealism, and as late as 1933, in his *Essay on Philosophical Method*, he could still be regarded as reformulating an Idealist point of view. But in his *Autobiography* (1939) and in his *Essay on Metaphysics* (1940) he took up a sceptical or 'historicist' position arguing that philosophy cannot discover truth but can only record as matters of history, 'absolute presuppositions' which vary from one time to another.[30]

and, A. Boyce Gibson:

> the fact is indisputable: Collingwood did in one phase make of philosophy the handmaid of history ... he resorted to the view that ... Philosophy as a separate discipline is liquidated by being converted into history.[31]

On the other side, the voices of dissent are few in number. H. S. Harris, for example, has argued that Collingwood's entire thought may be viewed as in some sense a fulfilment of a programme first outlined in *Speculum Mentis*.[32] An even stronger claim in this direction has been made by E. W. F. Tomlin,[33] whose views have been further supported by at least one of Donagan's reviewers, W. J. Emblom. "We suspect," writes Emblom, "that there is the need to attempt to carry out Tomlin's suggestion completely."[34] But in spite of his recognition that Collingwood's work forms some kind of a total system Tomlin does admit the very point with which this book takes issue, namely, that mainly as a result of "an intervening preoccupation with the nature and purpose of historical thinking" a "change of fundamental importance" did occur with the appearance of *An Essay on Metaphysics*.[35] Tomlin, however, regards this change as temporary and inconclusive, and he argues that Collingwood was, towards the end of his life, on the verge of abandoning historicism and returning to the metaphysical position of *Speculum Mentis* and *An Essay on Philosophical Method*.[36] Finally, there is the recent work of Louis O. Mink who argues in favour of viewing Collingwood as a "systematic philosopher of sorts" whose books "to an unusual degree complement and explain each other."[37] But whereas Mink supports his argument by appealing to Collingwood's theory of mind as expounded in the *Principles of Art* and the *New Leviathan*, it is my contention that Collingwood's thought should be evaluated according to the scheme laid down in *Speculum Mentis*. This does not mean that I believe Collingwood's later thought to have taken a wrong turn. It is rather that I do not regard the philosophy of mind expounded in the later writings as having superseded for the doctrines of *Speculum Mentis*. The two doctrines are in fact addressed to quite different sets of questions. But the questions to which the *Principles of Art* and the *New Leviathan* are addressed do not properly arise until the questions raised by *Speculum Mentis* have been dealt with. In particular, I would contend, the matter of Collingwood's alleged conversion to historicism cannot be settled except by appeal to the conceptual framework laid down in *Speculum Mentis*.

I will therefore argue, against the many supporters of the radical conversion hypothesis and in support of the dissenting voices, that Collingwood's thought can be viewed as a system, that his later thought is a dialectical outgrowth of his early thought, and that at no time did he subscribe to the doctrines of radical historicism.[38] It is true that he accepted philosophy in one of its aspects as being concerned with the methodology of history; and it is true that his later writings place more emphasis on the importance of history; but it does not follow that because of this he ceased to recognize the autonomy of philosophy. On the contrary, the existence of an autonomous philosophical activity remains for him an absolute presupposition of any historical science. The rapprochement at which Collingwood's thought aimed is one which, once achieved, would guarantee the autonomy of both history and philosophy.

Collingwood of course subjected the doctrine of rapprochement to a variety of interpretations. And this has tended to obscure the real meaning of the doctrine. In *Religion and Philosophy* he accounts for it in terms of a theory of "concrete identity." In *Speculum Mentis* and

An Essay on Philosophical Method the notion of concrete identity is further interpreted as a dialectical scale of overlapping forms. Finally, there is the controversial interpretation expounded in *An Essay on Metaphysics*. But this, as I hope to show, is substantially a restatement – albeit a rather clumsy one – of the theory of dialectical rapprochement.

I will argue therefore that the history of Collingwood's thought is not characterized by a radical conversion from "idealism" to "historicism," but, rather, that the rapprochement which he set out to accomplish in 1916 was actually achieved in *Speculum Mentis* and *An Essay on Philosophical Method* and subsequently applied, in the remainder of his writings, to the interpretation of numerous philosophical problems. My book is an attempt, in other words, at meeting the need of viewing the bulk of Collingwood's thought as an expression of the programme laid out in *Speculum Mentis*.

But finally, it will be my contention that if Collingwood is to be identified with historicism at all it can only be with what I shall hereafter refer to as the tradition of transcendental historicism, according to which philosophic truth, while admittedly grounded in history, is nevertheless not entirely historical in character. That is to say, although it is only through the historical process that truth brings itself into existence, and only through historical thinking that it reveals itself to thought, what is revealed at any given time in history is nevertheless absolute and transhistorical, a permanent aspect of the self-completing and infinite 'absolute' standpoint or concrete universal, whose final revelation, once achieved, would coincide with the end of all time.

Representing the tradition of transcendental historicism, which takes a firm stand against the relativism of radical historicism, are such philosophers as Hegel, Husserl, Rickert, the early Heidegger, and Cassirer. A more recent defence of this position is E. L. Fackenheim's *Metaphysics and Historicity*.[89] Husserl's critique of historicism provides a definition of transcendental historicism with which Collingwood would most certainly agree. Husserl wrote:

> It is easy to see that historicism, if consistently carried through, carries over into extreme subjectivism. The ideas of truth, theory, science, would then, like all ideas, lose their absolute validity. That an idea has validity would mean that it is a factual construction of spirit, which is held as valid and which in its factual validity determines thought. There would be no unqualified validity, or 'validity-in-itself', which is what it is, even if no one has achieved it and though no historical humanity will ever achieve it. Thus too, there would be no validity to the principle of contradiction nor for any logic, which latter, nevertheless is still in full vigour in our time. The result will be that the logical principles of non-contradiction will be transformed into their opposites. And to go even further,

all the propositions which we have just enunciated and even the possibilities that we have weighed and have claimed as constantly valid would in themselves have no validity.[40]

Like Husserl, Collingwood too recognized that a rational and scientific assessment of the historicity of thought presupposes criteria which are themselves non-historical or transcendental. Such criteria, however, cannot themselves be determined by a strictly empirical (i.e. historical) science without presupposing what this science seeks to prove. A strictly historical science, in other words, cannot itself validate the criteria according to which it proceeds: neither can it refute the possibility of a strictly non-historical philosophical science. Such refutations are only possible by presupposing what historicism seeks to deny – namely, the existence of "scientific philosophy." Indeed, as Husserl puts it, it is clear that any kind of rational criticism – and this is the essence of culture – "in so far as it is really to lay claim to validity implies the ideal possibility of a systematic philosophy as a strict science.[41]

Collingwood makes much the same point in his critique of the "propaganda of irrationalism" in the *Essay on Metaphysics* (81–180) where he outlines the consequences of abandoning the logical principles of scientific thinking in favour of pseudo-scientific principles which virtually undermine the very ideas of truth and validity. But this is precisely what happens when radical historicism takes hold of thought. Thus I do not see how it is possible for Collingwood to have given such a lucid critique of "irrationalism" while at the same time professing allegiance to the doctrines of radical historicism.

Husserl's antidote to radical historicism was a phenomenologically oriented theory of essence "which alone can provide the basis for a philosophy of the spirit."[42] Collingwood's antidote for "irrationalism" is his so-called "reform of metaphysics." But if Collingwood's metaphysics is to be compared with Husserl's phenomenology, it is only because both proceed from a firm commitment to the need for a transcendental philosophy of the spirit or mind. For Collingwood, as for Husserl, metaphysics is not simply an inquiry into the abstract transcendentality of being *qua* being but an inquiry into the process whereby being constitutes itself within the life of mind. The object of metaphysics, being *qua* being, is not simply an abstract and static self-identity but a concrete and dynamic identity in difference. Collingwood's entire philosophy, like that of Husserl, was an attempt to uncover the transcendental structure of mind. A large measure of his genius lay in his ability to show how not only philosophy, but art, religion, science, and history, contribute towards such an end. Hence his lifelong interest in the need for rapprochement.

6 THE IDEA OF PHILOSOPHY AS A SCALE OF FORMS: A NEW INTERPRETATION OF COLLINGWOOD'S THOUGHT

The interpretation which I now propose to defend amounts to a somewhat elaborate attempt to support Collingwood's own interpretation in the *Autobiography*. Collingwood claimed at the very outset of his career (in *Speculum Mentis*, for example, and again in *An Essay on Philosophical Method*) that philosophy is necessarily systematic. *Speculum Mentis* not only alleges a commitment to the idea of a system but confesses "the crime of offering the reader ... a crude sketch of such a system" (SM, 9). This commitment was reaffirmed ten years later when he wrote *An Essay on Philosophical Method*: "I think it can be shown that in some form or other the idea of a system is inevitable in philosophy, and that no attempt to deny it can succeed unless it is pushed to the point of denying that the word philosophy has any meaning whatever" (EMP, 186); "philosophy must think of itself as systematic." (EMP, 198)

In the *Autobiography*, it is true, the idea of a system is never explicitly discussed. Yet, as we have already noted, Collingwood there affirms that his whole philosophy has been "in the main an attempt to bring about a *rapprochement* between philosophy and history" (A, 77). The most effective way of accomplishing this task would be through the systematic attempt to unify the various forms of experience in which both philosophy and history participate. Collingwood himself points out in the *Autobiography* that early in his attempt to lay the foundations for a philosophy of history, he was driven to acknowledge the need for a new kind of philosophy (A, 77). And what else could this new philosophy be except a newly conceived philosophy of mind, a "critical review of the chief forms of human experience," as set forth in *Speculum Mentis*, and which, according to Collingwood, is the only philosophy that can exist? (SM, 9) It would seem reasonable, then, to suggest that *Speculum Mentis* was Collingwood's own response to what, in the *Autobiography*, he called the need for a new philosophy. Indeed, would not the date at which *Speculum Mentis* was composed (sometime before 1923) coincide roughly with the date at which, according to the *Autobiography* account, the need for a new philosophy was felt?

The main purpose of *Speculum Mentis* is to organize the various forms of experience into a dialectical scale of forms – the logical principles of which were later worked out in *An Essay on Philosophical Method*. This task is accomplished from the standpoint of absolute knowledge, which is philosophy without presuppositions. Collingwood conceived it to be the proper task of absolute philosophy to re-examine and reconcile to itself (i.e., place on a scale of forms) the various phases of experience which are not absolute (although they may mistake themselves to be) and do involve presuppositions. This conception of philosophy suggests the following possibilities concerning the structure of Collingwood's own thought; that Collingwood's own philosophy is an attempt to fulfil the requirements of this system; that his own philosophical development exemplifies the logical structure of that system; and that all of his writings occupy various places on a scale of forms. I shall therefore attempt first of all to take seriously Collingwood's own claim to have produced a system, and secondly to explore the consequences of entertaining the hypothesis of viewing the whole of Collingwood's philosophy as a projection of the programme outlined in *Speculum Mentis*.

The conclusions of *Speculum Mentis* are important in two specific areas: (a) concerning the idea of philosophy as a system, and (b) concerning the rapprochement between philosophy and history which underlies Collingwood's concept of this system.

A *The Idea of Philosophy as a System*

Speculum Mentis is an analysis of experience with a view to disclosing the basic presuppositions which underlie each of its forms. The relation among the forms constitutes a dialectical history of errors. In this respect the book bears a strong resemblance to Hegel's *Phenomenology of Mind*. Like the latter, *Speculum Mentis* is a prolegomena to all future philosophizing. Its main purpose is to explain how philosophy becomes a science, that is to say, comes into existence. What comes into existence, however, is not philosophy as a finished product, in abstraction from the rest of experience, but a self-perpetuating activity which is continually turning back and re-examining each of the other forms with a view to organizing them into a scale of internally related and overlapping life worlds.

But *Speculum Mentis* aims at something more than being a philosophy of life worlds. The phenomenology of experience is a stage through which philosophy passes in order to gain insight into the transcendental structure of mind or consciousness, and through this, into the structure of being itself. By being Collingwood does not, as I have already noted, mean pure abstract being, or substance. This concept of being was rejected as early as 1916 in *Religion and Philosophy*. Being is a concrete set of activities, whose essence, rather than transcending these acts, is, on the contrary, identical with them. But this identity is achieved without a total loss of transcendence. Since the acts through which being constitutes itself are acts of mind (i.e., acts of self-knowledge), being may therefore be defined as the synthesis of the mind's acts of self-knowledge; art, religion, science, history, and philosophy (RP, 34, 100, 116; SM, 396, 315).

Philosophy, conceived of as a *mode* of being, poses difficulties for itself not shared by the other sciences. This is because of philosophy's peculiar role as not only the critic of experience but also one of the experiences criticized. In so far as philosophy is the critic of the other forms, it is the philosophy of the modes of being; being *qua* art, religion, science, and history. But in so far as it is the critic of its own activity (the philosophy of philosophy), it is the philosophy of being as such, being *qua* being – the highest achievement of which is the philosophy of the mind as pure act (*speculum speculi*), or absolute philosophy. The pure act – a term which Collingwood borrowed from Gentile – is not, as we have already noted, a separate activity, abstracted from the rest, but a product of the historically grounded philosophies of the separate standpoints or modes of being. The latter are concrete experiences; attitudes which the mind takes towards itself in relation to certain objects, such as art, nature, God, history, and so on. Collingwood's name for the thought which investigates the structure of these attitudes or standpoints is metaphysics, defined as the science of absolute presuppositions.

To completely understand this conception of metaphysics it is necessary to introduce, on Collingwood's behalf, two sets of distinctions. The first is a distinction between (a) metaphysics as the phenomenological analysis of consciousness per se (metaphysics sense I), and (b) the more specifically historical analysis of the presuppositions of past and present thought (metaphysics senses II and III). The former I will call phenomenology; the latter I will call metaphysics proper. Phenomenology, as exemplified by *Speculum Mentis*, is the analysis of mind as a system of necessary categories, or, to use a term which Collingwood himself sometimes uses, "habits," such as "imagination" (art), "faith" (religion), "understanding" (science), and "reason" (history and philosophy). But while the subject matter of phenomenology is the categorial aspects of mind which are transcendental and transhistorical, the activity of metaphysics is historical in the sense that it must be done anew by each generation.

Metaphysics proper, whether of past or present thought, is an historical analysis of the presuppositions and claims of each of the separate sciences to which the categorical habits of mind give rise: claims which are often erroneous and which change from generation to generation.

The *Idea of History* (parts I–IV), for example, and almost the whole of the *Idea of Nature* are exercises in the metaphysics of past thought (metaphysics sense II), while the Epilegomena of the *Idea of History* and the *Principles of Art* are examples of the metaphysics of contemporary thought (metaphysics sense III). The ideal limit of the metaphysics of contemporary thought is the philosophy of philosophy, the systematic evaluation of the transcendental presuppositions of critical thought itself, as exemplified by *An Essay on Philosophical Method*. The philosophy of philosophy is the point at which the historically grounded metaphysics of past and contemporary thought and the phenomenology of consciousness per se coincide. It is also the ground of the unity of the transcendental philosophy of being *qua* being (the philosophy of the mind as pure act) and the historically grounded philosophies of the modes of being. The life of philosophy, in other words, is a single act which is at the same time a plurality of distinct acts. The unity of philosophy is the unity of a "concrete universal" – a concept which is indispensable to the understanding of Collingwood's thought. Every question raised by philosophy at one level carries implications at every other level. Thus, for example, an answer to the question, What is art? has implications concerning not only each of the other forms, but also concerning the structure of consciousness itself. An appreciation of the interdisciplinary character of philosophy is another prerequisite to the understanding of Collingwood's thought.

In addition to the distinction between phenomenology and metaphysics proper there is implicit in Collingwood's thought a further distinction according to which both of these philosophical acts may be seen to operate on three distinct but related ontological levels.[43] At the first level, consciousness assumes an absolute distinction between subject and object, and views the whole of reality as an expression of whatever experience it is presently identified with. Thus, for example, first-level philosophy of art elevates itself into an "aesthetic" philosophy when it begins to view the whole of reality according to the characteristics which belong primarily to art. At the second level, the distinction between subject and object remains but each experience now regards itself as only one among a variety of equally valid standpoints. At the third level the subject-object distinction has been finally overcome and some recognition is given to the fact that the forms of experience, rather than being coordinate species of a genus, are on the contrary a scale of overlapping forms.

On the basis of these distinctions the implicit rationale of Collingwood's published works may now be reconstructed. According to this reconstruction each work may be seen as exemplifying one or another type of philosophy operating on one or more of the three levels of experience. *Speculum Mentis*, for example, in addition to being a phenomenological analysis of the universal and necessary forms or categories of experience is at the same time a third-level critique of the metaphysics of the separate standpoints in so far as they exist at the first ontological level. Examples of reflection at the second level may be found in *Religion and Philosophy* (1916), *Outlines of a Philosophy of Art* (1925), "Are History and Science Different Kinds of Knowledge?" (1922), and "The Nature and Aims of a Philosophy of History" (1925).

In 1932, after having reflected primarily on the structure of such forms as art, religion, and history, Collingwood turned his attention to the transcendental presuppositions of philosophy itself. *An Essay on Philosophical Method* is an example of what may be regarded as the metaphysics of third-level philosophizing. In this work Collingwood outlines what he calls the doctrine of the overlap of classes and the theory of the scale of forms which together define the theoretical presuppositions according to which the philosophy of the separate standpoints ought to proceed if it is to be consistent with the spirit of the age. To behave otherwise was not only an anachronism but a sign of cultural decadence.

The principles stated in *An Essay on Philosophical Method* are the principles underlying Collingwood's own thought even before he wrote the essay on method. In 1927 and 1928, for example, he wrote two papers on the relation between faith and reason in which these very principles are implicit. These papers may therefore be regarded as genuine examples of third-level philosophy applied to the analysis of faith. In 1933 he turned his attention to what in *Speculum Mentis* he called the first stage of reason, namely, science. The results of these reflections, carried out over a period of years, were published posthumously in 1945 as the *Idea of Nature*. At the end of this work Collingwood repeats a point already made in *Speculum Mentis*, which is that science can be properly understood only in the context of history. He therefore declares that we must proceed from the idea of nature to the idea of history (IN, 177).

This is precisely what Collingwood himself did when in 1936 he wrote the first draft of what later became the *Idea of History*. His reflections on history were interrupted, however, when on several occasions he felt obliged to respond to various cultural crises. In 1937, for example, he wrote the *Principles of Art* in response to what he regarded as a serious aesthetic and moral crisis which he feared would lead to a corruption of European consciousness. And in 1939 he wrote *An Essay on Metaphysics* in response to positivism which he regarded as a further threat to the survival of culture.

Shortly after his encounter with positivism Collingwood returned to the philosophy of history. He now began working on what he no doubt hoped would be his major achievement, the *Principles of History*, a systematic metaphysical analysis of the absolute presuppositions which lay at the basis of his own experience as an historian. The aim of this analysis was to represent the contemporary idea of history as a "self-dependent, self-determining, self-justifying form of thought" (IH, 249). But this work was never completed and only parts of it have been published as sections of the *Idea of History* (pt. III, s. 8 and pt. V, ss. 3 and 6). Perhaps the reason why the *Principles* was never completed is that in 1940 Collingwood interrupted his work once again in order to begin work on the *New Leviathan*, which is also addressed to a cultural crisis, in this case the political manifestoes of Fascism and Nazism, which Collingwood regarded as forms of cultural barbarism. The *New Leviathan* (1942) was the last work published during Collingwood's lifetime. He died in 1943.

B *The Relation between Philosophy and History*

Speculum Mentis provides the clue not only to the plan or architechtonic of Collingwood's system but also to the relation between philosophy and history which underlies the exposition of that system. The *Essay on Metaphysics* argues for an identity between philosophy and history. The *Autobiography* argues that this identity was established early in Collingwood's philosophical career. Collingwood's critics reject this claim on the grounds that in his early thought he favoured the autonomy of philosophy whereas his later thought gives a clear-cut priority to history. They do not understand, in other words, how philosophy and history can be identical and yet distinct. But *Speculum Mentis* explains how in 1933 Collingwood could reconcile the identity of philosophy and history with the autonomy of philosophy and in 1939 employ the very same identity as a basis for elucidating the historicity of philosophy. Using *Speculum Mentis* as a guide, then, it is possible to show that there is no essential inconsistency between *An Essay on Metaphysics* and *An Essay on Philosophical Method*.

7 THE AIM AND PLAN OF THIS BOOK

The precise aim of this book may now be stated. It is not my purpose to concentrate on a critical appraisal of Collingwood's thought, either in whole or in detail, by showing whether and to what extent his thought satisfies the criteria laid down by the other dominant philosophical trends of our time. There will be little *ab extra* criticism of this kind. My aim is rather to examine *ab intra* the various stages through which Collingwood's thought developed in his attempts to establish a rapprochement between philosophy and history, to show how in terms of this rapprochement his philosophy may be exhibited as a system, and finally, to evaluate the extent to which his thought contributes to an elucidation of the problems with which he was concerned centrally, and which are still problems for us today. Since to consider all of Collingwood's writings in this way would be too ambitious for a project of this kind I shall limit myself primarily to the relations which exist among *Speculum Mentis, An Essay on Philosophical Method, An Essay on Metaphysics*, the *Autobiography*, and the *Idea of History*, as well as a series of papers published between 1920 and 1930. References will, of course, be made to other works, but only for the purpose of elaborating and illuminating themes which have been suggested by the first group of works. This means excluding from consideration many of the problems to which Collingwood devoted a great deal of attention: his theory of imagination, his critique of psychology, his theory of language, his philosophy of religion, and his own positive synthesis of psychology and political science in the *New Leviathan*.[44] But, I would contend, no real understanding of these problems is possible except on the basis of a prior insight into the relation between philosophy and history and its effect on the "reform of metaphysics" which is the main concern of this book.

Accordingly, in chapter II, I shall examine the relation between philosophy and history as it first appeared in *Religion and Philosophy* and other writings prior to the publication of *Speculum Mentis*. The attempt at rapprochement is here described in terms of what I shall call 'the univocal theory of the relation of the sciences.' Chapter III is devoted to an exposition of the doctrine of the role of philosophy in *Speculum Mentis*. The latter is interpreted as an attempt to render explicit the implicit presuppositions of *Religion and Philosophy*, thereby correcting the 'philosophical errors' upon which the earlier work is founded. The identity of philosophy and history which is achieved in *Speculum Mentis* is described as a 'dialectical' one – the basis of which, as we have already noted, is the dual nature of philosophy itself as a series of historical dogmatisms or metaphysics on the one hand, and as transhistorical or transcendental philosophy on the other. The latter is of course immanent in the former. Dogmatic metaphysics, as I have already indicated, is described as existing on three distinct but related levels, corresponding to a tripartite distinction within experience itself. Chapter IV concentrates on the dialectic of experience before it has been systematized by thought, while chapter V is concerned with the scale of dogmatic philosophies which arise after experience has been systematized by thought, and which constitute, therefore, the reflective moments of experience. In both chapters the doctrines of *Speculum Mentis* are related to various other writings which appeared both before and after the publication of *Speculum Mentis* but which exemplify the doctrines which the latter expounds.

In chapter VI the presuppositions of the metaphysics of the particular sciences, as laid down from the absolute standpoint, are examined under the following heads: (a) the theory of the concrete universal, (b) the logic of the overlap of classes, and (c) the doctrine of dialectical necessity. In so far as philosophy proceeds according to these presuppositions Collingwood describes it as "categorical thinking." Categorical thinking is of two kinds, categorical universal and categorical singular. The latter is the instrument of history, the former of philosophy. Chapter VII is devoted to an exposition of the theory of philosophy as categorical universal judgment. An attempt is made here to defend Collingwood against certain realist views put forward originally by Gilbert Ryle and repeated more recently by Alan Donagan concerning the very possibility of categorical universal judgments. The controversy between Collingwoodian and realist logic is examined with reference to an unpublished correspondence between Collingwood and Ryle which took place in the spring of 1935.[45] The argument is advanced that, in spite of prima facie evidence to the contrary, there is no incompatibility between the categorical universal and the categorical singular judgment, and that a proper understanding of either would require recognizing that the two forms of judgment are not two species of a genus but are overlapping forms on a scale: in other words, the two forms of judgment constitute an 'identity in difference.' *An Essay on Philosophical Method* is represented as exploring one aspect of this identity; *An Essay on Metaphysics* is represented as exploring another aspect.

Chapter VIII applies the conclusions of chapter VII to the interpretation of *An Essay on Metaphysics*, in which Collingwood outlines his reform of metaphysics. It is argued that the prima facie historicism of this work is the result not of a radical change in outlook but rather of other more practical causes. In 1936, for example, A. J. Ayer published *Language, Truth and Logic*. By 1939 the influence of this book on British philosophy had become considerable and Collingwood interpreted this as a sign of crisis. *An Essay on Metaphysics* was Collingwood's response to this crisis. On previous occasions, however, whenever he had entered into philosophical dispute with his colleagues, Collingwood felt that he had been consistently misunderstood. This time, chiefly because of the urgency of the situation, he did not intend to run this risk. He therefore attempted to express the doctrines which lay at the basis of his earlier writings in a language which he thought would be more acceptable to his audience. In particular, he hoped to rescue these doctrines from positivist criticism by showing that the latter simply did not apply. Whether or not this attempt was successful is a matter for dispute. In my opinion it was a failure because Collingwood succeeded, not in stemming the tide of positivism, but in contributing to a misunderstanding of his own views.

It will therefore be denied that Collingwood's intention in *An Essay on Metaphysics* was to compress philosophy into history. It will also be denied that the *Essay* was the logical consequence of certain sceptical tendencies which lie deep in the early history of Collingwood's thought. I will argue to the contrary that Collingwood's real aim in this work was to expound anew the rapprochement already implicit in *Speculum Mentis* and that, mainly as a result of his effort to meet positivism on its own terms, he found himself in the absurd position of trying to defend his philosophy from a standpoint which he had already explicitly and emphatically repudiated. But once the reform of metaphysics is properly understood the conception of metaphysics as an historical science can be shown to rest on the very duality of philosophy as categorical-universal–categorical-singular judgment which underlies the central arguments of *Speculum Mentis* and *An Essay on Philosophical Method*.

One of the features of categorical thinking as outlined in chapter VIII is that it is a form of self-knowledge. Chapter IX is therefore devoted to an exposition of the first moment of categorical thinking, history conceived as a form of self-knowledge. The emphasis in this chapter is on the *Idea of History*. After relating this work to the plan of *Speculum Mentis* and characterizing it as an example of contemporary or systematic metaphysics operating at the third ontological level, the idea of history as self-knowledge is examined in the light of the historicity of human nature.

The argument is brought to a conclusion in Chapter X with an examination of the relation between historicity and absolute philosophy. Attention is now given to the idea of philosophy as self-knowledge; and the rapprochement between philosophy as self-knowledge and history as self-knowledge is finally explained in terms of the theory of mind as "pure act," a theory which Collingwood borrowed from Gentile. It will be my claim that the latter is not only the unifying theme of *Speculum Mentis*, but the foundation of Collingwood's entire philosophical system and that failure to recognize this has resulted in an inability to perceive Collingwood's thought as a systematic unity in which every moment has been systematically anticipated from the very beginning.

II

The Relation between
PHILOSOPHY AND HISTORY
in Collingwood's Early Writings:
1916-1922

Collingwood's views concerning the relation between philosophy and history were first presented in *Religion and Philosophy* (1916). In this book Collingwood argued that "History and philosophy are ... the same thing" (RP, 51). By this he meant (a) that history and philosophy depend upon each other and (b) that they are simultaneous activities, that is, that all attempts to distinguish them in terms either of their objects or of their activities are invalid. "We seem therefore," writes Collingwood, "to have here a distinction within the region of the intellect parallel to that of intellect and will in the mind as a whole" (RP, 46).

I THE INTERDEPENDENCE OF PHILOSOPHY
  AND HISTORY

Collingwood rightly points out that history cannot exist without philosophy – in the sense that it cannot proceed without philosophical presuppositions of a highly complex character. In the first place it deals with evidence and therefore makes epistemological assumptions concerning the status of evidence. In the second place, it describes the behaviour of historical agents in terms whose meaning is fixed by ethical thought. And finally, it has continually to determine what events are possible, and this can only be done "in virtue of some general metaphysical conclusions" (RP, 47).

Philosophy is also said to presuppose history. Collingwood's chief reason for making this claim is that any theory must be a theory of the facts, and all facts are historical. This may be interpreted to mean either that, since the facts of history are the product of historical development, philosophy is therefore the necessary product of its own past, or that philosophy must wait for the facts of history to present themselves before it can interpret them (RP, 47–8). On the first interpretation philosophy is historicized; Collingwood describes it as "historical positivism" (RP, 38). On the second it is given a purely empirical basis; Collingwood calls this "empiricism" (RP, 48). But Collingwood denies that either of these interpretations can explain what is meant by the necessity of history to philosophy. Against the first view he argues that "philosophy is a human activity not a mechanical process; and is therefore free and not in any sense necessitated either by its own past or anything else" (RP, 47). Against the second view he argues, rather dogmatically, that the very idea of a theory based solely on the accumulation of the facts is an error (RP, 49):

> For it is incorrect to say that philosophy is theory *based upon* fact; theory is not something else derived, distilled, from facts but simply the observation that the facts are what they are. And similarly the philosophical presuppositions of history are not something different from the history itself: they are philosophical truths which the historian finds historically exemplified. (RP, 51)

Collingwood concludes, therefore, that history *a parte objecti* must be regarded neither as a mechanical process, nor as a gradual accumulation of facts, but simply as "objectivity" – as the "real fact of which we are conscious." History is that which actually exists: fact, as something independent of my own (or your) knowledge of it. In this sense there can be no philosophy without it, for "no form of consciousness can exist without an object" (RP, 49). Philosophy presupposes history, then, in the sense in which any form of knowledge presupposes an object. The "facticity" of the object of philosophy, which is the ground of the latter's historicity, is of a primarily metaphysical nature; it has to do with the very nature of reality per se rather than with the mere contingencies of experience.

Collingwood's analysis of the so-called false interpretations of the thesis that philosophy presupposes history, while interesting, is actually incomplete. There is no explicit reference to what I have previously called radical historicism, the thesis that philosophical theorizing not only has a history (which is one way of historicizing philosophy), but also is itself a fact about which we cannot raise further transhistorical questions. But this is clearly the most radical and hence most serious form of historicism, and the one which Collingwood, in order to defend the thesis of *Religion and Philosophy*, would be the most concerned to repudiate.

Of course one might argue that the very fact that he does not explicitly repudiate it suggests that he may after all have subscribed to it himself. But this suggestion is ruled out by the fact that it is simply inconsistent with the main thesis of *Religion and Philosophy*, which, if I understand it correctly, rather than affirming radical historicism, necessarily denies it. Such a denial is at least implicit in Collingwood's criticism (in the course of a discussion concerning the status of historical knowledge in general) of what he calls "anti-historical scepticism" (RP, 44-5) – the view that for methodological reasons the conclusions of history are too uncertain to be taken seriously and called knowledge. It is true that this conclusion follows from a variety of arguments which are concerned primarily with methodology and the reliability of evidence: arguments which are independent of the conclusions of radical historicism which have to do with the ontological conditions of truth and historicity. The fact is, however, that if Collingwood is not prepared to accept, as a conclusion about the status of historical knowledge in general, what he calls anti-historical scepticism, then he is certainly not likely to accept the implications of radical historicism (that for ontological reasons, neither the conclusions of history nor philosophy can be judged by transhistorical or objective standards, and must therefore be denied the status of knowledge). Collingwood's ontology, as I hope to demonstrate throughout, recognizes the historicity of being and truth but does not deny the possibility of a transhistorical or transcendental standpoint from which to comprehend the historicity of truth.

A refutation of radical historicism is also implicit in Collingwood's discussion of what he calls pure "immanent pantheism," the doctrine according to which man and God are absolutely identical (RP, 149 ff.). Such a view presupposes the same abstract identity between reality and its appearances as does radical historicism. Thus Collingwood's rejection of immanent pantheism is also an implicit rejection of the identification of being and time, or truth and historicity, which characterizes radical historicism. Finally, a repudiation of radical historicism seems implicit in his description of history as that which actually exists, as fact independent of my own or your knowledge of it (RP, 49).

The same argument concerning the interdependence of philosophy and history was again put forward a few years later in "Croce's Philosophy of History" (1921), the purpose of which was to review critically Croce's recently published *Teoria e storia della storiografia* (1917). One of the views which Collingwood attributes here to Croce resembles closely the position which he expounds himself in *Religion and Philosophy*. Indeed it is quite clear that in discussing Croce's views Collingwood is doing more than simply describing them; he is defending them as well. Concerning the relationship between philosophy and history he writes, following Croce: "Each without the other is a lifeless corpse: every piece of real thinking is both at once" (CPH, 276). And his description of the basis from which Croce proceeds could apply with equal force to the argument of *Religion and Philosophy*:

> History without philosophy is history seen from the outside, the play of mechanical and unchanging forces in a materialistically conceived world; philosophy without history is philosophy seen from the outside, the veering and backing, rising and falling of motiveless winds of doctrine ... But history fertilized by philosophy is history of the human spirit in its secular attempt to build itself a world of laws and institutions in which it can live as it wishes to live; and philosophy fertilized by history is the progressive raising and solving of the endless intellectual problems whose succession forms the inner life side of this secular struggle. Thus the two studies which, apart, degenerate into strings of empty dates and lists of pedantic distinctions ... become, to-gether, a single science of all things human. (CPH, 264)

2 THE SIMULTANEITY OF PHILOSOPHY AND HISTORY

The argument for the interdependence of philosophy and history does not, of course, demonstrate that they are therefore "the same thing," in the sense of being simultaneous. Granted that they are interdependent, what more can Collingwood say to show that they are identical? By calling them identical he apparently means no more than that they are equally valid forms of knowledge, in which case the relation between them may be described as 'univocal.' The criterion on the basis of which Collingwood establishes the identity of philosophy and history is that they cannot be distinguished either in terms of their objects or in terms of their activities.

To begin with, Collingwood argues, it is customary in some quarters to treat the object of philosophy as the universal, the necessary, and the eternal, while the object of history is defined as the contingent and the temporal. But every truth is temporal and every fact independent of time. The difference between a timeless truth and a temporal event is the difference between two aspects of the same thing. Thus both history and philosophy have as their object the same thing: the one real world, the totality of existence. And this is the historical fact. History *a parte objecti*, the reality which historical research seeks to know, is nothing else than the totality of existence; and this is the object of philosophy as well.

Neither can philosophy and history be distinguished epistemologically in terms of their activities. Collingwood's reason for this, however, amounts to no more than a repetition of the conclusion of the first argument; history and philosophy are the same activities because they have the same object: "History *a parte subjecti* – the activity of the historian – is the investigation of all that has happened and is happening, and this is philosophy too" (RP, 51).

It is clear, then, that Collingwood has used only one criterion – the criterion of being about the same object – as a basis of establishing the identity of philosophy and history. And if we allow him this criterion it follows that the distinction between philosophy and history is purely abstract, *a distinctio rationis*. Objectively, there is only one object, the concrete historical fact, which, looked at from one point of view reveals historical facts, and looked at from another reveals philosophical principles. Subjectively, there is only one judgment which, abstracted one way, leads to the historical point of view and, abstracted another way, leads to the philosophical.

It is interesting to note that the same criterion is used throughout *Religion and Philosophy* in order to establish other rapprochements. Concerning the relation between religion and philosophy, for example, Collingwood writes:

If religion and philosophy are views of the same thing – the ultimate nature of the universe – then the true religion and the true philosophy must coincide, though they may differ in the vocabulary which they use to express the same facts [RP, 18] ... Since religion, on its intellectual side, is a theory of the world as a whole, it is the same thing as philosophy; the ultimate questions of philosophy are those of religion too. (RP, 19)

Finally, it is made the basis of a doctrine of intersubjectivity, the doctrine that all minds are united in one mind (RP, 104 ff.).

Collingwood's discussion of the metaphysics of intersubjectivity is especially helpful for an understanding of the doctrine of concrete identity in difference. Intersubjectivity is established in *Religion and Philosophy* according to the criterion that if two minds are identical with the same object then they are identical with each other: "Union consists of the fact that both are dealing with the same problems; for in so far as any two minds are conscious of the same reality, they are the same mind" (RP, 161). In any act of knowing there must always be a concrete identity between my mind and its object in the sense that my thought about the object is not something "like" the object but "is" the object *as I know it*. Since the *esse* of mind is not *cogitare* simply, but *de hac re cogitare* (RP, 100), mind is therefore identical with its thoughts and, to the extent to which these thoughts are therefore identical with their objects, the identity between mind and object is established. This is the basis from which Collingwood eventually developed his famous doctrine of history as the "re-enactment of past thought" (IH, 282 ff.; A, 111), and it must therefore be taken into account if we are to understand fully what Collingwood means by such statements as, "the historian of a certain thought must think for himself that very same thought, not another like it" (A, 111; cf., IH, 283–302). Collingwood writes, in *Religion and Philosophy*:

> My thought of the table is certainly not something "like" the table; it is the table as I know it. Similarly, your thought of the table is what you know of the table as known to you; and if we both have real knowledge of the table, it seems to follow that our thoughts are the same, not merely similar; and further, if the mind is its thoughts, we seem to have, for this moment at least, actually one mind; we share between us that unity of consciousness which was earlier [RP, 99] said to be the mark of the individual. (RP, 101)

This doctrine of intersubjectivity tends partly to explain why Collingwood believed that the historical study of the past was one way of overcoming the fragmentation of modern life and establishing a genuine community of spirit.

Intersubjectivity is achieved not only through knowledge of the same objects but also through the intentional act of willing the same ends (RP, 104, 105). In this case what constitutes intersubjectivity is not just that each wills the same thing, but that each does so in a state of perfect freedom, as a matter of choice. But this very freedom to will, which is the source of unity, is also the source of disunity; for, just as the mind is free to maintain the harmony of unity so the same mind is free to dissolve the relationships through its own self-betrayal (RP, 105). The risk of disunity, which perpetually threatens whatever unity has been achieved, and which creates, therefore, an immanent and inescapable tension, is the ground of difference on the side of the subject. Indeed, the fact that unity is accomplished not as a fixed and unchangeable state of affairs but only through the continuous exercise of free will is what saves the intersubjectivity of minds from being a mere abstract self-identity.

There is also, according to Collingwood, a source of differentiation on the side of the object – although this too turns out to have its ultimate ground in the conditions of subjectivity. What stands out about the object of mind *qua* mind is the fact that it is never merely abstract and undifferentiated, a pure uninterpreted datum. If there were such objects then the relation between any two minds knowing them would be a blank unity without difference. But, Collingwood declares:

> Any truth or ideal of conduct expresses itself under infinitely various aspects. A single truth never means quite the same thing to different minds; each person invests it with an emphasis, an application, peculiar to himself. This does not

mean that it is not the same truth; the difference does not destroy the identity any more than identity destroys difference. It is only in the identity that the difference arises. (RP, 106)

In this statement Collingwood combines the epistemological doctrine that all knowledge is mediation with the metaphysical doctrine of the concrete universal. The latter is particularly evident in Collingwood's claim that the object of any particular mind is only one moment of a totality which includes the contributions of other minds. Indeed, the object's very existence as an object for me depends upon the existence of all the other moments. Thus Collingwood declares: "I desire the existence of a whole to which I can only contribute one among many parts. The other parts must be contributed by other people; and therefore in willing my part I will theirs also." (RP, 106)

There is finally, in this discussion of intersubjectivity, a clear anticipation of the later doctrine, found in *Speculum Mentis*, that truth, the perfect state of freedom, the concrete identity, must be achieved by means of a progressive development through a scale of errors. Collingwood writes in *Religion and Philosophy* that unity or concrete identification is not the starting point but the goal of human endeavour. But in achieving this goal the mind advances "like the spiral tunnel of an Alpine railway; it ends, if not where it began, at least immediately above it. The end is not the antithesis of the beginning, but the same thing raised to a higher power" (RP, 107; cf. OPA, 94–5; SM, 317, 293).

Again it must be emphasized that this identification of philosophy and history should not be confused with radical historicism which achieves this identity by assimilating philosophy to history. I have already pointed to several places in *Religion and Philosophy* in which there is at least an implicit refutation of radical historicism. To these may be added a more explicit refutation from "Croce's Philosophy of History" (1921). It is true that most of this essay consists of a defence of Croce's doctrine of the interdependence of philosophy and history. It concludes, however, with a sharp criticism of another view which, according to Collingwood, Croce also held alongside the first – the view that philosophy is a mere subordinate part of history. Collingwood interprets this as meaning that historical thought is the concrete synthesis of "philology," the pure study of fact, and philosophy, the pure interpretation of facts. Neither philosophy nor philology can stand alone; both must be combined and hence converted into the more perfect form of history:

Croce here shows, if I read his meaning aright, that he is gradually deserting philosophy for history. He appears to have come to the conclusion that philosophical truth is to be attained not by direct fire – by the study of philosophy in the ordinary sense, which he now pronounces a delusion – but indirectly, as a product of ordinary historical work. Philosophy in his mind is being absorbed into history; the two are not poised in equilibrium, as with Gentile, but the one is cancelled out as already provided for by the other. (CPH, 277)

Exemplary of this view is Croce's statement in the appendix to *Teoria e storia della storiografia* that philosophy is nothing "but the *methodological moment of historiography*: an explication of the categories constitutive of historical judgments, or of the concepts that direct historical interpretation."[1] And this, according to Croce, is an immanent methodology which goes on within the process of history itself. Thus Croce, the historicist, interprets the relation between philosophy and history in the same way that positivism interprets the relation between philosophy and natural science.

As represented by Collingwood, Croce appears to be putting forward the following argument: philosophy is the methodology of history, therefore philosophy is an inferior form of thought requiring history to complete it. It is not at all clear, however, that the second claim, concerning the inferiority of philosophy, logically follows from the first claim, that philosophy is methodology. Indeed, Collingwood himself does not seem to recognize that these are in fact two separate claims requiring some further argument to justify deriving the latter from the former. For to say simply that philosophy is the methodological moment of history does not yet absorb philosophy into history. There is no reason why philosophy cannot be the methodological moment of history and still be autonomous and transhistorical. In other words, a more complete reconstruction of Croce's argument must point out that the absorption of philosophy into history means something more than that philosophy is the methodology of history; it must mean, for example, that methodological thinking is itself an historical fact about which no further transhistorical statements can be made. Only then can Croce be accused justly of deserting philosophy for history.

Collingwood's chief complaint against Croce's historicism is the charge that, ironically enough, the assimilation of philosophy to history marks a victory of the very naturalism which Croce was trying to avoid over the idealism he was trying to profess:

The naturalist triumphs over the idealist because the synthesis of philosophy and philology in history implies the naturalistic conception of philosophy and philology as two different and antithetical forms of activity, which again implies that ideas or categories, or whatever is the subject-matter of philosophy, are something different from facts, the subject-matter of philology. Such a dualism of idea and fact is wholly impossible to an idealist; and yet only on this assumption can it be maintained that philosophy is immanent in history while history is transcendent with reference to philosophy. (CPH, 277)

Thus Collingwood is here refuting Croce's historicism by means of the same arguments with which he refuted the alleged separation of philosophy and history in *Religion and Philosophy*; he denies that history and philosophy can be distinguished either in terms of their activities or in terms of their objects. Collingwood is claiming, in other words, that both historicism, which asserts a false identity between philosophy and history, and naturalism, which asserts a false separation between them, are guilty of the same error — the error of treating observation and interpretation (*verstehen*) as co-ordinate species of explanation (*erklären*). In *An Essay on Philosophical Method* Collingwood describes this error as the fallacy of false disjunction (EPM, 49).

3 THE RELATION BETWEEN HISTORY AND SCIENCE

As an indication of Collingwood's drive towards system, even as early as the period of *Religion and Philosophy*, it is interesting to note that he was able at this time to employ the very arguments by which he had attempted to relate history and philosophy to the solution of other problems. Thus, for example, in 1922, in an article entitled "Are History and Science Different Forms of Knowledge?"[2] Collingwood employs the same criterion of being about the same object as a basis for denying the distinction between history and science. There is no such thing, he argues, as a distinction "between two kinds of entity, a *particular* and a *universal*, such that any cognition may be knowledge of the one in isolation from the other" (HS, 444). In the first place, any attempt to distinguish history and science in terms of their activities is illusory. But any attempt to distinguish them in terms of their objects is also illusory. Collingwood therefore argues that to employ this contrast between generalization and particularization as a basis for distinguishing between science and history is incorrect. Science, he argues, is not merely concerned with generalizations but with the interpretation of data in terms of generalizations — that is to say, with the interpretation of individual facts by means of general concepts. Interpretation, however, is not

the employment of a previously-constructed tool (concept) upon a separately-given material (fact) : neither the concept nor the fact is 'possessed' (*thought* and *observed* respectively) except in the presence of the other. To possess or think a concept is to interpret a fact in terms of it: to possess or observe a fact is to interpret it in terms of a concept. (HS, 447)

In other words, it is Collingwood's contention that the scientist apprehends not simply the universal but the particular concrete fact as well, and the abstract distinction between the universal and the particular is repudiated. The real work of science is the interpretation of the individual fact – precisely the same task as that of history (HS, 449). Thus the rapprochement between history and science, like the rapprochement between history and philosophy, is founded on the philosophical principle of the identity of objects.

Collingwood's position here may be further illustrated by his discussion of what he regarded as "the fallacy of inductive logic." The inductive logician, according to Collingwood, assumes that the task of science is to generalize, to frame universal laws, and that its starting point is the facts of ordinary observation. The question for inductive logic then is, How do we infer universal laws from the particular facts? The logician answers this question by describing the process in detail, but when he has done so one cannot help seeing that the alleged particular from which he started was never a pure particular but was already steeped in universality. The process ought to have begun with the pure uninterpreted sense datum. It never does, however, for two very good reasons. First, such a pure sense datum does not exist except as an abstraction, and cannot therefore be the concrete starting point of a process; and secondly, even if one did exist we could never get beyond it to reach the universal. The inductive logician, therefore, in order to bridge the gap between the particular and the universal, begins with "the carefully staged" or controlled "experiment" which pretends to consist of "intelligently recorded observations" which are already "bristling with conceptual interpretations." But the inductivist, ignoring the fact that his very starting point presupposes and contains a conceptual framework, proceeds to "reduce" (or induce) the concept he has surreptitiously presupposed, thus committing the fallacy of *petitio principii* (HS, 448).

Collingwood therefore declares that the aim of the scientist is not simply to derive universals from particulars but to comprehend more fully the concrete individual: "to interpret intuitions by concepts or to realize concepts in intuitions" (HS, 448). And this means that, so far as the relation between science and history is concerned, "the analysis of science in epistemological terms is thus identical with the analysis of history, and the distinction between them as separate kinds of knowledge is an illusion" (HS, 450).

This argument against the so-called fallacy of inductive logic seems to rest, however, on a fundamental confusion between two levels of universality, thus conflating separate problems. Collingwood begins by questioning the alleged inference from particulars to universal laws.

Instead of questioning this on purely logical grounds, however, he points out that in fact one cannot even perceive a particular without the mediation of universal concepts. But this is a fact about perception rather than about the logic of induction – the claim of inductive logic is not that from particulars we derive concepts but that from particular instances we derive universal laws.

Hence to emphasize the role of mediation in perception does not necessarily invalidate the claims of inductive logic. Collingwood's failure to separate these distinguishable problems tends in fact to weaken the force of his argument. But, once it is recognized that his real interest is not the logical problem of induction but the epistemological relation between various acts of knowing (which is a problem of perception) the force of his argument begins to be felt. The question he is really asking is whether the distinction between science and history rests upon the distinction between perception of universals and perception of particulars. Collingwood's answer is that it does not. All perception contains elements of mediation, and a careful analysis of what is really involved in perception would demonstrate this overlap. If there is a fallacy, then, it is a fallacy of perception, not induction; and it is surely, and almost exclusively, on the basis of this analysis of perception that Collingwood is able to draw the conclusion, already cited, that "The analysis of science in epistemological terms is thus identical with the analysis of history and the distinction between them as separate kinds of knowledge is an illusion" (HS, 450).

4 COLLINGWOOD'S CLASSIFICATION OF THE SCIENCES

Collingwood was intent from the very outset of his philosophical career upon establishing a new basis for the classification of the sciences or forms of life which would demonstrate, against popular conceptions, that all distinctions among ways of knowing are illusory and abstract. Of central importance both in his early and later writings is a rejection of the mythology of dualism – the claim that there are two separate worlds, the one unchanging and self-identical, known only to philosophy and science, and the other subject to change and development, known only to history. This bifurcation of reality leads, in Collingwood's opinion, to serious difficulties, particularly when applied to human nature. Ultimately it leads either to radical scepticism or to rigid dogmatism. Scepticism arises not only from failure to bridge the gap between appearance and reality, permanence and change, but also from the tendency to bridge this gap by postulating change as the only reality. Dogmatism is a consequence of denying altogether the reality of change and postulating the world of permanent and unchanging truths as the only reality. Collingwood was therefore dedicated to the abolition of all such false distinctions.

This does not mean, of course, that he recognized no differences at all. On the contrary, it was clear to him from the very beginning that the problem of the unity of science could not be solved by postulating some kind of Parmenidean self-identity. A world of "mere self-identity," he writes in *Religion and Philosophy*, "would be as inconceivable as a world of mere change" (RP, 51). Indeed, Collingwood clearly recognized that all abstract distinctions have a tendency to turn into their logical opposites. The very notions of abstract separation and abstract identity are internally related by an inescapable dialectic which continually reduces the one to the other. He therefore postulated, as the metaphysical basis of his new classification of the sciences, a synthesis of permanence and change in which reality was defined, after the fashion of Bradley, as the totality of its appearances. In short, according to Collingwood, the doctrine of the unity of science can only be derived from the metaphysical doctrine of the identity of unity in difference.

In *Religion and Philosophy* the concept of identity in difference is presented as a concrete activity which necessarily presents itself under the aspect of innumerable differences, and which through a process intrinsic to its very nature overcomes these differences without totally abolishing them (RP, 115 ff., 148 ff.). Some years later, in *Speculum Mentis*, this concept of identity is further explicated in terms of dialectical logic, and subsequently applied to the organization of the various sciences and forms of life into a concrete system. Underlying the programme of *Speculum Mentis* is the metaphysical conviction that each of the disciplines or sciences expresses the essential structure of a specific category or "habit" of mind. Thus, for example, what we call "art" is a controlled expression of the "Imagination," the "habit" of endowing the world with properties, while what we call "religion" is made possible by "Faith," the mind's natural tendency to accept the products of its own imagination as truths to be believed. But while each of the specific categories or habits are distinct they are far from being separate. Each interacts and overlaps with the rest. Taken together they form what Collingwood calls, in *An Essay on Philosophical Method*, a "scale of overlapping forms." The relations between the forms are "dialectical," that is to say, the overlap follows a natural or "serial" order from imagination to reason, in the sense that reason not only complements and completes but arises out of imagination.

The categorial scale of forms thus forms a basis for the unity of the disciplines which are derived from the categories. The various sciences are now seen to constitute a scale of overlapping forms rather than either a series of mutually exclusive classes, conceived as co-ordinate species of a common genus, or a system of distinct but equivalent sciences, each treating different aspects of the same subject matter, or different attributes of the one substance. By contrast with the species of a genus the forms on a scale are organized in such a way that each successive form penetrates more *deeply* than the last into the essence of its subject matter, thus expressing the nature of the one substance more *adequately* (EPM, 189). Hence just as there is no act of mind which is not as much an expression of "Imagination" and "Faith" as it is an exercise of "Reason," so there is no purely scientific or philosophical judgment which is not also historical and aesthetic, no purely particular judgment which is not also universal, and so on. And just as "Reason" is a more adequate source of truth than "Imagination" or "Faith" so the disciplines derived from Reason (namely, history, science, and philosophy, in that order) are more adequate embodiments of truth than are the disciplines derived from both Faith (religion) and Imagination (art). This ontological conception of reality as a dialectical scale of distinct but not separate forms – which is virtually a restatement of the idealist doctrine of the "concrete universal" – is the ultimate basis of Collingwood's philosophy of rapprochement.

Beginning, then, with *Speculum Mentis*, the act of knowing is conceived as a "concrete universal" expressing itself through a variety of distinct but dialectically related forms. Accordingly, the task of philosophy is defined as the systematic attempt to locate and expound the presuppositions which define the various forms of thought, with the two-fold purpose of vindicating the autonomy of the separate standpoints, on the one hand, and of exposing their interconnections and concrete identity, on the other.

5 IDEALISM AND THE DOCTRINE OF UNIVERSAL JUDGMENT

Collingwood's views concerning the relation between philosophy and history were strongly influenced by the idealist doctrine of judgment, as held by Bradley and Croce. Collingwood credits Bradley with stating for the first time "the identity of the universal and individual judgment, which, as Croce was to explain twenty years later, is the definition of historical knowledge" (IH, 140).[8] Croce's influence on Collingwood becomes especially apparent when we begin to take notice of the similarity between Collingwood's early views and the doctrines which in various places he attributed to Croce. In particular the thesis of *Religion and Philosophy* concerning the mutual interdependence of philosophy and history seems identical to the one which Collingwood, in *The Idea of History*, describes as "Croce's doctrine of the mutual implication of the universal or definitive judgement and the individual or historical judgement" (IH, 196), which, according to Collingwood, is Croce's solution to the problem of how philosophy is related to history.

Collingwood's reconstruction of Croce's thought is set forth mainly in *The Idea of History* and in a pamphlet of 1930 entitled "The Philosophy of History." As represented by Collingwood, Croce's main contribution is seen to lie in his criticism of the traditional doctrine that all judgments may be divided into universal and particular (corresponding to a priori and a posteriori) cognitions, as though they were mutually exclusive. Croce argues, and Collingwood would seem to concur, that such a division is false. Matters of fact cannot be absolutely distinguished from matters of reason. Necessary or eternal truths and contingent or individual truths are not two separate kinds of cognition but inseparable elements in every cognition. In short, a universal is a genuine truth only in so far as it is realized in a particular instance; it must be incarnate in the individual.

Collingwood illustrates Croce's thesis with the following example. Take any judgment which appears to be purely universal, such as J. S. Mill's definition of a right act as one which produces the greatest happiness for the greatest number. At first this looks purely universal and non-historical. But if we examine it we will find that it contains an historical element. This is because the definition has been framed by an individual historical thinker to meet a problem which has arisen in a particular way. In other words, what Mill was doing when he formulated this definition was to describe what *we* mean when *we* call an action "right," the *we* being nineteenth-century Englishmen with the moral and political ideas of their time (IH, 195; PH, 12–13).

At the same time, according to Collingwood, the individual or historical judgment is no mere intuition of a given fact, it is a judgment with a predicate or concept. This concept is present as a universal idea in the mind of the person who makes the judgment; so that if he understands his own thought, he must be able to give a definition of it. Thus, there is really only one kind of judgment, which is both universal and individual: individual in so far as it describes an individual state of affairs, and universal in so far as it describes it by thinking it under universal concepts.

Take for example the following historical judgment: "It must not be forgotten that monarchs such as Louis XI and Ferdinand, notwithstanding their crimes, completed the national work of making France and Spain two great and powerful nations" (IH, 195). This judgment presupposes that both the writer and the reader understand such terms as "crime," "nation," "powerful," etc., in the same way. In other words, the writer and reader possess in common a certain set of political ideas, and the statement assumes that these ideas are coherent and logically defensible – that is, they presuppose an ethical and political philosophy. Again, when we say "Alexander VI was unscrupulous" (PH, 13), there is a whole system of moral philosophy contained in "unscrupulous." It is through such ethical and political philosophies, Collingwood declares, that we grasp the historical reality of Louis XI and Alexander VI, and conversely it is only because we find the concepts of these philosophies realized in Louis and Alexander – the historical facts, as it were – that we can even grasp what these concepts are.

This is precisely the thought contained in Collingwood's remark in *Religion and Philosophy*, cited above, that "the philosophical presuppositions of history are not something different from history itself: they are philosophical truths which the historian finds historically exemplified" (RP, 51). The latter extends further the principle (also cited above) from "Are History and Science Different Forms of Knowledge?" that concepts can be apprehended only through the interpretation of facts, while facts can be interpreted only through the mediation of concepts (HP, 447). Collingwood is obviously trying to explain that the true universal is no mere abstraction but exists only in the shape of its concrete universality; that is to say, as an historical individual. Thus his concluding remarks in *The Idea of History* concerning the implications of the Crocian doctrine of judgment for history could just as well have been written about his own rapprochement between philosophy and history, as developed in the period of *Religion and Philosophy*:

> Instead of trying to place philosophy and history outside one another in two mutually exclusive spheres, and thus making an adequate theory of history impossible, he brings them to-gether into a single whole, a judgement whose subject is the individual while its predicate is the universal. History is no longer conceived as mere intuition of the individual; it does not simply apprehend the individual, in which case it would be art; it judges the individual; and hence the universality, the *a priori* character, which belongs undefeasibly to all thought, is present in history in the form of the predicate of the historical judgement. What makes the historian a thinker is the fact that he thinks out the meanings of these predicates, and finds these meanings embodied in the individuals he contemplates. But this thinking-out of the meaning of a concept is philosophy; hence philosophy is an integral part of historical thinking itself; the individual judgement of history is a judgement only because it contains in itself, as one of its elements, philosophical thinking. (IH, 196)

III

Speculum Mentis: Philosophy and the TRANSCENDENTAL STRUCTURE of Experience

1 TRANSITION FROM RELIGION AND PHILOSOPHY TO SPECULUM MENTIS

The conclusion of *Religion and Philosophy* concerning the relation between history, philosophy, and the other sciences, is that they are "the same thing." This identity is achieved according to what appears to be a single criterion, the criterion of their being about the same object, variously described as the one real world, the totality of existence, and the historical fact. By means of this same criterion Collingwood arrived at a theoretical basis for establishing the unity of the sciences. But this required treating the sciences as 'univocal' expressions of the single act of knowing.

In *Speculum Mentis* the identity of the sciences is reaffirmed but the criterion according to which it is established is reinterpreted to take more adequate account of specific differences. The result, as we have already noted, is that the more abstractly conceived system of univocal relations, which tends to characterize the standpoint of *Religion and Philosophy*, gives way to a dialectical system according to which the various sciences form a logical hierarchy or scale of overlapping forms. The latter reflects, in ways which have yet to be explained, the dialectical growth of consciousness itself.

The conception of different philosophical sciences as treating distinct aspects of the same subject-matter, or expressing distinct attributes of one substance, will be modified by conceiving them as terms in a scale, each penetrating more deeply than the last into the essence of its subject-matter and expressing the nature of the one substance more adequately. (EPM, 189)

According to this new theory, the sciences are still about the same objects but this time differences are not reduced merely to the fact that each takes an equally valid view of one aspect of the object. Collingwood repudiates this notion at the very outset of *Speculum Mentis*:

There is an obstacle which we must here remove from our path. This is the theory of art, religion and the rest as co-ordinate species of knowledge, species of a genus, each valid and autonomous in its own sphere but each limited to a single aspect of reality, each constituting a single aspect of mind. (SM, 46; cf. also, EPM, 35, 40)

At first sight this appears to be a repudiation of the very views which Collingwood had earlier defended in *Religion and Philosophy*. It must be pointed out, however, that there is in *Religion and Philosophy* an implicit contradiction between what is intended and what is in fact accomplished. It is clear, for example, that while Collingwood's intention was to establish a "concrete identity" among the various sciences, his actual achievements fell far short of this. The explicit achievements of *Religion and Philosophy* amounted, in fact, to a philosophical error, the error of falsely conceiving the forms of knowledge as species of a genus. But every error contains an implicit truth, and *Speculum Mentis* may be regarded as the attempt to explicate this truth which, in the case of *Religion and Philosophy*, is that the very act through which each form identifies itself with every other form is at the same time a source of differentiation. Or, to put it another way, the implicit truth of *Speculum Mentis* is that the generic essence rather than simply transcending the specific differences which are univocally related to it, is, on the contrary, identical with these differences which co-exist in a perpetual state of tension, so that the universal itself is also in a state of perpetual tension.

Thus *Speculum Mentis* is not simply a repudiation of *Religion and Philosophy*; it is also an attempt to supply the conceptual framework from which the explicit aims of *Religion and Philosophy* may be finally realized. In short, *Religion and Philosophy* is not simply negated but is rather superseded by *Speculum Mentis*. This interpretation may be supported by Collingwood's own remarks in *Speculum Mentis* concerning *Religion and Philosophy*. In *Religion and Philosophy*, he writes, the identity of the forms of experience is too "abstract" and does not account for the important "concrete" distinctions which exist between them. This error may be overcome, however, through the application of what Collingwood calls the principle of "the distinction between explicit and implicit" (SM, 85).

I contended throughout that religion, theology, and philosophy were identical, and this I should not so much withdraw as qualify by pointing out that the 'empirical' (i.e., real but unexplained) difference between them is that theology makes explicit what in religion as such is always implicit, and so with philosophy and theology. (SM, 108 fn. 1)

Collingwood explains what he means by the distinction between explicit and implicit in this manner. In every experience there are certain principles, distinctions, and so forth, of which the person whose experience it is is consciously aware; these are the "explicit features of the experience in question." Thus, for example, a moral agent *qua* moral agent is necessarily and explicitly aware of the distinction between right and wrong. On the other hand, an observer studying a certain form of experience often finds it impossible to give a rational account of it without stating certain principles and distinctions whether or not they are consciously made by the person whose experience he is studying. Thus, to cite an example for Collingwood, if you wish to describe the world view of primitive man you must first point out that to the primitive mind 'all things are full of gods' (the principle of polytheistic animism) and that for this reason the epistemological relation which best characterizes man's attitude to nature is not the relation of subject to object (I-it) but the relation of subject to subject (I-thou). Only by means of such principles can the experience of primitive man be rendered intelligible. Collingwood holds that such principles are "unconscious," by which he means only that they are *implicit in the experience in question* (SM, 85, 93). Translated into the language of his later philosophy this would seem to mean that the observer or historian of any given form of experience can give an account of this experience only in terms of the "absolute presuppositions" which are implicit in the experience in question.

How does this new distinction affect the theory of the classification of the sciences? To begin with, the standpoints, and hence the sciences, form a natural or serial order of their own. The order is such that each logically renders explicit what is implicit in the previous standpoint; that is, it resolves the contradiction between what the previous standpoint claims to be and what it really is. In so doing, however, a further error is committed and a new contradiction emerges which requires resolution at a higher level. This leads to the creation of a new standpoint. Since for Collingwood there can be no such thing as a pure or total error – the truth being to some degree present even in the most egregious error (EPM, 83) – the basis of this new standpoint is therefore implicit in the old standpoint which it supersedes. Thus religion renders explicit what is implicit in art, science what is implicit in religion, history what is implicit in science, and philosophy what is implicit in history (SM, 108).

Implicitly, then, all of the sciences are about the same object. In this sense they are identical. This identity, however, becomes explicit only through the logical and phenomenological development of consciousness in the course of which philosophy gradually emerges. Philosophy is therefore not just one among the variety of sciences but the ground of the unity of this variety.

This view of philosophy as the organon of the other standpoints is present as early as *Religion and Philosophy* where philosophy is presented as the basis through which the unity of Christianity may be restored. "Christianity," he writes, "is approached as a philosophy, and its various doctrines are regarded as varying aspects of a single idea which according to the language in which it is expressed, may be called a metaphysics, an ethic, or a theology" (RP, xiii). Thus any particular form of life, whether it be religion, or science, or art, or history, etc., which comes to reflect upon itself, will recognize itself as a necessary part of the life of philosophy (RPS, 2). Philosophy is the basis from which all diversity in knowledge both proceeds and returns; it is, to borrow for Collingwood a phrase of Aristotle, the act to which all other forms of knowledge are related *pros hen legomena* (i.e., as things directed towards a single end).[1]

One might even apply the distinction between implicit and explicit to the interpretation of Collingwood's own writings. Indeed, I have already argued that *Speculum Mentis* renders explicit what is implicit in *Religion and Philosophy*, in the same sense that philosophy, for example, renders explicit what is implicit in each of the other forms. The dialectical relation between *Religion and Philosophy* and *Speculum Mentis* may now be further explicated by seeing how the very definition of reality which is explicit in *Religion and Philosophy* would, if developed in terms of certain implicit assumptions concerning the nature of mind which Collingwood appears to accept, lead straight to the position of *Speculum Mentis*. In the former work, reality is defined as the object of all the sciences – in effect, as the whole forming a univocally related system of appearances. But what kind of reality can possibly satisfy this criterion of completeness, and how can such an object be characterized? I would suggest that it was in the attempt to answer this question that Collingwood advanced from the position of *Religion and Philosophy* to the position of *Speculum Mentis*.

Under the influence of Bradley and Hegel, Collingwood's thought would most likely have taken the following direction. Reality is not something other than appearance but is appearance itself. Appearances, however, can only constitute themselves within the experience of consciousness or mind. Thus the answer to the question, What is reality? presupposes an answer to the question, What is mind? Given a variety of assumptions about the nature of mind which, even in *Religion and Philosophy*, Collingwood appears to accept – that it is identical with its acts, that it makes itself through these acts; in effect, that it undergoes dialectical development – it follows that reality itself, and truth, must be subject to the same dialectic of self-making. Thus the appearances of mind (and consequently the sciences which are founded upon these appearances), rather than being univocally related, are, on the contrary, related according to a dialectical system, so that one form of knowledge grows out of another as a result of internal stresses and strains.

This is precisely the position of *Speculum Mentis* which is explicitly described as an analysis of experience, conceived as a system of appearances, a series of successive attempts on the part of mind to mediate itself through the construction of external worlds, such that each successive stage is the dialectical product of a previous one and the presupposition of a further one. This process requires, however, that each particular standpoint presents itself as absolute and therefore as standing in opposition to every other standpoint. For, writes Collingwood, "Every person who is actually absorbed in any given form of experience is by this very absorption committed to the opinion that no other form is valid, that his form is the only one adequate to the comprehension of reality" (SM, 307). What is more, it is only the philosophical error of thinking that there are such distinctions that gives rise to the sciences in the first place and makes them what they are (SM, 309).

From the absolute standpoint philosophy recognizes that there are "no autonomous and mutually exclusive forms of experience" (SM, 306). But this transcendental insight is available only to philosophy and must be achieved by each generation for itself. The necessity to work towards transcendental insights through error – that is, by first attempting to vindicate the autonomy of the separate standpoints – is the ground of the finiteness and historicity of philosophy. Yet, insofar as this insight has been obtained at all, it is transhistorical and infinite. "A mind which knows its own change," writes Collingwood, "is by that very knowledge lifted above change" (SM, 301). The self-development of man as finite (the achievement of the historical sciences) is at the same time the assertion of himself as infinite (the achievement of absolute or transcendental philosophy). Transcendental philosophy, however, is itself the product of a dialectic which proceeds through a series of errors or misrepresentations concerning the way in which philosophy operates as the organon of experience in general and of each finite form in particular.

2 PHILOSOPHY AND THE PHENOMENOLOGY OF EXPERIENCE

The foundation of Collingwood's rapprochement was his belief that each of the disciplines expresses, in a highly formalized way, the essential structure (or what I would prefer to call, after Husserl, the *noetic* content) of a specific category or "habit" of mind (such as, for example, imagination, faith, and reason). He therefore contended that just as the various categories or habits of mind can be shown to interact and overlap, so will the formalized disciplines constitute a scale of overlapping forms. Hence, just as there is no act of mind which is not as much an expression of feeling and imagination as it is an exercise of reason, so there is no purely scientific or philosophical judgment which is not also historical and aesthetic, no purely universal judgment which is not also particular, and so on. But to understand fully this doctrine, which represents both experience and thought as a scale of forms, it is first necessary to have a clear picture of Collingwood's theory of the relationship between philosophy and the primordial structure of experience, which in turn revolves around his notion of philosophy as a master critic of experience. It is from the attempt to represent the natural dialectic of experience (or, again to use Husserl's language, to reveal the *noetic* structure of experience through a phenomenology of its *noematic* or phenomenal appearances) that the conceptual framework for Collingwood's rapprochement philosophy draws its decisive character.

Collingwood's theory of philosophy begins with a distinction between "primary" experience and the "reflective" moment of that experience. The latter is the origin of philosophy and bears a relation to the former which is analogous to the relation which exists between what is known explicitly and what is known implicitly. Primary experience, writes Collingwood, is "the apprehension of the object," while reflective or secondary experience is "the return of the mind upon itself to study its own primary experience" (SM, 255). Ideally, the philosophy of an experience seeks to render explicit the thought which is already implicit in the experience in question, so that philosophy has the task not only of expounding an experience from within in a reasoned, orderly, and systematic manner but of asking itself whether the theoretical constructions it comes up with really do "agree with what we find in actual experience" (EPM, 164).

One of the most articulate statements concerning the relation between philosophy and experience (which underlies the thought of *Speculum Mentis*) occurs in *An Essay on Philosophical Method*. This book is largely a commentary on what might well be regarded as the most fundamental principle of Collingwood's entire philosophy:

> the principle that in philosophical inquiry what we are trying to do is not to discover something of which until now we have been ignorant, but to know better something which in some sense we knew already; not to know it better in the sense of coming to know more about it, but to know it better in the sense of coming to know it in a different and better way – actually instead of potentially, or explicitly instead of implicitly, or in whatever terms the theory of knowledge chooses to express the difference. (EPM, 11)

The same principle is described in the *New Leviathan* as the distinguishing characteristic of the sciences of mind as opposed to the natural sciences: "whereas from a natural science a man often learns something utterly new to him, the sciences of mind teach him only *things of which he was already conscious*" (NL, 5–6). From this conception of philosophy as re-affirming a knowledge already possessed in substance before we begin to philosophize, Collingwood draws a number of implications.

To begin with, if the substance of philosophical knowledge is known to us, however dimly and confusedly, before philosophical reasoning begins, the purpose of that reasoning can only be to present it in a new form, a "reasoned" form: the form of a system constructed according to certain principles (EPM, 164). In effect, Collingwood is here repeating Aristotle's rule that philosophy translates the mere 'fact' of experience into the 'reasoned' fact (or, to use Aristotle's own language, philosophy is the formal cause of a process in which experience is the material cause). And this really means, as Aristotle also made clear, that unless the facts are there in the first place, no philosophical account can be given of them. Philosophy, in short, is not like pure imagination – the creation *ex nihilo* of a web of ideas – but is the expression of the results of the philosopher's own experience and that of other people, in a reasoned and orderly shape. The philosopher must determine, therefore, not only what is presupposed by an experience but also whether the results agree with the facts (EPM, 164). Thus when we ask, for example, whether a given moral theory tallies with moral experience itself, we are asking whether the theory makes intelligible the moral experience which we actually possess (EPM, 172). But this question can only be answered by means of criteria derived from a higher standpoint. In other words, rather than simply imposing universals *ab extra* upon the world of experience, forcing particulars to conform to universals, the universal itself must be made to conform to experience. Indeed, its very validity as a theoretical (i.e. descriptive-evaluative) concept depends upon its being rooted in the experience which it claims to account for.

Thus Collingwood claims that although "philosophy aims at determining a priori the characteristics which belong of necessity to its concepts as such in their true universality," every statement of this kind is merely tentative until it has been verified by reference to the facts: "a philosophical theory must show that what it claims as necessary in the concept is possible in every specification of the concept and actual in its instances" (EPM, 116). One way of showing this would be by providing evidence that the characteristics assigned to any given concept are in fact presuppositions of whatever experience exemplifies that concept. To say, for example, that the concept of causality implies necessary connection requires the further step of showing not only that it is *possible* to so define causality but that *in fact* the actual experience of causality (an experience which must always be finite and historically grounded) rests upon this presupposition. This, of course, is the source of the historicity of philosophy.

There is also implied by this doctrine of the unity of thought and action the further doctrine that since the experience from within which any given philosophical system arises is historically situated, and hence subject to change, the 'truth' of the reflective moment of this experience is also historically situated and subject, therefore, to corresponding changes. This means that the reasoned vindication of a concept is essentially a synthesis of conceptual (or a priori) and empirical-historical techniques of analysis.

The relation between philosophy and experience may be further characterized by distinguishing the philosophical process from the inductive and deductive techniques of the natural sciences. In the latter, universal propositions are derived from certain facts or data which are unchanged by whatever conclusions are drawn from them. Likewise the logical principles, assumptions, and rules of procedure are in no way altered or confirmed by the successful conduct of the arguments based on them. Either they are certain from the beginning, such as the rules of logic, or they are mere assumptions from beginning to end, like the principle of the uniformity of nature.

In philosophy, however, our initial facts are never mere facts, but potentially universal propositions. In empirical science we begin by perceiving *that* the facts are so and so and go on to form a theory of *why* they are so and so. But in adding this new theory to the old facts we do not come to know the facts in a different way, we only come to have something new in our minds alongside the old knowledge. The process is a special kind of accumulation. In philosophy, on the other hand, the knowledge *why* things are so makes a difference to the knowledge *that* they are so; it also affects or changes the object known. The new knowledge imparts a new quality to the old; in seeing why things are thus, we are not merely adding one piece of knowledge to another, we are coming to know the old better. This means that whereas scientific statements may properly be regarded as descriptive hypothetical universals, philosophical statements must be regarded as normative or categorical universals. The philosophical significance of this distinction will be further discussed in chapter VII.

This argument may appear, at first sight, to betray a general lack of sophistication concerning the nature of scientific explanation. It is certainly not at all clear that there is no difference (even according to scientists themselves) between the fact as such, and the same fact as explained by a general law or by a theory. That Collingwood himself knew better is indicated by his general treatment of science in *The Idea of Nature*, in which he seems virtually to deny the very distinctions between science, history, and philosophy which he now appears to be making. I would argue, however, that, from the point of view of the system, this apparently naive attitude can be reconciled with the more sophisticated attitude of the *Idea of Nature*. The view which science takes of itself in *Speculum Mentis* and *An Essay on Philosophical Method* exists at the lower end of the scale which exemplifies the dialectical development of the idea of natural science. It is not, therefore, to be confused with the one which Collingwood himself held, nor does it follow that Collingwood believed it to be typical of top-level scientific thinking. It is rather the view which, although it is implicit only at the most primitive level of scientific experience, has in some quarters been elevated to the rank of a dogma concerning the truth about science in general and applied with disastrous results to the method of philosophy itself. On this point Collingwood himself, in a passage from *An Essay on Philosophical Method* in which he seems to anticipate the very objection which I have just attempted to answer, declares:

I have illustrated the idea of exact science from elementary mathematics, and the idea of empirical science from zoology, botany, and other natural sciences. Perhaps a mathematician, if I am fortunate enough to number mathematicians among my readers, may say to me: Your account of the method used in exact science is altogether beside the mark; modern mathematical theory has changed all that, and you are tilting at a man of straw. If so, I shall reply that my contentions, so far from being invalidated, are confirmed precisely in that quarter where confirmation is most welcomed. For what I am discussing when I distinguish philosophical method from that of science, is not mathematics itself but a certain method, often mistakenly used in philosophy, which is believed to be that of mathematics ... A corresponding answer would apply to a scientist who objected to my account of inductive science. (EPM, 9–10)

I would further suggest, in keeping with Collingwood's systematic interests, that the point which he really wants to make concerns the contrast between two basic attitudes towards the relation of subject to object. According to one attitude, knowing makes no difference to the object known. This is the attitude of philosophical realism. There is another attitude, however, favoured by Collingwood himself, according to which knowing does make a difference to the nature of the object known. This "existential" attitude, which asserts that there is a "feedback" between the act of knowing and the object known, is well illustrated by the central doctrine of *Speculum Mentis*: that the philosophical knowledge which mind has of itself affects the behaviour of mind in such a way as to alter its very nature. This feed-back theory of knowledge is an important part of the theory of the relation of philosophy to experience. Thus when Collingwood says, in *An Essay on Philosophical Method*, that philosophical knowledge does not simply accumulate but develops, improves as well as increases, becomes deeper as well as wider, and therefore vanishes in its original form to reappear in a new way (EPM, 168–70, 174), he is presupposing the whole doctrine of the theory of the forms of error which is given detailed exposition in *Speculum Mentis*.

Collingwood's views on the relation between philosophy and experience may now be summarized. In the first place, there is an intrinsic continuity between philosophy and experience: philosophy is nothing but the experience itself, with its universality further insisted upon, its latent connections and contradictions brought into the light of consciousness. Secondly, successive levels of philosophizing constitute a scale of forms. At every point in this scale there is a datum or body of experience – let us take art for example – which represents the stage that has actually been reached. Then there is the problem of explaining this experience by constructing a theory of it, which is nothing but the same experience raised by more intense thought to a higher level of rationality. The accomplishment of this task, however, is only the continuation of a process already begun; for it was only by thinking and reflecting upon a previous form of experience that we arrived at the experience we presently enjoy. Thus even though the experience upon which we are reflecting is the single experience of art, each successive stage of reflection necessarily differs from every other one. For example, our present thought differs from previous stages by employing new principles and criteria which supersede the principles and criteria of past stages. The new stage, regarded as a theory, is therefore a theory criticized and refuted; what stands firm is not its truth as theory but the historical fact that it has actually been reached, which means, of course, that we have actually experienced it, which is the basis of its historicity. Thus, even though we may criticize and demolish it as a theory, we are nevertheless confirming and explaining it as an experience (EPM, 173). Philosophy is therefore a continual negation of its own theoretical achievements. By subjecting these theoretical achievements to the test of the experience from which it originally sprang philosophy generates the need for new and more adequate theoretical standpoints.

These reflections concerning the nature of philosophy and its relation to experience, as set forth in *An Essay on Philosophical Method*, provide a good introduction to a discussion of the theory of philosophy in *Speculum Mentis*.

According to *Speculum Mentis*, philosophy, as the master critic of experience, is a twofold process. On the one hand, it is a form of internal criticism, the purpose of which is to reveal and defend the presuppositions of any given standpoint (SM, 100). Of everything that the mind does it gives itself an account as it does it, and this account is inseparably bound up with the doing of the thing (SM, 84). Thus arise the philosophies of art, religion, science, and history. In general, the philosophical critique of a given standpoint may be described as the vindication of that science from its own point of view (SM, 272). In the case of religion this form of criticism is called theology; in science it is called logic and metaphysics (SM, 255). But although, as in the later *Essay on Metaphysics*, Collingwood explicitly employs the term metaphysics in this, its narrow sense, as the philosophy of natural science (the classical theory of metaphysics as the theory of abstract being having been expressly repudiated [SM, 274]), it is clear, as I hope to show, that there is implicit in Collingwood's thought a more general sense according to which metaphysics may be regarded as the philosophical critique of any and every standpoint. And since all such criticism, according to Collingwood, is subject to the principle that "to embrace a particular form of experience and to believe in its validity are the same thing" (SM, 43, 307), the critical philosophies of art, religion, science, and history are characterized in *Speculum Mentis* as cases of "dogmatic" philosophy. On this reasoning, metaphysics (in both its narrow and general senses) is really another name for dogmatic philosophy.

There are certain features which all forms of criticism share. Foremost among these is historicity. At first the critic's business is thought to be no more than the description of the abstract principles of the genesis of any given standpoint. The truth, which is yet to be discovered, is that these principles are, on the contrary, always concrete historical facts (SM, 100). Criticism, therefore, whether it be criticism of art (aesthetics), the criticism of religion (theology), or the criticism of science (logic and metaphysics), is implicitly an historical activity, an activity of historical reconstruction.

A second common aspect of the twofold process of criticism is that the interrogation is conducted from the absolute standpoint; that is to say, according to criteria which transcend every particular standpoint. And since this transhistorical standpoint is immanent in each historical standpoint, history may subsequently be shown to be implicit philosophy. The chief philosophical criterion according to which criticism is conducted is variously described as the criterion of the "complete and undivided life" (SM, 36), the criterion of "possibility and consistency," and the criterion of "system" itself (SM, 44–5). Philosophy, however, has the task not only of employing such criteria in the examination of standpoints but of deriving them as well. There is, therefore, in addition to the philosophies of art, religion, science, and history, a philosophy of philosophy. The latter is concerned with the transcendental presuppositions of all critical thought.

The critic, then, attempts to reveal the structure of a given standpoint, according to criteria which derive from the absolute standpoint. But since, as we have already noted, to embrace a particular form of experience and to believe in its validity are one and the same thing (SM, 43), the critic, in attempting to reveal the structure of a given standpoint, attempts to defend it as well, with the consequence, as we have seen, that philosophy passes into a form of dogmatism and becomes the reasoned vindication of the claim to absolute truth for a particular standpoint. This brings us to the central paradox of philosophy conceived of as a science of criticism. It is only in the attempt to defend the truth of a given standpoint that the inconsistencies of that standpoint are revealed. To recognize these inconsistencies is the task of absolute philosophy which is always immanent in dogmatic historical criticism. Once the inconsistency of a given standpoint is recognized and discovered a new standpoint arises which serves as the solution to the rift created within the original one.

Thus, the dogmatic affirmation of the claim to truth of an erroneous standpoint is a necessary stage in the therapeutic process which begins with the discovery of an error and ends with its correction: a process which is characteristic of a dynamic dogmatic philosophy. But while the progress of consciousness from one standpoint to another is necessary – in a sense which will be discussed in more detail in chapter VI – it is nevertheless possible for consciousness to resist the course of its own immanent logic and refuse to move on to a higher standpoint. A consciousness which so arrests itself can only be described as corrupt, and the philosophy which attends this process ceases to be therapeutic and becomes a corrupt or unhealthy form of dogmatism, the pursuit of which, according to Collingwood, is a threat to the survival of culture (SM, 280-1; PA, 215-21; EM, 46, 244).

The task of the critic is therefore twofold. On the one hand, *qua* historian he must disclose the presuppositions which lie at the basis of any given standpoint. At the same time, *qua* philosopher he must act as judge and reveal the error upon which these presuppositions rest. The disclosure of this error becomes the basis upon which a new standpoint can arise.

The principle according to which the system of standpoints is ordered is described by Collingwood thus: "each term is ... built upon or derived from its predecessor and therefore does not start *in vacuo*, is not a wholly fresh embodiment of the universal, but is essentially a modification of the term before" (SM, 55). Later Collingwood describes this principle as the principle of "dialectical development":

> It is the very essence of a dialectical development that each phase in it should contain the next implicitly, and it is this implicit presence of elements which are, as it were, submerged in the immediacy of a particular phase. Every phase of experience is implicit in its predecessor, and therefore it is not surprising that science should be implicit in religion; but the scientific content *in tabu* and the like is felt not as science but as religion. (SM, 164)

In the *New Leviathan* he speaks similarly of philosophy as a "catalogue" of the "functions," of consciousness "as exemplified in its practical and theoretical working" (NL, 62), and organized or arranged "serially" so that "each term should be a modification of the one before it" (NL, 63).

In more metaphorical terms the twofold critical process described above may be characterized by what Loewenberg (with reference to Hegel) has described as an "iconoclastic" rhythmic alternation between the viewing of a standpoint *ab intra* and the viewing of it *ab extra*.[2] The first moment is essentially "histrionic," having as its goal the description of what the standpoint is *ab intra* in itself. The second moment is primarily "negative" having as its goal the description of what the standpoint is *ab extra*, that is, for the absolute. The whole project is somewhat like a drama in which standpoints rise and fall and in which truth develops through a succession of self-annihilating, self-creating moments. The dramatis personae – art, religion, science, and history – are questioned until the histrionic effort leads to the discernment that the type of cognition under examination is inherently erroneous. To speak of the growth of knowledge is to imply that new thoughts and new facts are perpetually coming to consciousness (SM, 90).

The above distinction between *ab intra* and *ab extra* is offered in part as a more adequate rendering of a distinction, which Collingwood himself introduces in *Speculum Mentis*, between the crude but popular conception of dogmatic philosophy and the more sophisticated conception of critical philosophy (SM, 254; see also EPM, 217–20). Dogmatic philosophy, writes Collingwood, is generally regarded "as the procedure of thought without inquiry into its own powers," while critical philosophy is "the investigation by thought itself of the limitations of its capacity" (SM, 254). Collingwood's comments on the usefulness of such a distinction, however, suggest that he might have been happier with the convention here adopted of viewing the two processes of dogmatic and critical philosophy (as defined above) as dialectically related aspects of the *ab intra* and *ab extra* moments of the single process of critical philosophy. The *ab intra* moment gives rise to the erroneous and abstract activity of dogmatic philosophy in its narrow sense, while the *ab extra* moment is the source of the more dynamic and critical activity which transcends the former by exposing and recognizing its limitations.

It should now be obvious that the "iconoclastic dialectical" approach of *Speculum Mentis* resembles strongly that of Hegel in the *Phenomenology of Mind*, an approach which Loewenberg has aptly described as "comic." The aim of all comic art, as Loewenberg points out, is to render ridiculous situations or characters that are out of joint. The reason for this is not entirely negative, however, for the logical absurdity inherent in comic figures, when made manifest by faithful impersonations, furnishes its own logical catharsis. The very recognition of a self-contradictory situation must lead to its abandonment. This basic postulate of rationalism is at the same time the very principle which governs the construction of all genuine comedy. It is also the principle which dominates the phenomenology of *Speculum Mentis*. *Speculum Mentis*, in other words, is a comedy of errors enacted from the absolute standpoint. Instead of showing us the absurdities of men and women inflicting evil upon themselves and each other in their blindness and self-delusion, as does the comic poet, the comic philosopher, with his weapon of dialectical logic, uncovers the antithesis of ideas and beliefs.

Speculum Mentis, therefore, takes the form of successive impersonations of types of cognitions with the purpose of betraying to us the contradictions hidden from their adherents. At each stage in its development consciousness adopts a particular standpoint which, upon critical examination, turns out to be unsatisfactory. This leads to the adoption of a new standpoint. But each time it adopts a new attitude it forgets what has transpired before, and hence each new assertion is as dogmatic as the last; disappointment awaits every overconfident assertion.

The comic element is equally present in the fact that while our philosophical critique has the task of exposing the inconsistencies which lie at the basis of the various standpoints, this task, as I have already indicated, is not entirely negative. For although the recognition of error is synonymous with its negation, negation is "determinate" – that is, it destroys only what is illusory, retaining what is permanent and enduring. Thus, according to the terms of determinate negation, the act which on the one hand is responsible for the destruction of a standpoint is at the same time the vindication of the very standpoint it refutes (SM, 45; cf. also, ch. VI, s.4, below).

The therapeutic character of philosophy, as described in *Speculum Mentis*, may be compared with what Collingwood says in *Religion and Philosophy* about evil, punishment, and redemption. Punishment plays the same role in the moral life as criticism does in the life of the intellect. To begin with, the condemnation of evil is a necessary manifestation of good wills in so far as they are grounded in the absolute standpoint (RP, 177). Punishment, like criticism, is not simply negative but has, as its positive goal, forgiveness and redemption (RP, 176, 179). Punishment, in other words, is not sheer negation but determinate negation, the medium through which finite mind redeems itself. More than this, it is the medium of infinite redemption as well. "God's punishment of man is man's punishment of himself, and man's repentance is God's repentance also" (RP, 187). Thus, in *Speculum Mentis*, philosophy like punishment has the task of overcoming error and thereby redeeming an otherwise corrupt society by restoring the existential unity of life. This it does by undermining the claims of each standpoint for total independence from every other standpoint and by exposing to absurdity the claims of each to be in possession of absolute truth. In destroying the false autonomy of each standpoint, which rests on separateness and mutual exclusiveness from every other standpoint, the philosopher has provided a more genuine basis of autonomy by exhibiting each standpoint as a necessary stage in the dialectical development of mind.

Our map is now beginning to take shape. It is to be a statement of the essential nature or structure of each successive form of experience, based on actual knowledge of that form from within, and concentrated upon the search for inconsistencies, rifts which when we come to put a strain on the fabric will widen and deepen and ultimately destroy it. (SM, 46)

This process is later described as a dialectical criticism of errors, a term which applies with equal force to the idea of metaphysics as expounded in *An Essay on Metaphysics*.

> In its actual course, thinking moves by the dialectical criticism of errors – the criticism of an error by itself, its break up under the stress of its internal contradictions – to their denial: this denial is a truth, so framed as to negate the error just exploded, but generally falling into a new and opposite error by an exaggerated fear of the old. Any element of error in this new truth will, if thinking goes vigorously forward, initiate a new dialectical criticism and the process will be repeated on a higher plane. Thus thought in its progress – a progress not mechanical or predestined but simply effected by the hard work of thinking – moves through a series of phases each of which is a truth and yet an error, but, so far as the progress is real, each is a triumph of truth over a preceding error and an advance to what may be called a truer truth. (SM, 289)

In *An Essay on Metaphysics*, metaphysics is defined as "thinking systematically about what presuppositions are actually in use" (EM, 197). Such thinking is essentially historical. But the presuppositions which are the objects of historical thinking are not themselves the mere products of historical experience. "Absolute presuppositions," writes Collingwood, "are not 'derived from experience', but are catalytic agents which the mind must bring out of its own resources to the manipulation of what is called 'experience' and the conversion of it into science and civilization" (EM, 197). In other words, the absolute presuppositions which underlie historical experience have a transcendental ground in the structure of mind.

If we wish to understand how presuppositions act as catalytic agents we must return to *Speculum Mentis* where Collingwood explains how the dialectical criticism of errors is both a transcendental philosophy of mind and a catalytic source of new experiences. Like metaphysics, dialectical criticism is historical (SM, 100), and like metaphysics it is the medium through which mind makes itself. Collingwood describes the dialectical history of the mind's attempt to achieve self-knowledge as a "dialectical drama in which every phase has grown out of its predecessor with a kind of dramatic inevitability" (SM, 289). And I would argue that the "manipulation of experience and the conversion of it into science and civilization" which is referred to in *An Essay on Metaphysics* is also a dialectical drama exhibiting "a kind of dramatic inevitability."

This inevitability, however, must not be confused with either logical deduction or metaphysical predeterminism. Dialectical inevitability is a form of creative rationality. Dialectical history not only recounts the errors of the past but engages in the much more creative enterprise of

66 THE TRANSCENDENTAL STRUCTURE OF EXPERIENCE

showing how each "has contributed something to the state of knowledge to-day: a *felix culpa*, in so far as it has been the occasion of our rise to higher things" (SM, 290).

The ontological counterpart of this conception of dialectical history is the conception of the historical process, *a parte objecti*, as a rational process which exhibits both regularity and novelty. But the novelty of history is not the novelty of a sheer flux of unique and disconnected events. Nor is the regularity of history the regularity of a barren cyclical repetition of the same pattern over and over again; still less is it a shuffling of rearranged units like repeated throws of dice such that every new event is no more than an arbitrary selection from a given number of possibilities. The regularity of history lies in the continuity which underlies the fact that history is "a process in which every phase, while it grows out of the preceding phase, sums up implicitly the whole of previous history" (SM, 56). But the novelty of history lies in the fact that "every such summation is a new act"; that is to say, the past is not simply summed up, but superseded.

3 THE ONTOLOGICAL STRUCTURE OF CONSCIOUSNESS AND EXPERIENCE[3]

In the previous section philosophy was defined in terms of a twofold methodological distinction between viewing the subject *ab intra* and viewing it *ab extra*. But the theory of philosophy which is given in *Speculum Mentis* is more complex than this. For superimposed upon this methodological distinction is a further one according to which the former appears to operate on at least three distinct but related ontological levels, or, to use a term from the *New Leviathan*, "soundings" (NL, 63–4).[4] These levels are not simply three self-contained types like the co-ordinate species of a genus, nor are they three pigeon holes into which experiences may be conveniently sorted. They are, on the contrary, a scale of dynamically changing and overlapping forms, having a natural order of their own and subject to a special set of rules. Experience, in other words, undergoes a logical and dialectical development not only from one form of experience to another (from art to religion, for example) but also, *within* each of the five major forms of experience, from one level to another.

The designation of five as the number of general forms and three as the number of the levels of consciousness is not to be taken as exhaustive, because, as Collingwood himself declared in *Religion and Philosophy*, "no list of faculties or activities can ever ... be exhaustive" (RP, xvi). Nevertheless, he admits, there is no harm in employing such schemes whose main virtue is simply to give us a convenient starting point for illustrating the all-important fact that series means concrete novelty, the denial of both abstract repetition and abstract change (SM, 56–7). But, Collingwood warns, it is only harmless so long as we recognize that it is provisional: "the life of mind is not the rotation of a machine through a fixed cycle of fixed phases but the flow of a torrent through its mountainbed, scattering itself in spray as it plunges over a precipice and pausing in the deep transparency of a rock-pool, to issue again in an ever-new series of adventures" (SM, 57). Or, more precisely, to cite a passage from the *Outlines of a Philosophy of Art*:

Life is not a mere rotation of three ... categories in a rhythmical monotony. The triple rhythm is present in all life, but is never twice alike; its whole character is altered by the specific differences of the experience in which it is embodied. These differences emerge in the course of a process which on its theoretical side may be called the spirit's attempt to know itself, on its practical side the spirit's attempt to create itself. To know itself means also knowing its world, and to create itself means creating its world; its world in the former case means the world of which it is aware, in the latter case the world in which it can live. There is a theoretical rhythm in the spirit's life, which consists of an alternate concentration on the external world and on its own nature, and a practical rhythm, which consists of an alternate adaptation of itself to the world and of the world to its own needs. (OPA, 88–9)

At the first ontological level each of the particular forms makes an unequivocal and dogmatic interpretation of its own essential nature. This interpretation turns out, when criticized, to be based on a false and arbitrary distinction. For example, the essence of art is defined *ab intra* as pure imagination, imagination without assertion. When criticized *ab extra* from the absolute standpoint it is shown to rest on an erroneous and arbitrary distinction between imagination and reason. Religion is defined *ab intra* as pure faith. *Ab extra* it is described as metaphor mistaking itself for literal assertion and its claim to autonomy turns out to rest upon a false distinction between faith and reason. Science, meanwhile, is an affirmation of the abstract universal conceived as the whole of reality. *Ab extra* this is shown to presuppose a false distinction between appearance and reality. And so on.

First-level dogmatism rests on two fundamental presuppositions. The first is that each form has a fixed and given self-identical nature. The second is that the particular conception of reality implied by any given standpoint is the only true and valid one, which itself presupposes that there is only one true view of reality (SM, 41). The theoretical moment of each standpoint, in other words, presents itself not simply as a dogmatic *Weltanschauung* but as a *Weltanschauungslehre*. Thus, for example, not only does art assert itself as pure imagination, but the qualities which define the objects of imagination are extended to the entire world of reality. It is not surprising, then, that such philosophies as exist at this level tend to assume an attitude of total indifference, if not intolerance, to any other interpretation of reality.

As a consequence of the dialectical interplay between the *ab intra* and *ab extra* approaches, however, consciousness is forced to the recognition that the absolute presuppositions of the first level of criticism are inconsistent. Once it is realized that each standpoint, as defined at the first level, rests upon a false distinction, consciousness is obliged to redefine the nature of each standpoint and start anew. Each standpoint will now conceive of itself as only one of a number of equally valid standpoints and proceed to define itself accordingly. Thus art, for example, which at the first level posits itself as the only fundamental mode of existence, co-exists at the second level with other forms whose validity and claims to knowledge it no longer denies. Likewise, each of the other forms conceives of itself as one of a number of equally valid and true standpoints, which arise as a result of the various ways in which mind views what is essentially the same object. At the same time each form recognizes that it has a history which to some extent exemplifies the influence which the other forms have had upon it.

But the philosophy or reflective-theoretical moment which seeks to justify this point of view is characterized by two peculiarities which set it apart from the third level. In the first place, at the second level, consciousness has not yet overcome the subject-object distinction – the negation of which is the differentia of absolute philosophy. It therefore continues to posit the object of each form as an independently existing entity. In the second place, second-level consciousness treats each form as though it were the species of a genus, and any overlap which exists is therefore treated as a mere overlap of extension between classes – that is, the forms are externally related through the simple mediation of the universal genus.

But again, as a result of the dialectical interplay between the *ab intra* and the *ab extra*, consciousness transcends itself. The relation between subject and object becomes one of dialectical identity while the relation among the forms becomes one of rapprochement. The result is the discovery of a new and higher level of existence in which philosophy treats each form not as the species of a genus, but as a member of a scale of forms whose overlap is an overlap of intension between concepts or categories rather than an overlap of extension between classes. As Collingwood himself puts it in *An Essay on Philosophical Method*, each category in its degree specifies its "generic" essence, but each embodies it more adequately than the one below. Or, to put it another way, according to the logic of the overlap of classes the generic essence is immanent in or identical with the variable element (EPM, 92–103). This, in effect, is the principle of rapprochement philosophy, which Collingwood elsewhere describes as the principle:

that our five forms of experience are not five abstractly self-identical types of event which, by their recurrence in a fixed or changing order, constitute human experience; but types whose recurrence perpetually modifies them, so that they shade off into one another and give rise to new determinations at every turn. (SM, 86)

And this means, among other things, that each particular form within the total system of forms is itself a scale of forms, having its own logical and historical development. To cite once again the case of art there will be an aesthetic, a religious, a scientific, an historical, and even a philosophical form of art. The same applies for each of the other forms. Thus the third level introduces for the first time the possibility of a genuine philosophy of history, mind, and nature, and so on. It is also the level at which morality and social relations can be shown to transcend both the vicious dogmatism of prejudice and intolerance and the pseudo liberal-humanism of "toleration," for the more genuine community of "intersubjectivity."

This threefold distinction – which is crucial not only for the purpose of reconstructing and understanding Collingwood's thought but also for establishing a continuity between his early and later writings – is not one which is explicitly formulated by Collingwood himself. It is justified, however, not only by implication but by certain distinctions which Collingwood does make in various places for the purpose of elucidating his subject matter.

In particular the present threefold distinction bears a strong analogy to Collingwood's description, in *Speculum Mentis*, of the various ways in which the five forms of experience are said to compete for the prize of truth (SM, 42–4). A prize, writes Collingwood, can be dealt with in three ways. It can be given to one competitor and denied to the others; it can be divided between two or more of the competitors; or, it can be not awarded. Thus, he continues, either one of the five forms is the one which gives us real knowledge, or each gives us one type of real knowledge, or all are delusions. The first alternative resembles the dogmatic approach of the first level of consciousness. At this level each competitor claims – to cite a passage from another context – "not only to give truth, but to give the absolute or ultimate truth concerning the nature of the universe, to reveal the secret of existence, and to tell us what the world really and fundamentally is" (SM, 41). The second alternative, dividing the prize between two or more of the competitors (SM, 42), resembles our second level of existence, the level which treats the forms as co-ordinate species of a genus – a notion which Collingwood criticizes quite severely (SM, 46–7).

The final alternative, that all forms of so-called knowledge are delusive, actually comes closest to the truth and resembles, with some qualifications, the mark of the third level; for one of the main features of third-level philosophy is the recognition that the argument for the separation of the forms is illusory. This is not, however, the only purpose of third-level criticism. For, as we have already noted, the negative moment of criticism is only a stage on the way towards a more positive achievement. Collingwood himself seems to recognize this when he points out that if revealing the illusory nature of each claim to truth were all that was accomplished then the person who disclosed these errors would himself be claiming to have a sixth form of knowledge (SM, 42); which means, in effect, that the so-called "third alternative" paradoxically presupposes the first which it claims to have repudiated. But this would virtually destroy the process of thought by arresting it in a circle of self-contradiction. If criticism is to survive this paradox it must clearly make a "new beginning." The "new beginning," however, is not just a fourth alternative but is more like a synthesis which both rejects and preserves what has gone before. The characteristics of this new beginning, which resemble the more positive features of what I am calling the third level, derive from the insight that the recognition of the illusory nature of each form must be accompanied by the realization that the truth has after all been implicit from the start, and that the five types of experience constitute an overlapping scale of forms, each exemplifying the truth to a degree by embodying it more adequately than the one below (SM, 50, 55, 56). Criticism, in other words, is not merely destructive:

> It is a vindication of the very experiences which it refutes, for it exhibits them not as strange and inexplicable perversions of the mind, morbid types of thought indulged in by the foolish and depraved, but as stages through which the critic has himself passed, and which he can confess without forfeiting his claim to rationality. (SM, 45)

Thus the recognition (and hence destruction) of the illusory claims to truth is only the negative moment of a total process for which the systematic organization of these claims into a scale of forms is the positive moment.

Other sources for this tripartite conceptual scheme can be found in *Religion and Philosophy* and *An Essay on Philosophical Method*. In *Religion and Philosophy* he carefully distinguishes between various kinds of abstract identity on the one hand and a more genuine concrete identity on the other (RP, 104 ff.). Concerning the relation between man and God, for example (which parallels the discussion in *Speculum Mentis* of the relation between the sciences and truth), he points out that there are several ways of interpreting it. There is first of all the position of "absolute transcendent theism" according to which only one man is truly divine (RP, 149, 163), an attitude which corresponds to the first level of dogmatism. In the second place, there is the doctrine of "immanent pantheism," according to which all men are equally divine (RP, 148–9, 162). Another version of this latter view which corresponds to the second level of dogmatism, is materialism which represents God as a whole composed of separate and mutually exclusive parts (RP, 152).

In *Religion and Philosophy,* Collingwood advances various criticisms of these two views. In the first place, he points out that they both proceed from the same logical error of postulating an abstract separation between God as universal and man as particular. "These two tendencies of false logic," he writes, "the tendency to elevate one particular into the standard and only real instance of a universal" (RP, 163), and the tendency to regard every man as "equally an instance of that nature and a manifestation of the essence of God" (RP, 164), both assume that "God is the universal of which man is the particular." This assumption is part of the logic of the abstract universal, or the logic of genus and co-ordinate species. But, Collingwood declares, the logical conception of the universal, or, the logic of genus and species, "is in fact inapplicable to the relation between God and other minds." "And therefore we cannot argue that any particular mind shows the nature of God as well as any other. The question to be asked about mind is not what it is, but what it does; a question with which the logic of things does not deal" (RP, 165). Against these false views of the relation between the universal and the particular Collingwood advances an alternative interpretation which introduces the concept of a "concrete identity in difference" (RP, 151 ff.). The latter is essentially an "identity of intension" (RP, 158): a concept which is only imperfectly worked out in *Religion and Philosophy* but which is given a more definitive expression in *Speculum Mentis* and *An Essay on Philosophical Method*.

Similar arguments against the logic of the abstract universal can be found in *An Essay on Philosophical Method*. Here again, this logic is shown to give rise to the two levels described above. Collingwood argues, for example, that there are three types of universal judgment which, however appropriate they may be in science, are inappropriate to philosophical analysis. The first type of judgment is the generalization in which the content of the universal is determined by the act of generalizing from instances. Thus, for example, it might be noticed that many individual right acts promote happiness – from which it is presumed that their being right is either identical or in some way especially connected with their "felecific" property. This judgment corresponds to the tendency of first-level dogmatism to define the whole of the genus in terms of only one of its species (EPM, 112–13). The second type of judgment "treats the concept or universal as a genus, distinguishes its various species, and looks for the generic essence in the shape of something common to these species and indifferently present in all of them" (EPM, 113 and 37 ff.). This corresponds clearly to the second level of dogmatic philosophy. The third type of judgment, however, differs from the second only in the sense that the universal element which binds the species together, rather than deriving from an empirical survey of the species themselves, follows by definition from the a priori nature of the universal. In effect, however, its consequences are the same – namely, the species are univocally related to the generic concept whose essence transcends the specific variables.

Against these fallacies Collingwood offers in *An Essay on Philosophical Method* a "fourth" way of arranging the elements of judgment which at the same time preserves traces of the other three. This "fourth" way, which is really a synthesis of the first three, proceeds by "arranging the species in a scale and showing that the features of the generic essence shine out more clearly as the scale reaches its culmination" (EPM, 115–16). It is clear, then, that the fourth interpretation of judgment in *An Essay on Philosophical Method* is virtually the same as the "new beginning" of *Speculum Mentis*, which in turn is a fuller development of the doctrine of concrete identity in difference first described in *Religion and Philosophy*. Although, as I have already pointed out, the insights of *Religion and Philosophy* are obscured by the tendency throughout that book to misrepresent the "concrete identity of difference" as a series of distinct but equally valid (or univocal) expressions of the same subject matter.

4 TOWARDS A RE-INTERPRETATION OF COLLINGWOOD'S THOUGHT

The tripartite dialectic of experience outlined above provides a new conceptual framework for the interpretation of Collingwood's thought. On the basis of this conceptual framework, for example, the following conclusions concerning the structure of the argument in *Speculum Mentis* can be drawn. In the first place, while the main purpose of *Speculum Mentis* is to explicate the structure of the first and most primitive level of consciousness, there is nevertheless implied by this analysis the need for the further critiques of second- and third-level consciousness. Thus *Speculum Mentis* must be treated not simply as one of the early juvenilia which have been rendered obsolete by the later and more mature writings, but as a necessary prolegomenon to the various critiques of second- and third-level consciousness exemplified by Collingwood's other philosophical writings. From this hypothesis it follows that the apparent inconsistencies between *Speculum Mentis* and the later writings have in fact already been anticipated by the plan of *Speculum Mentis* and are the result therefore not so much of the fact that Collingwood changed his mind as of the fact that his own philosophical development obeys the very rules laid down for philosophy by the theory of *Speculum Mentis*; the theory, namely, that philosophy consists of a scale of overlapping forms which admit of discontinuities as well as continuities. Thus such differences as may appear as either a series of irreconcilable inconsistencies or as evidence of significant changes of outlook will emerge, when regarded from the standpoint of the logic of the overlap of classes, as forms on a scale – that is, as systematic differences (or errors) which not only have been anticipated from the start but which perform a dialectical function in the system as a whole.

This claim may be tentatively explained as follows. *Speculum Mentis* is a general phenomenology of mind, conducted from the absolute standpoint. As such its task is to organize and relate the various categories or habits through which mind expresses its universal or generic essence. At the same time, with a single exception, it is a third-level critique of a series of first-level standpoints. The exception is philosophy, which is described not only as a series of first-level dogmatisms but also as a third-level activity, the philosophical examination of its own presuppositions. The latter discloses the presuppositions according to which the third-level critique of the first-level dogmatism is conducted. Each of the main categories of mind gives rise to a series of first-level dogmatisms which are expounded *ab intra* and then criticized *ab extra*, so that developments within each single form, from level to level, while not explicitly described, are at least implicit. For example, the clue to the future development of art, from the first to the third levels, is provided by the phenomenological transitions within mind itself from imagination (aesthetic consciousness) to faith (religious consciousness) to understanding (scientific consciousness) to reason (historical and philosophical consciousness). Thus, third-level art, while not explicitly expounded, is nevertheless implicit in philosophy's third-level account of itself which runs throughout the whole of the book. The same considerations apply to each of the other standpoints.

Speculum Mentis confronts us, therefore, with a dramatic portrayal of the conflict between the presuppositions of the third level and the presuppositions of the first level: a conflict which is further exemplified by the differences between the first-level accounts of art, religion, science, and history in *Speculum Mentis*, and their third-level accounts in the later writings, so that the so-called discrepancies between the early and the later writings turn out to have been clearly anticipated by the phenomenological structure of *Speculum Mentis*.

My task in the remaining chapters is to apply such distinctions as have been drawn above to the interpretation of Collingwood's various publications, with particular attention to the relation between philosophy and history. I shall attempt, in succeeding chapters, to disclose and comment upon the dialectic of experience which, when expounded *ab intra* and criticized *ab extra*, leads not only to developments from one form to another (from art to religion for example) but to developments within each particular form from one level of consciousness to another. I shall argue, moreover, that, whereas *Speculum Mentis* concentrates almost exclusively on what I have called first-level consciousness, the later writings belong to the second and third levels. And this means that, in order to fulfil the double aim of this analysis, I will be required to introduce into the discussion of *Speculum Mentis* materials which are drawn from some of the later writings. Chapters IV and V will accordingly attempt to relate the dialectic of the first level of experience, as expounded in *Speculum Mentis*, to the dialectic of the second and third levels, as exemplified in the other writings.

One final word of explanation concerning the structure and organization of chapters IV and V is required. At the risk of some repetition – which is to a certain extent a necessary requirement of any attempt to expound a dialectical system – I have chosen to follow Collingwood's own example and separate the discussion of experience per se (in chapter IV) from the discussion of the philosophy of experience (in chapter V). But although the ostensible subject of chapter IV is the dialectic of experience per se, it must be remembered that once any experience attempts to express itself at all it can no longer avoid the mediation of thought, and the distinction, therefore, between experience per se and the philosophy of experience breaks down. As Collingwood himself puts it, "the supposedly non-philosophical or pre-philosophical knowledge from which this process began is only in a relative sense non-philosophical" (EPM, 171). The dialectic of philosophy, in other words, is already implicit in the dialectic of experience (SM, 255). Chapter V may therefore be regarded as a more systematic and explicit account of what has already been accomplished in chapter IV. But in order to minimize repetition, I shall adopt the following conventions; chapter IV will illustrate the dialectic per se by attending to all five forms while chapter V will illustrate the dialectic of the philosophy of experience by concentrating almost exclusively on the form of history alone.

⁓ IV ⁓

History as
IMPLICIT PHILOSOPHY

I THE PHENOMENOLOGY OF EXPERIENCE

A *Art*

The first stage in the phenomenological development of consciousness is aesthetic consciousness, from which arises the standpoint of art. Art, like every other standpoint, begins by making an unequivocal claim to absolute knowledge and truth (SM, 49). In so doing art discloses itself as an activity of pure imagination, that is to say, as sheer supposal or questioning. Against art, religion will assert the priority of pure faith, science the priority of the abstract universal, history the priority of the concrete fact, and philosophy (which seeks to transcend all other standpoints) the priority of concrete mind.

Taken as a whole, imagination, faith, abstract and concrete thinking are all implied by any given act of thought. Abstracted from the whole, however, each may be made the basis of a separate standpoint which is founded therefore on an implicit error – the error (among others) of conceiving itself in isolation from every other standpoint. Thus the aesthetic element, for example, which is a part of every cognitive judgment, being no more than the questioning moment of the question and answer process which characterizes all knowledge (SM, 83), becomes, when it is made the basis of an entire world view, a separate standpoint which calls itself art. The separate standpoint of philosophy is similarly founded on the error of conceiving itself as "... one specialized form of experience, instead of realizing that it is merely the self-consciousness of experience in general" (SM, 256). The very same considerations apply to the origins of each of the other separate standpoints.

Once art as a separate science has emerged, however, philosophy has the task of revealing the presuppositions which lie at the basis of that standpoint and of testing them for consistency. In performing this task, the critic (who operates, as I have already suggested, on three ontological levels) aims not only at revealing the basic presuppositions of the idea of art as such, as opposed to, say, the idea of religion or the idea of science, but at disclosing as well the historical processes through which these presuppositions came into being.

But the history of art is paradoxically one of the main sources of the negation of the idea of art. As Collingwood describes it, art as pure imagination can have no history. This is because in so far as the work of art is the mere product of the imagination, every work of art is necessarily a "windowless monad," internally coherent and independent of all other works (SM, 71). There can be, therefore, no legitimate attempt on the part of aesthetic consciousness to compare present works of art with past works, or even presently existing works with one another. When this aesthetic monadology is elevated to the level of a general philosophy or world view we arrive at the dogmatic assertion that reality consists only in what is immediately (i.e., presently) imagined. *A parte subjecti, 'esse est imaginare'*; *a parte objecti, 'esse est imaginari'* (SM, 65).[1]

At the same time, however, art is implicitly a process of mind, and mind is not pure imagination. What art does not realize is that it is of the very essence of mind that it not only act but that it give an account of itself at the same time, an account which is in essence both historical and philosophical. Indeed, for Collingwood, the capacity of mind to provide such an account for itself is the basis of the distinction between mind and nature. For these reasons the history of art, which is part of the art process itself, is an explicit negation of the idea of art because history is a denial of the monadism upon which art as pure imagination rests. The idea of art as pure imagination must therefore dissolve when it has realized that it has all along been presupposing what it has explicitly denied: either this or it must reconstitute itself in such a way that it reconciles the inherent contradiction. The refusal of art to compromise, which is the characteristic of first-level consciousness, is the negative moment of the dialectical transition from art to religion. But the willingness of art, on the other hand, to retain its integrity by reconstituting itself in the required and prescribed manner, means the rebirth of aesthetic consciousness on a new and higher level.

There are other more systematic reasons why art as pure supposal is impossible (SM, 77-8, 100).[2] Supposal cannot exist except in a context of assertion: in this case, assertions concerning the nature of the aesthetic process. These assertions are implied by the fact that at any moment in the process of creation the artist has in mind a criterion which enables him to distinguish between the right and the wrong way of continuing that process of creation. In short, aesthetic creation is necessarily self-critical, and the criticizing moment or concept, the idea of structure or relevance, is always in advance of the criticized moment, the flow of imaginations which it controls (SM, 97).

The priority of assertion over supposal, of the concept or "idea" over the imagination, is particularly evident in the contradiction which emerges between the claim of art to be pure metaphor, expression, or intuition, on the one hand, and its claim to be absolute truth on the other. As in the case of artistic creation in general, the criterion according to which art establishes itself as truth is neither intuitive nor devoid of meaning (i.e., it is not itself an act of sheer supposal); it is conceptual and philosophical. Art *qua* art *says* what it means but to *know* what it means is philosophy (SM, 89–90).

By means of the criticism which is implicit within the very process of creation itself, consciousness has become aware of the contradiction which lies at the basis of art, the contradiction between supposal and assertion. Consciousness must now recognize that in addition to presupposing a history, art presupposes as well a context of universal and categorical assertions. Thus, not only has art been shown to be implicit history, it has been shown to be implicit philosophy as well. In other words, art turns out to be precisely the opposite of what it claims to be: thought instead of pure imagination. Consciousness is therefore forced to abandon the standpoint which asserts an absolute separation between supposal and assertion.

Although Collingwood did not quite put it in these terms, it might be said that the consequence for art of this 'shock of recognition' is 'death,' for to abandon its claim to be pure imagination is to abandon the very basis of its autonomy. To put it in more metaphorical terms, and to employ once again the analogy, which runs throughout much of Collingwood's philosophy, between philosophy and psychoanalysis, if the claim on the part of consciousness to be art can be likened to the having of a neurosis, the 'catharsis' of recognizing that art is really philosophy and history results in the overthrow of that neurosis.

But, in fact, consciousness does not abandon its neurotic claim to be art so easily. Collingwood himself declares that in every dialectical transition the implicit is made explicit only in the teeth of a certain resistance. It is only unwillingly that art realizes its own immanent logic. This is because the stability of these activities depends upon their refusal to face these facts about their own nature (SM, 246). Indeed, it is at this point that consciousness runs the risk, by refusing to face the facts, of sinking into that corrupt and narrow form of dogmatism mentioned earlier (ch. III, s. 2). In effect then, aesthetic consciousness is faced with the following dilemma; either it faces up to the facts and consequently destroys itself as a separate standpoint, or else it refuses to face up to the facts and thereby becomes corrupt or deranged.

Yet this dilemma is far from being insoluble. It is true that the self-knowledge which arises from art leads to the creation of a series of further standpoints. But, as we have already noted, the negation through which art is transformed into these other standpoints – into religion, for example – is 'determinate.' What is destroyed is the claim of art to be *pure* imagination, rather than the idea of art in general. Indeed, the destruction of this most primitive and dogmatic interpretation of art liberates aesthetic consciousness so that it may now progress through the scale of art forms. Thus, with the arrival on the scene of religion, science, history, and philosophy, the life of the imagination continues to flourish and in so doing exhibits, under the influence of these other forms of knowledge, a variety of new interpretations concerning the nature of imagination and the creative process. In terms of our earlier distinction, the so-called 'death' of art is really only the death of the first level of experience, and through the agency of that death we are brought to the threshold of the second and third levels of experience.

The question which gives rise to the two higher levels of experience is, What must be the nature of art after the appearance of the other forms of knowledge? How, in other words, do religion, science, history, and philosophy (which logically supersede the form of art) affect the idea of art as such?

An example of second-level consciousness and the criticism which attends it is to be found in a small book which Collingwood published in 1925 entitled *Outlines of a Philosophy of Art*. This book is presented as an attempt to carry out the programme of *Speculum Mentis*, not by simply repeating what has already been said in the earlier book but by developing its implications (OPA, 4). If this programme is to be taken seriously, we must recognize that the idea of art which is examined in the *Outlines* is the idea with which the analysis of *Speculum Mentis* concludes rather than the idea with which it began.

First-level aesthetic consciousness is accompanied by an aesthetic philosophy which recognizes no other form of knowledge. According to this "aestheticism" the distinction between imagination and reason is absolute. At the higher levels, however, aesthetic consciousness recognizes that it is only one of a number of standpoints which consciousness adopts towards its object. Thus, contrary to the aestheticism of the first level, aesthetic experience now realizes that it can only answer the question of what art is by placing itself in relation to the other activities, and Collingwood therefore admits at the very outset of the *Outlines* that "... the only possible philosophy of art is a general philosophy of man and his world and with special reference to man's function as an artist and his world's aspect of beauty" (OPA, 8). In effect, then, Collingwood is declaring that philosophy of art can only be conducted against the background of a 'philosophical anthropology.' We cannot answer the question, What is art?, until we have answered the prior question, What is the nature of consciousness that it is capable of giving rise to the activity of art?

This conclusion, however, which is laid down from the absolute standpoint, is only implicit in second-level consciousness, whose behaviour is not yet commensurate with the theoretical insights of absolute philosophy. For the idea of philosophy of art as philosophical anthropology is in fact only an ideal limit which is more adequately exemplified at the third level of experience and only fully exemplified at the absolute standpoint. Thus, although second-level aesthetic consciousness accepts itself as one among a number of standpoints, it experiences its relation to these other standpoints according to the model of genus and co-ordinate species: each species, rather than make for itself an unequivocal claim to truth, simply accepts itself as one species among many, differing from the others in certain specific ways. Thus second-level aesthetic experience, through the instrument of philosophy of art, proceeds *ab intra* to justify second-order aesthetic consciousness in terms of a logic of genus and species, which, when its implications are fully understood, makes a genuine philosophical anthropology impossible.

This interpretation is implicit in Collingwood's own statement at the outset of the *Outlines*:

Art, religion, science, and so forth, which are here treated as species of a genus called activity, are in reality related to one another in a way which is not exactly that of co-ordinate species ... For the present it is sufficient to point out that the logic of genus and species is at this stage of the inquiry used as the first approximation to a truth which it does not exhaust. (OPA, 11)

As a result, art is once again defined as imagination divorced from reason; imagining is distinguished from thinking and the imaginary world is distinguished from the real world (OPA, 13). But, whereas at the first level consciousness commits the category mistake of confusing the mere differentia of the species – pure imagination – with the generic essence itself (so that the genus is in fact completely equated with one of its species), second-level consciousness, as described in the previous chapter, is fully aware of the fact that it is only one of a number of equally valid species. In other words, while first-level aesthetic consciousness demands the prize all for itself, second-level aesthetic consciousness, which is the subject of the *Outlines*, is willing to share the prize with the other forms of knowledge.

The significant feature of second-level consciousness, so far as its general behaviour is concerned, is the fact that it has not yet overcome the distinction between subject and object which is the differentia of absolute consciousness. As a result, the philosophy which attends this level of consciousness is unable, as yet, to employ the logic of the overlap of classes which, from the absolute standpoint, is known to account for the unity of the various forms. For just as mind experiences itself and its object as separate and mutually exclusive entities so the object by itself, as well as the activity through which this object is apprehended, is classified and divided according to this same paradigmatic notion. Thus arises the philosophical concept of a plurality of separate activities, related as co-ordinate species of a genus, having a plurality of objects, related similarly as co-ordinate species of a genus.

A more explicit feature of second-level experience, and one which it shares with third-level consciousness, is its historical character – a fact which is not, of course, recognized at the first level, which thinks of itself as rigidly a priori. Understanding any activity means reflecting on a given mass of experience related to that activity. This experience can only be acquired through the long and specialized pursuit of that activity itself, and this is primarily an historical process. Only after this experience has been acquired is it possible to reflect upon it and bring to light the principles underlying it. To expound the principles which lie at the basis of a given form of experience, then, does not mean deducing these principles a priori and in abstraction from actual experience. What the philosopher of experience is really trying to do is to communicate his reflections upon his own experience to readers who have the same experience themselves (OPA, 9). Or, in the language of his later philosophy, what Collingwood appears to be saying is that aesthetic theory is not an attempt to investigate and expound eternal verities concerning the nature of an eternal object called art (PA, vi), but an attempt to uncover the "absolute presuppositions" which are being made by those persons who are actually engaged in this activity (EM, 47).

For a variety of reasons, having mostly to do with the inadequacies of the extensional logic of genus and species, the analysis of art at the second level is not sufficient, and consciousness is therefore driven to re-examine itself at a higher level. Thus arises the experience of third-level aesthetic consciousness which is the subject of analysis in the *Principles of Art*.

At the third level, consciousness has learned to experience the unity of subject and object, and aesthetic philosophy now reconstitutes itself in terms of a rapprochement between subject and object. The new aesthetic experience and its accompanying philosophy of art is guided by the intensional logic of the overlap of classes, and the imagination may now be analyzed in terms of its rapprochement (i.e., dialectical overlap) with reason. As a result, the contradiction between supposal and assertion which characterizes the first level is to some extent reconciled. In general, third-level aesthetic philosophy is the logical outcome of the discovery that art is implicit philosophy. It may therefore be characterized as 'philosophical aesthetics,' which is the reflective moment of third-level aesthetic experience.

The *Principles of Art*, like the *Outlines* and *Speculum Mentis*, describes aesthetics or the philosophy of art as the analysis of the presuppositions of an historically changing standpoint. The *Principles* is therefore concerned with the analysis of the aesthetic standpoint as it exists "here and now" in 1938 in England: "For I do not think of aesthetic theory as an attempt to investigate and expound external verities concerning the nature of an eternal object called Art, but as an attempt to reach, by thinking, the solution of certain problems arising out of the situation in which artists find themselves here and now" (PA, vi; see also PA, 325).

But, although the subject matter of the *Principles* is a body of historically situated thought, the presuppositions according to which the philosophical critique of this thought takes place are both historically grounded (in the sense that they are revealed not to mind *qua* mind but only to a mind engaged in the act of historical reconstruction) and transhistorical (i.e., they are derived from the transcendental principles underlying the course of any critical thought whatever – whether that thought be directed towards the analysis of art, religion, science, history, or even philosophy itself). The nature of these principles, which are both transcendental and yet historically grounded – a special kind of synthetic a priori – will be further discussed in chapter VI. Foremost among these presuppositions, however, are the principles that 'All thought exists for the sake of action,' and 'The philosophical analysis of any single form of life has serious existential implications for culture as a whole.' Collingwood therefore argues in the *Principles* that the philosophy of art is no mere intellectual exercise, but has practical consequences bearing on the way in which we ought to approach not only the practice of art but (because a philosophy of art is a theory about the place of art in life as a whole) the very practice of life itself (PA, vii).

Art is now described as a form of self-knowledge (which in turn is described as the foundation of all life) arising from the attempt of consciousness to apprehend the truth. Good art, Collingwood argues, derives from a "truthful" (one is tempted to say 'authentic') consciousness, and is not a luxury; bad art derives from a "corrupt" consciousness, and is not a thing we can afford to tolerate (PA, 284). The corrupt consciousness, from which bad art proceeds, is the source of untruth in every other sphere of life as well. Such a consciousness supplies the false presuppositions on the basis of which intellect, as well as imagination, proceeds towards the creation of empty and useless structures; moral ideals are castles in the air, political and economic systems are mere cobwebs;

I do not speak of these grave issues in order to magnify the office of any small section in our communities which arrogates to itself the name of artists. That would be absurd. Just as the life of a community depends for its very existence on honest dealing between man and man, the guardianship of this honesty being invested not in any one class or section, but in all and sundry, so the effort to overcome corruption of consciousness, is an effort that has to be made not by specialists but only by everyone who uses language, whenever he uses it. Every utterance and every gesture that each one of us makes is a work of art. It is important to each one of us that in making them, however much he deceives others, he should not deceive himself. If he deceives himself in this matter, he has sown in himself a seed which, unless he roots it up again, may grow into any kind of wickedness, any kind of mental disease, any kind of stupidity and folly and insanity. Bad art, the corrupt consciousness, is the true *radix malorum*. (PA, 285)

This passage, incidentally, would make little or no sense unless it were assumed that aesthetic consciousness is implicit in and presupposed by each of the other forms of consciousness (which, in the language of *Speculum Mentis*, dialectically supersede it) so that a corruption at this, the most basic level of consciousness, would necessarily imply corruption at every other level as well. This is an affirmation of the principle, laid down from the absolute standpoint, and having the status therefore of a transcendental presupposition, that art – to cite a passage from the *Outlines* – 'is the primary and fundamental activity of the mind, the original soil out of which all other activities grow' (OPA, 14). Thus, not only is it impossible to have bad art in a healthy and well-ordered society, it is likewise impossible to have good art in a bad or corrupt society.[3]

Most students of Collingwood seem scarcely to have realized that the description of the corrupt consciousness in the *Principles* closely parallels the account of the development of mind in *Speculum Mentis*. Indeed, one might treat the description of the corrupt consciousness as a commentary on the following passage from *Speculum Mentis*:

... the mind, having formed a false conception of itself, tries to live up to that conception. But the falseness of the conception just means that it cannot be 'lived up to'. There is therefore a permanent discord between what the mind thinks it is and what, on the strength of that conception, it does: even though this behaviour is not at all the same thing as the behaviour of a mind that knows itself truly. The result is an open inconsistency between theory and practice; and this inconsistency, as ground for dissatisfaction, is the starting-point of the attempt at truer self-knowledge. (SM, 250)

The life of thought in *Speculum Mentis* may therefore be described as a risk. For it must continually face the prospect of arresting the mental process entirely by sinking into any one of the series of errors through which mind moves in the course of its natural development. At the same time, however, mind enjoys the freedom to project beyond any given error towards a truer self-knowledge.

In the *Principles*, Collingwood makes a point of explaining that corruption, in whatever form, is not due to a deliberate lie on the part of consciousness; consciousness does not deliberately and wilfully destroy itself in this way. On the contrary, the error or untruth which is embraced by it and results in its downfall is, in the language of *Speculum Mentis*, "unconscious" or "implicit." But once the corrupt consciousness explicitly recognizes the error upon which it is based, the corruption ceases to be a corruption (PA, 219). Thus the *Principles of Art* continues to draw on the analogy (first used in *Speculum Mentis*) between psychoanalysis and the philosophical detection of the untruths of the corrupt consciousness.[4]

The *Principles of Art* is an attempt on Collingwood's part to overcome the corruption, resulting from a breach of the unity of thought and action, which he fears lies at the basis of contemporary aesthetic experience. The arts are in a state of general decay. To save itself art must re-establish its lost contact with its audience: "The kind of contact that is required is a collaborative contact in which the audience genuinely shares in the creative activity of the artist" (PA, 331). In order to accomplish this the artist must give up the idea of "pure" art and substitute for this the theory of art as action. This is precisely the difference between first- and third-level consciousness: between the theory of pure art (religion, science, etc.) and the theory of art (religion, science, etc.) as action.[5]

One important consequence of this change in outlook obtains at the level of "choosing a subject." The artist who believes in the theory of pure art insists upon the right to choose his own subject. But the artist who accepts the theory of art as action will allow his subject to choose him. He will, in other words, spontaneously share the interest which people around him feel in a certain subject and allow that interest to determine what he likes. In so doing he implicitly accepts the collaboration of his public from the very inception of his work, and the public, thus accepted as collaborators, will inevitably become his audience (PA, 332). In this respect the artist ceases to be the contemplator of a separate and eternal world of aesthetic truths and becomes instead the prophet and critic of culture (PA, 325). Likewise, the philosopher of art ceases to be a mere aesthetic monadologist and becomes instead a philosophical anthropologist:

> The artist must prophesy not in the sense that he foretells things to come, but in the sense that he tells his audience, at risk of their displeasure, the secrets of their own hearts. His business as an artist is to speak out, to make a clean breast. But what he has to utter is not, as the individualistic theory of art would have us think, his own secrets. As spokesman of his community, the secrets he must utter are theirs. The reason why they need him is that no community altogether knows its own heart; and by failing in this knowledge a community deceives itself on the one subject concerning which ignorance means death. For the evils which come from that ignorance the poet as prophet suggests no remedy, because he has already given one. The remedy is the poem itself. Art is the community's medicine for the worst disease of mind, the corruption of consciousness. (PA, 336)

There is implied in this passage a second level at which the artist restores contact with his audience; namely, the recognition (on the part of the artist) that his activities overlap with those of the other sciences. "The scientist and historian and philosopher must go to school with the man of letters ... The literary man must go to school with the scientist and his likes, and study to expound a subject instead of merely exhibiting a style" (PA, 299). The theory of art which is outlined in the *Principles* is, therefore, the theory of art as action. It is true that Collingwood still defines art as imagination: "The aesthetic experience, or artistic activity, is the experience of expressing one's emotions; and that which expresses them is the total imaginative activity called indifferently language or art" (PA, 275). But the theory of art as imagination in the *Principles* is quite distinct from the theory of art as pure imagination in *Speculum Mentis*. In the latter work aesthetic consciousness explicitly asserts an absolute and abstract distinction between imagination and reason. The *Principles* however, establishes a rapprochement between imagination and reason. The maxim which perhaps best describes the course of Collingwood's thought in the *Principles* is Kant's famous dictum: intuitions without concepts are blind, concepts without intuitions are empty.

This new rapprochement is reflected in the attempt throughout the *Principles* to reconcile the discrepancy between the theory of the "idea as a feeling not interpreted by thought" and the theory of the "idea as a feeling perpetuated and dominated by consciousness" (PA, 212). The conclusion of this argument is the conception of the imaginative process as being under the firm control of the intellect (PA, 235). Further examples of the 'intellectualization' of the imagination are provided by the various descriptions of art as an expression of mind. The work of art is said to exist only in the artist's mind and, therefore, appreciating it means imaginatively reconstructing for yourself the object which exists in the mind of the artist (PA, 139). The imaginative process of reconstruction – which resembles, incidentally, the imaginative reconstruction of history – must be guided by principles derived from reason. Finally, art is described as not simply the expression of emotions pure and simple, but of the emotions of a thinking being (PA, 252).

The explicit rapprochement between imagination and reason which presumably distinguishes the *Principles* from *Speculum Mentis* is of course implicit in *Speculum Mentis* from the start.[6] Indeed, it is my claim that the *Principles* is a continuation of the analysis of art which is begun in *Speculum Mentis*(just as I hope to show later that the *Idea of Nature, An Essay on Metaphysics,* and the *Idea of History* are continuations of their corresponding standpoints in *Speculum Mentis*) : it constitutes, in fact, the third level of criticism which is implicit in the actual critique of *Speculum Mentis*. The latter brings art to the point of self-awareness; aesthetic consciousness realizes that it has all along presupposed a false distinction between imagination and reason. The *Principles* is an attempt to expound the idea of art which has accepted the requirement of *Speculum Mentis* for a rapprochement between imagination and reason. The *Principles* shows how, in keeping with the principle of determinate negation, the unity of imagination and reason can be preserved without having to pass over entirely into religion; without, in other words, destroying the aesthetic standpoint altogether.

What the *Principles* does not do, however, is explain how the new conception of imagination as the synthesis of sensation, feeling, and reason, is nevertheless distinct from the thought and activities of science, history, and philosophy. It does not show how art can accept the implication of its discovery of the false basis of its claim to be a unique and separate form, and yet preserve a sufficient degree of autonomy to remain distinct from the other sciences.

Similar problems arise, of course, for each of the other activities. For it was the peculiar feature not only of the *Principles* but, as we shall see, of the *Idea of History* and the *Idea of Nature* as well, to confine the analysis to the *ab intra* vindication of any given standpoint "... regarded as a special type or form of knowledge with a special type of object, *leaving aside, for the present, the further question how that inquiry will affect other departments of philosophical study*" (IH, 7, my italics).

B *Religion*

At the first level of consciousness the failure of art conceived as a self-consistent whole is due to the fact that it is pregnant with a message it cannot deliver (SM, 110). The problem which art gives rise to is the problem of recognizing the need of imagination to assert what it imagines as true. Consciousness must move from the category of the purely aesthetic to the category of the aesthetic-logical (a transition which, as we have seen, is already implicit in the art process itself). The solution to this problem is achieved when consciousness brings expression and assertion together into one act, and thereby adopts a standpoint which not only asserts what it imagines as true but believes in the reality of this assertion as well (SM, 111). This new standpoint is religion.

In adopting the standpoint of religion, consciousness is affirming the identity in difference of religion and art. The basis of this identity is the fact that religion is implicit in art from the beginning: it is the implicit (though incomplete) resolution of the contradiction which lies at the basis of art. At the same time art and religion are different because religion not only brings together what art has rent asunder but explicitly elevates this new synthesis to the rank of a dogma. Thus religion as a separate and distinct form of life emerges.

But while religion is explicitly assertion, it is assertion which absolutely refuses the responsibility of justifying itself against criticism. The attitude which accompanies this form of assertion is "faith" (SM, 132), and the differentia of religion is therefore the distinction between faith and reason. Accordingly, the history of religion is the history of the various ways in which consciousness tries to assert truth as an object of faith. The interpretation may vary from age to age but the basic distinction between faith and reason remains permanent. At the same time, of course, the distinction becomes more and more concrete until what began, at the first level of consciousness, as a basic antithesis becomes, at the third level, a rapprochement.

Judged from the absolute standpoint the theory of pure faith, like the theory of pure imagination, is shown to be illusory. As in the case of art there is at the basis of religion a contradiction between what is said and what is meant. The explicitly affirmed distinction between faith and reason is implicitly denied. This is evident in the fact that religion not only asserts a truth but implicitly claims to defend it as well. God the holy, the object of faith, becomes God the concept, the object of reason.

Thus we pass from the realm of the "holy" to the realm of "reality." When this implicit interpretation of God as "reality," the object of thought, is rendered explicit we pass from religion as such to theology which, as a form of criticism, is essentially philosophical. Theology is, in fact, the science of the presuppositions of the religious experience and exists therefore on three levels. At the first level it is the dogmatic religious philosophy which recognizes no other form of knowledge. At the second level it is the analysis of faith as one of a number of possible attitudes which the mind takes toward reality. At the third level it seeks to establish a rapprochement between faith and reason and becomes philosophical theology.

The failure on the part of religion to maintain the separation of faith and reason, which religious consciousness claims *ab intra* to be its differentia, rises from confusion between symbolic and literal thinking. Religion makes claims about the nature of reality which it expresses by means of symbols and metaphors. There is, therefore, a distinction between what religion says and what it means. But religion *qua* religion confuses the two, with the consequence that there is a contradiction between what religion claims to be and what it really is. *Ab extra*, religion is characterized as metaphor mistaking itself for literal thinking with the result that it asserts the reality of what is only a symbol and thereby treats the symbol as though it were a concept (SM, 153).[7] The differentia of religion, then, even though it constitutes what amounts to a philosophical error, lies in the identity of symbol and meaning.

Collingwood's example is the church, a symbol whose meaning, "worship," can be expressed in a variety of different ways. In the content of a specific religion the church is not just a symbol of worship but the *only form* of worship. The church, in other words, becomes the very meaning which it ostensibly seeks only to symbolize – which is a category mistake of the same kind as the definition of the genus in terms of only one of its species. Since the distinction between symbol and meaning is the basis of the distinction between faith and reason, the kind of confusion between symbol and meaning which results in their being identified has the consequence of denying the more general distinction between faith and reason. Religion says: 'You cannot criticize my assertions because what I assert is an image, not a concept; and criticism applies only to concepts.' But at the same time it demonstrates in its actual behaviour the contrary position by treating the images it asserts as though they were concepts, and in this way the language of religion becomes a rational language seeking not only to disclose an interpretation of truth but to defend it as well.

But the language and categories of justification must lie outside religion, just as the criterion of relevance lies outside art. The very existence of religion, in other words, implies the existence of a non-religious truth. To recognize this would mean to pass beyond metaphor and symbol and concentrate on meaning, which involves treating the language of expression for what it is, mere metaphor or symbol, thereby creating another language with which to describe meaning. This, in effect, is what theology does when it seeks to explain the entire mass of religious *imagery* in terms of the *concept* of God. This procedure of explaining imagery in terms of concepts, while it is the very negation of the religious outlook, is at the same time the basis of a new standpoint which is called natural science. The latter is founded on the explicit recognition of a distinction between language and meaning – a distinction which expresses itself for science in terms of the distinction between particular and universal, appearance and reality, events and their causes, phenomena and the laws of their behaviour. When this distinction is rendered abstract and absolute (that is to say, elevated to the rank of a dogma) science as an autonomous form of life emerges as the first stage in the life of thought as such.

The birth of science does not, of course, mean the death of religion in any absolute sense of the term. But it does, together with the birth of history and philosophy (both of which are implicit in science), seriously affect the basic structure of the religious consciousness which must now reconstitute itself in terms of a rapprochement between faith and reason. The birth of science, in other words, is the occasion upon which religious consciousness advances towards the second and third levels of existence; an advance which cannot be completed, of course, until the appearance of history and philosophy. The history of religion may therefore be viewed as a scale of forms developing on three levels, each exemplifying to a degree the rapprochement between faith and reason which is the ideal limit towards which religious consciousness aims.

To destroy the natural dialectic by using the rise of science as an excuse for disposing of religion is a mistake whose consequences are disastrous for the whole of human culture. The suppression of any form of life in favour of another was for Collingwood an irrational and pathological activity. Just as no society can be expected to survive without art so no society can prevail without religion. Religion, he declared in his essay "Facism and Nazism" (1940), is the passion which inspires a society to persevere in a certain way of life and to obey the rules which define it. Without a conviction that this way of life is a thing of absolute value, and that its rules must be obeyed at all costs, the rules become dead letters and the way of life a thing of the past. The civilization dies because the people to whom it belonged have lost faith in it. They have lost the spiritual motivation to keep it going. They no longer feel it as a thing of absolute value. They no longer have a religious sense of its rules as things which at all costs must be obeyed. Obedience degenerates into habit and by degrees the habit withers away.

This is precisely, according to Collingwood, how the Graeco-Roman civilization came to an end: "It died because the religious passion that provided its driving force had ceased to exist" (FN, 168). In the course of time, civilization was revived by Christianity which built a new heaven and a new earth: the earth of modern politics and the heaven of modern physical science. It was Collingwood's contention that the very idea of freedom itself – free speech and free thought for everyone; free inquiry and free discussion in science, free inquiry and free discussion in politics – had been distilled from the doctrines and practice of Christianity.

> The real ground for the "liberal" or "democratic" devotion to freedom was religious love of a God who set an absolute value on every individual human being. Free speech and free inquiry concerning political and scientific questions; free consent in issues arising out of economic activity; free enjoyment of the produce won by a man's own labour – the opposite of all tyranny and oppression, exploitation and robbery – these were ideals based on the infinite dignity or worth of the human individual; and this again was based on the infinite, on the fact that God loved the human individual and Christ had died for him. The doctrines concerning human nature on which liberal or democratic practice was based were not empirically derived from research into anthropolitical and psychological data; they were a matter of faith; and these Christian doctrines were the source from which they were derived. (FN, 170–1)

But the liberal-democratic tradition, at the time of Collingwood's maturity, found itself under attack. The success of this attack, through the activities of Fascism and Nazism, derives from the disappearance of religion and its replacement by a cult of emotion. It was Christianity which supplied the driving force of the habit of freedom. But once the habit becomes a mere habit it has no punch. And having lost its punch – that is, its religiosity – the habits of freedom, liberty, and democracy can no longer resist the destructive forces of irrationalism. Just as barrenness of thought is the price one pays for a dogmatism that suppresses the religious dimension of thought, so barbarism is the ultimate destiny of any society which suppresses the religious dimension of life. Thus Collingwood declared, at the conclusion of "Fascism and Nazism,"

> The time has long gone by when anyone who claims the title of philosopher can think of religion as a superfluity for the educated and an "opiate for the masses." It is the only known explosive in the economy of that delicate internal-combustion

engine, the human mind. Peoples rich in religious energy can overcome all obstacles and attain any height in the scale of civilization. Peoples that have reached the top of a hill by the wise use of religious energy may then decide to do without it; they can still move, but they can only move downhill, and when they come to the bottom of the hill they stop. (FN, 176)

Collingwood's interest in a rapprochement between faith and reason goes back to *Religion and Philosophy*. Indeed, one might regard this book as an examination of second-level religious consciousness on its way to becoming a third-level experience. Collingwood's purpose in *Religion and Philosophy* is to treat religion, and Christianity in particular, "... not as dogma (this is the mark of a first-level experience) but as a critical solution of a philosophical problem (which is the mark of the second and third levels)" (RP, xiii). This can be accomplished only if religion is regarded not as "the activity of one faculty alone," but as "a combined activity of all elements in the mind" (RP, xvi). He sets out, therefore, to establish an identity between religion and the other major forms of experience, such as science, history, and philosophy. The identity which Collingwood wanted, of course, was a concrete identity, but the identity he achieved, as I have already pointed out, was a mere abstract identity: the identity which characterizes a plurality of forms which are all coordinate species of the same genus called knowledge. And this, as we have seen, is the mark of second-level consciousness: the level which implies what I have previously referred to as the abstract theory of the relation of the sciences.

The theoretical plan of *Religion and Philosophy* derives from a more practical concern to correct certain erroneous views concerning the nature of religious experience. In particular Collingwood was attacking the definition of religion as emotion, which was advanced by William James and Rudolph Otto. In this book Collingwood denied the legitimacy of contrasting religion, conceived of as an irrational and therefore inferior form of knowledge, with science, conceived of as a superior form having cognitive certainty. This contrast, he argued, is in fact founded on false premises. He therefore set out to demonstrate that religion is much more like philosophy, as far as its status as a form of knowledge is concerned. And history is the medium through which the identity between history and philosophy can be achieved. (Hence the pains which Collingwood took in this book to demonstrate that philosophical speculations upon the meaning of the Christian faith presuppose the existence and reality of the historical facts they are about. In other words, it makes a difference whether Christ really lived and acted as he is described [RP, 53-4].)

The failure of *Religion and Philosophy* to achieve its ostensible purpose is the failure of second-level consciousness in general, and it was therefore not until *Speculum Mentis* that a genuine rapprochement between faith and reason became possible. The conclusion of *Speculum Mentis* concerning the unity of the sciences is that genuine unity can be accounted for only in terms of 'the dialectical principle of explicit and implicit,' which is the basis of the logic of the overlap of classes which characterizes third-level consciousness. Thus when religious consciousness learns to experience its concrete identity with the other sciences it has begun to exist on the third level of consciousness.

The first explicit discussion of third-level religious consciousness appeared in 1927 in an article entitled "Reason is Faith Cultivating Itself."[8] In this article Collingwood cites Descartes' *Cogito* as an example of a rational certainty (i.e., a universal and necessary truth) which is at the same time a matter of faith in that it rests not on arguments but on direct conviction (RFCI, 8). Collingwood credits Descartes with the discovery that the foundation and source of all knowledge whatever is intuitive certainty or faith.

> This conception of Descartes solves the problem of the relation between faith and reason. Reason itself is henceforth seen to depend for its cogency on that immediate and indemonstrable certainty which is faith; faith is henceforth no longer severed from reason or given a field of its own to operate by itself, but becomes as it were the soul of which reason is the body. (RFCI, 9)

In our awareness of our own responsibility and spontaneity, of our timeless and eternal reality, and of the existence of an infinite mind upon which our finite nature somehow depends, we are, Collingwood argues, in possession of certainties of the same kind as Descartes' *Cogito*. They cannot be proved because they lie too close to us. They are the presuppositions of all proof whatever: not like the Aristotelian axioms which enter into particular arguments as their premises, but rather as the conditions of there being any arguments at all (RFCI, 9–10).

Not only is faith the ground and source of reason, but reason itself, according to Collingwood, is no more than the development of faith into an articulated system (RFCI, 12). Reason, in other words, is implicit in faith in the sense that (a) only through reason can faith reveal its own nature to itself and (b) all scientific and philosophical ideas, before they have been worked out in explicit intellectual terms, are present to men's minds in the form of religious beliefs (RFCI, 13):

> The faith that sets out in search of understanding is a faith already endowed with sufficient understanding to recognize its need for more. And in searching for more understanding it is searching not for an extraneous addition to itself, but

for a development and confirmation of its own nature ... reason is nothing but faith cultivating itself. (RFCI, 14)

If *Speculum Mentis* may be cited as an example of faith cultivating itself – in the sense that reason is there shown to render explicit what is already implicit in faith – then the identity which exists between faith and reason, and between religion and the other sciences, must be an identity in difference. Thus in rendering explicit in reason what is implicit in faith, concrete differences are introduced which may then become the basis for distinguishing the standpoint of faith from other standpoints.

These differences are given some attention in a pamphlet published in 1928 entitled *Faith and Reason*,[9] and which, in effect, relates and analyses the two forms according to the rules of the logic of the overlap of classes.[10] Faith is defined as our attitude towards reality as a whole, reason as our attitude towards its details as distinct from each other (FR, 24–6; 220–2).

Within the realm of faith itself further dialectical distinctions emerge. Conceived as an attitude towards the universe as a whole, faith may be either (a) theoretical, (b) practical, or (c) emotional. Theoretical faith is knowledge that the universe as a whole is rational. This is a basic and universal presupposition of science. Indeed, Collingwood will later describe it as an absolute presupposition. Practical faith consists in the certainty that life is worth living, in the belief that the world is open to possibilities, and in the knowledge that we are free. These are the absolute presuppositions of moral existence. Finally, the emotional aspects of faith are present in art, conceived as a feeling towards the universe as a whole (FR, 25–6; 221–2).

Corresponding to the dialectic of faith is the dialectic of reason. Reason, the scientific habit of mind, is the attitude which we take up towards things as parts of a whole, as finite things distinct from one another and connected with one another by a network of relations which it is the business of thought to trace out in detail. Theoretical reason treats things as objects to be studied. Practical reason selects particular ends to pursue. Finally, there is an emotional aspect in which everything excites in us a feeling proper and peculiar to itself (FR, 26–7; 222).

Thus the proper sphere of faith is everything in the collective sense, that is, everything conceived as a whole. The proper sphere of reason is everything in the distributive sense, every separate thing, all finite things. Reason, says Collingwood, cannot come into open conflict with faith because reason can only operate in a system whose general nature has first been determined by faith:

So far from a conflict between faith and reason being inevitable from the nature of things, they are in point of fact necessary to each other.

Faith cannot exist without reason. The infinite is not another thing which is best grasped by sweeping the finite out of the way; the infinite is nothing but the unity, or as we sometimes say, the "meaning", of finite things in their diversity and their mutual connections. (FR, 27; 223)

Thus is affirmed the interdependence of faith and reason, the structure of which is paradigmatic of the interdependence of art, religion, science, history, and philosophy. Faith cannot exist without reason, for faith must be accompanied by an attempt to embody itself in reason by developing its own assertions (which as undeveloped would be mere abstractions) into a system of thought and conduct (FR, 28; 224). Likewise, reason cannot exist without faith. Reason rests on presuppositions concerning the nature of the universe as a whole which are not scientifically discovered or ascertained but embraced by an act of faith (FR, 28–9; 224–5).

A person who sees that the whole of life, regarded as a whole, is the sphere of religion, and that the same whole, regarded as made up of details, is the sphere of science, must see that it is possible to be religious without ceasing to be genuinely scientific and scientific without ceasing to be genuinely religious. And a person who sees that the whole lives in the details, and the details in the whole, must see that it is only possible to be genuinely scientific by being genuinely religious, and vice-versa. (FR, 30; 226)[11]

c *Science: The Assertion of the Abstract Universal*

The breakdown of first-level religious consciousness is the result of an implicit and unresolved contradiction between meaning and symbol. *Ab intra* religion is the active worship of a 'truth' which is ostensibly an object of faith only. The experience of worshipping such an object finds expression in symbols and metaphors which religion will therefore employ only as a means toward celebrating in this faith. In its actual behaviour, however, the symbol is not only identified with its meaning, but the meaning itself is treated as a concept rather than as an object of faith, and defended moreover by reason. This contradiction is resolved when the principle implicit in the behaviour of religion is rendered explicit and made the basis of a separate standpoint. Thus arises natural science in which the tension between symbol and meaning is resolved into the distinction between appearance and reality, and the attitude of devotion which characterized religious consciousness is now recognized as an explicit affirmative judgment.

The first and most primitive stage in the development of science is 'abstract' science, which is simply the affirmation of the abstract universal as truth and reality. The abstractness which characterizes this attitude is the result, incidentally, not of a conscious and deliberate choice on the part of science but of the 'unconscious' control of an inheritance from religion: the belief, namely, that the object of worship is totally other than experience. In science this belief reappears in the dogma that reality (the object of thought) is totally distinct from thought itself. Thus science perpetuates the abstract distinction between subject and object which is implicit in religion and art.

Collingwood cites, as an example of abstract science carried to the extreme, the Greek model of an a priori deductive science. The basic presupposition of Greek science was the belief that the object of knowledge is the pure abstract concept, knowledge of which is purely cognitive and independent of experience; and science was therefore defined as knowledge by pure thought of the real world (SM, 163–9). As Collingwood describes Greek science it is clear that it represents an ideal example of first-level scientific consciousness, for the fundamental principle which lies at the basis of science is extended by the Greeks to the whole of reality, and the a priori deductive model is put forward as the only one which can make a legitimate claim to be knowledge at all.

The Greek idea of science, however, was false, and ideally its breakdown was implicit from the start. In claiming to be knowledge by pure thought of the real world, science was claiming to be what in principle it could not be. Even Plato, who defended this doctrine, realized that for science to be so defined it must necessarily presuppose itself before it even begins. In other words, Collingwood argues, only a mind which already possesses a knowledge of its object can rediscover this object in the a priori deductive manner outlined by Greek science. Knowledge presupposes knowledge.

There was a further inconsistency within Greek science between the theory of science and the actual practice of it. To the question, What is the origin of the concepts studied by science? the Greeks answered mistakenly that they were obtained a priori from a source untouched by sensuous experience. In practice, however, they were derived empirically. It was, therefore, only in theory and never in practice that the Greeks shut their eyes to the world of facts and experience (SM, 178).

While the breakdown of abstract science was dialectically implicit from the start, this breakdown did not occur historically until the close of the Middle Ages when the leading scientists of the Renaissance repudiated the a priori or deductive ideal and fought a battle which ought never to be necessary again, the battle for the recognition of facts.

Renaissance scientists thus rendered explicit the empirical element which was implicit even in Greek science. Observation and experiment, they argued, were the true sources of scientific knowledge and a priori reasoning was inherently inadequate (SM, 177).

The transition from a priori to empirical science was accompanied by the substitution of inductive for deductive logic. But even inductive science is not free of inconsistency. For the process of induction itself rests on a principle variously described as the uniformity of nature, the law of universal causation, and so forth, which, just because induction rests upon it, induction is powerless to establish. Such a principle, if it is to be established at all, can only be established by deduction. What is more, the principle of the uniformity of nature which, according to Collingwood, is presupposed by inductive and deductive science alike, is at the same time the main source of abstractness. For uniformity is nothing but the abstractness of the concept, its indifference to the variations of its own instances. Induction then, far from overcoming the fundamental abstractness of deduction, simply reasserts it, and the attempt on the part of scientific consciousness to flee from the a priori deductive model ends in failure.

Collingwood's account of the dialectic of science begins with the claim that the differentia of science, viewed *ab intra*, is the belief in the separation between universal and particular, and we have seen that scientific consciousness is torn by a tension between two opposing views concerning the manner in which knowledge of universals is to be had, namely, the deductive and inductive models. The deductive model was shown *ab extra* to rest on the paradoxical presupposition that knowledge presupposes knowledge. And the inductive model turns out *ab extra* to presuppose the deductive model. More than this, the inductive model implicitly denies the abstract separation between universal and particular which is the very definition of scientific consciousness. For unless the universal were immanent in the particular, the latter could never be used as evidence of the former, and induction would in principle be impossible. But to recognize this means abandoning the scientific standpoint for one which explicitly redefines the object as the concrete synthesis of universal and particular. In short, science is replaced by history.

Collingwood's argument concerning the transition from science to history will become particularly evident if we examine carefully some of the implications which derive from the discovery of the unity of universal and particular in the concrete fact. So long as universals are abstractly separated from particulars, it is possible to maintain a similar distinction between appearance (or illusion) and reality. It is easy to see why, according to this view, history, which is primarily concerned with particulars, can never attain the status of a science. But once it is recognized that the universal is immanent in particulars, the distinction between appearance and reality breaks down. Reality is now recognized to partake of particularity and to share in some of its characteristics; the truth ceases to be a world of pure unchanging and eternal truths and becomes instead a synthesis of permanence and change. The true object of knowledge now becomes, not the abstract universal, but the concrete fact; and this is the object of history. We are therefore left with the absurd conclusion that if science is knowledge of the universal then science cannot be science; or, to put it another way, if science is knowledge of reality then the definition of science as knowledge of the abstract universal is a contradiction in terms.

This conclusion can be avoided only by abandoning the view that the object of science (whatever it is) is a description of reality at all. This is precisely the path which, according to Collingwood, modern science has chosen in order to avoid the implications of the only other alternative which lies open to it: to abandon the view that reality is a permanent and unchanging substance. Thus the classical view of science as the study of reality was abandoned in favour of the view according to which the object of science is not the real but the possible and science is therefore regarded as being essentially hypothesis, not true but useful. But this, as Collingwood points out, only meant delaying the inevitable, for even the theory of science as hypothesis leads straight to history.

The theory of science as hypothesis may be summed up as follows. Science asserts not the actual truth but only what would be true if something else were true which is laid down as an hypothesis. It asserts not that S is P but only that if there were an S it would be P. Its procedure consists, therefore, first in making an assumption, secondly, in deducing the consequences of that assumption. Throughout this entire process it never consciously or explicitly makes an assertion in the sense of a categorical judgment at all. Its judgments are purely hypothetical. Thus, for example, the geometrician *qua* geometrician has no need either to raise questions concerning the existence of such things as points, lines, triangles, etc., or even to make categorical assertions that such things exist (which, Collingwood seems to imply, is the job of the metaphysician [SM, 183]). For the geometrician *qua* geometrician it is sufficient simply to point out what would happen if there were such entities. Science, in other words, is a pure tissue of hypothetical implications, none of which are asserted as facts.

This theory of science as fundamentally an act of supposal or hypothesis contains implications which, according to Collingwood, force the dialectical transition from science to history, a transition which embodies what has already occurred in the transition from art to religion. As in the case of art, so in the case of science, supposal cannot exist except against a background of assertion; science presupposes metaphysics. Thus, just as a work of art presupposes a criterion of relevance which is an assertion, so an hypothesis presupposes something which is non-hypothetical, namely, the categorical assertion of a fact. Collingwood cites as a primary example of the categorical basis of hypothesis the fact of our own freedom and competence to frame hypotheses at all. You cannot, he argues, simply suppose that you are free to suppose; you must assert that you are both free to suppose and actually supposing. The very act of framing an hypothesis, in other words, is a concrete historical fact, and the historical fact is therefore the concrete basis of all scientific abstraction.

What Collingwood is saying, in other words, is that the activity of science is really no more than the questioning attitude which forms the cutting edge of history. What has happened is that consciousness has abstracted what is only a moment of experience and has equated this with the whole of experience. The scientist thinks that he is dealing either with a world of pure concepts or else with a world of hypotheses. In fact, he is working at the determination and elucidation of historical facts, and if he calls himself a scientist instead of an historian that is only because he is in error as to the nature of his work.

Collingwood declares, however, that the time is rapidly approaching when science will feel the need of absorbing itself bodily into history, reshaping its problems in historical terms, and resolving scientific method into historical method (SM, 188). This could very well be a clear and unequivocal reference to the existence of scientific consciousness at the second and third levels.

The transition to second- and third-level scientific consciousness is implicit in the presuppositions which lie at the basis of the phenomenological transition from science to history: in particular, in the presupposition that science and history are identical. But the birth of history does not mean that science must perish completely. On the contrary, it is simply the occasion for science to reconstitute itself in order that it may continue to exist. It is possible, in other words, for science to accept the implications of its identity with history without necessarily destroying itself as a standpoint. Two examples of how this may be done, chosen from Collingwood's own writings, will be offered; the first is intended to illustrate the second level of scientific consciousness; the second is intended to illustrate the third level.

The first example is the theory, already discussed, which is expounded in *Religion and Philosophy*: the theory, namely, that science and history are each co-ordinate species of the same genus, two equally valid ways of viewing the same subject matter. This view which, according to Collingwood, was first expounded by Croce, is developed in detail in the the 1922 paper entitled "Are History and Science Different Forms of Knowledge?" And since this paper has already been discussed in chapter II (s.3) above, we need only, at this point, remind ourselves of Collingwood's conclusion that "the analysis of science in epistemological terms is ... identical with the analysis of history, and the distinction between them as separate kinds of knowledge is an illusion" (HS, 450). It is clear that this view has all the marks of second-level consciousness.

By contrast with this view there is the theory of science which is expounded in the *Idea of Nature*:

I conclude that natural science as a form of thought exists and always has existed in a context of history, and depends on historical thought for its existence. From this I venture to infer that no one can understand natural science unless he understands history: and that no one can answer the question what nature is unless he knows what history is. (IN, 177)

Presupposed by this conclusion is the view that the identity of history and science is not just one in which both are equally valid co-ordinate members of a common genus called knowledge or judgment. It is rather an identity in which history 'overlaps' with science, as a higher form overlaps with the lower which it has superseded, and science overlaps with history, as the lower form overlaps with the higher which has superseded it. The result is a form of scientific consciousness which has been 'historicized' but not destroyed or annihilated.

The general features of this new level of scientific consciousness are outlined in the *Idea of Nature*. To begin with, the *Idea of Nature* affirms the conclusions of *Speculum Mentis* that history brings about the realization on the part of science that what it studies is not abstractions but real concrete processes subject to change and development:

History had by now established itself as a science, that is a progressive enquiry in which conclusions are solidly and demonstratively established. It had thus been proved by experiment that scientific knowledge was possible concerning objects that were constantly changing. Once more, the self-consciousness of man, in this case the corporate self-consciousness of man, his historical consciousness of his own corporate doings, provided a clue to his thoughts about nature. The historical conception of scientifically knowable change or process was applied under the name of evolution, to the natural world. (IN, 13)

History, in other words, is affirmed as the organon of science (cf. IN, 175, 176, 177).

Collingwood illustrates the dependence of science on history with the following considerations. In the first place, science must rely upon history for its method. The reason for this is that natural science consists of facts and theories. A scientific fact is an event in the world of nature. A scientific theory is an hypothesis about that event which further events will either verify or disprove. Since an event in the world of nature becomes important for the natural scientist only on the condition that it is observed, it is necessary that the scientist understand the conditions under which observation is possible, particularly since he is often required to consult and interpret the record left by another scientist in such a way as to satisfy himself that the man whose work it records really did observe what he professes to have observed. This consultation and interpretation of records is the characteristic feature of historical work: "Thus a 'scientific fact' is a class of historical facts; and no one can understand what a scientific fact is unless he understands enough about the theory of history to understand what an historical fact is" (IN, 177). Virtually the same point is made in the *Autobiography* when Collingwood declares that since all scientific knowledge involves (and indeed rests on) an historical element, "any philosopher who offered a theory of 'scientific method', without being in a position to offer a theory of historical method, was defrauding his public by supporting his world on an elephant and hoping that nobody would ask what kept the elephant up" (A, 87).

There are other ways in which the *Idea of History* has affected the idea of nature. Take, for example, the abandonment of the mechanical conception of nature according to which the only kind of change was "breaking down." In the old view the world of nature was merely a machine, or a collection of machines, in which everything that happened to it was the result of efficient causes. For an evolutionary science of nature, however, the *esse* of anything is its *fieri*; and a science of that kind must therefore rest upon the proposition that everything in nature tries to persevere in its own becoming – to continue the process of development in which, so far as it exists at all, it is already engaged (IN, 15–16).

The principle that the *esse* of a thing is its *fieri* requires a somewhat extensive reform in the vocabulary of natural science, to replace all words and phrases descriptive of structure or substance by words and phrases descriptive of function. Thus Collingwood declares that if nature is a machine, "the various motions of its parts will be motions of things which have structural properties of their own independent of these motions and serving as their indispensable requisites" (IN, 16).

In other words, in a machine, and therefore in nature (if nature is a machine), structure and function are distinct, and function presupposes structure.

In the world of human affairs regarded as an object of history there is no such distinction and a fortiori no such priority. Structure is resolvable into function. When historians talk about the structure of feudal society or of capitalist industry or of the Greek city state, they are in fact describing various complexes of function, kinds of ways in which human beings behave. Thus, to say, for example, that the British constitution exists, is to say simply that certain people are behaving in a certain kind of way (IN, 16–17).

In an evolutionary view of nature a logically constructed natural science will follow the example of history and resolve the structures or objects with which it is concerned into different kinds of function. Nature (like mind) will be understood as consisting of processes, and the existence of any special kind of thing in nature will be understood as meaning that processes of a special kind are going on there. The properties of nature will be understood not as structural properties but as modes of behaviour (IN, 17). Facts, in other words, will be treated as functions.

Another area where the idea of history affects the idea of nature may be discussed under the principle of minimum space and minimum time. According to the principle of minimum space, wherever there is a natural substance S_1 (such as water), there is a smallest possible quantity of it (the molecule of water), anything less than which will not be a piece of that substance but a piece of a different substance S_2 (hydrogen or oxygen). According to the principle of minimum time, there is a minimum time t, during which the movements of the (oxygen and hydrogen) atoms within a single molecule (of water) can establish their rhythm and thus constitute that single molecule. In a lapse of time smaller than t the (oxygen and hydrogen) atoms exist, but the molecule does not exist. There is no S_1, there is only S_2, the class of substances to which hydrogen and oxygen belong (IN, 22). Thus, just as the shape of history depends on the point of view of the observer (the historian) so the shape of nature depends upon the "time" and "space" under which it is observed.

This description of the evolutionary view of nature (which regards nature as historical) appears, at first sight, to conflict with what Collingwood says in the *Idea of History* where he seems to reject the idea of evolution as a model for history.

This evolutionary conception of nature ... might seem at first sight to have abolished the difference between natural process and historical process, and to have resolved nature into history and if a further step in the same resolution were needed, it might seem to be provided by Mr. Whitehead's doctrine that the very possession of its attributes by a natural thing takes time ... But just as history is not the same thing as change, so it is not the same thing as 'timefulness', whether that means evolution or an existence which takes time. Such views have certainly narrowed the gulf between nature and history ... but in order to decide whether the gulf has been really closed and the distinction annulled, we must turn to the conception of history and see whether it coincides with this modern conception of nature. (IH, 211–12)

How can this passage from the *Idea of History* be reconciled with the conclusions of the *Idea of Nature*? This is a difficult question and one for which Collingwood himself offers no explicit advice. But there is an implicit answer which is suggested by an important distinction underlying the whole of Collingwood's thought between the concept of an activity as a general habit of mind and the concept of that same activity as a specialized discipline.

The term "habit of mind" is explicitly used in *Faith and Reason* (195), and "Ruskin's Philosophy." It is also implicit in "Aesthetic" and "The Place of Art in Education." In "Ruskin's Philosophy" Collingwood distinguishes between the "historical habit of mind" and the "logical habit of mind." The former looks for individual facts, the latter for historical general laws (RUP, 11). Each of these habits gives rise to what is in effect a first-level dogmatism: "logicism" and "historicism" consist in the dogmatic application of their respective ideals to all forms of mental activity (RUP, 13–14). And although Collingwood continues to use the term "habit" to describe even these dogmatic activities the distinction between habits as necessary aspects of mind *qua* mind and dogmatic or specialized habits is clearly implicit.

Similarly, in "The Place of Art in Education" Collingwood implicitly distinguishes between the concept of art as a necessary aspect of mind *qua* mind (i.e., as a habit) and the idea of art as a specialized function. The former is necessary for the preservation of life in general; the latter leads to a form of specialized vocational and professional training.

A further discussion of this notion is found in "Aesthetic" which concentrates again on the distinction between art as a general habit of mind (or category of things in general) and its more specialized activities. The differentiae of the former are "the constructive spontaneous power" which every mind possesses (AE, 215), the absence of utility as a guiding principle in construction (AE, 219), and the ability to view something as an individual without classifying or relating it to anything else (AE, 255, 232). Accordingly, anything may be viewed as a work of art (e.g., a machine or scientific theory) in so far as it is simply an "ordered and harmonious system of lines and masses, colours and sounds," or even ideas. Anything, in other words, may be viewed as a work of art which looks or sounds constructed (AE, 223). And "Everything may be treated as a work of fine art by a simple process of ignoring its reference to anything outside itself [AE, 225] ... by being cut off from its surroundings and being treated as an individual whole" (AE, 226). Finally, so far as the specialized arts are concerned, they are defined by the familiar rules of painting, sculpting, dancing, music, and so on.

If history, like art, is distinguished into a general category of mind, on the one hand, and the specialized activity or discipline, on the other, the apparent discrepancy between the account of the relation between history and nature in the *Idea of History* and that in the *Idea of Nature* may be reconciled. For example, we must ask to what conception of history is Collingwood comparing the evolutionary views of nature in the *Idea of History* and the *Idea of Nature* respectively? I will suggest that in the *Idea of Nature,* as in *Speculum Mentis,* Collingwood is assimilating the idea of nature to the idea of history regarded as a general habit or category of thinking. The latter is simply the capacity to experience the "facticity" of things. Thus the historicity of nature would seem to follow from the definition of historicity as facticity. In other words, given the characteristics which in *Speculum Mentis* are assigned to historicity as a general category, it follows that natural science would eventually regard itself as historical.

This view of historicity does not, however, supply the differentia of history regarded as a special science, having a special object. But this is precisely what the idea of re-thinking is intended to do. Re-thinking is the differentia of third-level history. And it is with the latter that the evolutionary theory of history is compared in the *Idea of History.* Just as history as a general habit or category must not be confused with history as a specialized discipline, so the historicity of nature must not be confused with the historicity of thought. To deny, in the *Idea of History,* that nature is historical, in the sense in which it is historical in the *Idea of Nature* and *Speculum Mentis,* is not a contradiction if it is realized that both the assertion and the denial take place at different points on a dialectical scale of questions and answers. In short, to use Collingwood's own "logic of question and answer," the statements "nature is historical" and "nature is not historical" in the *Idea of History* and the *Idea of Nature,* respectively, are not contraries because they are not answers to the same questions. They are rather different answers to different questions, arising at different points on a developing scale.

The former is an answer to the question, What is the relation between the modern view of nature and the idea of history as a general habit or category of mind which is necessarily involved in any and every act of cognition? The latter, however, is an answer to the question, What is the relation of the modern view of nature to the modern view of history regarded not as a general category but as a specialized and autonomous discipline?[12]

Collingwood's purpose in the *Idea of Nature* is to explicate the idea of nature as a third-level concept, and he does this by exposing the overlap between nature and history. But now a question arises which asks whether the theory of science expounded in the *Idea of Nature* is in fact an example of third-level scientific consciousness. According to my argument, third-level consciousness is predominantly philosophical, so that what we really want is an example of 'philosophical' science. Instead we are given an example of 'historical' science: "... the modern view of nature ... is based on the analogy between the processes of the natural world as studied by natural scientists and the vicissitudes of human affairs as studied by historians" (IN, 9). But this objection only illustrates how misleading our tripartite classification can be when it is applied too rigidly. For while it is true that third-level consciousness is primarily philosophical, philosophy is identical with history, and to the extent to which history is philosophical, so 'historical' science is, in its turn, 'philosophical.' If we do not forget that our scale of forms is dynamic rather than static, the difficulty will be overcome. The history which has 'superseded' science is a history which has in turn been superseded by philosophy, and the characteristics which are bestowed by history upon science are derived therefore from philosophy. Notice, for example, that 'historical' science has not only given up the abstract distinction between subject and object, but the philosophy which accompanies it is one which accepts the implication of a logic of overlapping classes (at least in so far as the relation of the sciences is concerned). In these respects, historical science has satisfied the criteria of third-level consciousness.

But the most important thing to realize is that third-level scientific consciousness has its own scale of forms, a scale within a scale, and is subject therefore to logical and historical development. In the course of this development the ideal limit of third-level scientific consciousness – whatever that may be – is more and more exemplified, given more and more concrete embodiment. 'Historical' science exists, no doubt, near the bottom of that scale, and will be superseded by higher and more 'philosophical' forms. But that it belongs on the scale at all cannot be denied. It was Collingwood's belief that although philosophy had already arrived on the scene, the age in which he lived was predominantly an 'historical' one, to be superseded in time by a philosophical age (SM, 54). It is appropriate then that third-level scientific consciousness should take the form that it does. Perhaps we cannot help wondering about the precise features of those more advanced, more 'philosophical,' forms of science which are yet to be developed. Wonder as we may, however, we cannot predict with any accuracy the future course of science. Indeed we can only cite Collingwood's warning at the end of the *Idea of Nature,* when he quotes with approval Hegel's famous saying at the end of his treatise on the philosophy of history: "That is as far as consciousness has reached" (IN, 174):

Similarly, I must say now, 'That is as far as science has reached'. All that has been said is a mere interim report on the history of the idea of nature down to the present time. If I knew what further progress would be made in the future, I should already have made that progress. (IN, 175)

2 HISTORY AS THE ASSERTION OF CONCRETE FACT: THE CATEGORICAL SINGULAR JUDGMENT

The basis of the transition from scientific consciousness to history lies in the recognition that the perception which characterizes all scientific thinking is historical and that the true object of thought is therefore not the abstract but the concrete universal. When this insight is rendered explicit and made the basis of a new standpoint, history as a separate and autonomous form of experience arises.

History is that cognitive activity which thinks the concrete universal, the unity of particular and universal, which is not a bare indistinguishable identity but an identity to which difference is organic and essential, a union in which the two sides can be distinguished but not separated.[13] Collingwood characterizes this activity as "reason" as opposed to "understanding," the act of thinking the abstract universal (SM, 196). "The antithesis of understanding and reason, or abstract and concrete thinking," writes Collingwood, "is the antithesis of science and history" (SM, 198). But he then goes on to say that "the separation of understanding from reason is itself an act of understanding, which reason is bound to repudiate" (SM, 198). The difficulties created by these statements may be resolved by interpreting them and other similar passages in terms of the previously drawn threefold ontological distinction. For then it will be clear that the antithesis between understanding and reason exists only at the first level of consciousness, while the repudiation of this distinction is characteristic of second- and third-level consciousness.

There is a difference, in other words, between reason operating at the first level and reason operating at the second and third levels. At the first level, reason is governed by the principle, already cited, that to be actually absorbed in any given form of experience is by this very absorption to be committed to the belief that no other form is valid (SM, 307) – a principle which we now recognize to apply at the first level of consciousness only. As a result, reason is not yet fully reason and it therefore occupies a place at the bottom of its own scale of forms.

Understanding, or scientific consciousness, is likewise committed by its original error at the first level to denying its own identity with history (SM, 198). In so far as it lives its life only at the first level, it is committed to the view that "... science is the only form of thought, and history does not exist at all" (SM, 199). Indeed, so long as we remain at the first level of consciousness, Collingwood is perfectly justified in declaring: "From no point of view ... can science and history be regarded as co-existent and equally rational or defensible manifestations of thought" (SM, 198–9). But once reason has freed itself from first-level dogmatism it recognizes that in fact the separation of understanding and reason is a false abstraction, that in truth the two are identical (SM, 198).

This identity, however, which is characteristic of higher level consciousness, must be distinguished from another kind of identity, also referred to in this passage, in which history simply 'subsumes' science under it; the view according to which science exists only as an element within the body of history itself, as a mere weapon or tool of historical thinking (SM, 199). This is an equally misleading form of first-level dogmatism, which is no different in kind from the 'scientism' which, under the banner of positivism, subsumes all activities under the activity of science, or from the 'historicism' of Croce (which Collingwood rejected in 1920) which makes philosophy no more than the methodological moment of history. The identity which raises reason to a higher level of existence must be one which, when interpreted in terms of the model of genus and co-ordinate species, leads to the view of *Religion and Philosophy* and the 1922 essay on the relation between history and science, but which, when interpreted in terms of the logic of the overlap of classes, leads to the theory of the 'dialectical' relation of science and history. In a passage which would otherwise make very little sense Collingwood explicates the latter condition as one in which "... one tries to be what the other is, one implies what the other expresses, one questions where the other answers, one overlooks what the other recognizes;

and of which therefore the more primitive is absorbed without residue in the more advanced" (SM, 200).

The idea of history as concrete thought, having as its object the concrete fact, is the product of a long historical development. In keeping with the principle established at the outset of *Speculum Mentis* that the natural or logical order of the forms of experience is exemplified in the history of mankind (SM, 51), and that each particular form is itself a scale of forms exhibiting the same natural order (SM, 56), history, in so far as its historical development is concerned, can be expected to reflect the influence of the major forms which both precede and supersede it. There is, therefore, an aesthetic, religious and scientific history, as well as a philosophical history.

The most critical stage through which history must pass is the scientific stage. Indeed, Collingwood declares on various occasions that the greatest ordeal which the idea of history has to face is the attempt to assert its autonomy against the tyranny of natural science (IH, 193).[14] This theme is taken up in more detail in the first four parts of the *Idea of History*. Thus history, like science and art, must pass through a complete dialectic of its own in which the conflict between its own abstractness and the concreteness of the facts upon which it rests is resolved. For this reason the origin of history during the Renaissance was only an implicit origin. It is true, Collingwood argues, that Renaissance historians finally recognized that the object of historical knowledge was the 'fact.' At the same time, however, they mistakenly conceived the fact as a mere abstract instance of an abstract law, as a mere particular rather than an individual, and the idea of history was therefore distorted in order to bring it into line with the abstractions of natural science (SM, 203).

Yet implicit in scientific history is the ultimate form of historical thought, which is perception. Indeed, Collingwood asserts categorically that "perception and history are identical" (SM, 204). The identification of history with perception is perhaps the most significant feature of this early phase of Collingwood's philosophy of history. Indeed the argument of *Speculum Mentis* would almost lead us to believe that the history of the idea of history is synonymous with the development in consciousness of interpretations of perception. History, Collingwood writes in an article in 1925 (which expands the view of *Speculum Mentis*) is "perception raised to its highest level" (NAPH, 167). In short, the dialectic of the history of historiography is the dialectic of perception.

Collingwood's identification of history with perception in *Speculum*

Mentis and "The Nature and Aims of a Philosophy of History" has been a source of confusion concerning the relation between the early and later writings. The most serious difficulty is the problem of reconciling the doctrine which identifies history and perception with the doctrine of the *Idea of History*, which tends to draw a sharp distinction between history and perception (IH, 233, 307–8). This apparent change in attitude tends to confirm prevailing notions that Collingwood's thought is subject to radical discontinuities. Nathan Rotenstreich, for example, contrasts Collingwood's early preoccupation with the "facts" or "objects" of history, with his later interest (characteristic of the *Idea of History*) in the more subjective factors connected with the act of historical thinking.[15] The latter, according to Rotenstreich, betrays a general shift in Collingwood's philosophy away from epistemological realism and towards some kind of Hegelian Idealism,[16] and he cites "The Nature and Aims of a Philosophy of History" (1925) as the precise point at which this transition occurred. Since Rotenstreich regards this transition as the result of a change in Collingwood's general philosophical outlook rather than as a stage in the systematic exposition of the idea of history, he therefore declares that "There is a lack of symmetry in Collingwood's theory of history."[17]

A somewhat different account of Collingwood's radical shift from one view of history to another is given by Alan Donagan.[18] Donagan argues that in *Speculum Mentis* as well as in "The Nature and Aims of a Philosophy of History" (1925) Collingwood advances the doctrine, derived from the identity of history with perception, that since objects of perception in general are objects in the flow of feelings which have been raised to consciousness, the objects of history must likewise have their place in the flow of immediate consciousness.[19] This doctrine, "that history, as a specific form of experience, is identical with perception," was asserted, according to Donagan, together with its derivative doctrine "that to historians past thoughts are an objective spectacle." Both doctrines, Donagan continues, are false. Indeed, if either were true, "scepticism would be inevitable." Donagan then argues that Collingwood himself realized this and went on in the *Idea of History* to redefine history *a parte subjecti* in terms of the notion of "re-thinking." As represented by Donagan, the *rationale* of Collingwood's conversion from realism to idealism may be characterized as follows. Either the objects of history are mere facts which exist independently of their being known, or else they are thoughts. They cannot be mere facts because this leads to scepticism. But if they are thoughts they cannot be objects of perception. You cannot become aware of the thoughts of others except by re-thinking them for yourself.[20]

Finally, Collingwood's critics will no doubt argue, it was Collingwood's attempt to account for the possibility of re-thinking that forced him to accept the doctrines of radical historicism. For, since re-thinking must occur within the context of the historian's own mind, and since the historian's mind is subject to the conditions of historicity, the results of re-thinking must therefore be subject to the same conditions.

These interpretations by Rotenstreich and Donagan raise questions of fundamental importance. Does the shift from realism to idealism in Collingwood's philosophy of history constitute a conversion or radical change in outlook? Or, can it be alternatively regarded as a dialectical transition within the systematic exposition of the idea of history? And is it furthermore the case that Collingwood's preoccupation with the subjective factors of the act of knowing or re-thinking leads straight to the doctrines of radical historicism? The answers lie in a careful appraisal of Collingwood's various accounts of perception.

Collingwood begins in *Speculum Mentis* by defining perception as the standpoint in which we are immediately aware of an object, namely, the concrete historical fact. He is quick to point out, however, that the immediacy of perception "does not exclude mediation" (SM, 204). Perception, he argues, "... is not abstract immediacy (sensation) but implicitly contains an element of mediation (thought)" (SM, 204). This view had already been elaborated in a paper published in 1923 entitled "Sensation and Thought." The thesis advanced there is that perception involves mediation as well as immediacy and the element of mediation predominates. The argument is really no more than a commentary on Kant's dictum: "intuitions without concepts are blind, concepts without intuitions are empty." Perception is fundamentally mediation or interpretation because every starting point of thought no matter how simple must already be the product of thought (ST, 74-5). One is reminded of Hegel's comment in the *Phenomenology* that "... behind the so-called curtain, which is to hide the inner world, there is nothing to be seen unless we ourselves go behind there, as much in order that we may thereby see, as that there may be something behind there which can be seen."[21]

Collingwood recognizes, however, that by perception people usually mean something which is quite different, something more akin to sensation, and he goes on to warn us against such an error by demonstrating how the analysis of perception reveals inevitably the presence of thought and mediation.

Against Donagan I will contend that if perception itself is viewed in terms of what Collingwood called a scale of forms (or, more precisely, a series of philosophical errors) then it follows that the kind of perception which he claims Collingwood is talking about in *Speculum Mentis*, and which (according to Donagan) is rejected as a model for history in the *Idea of History*, while it indeed occupies a place on the scale, is nevertheless superseded by higher forms of perception. It would be a consequence of this interpretation, therefore, that when in *Speculum Mentis* Collingwood identifies perception with history he is referring to the perception of reason not the perception of understanding. On the other hand, when in the *Idea of History* he separates history from perception (IH, 233) it is precisely the perception of the understanding that he has in mind.

The first stage in the scale of forms which constitutes perception is, according to Collingwood, aesthetic perception. Its corresponding form of history is mythology and fable (SM, 209). The next form is religious perception (for example, the world view of primitive man) in which the 'fact' appears to consciousness as the will of God (SM, 209). Implicit in this standpoint is a denial of the concreteness of the fact and its subordination to an abstract transcendent cause, conceived as an object of imagination, namely, the supreme being of God. Thus arises the next stage of perception in which the transcendent cause of religious perception becomes the abstract law. In the form of history corresponding to this stage, the fact becomes the mere abstract instance of an abstract principle. Collingwood is here referring to the dogma of positivism and its programme for the "elevation of history to the rank of a science" (SM, 208).[22] Conceived as the science of 'mere facts' a positivistic historical explanation requires to be supplemented from outside by the so-called 'laws of history,' the discovery of which lies with sociology, economics, and the other social sciences; historical facts become therefore so much fuel for the engine of social science (SM, 208).[23]

Each of the above interpretations of history – the mythical, the religious, the scientific – is founded on a philosophical error which produces an unreconciled opposition. Aesthetic history creates a world of metaphor and myth whose opposite is the unromantic light of common day. Religious history finds its opposite in 'nature' or whatever it may call those facts which it cannot reconcile with its notion of divine providence. Such natural phenomena are, from the point of view of religion, "diabolical intrusions," "enemies of God," and so forth, against which God's actions stand out as miracles (SM, 209–10). Finally, scientific history "finds its opposite in the 'contingent', a derogatory name invented by it to describe those facts which it cannot force into its abstract schemes" (SM, 209).

With the emergence of a more genuine form of history, the possibility of a synthesis of all these opposites is created. Genuine history therefore reconciles drama with fact, providence with chance, necessity with contingency (SM, 210). Moreover, in negating and superseding the other forms of historical experience, genuine history does not of course simply discard them. On the contrary, a dialectical mediation, as we have already noted, involves not only asserting as true something which in the previous term was wrongly denied, but retaining as well the implicit presupposition of that term. Thus in the genuinely historical perception of the fact, the object is mediated through all of the other forms. The historical process is therefore seen as a drama working according to a rational principle on the one hand, and mysterious forces on the other, and as combining in its method both a priori and a posteriori elements. It is only when what is in reality but one moment of a total experience is abstracted and elevated to the rank of a dogma, asserting itself as an independent and autonomous form of experience, that the dialectic is arrested and an error is committed (SM, 210).

Historical perception, that is, perception raised to its highest power, is ideally the attempt to grasp the object as a whole in a synthesis of "front and back," "top and bottom," "past," "present," and "future." This means literally "seeing what we do not see": using the data immediately present to reconstruct the whole of which it is a part. Whereas the scientific historian – to cite only one example – is content to describe merely what happens and has happened, the genuine historian "must investigate causes and inquire into motives, discerning the right from the wrong" (SM, 217). The question therefore arises, What must the nature of fact be in order to satisfy these conditions?

The answer implicit in *Speculum Mentis* may be re-constructed as follows. The only object which when known describes not only what happened but why it happened is the concrete fact. The concrete fact contains within itself the grounds of its own explanation. Historical perception makes no distinction, in other words, between what happened and why. The latter is the mediating factor by means of which the fact is perceived. The object of history is not therefore the fact or event apprehended independently of its causes (as Taine, for example, declared when he wrote, "Après la collection des faits la recherche des causes") ;[24] nor is it the causes by themselves viewed as abstract laws "brooding above the flow of historical events" (SM, 218) ; it is simply "these events themselves as purposed and planned by the agents" (SM, 218).

The act of historical perception is thus, according to Collingwood, an act of judgment; indeed, judging the causes of action is a necessary requirement of the standpoint as such. The judgment is not an alien act performed by the historian for motives outside his historical work; it is part of that work which cannot be omitted without turning the whole into a process of false abstraction, thus separating the event from the act. In this sense, writes Collingwood, the evaluation of the historical act is identical with its determination, and it is true that "die Weltgeschichte ist die Weltgericht" (SM, 218).

If this is the view which is defended in *Speculum Mentis*, then it seems like a short enough step to the doctrine of the *Idea of History*:

> The historian, investigating any event in the past, makes a distinction between what might be called the outside and the inside of the event. By the outside of the event I mean everything in it which can be described in terms of bodies and their movements ... By the inside of the event I mean that in it which can be described in terms of thought ... The historian is never concerned with either of these to the exclusion of the other. (IH, 213)

Yet, as critics of Collingwood will invariably argue, the positions of *Speculum Mentis* and the *Idea of History* are in fact vastly different and have often been held to be irreconcilable. When seen in the proper perspective, however, these apparent differences may be reconciled.

The real difference between the *Speculum Mentis* account of perception and that of the *Idea of History* is to be found by analysis of the various criteria according to which the object of perception (in each work) is defined. There is first of all the criterion, described above, according to which the object becomes more and more concrete. In this respect there is no explicit difference. Within this process, however, there are other criteria, such as whether the object is temporal or extra-temporal, past or present, thought or non-thought. In the *Idea of History*, for example, science is defined as the perception of the here and now in terms of laws or causes (i.e., abstract universals which are "... in one sense everywhere and in another nowhere, in one sense at all times and in another at no times ..." [IH, 234]). In short, science is the perception of the temporal through the mediation of the extra-temporal. This gives it an abstract character, and it follows that the mediating factor is not intrinsic to the scientific fact itself. This is the attitude which Collingwood called perception in the *Idea of History*. It is certainly not the perception which in *Speculum Mentis* is identified with history, for the mediating factors in this form of perception are intrinsic to the fact itself.

But while the object of historical perception in *Speculum Mentis* is described as the concrete fact (i.e., as that which is apprehended not in terms of external laws or causes but in terms of other concrete facts) (SM, 218), no special attention is given to the insight that it is only the past as thought which in the end can be such an object. On the contrary, the impression is given in *Speculum Mentis* that everything which is apprehended as concrete is by definition historical. In the *Idea of History*, however, the object of history is explicitly defined not simply as the concrete fact (IH, 234), but as "thought" (IH, 317; A, 110), and as "events which have finished happening, and conditions no longer in existence" (IH, 233). Thus, if by perception we continue to mean the perception of the mere facticity of all things, then historical knowledge of past thought, as defined in the *Idea of History*, is not perception.

In so far as we treat these works as answers to the question, How is knowledge of the past possible? the distance between *Speculum Mentis* and the *Idea of History* thus seems vast. But the reasons for this are systematic and not, as Donagan has suggested, because of a radical change in Collingwood's thought. In *Speculum Mentis*, the historical attitude is presented not only as a special form of knowledge, but as an element which enters into all knowledge (not only history, but science, religion, art, and even philosophy). The latter, the concept of history as a category or habit of mind, provides a basis for explicating the meaning of Collingwood's statement that "the fact, as historically determined, is the absolute object" (SM, 218). This means that we have historical knowledge of tables, chairs, and even nature as well as of historical events; for, as we have already seen, the perception of any fact is historical. But how can this universalizing of history in *Speculum Mentis* be reconciled with the explicit claim in the *Idea of History* that there can be historical knowledge only of events which take the form of past thought?

This too is a difficult question which draws attention to what is perhaps the greatest single weakness in Collingwood's system. The difficulty stems from Collingwood's failure in *Speculum Mentis* to distinguish clearly between a given form of knowledge conceived as a general habit of mind (or category), and the same form conceived as a special science. This very distinction, which has already been dealt with above, is implicit throughout *Speculum Mentis*, and had Collingwood himself drawn attention to it he might have been spared a great deal of criticism; for in order to make sense of much of what he says throughout *Speculum Mentis*, it is necessary to employ this distinction.

For example, in the case of history viewed as a habit of mind only, it is true that the concreteness of the fact is what makes it historical. In this respect the whole world is an *historical* fact simply because it is a *fact*. Our knowledge of the facticity of things, in other words, is what makes our knowledge of all things historical. It is an error, however, to raise this habit of mind to the rank of a general dogma (as in the case of realism or first-level dogmatic historical philosophy which is the elevation of the historical habitus, as described in chapter VI of *Speculum Mentis*, to a universal world view). It is also an error to mistake this habit for the idea of history as an autonomous form of knowledge having a special object of its own. For while it is true that the discipline of history is derived from the historical habit of mind, the differentia of this discipline cannot be strictly deduced from the formal structure of the habit.

Thus, from the concept of the historical habit of mind as the knowledge of the facticity of all things we can deduce neither the idea of history as the perception of facts nor the idea of history as the re-thinking of past thought. But once consciousness commits the error of identifying the discipline with the habit from which it is derived, the first step has been taken in the self-correcting dialectical process which advances through various interpretations from the idea of history as the perception of facts to the idea of history as the re-thinking of past thought.

The criteria according to which this development occurs are supplied by philosophy which, as we have already seen, undergoes its own peculiar development. The theory of perception, in other words, should be evaluated according to the tripartite conceptual framework introduced above (ch. III, s. 3). Thus perception, like every other act of mind, must be regarded as operating on three distinct but related levels. At the first level, therefore, perception will assume an absolute separation of subject from object, as well as dogmatically assuming that there is only one genuine way of apprehending that object. This level is represented by realism, which presents itself as the first stage in the philosophy of history.

At the second level, in keeping with the requirements of our tripartite model, the distinction between subject and object is retained but consciousness now believes that there are a variety of different but equally valid ways of viewing the object. History, the perception of facts as concrete individual events, is one of these ways. This is the standpoint of "The Nature and Aims of a Philosophy of History."

Finally, as a result of internal dialectical tensions this stage in turn gives rise to the third-level interpretation of the *Idea of History*. This transition (whose dialectic will be more thoroughly examined below) is primarily effected by the philosophical insight that the object of history cannot be totally independent of the perceiving subject and yet concrete. If history is to be categorical knowledge of the concrete then there can no longer be any separation between subject and object. Thus third-level historical consciousness denies the distinction between subject and object. But to do this is also to deny the separation of the various forms of knowledge. History no longer conceives of itself as one of a number of co-ordinate species. Instead it seeks membership on an overlapping scale of forms. And, since only mind can satisfy the criteria of knowledge in which there is no longer any distinction between subject and object, history is therefore defined as the mind's self-knowledge of itself in the form of past thought.

Thus the transition from the standpoint of history as the perception of independently existing facts to the idea of history as the re-thinking of past thought is already implicit in the phenomenological development of mind (conceived as a system of habits or categories) from the habit of history to the habit of philosophy and within each habit from the first to the third level. The standpoint of the *Idea of History* must therefore be regarded as the dialectical outcome of the position of *Speculum Mentis*, rather than as an entirely new beginning which repudiates all earlier standpoints.

Unfortunately, Collingwood's own exposition of history in *Speculum Mentis* does not make explicit use of such distinctions as have been drawn above. He therefore writes at different levels in different places without explicitly acknowledging it, and it is unhappily left to the reader to decide on which occasions he is referring to history as a general habit of mind and on which occasions he is referring to it as a special discipline, that is, as a science (and if the latter at what level). Thus, for example, when Collingwood declares that history is identical with perception (SM, 204, 205) and that "There is thus no feature of experience, no attitude of mind towards its object, which is alien to history" (218), he is referring to history as a general habit of mind. But when he declares that the historian's goal is "the knowledge of the infinite world of facts" (231) – a knowledge which is characterized by "objectivity" (237) so that "As long as we pretend to write history, we must claim access to the fact as it really was" (238) – and that the business of the historian is to determine not only "what happened" but "why it happened" by investigating "causes" and inquiring into "motives, discerning the right from the wrong" (217), he is referring to history as a special (but erroneously conceived) discipline. Likewise, when Collingwood writes, "History as a form of knowledge cannot exist" (238) he is referring not to the habit as such nor even to the discipline as such, but rather to the habit mistaking itself for a strict discipline. The latter is a dogmatic error which, when exposed, provides the dialectical basis not only for the transition from history to philosophy but for the transition within historical consciousness itself from one level to another: and hence the rebirth, in a new form, of the idea of history as a special and autonomous activity.

It is clear then that the discrepancy between the *Speculum Mentis* account of history and that of the *Idea of History* is the result not only of Collingwood's failure to acknowledge explicitly the distinctions implicit in his actual account of history, but also of the very nature of the dialectical distinction which exists between the two works. There is, as I have already suggested, a basic contradiction in *Speculum Mentis* between subject and object. It is partly because of the latter that consciousness confuses history as a general habit of mind (for which a distinction between subject and object is appropriate) with history as a special form of knowledge (for which, at its highest level, such distinctions are overcome). From the standpoint of history conceived as a general habit of mind, facts are objects to be acquainted with and the terms of reference within which acquaintance occurs make any such identity between subject and object as is required by historical knowledge impossible. Collingwood therefore declares in the *Idea of History* that: "All theories of knowledge that conceive [historical knowledge] as a transaction or relation between a subject and an object both actually existing or compresent to one another, theories that take acquaintance as the essence of knowledge, make history impossible" (IH, 233).

The acquaintance theory of knowledge, and its implied separation between subject and object, is a characteristic of all standpoints expounded *ab intra* at the first level – which is precisely the level at which the *Speculum Mentis* account of history exists. At this level the distinction between knowing mind and concrete fact becomes, when elevated to the rank of a general dogma, a kind of 'historicism' whose implicit philosophy is philosophical realism. There is therefore created a dialectical tension between the implicit idealism of the doctrine of perception and the explicit realism of the theory of history which is actually advanced. This tension is the basis upon which history is finally superseded by philosophy (which is a consequence of the discovery that history is implicit philosophy).

But in keeping with the basic principle of *Speculum Mentis*, the idea of history, like the ideas of art, religion, and science, is itself a scale of forms, and this implies that the negation of history by philosophy is the occasion upon which history re-constitutes itself. This gives birth to philosophical history for which the distinction between subject and object is gradually overcome. From the philosophical standpoint mind recognizes that what it takes to be its object is in reality only an appearance of the subject which is substantially altered by the act of its being known.

Thus, when Collingwood declares that the concept of the world of fact as a "concrete universal (SM, 221) ... compels us to recognize an object to which the subject is organic, in the sense that the subject's consciousness of it makes a real difference to it as a whole and to all its parts" (SM, 244) and that "the world of fact which is explicitly studied in history is therefore implicitly nothing but the knowing mind as such" (SM, 245), he is laying the foundations for a higher-level account of 'philosophical' history. Under the influence of philosophy the question which higher-level philosophical history poses for itself must therefore be, What are the characteristics of the idea of history for whom the object is the concrete fact whose nature is such that it is essentially altered by the fact of its being known? The answer to this question is given in the *Idea of History* which is an analysis of the highest level of historical consciousness, the level at which the long-sought-for rapprochement between history and philosophy has finally been achieved. At this level the philosophical historian knows what the historian of *Speculum Mentis* does not know: that his own knowledge of facts is organic to the facts themselves, that his mind is these facts knowing themselves and these facts are his mind knowing itself. History is now defined as the science of mind par excellence and is indeed perception raised to its highest power; a perception which, having transcended the subject-object distinction, may now be more properly described as 'imaginative re-construction' or 're-thinking,' "a process in which man creates for himself this or that kind of human nature by re-creating in his own thought the past to which he is heir" (IH, 226) and in this way achieves for himself a state of genuine freedom (SM, 222; IH, 315–20).

3 THE NEGATION OF HISTORY

Ideally, the object of first-level history is the absolute whole, the infinite world of fact. Thus, historical consciousness requires *ab intra* that the perception of any single fact presupposes a knowledge of the whole context. But (and this is the point at which historical consciousness runs the risk of relapsing into scepticism) since this context is a continually changing dynamic process which is always in principle incomplete, it necessarily follows *ab extra* that we can never know any single part as it actually is (SM, 231). It follows, therefore, that if universal history is defined as an absolute and perfectly organized individual whole such that every part in it determines every other part, there is no escape from the conclusion that ignorance or error concerning any one part involves an essential and radical ignorance or error concerning every other part (SM, 232).

To avoid this inference it is necessary to postulate a new conception of historical fact, namely, the concept of fact as atomic rather than systematic, which involves, of course, the substitution of external for internal relations. Each fact is what it is, irrespective of all the others, and is knowable by itself as though it were a perfectly isolated atom whose nature is unaffected by the existence of other atoms to which it is only externally related. This means that we can apprehend the atomic facts of history one by one and thus build up structures of fact which have nothing to fear from any unrevealed fact that may lurk in the surrounding darkness. The possibility of historical knowledge is therefore saved.

But the price of this salvation is the destruction of the historical standpoint. Historical atomism plunges history back into scientific consciousness by destroying the differentia which separates history from science. The theory of external relations which historical atomism presupposes may be true for science, but it is false for history. History, if it is to defend its autonomy at all, must conceive of itself primarily as the perception of the concrete fact to which the context in which it exists is not irrelevant but essential.

We are therefore left with the following dilemma. If history (as defined in *Speculum Mentis*) exists, its object is an infinite whole which is unknowable and renders all its parts unknowable. If, on the other hand, the facts of history are atomic facts then history as a separate and autonomous form of knowledge does not exist and we are thrown back on science, whose bankruptcy we have already accepted (SM, 234).

History then, like every other form of knowledge, rests upon a contradiction between what it ideally is and what it actually is. The basis of this contradiction lies in an error which history shares with every other standpoint, namely, the explicit affirmation of the distinction between subject and object. In the language of *An Essay on Metaphysics*, the distinction between subject and object which underlies each standpoint in *Speculum Mentis* (with the possible exception of absolute philosophy) may be characterized as an "absolute presupposition." In so far as history is committed to the separation of subject and object, consciousness appears to have achieved the final alienation of the mind from its object. Yet it is only in history that the indispensable condition of the possibility of knowledge is for the first time realized. For we know implicitly in history what we never knew before, namely what kind of an object it must be that is alone knowable. It must be an object not merely of the imagination, like a work of art, but of thought; yet like the work of art it must be concrete and individual. It must, like the object of religion, be absolute and eternal; yet, unlike this again, it must be a real object and not the imaginative or metaphorical presentation of an object. It must be capable of being conceived, like the object of science, yet it must not be an abstraction. Finally, like the object of history, it must be a fact, an absolute concrete individual; but it must be accessible to the knowing mind (SM, 238–9).

The fundamental difficulty which faces history is that the very condition of the possibility of knowledge appears to be denied in the act of knowing *per se*. For if knowledge is the apprehension of *what is, as it is*, then we must either know it in its totality or not at all. To know it only partially is not to know it as *it is in itself* but only as it is *for the knowing subject*. Since knowledge proceeds by error, it follows that the object of knowledge will be itself an error; it will never, in the growth of knowledge, coincide with the object in itself. If knowledge is to be possible, then there must be an object which is *in itself* only what it is *for another*; or, to use Hegel's expression, which is *per se* only what it is *per se* for consciousness.[25] We are thus presented with the concept of an object whose very nature is to be altered by being known, even if this alteration is an error; an object, in other words, whose very mode of existence is to be known erroneously.

The contradiction inherent in the separation of subject and object may be arrived at by taking a slightly different path. Implied by the separation in question is the assumption that knowing makes no difference to the object known. This statement, however, is inconsistent with the original claim that for history the object of knowledge is the entire world of fact. For to claim that I know something (whether I know it implicitly or explicitly) is to establish a fact and this fact must therefore be added to the entire world of facts, in which case it follows that the entire world of fact is indeed changed by my coming to know it. In other words, the facts as I know them are by that very knowledge made different from the same facts as I do not know them. This applies as well to the conversion of knowledge from implicit to explicit. The universe of fact which is implicitly known becomes objectively different by being explicitly known because our knowledge of it is part of it. It follows then that the truth of history, when rendered fully explicit, is a denial of any absolute distinction between subject and object:

> The fundamental principle of history itself, namely, the concreteness of the object, thus makes it impossible for the object to ignore the subject, and compels us to recognize an object to which the subject is organic, in the sense that the subject's consciousness of it makes a real difference to it as a whole and to all its parts. The subject is thus no mere separable part of the world of fact, but an essential element which penetrates its whole fabric, a constitutive element in the object itself. Being known, whether truly known or erroneously known, must make a difference to the object; to deny this, we can now see, is to turn one's back on concrete thought and revert to the fallacies of abstraction. (SM, 244)[26]

The question now arises, What kind of an object is it which, on the one hand, can be conceived of as an absolute fact yet at the same time is such that knowledge of it is organic to the facts themselves, without excluding, of course, the possibility of error? The only object which, according to Collingwood, satisfies these criteria, is "mind" which is essentially an activity of self-knowledge proceeding through error and endowing itself in this way with a nature as such. Mind, writes Collingwood, *is* only what it *does* (SM, 241):

> ... a mind which is ignorant of its true nature does not in the fullest sense possess this nature. The true nature of the mind does not exist ready-made somewhere in the depths of the mind, waiting to be discovered. Till it is discovered it does not exist; but yet it does exist in a confused and distorted form, since the errors made about it are only partial errors, and the dialectical task of bringing it into existence or coming to know it (the two are the same) is simply the clearing up of these confusions, which appear as inconsistencies, conflicts between what, at a given stage, the mind finds itself to be and what it feels it ought to be. (SM, 207)

It may be thought that the reduction of the subject-object distinction to a dialectical identity, which is the mark of philosophy, will have the effect of transforming the world into a solopsistic product of imagination (SM, 244). This consequence, however, does not follow.[27] The products of imagination are, as we have seen, neither true nor false. The imagined object exists precisely as it is imagined. But the object of thought, even though its nature is to some extent determined by the erroneous view which thought itself has of it, does not, by means of this error, necessarily lose its true nature, which *qua* real object remains hidden behind the ostensible object. In other words, there is always a permanent discrepancy between what the object is *per se* and what the object is *for us*; and, when the object is recognized to be mind, this implies recognition of the fact that self-estrangement is a permanent feature of the human condition. If we call the object as it is *per se*, truth, and the object *for us*, error, then we must point out that the tension between them is a dialectical one in which truth is implicit in error. There is no such thing as pure error, and the erroneous judgment which the mind makes of its object is therefore inconsistent with itself.

Finally, since this inconsistency occurs in a rational mind, the very knowledge of it is a step in the direction of overcoming it:

> ... the mind having formed a false conception of itself, tries to live up to that conception. But the falseness of the conception just means that it cannot be 'lived up to'. There is therefore a permanent discord between what the mind thinks it is, and what, on the strength of that conception, it does: even though this behaviour is not at all the same thing as the behaviour of a mind that knows itself truly. The result is an open inconsistency between theory and practice; and this inconsistency, as ground for dissatisfaction, is the starting point of the attempt at truer self-knowledge. (SM, 250; cf. 84, 245)

We may now, with Collingwood, sum up the results thus far. Our task has been the search for an object of knowledge. We found that in art we could get no true object because the ostensible object, the work of art, points beyond itself to a different object of which art is only the symbol. In other words, art pretends to be pure imagination but is not; on the contrary, it is the implicit assertion of something which although it is not explicitly asserted is nevertheless the real object of art. But what the nature of this real object is, art cannot say. In the case of religion, too, we found that the ostensible object, God, was not the real object. The mythology of religion does not say what it means; it too points beyond itself to a concealed truth which is not stated. Religion claims to be pure faith but, like art, it rests implicitly on a content of assertions. Even in science the ostensible object, the abstract concept – indifferently called the physical or material world, the realm of abstract thought, pure being, or the like – is really no more than an arbitrary construction, a purely fictitious concept, and not the real object of thought at all. Only in history did we find a type of thought which, to all appearances, meant what it said when it pointed to facts as its real object. We therefore ventured to assume that fact, the real object of history, is the hidden and implicit object not only of science but of religion and art as well. But what is this fact? What is it about?

Throughout the whole process, we have assumed that the imagery of art, the mythology of religion, the mechanism of science, are successive veils hung between the mind and its object as it is in itself. In effect we have assumed, absolutely without any justification whatever, a distinction between subject and object; and not only a distinction, but a separation, a relation of difference without identity.

But difference without identity is an abstract concept, while the fundamental principle of history is concreteness for which there can be no separation. For, if both subject and object are concrete individuals (as opposed to abstract particulars) then each must be determined by the other. It is thus impossible for the object to ignore the subject. History by its own inner dialectic compels us to recognize an object to which the subject is organic, an object which can only be the knowing mind itself for, as we have seen, a mind's error actually deranges it and causes it to behave abnormally; and it is only by correcting this error that the mind can regain its true nature. Collingwood therefore reaches the ultimate conclusion that the "world of fact which is explicitly studied in history is therefore implicitly nothing but the knowing mind as such" (SM, 245).

History, then, conceives of its object as the concrete fact. To become conscious that the concrete fact is implicitly mind or thought is to leave the standpoint of history for philosophy. Philosophy is the study of thought *qua* thought, the standpoint in which the long-sought-for reconciliation between substances and subject has been achieved. In short, history poses a problem which only philosophy can solve, and the conclusion of *Speculum Mentis* is therefore that history is only implicit philosophy; or to put it another way, art, religion, science, and history are philosophical errors, unconscious philosophies of mind *nescientis se philosophari* (SM, 240). The declaration by philosophy that the other forms of knowledge are all implicit philosophy – a declaration which can only be made at the third level – introduces a philosophical concept of mind that "requires us to conceive the whole as *totum in toto et totum in quadlibet parte*, and the part as performing a function in the whole without which the whole would simply not exist" (SM, 300).[28]

V

Philosophy as a
SCALE OF FORMS:
Dogmatic Philosophy

Philosophy, as characterized by Collingwood, exists on a variety of levels. In chapter III a distinction was drawn between three ontological levels, each of which was in turn characterized by a methodological distinction between an *ab extra* and an *ab intra* approach. The latter distinction is the source of a further distinction between pure absolute philosophy, which in its ideal state transcends all particular standpoints, and the more historically grounded philosophy, which acts as the reflective moment of finite experience. Collingwood's name for the latter is "dogmatic philosophy" or metaphysics.

According to the terms of my exposition, the discrepancy between absolute and dogmatic philosophy is proportional to the place which the latter occupies both on the 'horizontal' scale which develops from the first to the third ontological levels and on the 'vertical' and more general scale which develops from art to philosophy. The differentia of absolute philosophy, conceived as a separate standpoint, is the explicit identity of subject and object (SM, 249). This identity, however, has been implicit from the very beginning in the dogmatic philosophies of art, religion, science, and history. The true object has always been the mind itself; it is only the ostensible object that is other than mind (SM, 249). Absolute philosophy is, therefore, an implicit presupposition of every other standpoint.

But although absolute philosophy is implicit in every other standpoint, its implicitness differs in kind from case to case. Indeed the absolute identity which is the chief differentia of philosophy is at best an ideal limit, characteristic only of the pure state of philosophy which exists at the top of the ontological scale. The latter, however, is achieved only as the conclusion of the dialectical development which characterizes the general scale of forms from art to philosophy. Philosophy, in other words, must be conceived as a scale exhibiting the stages through which its ideal limit is gradually realized: "... within philosophy we shall find an aesthetic philosophy, a religious philosophy, and an intellectual philosophy which splits up into scientific philosophy, historical philosophy, and philosophical philosophy" (SM, 56). And the stages through which absolute philosophy (which constitutes the *ab extra* moment of criticism) develops are synonomous therefore with the stages through which dogmatic philosophy (which constitutes the *ab intra* moment) develops.

I THE GENERAL CHARACTERISTICS OF DOGMATIC PHILOSOPHY

Dogmatic philosophy is the philosophy which is implicit in each of the separate standpoints. There are, therefore, as many cases of dogmatic philosophy as there are types of abstraction. Of crucial importance to my argument is my claim that implicit in the description of dogmatic philosophy in *Speculum Mentis* is a fundamental distinction between (what I have called for Collingwood) 'therapeutic' and 'corrupt' dogmatism. The former is healthy and virile, the latter is pathological.

Therapeutic dogmatism develops according to the threefold ontological distinction outlined in chapter III (s. 2) and is a necessary ingredient in the life of mind as such. Thus Collingwood writes, concerning therapeutic dogmatic philosophy in general: "... we ought to treat dogmatic philosophy with reverence ... For it is only by the gate of dogmatism that one can set forth upon the road to philosophy ..." (SM, 260). The same point is made later on in a passage dealing specifically with scientific dogmatism. The latter, he writes, "is not altogether an error":

It is a discipline. Hegel said that every philosopher ought to pass through a phase of Spinozism, which is little but a scientific dogmatism of a peculiarly rigid kind. So the technicalities of abstract thought, though they are not philosophy, are a gymnastic without which the philosopher is likely to be a slack-jointed and flabby creature. (SM, 281)

There is a point, however, at which a dogmatic standpoint like this ceases to be relevant and appropriate. On such occasions the mind, if it is to maintain a healthy life, must move on to a higher and more enlightened standpoint. "A mind's error about itself," writes Collingwood "... actually deranges it and causes it to behave abnormally; and it is only by correcting this error that the mind can regain its true nature" (SM, 245). Failure to do so may lead to 'corrupt' dogmatism. The latter, which is the product of the 'corrupt consciousness,' is the refusal of mind to advance from the first to the second and third ontological levels; and this, according to Collingwood, constitutes a serious threat to the very stability of culture and civilization. Thus Collingwood declares, concerning the role of scientific dogmatism in modern thought, in a passage which applies with equal force to all first-level dogmatic philosophies which have resisted the necessity to advance: "... scientific philosophy is an anachronism; but an anachronism that still walks the street and seems in no haste to die [SM, 280] ... In fact, it is the prime obstacle to the healthy development of modern philosophy." (SM, 281)

The distinction between therapeutic and corrupt dogmatism may be further illustrated by means of the analogy, previously employed, from psychoanalysis. The development of consciousness is essentially a history of errors, and the distinction between therapeutic and corrupt dogmatism is a distinction, therefore, between two types of error. There is, in effect, a 'pathology of normalcy' as well as a 'pathology of abnormalcy.'

The concept of a distinction between a healthy and a corrupt consciousness is explicitly introduced in "Aesthetic" (1927). This essay is an example of a third-level analysis of the concept of imagination regarded as a general habit of mind. In this essay Collingwood is interested in exploring the relation between the psychoanalytical theory of imagination and the philosophical analysis of it. The latter, which he calls "aesthetic," is virtually a metaphysic of the aesthetic or imaginative activity *qua* imaginative. Contemporary psychology, according to Collingwood, has come to the conclusion that all human activities derive from the imagination which is recognized to exert a strong influence on the processes of perception. But at the same time psychology regards the imagination as fundamentally diseased, so that all of its activities are regarded as pathological. On this view the theory of the imagination must necessarily take the form of a pathology (AE, 237).

It is Collingwood's contention, however, that by approaching the imagination from the standpoint of aesthetic, the conclusions of psychoanalysis may be seriously modified. What the latter does not realize is that there is a distinction between the "right" and the "wrong" activities of the imagination. "Psychoanalysis," he writes, "possesses no criterion for distinguishing the healthy from the unhealthy imagination" (AE, 238). Now Collingwood might have gone on to declare that while even the healthy imagination is subject to error – in which case the study of it is also a pathology – there is a difference between the pathology of the healthy imagination (phenomenology and metaphysics) and the pathology of the corrupt or unhealthy imagination (psychology, psychoanalysis, etc.). This is precisely the distinction which in various places throughout this book I am claiming to derive from the behaviour of philosophy in *Speculum Mentis*. But Collingwood does not do this. He adopts instead what I would regard as the less promising convention of simply defining pathology as the science of the unhealthy imagination and aesthetic as the science of the healthy imagination. He was not interested in taking the further step of explaining the development of the healthy imagination according to a phenomenology of error (in which case it would follow that the distinction between the two types of imagination would rest upon a distinction between two types of error).

Finally, on the basis of such distinctions as he has made, Collingwood proceeds to characterize the general difference between the two sciences of mind. Any product of the imagination may be either healthy or morbid. If it is healthy, it is a work of art; if morbid, it is regarded as an object for pathology. It is for aesthetic (the metaphysic of the imagination) to say which it is. If it is to be regarded as a work of art, aesthetic may continue to explore its nature. If, however, it turns out to be pathological, it must be handed over to psychoanalysis (AE, 239). The art critic explains *that*, and according to *what criteria*, a given piece of art is to be regarded as bad; the psychoanalyst sets out to determine *why* it has become bad (AE, 240). The psychoanalyst, in other words, aims to provide a causal account which investigates the origins of aesthetic disorder. Collingwood therefore concludes that:

> the science of aesthetic demonstrates the existence of an activity called imagination, an activity which, being indifferent to the reality or unreality of its own objects, could be nothing but a morbid pathological factor in a life of mind whose sole business was to cognize and manipulate external things. (AE, 243)

But, he continues,

> Aesthetic [also] demonstrates that this imaginative activity is in point of fact capable of perfectly healthy and normal functioning, and, as so acting, gives their special character to all those highly various functions which we call the arts; and that it operates in a pure form in what we call the fine arts. I have pointed out that it is a pathological as well as a healthy activity, and that we are indebted to modern psychology for a vast store of information concerning this side of its operations; but that since this psychology has inherited a view of the mind which implies that all imagination is a morbid thing, it is unable to distinguish between a healthy and a diseased imagination. (AE, 243-4)

The distinction between a healthy and a corrupt consciousness is analogous to the distinction between the healthy and the pathological imagination. But I have suggested that since even a healthy consciousness is subject to error – in fact necessarily develops through error – one might conceive of there being a pathology of 'normalcy' as well as a pathology of 'abnormalcy.' And I am therefore suggesting that phenomenology, which is primarily concerned with the logical development of thought, may be properly regarded as a pathology of normalcy, and the analysis of dogmatic philosophy in *Speculum Mentis* may therefore be regarded as a clear example of such a pathology. When consciousness becomes corrupt, however, the dialectic ceases to operate; the processes of mind become irrational and a new set of categories is required to understand them.

There are certain features which all forms of healthy dogmatism share. Of most importance is the fact that all dogmatic philosophy is characterized by a distinction between dogmatic philosophy conceived as a direct expression of consciousness (as art, religion, science, etc.) and dogmatic philosophy as a philosophical reflection upon these forms of consciousness; or, to use Collingwood's own language, between "direct," "primary" experience (the actual act of apprehending the object) and "reflective" or "secondary" experience (the return of the mind upon itself to study its own primary experience) (SM, 255). This distinction between primary and secondary experience which is the "infallible mark of dogmatism in all its varieties" (SM, 255) is the form in which the subject-object distinction appears in dogmatic philosophy.

Absolute philosophy, for which the distinction has been overcome, realizes what dogmatic philosophy does not, namely, that the distinction between first- and second-order thinking is the result of a general philosophical error, the error of the mind mistaking itself for an object other than mind. It is this error which gives rise to the distinction between subject and object, on the one hand, and between knowledge of subject and knowledge of object, on the other. It is the same error which, operating within primary consciousness, gives rise both to the subject-object distinction which characterizes each particular standpoint and to the belief in the diversity and separateness of the particular standpoints. Historicity is a second general feature of dogmatic philosophy. Dogmatic philosophy, as we have seen, is a scale which includes philosophy of art, philosophy of religion, philosophy of science, and philosophy of history. But each form on the scale is itself a dynamically changing scale. There is, therefore, a history of the philosophies of art, religion, science, and history. As fundamental changes within each primary form occur, so changes arise at the level of reflection. Dogmatic philosophy must therefore be rewritten by each generation. While both of these features apply to all three ontological levels of dogmatic philosophy, it is only at the second and third levels that the historicity of dogmatic philosophy is consciously accepted. At the first level it is, if anything, explicitly denied.

Philosophy at this level thinks of itself as an exposition of eternal truths.

A third feature of dogmatic philosophy lies in its description as the reasoned vindication of a given point of view (SM, 272). The mind gives itself an account of everything that it does. Dogmatic philosophy is therefore a 'logos' of the mind's various activities. As such, it is subject to a fundamental duality which I have previously distinguished as a purely descriptive *ab intra* activity – this is the narrow sense of the term – and a more critical *ab extra* approach. Both are necessary moments of the dynamic and concrete activity which is dogmatic philosophy proper.

Finally, since there are three levels upon which dogmatic philosophy operates, there will be three levels of 'logos,' three different senses in which reason vindicates a given point of view. Although Collingwood's discussion of dogmatic philosophy in *Speculum Mentis* is confined for the most part to the first level, only the other levels are clearly implied. It will therefore be my purpose in this book to dig out the programmes of second- and third-level dogmatic philosophies which are implied by the discussion of the first level.

The first and most primitive level is characterized by a blind and uncritical adherence to the principle (already cited) that to embrace a particular point of view and to believe in its validity are one and the same thing. At the first level 'believing in the validity of a standpoint' is equivalent to 'unequivocally assuming its truth.' Having assumed the truth of a standpoint, dogmatic philosophy is then concerned to reveal the basic presuppositions upon which that standpoint is based. The interesting thing about this procedure is that the truth which is assumed to apply to the standpoint in question is not itself arrived at by means of a philosophical argument. On the contrary, this assumption is guaranteed by an entirely different source whose infallibility philosophy simply takes for granted. It therefore follows that the business of dogmatic philosophy (in the narrow sense of the term) is to expose the presuppositions of a given standpoint rather than to establish their truth (SM, 257). Or, to put it another way, the business of philosophy is to analyse *ab intra* the meaning of propositions leaving aside the *ab extra* question whether or not these propositions are true: "This is the programme of all dogmatism. An infallible, non-philosophical source vouchsafes a revelation of absolute truth ... which philosophy is not asked to justify and is not allowed to criticize; and philosophy is granted the privilege of expounding and commenting on this revelation" (SM, 257).

According to my interpretation, the above statement applies specifically to the *ab intra* moment of dogmatic philosophy conceived in its narrow sense. But, as I have already pointed out, the separation of this purely descriptive activity from the normative and critical activities of a more dynamic dogmatic philosophy is at best tentative and without any real validity. Granted these qualifications, the notion of descriptive dogmatism is further elucidated by recognizing that although the priority of 'meaning' over truth applies at all three levels, it does so in different ways. At the first level the truth which is assumed is thought to be permanent and eternal, applying to the whole of reality. At the second level, it is recognized as the truth of a standpoint only. At the third level it is recognized as a necessary error which can be properly illuminated only through a general philosophy of man.

The forms of first-level dogmatic philosophy are "aesthetic philosophy," "religious philosophy," "scientific philosophy," and "historical philosophy." Aesthetic philosophy accepts the infallibility of art and attempts to vindicate not only the aesthetic experience but the interpretation of the whole of experience in terms of it (SM, 260). Religious philosophy similarly assumes the infallibility of religion and, accepting that as its fixed point, constitutes itself the *ancilla fides*. Scientific philosophy, or "metaphysics" in the narrow sense of the term, is the vindication of science from its own point of view, *scientia scientiarum*, the scientific theory of science (SM, 272). Historical philosophy, the last of the dogmatisms, is the reasoned vindication of historical consciousness and the attempt to apply this to the interpretation of the whole of experience. As described by Collingwood, scientific philosophy bears a striking resemblance to what in his day was known as scientific positivism while historical philosophy bears a strong resemblance to philosophical realism (SM, 281).

The general nature of first-order dogmatism is implicit in Collingwood's critique of 'aesthetic philosophy.' We have already, of course, encountered this dogmatism during our discussion, in chapter IV, of first-level aesthetic consciousness. Indeed, as we have already noted, in the concluding remarks to chapter III, it is in fact impossible to maintain in practice the distinction between primary experience and the philosophical reflection upon it; the very moment the former attempts to express itself at all it passes over into the latter.

Aesthetic philosophy vindicates the autonomy of art by asserting the supremacy of immediacy and denying the validity of thought. Its maxim is "Don't think, feel" (SM, 263). What aesthetic philosophy does not realize, of course, until it is viewed *ab extra* from the absolute standpoint, is that this wholesale denial of thought, on the one hand, and assertion of non-thought on the other, is itself based on logical presuppositions which are precisely those of the scientific intellect which is denied (SM, 262). It therefore follows that the denial of thought is self-contradictory. If, as aesthetic philosophy declares, feeling were enough, the explicit principles which recommend feeling would be unnecessary (SM, 263). Aesthetic philosophy, like every other dogmatic philosophy, is therefore the formal denial of its own existence. But this denial is paradoxically an implicit affirmation of its existence; for it shows itself, by its denial, to be doing precisely what it denies it is doing, namely thinking. Aesthetic philosophy is thus a living example of the so-called fallacy of "pseudomenos" and, like all forms of that fallacy, "it is dissipated by the discovery that its very denial is implicitly an assertion" (SM, 263).

Collingwood insists that there is no dialectical transition from one form of dogmatic philosophy to another, from aesthetic to religious philosophy, for example (SM, 263). Here again it is necessary to resort to my earlier distinction between dogmatism in its narrow sense, as the purely descriptive *ab intra* vindication of experience, and the more dynamic and concrete dogmatic philosophy which includes a critical *ab extra* moment. In the light of this distinction, Collingwood's claim that there is no dialectic of dogmatic philosophy must be interpreted as meaning that the dialectic is at work only in the concrete and dynamic process of therapeutic dogmatic philosophy and not in the narrow activity of corrupt dogmatism which, by virtue of its pathology, is no longer open to change. The same considerations apply to the development within any given form of dogmatic philosophy from one level to another. What is developing is the total shape of experience from which the narrow form of dogmatic philosophy is again only an abstraction. Thus whenever in future I speak of the development of dogmatic philosophy, I shall take for granted the fact that this development is occurring only within the complete and dynamic activity of therapeutic dogmatic philosophy.

The concept of dogmatic philosophy as a development through three ontological levels of existence throws light on a number of otherwise obscure Collingwoodian dicta. During the course of his discussion of the general character of dogmatic philosophy Collingwood writes that dogmatic philosophy is nothing but a single, blind, abstract act of will: it is the determination to remain within the circle of a specific form of experience. Religious dogmatism only consists in repeating to oneself, "I will remain at the religious point of view," and in reasserting this point of view in its abstractness against all comers. Modern realism says to itself, "I will on every occasion separate the subject from the object"; and that is all it does (SM, 259). This is a clear description of what we have called the first ontological level. Later on, while discussing aesthetic philosophy, he speaks of a development from "the talk of artists about art" (SM, 261) to a philosophy of "intuitionism" (here Collingwood doubtless had Bergson and Blondel in mind) and finally to a "... philosophy which places the aesthetic side of knowledge in its right place, and this can only be a complete philosophy of knowledge" (SM, 261; cf, OPA, 8). This latter stage in the development, which is a clear reference to the third ontological level, is the ideal limit towards which therapeutic dogmatic philosophy aims and is the point at which dogmatic philosophy passes over into absolute philosophy in its dual function of phenomenology (as exemplified by the attempt to produce a *"speculum mentis"*) and *"speculum speculi"* (which is the pure act of knowledge itself).

Against the background of this discussion of the three ontological levels the following characteristics can be assigned to dogmatic philosophy.

First-level dogmatic philosophy is the reasoned vindication of a standpoint from within as though (a) no other standpoint existed and (b) the standpoint being defended had a permanent and unchanging essence which applies not just to this standpoint but to the whole of reality. At the second and third levels philosophy continues to expose the standpoint from within. This time, however, there is explicit recognition that the standpoint in question is only one of a number of possible standpoints, each of which has its own history, and all of which, when related together, constitute a general history of mankind. At these levels, particularly at the third level, dogmatic philosophy will conceive of itself as only one aspect of a total process whose aim is to provide a complete philosophy of knowledge: that aspect, namely, which seeks, at any given time, to reveal the presuppositions of a single standpoint and to relate them to the presuppositions of other contemporary standpoints. Aesthetic philosophy will therefore become the historical analysis of the presuppositions of aesthetic consciousness past and present; religious philosophy will become the historical analysis of the presuppositions of religious consciousness, both past and present; scientific philosophy will become the historical analysis of the presuppositions of scientific thought, past and present. And so on.

Collingwood himself provides an example of third-level dogmatic philosophy during the course of his critique of philosophical idealism (conceived as a total refutation of the material world). Against this false form of idealism, he declares:

We hold that the scientist's world, so far as it exists, really is material, in the sense that, so far as he is a scientist, he believes in its reality as material, and that, so far as he succeeds in being a scientist he is right so to believe. But we hold that this material world, regarded as material, is not fully intelligible, and that to describe it as the object of scientific thought is to fall into the error of supposing that scientific thought can maintain itself as a stable attitude towards a real object. (SM, 267)

In this passage Collingwood is doing two things. On the one hand, he is doing straight third-level metaphysics, revealing the basic assumptions of twentieth-century scientific thought. At the same time he approaches the ideal limit of third-level dogmatic philosophy, the point at which it passes over into absolute philosophy, when he comments on the relation of the presuppositions of science to the world of knowledge as a whole. The first moment corresponds to the *ab intra* approach, the second to the *ab extra*.

2 DOGMATIC PHILOSOPHY OF HISTORY AS A SCALE OF FORMS

The distinction between first-, second-, and third-level dogmatic philosophy has to some extent already been exemplified. In chapter IV, for example, I was concerned not only with the primary experiences of art, religion, science, and history, but with the secondary experiences of dogmatic philosophy as well. In the course of this discussion I adopted a convention which I shall continue to follow in the present chapter. This was the convention of referring to first-level dogmatic philosophy as 'aesthetic philosophy,' 'religious philosophy,' 'scientific philosophy,' and 'historical philosophy'; second-level dogmatic philosophy as 'philosophy of art,' 'philosophy of science,' 'philosophy of religion,' and 'philosophy of history'; and third-level dogmatic philosophy as 'philosophical aesthetics,' 'philosophical theology,' 'philosophical metaphysics,' and 'philosophical history and historiography.' I have also suggested that while *Speculum Mentis* was primarily concerned with first-level dogmatic philosophy, most of Collingwood's writings after this exemplify the second and third levels. Finally I have suggested that all of this is in accordance with the master plan laid out in *Speculum Mentis*. Thus I cited the *Outlines of a Philosophy of Art* as an example of second-level dogmatic 'philosophy of art' and the *Principles of Art* as an example of third-level 'philosophical aesthetics.' Similarly, the *Idea of Nature* was cited as an example of third-level metaphysics (or philosophy of science).

Since my main concern in this book is Collingwood's theory of the historicity of philosophy, I shall attempt to elucidate the notion of history by means of the same distinctions which have hitherto been applied to the other major forms of experience. And this means exhibiting Collingwood's theory of history as a scale of forms beginning with *Speculum Mentis* (which presents the theory of history at the first level:

the level at which it first arrives on the scene, as it were) and ending with the *Idea of History* (which is an example of third-level philosophical historiography).

A *Historical Philosophy and Philosophy of History: First- and Second-Level Dogmatic Philosophies*

The distinction between first- and second-level dogmatic philosophy may be illustrated by comparing the 'historical philosophy' expounded in *Speculum Mentis* with the 'philosophy of history' expounded in "The Nature and Aims of a Philosophy of History" published in 1925. In *Speculum Mentis* consciousness reached the conclusion that the true object of knowledge was the "concrete fact": an insight which is the characteristic mark of historical knowledge. In reaching this insight, however, consciousness is the victim of two fundamental errors: that of distinguishing between subject and object, and that of refusing to recognize the existence and validity of other claims to knowledge. The principles relating specifically to historical knowledge are thus raised to the level of a general philosophy of knowledge and existence; the characteristics of historical facts in particular become the characteristics of facts in general; all knowledge becomes a species of historical knowledge. Thus arises the philosophy of modern realism.

The two main principles of realism are, according to Collingwood's account, the assertion of the concrete fact as ultimately real and the denial that the object is conditioned or affected by its being known (SM, 282). Both claims lead to self-contradictory conclusions. We have already seen, in our discussion of historical consciousness, that since concrete facts are internally related, knowledge of any one presupposes knowledge of the whole. Since the latter is a condition which can never be realized, historical knowledge is rendered impossible. This sceptical conclusion can be avoided only by falling back into a form of atomism which is, of course, a regression to scientific dogmatism. The separation of subject and object is equally misleading. For if, according to the first principle, reality is one all-embracing system of concrete fact, then either the knower falls inside the absolute whole or he does not. If he does, then differences in his thought about it make a difference to it, and the more completely 'real' it is – that is, the more organized and interconnected it is in all its parts – the more fundamental these differences will be and the more completely the positivity of fact is lost (SM, 283–4, cf. A, 44).

Consciousness cannot remain at this level of experience without suffering corruption. It is forced, in order to avoid moving about in a vicious circle (which is the unhealthy solution to the problem and is equivalent in psychoanalytical terms to repression), either to regress to a more primitive standpoint (e.g., scientific consciousness) or to advance to a higher level of historical consciousness. This advance to a higher level of historical consciousness must be understood, incidentally, as part of a wider transition to an entirely new shape of experience, which is philosophy. Philosophical history is, therefore, the preservation of the historical consciousness within the general boundaries of the philosophic form of life, and philosophical historiography is the reflective moment of this rapprochement. At this new level the reasoned vindication of the historical standpoint does not lay claim to being a general philosophy of all knowledge and existence. On the contrary, philosophy recognizes the existence and validity of the other forms of knowledge and professes only to expound the way the world looks from this given standpoint and no other. It even recognizes that while the basis of this standpoint is erroneous, the error is rooted in necessity. Historical philosophy becomes now a more genuine philosophy of history and renders explicit what is already contained in the critical moment of the first-level historical standpoint.

The first stage in the critical self-development of historical consciousness is exemplified by the 1925 essay entitled "The Nature and Aims of a Philosophy of History," which I have previously cited as an example of second-level historical consciousness.

In the first place, the essay, in keeping with the conclusions of *Speculum Mentis*, affirms the logical doctrine of the overlap of classes. "The various forms of thought," writes Collingwood, "are not species of a genus" (NAPH, 166). On the basis of this claim Collingwood expounds a theory of the relations of the forms of knowledge in terms similar to those of *Speculum Mentis* – in terms, that is, of the principle of identity in difference (SM, 166-7). This, however, is laid down *ab extra*. *Ab intra* philosophy deals with history as though it were the species of a genus, differing from other forms of knowledge in certain specific ways. The reason for this is the fact that the behaviour of second-level historical consciousness is not yet perfectly consistent with the theoretical conclusions of absolute philosophy; it is not until we reach the ideal limit of the third level that the rift between theory and practice is breached.

In the second place, a distinction is made between the actual practice of historical thinking and philosophical reflection on this practice (NAPH, 161); or, to put it another way, between 'primary' and 'secondary' thinking; a distinction which, according to *Speculum Mentis*, is the infallible mark of dogmatism. In keeping with the requirements of the second level, historical thought is described as "one among a number of attitudes taken up by the mind towards the objective world; it is an attitude which assumes that there exists a world of facts – not general laws but individual facts – independent of their being known ..." (NAPH, 161-2).

At the first level, consciousness also postulates the concrete fact as the true object of history. But, as we have seen, by asserting this in the context of an abstract and absolute distinction between subject and object, historical consciousness implicitly leads to scepticism. At the second level, however, the concrete fact is placed in its proper context. The scepticism which prevailed in the *Speculum Mentis* account is here replaced by a more critical acceptance of the limitations of historical knowledge. Historical consciousness itself recognizes that "it is possible if not wholly to discover these facts, at any rate to discover them in part and approximately" (NAPH, 162), and philosophy of history will show that this recognition does not necessarily invalidate history's claim to be knowledge.

Given this definition of historical thought, philosophy of history is described as a "critical discussion of this attitude, its presuppositions and its implications: an attempt to discover its place in human experience as a whole, its relation to other forms of experience, its origin and validity" (NAPH, 162). This is second-level dogmatic philosophy of history.

Support for this interpretation of the essay as an example of second-level dogmatic philosophy is provided by some of Collingwood's own comments. For example, he is careful to distinguish the level of philosophy of history which is exemplified in the essay under consideration from certain other 'dogmatic' philosophies which

> not only assume the validity of historical thought, which the historian himself assumes, but, *plus royaliste que le roi*, they assume that the fruits of this thinking have a certainty and finality which no historian would attribute to them; and on this basis they try to construct a hybrid view of the objective nature of historical fact which is at once bad history and bad philosophy. (NAPH, 162)

A genuine philosophy of history, he continues, does not swallow whole whatever it thinks (and perhaps wrongly thinks) it has heard historical consciousness say (this is the infallible mark of first-order dogmatic philosophy), but is a critical attitude, which undertakes the task of inquiring not only into the results of a certain type of thought but into the presuppositions and implications of that type of thought itself: "an attempt to discover its place in human experience as a whole, its relation to other forms of experience, its origins, and its validity" (NAPH, 162).

Collingwood cites as examples of dogmatisms which are to be rejected (a) the attempt to discover general laws which govern the course of history, where such laws are conceived as eternal and unchanging truths of which the various events recorded in history are instances (NAPH, 151), and (b) the attempt to discover in history not so much an exemplification of eternal abstract laws as the progressive working out of a single concrete plan and to show how the various phases of historical change, as known to us, have tended towards the realization of this plan (NAPH, 152). The first of these dogmatisms is quite clearly a conclusion of scientific philosophy, the second of religious philosophy.

Against such dogmatisms, Collingwood asserts a theory of history which may be summed up as follows. *A parte objecti* history is the real individual as opposed to the imaginary individual of art and the abstract universal of science. *A parte subjecti* history is perception raised to its highest power (NAPH, 167). History is therefore a form of judgment which, since its object is the real individual concrete fact, may be described as "categorical," as opposed to the abstract thinking of science which is "hypothetical" (NAPH, 163).

As in the case of first-level history (already described), the most significant feature of second-level philosophy of history is the identification of history, as a form of knowledge, with perception. But although this identity was also asserted in *Speculum Mentis* to be a feature of first-level historical consciousness, it was asserted there in a different context. First-level consciousness is permeated by a basic inconsistency between its avowed realism (which appears in the very definition of history as the science of concrete individual facts as well as in the separation of subject and object) and its implicit idealism (which appears in the description of perception as a form of mediation). This inconsistency is not recognized either by first-level historical consciousness or by first-level historical philosophy. At the second level, although historical consciousness is still dominated by realism, philosophy of history moves towards idealism (which is demonstrated by the fact that, having recognized this inconsistency, philosophy allows the implications of the doctrine of perception to take priority over the explicit realism of the doctrine as a whole).

Second-level philosophy of history (looked at according to my interpretation) accomplishes two things. On the one hand, it reconciles the inconsistency between realism and idealism which exists at the first level. On the other hand, it provides a basis for dealing with the scepticism with which the first account concludes. The latter is a logical consequence of the former.

What precisely is the meaning of the second-level doctrine that history is perception raised to its highest power? At the lowest end of the scale perception appears as the apprehension of the immediately given. As we move up the scale, however, we realize that in fact neither is perception immediate nor is the object given. For in all perception we are making a judgment, trying to answer the question what it is that we perceive, and all history is simply a more intense and sustained attempt to answer the same question. One might in fact argue that the past which the historian brings to light is revealed only in the attempt to understand the world actually present to his senses (NAPH, 168). Indeed, as we have already seen, the identification of perception with sheer immediacy is based on the philosophical error of confusing the whole with its parts: perception is confused with sensation. What is more, sensation, the apprehension of the pure datum, is a mere abstraction. In actual fact we never get a pure datum: whatever we call a datum is already interpreted by thought. The only difference between what we ordinarily call perception and what we ordinarily call historical thinking is that the interpretive work which in the former is only implicit and only revealed by reflective analysis is in the latter explicit and impossible to overlook.

Second-level historical consciousness, which recognizes itself as perception raised to the highest power, retains at the same time the first-level distinction between subject and object. This distinction appears in "The Nature and Aims of a Philosophy of History" as the distinction between the actual and the ideal. What the historian *actually* knows is only an approximation to what *ideally* exists – the infinite world of fact which is the real object. Speaking on behalf of the historian for whom this distinction is taken as real, Collingwood therefore writes that each historian sees history from his own centre. No one historian can see more than one aspect of the truth, and even an infinity of historians must always leave an infinity of aspects unseen. Historical study is inexhaustible, and all history at its actual best is the provisional and tentative answer to a question which remains at bottom unanswered (NAPH, 172). The conclusion is that the "fact" as such is in reality unknowable.

Thus historical consciousness is still haunted by the realism which dominated its existence at the first level. In both cases the belief in an ideally existing world of fact which history attempts to approximate leads to scepticism. But this belief is plainly inconsistent with the interpretation of perception which is explicitly acknowledged. At the first level, neither historical philosophy nor historical consciousness faces up to this inconsistency, with the result that history, as an autonomous form of knowledge, breaks down in favour of philosophy. At the second level, however, while historical consciousness tries to accept both the realist distinction between subject and object and the idealist theory of perception, philosophy of history recognizes the nature of this inconsistency and transcends it. This happens, according to Collingwood, "when thought returns upon itself and faces the question of its own relation to its object"; "by criticizing the point of view from which it has regarded that object it transcends this point of view" (NAPH, 173). Hence to philosophize about historical thinking is to transcend the monadism of historical thought, to desert monadism for monadology. Philosophy realizes what in historical consciousness is only implicit, by achieving a logical solution to the inherent contradiction between the distinction of actual and ideal, on the one hand and, on the other, the theory of perception as mediation, which holds there is no ideal or real world as opposed to the actual world; there is only the system of appearances. Appearance is reality (NAPH, 173-4). The philosophy of second-order consciousness is the moment, therefore, at which the idealism of the doctrine of perception prevails over the realism of the subject-object distinction. When the implicit principle of historical consciousness, which second-level philosophy of history has raised to explicit consciousness, is consciously and explicitly adopted by history itself, we have reached the point of transition from second- to third-level historical consciousness.

The transition is exemplified in an essay of 1928 entitled "The Limitations of Historical Knowledge."[1] This essay forms a logical bridge from the 1925 essay to *The Idea of History*. In the main, the 1928 essay is an attack on the realism which seems to characterize the portrait of history which is drawn in *Speculum Mentis* and, to some extent, the 1925 essay. This does not mean, if my interpretation is sound, that in 1928 Collingwood suddenly changed his mind about the nature of historical knowledge. It means rather that the 1928 essay brings the scale of forms which constitutes philosophy of history a step higher by rendering explicit the solution to the conflict which lies at the basis of the realist theory of history. It would be misleading to suggest that the realist theory advanced in *Speculum Mentis* was Collingwood's own answer to the question, What is history? It is, on the contrary, no more than what is logically implied by the level of mind which in *Speculum Mentis* is called historical consciousness and which philosophy is bringing into question. If we want to know Collingwood's answer to this question we must look not to the philosophy being brought into question but to the philosophy which is doing the questioning. What is the theory of history which is implied by the criticisms which are brought to bear on the realist theory of history?

It is my contention that the answer to this question constitutes a scale of forms which is exemplified by the various writings on history which appeared after *Speculum Mentis*. The latter brings historical consciousness to the point where, under the influence of philosophy, it is prepared to reconstitute itself. This it does to some extent in the 1925 essay. But even here the discrepancy between the behaviour of consciousness and its theoretical presuppositions is pronounced. History has not yet been purged of its neurotic tendencies. A step in this direction is taken in the 1928 essay which goes a long way towards alleviating the breach within consciousness: but only by following out the implications of what is already contained in the standpoint of 1925. I am suggesting, in other words, that Collingwood's own philosophical development may be interpreted according to the pattern laid down for philosophy in *Speculum Mentis*.

"The Limitations of Historical Knowledge" is a critical examination of the presuppositions of actual historical consciousness as it passes from the second to the third level of existence. The philosophy of this experience is therefore an example of dogmatic philosophy of history which exists somewhere between the second and third levels – an illustration, incidentally, of the fact that the three levels constitute a scale of overlapping forms.

The basic principle of 'contemporary' historical consciousness, according to the 1928 essay, is that you cannot say anything, however true, for which you cannot produce evidence (LHK, 218). Of course, what is meant by producing evidence is subject to a variety of interpretations. According to realism, for example, the historical past is the sum total of events that have happened and may therefore be considered a thing-in-itself. The historian aims at finding out this past, and the value of evidence lies in its ability to reconcile the historian's contentions with what really happened (cf. SM, 237). But this, as we have already seen, is an ideal which can never be realized and we are led straight to the sceptical conclusion that knowledge of facts is impossible. We are therefore left in the absurd position of claiming that if history is knowledge of facts then history as a form of knowledge is not possible: which is, of course, the very paradox which lies at the basis of the *Speculum Mentis* account of history. From a logical point of view this is equivalent to affirming both A and non-A at the same time.

This is not the only absurdity which is implied by historical realism. If, as realism argues, every historian as such ought to know the whole past in order properly to know any part of it, then it also follows that (a) there is no validity to the idea of specialization, (b) the quality of historical scholarship is to be assessed in terms of the quantity of facts known, and (c) there are no limits to historical enquiry. This latter conclusion involves the absurdity of thinking, for example, that the question what Julius Caesar had for breakfast the day he overcame the Nervii is as genuinely historical a problem as the question whether he proposed to become king of Rome (LHK, 220). All of this follows from the absurdity of conceiving the past as a dead past existing by itself in a νοητὸs τόπos of its own.

The conclusions of realism can be avoided, according to Collingwood, only if the historian accepts the view that the game is won not by the player who can reconstruct "what really happened" but by the player who can show that his view of what happened is the one which is supported by the evidence accessible to all players (LHK, 218). In short, there is no way of knowing what view is "correct" except by finding what the evidence proves when critically interpreted.

According to Collingwood, not only is this rule "accepted by every player of the game without protest or question, but anyone can see it to be reasonable" (LHK, 218): which is, incidentally, a clear indication that he definitely considers the philosopher of history to be disclosing the presuppositions of actual historical consciousness. The so-called rules of the game, which seem to control the behaviour of historians, are really the definition of what historical thinking is. For historical thinking means nothing else than interpreting all the available evidence with the maximum degree of critical skill. It does not mean discovering what really happened if "what really happened" is anything other than "what the evidence indicates"(LHK, 219). There is therefore no longer any contrast between the historian's picture of the past and the real past. The historian's picture of the past, so far as it is historical at all (i.e. conforms to the criteria of historical thinking), is the real past.

Historical consciousness has now eliminated the "thing-in-itself" which haunts first- and second-level historical consciousness. Yet, if we accept the dialectic of *Speculum Mentis,* we must recognize, paradoxically enough, that it is only by affirming and attempting to defend a realist theory of history that the implicit error of realism can be discovered and steps taken to correct it. This is because – as Collingwood himself points out in this essay – there is a permanent tendency in all thought (which Collingwood sometimes calls "the plain man's realism") to think of the object as a thing existing in itself and by itself out of all relation to the knowledge of it (LHK, 219). *Speculum Mentis* has shown what happens when this "permanent tendency" is abstracted from its proper context and transformed into a general dogma.

But it also shows how abstracting itself thus may be regarded as a necessary stage in the growth of consciousness as such. According to the terms of the methodological distinction (introduced during the earlier discussion of *Speculum Mentis*) between the *ab intra* and the *ab extra* approaches, it is clear that while realism is the *ab intra* moment of first- and second-level historical consciousness, scepticism is the negative moment – the moment through which consciousness achieves a dialectical development from one stage to another. This may explain Collingwood's statement in this essay that "historical scepticism may now be seen in its proper function, as the negative side of the definition of historical knowledge" (LHK, 219). If by negative is meant the determinate negativity of the dialectic of *Speculum Mentis* then it is only through the experience of this scepticism that the realist discovers the implicit error upon which his standpoint rests. In more precise terms, the experience of scepticism leads the realist philosopher to the realization that "he does not want a real past at all"; or rather, he only wants it in his moments of crude realism. In his moments of scepticism, however, he discovers that he does not possess it, and reflection shows that he gets along very well without it (LHK, 221). This is almost like saying (if my interpretation is sound) that the position of the 1928 essay, which places a new interpretation on the nature of the historical past, is the dialectical product of the internal strains which lie at the basis of the realist view which is advanced in *Speculum Mentis* as well as in "The Nature and Aims of a Philosophy of History." It is also clear that the new theory of history is consistent with the general principles according to which the phenomenological analysis of *Speculum Mentis* is conducted, in particular the principle which denies the absolute distinction between subject and object and the existence of a thing-in-itself over and above its appearances.

What precisely is the new theory of the historical past which is implied by the level of historical consciousness which has purged itself of its realism? In "The Limits of Historical Knowledge" Collingwood provides only a summary sketch. In the first place, the historian does not want a real past. Rather, he wants a real present, a world of things perceived and perceivable, and he wants to "reconstruct in his mind" the process by which *his* world – the world of his present experience – has come to be what it is. This is a process, however, which is not now going on. It is not an object with which we can be acquainted; it is not a fact in the realist's sense of fact; it is not something which can be apprehended in the natural sense of the word apprehended. Collingwood is here affirming a point, which he laboured at some length in the *Autobiography,* concerning the need for a new theory of knowledge " ... devoted to the special problems raised by historical thinking ... problems such as one might group together under the question 'how is historical knowledge possible?' " (A, 77)

But this demand for a new theory of knowledge, Collingwood argues,

soon developed into the demand for a new kind of philosophy (A, 77).
It was clear to him that within the universe of discourse dominated by
realism what passed as a theory of knowledge had been devised with
special reference to the methodology of natural science, and that anyone
who attempted the application of it to history found, if he knew what
historical thinking was like, that no such application was possible
(A, 85). It is almost certain that Collingwood, as the *Autobiography*
suggests, arrived at this opinion before he wrote *Speculum Mentis* and
the realist theory which is outlined there is presented with the sole purpose of expressing its limitations and preparing the ground – as all
genuine philosophical dialogue must do – for a further discussion of
history at a higher level.

The question therefore arises, Under what categories can knowledge
of such an object as the historical past be accounted for? The complete
answer to this question – which Collingwood summarizes in chapters IX,
X, and XI of the *Autobiography* – is not given until the *Idea of History*.
But this answer is almost anticipated in "The Limits of Historical
Knowledge" when Collingwood redefines the historical past as the past
as it appears from its traces in the present. The past, in other words,
is present in the very world which the historian perceives around him
(LHK, 221). From this it follows that if all historical thought is indeed
the historical interpretation of the present, then the central question of
history is, "How has the world as it now exists come to be what it is?"
(LHK, 222)

Implicit in these remarks is what Collingwood called in the *Autobiography* the "first principle of a philosophy of history": "that the past
which an historian studies is not a dead past, but a past which in some
sense is still living in the present" (A, 97). What is more, in describing
the nature of the historian's knowledge of this object, the 1928 essay
seems to be on the very verge of the doctrine of imaginative reconstruction. If "imagine," he writes, "is our only term for the 'apprehension'
of a non-existent object, he is imagining it" (LHK, 221). It is true that
Collingwood immediately qualifies this remark by pointing out that
even the term imagination is misleading because imagination knows
nothing of the difference between truth and error, and the historian,
he argues, is doing his best to avoid error and achieve truth. But this
problem only arises, as Collingwood himself should have realized, if by
imagination is meant the pure imagination which is the first category
of *Speculum Mentis*. Once it is realized that imagination and reason
'overlap' – or, to put it another way, once a rapprochement between
imagination and reason has been achieved – it will be possible to apply
the categories of imagination to the rational process of historical think-

ing, as Collingwood does in the *Idea of History*, without losing either art in history or history in art.

The theory of the past as the product of an 'imaginative' interpretation of the present according to the 'rules' of historical thinking, which is advanced in "The Limits of Historical Knowledge" (and which anticipates the doctrine of 're-thinking' which appears in the *Idea of History*), was originally defended as early as 1926 in an essay entitled "Some Perplexities about Time."[2] Indeed, if my interpretation of the logical origins of Collingwood's mature thought is sound, I might go as far as to argue that the seeds of this paper were already present in Collingwood's mind at the time he wrote *Speculum Mentis* – as the following passage from *Speculum Mentis* would seem to testify: "In the absolute process of thought the past lives in the present, not as a mere 'trace' or effect of itself in the physical or psychical organism, but as the object of the mind's historical knowledge of itself in an eternal present" (SM, 301–2).

These two papers are to some extent commentaries on this passage from *Speculum Mentis*. "Some Perplexities about Time" begins with a distinction between 'existential' and 'non-existential' modes of being, corresponding to a further distinction between actual and ideal being.[3] Ideal being, while it is a proper object of thought in general, is nevertheless non-existential, and judgments about it are therefore (to carry Collingwood's thought a little further than he did himself) hypothetical rather than categorical. Into this class, Collingwood places the future which is possible but not necessary, and the past which is necessary but not possible. The actual or real, on the other hand, is the present conceived not as a mathematical point between future and past, but as the existential union of the present and past in a duration or permanence which is essentially bound up with change. In short, neither the past *qua* past (i.e., as ideal necessity) nor the future *qua* future (i.e., as ideal possibility) have any real existence. This is reserved exclusively for the past as living in the present and the future as germinating in the present (SPT, 149).

The problem which arises for philosophy of history, concerning the conditions under which such an object as the historical past can be made an object of knowledge, is one to which Collingwood devoted a great deal of attention. On the one hand the past is identical with the present. On the other hand, it is different from the present. Unless it is somehow identical with the present it can never be known at all: this is the lesson implied by the critique of realism. At the same time, unless it is somehow different from the present, knowledge of it cannot be distinguished from present knowledge, and history as an autonomous form of knowledge is denied. But what precisely is this difference in identity? "No question in my study of historical method," writes Collingwood, "ever gave me so much trouble ..." (A, 112). Indeed, it is in terms of this problem that Collingwood wrote the history of nineteenth- and early twentieth-century historiography, and his major criticism of such philosophers as Bradley and Oakeshott in England, and Dilthey and the historicists in Germany, is that they simply failed to solve this problem.

Collingwood's solution to the problem of historical knowledge took the form of what he calls in the *Autobiography* the 'principle of incapsulation': "Historical knowledge is the re-enactment of a past thought incapsulated in a context of present thoughts which, by contradicting it, confine it to a plane different from theirs" (A, 114). But while it no doubt took him many years to work out the details of this solution (to be discussed more fully in chapters VIII and IX) it would seem to have already been implicit in the 1926 essay and even to some extent in *Speculum Mentis*.

Let us look more carefully at some of the implications of "Some Perplexities about Time" and its relation to the central doctrines of *Speculum Mentis*.

The conception of the present as the synthesis of past and future implies a doctrine of time which views the past as both 'immanent' in and yet 'transcendent' of the present. The immanence-transcendence of the past in the present is clearly implied in the claim that the distinction between the ideal and real, like all true distinctions, is not absolute. On the contrary, so the essay seems to suggest, the relation between the two must be understood in terms of what Collingwood later came to call 'the logic of the overlap of classes.' Thus anything which is real is implicitly ideal. The historical past, therefore, while it is 'existentially' real in so far as it is incapsulated in the present, is at the same time 'ideal' in so far as it can be reconstructed and made an object of thought. Thus Collingwood characterizes the past as an object which has been called into being "by recollecting and by thinking historically ... by disentangling [the past] out of the present in which it actually exists, transformed and re-transforming it in thought into what it was" (SPT, 150). What prevents the past, so conceived, from becoming a mere mode of present experience is its quality of 'transcendence,' while what prevents it from being a mere object of 'acquaintance' is its quality of 'immanence.' The 'immanence-transcendence' of the past in the present which is implied in the 1926 paper bears a strong analogy to the central doctrine of *Speculum Mentis* concerning the immanence-transcendence of the absolute mind. Indeed, this doctrine which synthesizes all the principles upon which *Speculum Mentis* proceeds (e.g., the dialectical logic of the overlap of classes and the scale of forms, the doctrine of the concrete universal), is implicitly recommended in the closing paragraph of "Some Perplexities about Time":

> ... this conception ... the only one I can discover which gives any hope of escape from my perplexities about time, is only open to a logic which conceives the real as a synthesis of opposites and a metaphysic which has abandoned the hopeless attempt to think of all objects of thought as existent. If we must regard the real as a collection of elements each of which is real by itself and in its own right, we must give up the solution which I have attempted to sketch and find another, if we can. (SPT, 150)

By "a logic which conceives the real as a synthesis of opposites" is meant the dialectical logic of the overlap of classes, or the scale of forms, which is employed in *Speculum Mentis* and systematically expounded in *An Essay on Philosophical Method* (1933). By "a metaphysic which has abandoned the hopeless attempt to think of all objects as existent," is meant the doctrine of 'immanence-transcendence' which characterizes *Speculum Mentis* and was Collingwood's answer to philosophical realism. The new metaphysic repudiates the realist doctrine of external relations and asserts instead the internal relations of the concrete universal. It is only in terms of this doctrine that an answer can be provided to the question posed earlier, Under what conditions can the past be made an object of knowledge? This is an answer which avoids both the 'Scylla' of portraying an unknowable ideal past and the 'Charybdis' of radical historicism. Thus the notion of 'incapsulation' which lies at the basis of the doctrine of re-thinking is derived from, and remains founded on, the central doctrines of *Speculum Mentis* and *An Essay on Philosophical Method*.

B *Third-Level Dogmatic Philosophy*

I have already suggested that the description of dogmatic philosophy in *Speculum Mentis*, particularly when viewed from the third ontological level, provides a basis for linking *Speculum Mentis* with some of the later writings. Thus the *Principles of Art*, the *Idea of Nature*, and the *Idea of History* are all cases of third-level dogmatic philosophy.

An Essay on Metaphysics, although it contains some examples of the latter, especially in the domain of natural science, is primarily an exposition (from the absolute standpoint) of the presuppositions of third-level dogmatic philosophy in general. For, although the term metaphysics is employed there, as it is in *Speculum Mentis*, as the name for the critique of natural science, it is clear that the term can be (and is in fact) extended to cover all other critiques as well. The *Principles of Art* is, therefore, an example of the metaphysics of art, the *Idea of Nature* is an example of the metaphysics of science, and the *Idea of History* is an example of the metaphysics of historiography. *An Essay on Metaphysics* provides further examples: the ontological argument, for example, illustrates the metaphysics of religion and natural science together, while the analysis of causation illustrates the metaphysics of history and natural science.

The significant thing about these examples is that they illustrate in some detail the level of consciousness which is implied by third-level analysis. Thus, for example, the critique of the ontological argument illustrates the rapprochement between religion and science by demonstrating that statements concerning the existence of God are at the same time absolute presuppositions of natural science, and the analysis of causation explains the similarities as well as the differences between natural and historical causation.

The infallible mark of dogmatic philosophy operating on all three ontological levels is, according to *Speculum Mentis*, the distinction between primary and secondary experience. This distinction is one of the main criteria for linking *Speculum Mentis* with some of the later writings; for if this is indeed the infallible mark of dogmatic philosophy, then the *Idea of Nature* and the *Idea of History* are, by their own admission, cases of dogmatic philosophy.

At the outset of the *Idea of Nature*, Collingwood distinguishes between the detailed work of science, on the one hand, and the philosophical reflection on it, on the other. The latter, he adds, is necessary to the progress and future of the former:

... for when people become conscious of the principles upon which they have been thinking or acting they become conscious of something which in these thoughts and actions they have been trying, though unconsciously, to do: namely to work out in detail the logical implications of these principles. (IN, 2; cf., below, ch. VII, s.7, ch. VIII, s.10)

The very same distinction appears at the outset of the *Idea of History*, where philosophy is explicitly described as "thought of the second degree," "thought about thought" (IH, i).

The characteristic feature of third-level dogmatic philosophy is the fact that while it is forced for methodological reasons to proceed *ab intra* by making distinctions which from the absolute standpoint are recognized to be illusory, it nevertheless recognizes and accepts the implications of the logic of the overlap of classes. This means that philosophy sets for itself the task not only of expounding a standpoint from within but of relating this standpoint to all other standpoints as well, with the ultimate aim of arriving at a complete theory of knowledge, which, as *Speculum Mentis* suggested, is the ideal limit of dogmatic philosophy.

This programme is explicitly stated at the outset of the *Idea of History*. Philosophy is here distinguished into two stages. The first stage is the critical examination of the presuppositions of a standpoint, "regarded as a special study of a special problem" (IH, 6); it is at this stage that a variety of abstract distinctions may have to be employed. The second stage involves working out the connections between these presuppositions and those of the other standpoints; and this must be done strictly according to the logic of the overlap of classes. The first stage is primarily *ab intra*; the second, which is primarily *ab extra*, is governed by the principle that "Any addition to the body of philosophical ideas alters to some extent everything that was there already, and the establishment of a new philosophical science necessitates a revision of all the old ones" (IH, 6–7). And implicit in this statement is one of the central principles of *Speculum Mentis*, already cited:

... that our five forms of experience are not five abstractly self-identical types of events which by their recurrence in a fixed or changing order, constitute human experience; but types whose recurrence perpetually modifies them, so that they shade off into one another and give rise to new determinations and therefore new types at every turn. (SM, 56)

c *Philosophy and Philosophical Historiography*

Another characteristic feature of third-level dogmatic philosophy derives from the influence upon it of philosophy. Philosophical history is the natural outcome of the discovery on the part of mind that history is implicit philosophy; it is the solution which mind offers in order to escape from the dilemma of either relapsing back into a more primitive standpoint or else passing over entirely into philosophy. Philosophical history, therefore, occupies a place at the top of the scale of forms which is history, and is the point at which the form of history and the form of philosophy overlap. We have already noted that included within the scale of forms which is history are aesthetic history, religious history, scientific history, and historical history. With the arrival on the scene of philosophy, the scale expands to include philosophical history, and just as philosophy logically supersedes history so philosophical history supersedes historical history. This means, of course, that the former, which is characteristic of the *Idea of History*, is already implicit in the latter, which is the standpoint of *Speculum Mentis*. Thus the transition from history to philosophy, rather than resulting in the destruction of history, means instead that history appears again on a new level of experience.

The characteristic feature of second-level history (and historiography) is, as we have already noted, the implicit conflict between two incompatible beliefs: the belief, on the one hand, in the separation of subject and object (which becomes translated into a distinction between the past as the historian knows it and the past as it really is), and the belief, on the other hand, that historical knowledge is perception raised to its highest power. When the implications of the latter are taken to their logical conclusions, they supersede the implications of the former belief, and a new level of historical consciousness emerges.

The basic differentia of third-level historical consciousness is its attitude towards the subject-object distinction. Whereas the historian of *Speculum Mentis* and "The Nature and Aims of a Philosophy of History" assumes that there is a world of fact independent of his knowing mind, a world which is revealed but not constituted by the historian's thought, the philosophical historian (and historiographer) of the *Idea of History* explicitly acknowledges the fact that historical knowledge is not only the mind's knowledge of itself, but is also a form of historical action – a view which is an extension at the level of history of the philosophical insight achieved at the end of *Speculum Mentis* that the true object of knowledge is one which is altered by its being known, which exists per se only as it exists for us. The 'historical historian' is abstractly separated from his object; he therefore fails to realize the unity of thought and action. He is a mere spectator who does not modify the world but merely apprehends it (OPA, 93); his object, *res gestae*, is always the object of his thought and never that thought itself. The relation between the historian's mind and the mind of the agent he is studying is a relation at most of ὁμοιουσία, never of ὁμοουσία. He is therefore always the spectator of a life in which he does not participate: he sees the world of fact as if it were a gulf which, as a historian, he cannot bridge. So defined, history can never be a form of self-knowledge (NAPH, 165).

This abstractness is overcome only in philosophy. The object of philosophy is a reality which includes both the fact of which the historian is aware and his awareness of that fact (OPA, 93; NAPH, 165). The philosopher is not, like the historian, outside his own picture; he sees himself as part of the historical process which he studies. Part of his problem, therefore, is to understand how he himself has been produced by the same historical process he is seeking to know: he who is at once a product and the spectator of it. With this clue in hand he is able to re-interpret that process itself, and to see in every phase of it a nisus towards self-consciousness. And in realizing that history is the emergence of the spirit's consciousness of itself he is actually achieving that consciousness, and bringing into existence, in his own person, that awareness of himself which he finds to be the fundamental characteristic of spirit: "His knowledge is, therefore, explicitly action; he is creating himself by knowing himself, and so creating for himself an intelligible world, the world of spirit in general" (OPA, 94).

This distinction between philosophy and history is a distinction which exists at the second level. When history re-constitutes itself, under the influence of philosophy, as a legitimate form of self-knowledge, abolishing the abstract separation between subject and object, the distinction between philosophy and history is abolished as well; or, at least, the distinction is raised to a higher level. At the level of philosophical history the object of history no longer exists independently of the historian's attempt to know it, and the distinction between philosophy and history is no longer as simple and straightforward as it was at the second level. The third level affirms the identity of philosophy and history. Yet, even at this level, the identity must be qualified by a special distinction between historical consciousness as such and the philosophical reflection upon this consciousness; for the identity in question is a case of identity in difference. The precise nature of this distinction will be explained in chapter x in terms of the doctrine of immanence-transcendence. I will argue that the latter is Collingwood's way of avoiding the historicism which appears at first glance to be a consequence of any doctrine which identifies philosophy and history.

VI

Philosophy as
ABSOLUTE KNOWLEDGE

Thus far our discussion has centred around the idea of philosophy conceived as the critic or interrogator of experience. As such, philosophy comprises a scale of forms – aesthetic philosophy, religious philosophy, scientific philosophy, and historical philosophy – each of which is itself a scale of dogmatic philosophies existing primarily on three ontological levels.

Philosophy, however, is more than this scale of historical dogmatism. There is also a 'philosophical philosophy,' the standpoint of absolute knowledge which underlies the historical scale of dogmatic philosophies. Absolute philosophy is the mind's knowledge of itself, the identity of 'act' and 'fact.' As such it takes two distinct but related forms. On the one hand it is 'immanent' in all other standpoints, providing the criteria according to which the *ab extra* critique of the forms of experience proceeds. And although the criteria, or absolute presuppositions, of the science of the historically relative absolute presuppositions (which underlie the particular standpoints) are themselves historically grounded, they are nevertheless a priori: they derive from the categories of mind.

At the same time philosophy is the activity, sometimes referred to by Collingwood as the "pure act," towards which all other activities aim and through which the illusory character of these standpoints is exposed in order that their essential unity one with the other may be affirmed. As pure act, philosophy is the identity of subject and object, the mind's knowledge of itself which is at the same time the conscious self-creation of mind – "no mere discovery of what it is, but the making of itself what it is" (SM, 296). It is this activity which, on the one hand, as pure act, transcends all particular standpoints, and on the other, is the immanent goal towards which all the particular standpoints aim; for each particular standpoint has as its immanent goal the mind's knowledge of itself, and it is only the error of confusing the nature of its true object that occasions the rise of a particular standpoint at all (SM, 309). Thus Collingwood argues that, on the negative side, philosophy is the progressive reduction of art, religion, science, and history to philosophy – or as Hegel put it, philosophy is "the conscious insight into the untruth of the phenomenal knowledge."[1]

On the positive side, however, the progressive reduction of the special sciences to philosophy is a vindication of their autonomy (SM, 45); what is destroyed is only the false claim to autonomy based on an erroneous and dogmatic claim to absolute knowledge and mutual separation. Philosophy demonstrates the falsity of the abstract theory of the sciences which regards them as separate and autonomous species of the genus 'knowledge.' Contrary to the latter conception, philosophy shows each form to be implicitly identical with every other form, and it is only an error that makes some people ignore one element of their experience and others ignore another, thus coming to the conclusion that their experiences are of a fundamentally different kind (SM, 308).

Philosophy thus realizes what no other standpoint does, namely, that it is only the error of asserting its abstract autonomy which gives a standpoint its distinct character (SM, 309). It is only because science, for example, asserts its truth against the falsity of all other standpoints that there is such a thing as scientific consciousness at all. "Every person who is actually absorbed in any given form of experience," writes Collingwood in the critical passage already cited, "is by this very absorption committed to the opinion that no other form is valid, that his form is the only one adequate to the comprehension of reality" (SM, 307). Thus the truth of science, that it is really implicit history and philosophy, is a truth for philosophy alone, and science *qua* science is denied insight into its essential nature. The quarrel between philosophy and science is therefore shot through with irony: it is only because science is implicit philosophy that it can challenge the authority of philosophy at all and declare its superiority against all other forms of experience; philosophy knows this, but science does not. The history of science, in so far as it exists primarily at the first two levels, is the history of the varying interpretations which science has placed upon its separateness from all other forms of experience, while the history of the philosophy of science is the history of the general realization, culminating in third-level 'philosophical' philosophy of science, that the basis of this autonomy is illusory, and that in fact science is identical with all other forms of knowledge.

In denying the abstract autonomy of the particular sciences, philosophy is implicitly asserting their genuine autonomy by exhibiting each form as one aspect of a scale of forms, or one moment of a concrete universal. As a result of this revelation there is created, as we have seen, the possibility of a new level of existence for each of the major forms of experience: philosophical aesthetic experience, philosophical religious experience, philosophical science, and philosophical history. At this level a new scale of dogmatic philosophies emerges: philosophical aesthetics, philosophical theology, philosophical philosophy of science, and philosophical historiography. In contradistinction to the lower levels of dogmatic philosophy, this new level speaks, not the language of the logic of genus and species exclusively, but the logic of the overlap of classes as well. It is true that even at this level there are differences among the sciences; differences which, because they are sometimes explained in terms of an abstract logic of mutual exclusion, are therefore of an illusory nature – for example, the distinction between nature and history which runs throughout much of *The Idea of History*. It is nevertheless the case that at this level each science is that much closer to the realization of its immanent goal, which is the life of philosophy conceived as absolute knowledge, the standpoint at which, having transcended its historicity, philosophy now grasps itself *sub species aeternitatis*.

I THE TRANSCENDENTAL PRINCIPLES OF PHENOMENOLOGY

The phenomenological critique of experience proceeds, as I have already pointed out, according to the twofold method of viewing the subject *ab intra* and then criticizing it *ab extra*. The criticism of a standpoint *ab extra* is conducted according to a set of criteria, which constitute the transcendental presuppositions of the phenomenological analysis of experience, and may be generally described as 'the metaphysical doctrine of concrete mind.' In so using the term 'metaphysical' it may appear that I am departing from Collingwood's own usage, for he seems to reserve the term for the analysis of historically changing standpoints and explicitly denies the existence of such a priori truths as I now claim to be examining. But, as we shall see in more detail in chapters VII and VIII, Collingwood's denial of the existence of a science of being *qua* being is misleading. For the moment we need only point out that what he really denies is the science of being *qua* abstract being – which is, to use the familiar language of Spinoza, *ratio* proceeding according to the abstract analysis of classification and division. Collingwood does not deny, however, that there is a science of being *qua* concrete (or absolute) being, which aims at *scientia intuitiva*. On the contrary, he explicitly affirms the existence of such a science.

By a science of absolute mind Collingwood does not mean, of course, a standpoint of sheer unmediated intuition. Indeed, we have seen how absolute mind must posit itself as art, religion, science, and history in order to know itself as philosophy. The life of absolute mind is not

> ... the static contemplation by mind of its own fixed given nature – mind has no fixed given nature – but ... the self-creation of this nature is a perpetual discovery of fact which is at the same time the creation of fact: the creation of the fact of its discovery ... The life of absolute knowledge is thus the conscious self-creation of the mind, no mere discovery of what it is, but the making of itself what it is. (SM, 296)

The nature of this self-making process is essentially historical. Yet the science which organizes and arranges the results of this creative process into a philosophical system proceeds according to principles which have the status of a priori truths. These principles constitute the presuppositions according to which the science of historically relative presuppositions proceeds. If the latter is called 'metaphysics' then the former may perhaps be referred to as 'meta-metaphysics.' The metaphysical doctrine of concrete mind is meta-metaphysics, so conceived. If the life of concrete mind is the act through which mind creates itself by knowing itself, and if this self-knowledge is achieved through the construction and destruction of the external worlds of art, religion, science, and history, then the metaphysics of concrete mind is simply the science of the presuppositions according to which this construction and destruction of external worlds proceeds. We shall find that the same principles which govern the relations of the five major forms of experience govern as well the stages through which each particular form develops. In short, the principles of phenomenology (the science of concrete mind) are the same as the principles of 'metaphysics' proper – that is, the historical-philosophical analysis of the presuppositions which lie at the basis of any particular experience.

The metaphysical presuppositions of phenomenology may be analysed under three distinct but related headings. There is first of all the theory of the concrete universal; this is the most general level at which the presuppositions of phenomenology may be discussed. There is secondly the logic of the overlap of classes which reveals the morphology of the concrete universal and is the point at which Collingwood's version of the concrete universal differs from those of his idealist predecessors. Finally, there is the principle of dialectical necessity, which defines more precisely the way in which the members of the scale of forms (i.e., the moments of the concrete universal, mind) are related one to another. A definition of mind *per genus et differentia* has now been reached; mind is a concrete universal, exhibiting itself as a scale of overlapping forms, each related to the others by means of dialectical necessity.

2 THE THEORY OF THE CONCRETE UNIVERSAL

The theory of the concrete universal is presupposed throughout the whole of Collingwood's philosophy. It is, for example, the basis upon which he launched his lifelong attack on philosophical realism and the theory of the abstract universal. The main features of realism have already been referred to. They are (a) the assumption of a distinction between subject and object and (b) the assumption that knowing makes no difference to the object known. Implied by these principles is a theory of knowledge which makes acquaintance the essence of knowledge. Underlying the acquaintance theory of knowledge is the logic of propositions and the metaphysical theory of the abstract universal.

Realist epistemology postulates the existence of a world of independently existing facts. Knowledge of these facts is expressed in propositions, regarded as the only genuine units of thought, and truth can only mean the 'correspondence' of propositions to facts. It follows, then, that the main philosophical problem for such a logic is to establish criteria according to which this correspondence can be measured.

A correspondence theory of truth can have meaning only if it is assumed that the 'facts' to which propositions conform are permanent and eternal. Thus all philosophical systems, of ethics, politics, logic, and metaphysics, are regarded as no more than successive attempts to describe these self-identical facts, and the history of philosophy may therefore be viewed as the history of different answers to the same question.

In the *Autobiography* Collingwood discusses an application of this view to the history of political theory. The example presented is presumed to be typical of philosophical realism.

Suppose we are interested in comparing Plato's *Republic* and Hobbes' *Leviathan*, or Aristotle's *Ethics* and Kant's *Critique of Practical Reason*. According to realism the two former works are different answers to the question, What is the ideal nature of the state? while the latter are different answers to the question, What is duty? While it is the task of the historian to determine *what* these answers are, the philosopher decides which is true – that is, corresponds to the facts. In other words, the historical question, What was so-and-so's answer to this question? is clearly distinguishable from the philosophical question, Is it true? (A, 59)

But it was Collingwood's firm belief that the philosophical question concerning the truth of a particular philosophy cannot be separated from the historical attempt to reconstruct it;[2] the truth, rather than lying in the correspondence of propositions with facts, is more properly determined by such criteria as whether the question has really been answered, and whether the answer was relevant. What is important is whether the answer makes a positive contribution to the continuation of the historical dialogue in which the question under consideration must be continually posed. The philosopher's task is not to determine whether Plato's *Republic* or Hobbes' *Leviathan* is *the* truth. They may both be true or they may both be false. What the philosopher wants to know is whether the *Republic* is an appropriate answer to the question which it intends to answer, and whether the same is true of the *Leviathan*. Only if we commit the error of assuming that both are answers to the same question are we obliged to ask which is true and which is false.

To assume otherwise, according to Collingwood, is to fall into a kind of "... historical myopia which, deceived by superficial resemblances, failed to detect profound differences" (A, 61). The fact is that the *Republic* is an account of the 'polis' of the fifth century BC while the *Leviathan* is an account of the absolute monarchy of the sixteenth and seventeenth centuries in England. It is true that both the 'polis' and the 'absolute monarchy' are 'states.' But the 'state' is not an eternal and unchanging substance; it is an historically changing dynamic process which recognizes profound and essential differences between one historical manifestation and another. As Collingwood puts it in *Speculum Mentis*, summing up the whole matter: "The state is an historical, not a scientific conception – a concrete, not an abstract universal" (SM, 174).[3]

This conception of the state as a concrete universal is explored further in an article of 1929 entitled "Political Action."[4] The state, Collingwood argues, is generally conceived as a substance having an essence and attributes. This is the concept of the state as an abstract universal. Following this concept, political theory conceives itself either as an attempt to deduce a priori the implications of this essence, or as an inductive inquiry about the various attitudes of sovereignty found to exist in various states. All such theories, deductive or inductive, are agreed in accepting the limitations of the category of substance and attribute (PA, 155). Collingwood proposes to approach political theory from a different angle. Instead of putting the central issue in the form of the question, "What are the attributes of the state?" he proposes to put it in the form of the question, "What is political action?": "That is to say, I propose to take my stand, not on the category of substance and attribute, but on the category of action" (PA, 155).

Collingwood's quarrel with the doctrine of substance is bound up with his rejection of the abstract universal. In repudiating substance in favour of action, he commits himself to a theory of the concrete universal. In place of a plurality of abstract essences each constituting one species of knowledge, Collingwood proposes, on the side of the subject, a scale of historical activities, art, religion, natural science, political science, economic science, history, and so on, having as their objects a scale of corresponding activities: the relation of subject and object being in each case such as to constitute a fundamental 'unity,' each of which is a concrete universal, and all of which together constitute the moments of the concrete universality (i.e., activity) of mind.

What does it mean to say that the state is a concrete, not an abstract universal? A concrete universal is not a universal substance whose nature is shared in common by its instances. It is, on the contrary, a kind of synthesis which embraces differences as well as similarities. The instances of a concrete universal do not belong to that universal in the sense that they all possess, in precisely the same way, the same abstract characteristics which are the essence of that universal. If this were the case, then differences would be accidental and unimportant. And since differentiation and change are precisely those features which distinguish history from nature,[5] while there can be scientific, there cannot be historical, knowledge of abstract universals. The genuine universal, however, does not enjoy the separate existence of the abstract universal. Apart from its members, or instances (or, as Hegel preferred to call them, its 'moments'), it does not exist at all; its essence does not transcend the particularity of its instances like the essence of an abstract universal. One might almost say that the instances of a concrete universal, rather than sharing a common abstract characteristic, possess – to borrow Wittgenstein's phrase – "family resemblances"; and it is in virtue of these "family resemblances" that the various moments of the universal are recognized to belong to the same class.

The important thing about the concrete universal is that it treats differences as essential. Each 'moment' of a concrete universal expresses a different yet identical aspect of the whole, and in so far as it is different contributes essentially to the unity of the whole. Bosanquet, a contemporary of Collingwood, described the concrete (or "logical") universal as follows:

A world or cosmos ... a system of members, such that every member, being *ex hypothesis* distinct, nevertheless contributes to the unity of the whole in virtue of the peculiarities which constitute its distinctness ... the important point ... is the difference of principle between a world and a class. It takes all sorts to make a world; a class is essentially of one sort only. In a word, the difference is that the ultimate principle of unity or community is fully exemplified in the former, but only superficially in the latter. The ultimate principle, we may say, is sameness in the other; generality [i.e., abstract universality] is sameness in spite of the other; universality [i.e., concrete universality] is sameness by means of the other.

Thus the true embodiment of the logical universal takes the shape of a world whose members are worlds ... for the same reason which made it inevitable for the mere generality [i.e., abstract universal] to be defective by the omission of contents which differentiate the class-members from one another. The universal in the form of a world refers to diversity of content within every member, as the universal in the form of a class neglects it. Such a diversity recognized as a unity, a macrocosm constituted by microcosms, is the type of the concrete universal.[6]

To say then that the state is a concrete universal is to say that its nature or essence can be found only in the total system of its developing moments, and a complete understanding of its nature presupposes a knowledge of each stage of its development. Concerning this development two kinds of knowledge are possible. The first is historical knowledge of the past; the second, which follows logically from the first, is an imaginative construction of what the universal could ideally become – although it must be pointed out that from the latter nothing follows concerning its actual course; that is, it is not possible on the basis of this imaginative construction to make predictions. Collingwood would therefore agree with Hegel that since the temporal development of the 'Idea' is historical, knowledge of the concrete universal, even as pure Idea, must be mediated by an actual knowledge of its history.

Thus the question, What is the ideal nature of the state? can only be answered by studying the history of its development in the form of political activity or political experience; for in the long run the concrete universal is recognized to be identical with experience. And since the development of this experience is the development of a concrete universal, the history of theories of the state is the history not of different answers to the same question but the history of a problem which was more or less constantly changing, whose solution was changing with it. What is therefore usually regarded by realism as a permanent problem P is really, on Collingwood's account, a number of transitory problems P_1, P_2, P_3 ... whose individual peculiarities are blurred, he says, "by the historical myopia of the person who lumps them together under one name P" (A, 69):

> The 'realists' thought that the sameness was the sameness of a 'universal' and the difference the difference between instances of that universal. But this is not so. The sameness is the sameness of an historical process, and the difference is the difference between one thing which in the course of that process has turned into something else, and the other thing into which it has turned. (A, 62)

Presupposed by these statements in the *Autobiography* is not only the theory of the concrete universal but, as the following considerations will demonstrate, the theory of therapeutic dogmatic philosophy expounded in *Speculum Mentis*. To begin with, *qua* concrete universal, the state (to pursue the example from political philosophy) develops historically through the political experience of the people. Political philosophy is the reflective moment of this experience and is concerned, not with the exposition of eternal truths, but with the presuppositions of that experience as it is enjoyed by the persons who are part of it. Political theory is therefore dogmatic philosophy or the 'metaphysics' of political experience. On this view, Plato's *Republic* must be understood as an answer to the question, What is the nature of the 'polis'? which is a fifth-century BC question posed by Greeks who are experiencing the kind of thing they are bringing into question, and is not at all equivalent to the seventeenth-century question, What is the ideal nature of absolute monarchy?

Now it is true that Plato may have thought that in answering this question he was speaking for all time and eternity – in which case he would be behaving like a first-level dogmatic philosopher. The fact is, however, he was giving expression only to the Greek ideal of a human society: an ideal which was implicit in the experience of his contemporaries. Hobbes' *Leviathan*, on the other hand, is an answer to the question, What is the ideal nature of the absolute state? the absolute state being in this case relative to the experience of Hobbes' contemporary society. The *Leviathan*, like the *Republic*, is therefore a further example of dogmatic philosophy.

What does it mean then to say that the 'absolute' state and the 'polis' are both 'states'? Granted there are essential differences between them, what is the basis of their unity? Collingwood's answer is that they are *not* the same in the sense that they are both species of the universal, state – that is, their unity does not derive from the fact that they share the same abstract essence. They are the same only in the sense that the latter grows dialectically and historically out of the former. The *Republic* was Plato's answer to a question which arose from within the Greek political experience. Once the answer was given, however, its effect on experience was such as to force new questions to arise – in much the same way as philosophy, for example, forces each standpoint in *Speculum Mentis* to examine the basis of its existence. In revealing the structure of Greek political experience, philosophy (to use once again the language of *Speculum Mentis*) has brought consciousness to the point where it is now aware of those limitations and errors in its thinking of which it had hitherto been 'unconscious.' Once consciousness has become aware that the standpoint upon which it has been acting is erroneous, it is cured of its 'neurosis' as it were, and is now in a position to re-experience itself in such a way that it is virtually reconstituted: which gives rise, of course, to new problems demanding new solutions, until we reach the *Leviathan*.

The *Leviathan* is, therefore, in the language of dialectical logic, the product of a series of mediations each leading necessarily to the next. Since in the development from the 'polis' to the 'absolute state,' differences essential to the nature of the whole are introduced, the concept of the state consequently undergoes continual revision as these differences are introduced.[7]

The question, What is the state? is not therefore a separate question asked at a separate time, nor is it a sustained question which philosophers continue to ask throughout history. It is really only a kind of summary of all the particular questions which have been asked from time to time, such as, What is the polis? What is the absolute state? and so on. In so far as the state is concerned then, there is no such thing as a complete and final definition of it; there is only "... a living thought whose content, never discovered for the first time, is progressively determined and clarified by every genuine thinker" (SM, 13).

The doctrine of the concrete universal is thus a necessary presupposition of every genuine theory of history. It is in fact one of the criteria which historiography must employ in order to distinguish history from nature; for the difference between historical and scientific thinking (in general) is precisely the difference between thinking about the concrete and thinking about the abstract universal. Thus Collingwood writes in *Speculum Mentis*:

Reason is concrete thought, thought which does not arbitrarily create to itself, by abstraction, any object it pleases for the sake of ease in thinking it, but sets out to study facts as they are, and to conceive a universal which is truly the universal of its own particulars. Hence reason thinks the concrete universal, not the bare self-identity of science which leaves all differences outside itself but the identity to which difference is organic and essential. Understanding hypostatizes the concept into an object of intuition by itself, outside its own particulars; and this object is nothing real, but simply the fruit of an error. Reason finds the concept in the particulars, forming with them an inseparable unity. (SM, 196)

... concrete universality is individuality, the individual being simply the unity of the universal and the particular. The absolute individual is universal in that it is what it is throughout, and every part of it is an individual itself. On the other hand it is no mere abstraction, the abstract quality of individualness, but an individual which includes all others ... The principle of its structure is not classification, the abstract concept, but the concrete concept which is relevance, or implication. The only reason why this notion of a concrete universal is thought puzzling or paradoxical, is that our attempts at philosophical theory suffer from the obsession of regarding science as the only possible kind of knowledge. (SM, 229-31)

The same view was expressed by Collingwood some eleven years later in his inaugural lecture "The Historical Imagination" (1935):

> ... whereas science lives in a world of abstract universals, which are in one sense everywhere and in another nowhere, in one sense at all times and in another at no time, the things about which the historian reasons are not abstract but concrete, not universal but individual, not indifferent to space and time but having a where and a when of their own, though the where need not be here and the when cannot be now. History, therefore, cannot be made to square with theories according to which the object of knowledge is abstract and changeless, a logical entity towards which the mind may take up various attitudes. (IH, 234)

Underlying the distinction between reason and understanding, concrete and abstract universal, is a basic ontological distinction between historical and natural being. In the world of nature, individuals or particulars exist in external relations with one another. Each, according to Collingwood, is cut off from the other by a sharp boundary distinguishing clearly what is within from what is outside: "The inner and the outer are mutually exclusive." This is the kind of abstract individuality possessed by a mere object or thing, such as a stone or any other material body:

> It is the primary characteristic of the world of nature, and distinguishes that world from the world of mind, where individuality consists not of separateness from environment but of the power to absorb environment into itself. It is therefore not what individuality means in history, so far as the world of history is a world of mind. (IH, 162-3)[8]

Collingwood's conclusion, then, concerning the nature of historical explanation is clear and unequivocal: "... the concrete universal is the daily bread of every historian, and the logic of history is the logic of the concrete universal" (SM, 221).

3 THE LOGIC OF THE OVERLAP OF CLASSES

The logic of the concrete universal, referred to in *Speculum Mentis*, is no other than the logic of the overlap of classes which is systematically expounded in *An Essay on Philosophical Method* (1933). Indeed the latter clearly underlies the theory of the scale of forms which characterizes the thought of *Speculum Mentis*, in which the concrete universal is portrayed as a gradually developing system of overlapping forms.

The ostensible purpose of *An Essay on Philosophical Method* is to contrast the method of philosophical analysis, which has for its object the concrete universal, with the method of the natural sciences, which has for its object the abstract universal. As contrasted with philosophy, science proceeds by means of the abstract logic of genus and species, also referred to as the logic of classification and division. A criticism of this logic, with a view to demonstrating its self-contradictory character, had already been given in *Speculum Mentis*. Ostensibly, the aim of the logic of genus and species is to guarantee complete autonomy to each part of the whole, that is, to each species of the genus. But to treat the parts of a whole as though they were the species of a genus, or modifications of a common principle, means that to assert one is implicitly to assert the others as well (SM, 48). For, since each partakes of the same essence, to assert the essence of one is to assert the essence of all. The result is that the explicit pluralism of abstract logic implies its own opposite, namely, monism.

This same inconsistency arises when the logic of genus and species is applied to the classification of the sciences. Pushed to its logical conclusion the doctrine allows the admission of only one science having several branches. Collingwood is particularly concerned with the implication that, since the doctrine of genus and species is a logical doctrine, logic is to be regarded as a master science having jurisdiction over the whole field of science. This is especially implied by the fact that the same logical standards apply to each form of knowledge. If being a science means satisfying certain criteria, then there is really only one science, describable in terms of a static logic which is directed indifferently upon each form of experience. The logic of genus and species asserts, almost without realizing it, the absoluteness of formal logic and reduces all alike to that Procrustean standard: "This is pure intellectualism, and leads us to look for syllogisms in music, inductions in religion, and so forth: which precisely contradicts the thesis with which this view began, namely the independence of these various fields of thought" (SM, 49).

Substantially the same criticism is launched in *An Essay on Metaphysics* against the science of being *qua* being. Collingwood's main objection to a science of being *qua* being is that its subject matter would be an entity devoid of peculiarities – which means that it would contain nothing to differentiate it from anything else or, for that matter, from sheer nothingness:

The universal of pure being represents the limiting case of the abstractive process. Now even if all science is abstractive, it does not follow that science will still be possible when abstraction has been pushed home to the limiting case. Abstraction means taking out. But science investigates not what is taken out but what is left in. To push abstraction to the limiting case is to take out everything; and when everything is taken out there is nothing for science to investigate. You may call this nothing by what name you like – pure being, or God, or anything else – but it remains nothing, and contains no peculiarities for science to examine. (EM, 14)

This attack on the science of pure abstract being does not mean, as Knox has suggested, that Collingwood has betrayed his early philosophical beliefs. The conception of a pure undifferentiated being is only a more metaphorical way of describing the logic of the abstract universal which was a target of criticism from the very beginning of Collingwood's philosophical career. For Collingwood there is only one kind of being which can be made into an object of science, and that is the concrete being of mind. This is the view with which Collingwood's philosophy began and this is the view with which it ended.

An Essay on Philosophical Method repeats the arguments which have already been advanced in *Speculum Mentis*. Asserting the autonomy of co-ordinate species is now said to be committing "the fallacy of false disjunction": "I call this the fallacy of false disjunction, because it consists in the disjunctive proposition that any instance of a generic concept must fall either in one or in another of its specific classes ..." (EPM, 49). At the same time, the doctrine of genus and species implies another fallacy which denies the very autonomy which the doctrine sought to safeguard in the first place. This is the "fallacy of identified co-incidents" (EPM, 48–9), according to which, since every instance of a concept belongs to it in exactly the same way, the essence of each will be the same abstract characteristic, and the instances cannot in the end really be separated. We are thus confronted once again with the fallacy of pseudomenos – namely, that the very affirmation of a given standpoint implicitly presupposes its complete denial.

But while Collingwood has argued that the generic doctrine of classification and division is inappropriate to the classification of the sciences in general, he does admit that within the boundaries of the natural sciences it plays a vital and useful role. Indeed, it is perhaps the only logic that is useful at all. This is because, as in *Speculum Mentis*, Collingwood accepts the abstract universal as the proper object of science, and an examination of the concepts of mathematics, physics, chemistry, etc., will demonstrate that they obey and conform to the rules of classification and division as laid down by logicians. Indeed, Collingwood goes so far as to suggest that the very *conditio sine qua non* of the validity of the methods of the natural sciences lies in this general conformity to the rules of classification and division.

So long as the logical doctrine of classification and division remains within the general boundaries of the natural sciences no serious error is being committed. It is only when this method of analysis is applied to concepts which more properly belong to philosophy that serious difficulties arise which cannot be resolved by means of a logic of genus and species. For example, the doctrine of classification involves the paradoxical assumption that, although a certain generic nature can be realized in various specific ways, no instances of it can realize it in two of these ways at once. Such an assumption makes classification in some cases virtually impossible, as in the case of art. Suppose we have divided art into its specific classes: poetry, music, painting, etc. What happens when we come to a song, or an opera? How are we to classify these? It would be paradoxical to treat them either as two separate works of art, for instance, a poem and a piece of music going on at once. It would be even more paradoxical to describe them as belonging to a third species, which is neither music nor poetry. The truth of the matter, according to Collingwood, is that they are "both poetry and music, a single work of art containing the two specific forms" (EPM, 29).

Similar difficulties arise when we attempt to apply this doctrine to those concepts pertaining to human nature and the human condition. This is because there is an essential difference between the logical structure of the concepts of science and the logical structure of the concepts of philosophy: "The specific classes of a philosophical genus do not exclude one another, they overlap one another" (EPM, 31). It is this notion of the overlap of classes which is the clue to the nature of philosophical method: "In the argument of this essay the overlap of classes is to serve as the clue to the discovering of the peculiarities that distinguish philosophical thought from scientific" (EPM, 31).

Collingwood further illustrates the doctrine of the overlap of classes with the following examples. To begin with let us take the concept 'thought,' and its two species, 'judgment' and 'inference.' Are these mutually exclusive, co-existing, or co-ordinate species? To separate them is to affirm the possibility that each can be defined without reference to the other, which is of course impossible. Take 'judgment' alone, and divide it into the species 'affirmative' and 'negative.' If the theory of classification were relevant to thought then it ought to be possible first to define the generic nature of 'judgment' without reference to its species (as, for example, a triangle may be defined without reference to its species, equilateral, isosceles, and scalene), and then to add the differentia of the two species separately. But in fact the notion of judgment can never be defined without reference to affirmation and negation.

According to the doctrine of classification, not only can the genus be defined independently of its species, the species themselves can be defined independently of each other. This is because each species completely exhibits the generic nature of judgment in the same way that a straight line and a curved line each exhibits the complete nature of line. But how can a negative judgment be defined independently of an affirmative judgment, or vice versa? (EPM, 36–9)

The same considerations obtain among moral concepts. Take, for example, the concept of goods. These have been traditionally divided into three species: the pleasant, the expedient, and the right. No one has ever suggested that these are mutually exclusive kinds, for this would imply that whatever is pleasant must therefore be both inexpedient and wrong, and whatever is expedient must be both wrong and unpleasant, while whatever is right is both unpleasant and inexpedient. On the contrary, the doctrine of the overlap of classes is at the basis of all serious ethical theories: "These and similar considerations make it clear that in our ordinary thought about moral questions, whether we call this thought philosophy or common sense, we habitually think in terms of concepts whose specific classes, instead of excluding one another, overlap" (EPM, 42–3).

From the principle of the overlap of classes it follows that "no method can be used in philosophy which depends for its validity on their mutual exclusion" (EPM, 46). Thus the principle which states that whenever a generic concept is divided into its species there is a corresponding division of its instances into mutually exclusive classes is false when applied to philosophy and leads, as we have already seen, to the "fallacy of false disjunction" (according to which any instances of a generic concept must fall either into one or the other of its specific classes). Applied positively this may lead to the "fallacy of precarious margins," according to which, since there is a distinction between two concepts, and if every concept has its own instances, there must be a difference between their instances (EPM, 48–9).

The first rule of philosophical method then will be to avoid false disjunctions and to assume that the specific classes of a philosophical concept always overlap, so that two or more specifically differing concepts may be exemplified in the same instances. A useful reminder of this rule, writes Collingwood, is Aristotle's formula for the overlap of classes, namely, that two concepts are 'the same thing' in the sense that a thing which exemplifies the one exemplifies the other also, but their 'being' is not the same in the sense that being an instance of one is not the same as being an instance of the other (EPM, 49–50).

Collingwood's account in the *Essay on Philosophical Method* of the differences in method between philosophy and science needs to be supplemented by the argument of *Speculum Mentis*. According to the latter, the main reasons for the differences in method have to do with the ontological nature of the subject matter as well as with the logical form that knowledge of the subject matter must take. The subject matter of science is something abstract and hypothetical: the scientist is not so much concerned with its existence as with whether or not it conforms to the rules of method. And since the most fundamental principle of nature is uniformity, classification and division are appropriate.

Philosophy, on the other hand, analyses the concrete universal; its judgments are therefore categorical. Real existence as opposed to hypothetical existence is dynamic, subject to variation and change, and this change is not extraneous to the generic essence but is, on the contrary, identical with it (EPM, 60). Variations or expressions of this existence constitute, therefore, not a collection of co-ordinate species, or mutually exclusive classes, but a system of overlapping classes, or, to use another term which Collingwood employs, a philosophical scale of forms, such that each form sums up the whole scale to that point (EPM, 89). This is precisely the conclusion of *Speculum Mentis* concerning the philosophical examination of the forms of experience:

> Beginning, then, with our assumption of the separateness and autonomy of the various forms of experience, we have found that this separateness is an illusion. Each form is at bottom identical with all the others. It is only an error that makes people ignore one element of their experience and others ignore another, and thus come to the conclusion that their experiences are of a fundamentally different kind. They are different, but it is only the error of thinking they are different that makes them different. Artists and scientists must fight; it is their nature to; – but they have acquired this nature by committing themselves to the error of regarding art and science as separate things. (SM, 308-9)

The species of a philosophical concept such as the life of spirit or mind, are not co-ordinate species of a genus. On the contrary, they constitute a logically developing series in which the variable element and the generic essence are the same, the generic essence being that which is successfully displayed by the specific forms in continuously increasing fulness. Each form, in other words, will occur at a critical point in a scale. The higher term, while it is of the same genus as the lower, differs in degree (as a more adequate embodiment of the generic essence) as well as in kind (as a specifically different embodiment). This implies that the specific forms are both opposites and distincts; the higher is distinct from the lower as one specification from another, but opposed to it as a higher specification to a lower, a relatively adequate to a relatively inadequate, a true embodiment of a generic essence to a false embodiment (EPM, 88) – just as the feelings of heat and cold, for example, are not only distinct feelings but opposite feelings, and at the same time gradations on a scale of feelings; or as goodness and badness are at once distinct and opposite moral conditions and gradations on a scale of moral worth.

It is also implied that the higher form, in superseding the lower, preserves nevertheless the truth of the lower. In other words, the higher form possesses not only its own specific character but also that which its rival falsely claimed. The higher then 'negates' the lower and at the same time re-affirms it: negates it as a false embodiment of the generic essence and re-affirms its content.

Each term in the scale, therefore, sums up the whole scale to that point. Wherever we stand in the scale we stand at a culmination which is more than a mere culmination because the specific form at which we stand is the generic concept itself, so far as our thought yet conceives it. The proximate form, next below where we stand, while it continues to offer itself as the culmination of the concept, is, in fact, from our present point of view, an error whose truth nevertheless has been produced, preserved, and re-affirmed in the higher form (EPM, 89). No better example of a philosophical scale of forms can be found than in the five forms of consciousness which constitute the subject matter of *Speculum Mentis*:

> The five phases of spiritual life ... are not species of any common genus. They are activities each of which presupposes and includes within itself those that logically precede it; thus religion is inclusively art, science inclusively religion and therefore art, and so on. And on the other hand each is in a sense all that follows it; for instance in possessing religion we already possess philosophy of a sort, but we possess it only in the form in which it is present in and indeed constitutes religion. (OPA, 94)

As Collingwood explains it, we are confronted, in every case of overlap, not only with the overlap of the lower by the higher, but also with the overlap of the higher by the lower. The rules governing the former are somewhat different from the rules governing the latter. The higher overlaps the lower by including the whole of the positive content of the lower as a constituent element within itself. What is excluded is only the negative (i.e., erroneous) aspect of the lower which must of necessity be rejected by the higher. This negative element is constituted by the fact that the lower, in asserting its own content, denies that the generic essence contains anything more. This denial (whose similarity to the behaviour of all first-level standpoints cannot go unnoticed) is precisely what constitutes the falsehood of the lower form.

When it comes to the overlap of the higher by the lower, however, a slightly different principle obtains. The lower does not include the *whole* of the positive content of the higher; it adopts one part while implicitly rejecting the others. And this implicit rejection (which can be ascertained only after the fact), of a substantial part of the positive content of the higher, which supersedes it, is another source of the falsehood of the lower form.

In the *Essay on Philosophical Method* Collingwood offers, as an example of such an overlap, the relations between the various types of moral philosophy. Thus he declares, concerning the relation between utilitarianism and the higher form of the ethic of duty:

utilitarianism is right to regard expediency as one form of goodness; its mistake is to think that there is nothing in even the highest forms of goodness that cannot be described in terms of expediency; and therefore a better moral philosophy would re-affirm utilitarianism while denying one part, this negative part, of its doctrine. (EPM, 90)

At the same time, however, utilitarianism overlaps with the ethic of duty; it "claims much of the contents of better moral theories as sound utilitarian doctrine, but dismisses the rest as so much error or superstition" (EPM, 90). Duty therefore rejects expediency as an autonomous form of goodness but reaffirms it by integrating it with its own principles and hence appropriating it as a constituent element in its own make-up. Thus, Collingwood declares: "duty and expediency overlap: a dutiful action always has its own expediency and an expedient action to that extent partakes of the nature of duty" (EPM, 91).

What Collingwood seems to be saying (to return to the language of *Speculum Mentis*) is that the ethics of duty is implicit in the ethics of expediency, as history is implicit in science; moreover, the concept of duty is the logical solution to the contradiction which lies at the basis of the concept of utility. Thus 'deontic' ethics may be said to overlap with 'utilitarian' ethics in the sense that it is the logical and phenomenological product of it. Duty is both the negation of utility and its reaffirmation in a higher, more adequate context. Utilitarianism overlaps with deontic ethics in the sense that to expound the former *ab intra* and then criticize it *ab extra* discloses a contradiction whose resolution can only be achieved by means of the latter. "Our dialectical series of forms of experience," writes Collingwood "moves in a sense forward, in a sense backward" (SM, 206; see below, ch. VI, s. 4). Looking backward from the standpoint of duty, the overlap between duty and utility would be explained in terms of a reverse or backward dialectic. Looking forward from the standpoint of utility, the overlap would be explained in terms of a forward dialectic.

An even better example of the application of the logic of the overlap of classes to the explanation of ethical behaviour is provided in the *New Leviathan*. The example not only illustrates the practice of philosophy as outlined in *Speculum Mentis*, it illustrates as well the method of philosophical history for, as *Speculum Mentis* points out, the purely philosophical analysis of a concept cannot be divorced from the historical analysis of the experience which exemplifies that concept.

The example in question concerns the relations between the criteria according to which human behaviour may be analyzed. On any occasion when a modern European is asked the question, Why did you do that? writes Collingwood in the *New Leviathan*, he will likely give one or other of three possible answers: (a) because it is useful, (b) because it is right, (c), because it is my duty. A realist employing the abstract logic of classification and division would no doubt treat these answers as though they were in competition with one another. Since the truth of any one mutually excludes the others, the realist would proceed to determine which of the three answers was the true one. But this would involve committing the fallacy of false disjunction and would lead also to the fallacy of identified coincidents, which is the complete negation of what we presupposed at the outset. A more adequate philosophical approach would deal with these answers in terms of the logic of the overlap of classes. The latter would not treat the concepts of 'utility,' 'right,' and 'duty' as co-ordinate species of an abstract genus. It would, on the contrary, exhibit them as a scale of the forms of moral experience; each would be shown to embody the whole in such a way that it explicitly renders forth the essence of the form which precedes it, and implicitly contains the next form which supersedes it.

This is precisely what Collingwood does in the *New Leviathan*. The three concepts are exhibited as a scale of forms beginning with utility and ending with duty. Utilitarian ethics is an answer to a question which presupposes that the meaning and value of an action lies in the end or purpose it achieves. The action is therefore judged according to whether or not it is useful in achieving a desired end. But merely to explain the action by showing how it realizes a certain end does not account for the *choice* of this particular act from among the totality of those which would have achieved the same end. The utilitarian model requires only that a type of deed is necessitated by a type of plan. But from a mere statement concerning the logical relations between means and ends nothing can be deduced concerning the problem of choosing from among the several ways in which the antecedent conditions can be satisfied; nor can anything be said about the choice of pursuing such ends in the first place. On a purely utilitarian account such choices are left to caprice (NL, 108).[9] Thus arises a question, concerning the choice of means, which presupposes that from among the many actions through which a given end can be realized only some are appropriate. To the question, Why do I do x? the answer is now, Because it is *right*. Not every action which is useful is right, only those which conform to the rules (NL, 111).

Yet even a regularian explanation never fully explains why just this action and no other is done. This is because the rules to which we appeal are generalizations admitting of alternative realizations. A rule only specifies *some* act of a certain kind. But which of the many particular acts of this kind ought I to do? Or is the choice between alternatives again a matter of sheer caprice? (NL, 115–16) Thus the regularian model, like the utilitarian model, is incomplete. As a result of this incompleteness, and in order to avoid the charge of capriciousness, it is necessary either to fall back on the utilitarian model (which means introducing a plurality of subordinate or secondary ends) or else move on to a higher standpoint in which the limitations of the previous two standpoints are overcome. Why, of all the possible things which I could have done, did I do this? The concept implied in the answer to this question is the one which most adequately embodies the essence of the moral life. This concept is no other than duty. To say that I have a duty to do x is to say that I have incurred an obligation to do so.

The special characteristics of duty are "determinacy" and "possibility." According to the former, whatever is my duty is an *individuum omnimodo determinatum*; there is only one of it; it is not one of a set of alternatives; there is nothing else that will do as well. According to the latter, whatever a man is under an obligation to do is an act which that man is here and now *able* to do. For these reasons, Collingwood argues, of the three kinds of ethical action, dutiful action is the only one that is completely rational in principle, the only one whose explanations really 'explain' (NL, 121–2) : "*A man's duty on a given occasion is the act which for him is both possible and necessary: the act which at that moment character and circumstances combine to make it inevitable, if he has a free will, that he should freely will to do*" (NL, 124).

The concept of duty may be further explicated by a passage in *The First Mate's Log* (1940) in which Collingwood is again criticizing the ethic of utilitarianism. The theory that the good is pure utility, writes Collingwood, is self-contradictory: "Sooner or later, the judgement that something is good because it is useful rests on the judgement that something is good in itself" (FML, 150). Indeed, he declares, "it is only because some things are good in themselves that anything can be useful" (FML, 151). Although in this passage Collingwood does not specifically mention duty, it is not unreasonable to assume that goals which dutiful actions hope to achieve are the same as ends which are good in themselves, and that as compared with such obligations as may arise within utilitarian and regularian ethics, the obligations of the ethic of duty are obligations to do what one regards as having "intrinsic worth." Or, to put it another way, there are some commitments which although they cannot be justified by an appeal to either utilitarian or regularian ethics are nevertheless regarded as genuine duties which one is obliged to pursue. Such ends have, in effect, the status of fundamental beliefs resting on certain absolute presuppositions to which one is 'existentially' related (in a manner to be discussed in more detail in chapters VII and VIII below).

The differentia of duty, as Collingwood describes it, is "conscience." But even this, like the 'rule' of the regularian ethic and the 'purpose' of the utilitarian ethic, prescribes only something in general. The fact is, Collingwood declares, when a man acts from duty he does more than obey a general dictate of conscience. It is at this point that the possibility of an even higher ethic than the ethic of duty arises. Collingwood does not describe this higher ethic in the *New Leviathan* but he does provide a clue to its general nature; indeed to discover it we need only follow through the course of the dialectic which has already produced the concepts of utility, right, and duty.

Behaviour according to duty is described as being the logical and rational consequence of a process of deliberation which has led the agent to one specific course of action; but such behaviour, writes Collingwood, is the mark of historical action. Not only is behaviour according to duty a form of historical action, it is, Collingwood suggests, the highest point on the scale of historical action:

> The consciousness of duty means thinking of myself as an individual or unique agent, in an individual or unique situation, doing the individual or unique action which I have to do because it is the only one I can. To think historically is to explore a world consisting of things other than myself, each of them an individual or unique agent, in an individual or unique situation, doing an individual or unique action which he has to do because, charactered and circumstanced as he is, he can do no other. (NL, 128)

The ethic of duty then is grounded in the principle of 'rational necessity' which, as the *Idea of History* explains, is an a priori principle of history. A truly historical view of human history, writes Collingwood, "sees everything in that history as having its own *raison d'être* and coming into existence in order to serve the needs of the men whose minds have corporately created it" (IH, 77).

To say that the human events of history are determined by *rational* necessity is not, of course, to imply that they could not have been otherwise. It is only in nature that we have laws which cannot be broken. Thus, whenever we have a violation of natural law we call it a miracle. In the realm of history, however, any act is rationally necessary if it is the thing to have done, the principles of reason being what they are.[10] This is an expression of the dialectic of a healthy consciousness. If in spite of this the agent does otherwise we call it a stupidity, a mistake, an irrationality, or possibly even an expression of a corrupt consciousness.

This does not mean that *only* mind is rational, but that the rationality of mind is quite distinct from that of nature. It is of the very essence of nature to obey laws which at the same time define that essence. The essence of nature may be said to be fulfilled but in no sense altered by that behaviour. It is of the very essence of nature, in other words, to coincide with itself at all times.

In history, on the contrary, whenever the agent acts according to reasons, the sphere in which these reasons are actualized is altered. This is why the historical situation can never coincide with itself. It is always implicitly other than itself, always on the verge of giving rise to new and unpredictable problems. Within this situation the agent's behaviour is similarly one of self-making. The essence of nature is affected neither by its behaviour nor even by that behaviour being made an object of understanding. In the case of man, however, his nature is affected by its being understood. Self-understanding is a condition of self-making, in the sense that as the self renders explicit the reasons underlying its actions it endows itself with a capacity for new and unpredictable forms of behaviour which in turn give rise to new and unpredictable historical situations (IH, 85).

The future of deontic ethics is thus bound up with the future of history. History, writes Collingwood, is to duty what modern science is to right, and what Graeco-Mediaeval science was to utility (NL, 128). The clue has now been disclosed. The dialectic of the ethical life is the dialectic of the life of mind as a whole. The ethic of duty supersedes utilitarian and regularian behaviour in the same way that history supersedes science. And in the same way as philosophy supersedes history so will the ethic of duty be superseded by a philosophical ethic which is both the negation and the affirmation of the previous forms of ethical behaviour. This philosophical ethic will be the form in which the whole shape of moral existence is given the most adequate embodiment. But, we must ask, What is the form that this higher ethic will take? How can it be described?

The answer to this question is found in *Speculum Mentis* in which the dialectic of the ethical life was first outlined. Utility is here assigned to the scientific consciousness, while duty finds its place within the context of historical consciousness, which is the discovery of individuality and freedom (SM, 222). But, as in the *New Leviathan*, so in the earlier *Speculum Mentis*, the historically grounded ethic of duty has limitations which require that it be superseded by some higher ethic in order that the potentialities of the moral life can be given their most adequate embodiment (SM, 223–1). This higher ethic is described in *Speculum Mentis* as "absolute ethics," the ethic of universal love (SM, 304), the characteristics of which are derived from the characteristics of the philosophic life itself. The resolution of the distinction between subject and object becomes, when elevated to the level of ethical action, the dissolution of the alienation between one individual and another, between the individual and society, and hence between the individual and himself; we have therefore transcended the subject-object dichotomy for the standpoint of 'intersubjectivity' which is genuine freedom (SM, 304–5):

> In absolute ethics the agent identifies himself with the entire world of fact, and in coming to understand this world prepares himself for the action appropriate to the unique situation. This is not an act of duty, because the sense of an objective and abstract law, whether lodged in the individual 'conscience' or in the political 'sovereign,' has disappeared. The agent acts with full responsibility as embodying and identifying himself with the absolute mind, and his act is therefore the pure act of self-creation. This act is identical with self-knowledge, and thus the abstract distinction of the will and the intellect is transcended. (SM, 305)

A still further example of the application of the logic of the overlap of classes to the solution of a philosophical problem is "What is the Problem of Evil."[11] The problem arises, according to Collingwood, from the fact that evil is usually posited along with goodness and omnipotence as though these three concepts were mutually exclusive – that is, as though they were three classes of externally related entities. But the employment of an abstract logic of classification and division gives rise to the following "dilemmatic" argument: If God wills the evil which exists, He is not good; if He does not will it, He is not omnipotent. But since it certainly exists, He either wills it or does not will it. Therefore He is either not God or not omnipotent. The "problem" consists in the attempt to refute this dilemma without denying the reality of any of the three terms, since neither can be denied without the destruction of our religious beliefs (PE, 67). In effect, then, Collingwood will apply what he later came to call the logic of the overlap of classes to the solution of this problem: a course which involves manipulating the terms of the dilemma by a criticism and re-exposition of the conceptions involved, in the hope of so reinterpreting them that they are no longer incompatible and irreconcilable (*ibid.*).

In keeping with the spirit of *Speculum Mentis* and the *Essay on Philosophical Method*, Collingwood declares that the problem of evil – like all speculative problems – is in one sense insoluble (i.e., in the sense that it can never be solved definitively, so that it need never be reconsidered in the light of new thought); but in quite another sense it *is* soluble (i.e., in the sense that every attempted solution sums up the problem thus far). Part of the difficulty in reconciling evil with the other concepts lies in the identification of pain with evil. So long as pain is regarded as evil the existence of pain will serve as a refutation of the goodness of God. This identification, however, rests on a philosophical error or fallacy (the fallacy of false identity): the responsibility for which rests with utilitarianism which bestows goodness upon consequences, events, things, or conditions, rather than, as Kant had emphasized, on will. For utilitarianism, the goodness of the will is secondary; it is merely the goodness of a means to an end. Collingwood contrasts utilitarianism with what he calls the "ethical outlook." The ethical (or Kantian) outlook recognizes that the problem of evil can never be solved so long as we continue to judge evil and goodness in terms of their consequences. A solution to this problem can be forthcoming only if the problem of goodness is treated as the problem of the good will and the problem of evil as the problem of the evil will (PE, 70). For the ethical habit of mind the division of evil into both pain and sin is fallacious. In fact, only the latter – sin – has a right to be discussed. (PE, 71).

The question with which we began was, How can a world created by God's will contain evils? According to the ethical standpoint, it makes a difference whether we are using the terms good and evil in their strictly moral sense or in the utilitarian sense. According to the former, which is the proper one, God's will is good in itself, as are the evils we speak of. Evils are acts of *sin*, that is, acts of the evil will (PE, 71). To call a thing evil is, therefore, to call it *an act of somebody's will*. Nothing that merely exists or merely happens can be called evil. Evil applies only to things done, to actions. Mere events, by themselves, have no moral predicates. Thus the question, Is pain an evil? when raised from the ethical standpoint, presupposes that pain is the product of somebody's will (PH, 72). In saying that pain is evil, then, we are saying that God (or the Devil) creates pain by an act of will, which is a wicked action. In other words, the goodness or badness of a thing is a reflection of the character of the volition. Taken by itself, pain is neither good nor evil. When it results from an evil will it is evil. But when it is willed by a good will, it is good. There is therefore no contradiction in supposing that pain is caused by a good will, or in believing that it may be good for us to have pain. It is only when things are judged solely by their consequences that a contradiction between pain and goodness obtains.

Not only does Collingwood propose a solution to the problem of evil by showing that in fact the concepts of pain and goodness overlap, but he argues as well that the antithesis between the utilitarian and the ethical points of view can itself be resolved by placing each on a scale of forms, instead of viewing them as competing answers to the same question. These standpoints are not, he declares, co-ordinate species of a common genus. They are, on the contrary:

> alternative presentations of the entire problem from opposing points of view. From the ethical point of view the problem is solely the problem of sin; the problem of pain is seen to be a quite different problem presenting a quite different character. From the utilitarian point of view the real problem is the problem of pain; the problem of sin is either simply solved by the conception of human freedom, or else remains as a particular case of the problem of pain. If we regard the will as means (utilitarian view) the problem of the bad will disappear into the problem of bad events or states of things, typified by pain. If we regard the will as end (ethical view) the problem of undesirable things or events, such as pain, is swallowed up in the problem of the evil will. But if instead of adopting either of these two views, we merely halt between two opinions, then our treatment of the problem of evil will fall into the two heads which we have enumerated. (PE, 73)

In effect then Collingwoood has ruled out what I have here called the first and second levels of dogmatism: the totalitarian claim that the whole of the problem of evil must be viewed from one or other of a set of mutually exclusive standpoints, and the more democratic claim that it can be looked at from both standpoints together. He proposed instead what he calls here a synthesis – involving a logic of the overlap of classes (as opposed to a logic of classification and division into genus and co-ordinate species). Thus, he declares: "Pain and sin ... are not two kinds or divisions of what evil is. To treat them as co-ordinate heads of one and the same problem is to stand in self-confessed contradiction as to the fundamental nature of the problem at issue." (PE, 74)

In other words, according to Collingwood, each is a different problem requiring a different solution, and as such gives rise to different questions demanding different answers.

It is not my purpose to expound in any detail Collingwood's ethics. It is nevertheless of interest to note the continuity between the treatment of ethics in *Speculum Mentis* and its treatment in the *New Leviathan*; for this continuity is symptomatic of the continuity which unifies the whole of Collingwood's thought. My main interest in this chapter has been to show how an overlap of classes is possible, and to make it clear precisely what this overlap is. Ethics is the subject I chose to exemplify it because this is the example Collingwood himself chooses in *An Essay on Philosophical Method*, and I have expanded his discussion there in the light of what he wrote elsewhere. What Collingwood showed in the essay on method was that dutiful action, when looked at in terms of the logic of the overlap of classes, is the point at which the falsity of both expedient and regularian behaviour is superseded and their implicit truth is reaffirmed. All dutiful actions are expedient because duty, as the higher specification, always and necessarily, re-affirms the lower; and the lower not sometimes but always partially and incompletely affirms the higher. "The overlap consists in this," writes Collingwood, "that the lower is contained in the higher, the higher transcending the lower and adding to it something new, whereas the lower partially coincides with the higher, but differs from it in rejecting this increment" (EPM, 91). The overlap is therefore not a mere overlap of *extension* between classes, but an overlap of *intension* between concepts, "each in its degree a specification of their generic essence, but each embodying it more adequately than the one below" (EPM, 91).

At the same time, as we have seen, the logic of the overlap of moral actions may be regarded as a logic of question and answer. Each of the three concepts of action arises in the context of a question-and-answer complex. Each is the answer to the same question, and yet each is the answer to a different question; or, to adapt a phrase from another context, each is the solution to the "eternal problem in a unique form" (THC, 444). Each of the three question-and-answer complexes rests on different presuppositions. The relations among these presuppositions however (and hence among the questions and answers to which they give rise) are such that the attempt to answer questions arising from the first set gives rise to stresses and strains which force the question-and-answer process on to a higher and more complete standpoint. But finally, the recognition that the overlapping forms of moral judgment are different answers to different questions (arising from different sets of presuppositions) provides a basis for a more tolerant attitude when judging the worth of particular forms of human behaviour. Thus an action (or way of life) which, looked at either from a strictly utilitarian or strictly regularian point of view, seems meaningless and unacceptable, may, when viewed as the response to an obligation based on duty, become endowed with meaning and value.

4 THE DOCTRINE OF DIALECTICAL NECESSITY

The relations among the forms of the overlapping scale which constitutes the concrete universality of mind – a system which is, of course, paradigmatic of all other scales of forms as well – are described by Collingwood as "dialectical." As Collingwood uses the term, the important point about dialectic is this: that in every dialectical process that which gives way to a new form does so because its nature is no longer adequate to the claims made upon it by the connected system within which it has its being.

At the centre of dialectic is the notion of 'determinate negation,' the sense of which is derived from Hegel's notion of *aufheben*.[12] To say that a form of consciousness has been 'negated' is to say that it has been reduced to 'nothingness': not to pure nothingness of course (τὸ μηδαμῶς ὄν, i.e., τὸ μηδὸν αὐτὸ καθ αὑτό), but to a nothingness with a content (τὸ μὴ ὄν εἶναι) – a content from which a new form of experience arises.[13] The point about negation is that the destruction of a standpoint is equivalent to its being transformed into a new standpoint; hence we do not say that the standpoint has been destroyed, but rather that it has been superseded.

For Collingwood, as we have already noted above, dialectic has both a forward and a backward movement. In its forward movement it is a progressive development from error to truth. But unless the truth were somehow present from the start there would be no possibility of discovering it at all. This point was well made by Hegel when he wrote at the outset of the *Phenomenology of Mind*:

> If the Absolute were only to be brought on the whole nearer to us by this agency, without any change being wrought in it, like a bird caught by a limestick, it would certainly scorn a trick of that sort, if it were not by its very nature, and did not wish to be, beside us from the start.[14]

This very thesis reappears in a passage already cited from *An Essay on Philosophical Method*:

> In a philosophical enquiry what we are trying to do is not to discover something of which until now we have been ignorant, but to know better something which

in some sense we know already; not to know it better in the sense of coming to know more about it, but to know it better in the sense of coming to know it in a different and better way – actually, instead of potentially, or explicitly instead of implicitly, or in whatever terms the theory of knowledge chooses to express the difference. (EPM, 11)

But although, according to both authors, the truth is with us from the start, it is not with us *as truth*, otherwise there would be no need to seek it. In so far as it is with us at all it is with us not *qua* truth but *qua* error. The prior existence of the truth *qua* error is the basis of the backward or reverse movement of dialectic, which may therefore be described as a regression from truth to error.

Collingwood illustrates the reverse notion of dialectic with the following example. A dialectical series of terms, he says, is one in which each term is an erroneous description of the next. Take the dialectical series, ABC. C is the truth, B a distorted account of it, and A a distorted account of B. Thus when C (which represents the true nature of mind) attempts to comprehend itself, the result is a mistake, B, which C makes about itself. This mistake, however, recoils upon C's own nature; for a mind which makes mistakes about its nature will find its conduct (which is in fact its nature) affected by these mistakes. Its nature will not be altered to coincide with the false conception, but it will be disturbed by that conception. From this then arises B, what the mind now thinks it is, and C_1 what it actually is (in the sense in which its nature has been altered or disturbed by its mistake).

Keeping in mind that, for Collingwood, the attempt on the part of C to know itself is always in the form of the positing of an object, there arises within consciousness itself an opposition between what the object is for *consciousness* (B), and what the object is *per se* (C_1). If we call C_1 the notion and B the object then experience consists in seeing whether the object corresponds with the notion. If in the attempt to do this consciousness commits another error, that is, fails even to render the notion of B coherent, then a downward step occurs which results in an even further distortion of the truth, namely, A. This still further lapse from truth in the experience of the mind C is now an error of the second degree, and therefore reacts in the second degree on the conduct and nature of the mind. It no longer behaves as C_1, but as B_1, which (since every alteration of the concept of the object for consciousness initiates an alteration of what the object is *per se*) is equivalent to C_2.

From the standpoint of the absolute, of course, the mind is still C although consciousness as such cannot know this. But it would be misleading to call it C, because it behaves not like C but like C_1 (SM, 206–7). Such a mind, says Collingwood, can only be described as follows:

> Implicitly it is C. But it is trying to conceive itself as B, although really there is no such thing as B; and even this error it has further confused so that it now thinks of itself as A. Its true nature C, overlaid by the successive misconceptions B and A comes out in the form C_2. It is, if we like so to distinguish, explicitly A, actually C_2, at bottom or ultimately C. (SM, 207)

Such then is Collingwood's description of the dialectic in reverse, which begins with what the mind in truth is, and follows the succession of errors which lead to its most primitive (i.e., erroneous) standpoint. In metaphorical terms Collingwood might have described this as 'the fall of consciousness.'

The very principles which lie at the basis of the reverse dialectic, in its descent from truth to error, are found also in the positive, forward movement of the dialectic in its ascent through error to truth. This may be described as 'the redemption of consciousness.' It is this forward movement which truly characterizes the natural course of mind and for this reason will be the path which philosophy will follow in its phenomenological exposition of the history of mind.

The forward path of the dialectic begins with the realization that the mind can achieve knowledge of itself only through mediation, that is, by positing itself as an object:

> The mind ... can only know itself through the mediation of an external world, know that what it sees in the external world is its own reflection. Hence the constructions of external worlds, works of art, religions, sciences, structures of historical fact, codes of law, systems of philosophy and so forth ... (SM, 315)

The external worlds of art, religion, science, and history are objectifications of forms of life which are related dialectically and which arise as the result of "a dialectical criticism of errors," which Collingwood describes as follows:

> In its actual course, thinking moves by the dialectical criticism of errors – the criticism of an error by itself, its break-up under the stress of its internal contradictions – to their denial: this denial is a truth, so framed as to negate the error just exploded, but generally falling into a new and opposite error by an exaggerated fear of the old. Any element of error in this new truth will, if thinking goes vigorously forward, initiate a new dialectical criticism and the process will be repeated on a higher plane. Thus thought in its progress – a progress not mechanical or predestined but simply effected by the hard work of

thinking – moves through a series of phases each of which is a truth and yet an error, but so far as the progress is real, each is a triumph of truth over a preceding error and an advance to what may be called a truer truth. (SM, 289)

Speculum Mentis is the enactment of this dialectical criticism of errors. Such a criticism will exhibit not only the purely 'serial' or 'logical' development of the concepts of art, religion, science, history, and philosophy; it will set forth as well the stages through which these forms have developed historically. This is because history is of the very essence of mind and it is only through history that the mind can mediate itself through error to truth.

The concept of mind as a dialectical process, as outlined above, is a presupposition of Collingwood's entire philosophy, and there is no evidence that this concept was ever abandoned. On the contrary, it is, as we shall see, implied at various levels throughout the *Idea of History* as well as in *An Essay on Metaphysics*.

Perhaps the best evidence in favour of the claim that the doctrine was never abandoned is the explicit discussion of this concept of mind in the *New Leviathan* (1942), the very last book which Collingwood wrote. In this work the mind is described as an "irregular" series of the following functions: appetite, passion, desire, and thinking. The development from one level to another is logical, but it does not proceed according to the same kind of rules which govern a "regular" series and according to which the continuation of the series can be predicted. The development of mind (and this is one respect in which mind differs from nature) is governed by a principle according to which, although each phase in the series is presupposed by another, there is nothing in any given term or in any given combination of terms on the basis of which we can predict what comes after it. Thus, for example, passion presupposes appetite, desire presupposes passion, reason presupposes desire, and so on. Yet there is nothing in, for example, feeling plus appetite which makes inevitable the emergence of passion, and so on. In short, "*the earlier terms in a series of mental functions do not determine the latter.*" This is called by Collingwood "the law of contingency" (NL, 65). What Collingwood obviously means to say here is that there is no purely 'deterministic' rule governing the logical development of mind, as would be the case, for example, in nature. He is claiming, in other words, that whatever causal relationships obtain between prior and posterior states of mind, they are not of the type normally applied to nature: the type which in *An Essay on Metaphysics* is described as sense III (EM, 313ff):

> Here that which is 'caused' is an event or state of things, and its 'cause' is another event or state of things standing to it in a one-one relation of such a kind

that (a) if the cause happens or exists the effect must happen or exist, even if no further conditions are fulfilled, (b) the effect cannot happen or exist unless the cause happens or exists, (c) in some sense which remains to be defined, the cause is prior to the effect ... (EM, 285–6)

This does not mean, as it may appear, that there cannot therefore be a 'logos' of the development of mind. On the contrary, such a logos is provided by the phenomenological analysis of *Speculum Mentis* which, having selected for its subject matter the intentionality of mind, presupposes a type of causality which is closer to that which in *An Essay on Metaphysics* is called sense I (EM, 285, 290–5). Such an account would, without presupposing that one function of mind leads inevitably to another, show forth, nevertheless, the development of mind as "the unfolding of a dialectical drama in which every phase has grown out of its predecessor with a kind of dramatic inevitability" (SM, 289).

Thus appetite would be shown to grow out of feeling, passion out of appetite, etc. The possibility of such an account presupposes an important distinction between two kinds of necessity: the necessity of what in *The New Leviathan* Collingwood calls a "regular" series, in which antecedent conditions necessarily determine consequent conditions (such that the latter are predictable solely on the basis of a thorough knowledge of the former), and the necessity of what he calls an "irregular" series (NL, 63), in which consequent conditions grow dialectically out of antecedent conditions (an example of which is the phenomenological logic of *Speculum Mentis* which explains how religion grows out of art, science out of religion, and so on – in which case the kind of prediction implied by a regular series is not possible. Predictability thus becomes a criterion according to which nature and mind can be distinguished; for, according to the terms of dialectical logic, mind, unlike nature, while necessary, is nevertheless "not predictable" (NL, 64). Indeed, as we shall see in more detail in chapter x, the unpredictability of mind is a consequence of the more comprehensive theory of the mind as pure act. The absolute mind, writes Collingwood, "has nothing over against itself as a necessity by which it is bound: not even the laws of its own nature" (SM, 300). The mind is not a substance whose nature transcends its activity. Its nature is nothing more than the product of that activity. Only to a mind which makes itself in this way can genuine freedom become a real possibility.

The principles which are implied both by *Speculum Mentis* and the *New Leviathan*, according to which one state of mind is modified into another, are (to use the language of the *New Leviathan*) the "law of contingency" (already referred to) and the "law of primitive survivals," which reads: *"When A is modified into B there survives in any example of B, side by side with the function B which is the modified form of A, an element of A in its primitive or unmodified state"* (NL, 65). What is here called "the law of primitive survivals" (elsewhere referred to as "the principle of incapsulation," A, 114, 140 ff.), sums up everything which is contained in the *Speculum Mentis* account of dialectical development. The essential identity of doctrine is well shown in the following passages from the *New Leviathan*:

... let *A* be consciousness and *B* second-order consciousness or reflection; and suppose that reflection is a modification of consciousness. Unless a man reflecting had in him a primitive survival of mere consciousness, he would have nothing to reflect on, and would not reflect. (NL, 65)

If appetite, passion, and desire form a series, each is a modification of the one before; but any individual example of passion contains, over and above the appetite which has been modified into passion an element of appetite pure and simple: any example of desire contains a primitive survival of passion and also one of appetite: and so, as the series goes on, the structure of the function grows more complex. (NL, 65-6)

It is only in terms of the laws of "contingency" and "primitive survivals" that we are able to understand the description of mind in *Speculum Mentis* according to which mind is "a dialectical drama in which every phase has grown out of its predecessor with a kind of dramatic inevitability" (SM, 289). By inevitability, of course, is meant not the abstract predetermined inevitability of nature, but rather the "contingent" inevitability of a "well constructed plot or fugue, the inevitability of concrete rational fact" (SM, 289). And this means, as we have already seen, that the plot of history can be grasped only 'after the fact' ("The owl of Minerva spreads its wings only with the falling of the dusk"):

A history of thought, then, gives a series of errors not exhausting the possibilities of unreason nor forming a predetermined scheme for thought, but recounting the errors that have actually been made and showing how each has contributed something to the state of knowledge today: a *felix culpa,* in so far as it has been the occasion of our rise to higher things. (SM, 290)

Throughout this whole discussion Collingwood has relied heavily on the criterion of non-predictability as a distinguishing feature of mind and history. It is necessary to point out, however, that the way in which he does so may possibly lead to a great deal of misunderstanding concerning the true nature of such knowledge as history makes possible vis-à-vis the development of mind. For to say that mind is unpredictable according to a certain model of prediction employed in natural science does not invalidate other models of predictability.

Indeed, Collingwood himself, although he does not explicitly acknowledge it, clearly prepares the ground for the possibility of other kinds of prediction. There is for example the imaginative reconstruction (already referred to) of what the future course of the mind's development might ideally be. There is also a kind of practical wisdom or 'historic sense,' which rules out the feasibility of pursuing certain courses of action because they are likely to lead to disastrous results. The latter is surely essential to the kind of knowledge which Collingwood continuously urged historians to acquire and without which the alleged rapprochement between theory and practice (which Collingwood claimed to be one of his major interests) would not be possible.

Collingwood describes the practical wisdom which history makes possible as "insight"; and the latter is contrasted with the "ready made rules for dealing with situations of specific types" which makes prediction possible in natural science (A, 101). The former is the basis upon which we act when we find ourselves in a situation in which our action is not determined according to a rule, and where the process is directly from "knowledge of the situation" to "an action appropriate to the situation" (A, 103). By "knowledge of the situation" is meant the kind of historical understanding which simply reveals what the situation is by showing up the less obvious features normally hidden from a careless and untrained eye (A, 100). By enabling us simply to "see the features of the situation," historical understanding provides the necessary insight according to which we can act without resorting to rules. Collingwood specifies two types of occasions upon which acting according to insight is necessary.

The first is when you find yourself in a situation that you do not recognize as belonging to any of your known types (A, 104). As a result, no rule can tell you how to act. But you cannot refrain from acting; you must do something. Given the necessary insight you may happen upon the right action which contains implicitly the rule appropriate to the occasion. This type of behaviour is a form of creative improvisation and is initiated primarily as a result of inexperience and ignorance. Over a period of time, however, success in such behaviour will result in an available body of rules with which to guide future behaviour and make creative improvisation unnecessary: which goes to show that even behaviour according to rules presupposes behaviour according to insight.

The second kind of situation is when you can refer the situation to a known type but are not content to do so because your desire is to cope with precisely those unique aspects of the situation which are not covered by its belonging to a type. This situation arises out of recognition of the limitations of what in the first example was called acting according to rules. Thus, for example, everybody has certain rules according to which he acts in dealing with his tailor (A, 104). These rules are based on genuine experience and by acting upon them a man will deal fairly with his tailor and thereby help his tailor to deal fairly with him.

But, Collingwood declares, so far as he acts according to these rules, he is dealing with his tailor only in his capacity as tailor and not as the unique human being John Robinson "aged sixty with a weak heart and a consumptive daughter, a passion for gardening and an overdraft at the bank" (A, 104). The rules for dealing with tailors do not enable you to come to grips with his humanity. In order to deal adequately with this it is necessary to go beyond the stage at which rules can be applied, to return to improvisation. Too strict allegiance to rules of conduct, like the consequences of regularian behaviour in general, keeps action at a low potential. If action is to be raised to a higher, more creative potential the agent must open his eyes wider and see more clearly the situation in which he was acting. Only the kind of insight which is made possible by a genuinely historical understanding of the nature of the situation being dealt with makes successful improvisation possible.

By a genuinely historical understanding Collingwood means, of course, knowledge of the present in which the past is incapsulated (A, 106). In short, historical understanding is the basis for what Collingwood has called action according to duty and, beyond this, action according to conscience. According to the latter, if my understanding of Collingwood is correct, no rule can tell me what my duty is, but I can certainly anticipate what actions are clearly not my duty; no rule can direct my conscience, but conscience can anticipate that obedience to certain rules may in certain circumstances be inappropiate. It is this kind of insight which, according to Collingwood, was lacking in the authors of the Treaty of Versailles. Their inability to anticipate the consequences of certain decisions resulted in what he describes as "an unprecedented disgrace to the human intellect" (A, 90). Lack of insight, he contends, was the reason for "their inability to control situations in which the elements are human beings and the forces mental forces" (A, 90).

But control of the human situation is not possible without some kind of intelligent forecasting, the kind made possible by history. In effect then, Collingwood has ruled out for history the kind of prediction (characteristic of the natural sciences) which is made possible by the strict application of rules, and has substituted instead the model of creative improvisation which proceeds not through the application of rules alone but by the elimination of inappropriate or false actions.

∞ VII ∞

Philosophy as
CATEGORICAL THINKING

I THE DISTINCTION BETWEEN CATEGORICAL AND HYPOTHETICAL THINKING

In addition to the doctrine of the overlap of classes and the scale of forms, Collingwood asserts, in chapter VI of *An Essay on Philosophical Method*, the conception of philosophy as categorical thinking. Categorical (as opposed to hypothetical) thinking is committed to the belief that its subject matter is something actually existing. And the latter, moreover, is exemplified by the very act of thinking itself. To think about thinking, for example, is itself an instance of what is being thought about. In this respect at least, Collingwood's notion of categorical thinking may be compared with Austin's notion of 'performative utterances.' As an example of hypothetical thinking, whose subject matter neither exists nor is exemplified by the act of thinking about it, Collingwood cites mathematics and empirical science. The distinction between categorical and hypothetical thinking is therefore made the basis of the distinction between philosophy and natural science in general.[1]

The distinction between philosophy and science can easily be misleading unless it is seen in its proper context. For at first sight it appears to violate the very principle of the unity of science which Collingwood's philosophy has all along been dedicated to upholding. This impression is vitiated, however, when the distinction is re-examined in terms of the doctrine of the overlap of classes and the scale of forms.

In the first place, it is only from the standpoint of the logic of species and genus that categorical and hypothetical judgments constitute mutually exclusive species of judgment. From the absolute standpoint the relation between them is one of overlap. Thus it is only to the extent that science conceives of itself as a separate and independent standpoint that it is necessarily committed to the belief that its judgments are purely hypothetical (even though this judgment is itself categorical). By contrast with science, philosophy is necessarily committed to the belief that its judgments are categorical. In recognizing its own judgments to be categorical, however, it must also recognize that *all* judgments, even hypothetical ones, are categorical, and that it is only an error which allows us to separate the hypothetical from the categorical and conceive of each in abstraction from the other. Indeed, to maintain an absolute distinction between philosophy and science would be to commit the fallacy of false disjunction. Thus, what Collingwood is doing in the first part of chapter VI, where he draws this distinction, is to contrast the way philosophy experiences itself with the way science experiences itself, but only so far as each conceives of itself as a separate and autonomous standpoint. But when viewed *ab extra*, from the absolute standpoint, philosophy, which is necessarily immanent in science, recognizes that in fact there is no absolute distinction between science and philosophy, between the hypothetical and the categorical judgment.

In support of this interpretation I will cite Collingwood's claim, at the outset of chapter VI (EPM), that although the mathematical and empirical sciences make only hypothetical assertions about their subject matter, a full account of such a science cannot be given without making reference to certain statements of a non-hypothetical nature. These latter statements, which Collingwood calls *conditiones sine qua non* of empirical science (EPM, 118), are presupposed, and can never, like the purely hypothetical statements which constitute the actual body of science, be demonstrated either a priori or a posteriori.[2]

The distinction within science between hypothetical statements and their *conditiones sine qua non*, may be characterized, if I understand Collingwood correctly, by means of the following examples drawn from empirical science. A scientist, after a certain number of observations, may come to the conclusion that 'There is a force, proportional to the product of the masses and inversely proportional to the square of the distance, acting between any two bodies.' Such a statement does not refer to anything actually existing, to actual bodies, for example; it refers, rather, to a set of ideal or standard conditions to which all particular bodies more or less conform. Likewise, when a scientist says, 'Force equals mass times acceleration,' he is referring not to anything actual, but rather to a set of ideal conditions to which actual things sometimes conform. The concepts contained in the above statements – force, gravity, acceleration, and so on – are not proper names; they are not 'referring' but 'fictitious' concepts: that is, they are not the names of actual entities, but descriptions of the ideal conditions under which certain observable things happen.

At the same time, however, such statements rest on a variety of what, for want of a better name, I shall call 'ontological commitments' or 'existential references': that is to say, beliefs which refer to something actual, something grounded in experience, such as, to cite Collingwood's own examples, the observation and recording of the facts of perception (EPM, 121), and my freedom to form hypotheses based on these observations (SM, 184).[3] Statements expressing these beliefs constitute what in *Speculum Mentis* is described as the context of assertion against which all supposal (whether it be the imaginative supposal of art, or the hypothetical reasoning of science) must exist. Thus, Collingwood declares toward the end of chapter VI, in a passage which, when seen in the proper context, makes the introductory remarks to the chapter seem more intelligible:

> Even in science, therefore, the overlap exists; and this I have already recognized by showing that the purely hypothetical propositions forming the body of science involve certain categorical elements which are necessary to their being but form no part of their essence *qua* science; these are, as it were, a solid structure of facts and truths, upon which the pliant body of scientific hypothesis leads a parasitic life. (EPM, 135)

This passage is written from the absolute standpoint, which, when it expresses itself as a philosophy of science, is the *ab extra* moment of third-level 'philosophical' philosophy of science. If science were to behave in accordance with the philosophical insights of the absolute standpoint it would enter the third level of existence – the ideal limit of which would be the point at which natural science would cease to experience its 'separateness' from the other sciences and would experience instead its unity with them. But there is a fundamental ambiguity, which affects science at all levels, between what the science is *ab intra* (science *qua* science, art *qua* art, etc.) and what it is *ab extra*. So long as philosophy constitutes itself as the reflective moment of the former, it will employ distinctions such as the one between categorical and hypothetical. But when philosophy constitutes itself as the reflective moment of the latter (which more closely approximates the ideal which philosophy has set before itself) it will declare that a complete theory of that standpoint must be a complete theory of knowledge which embraces all of the standpoints. These are precisely the reflections with which Collingwood concludes chapter VI of *An Essay on Philosophical Method*:

> A complete theory of knowledge ... would have to consider not only the formal distinction of philosophy from science, but the relation of each to the other

as substantive bodies of knowledge. It would have to ask whether the hypothetical element in philosophy is identical with science itself, or whether it is something peculiar to philosophy; and whether the categorical skeleton upon which are supported the hypothetical tissues of scientific thought proper is wholly or partly identical with philosophy. (EPM, 135-6)

Given this statement concerning the relation of philosophy and science when viewed *ab extra* we may now concentrate on the exposition of philosophy *ab intra* as categorical thinking

2 THE HISTORY OF THE CONCEPTION OF PHILOSOPHY AS CATEGORICAL THINKING

Collingwood begins his exposition of philosophy as categorical thinking by placing himself in the tradition of other philosophers. The aim of philosophy has always been to formulate its thought categorically. Thus Plato, discussing the difference between dialectic and mathematics in the *Republic* (511B), explains that whereas the starting points of mathematical reasoning are mere hypotheses, dialectic demands for itself a 'non-hypothetical starting point' ἀρχὴ ἀνυπόθετος. In a different way, Aristotle says the same thing, and he describes Plato's *ens realissimum* as τὸ ὄν ᾗ ὄν. Finally, the subject matter of philosophy is further qualified by Hegel's remark that the subject of philosophy is no mere thought and no mere abstraction, but *die Sache Selbst*.

Presupposed by these brief, all too general, comments, is an interpretation of the history of philosophy which would presumably place Collingwood in the main stream of the western philosophical tradition; for he always claimed that his own philosophy was no more than a repetition (with a difference, of course) of the essence of every great philosopher's teaching, *philosophia quaedam perennis* (SM, 13).
It is unfortunate that Collingwood was not able to write a history of philosophy along the lines of the first four parts of the *Idea of History* and the bulk of the *Idea of Nature*. The aim of this history would have been to trace the development of the idea of philosophy as 'categorical thinking'; and we might have expected it to end on the following note: 'How, or on what conditions, can the philosopher apprehend his object? My historical review of the idea of philosophy has resulted in the emergence of an answer to this question: namely, that the philosopher must conceive of his subject as something whose essence involves existence' (cf. IH, 282).

Collingwood did not himself provide us with a history of philosophy in terms of which he could view his own philosophical development, but the historian of Collingwood's thought cannot avoid reconstructing for himself the *philosophia quaedam perennis* of which Collingwood's own philosophy is a variation. Although such a project is actually beyond the scope of this study, it is sometimes helpful, in order to understand one philosopher's thought, to view it through the spectacles worn by other philosophers. Collingwood claims that the object of his philosophy is the being *qua* being of Aristotle, and the *deus sive natura* of Spinoza. To the extent to which we can clarify what each of these philosophers meant by their respective declarations we will approach a better understanding of Collingwood. The following reflections are offered as a mere starting point towards such a conclusion.

By 'being *qua* being' Aristotle meant not being *qua* abstract being, but being *qua* concrete being: he was affirming a concrete not an abstract universal. It follows, if this interpretation is accepted, that the expression το ὄν ᾗ ὄν is not tautological, in which case there is a difference between the meaning of τὸ ὄν and the meaning of ᾗ ὄν. This difference may be characterized by translating the phrase 'being *qua* being' into the phrase 'being *qua* modes of being,' and then treating the categories as a list of the various modes through which being expresses itself. The highest category is substance. But substance is itself a scale of forms, and we are led therefore to the notion of the highest substance. The ultimate nature of being *qua* being lies in the highest substance, which, in Aristotle's language, is the final cause (τέλος) or first principle (ἀρχή) of the universe. Since being is not a genus, the categories are not species each of which expresses the genus in precisely the same way; nor is substance a genus, dispersing itself into a plurality of substances. On the contrary the categories are a scale of forms each of which expresses the essence of being more adequately than the one below it.

The categories are related, according to Aristotle, *pros hen legomena,* with reference to the highest category; the substances are likewise related to the highest substance or first cause. It follows therefore that in order fully to understand the nature of the particular substances, one must first understand the nature of the highest substance, which for Aristotle is God. Philosophy then is implicit teleology which when rendered explicit becomes theology.

Aristotle's problem concerned the relation between God (the highest being), and the universe. His question was, Is the science of the highest being a separate science which is prior to and independent of all the other sciences which derive from it, or is the science of the highest being nothing more than the unity of the other separate sciences? If the former then how can this being who enjoys the existence of an eternal form be made an object of knowledge? If the latter then how is any particular science even possible except through the mediation of the absolute standpoint which knowledge of the separate sciences is supposed to achieve? Aristotle lacked the conceptual apparatus to solve his problem. He had made a good beginning. But he was unable to explain the conditions under which God could become an object of knowledge because he was still bound by the limitations of Platonic idealism which not only separated reality from the rest of the world but declared that it was a permanent and unchanging substance.

Aristotle's problem can be solved only when it is realized that being or reality is not a permanent and eternal substance but an activity which is constantly changing; and this activity, as Hegel realized, can only be the mind knowing itself. As a solution to Aristotle's problem Collingwood therefore places the object of knowledge within mind. Being is still, as it was for Aristotle, a plurality of activities, related *pros hen legomena* to the highest being. But this highest being is not, as it was for Aristotle, a separately existing, eternal substance. It is, on the contrary, an immanent-transcendent activity which Collingwood calls absolute mind.

The doctrine of *pros hen legomena* may be further regarded as the basis of Aristotle's solution to the problem of relating the 'manyness' of being with its 'unity.' The many are spoken of as one in the sense that they are all related, each in its own way, *pros hen*, to one central point. Being, he declares, is not itself a genus but is rather a group of genera. The term 'being' refers therefore both to the group as a whole and to what the members of this group share in common. Thus Aristotle declares: "There are many senses in which a thing may be said to 'be', but all that 'is' is related to one central point, one definite kind of thing, and is not said to be by mere ambiguity" (*Met*, 1003$_A$ 32–5). The question therefore arises, In what way is 'all that is' related to this 'one definite kind of thing'? In the *Categories* Aristotle distinguishes three types of naming, each of which may be regarded as the basis for a theory of relations. Things are said to be "equivocals" (τά σμωνυμα) when, though they have a common name, the definition corresponding with the same differs radically for each (*Cat*, 1$_A$ 1–5). In the *Nicomachean Ethics* Aristotle points out that things which are equivocals are so by chance alone (*EN*, 1096$_B$ 26). It is clear then that equivocation can hardly be regarded as a satisfactory basis for reconciling 'all that is' with the 'one.' In the second place, things are said to be named "univocally" (τά συνώνυμα) which have both the name and the definition answering to the name in common (*Cat.*, 1$_A$ 6–7). According to this type of relation, the differences among things would be accidental only; at the level of essence, everything would be identical. Thus, to solve the problem of relating the manyness of being with its unity in this way would be to reduce all differences of things *qua* being to bare abstract identity. Finally, things are said to be named "derivatively" (τά παρávυμa) which derive their name from some other name but which differ from it in "termination" (*Cat.*, 1$_A$ 12–14). On the basis of related passages in the *Ethics* (1096$_B$ 8–1097$_A$ 15), it would seem that 'all that is' cannot be related to the 'one' either by equivocation or by univocation (cf. also his criticism of the univocal theory of being in book Γ of the *Metaphysics*). There must therefore be a further alternative according to which the manyness of being can be reconciled with its unity, an alternative which will explain the ground of the unity of the different senses of being.

A clue to the nature of this alternative may be found in various passages of the *Ethics* (1096$_B$ 29–30) in which Aristotle describes certain types of relations which might account for the different senses of good. These are, according to Aristotle: (a) strict derivation (αφ ἑνός), (b) relation by virtue of contribution (πρὸς ἕν συντελεῖν), and (c) relation by analogy (ἀναλογιά). Examples of strict derivation are: the word 'grammarian' derived from the word 'grammar,' the word 'courageous' derived from 'courage,' and the word 'healthy' derived from 'health.' Examples of *pros hen* contribution are exercise, food, rest, and medicine, each of which is related to health in the sense that each contributes toward its maintenance as an end (τέλος). Finally, an example of analogy is such a relation as: 'the *eye* is to the *body* as *nous* is to the *psyche*.' Although Aristotle does not explicitly say so, it may be argued that of these three types of relation, the second, *pros hen syntelein*, provides the most promising basis for an interpretation of the teleologically oriented system of beings. On this interpretation, the concrete identity in difference (according to which the 'all that is' is related to the 'one definite kind of thing') is exemplified by a system of *pros hen* relations which may be regarded, therefore, as the ontological model according to which the many senses of being are related to the one kind of being. Each being is genuinely distinct and different from the others but shares in common with them the fact that it can contribute towards the same end.

Granted this interpretation of Aristotle's thought, a direct comparison may be entertained between it and Collingwood's philosophy. Compare, for example, the categories (regarded now as a system of *pros hen* relations) with the scale of forms. In the first place, Collingwood, like Aristotle, eliminates both the 'equivocal' and the 'univocal' theories of relations as possible models for explicating the basis of the unity of the scale of forms. The doctrine described in chapter III above as the dogma of first-level analysis has points in common with Aristotle's notion of equivocation, while the notion of univocation embodies what is described below as the dogma of 'second-level' analysis. At the first level each form is defined in total exclusion from the rest – they have nothing in common except their name. At the second level the forms are related (and indeed identified) as the co-ordinate species of a common genus. In place of these doctrines Collingwood substitutes the doctrine of the scale of forms, whereas Aristotle offered us the doctrine of things related *pros hen legomena* or, to be more precise, *pros hen syntelein*. Just as each of the categories may be regarded as contributing towards the activity of being *qua* being, so each of the forms on Collingwood's scale contributes, each in its own way, to the life of absolute mind.

But in spite of a resemblance between the two systems of thought, there are, of course, many important differences. In the first place, there is lacking in Aristotle any notion of dialectic by determinate negation. Secondly, whereas Aristotle's highest being is regarded as an eternal object whose existence and nature is in no sense dependent upon developments within the lower orders of being, for Collingwood the absolute, which is the point towards which the developing scale of forms is related *pros hen legomena,* is itself a product of the same self-making process which produces the many particular and finite forms. It would, however, seem reasonable to suggest, if this interpretation of Aristotle is granted, that Collingwood's scale of forms may be regarded as an historicist interpretation of Aristotle's doctrine of the categories.

In Spinoza there is also a concern to know the highest object, or *ens reale*. Spinoza distinguishes among the possible objects of knowledge *essentia formalis* and *essentia actualis*. The former is the *ens rationis* or object of *ratio*, the ordinary sciences. Its essence is prior to its existence, and can be expressed by means of definitions. Knowledge of it is purely hypothetical. *Essentia actualis,* on the other hand, is the object of *scientia intuitiva. Essentia actualis* is a being whose existence precedes essence or, to put it another way, whose existence is identical with its essence, and thinking about this is not only categorical but existential. It finds its expression in action: not only in the action of the subject but in the action of the object as well. This is the standpoint of *amor intellectualis Dei,* or intersubjectivity, which corresponds to the standpoint of *speculum speculi* or absolute knowledge in Collingwood's thought.

The distinction between *essentia formalis* and *essentia actualis* and their corresponding forms of cognition can be further explained by means of an examination of the various contexts in which these terms occur.

The term *essentia actualis* is employed in the *Ethics* in two places. It occurs first in part III, proposition vii, in the context of a discussion of *conatus*. Now, it is significant that when referring to *conatus* Spinoza uses the term *essentia actualis* and not *essentia formalis*. *Conatus* is described as "the actual essence of a thing" and as such it belongs to *natura naturans* and not to *natura naturata*. The second occurrence of *essentia actualis* is in part IV, proposition iv, where it is used to describe the actual essence of man in so far as it manifests the "actual power of God."

Essentia formalis, on the other hand, refers to a thing in so far as it can be rendered an object – that is, apprehended under the attributes of God (*Eth.* II, viii and note). "The truth and formal essence [*essentia formalis*]of things is what it is because it exists objectively [i.e., as an idea] in God's intellect" (*Eth.* II, vii, corollary and note). In effect, *essentia formalis* is used in the *Ethics* in the same sense as *essentia idealis* is used in the *Tractatus Theologico Politicus* – that is, as a description of that aspect of things which can be conceived independently of their existence (*Tract. Theo. Pol.* II, para. 2).

Corresponding to the ontological distinction between *essentia formalis* and *essentia actualis* is a further ontological distinction, employed in the earlier writings, between *ens rationis* and *ens reale* (*Cog. Met.*, I, i, para. 3; *Sh. Tr.*, II, iii, x). *Essentia formalis* is equivalent to what can be defined by *ratio* through common abstract notions which are *entia rationis*. But *essentia actualis* is the individuality, the very life of a thing; it is precisely that which escapes definition, the *ens reale* which is virtually beyond the bounds of reason (i.e., *ratio*).

For *ratio,* a thing is an object comprehended in terms of common and abstract notions which pertain to the essence of no individual thing; in effect, *ratio,* like the 'understanding' in Hegel and Collingwood, has for its object the abstract universal. *Ratio,* says Spinoza, "shows us indeed what a thing ought to be, but not what it really is. And this is why it can never unite us with the object of our belief" (*Sh. Tr.*, II, iv, para 2; see also, II, ii, xxii, xxvi). *Ratio* gives us knowledge of a thing in its kind and corresponds to what Collingwood calls hypothetical (as opposed to categorical) thinking. It follows then that if things are to be known in their individuality, as they really are (i.e., as *essentia actualis*, or, to use Collingwood's term, as a concrete universal) there must be another kind of knowledge which proceeds by methods other than the methods of classification, division, definition, deduction, and induction. Such knowledge must spring not from *natura naturata* but from *natura naturans* – that is, *conatus*, the effort by which every thing endeavours to persevere in its own being, which is nothing but the *essentia actualis* of the thing itself (*Eth.* III, vii).

To understand a thing as it really is, as it perseveres in its own being, is to understand it as it is relative to us, as we persevere in our own being. Such knowledge cannot be arrived at by the means enumerated above, by *ratio*. On the contrary, it can only be arrived at existentially (in a manner which corresponds to what Collingwood regards as a phenomenology of experience), through *intuitiva scientia*, the existential understanding of *conatus* which is nevertheless *sub species aeternitatis* (or, to use Collingwoodian language again, through a knowledge which is both historically grounded and yet transhistorical, or immanent and yet transcendent). Since *conatus* or the actual essence of things (which is what we are aware of through *intuitiva scientia*) is part of the infinite essence (i.e., the pure existence) of God, we are, through *intuitiva scientia*, brought into real and actual communication with the divine essence. In short, through the human experience of the individuality (i.e., *essentia actualis*) of things, "We feel and think eternity within us" (*Eth.* v, xxiii, note).

The highest effort of the human mind and its highest virtue is to understand things by *intuitiva scientia* (*Eth.* v, xxv), the knowledge of actual things relative to the experiencing subject. Through this knowledge man achieves his chief good, which is a knowledge of the substantial union of mind and nature (*De Intellectus Emendatione*, para. 6). *Intuitiva scientia* is therefore the standpoint which overcomes the abstract distinction between subject and object. It is the standpoint of intersubjectivity, an immediate union with the thing itself. To apprehend the universe *sub species aeternitatis* from the standpoint of *intuitiva scientia* is the fundamental presupposition of freedom and salvation which Spinoza calls *amor intellectualis Dei* (*Eth.* IV, xxviii; v, xxxvi and note).[4]

But, like Aristotle, Spinoza could not in the end reconcile the unity of being with the diversity of things and Collingwood would therefore be inclined to agree with Hegel that in the philosophy of Spinoza "all differences and determinations of things and of consciousness simply go back into the one substance ... all things are merely cast down into this abyss of annihilation ... His philosophy has only a rigid and unyielding substance, and is not yet spirit; in it we are not at home with ourselves."[5]

In Collingwood the ideal which was first put forward by Aristotle, and later by Spinoza, is again brought to life. But this time, mainly through the mediation of philosophers such as Hegel, Croce, and Gentile, the problems which in Aristotle and Spinoza are left unsolved are superseded. In Collingwood, Aristotle's *ens realissimum* and Spinoza's *ens reale* reappear as absolute mind, while *noesis noeton* and *scientia intuitiva* have their counterpart in *speculum speculi* or absolute knowledge.

But *obiter dicta*, as Collingwood himself admits, cannot decide philosophical questions. Indeed, he declares, if they could, there would be some plausibility in the notion that what we are discussing in philosophy is not *die Sache Selbst* but only thoughts, the thoughts that philosophers have had about it (EPM, 123–4). Collingwood is not, of course, rejecting the history of philosophy; he is rejecting the mere enumeration of past thoughts abstracted from the philosopher's experience: the kind of "scissors and paste" history which relies exclusively on authorities. He is really following his own rule to the effect that in philosophy the historical question, What was so and so's doctrine? is part and parcel of the critical attempt to establish the truth. Collingwood therefore sets out to establish the truth of philosophy's claim that the subject matter is something actually existing.

3 PHILOSOPHY AND THE ONTOLOGICAL ARGUMENT

Collingwood's proof consists mainly of a series of reflections on the so-called ontological argument. The latter amounts to a synthesis of two philosophical principles, the principle (derived from Plato) that to be and to be knowable are the same, and the neo-Platonic concept of God as a being of whom we can say *est id quod est*, a unity of existence, a perfect being (*pulcherrimum fortissimumque*) such that *nihil deo melius excogitari queat* (EPM, 124). Anselm, according to Collingwood, put these two thoughts together: the original Platonic principle that when we really think we must be thinking of a real object, and the neo-Platonic idea of a perfect being. It was by brooding about the latter thought, until he rediscovered the former as latent within it, that Anselm realized that to think of a perfect being at all was already to think of Him, or it, as existing.

A *Collingwood's Interpretation of Anselm*

Anselm's object is one that, ideally at least, completely satisfies the demands of reason: it is not a mere *ens rationis*. It applies, moreover, not to thought in general, but only to the thought of one unique object *id quo maius cogitari nequit*. In the special case of metaphysical thinking the distinction between conceiving something and thinking it to exist is a distinction without a difference.

What exactly does the ontological argument prove? As Collingwood represents it, it clearly does not prove the existence of whatever God the person who appeals to it happens to believe in. Between it and the articles of a particular creed there is no connection unless these articles can be deduced a priori from the idea of an *ens realissimum*. To treat the ontological argument as an affirmation of religious faith would be (to cite the argument of *Speculum Mentis*) a case of dogmatic religious philosophy which, in so far as it affirms God as its object, affirms as well the confusion between symbol and meaning, metaphor and assertion, which is the differentia of religious consciousness (SM, 264–5). What it does prove is that essence involves existence, not always, but in one special case: the case of God in the metaphysical sense:[6] the *Deus sive natura* of Spinoza, the τὸ ἀγαθόν of Plato, the τὸ ὄν ᾗ ὄν of Aristotle, the object of metaphysical thought. But this means the object of philosophical thought in general; for, writes Collingwood:

... metaphysics, even if it is regarded as only one among the philosophical sciences, is not unique in its objective reference or in its logical structure; all philosophical thought is of the same kind, and every philosophical science partakes of the nature of metaphysics, which is not a separate philosophical science but a special study of the existential aspect of that same subject-matter whose aspect as truth is studied by logic, and its aspect as goodness by ethics. (EPM, 127)

It therefore follows, according to Collingwood, "that, in so far as philosophy necessarily partakes of metaphysics, philosophy stands committed to maintaining that its subject matter is no mere hypothesis, but something actually existing" (EPM, 127).

B *The Ontological Argument and the Character of the Philosophical Sciences*

It may be further shown, Collingwood maintains, that this doctrine is deeply embedded in the whole fabric of the philosophical sciences as they actually exist, so that it is impossible to engage, however slightly, in the study of logic or ethics, for example, without committing oneself to the view that one is studying a subject matter that actually exists, and therefore aiming at a knowledge which is only expressible in categorical propositions (EPM, 128). Collingwood defends this claim by contrasting the actual behaviour of logic and ethics with the actual behaviour of mathematics, the latter being an example *par excellence* of hypothetical thought.

Mathematics devotes itself to expounding an ideal of what its subject matter ought to be but commits itself to no assertion that this ideal is anywhere realized. Mathematical statements may therefore be said to be heterogeneous with their subject matter: a statement about a triangle, for example, is not itself a triangle. But in logic the reverse is true. Not only is the subject matter of logic propositions and inference, but logical statements which are made about them are themselves propositions arrived at by means of inference. In short, logic not only discusses but provides examples of propositions and reasoning. And since the propositions and reasonings of which logic consists must conform to the rules which logic itself lays down, the claim can therefore be made that "logic is actually about itself" (EPM, 129).

Logic cannot, therefore, be in substance merely hypothetical. Mathematics can afford to be indifferent to the existence of its subject matter; so long as it is free to suppose it, that is enough. But logic cannot share this indifference, because it is itself an instance of its own subject matter. Thus, according to Collingwood:

> when we say 'all squares have their diagonals equal' we need not be either implicitly or explicitly asserting that squares exist; but when we say 'all universal propositions distribute their subject' we are not just discussing universal propositions, we are also enunciating a universal proposition; we are producing an actual instance of the thing under discussion, and cannot discuss it without doing so. (EPM, 129–30)

As opposed to the hypothetical propositions of mathematics, the propositions of logic are therefore categorical.

Collingwood further sums up this argument in a letter to Gilbert Ryle dated 9 May 1935:

> Logic not only discusses, it also contains reasoning; consequently, whenever a logician argues a point in the theory of inference, he is producing an instance of the thing under discussion; and, since he cannot discuss without arguing, he cannot discuss any point in the theory of inference without doing so. Consequently, in so far as it necessarily contains reasoning, the theory of reasoning cannot be indifferent to the existence of its own subject matter; in other words the propositions which constitute the body of that part of logic cannot be in substance hypothetical. *For example, if a logician could believe that no valid reasoning somewhere existed, he would merely be disbelieving his own logical theory.* (CRC, 1, 11–12)[7]

Moral philosophy reaches the same goal by a different path. Moral philosophy is "an account of how people think they ought to behave" (EPM, 132). The question how people think (which is descriptive and historical) is not, in any philosophical science, separable from the normative question whether they think rightly or wrongly; the historical and the philosophical questions are identical. Collingwood therefore declares that moral philosophy must face the responsibility of either holding that people are always right when they think they ought to perform some act, or of instituting some kind of comparison and criticism of moral judgments. Actually, this is a false alternative, and by putting it this way Collingwood is being misleading. I shall argue in chapter VIII that even for Collingwood an action can be both 'right' and yet 'subject to criticism.' In any case the point that Collingwood is trying to make is that, on the first alternative, the view is taken that the moral ideal already exists as an ideal in the minds of all moral agents (which is itself a value judgment); on the second alternative, it is presupposed that it partially so exists, and the more completely so as one tries to think out what one believes his duties to be (which is also a value judgment). In either case, the science is both normative and descriptive; it describes, not action as opposed to ideas about actions, but "the moral consciousness"; and this it is forced to describe as already being in some sense what it ought to be. Indeed, the moral philosopher would be unable to perform his task unless the criteria according to which he judges others were to some extent present in his own experience. Moral philosophy, in other words, is itself a form of moral action.

c *Categorical Thinking and the Logic of Modern Realism*

Collingwood's representation of philosophy as categorical thinking (i.e., as asserting universal and necessary propositions about something actually existing) has been the subject of much controversy.[8] A number of important and serious questions are raised by Alan Donagan who has examined Collingwood's theory in terms of the logic of *Principia Mathematica*. According to Donagan, Collingwood's claim that philosophical propositions are both universal (i.e., necessary) and categorical (i.e., existential) is inconsistent with "the logic which has come to dominate the schools since Collingwood's death," that is, the logic of Whitehead's and Russell's *Principia Mathematica*.[9] In particular, Donagan continues, none of the propositions with which Collingwood exemplifies the propositions of philosophy (i.e., Mind exists, Matter exists, God exists) can be accounted for in terms of the analysis of categorical or existential propositions provided by the *Principia*.[10]

As Donagan represents the alleged dispute between Collingwood and

Russellian logic, the reasons for the failure of Collingwood's propositions to conform to the rules of the *Principia* would seem to derive mainly from the following considerations. In the first place, according to the terms of *Principia Mathematica*, disregarding compound propositions (which Collingwood's examples clearly are not), all necessary propositions are hypothetical with respect to the affirmation of existence (i.e., they do not assert the existence of anything). In short, no existential propositions are necessary, and vice versa. But Collingwood's propositions are both necessary and existential. In the second place, according to the *Principia*, the simplest propositions which are categorical in Collingwood's sense (i.e., in the sense that to affirm a categorical proposition is to maintain that its subject matter is no mere hypothesis but something actually existing) are derived from sentences containing a logically proper name and a first order predicate. But, Donagan declares, none of Collingwood's propositions can be so derived. The reason for this – if I correctly understand Donagan's argument – is that the equivalents which *Principia* offers for such statements (and from which they would have to be derived) are particular and contingent, whereas Collingwood clearly regards them as universal and necessary. Thus, for example,[11] such a statement as, Mind exists, would have to be constructed from a statement of the form:

A Jones is a mind

in two steps. First replace the logically proper name, 'Jones,' by a variable, which can take any logically proper name as its value. This gives us,

A_1 x is a mind,

which is easily converted into a statement by 'quantifying over the variable,' thus giving us:

A_2 For some value of 'x', 'x is a mind' is true,

or, to use the more abbreviated form,

A_{2a} $(\exists x)$ x is a mind.

which means that there is at least one entity, x, which is a mind. But, on Collingwood's interpretation of statements such as, Mind exists, they could not possibly be so derived, because, being universal and necessary, their truth and meaning cannot be regarded as depending upon the existence of particular matters of fact. On the contrary, the meaning and truth of such statements depend on the existence of a universal and necessary being: a being which, unhappily, defies description according to the *Principia* account of existential categorical propositions. Thus Donagan declares:

In order to uphold his doctrine that, as well as being categorical, metaphysical statements like 'The *ens realissimum* exists' are universal and necessary, Collingwood had no choice but to propose an alternative to the analysis of categorical [i.e., existential] propositions in *Principia Mathematica*. Unhappily, having failed to appreciate Russell's revolutionary theory of quantification, which Frege had anticipated, he was not well equipped to improve upon it.[12]

It is Donagan's contention that Collingwood in fact failed to provide such an alternative; what is more, he knew he had failed, and when he came to write the *Essay on Metaphysics* he abandoned it altogether and was prepared to admit that metaphysical statements were not categorical universal. Yet, according to Donagan, Collingwood could not bring himself to believe that metaphysics is impossible. Under what conditions could it be possible then? Collingwood's answer was to regard metaphysics as a form of history. As history, the propositions of metaphysics cease to be categorical universal and become categorical singular or particular. (Donagan, with reference to Collingwood, uses the terms singular and particular interchangeably.)[13] Thus Donagan accounts for the historicization of philosophy in *An Essay on Metaphysics*.

But if, as Donagan suggests, Collingwood's reasons for giving up the doctrines of *An Essay on Philosophical Method* in favour of the doctrines of *An Essay on Metaphysics* had to do with the fact that he was unable to produce an alternative to the analysis of existential propositions in *Principia Mathematica*, then I fail to see how the solution which *An Essay on Metaphysics* offers could be any more satisfying; for such propositions as 'Jones believes, Mind exists,' or 'The Greeks believed that, Matter exists,' are surely no more easily accounted for than are the propositions, Mind exists and Matter exists. For this reason alone, I find Donagan's account of the rationale underlying Collingwood's alleged change of doctrine difficult to accept. To put it bluntly, if a proposition like Mind exists, means that there is an x such that x is a mind, and if, as Collingwood himself seems to suggest, explicating a presupposition means reconstructing the thought of the agent in meaningful terms, then the statement 'Jones presupposed that Mind exists,' when explicated by the metaphysician, can only mean 'Jones believed that there is an x such that x is a mind.' But this is far from exhausting what Collingwood, even in *An Essay on Metaphysics*, understood the presupposition to mean to anyone who ever held it, and I therefore fail to see why, by converting the logical form of the traditional claims of metaphysics into the form of statements about what someone else presupposed, Collingwood would have believed himself to have saved metaphysics. This at least tends to encourage me in my belief that the doctrine of the *Essay* is quite different from what Donagan claims it to be – though Donagan might well reply that it was precisely such dissatisfaction with the outcome of the *Essay* that led Collingwood to change his mind again in *The New Leviathan*.

The conclusions of Donagan's Russellian criticisms of Collingwood may be compared with the conclusions of a much earlier criticism by Gilbert Ryle, which appeared first in Ryle's paper "Mr. Collingwood and the Ontological Argument" and later in an unpublished correspondence which took place in the spring and summer of 1935. Ryle argues, if I understand him correctly, that in order for Collingwood *meaningfully* to claim that philosophical propositions are categorical (i.e., existential) then he "*must* mean" (my italics), to use language which is not Collingwood's, "... that philosophical propositions are or contain or rest on propositions embodying either at least one proper name or else at least one definite description which does in fact describe something." In short, Ryle declares, Collingwood must mean, by his theory of philosophy as categorical thinking, that "every philosophical proposition is or contains or rests on a genuine singular proposition"[14] – which means, as Ryle uses these terms, that it can be derived from a genuine particular proposition. According to this reasoning, to assert, for example, Mind exists, is to assert the existence of one or more matters of fact. Likewise, when Collingwood, with reference to logic, says, Essence involves existence (or, to be more precise, the existence of propositions is a necessary presupposition of the very idea of logic itself) he means no more than the perfectly general truth that a logical principle implies the existence of this and that proposition exemplifying it. Thus, according to Ryle, Collingwood has confused what is in fact no more than a general categorical proposition (reducible to a series of singular and particular propositions) for something he calls a categorical universal; and, for this reason, he was misled into thinking that philosophical propositions can be both categorical (i.e., existential) and necessary at the same time.

The sense of Ryle's argument is, therefore, to the effect that although Collingwood implicitly presupposes the very interpretation of categorical propositions which lies at the basis of Ryle's own logic, he nevertheless – either because he did not fully understand the implications of this position or (what is more likely) because he allowed himself to be misled by language – argued that there were some propositions which could be both universal and categorical at the same time. In the language of his earlier "Systematically Misleading Expressions," Ryle is in effect characterizing Collingwood as one of those metaphysical philosophers who are guilty of the sin of using "quasi-ontological" statements, and who, as if they were saying something of importance, "make 'Reality' or 'Being' the subject of their propositions, or 'real' the predicate. At best what they have to say is systematically misleading, which is the one thing which a philosopher's propositions have no right to be; and at worst it is meaningless."[15]

But Ryle's whole argument, as Collingwood himself points out, betrays a complete failure to appreciate the basic presuppositions upon which Collingwood's logic is built. Ryle's arguments are valid if and only if the presuppositions of Collingwood's logic of enquiry are the same as the presuppositions which underlie Ryle's propositional logic: such as, to cite Ryle's own description of them (in his letter to Collingwood dated 21 May 1935), that all universal judgments are hypothetical, that all categorical propositions are either particular existential or singular (which entail but are not equivalent to particulars), and that all affirmative existence (i.e., categorical particular) propositions are cases of matters-of-fact propositions; from all of which it follows that (as Ryle uses these terms) "No universal propositions are categorical" (i.e., no universal proposition is singular or particular, or, no universal propositions are or contain affirmative existential propositions (CRC, II, 11–57). The difference between Ryle's criticism and that of Donagan, then, amounts to the difference between the following claims. According to Ryle, if Collingwood is to mean anything at all then he must mean that metaphysical judgments are no more than general categoricals – that is, they either contain or rest on a genuine singular proposition which in turn entails a genuine particular proposition. According to Donagan, however, since Collingwood realized that he could neither bring his theory of philosophy as categorical thinking into conformity with the requirements of the prevailing theory of the logic of categorical propositions, nor provide an alternative account of such propositions, he abandoned the doctrine altogether for the more acceptable doctrine that all philosophical propositions are categorical singular (i.e., historical).

But, to repeat a point already made, if Donagan is right, then Collingwood is represented as trying to escape from one set of logical difficulties by becoming involved in yet another set of difficulties. If, on the other hand, Ryle is right, then in accepting the logical doctrine which posits general categoricals as well as categorical singulars and categorical particulars as the only existential ones (a doctrine which Collingwood refers to as "logical nominalism" [CRC, I, 28]), Collingwood might very well be forced into the position of accepting the associated metaphysical doctrine – sometimes referred to as 'logical atomism' – according to which what exists is an assemblage, or various assemblages of particular matters of fact.[16] Therefore, to say 'God exists,' or 'Matter exists,' or 'Mind exists' is to say that there are collections of individual facts which are instances of God, matter, and mind, respectively.

Or, to put it another way, the meaning of 'God exists' is reducible to a series of particular statements about individual facts, each of which must be verified by experience. To anyone (like Collingwood) who holds that logic implies ontology, this kind of 'ontological reductionism' is a direct consequence of the doctrine of logical nominalism. We are therefore left with the peculiar claim that since Collingwood is implicitly presupposing the doctrine of logical nominalism, he is also committed to the doctrine of ontological reductionism – that is, to the metaphysics of philosophical realism which (together with its "propositional logic as worked out by Bertrand Russell and A. N. Whitehead" [A, 45]) he had on several occasions repudiated – a doctrine which in the *Autobiography* he calls "the undischarged bankrupt of modern philosophy" (A, 45), engaged in building "card-houses out of a pack of lies" (A, 52), and founded, so he declares in the *Essay on Metaphysics*, on "human stupidity" (EM, 34).

That Collingwood could not (and indeed does not) accept the terms of reference with which Ryle criticizes his views is clear from his first letter to Ryle dated 9 May 1935. In this document Collingwood makes three declarations which sum up the main differences between the two points of view. The first concerns *the nature of universal propositions*; "... once more ascribing to me a doctrine which I do not hold and have in fact been at pains to repudiate, you assume that, when I said the universal judgments of exact and empirical science are merely hypothetical, I meant that *all* universal judgments are merely hypothetical" (CRC, I, 7). Such an interpretation on Ryle's part is an example (to use Collingwood's language) of the fallacy of *a dicto secundum quid* (from the universal judgments of science) *ad dictum simpliciter* (to universal judgments in general). Ryle himself might call it a category mistake. The second concerns *the existence of particular facts*:

> ... you ... assume that whatever really exists is a "particular matter of fact", and hence that whatever judgment asserts or implies existence asserts or implies some particular matter of fact. You not only assume this, but you ascribe the same assumption to myself; and hence you ascribe to me the view that the business of 'constructive metaphysics' is to establish particular matter of fact. This is in fact not my view. If there is any kind of thinking, as distinct from perceiving, whose business it is to establish particular matters of fact, that kind of thinking is according to me, historical thinking. I believe that such propositions as 'God exists', 'mind exists', 'matter exists', and their contradictions, do not assert or deny particular matter of fact; nor do I believe that they assert or deny anything

which can be adequately described as collections or classes of matters of fact. (CRC, I, 4) ... I do think that a philosophical proposition may be e.g. about thought or matter; and I dare say if I learned to use your language I could call thought or matter a designated entity; but I could never allow that it was either a particular matter of fact or a mere collection of particular matters of fact. (CRC, I, 6)

The third concerns the theory of types of propositions:

> I will admit for the sake of argument that there are any-propositions and every-propositions; but I contend that there are also all-propositions or, (as some logicians have called them) "true universals having a categorical character," i.e., they are not enumeratives, and yet they are not indifferent to the existence of the things to which they apply, but are of such a kind that their truth depends on that existence. I regard such propositions as especially characteristic of philosophy. I have not said that they are peculiar to philosophy; for the purpose of this essay all I am committed to saying is that they are found there and have there a high degree of importance. At the same time, I am committed to the view that the subject matter of philosophy is not a mere assemblage of matters of fact; once more, I have not said that the subject matter of e.g., empirical science or history *is* merely such assemblage, only that the subject-matter of philosophy is not. (CRC, I, 25–6)

In effect, Collingwood's reply to Ryle's criticisms suggests a dispute between two athletes who are playing different games, say football and baseball. The footballer is continually confessing confusion at the behaviour of the baseballer because the latter does not seem to be obeying the rules of football. The point of Collingwood's letter seems to be not so much to prove that his philosophy is right and Ryle's wrong, but to make it clear to Ryle that they are playing different games and won't he (Ryle) please stop judging him as though they were both playing the same game. In other words, he wants Ryle to realize that he (Collingwood) is not a bad player in the game of philosophy in which Ryle himself participates but is in fact a rather good player in an entirely different game, a game in which different kinds of philosophers participate.

The issue between Collingwood and *Principia Mathematica* (as represented by Donagan) and again between Collingwood and Ryle, is itself worth a separate and lengthy study, for as Ryle himself points out, "It is a very important question about the nature of philosophical theories, whether philosophical arguments can establish the existence of anything."[17] Of equal importance is the fact that the whole controversy reflects the central core of British philosophy during the first half of the twentieth century. But while these matters are serious, and deserving of more detailed and critical attention, my concern in this book is simply to examine the whole issue in the light of its bearings on the interpretation of Collingwood's philosophy. I shall therefore avoid such questions as whether Donagan correctly represents the logic of *Principia Mathematica*, whether and to what extent Ryle's views depart from the views of the latter, whether such a logic can be entertained independently of the metaphysics of logical atomism, or even whether such a logic is adequate at all. What is of immediate concern is the unquestioned assumption made by both Ryle and Donagan that failure to conform to the rules of propositional logic is identical with a failure to be logic at all.

In actual fact, Collingwood's logic of the overlap of classes (according to which categorical universal judgments are possible), can never be directly compared with the various propositional logics of realism. For, as Collingwood would be the first to declare, they are not species of a common genus, or answers to the same question. On the contrary, to use Collingwood's language, since each of the two types of logic rests on fundamentally different sets of presuppositions, each may therefore be regarded as an answer to a different question.

According to the logic of question and answer, the question to which *An Essay on Philosophical Method* is addressed arises from a belief that the nature of reality is dialectical, whereas the question to which the philosophies of Russell, Ryle, and possibly even Donagan, are addressed, arises from a belief that the world is composed of externally related facts. What kind of logic can adequately regulate the various ways of enquiring into the nature of the dialectical processes of mind? Collingwood's answer is the logic of the overlap of classes and the theory of philosophy as categorical thinking (which rests on the claim that philosophical propositions are a special kind of synthetic a priori). What kind of logic can best describe the world of externally related facts? Russell's answer was the logic of *Principia Mathematica*. On this view, the question for the historian of philosophy is not whether Collingwood's logic can be made to conform to the logic of realism, or vice versa. The real question is, What is the nature of Reality? Thus the real issue between Collingwood and the school of Russell, Ryle, and Donagan is not so much logical as metaphysical – which is precisely the point Collingwood himself makes in his two letters to Ryle.

4 CATEGORICAL THINKING AND METAPHYSICS

We are now in a position to determine more precisely what Collingwood means by the categorical thinking of philosophy and its relation to the ontological argument: a doctrine which when made explicit will provide a solid basis for challenging Donagan's claim that Collingwood's definition of metaphysical statements as categorical singular in *An Essay on Metaphysics* constitutes a repudiation of his earlier views in *An Essay on Philosophical Method*. This can be accomplished by pursuing certain clues provided by Collingwood's own example from logic and ethics and by his remarks to Ryle.

In the first place the examples cited from logic and ethics, both in *An Essay on Philosophical Method* itself and in his 1935 correspondence with Ryle, presuppose the principle of the unity of thought and action; more precisely, they presuppose implicitly the theory of the relation between philosophy and experience which is expounded in chapter VIII, s. 5, of *An Essay on Philosophical Method*. Philosophy, as we have already explained, is categorical in the sense that its very behaviour is itself a species of the subject matter under discussion. Philosophy, therefore, in providing a theory of its subject matter, is at the same time providing a theory of itself. This follows from the very notion of philosophy as the reflective moment of experience. No matter what the subject matter is, philosophy is obliged to produce, as constituent parts of itself, actual instances of thought which realize (at least to some extent) its own ideal of what the subject matter under discussion should be. Philosophy, in other words, is an activity in which the subject being brought into question is exemplified by the very act of questioning itself.

But what kind of subject can it be, which whenever it is brought into question, is exemplified by the questioning itself? It cannot be the subject of a 'proper name,' or a 'logical subject,' or a 'first-order predicate' – the kind of object denoted by the categorical propositions of Russellian or Rylian logic. Such objects are 'facts' whose existence is independent and unaffected by the knowing mind. It can only be an object whose being or existence is bound up with and determined by the very act of knowing itself: whose existence is, in a way, the answer to the questioning moment of experience. And such an object, as Collingwood has demonstrated in *Speculum Mentis*, is no other than mind, conceived as the product of a dialectical history of errors.

Implied by Collingwood's ontological argument, then, is the principle of the identity of thought and being, which Hegel described as "the most interesting idea of modern times."[18] Like Descartes, Collingwood finds the basis of philosophy in the *cogito*. I think therefore I am, and in so far as what I think about is my own experience, what I think about must actually exist. It is not that mind (which for Collingwood is identified with its acts, i.e., with experience) is only one of a number of possible objects for philosophy; *mind is the only possible object*. Thus, Collingwood argues in *Speculum Mentis* that a philosophy of the forms of experience "is the only philosophy that can exist" (SM, 9). This leads to another sense in which philosophy may be said to be categorical: philosophy is categorical not only in the sense that what it thinks about is something existing; it is categorical in the sense that what it thinks about are categories. Philosophy is therefore *categorical thinking about categories*. Categories are modes of being, that is to say, forms of experience; they are not classes or collections of particulars. Thinking about categories is different from thinking about classes. We cannot think categorically about either or both; we can only think categorically about categories.

To exist, then, means to exist as mind (whether finite or infinite). But we must not treat mind as though it were a mere entity, the subject of a logically proper name. That *would* be systematically misleading. The *ens realissimum* of the ontological argument is really no other than the absolute mind of *Speculum Mentis*, which is not a substance, but pure act. Since the being of absolute mind is identical with the activity of absolute knowledge, absolute mind is the identity of subject and object; and this is the concrete universal which is also the genuine historical fact (SM, 299). It is the object of metaphysical thought, and also the object of philosophy in general. In so far as mind thinks of itself as nature (in Fichtean language we could say, in so far as mind 'posits' itself as nature) it forms the subject of 'philosophy of science'; in so far as mind thinks of itself as art, it forms the subject of philosophy of art; and so on. This is not to suggest that there are no such things-in-themselves as nature, art, and so on, or even that intelligible things cannot be said about them; the claim is only that in so far as these things are things-in-themselves, they are not the objects of philosophical thought. The objects of philosophical thinking are never nature, art, history, etc., conceived as things-in-themselves. On the contrary, the subject matter of philosophy consists of the concrete experiences of nature, art, history, etc. The structure of being, in other words, cannot be separated from the structure of consciousness. Hence it is not nature, art, and history per se, but the ideas of nature, art, and history, which philosophers both think about and, through thinking about them, actually bring into existence.

This claim can be put even more precisely. Let us think of experience, say the experience of nature, as being basically of a twofold character. On the one hand, there is the raw sensuous encounter in which mind and nature immediately confront one another. Implicit in this immediacy, of course, is the reflective moment which is the source of mediation and provides the basis for the perceptual act. The perception of nature, which corresponds roughly to ordinary experience, contains implicitly the starting points of a more reflective standpoint from which the experience of perception is organized. This is the standpoint of understanding or science. Science is a particular way of organizing the mind's reflection upon its own experience of nature. This rational activity of the understanding which attempts to bring order into perceptual experience is the actual datum of philosophy. Thus, to repeat, the object of philosophy is not nature per se but the *experience* of nature.

Likewise, philosophy in general is the science of experience; and metaphysics, conceived as a particular philosophical science (philosophy of art, philosophy of nature, and so on), would be the science of absolute mind experiencing itself as absolute mind. But since absolute mind is no more than the unity (one is tempted to call it a transcendental unity) of the activities of mind constituting or positing itself as art, religion, science, and history, the so-called metaphysical study of mind can only be the study of mind *qua* art, religion, science and history. Thus Collingwood can say – as he does – that metaphysics is "not a separate philosophical science" (EPM, 127) but is identical with the philosophies of the particular standpoints.

We have now reached the definition of metaphysics as the science of particular experience; but this is the definition of dogmatic philosophy which was given in *Speculum Mentis*. Metaphysics is therefore, as I have previously claimed, dogmatic philosophy. The object of dogmatic philosophy is to explain the basis upon which experience reflects upon itself. And this it does by disclosing the presuppositions upon which this experience is organized.

Suppose it is the experience of nature which mind *qua* scientist is reflecting upon; metaphysics is therefore reflection upon the scientist's activity with a view to disclosing the presuppositions upon which the scientist's thinking proceeds; it is the science of the presuppositions of scientific consciousness. And this means that, in so far as the scientist's picture of nature – let us call this 'cosmology' – is rooted in his own experience of nature, that is to say his mind, the presuppositions according to which this experience is organized are derived, not from the real structure of nature conceived as a thing-in-itself (this would be realist cosmology), but from the structure of mind. That is why the history of science is bound up with the history of the growth of consciousness itself, and why the history of science is contingent upon the development not of nature but of the 'idea' of nature.[19]

But since the presuppositions according to which the scientist organizes his experience are rooted in experience, the metaphysician who uncovers them does not ask whether they are true, that is, whether they correspond with the actual facts of nature. The only question which the metaphysician can ask is whether they correspond to the actual facts of experience, or, to be more precise, to what the scientist really believes.

And this is an historical question. Metaphysics, then, is not only philosophical but historical. It is not only categorical universal but categorical singular. This is no contradiction, for it simply confirms the principle of the unity of sciences implied by *Speculum Mentis*. In particular it is no more than an affirmation of the rapprochement between philosophy and history already contained in the main conclusions of *Speculum Mentis*.

5 CATEGORICAL THINKING AND THE RAPPROCHEMENT BETWEEN FAITH AND REASON

Reflection on the history of the ontological proof, writes Collingwood, offers us a view of philosophy as a form of thought in which essence and existence, however clearly distinguished, are conceived as inseparable (EPM, 127). We have so far examined this claim in terms of the principle of the unity of thought and action, or theory and experience. There is another aspect of the ontological argument, however, which ought to be examined, this time in connection with the principle that knowledge presupposes knowledge. I am referring to the implication that the philosophical understanding of the identity of essence and existence, which is the conclusion of the ontological argument, presupposes a prior knowledge of it, albeit at a different level. This implication is affirmed for Collingwood in the correspondence between Anselm and Gaunilo in which Anselm admits that the ontological proof of the existence of God proves the existence of God only to a person who already believes it. Concerning this aspect of the argument Collingwood writes:

Thus Anselm, searching for a proof of God's existence, hit upon the famous ontological proof; and the odd thing is that when a kindly critic pointed out that his proof was logically conclusive only to a person who already believed in God, Anselm was not in the least disconcerted. "I believe" to quote his own words, "in order that I may understand; for this I know that unless I first believe I shall never understand." (FR, 18; 213)

This aspect of the argument points up the rapprochement between faith and reason: unless we already believed on faith in the existence of God, we could never receive a rational account of it. This is really a variation of the principle, *Nihil est in intellectu quod non fuerit in sensu*. If, following Collingwood's instructions in the earlier *Hibbert Journal* article of 1927, we read for intellect, 'scientific thought,' and for sense, 'religious intuition,' "we may say with substantial truth that the intellect discovers nothing that faith has not already known" (FRCI, 14). Indeed, Collingwood declares, we may view the whole life of man as *fides quaerens intellectum*. But this principle is paradigmatic of all other rapprochements, including that between 'essence' and 'existence.' Let us therefore read for *sensus* 'experience' or 'existence,' and for *intellectus* 'essence,' or whatever is the object of philosophical thought (not any thought, just philosophic thought). *Then nothing can be an object of philosophy which does not exist in experience.* And this is a further variation of the principle that philosophy renders explicit what is already implicit in experience – reveals, if you like, the presuppositions of experience. So far as our behaviour is determined by implicit presuppositions, which are perhaps 'unconscious,' we may be said to act on 'faith' or according to 'belief.' And for this reason it is perhaps appropriate to describe metaphysics, which is the act of translating these beliefs into reason, as the science of beliefs – in which case we are, I suppose, simply repeating Bradley's famous definition of metaphysics, as the finding of bad reasons for what we already believe on instinct.[20]

6 CATEGORICAL THINKING AND THE UNDERSTANDING OF THE HISTORICAL PAST

Collingwood's interpretation of what it means to exist as an object of philosophy may be further explicated by the criteria which he himself developed in his paper, "Some Perplexities about Time."[21] A comparison of *An Essay on Philosophical Method* with this paper will suggest that there is an analogy between the definition of the object of philosophy about which we make categorical statements, and the construction of the historical past about which we also make categorical statements. The force of this analogy should be to reinforce the claim already made that existence, whatever it is, is neither the object of mere perception nor the object of hypothetical thought.

As we have noted, in "Some Perplexities about Time" Collingwood distinguished between "actual" and "ideal" beings. The ideal is the *ens rationis*, or *essentia formalis*; the non-existent object of hypothetical thought. Into this class fall the objects of mathematics as well as the past *qua* past and the future *qua* future. Such objects have being for thought alone. The real, however, is that which exists as the subject of actual experience. In so far as an object like the past is to acquire real existence it must become part of actual experience: but not in the sense of being a mere object of perception, for then it would lose its character as past and become a mere mode of present experience.

The past then, as a genuine object of thought, is neither purely 'real' or purely 'ideal' but a synthesis of both; it is an aspect of real experience whose being is for thought alone. Collingwood therefore describes the past as "transcendentally real" to distinguish it from the mere objects of perception, on the one hand, and the mere objects of hypothetical thought on the other. It is the transcendentally real which is the object of categorical thinking. The transcendentally real is an object which is called into being by thought questioning itself; it is the product of a process in which thought transforms the mere data of experience into a rational structure. Thus nature, as a thing-in-itself, a mere object of perception, has 'real' but not 'ideal' existence. The scientist's knowledge of nature, which is derived from his observation of nature, is hypothetical; it has 'ideal' but not real or actual existence. But when the activity of framing hypotheses together with the experience on the basis of which these hypotheses are framed is itself made into an object of knowledge, we have arrived at an object which is 'transcendentally real,' and this is the object of philosophy. Thus the object of philosophy, like the object of history, is the 'transcendentally real.'

7 CATEGORICAL THINKING AS THE ANALYSIS OF THE PRESUPPOSITIONS OF EXPERIENCE

The notion of categorical thinking as the philosophical-historical analysis of the presuppositions of experience may be finally summed up by turning once again to the relation between philosophy and natural science – a relation which is paradigmatic of the relation between philosophy and any other form of experience. The scientist, as we have seen, infers from his real experience of nature to its ideal existence. The philosopher contemplates this first-order experience. The conclusions of science per se are statements about ideally existing objects and are therefore hypothetical. They are not, except implicitly, statements about the scientist's actual experience. But they presuppose other statements which, unlike the ostensible conclusions of science, are unverifiable and indemonstrable. These latter statements are the ultimate principles according to which the scientist's experience of nature is organized. They are derived, not from the observation of nature – for except by means of them there can be no observation – but, on the contrary, from the nature of mind. So far as nature is concerned they are regulative, but for mind they are constitutive. They are therefore categorical, that is to say, derived from the categories which describe the actual structure of mind.

In this respect Collingwood is a Kantian and what he is doing is restating Kant's concept of science according to which the hypothetical conclusions of science, which are ostensibly about nature conceived as a thing-in-itself, are paradoxically derived from categorical principles which are rooted in the nature of the human mind. But, whereas Kant viewed the mind as though it possessed a permanent and unchanging nature, Collingwood, in the tradition of Hegel and Dilthey, views mind as an historical process, and the categories as products of that process. This is why science has a history which reflects, in its own development, the history and development of consciousness itself.

It is at this point that, for Collingwood, philosophy enters the picture, for it is philosophy, conceived as the reflective moment of scientific experience, which is largely responsible for developments within that experience. Since the mind gives itself an account of everything it does, as it does it, and since this account is inseparably bound up with the doing of the thing, it follows that every activity is also a theory of itself: but not necessarily a true theory. It is often the case that the theory of an activity is inconsistent with the basic presuppositions implied by the actual conduct of that activity. And often by revealing these presuppositions both the theory is corrected and the actual practice of the activity altered. Philosophy, then, in its attempt to reconcile theory and practice, substantially alters the direction of action, hence creating the need for new theories.

Thus Hume and Kant, by disclosing the actual presuppositions which were implicit in scientific experience, changed not only the theory of science but the actual practice of it. They did this, however, not in their capacity as scientists, but in their capacity as philosophers. It is the philosopher who reveals the basic presuppositions of experience, and who contributes in this way not only to the theory of science but to the theory of mind as well. The philosopher's object is not nature, but the scientist's experience of nature, or 'first-order' experience which is something real and actual, something existing. Its existence, however, is transcendentally real; it is more than what is immediately present as an object of perception. It is something which must be reconstructed by thought. The philosopher not only describes the structure of scientific experience by formulating claims about the transcendentally real – claims like, 'Experience presupposes in its attempt to deal with nature, that nature is always and uniformly the same' – but, like the moral philosopher in *An Essay on Philosophical Method,* he must ask whether the theory he arrives at actually tallies with scientific experience, that is to say, makes intelligible the scientific experience which we actually possess (EPM, 172).

The philosopher's judgments may therefore be legitimized, in the sense that they may be shown to be implicit in the very structure of experience itself. They may also be called historical because the methods by which they are arrived at and the methods by which they are verified are basically historical. The *analysis* of presuppositions, then, is clearly both historical and philosophical. But what about the presuppositions themselves? *Qua* presuppositions they are neither legitimate nor illegitimate, because they are not yet rational; they are mere facts of experience which are often unconscious. It is not until they have been transformed into 'reasoned facts' that they can be questioned. In so far as they are *de facto* only, they are matters of faith or belief. The moment they are articulated, however, by a process which takes the form of a metaphysical archeology, they become judgments, that is to say they become candidates for *de jure* validation. What they both have in common is the fact that they are categorical, and the difference between *de facto* categorical beliefs and *de jure* categorical propositions is simply the difference between the implicitness of experience and the explicitness of theory.

VIII

Philosophy as HISTORY

1 CATEGORICAL THINKING AND THE PROBLEM OF UNIVERSALS

The theory of philosophy as categorical thinking having as its object existence or mind and expressing itself in judgments which are both universal and individual was consistently maintained from *Speculum Mentis* to *An Essay on Philosophical Method*. In the *Autobiography* and *An Essay on Metaphysics*, however, written in 1938 and 1939 respectively, Collingwood announced a programme for the reform of metaphysics and philosophy. Metaphysics, he declared, is no futile attempt to discover what lies beyond the limits of experience – this might better be described as "paraphysics" (A, 66). The so-called science of being *qua* being is described as pseudo-metaphysics and dismissed as nonsense. If metaphysics is to be a science at all it must claim its proper status as a purely historical enquiry in which the beliefs of a given set of people at a given time concerning the world's general nature are exhibited as a single complex of contemporaneous fact. And in the *Autobiography* he asserts that there is no branch of philosophy to which these considerations do not apply.

These comments have been interpreted by the majority of Collingwood's critics as evidence of a fundamental change in outlook: in particular, as a change from an 'idealist' to an 'historicist' outlook. (See above ch. 1, s. 4) John Passmore, for example, writes that "In his *Autobiography* (1939), Collingwood made public his conversion to historicism."[1] For T. A. Knox, as we have already noted, the *Autobiography* and the *Essay on Metaphysics* are logical outcomes of Collingwood's acceptance of the Crocian doctrines that "history is the only kind of knowledge" and "philosophy as a separate discipline is liquidated by being converted into history" (IH, xii, x). The official date of Collingwood's conversion, according to Knox, occurred somewhere between 1936 and 1938 (IH, xi). Then, having declared his intentions in the *Autobiography*, Collingwood set out on a campaign to 'historicize' the whole of philosophy. But such a project, according to Knox, could have only one ending: philosophical scepticism, which, in one form or another, was the price he paid for the endeavour to compress philosophy into history (IH, xi).

We have also noted Donagan's claim that, beginning with the *Autobiography*, Collingwood "implicitly abandoned ... [the] conception of metaphysical propositions as categorical and universal and substituted for it the doctrine that they are historical, i.e., categorical and singular."[2] Donagan sums up Collingwood's new theory of metaphysics as follows:

Metaphysics ... is not an attempt to establish categorical universal propositions about Being itself, but categorical particular propositions about what this or that people at this or that time have believed. As such it is 'purely historical' (A, 166). Kant had asked, 'How can metaphysics become a science?' Collingwood's answer, which in the *Essay on Metaphysics* he audaciously claimed to be 'the reform of metaphysics, long looked for and urgently needed,' was: 'By becoming more completely and more consciously what in fact it had always been, an historical science.' (EM, 77)[3]

In the light of what has been said in previous chapters, it is clear that we must seriously question any interpretation of Collingwood which argues that the doctrines of the *Essay*[4] are incompatible with the doctrines of *Speculum Mentis* and *An Essay on Philosophical Method*. But if such interpretations are erroneous the fault does not lie entirely with Collingwood's critics; for Collingwood chose in the *Autobiography* and the *Essay* to express himself in a most peculiar way, with results which could only be misleading. It is my contention that the *Essay* betrays a fundamental inconsistency between the theory of presuppositions expounded and the theory implicit in the examples cited by Collingwood as evidence of the former; there is, in other words, a contradiction between what Collingwood *says* and what he *means*. And I will argue that the latter, which is suggested by the examples, is not only compatible with the early philosophy but is precisely the standpoint already implied by the doctrines of *Speculum Mentis*. Metaphysics, as implicitly defined in the *Essay* and the *Autobiography*, is none other than third-level dogmatic philosophy.

But to thus overcome the apparent discrepancy between the *Essay* and the earlier doctrines does not yet answer the questions which arise from the description (in the *Essay* and the *Autobiography*) of philosophy as purely historical. This, of course, is not a new problem; it has been with us from the very beginning: ever since *Religion and Philosophy* declared that history and philosophy were the same thing. The solution to this problem is implicit, however, in *Speculum Mentis* and *An Essay on Philosophical Method* where philosophy is defined as categorical thought about the concrete universal – mind. The essence of mind is 'historicity,' which in Collingwood's view is neither pure universality nor pure particularity, but the concrete synthesis of universal and particular. Within the terms of dialectical logic, philosophical statements about this object are therefore both universal (i.e., necessary) and singular (i.e., particular). (So far as I can tell, there is, for Collingwood, no important difference between singular and particular.) But all such judgments are made from one or another finite standpoint, and in so far as mind adopts a given standpoint it must make, or assume, such distinctions as are necessary to the integrity of that standpoint. Thus historical understanding, which is a necessary aspect of the structure of every and any experience, explicitly regards itself (when it is transformed into a separate standpoint) as expressible in a body of categorical singular judgments. As we have already noted, they are categorical because, in the first place, the subject of these judgments is something actual, and, in the second place, in thinking about it the historian is actually exemplifying that subject itself. They are singular because they are concerned with unique events. Implicitly, however, the judgments of history are universal, because those so-called unique events which constitute the subject matter of history are in reality expressions of the universal and necessary structure of mind. Indeed, it is only because the individual is the embodiment of the universal that it can be a genuine individual at all.

We have also noted that an absolute separation between universal and categorical singular judgments can obtain only in a logic which treats all *existing* things as individual members of a class, that is, as matters of fact, and all necessary things as hypothetical (i.e., with respect to the affirmation of existence). And I am contending that to argue, as Donagan and Knox have done, that in the *Autobiography* and the *Essay on Metaphysics* Collingwood has abandoned his definition of metaphysics as categorical universal for the contradictory view that it is categorical singular, is implicitly to claim that he now accepts the standpoint of logical nominalism and its metaphysical corollary which denies genuine existence to universals: a standpoint which he had hitherto dedicated his life to repudiating.

But in fact, Collingwood at no time repudiates his belief in the existence of universals, which in his 1935 correspondence with Ryle he cites as the main difference between himself and Ryle. In his first letter, for example, Collingwood writes:

> It seems probable to me that the fundamental point at issue between us is concerned with the way in which we answer the question "what is a universal?" (I use that word as possibly affording a neutral ground between our vocabularies). It looks to me as if, in your logic, this question was answered by saying "a universal is a class"; i.e., that whenever we make a statement (assent to a proposition) about "all x", we are really making n statements about the n instances of x which exist. The theory of universals is thus, so to speak, resolved into the theory of classes. It seems to me that this analysis applies not only, as at first sight one might suppose, to enumerative or "every" propositions about classes of "matters of fact", but also (following Russell) to "any" propositions concerned with "relations between ideas"; the general doctrine being that any account of a "universal" can be analyzed without residue into an account of a "class". This would represent a line of thought more or less identical with logical nominalism.
>
> In my own view, this line of thought is so far from satisfactory that it inverts the necessary order of analysis and is thus a case of *obscurum per obscurius*. I am disposed to think that what makes a number of things instances of a class is their common possession of some common nature, and that this common nature (the so-called "universal") is thus the *ratio essendi* of the class as such. Instead of resolving the theory of universals into the theory of classes, I should therefore be inclined to take the opposite line, of resolving the theory of classes into the theory of universals. This, of course, is akin to logical realism.
>
> This difference would tend to produce the result that, when *you* speak of some kind of thing as existing, you would analyze your statement into something like this: "the class of x's, viz. $x_1\ x_2\ x_3$ ... exist"; whereas I, using the same language, would have to analyze it somehow more like this: "the universal x-ness exists and is instanced in various x's, $x_1\ x_2\ x_3$ ... "
>
> And this would produce a further difference, that whereas for you it is meaningless to talk of x-ness as existing unless you are prepared to enumerate the x's that exist (for the latter is, according to you, I fancy, the only possible meaning of the former) for me it is possible to talk of x-ness as existing without claiming any ability to make that enumeration: the existence of x-ness being for me sufficiently guaranteed by the existence of even a single x irrespectively of what others exist.
>
> So the question which most fundamentally seems to divide us appears to me to be the question: Is a universal simply a class, or is it that which makes a class a class? – where you take the first alternative and I the second. (CRC, 1, 28–9)

When judged from the standpoint of his over-all philosophy the above passage opens itself to the following interpretation. In the case of nature, universals are abstract and purely ideal, and scientific statements which attempt to relate them are therefore hypothetical. In the case of mind, however, the universal is concrete, and philosophical or historical statements about it are therefore categorical.[5] The concrete universal is itself a synthesis of 'individual' concrete universals, each of which is in turn further differentiated, and so on. Any categorical singular statement which has for its object one or more of these differentiations implicitly presupposes statements whose object is the universal itself. When this implicit universality is rendered explicit we have transcended history for philosophy, and the latter may now be said to have superseded the former. According to the theory of determinate negation, this means, of course, that philosophy is history at a higher level. Philosophy is the science of mind *qua* mind. But if we mean by this, mind *qua* concrete mind, then the achievement of the philosophical standpoint is no more than the recognition that the philosopher, in order to be a philosopher, must become an historian and study mind in each of its particular modes; for mind is nothing but its acts. The essence of mind lies in its history. The history of mind is therefore a fundamental aspect of the philosophy of mind; but, except through the mediation of the latter, the former is not possible. Thus, Collingwood writes in *The Idea of History* (Epilegomena, s. 5):

> The vague phrase that history is knowledge of the individual claims for it a field at once too wide and too narrow: too wide, because the individuality of perceived objects and natural facts and immediate experiences falls outside its sphere, and most of all because even the individuality of historical events and personages, if that means their uniqueness, falls equally outside it; too narrow, because it would exclude universality, and it is just the universality of an event or character that makes it a proper and possible object of historical study, if by universality we mean something that oversteps the limits of merely local and temporal existence and possesses a significance valid for all men at all times. These too are no doubt vague phrases; but they are attempts to describe something real: namely the way in which thought, transcending its own immediacy, survives and revives in other contexts; and to express the truth that individual acts and persons appear in history not in virtue of their individuality as such, but because that individuality is the vehicle of a thought which, because it was actually theirs, is potentially everyone's. (IH, 303)

It would appear, on the basis of these remarks, that the difference between the categorical singular and the categorical universal is the difference between two aspects of the same concrete process; the relation between them is dialectical, corresponding to the dialectical relation between history and philosophy itself. To specify an act of thought as categorical singular is not, therefore – if the object of this thought is the concrete universal – to deny its status as universal. Indeed, it is only by implicitly assuming the latter that the former can be asserted at all.

Philosophy, we have seen, must necessarily become historical, in order to fulfill itself as philosophy. The object of history is thought. The philosopher, however, is interested in a special kind of thought. The historian thinks about Napoleon's thought, the philosopher about the historian's thought about Napoleon's thought. He can also turn around and reflect on his own experience, thus giving rise to the philosophy of philosophy. The important thing, however, is to recognize that even the philosophy of history and the philosophy of philosophy are historical. This does not mean that philosophy as a separate discipline has been liquidated by history. It means only that there is a very special duality in all thought between the philosophical and the historical moments which constitute it. And the identity of philosophy with history must always preserve the differences between these inseparable but distinct moments.

Of special interest to the philosopher who has become the historian of a given mode of thought are the presuppositions and criteria according to which that form of thought proceeds. Among these presuppositions we may distinguish roughly two kinds. First there are those which can be verified and which constitute the body of that science proper, such as 'force equals mass times acceleration,' 'smoking is the cause of cancer,' 'variations in nature are due to natural selection,' 'power corrupts,' and so on. Secondly, there are those which are not themselves part of the body of that science, that is, which are not products of scientific reasoning and which cannot therefore be proven within the body of that science. These are the *conditiones sine quae non* of the science in question. The metaphysician is particularly concerned with the latter, which include such assumptions as 'God exists,' 'every event has a cause,' 'nature is uniformly and everywhere the same,' and so on. The metaphysician's task as an historian is to demonstrate simply that these presuppositions were in fact held. The results of such demonstrations take the form of categorical singular propositions. But the metaphysician is also a philosopher, and implicit in the categorical singular judgment is the categorical universal judgment about mind *qua* mind.

2 THE LOGIC OF BELIEF

What precisely is the difference between these two judgments? To answer this question for Collingwood, we must make a distinction between *asserting a fact about another's belief* and *asserting a fact about my own belief*: between asserting, for example, that 'Hegel presupposed that where there are no strains there is no history' (in which case I am the historian of Hegel's thought, but am not committed to accepting it myself) and asserting my consciousness of the fact that the principle of dialectical strains is a presupposition of my own experience. There is likewise a difference between being conscious of the fact that according to Kant man is a rational being, and recognizing that rationality is a necessary condition of my own experience and hence of experience in general. The second kind of statement has existential implications not shared by the first. And the clue to this difference, according to my interpretation of Collingwood, is provided by Collingwood's account of the ontological argument. For just as a person who recognizes that, in the case of one special kind of being, essence involves existence (with the consequence that he is necessarily committed to believing in the existence of this being) so the historian of his own thought is necessarily committed to believing in his own presuppositions (SM, 307), even though their conscious acceptance may well be the beginning of a process which results in their being overthrown. What is believed, moreover, is not just that these beliefs are presupposed but that they are universal and necessary conditions of experience in general. This means that the categorical singular judgment contains implicitly a categorical universal judgment to which I am necessarily committed.

This may give the impression that truth is something 'eternal' and 'permanent.' But in fact the existential implications of such truths change from generation to generation. It is only, for example, by becoming the historian of Hegel's thought that I come to realize that his belief in the rationality of history is also my belief. In becoming 'my' belief its content has, of course, acquired meanings not recognized by Hegel: my experience of the rationality of history is the same as Hegel's — yet different. But unless I first know Hegel, I cannot know myself. History is a necessary condition of self-knowledge. And since philosophy is the highest realization of self-knowledge, philosophy may therefore be said to be grounded in history. Thus, to repeat the point already stressed, the philosopher cannot escape the necessity of becoming an historian.

Failure to accept these conditions is an expression of the corrupt consciousness and leads, as Collingwood points out in the *Essay on Metaphysics*, to the deterioration of culture. Thus Collingwood charges that what destroyed the 'pagan' world was not barbarian attacks but "... its own failure to keep alive its own fundamental convictions" (EM, 225). The corrupt consciousness is also displayed in cases where, having failed to express the presuppositions which are actually alive in my experience, I deceive myself into thinking that I have done so, and falsely declare allegiance to principles which are not in fact genuine. Collingwood describes this as a form of "irrationalism"[6] and he cites as a prime example the anti-metaphysical tendencies of modern European civilization as exemplified by positivism and psychology.[7]

The nature of this corruption, which derives from an untruthful consciousness is further discussed in *The Principles of Art* where it is shown to be the source not only of bad metaphysics but of bad art as well (PA, xii, s. 3, 280–5):

> Art is not a luxury, and bad art not a thing we can afford to tolerate. To know ourselves is the foundation of all life that develops beyond the merely psychical level of experience. Unless consciousness does its work successfully, the facts which it offers to intellect, the only things upon which intellect can build its fabric of thought, are false from the beginning. A truthful consciousness gives intellect a firm foundation upon which to build; a corrupt consciousness forces intellect to build on a quicksand. The falsehoods which an untruthful consciousness imposes on the intellect are falsehoods which intellect can never correct for itself. In so far as consciousness is corrupted, the very wells of truth are poisoned. Intellect can build nothing firm. Moral ideals are castles in the air. Political and economic systems are mere cobwebs. Even common sanity and bodily health are no longer secure. (PA, 284–5)

In effect, then, philosophy leads a double life. On the one hand it is the historical reconstruction of past thought. On the other hand, it is the 'transhistorical understanding' of the universal principles of thought which are implicit in the historical reconstruction of the philosopher's own experience. *An Essay on Philosophical Method* is an attempt to record the latter experience, while *An Essay on Metaphysics* is an attempt to give systematic expression to the theory which is implicit in the former. As such, *An Essay on Metaphysics* may be regarded as an application of the theory of philosophy expounded in *An Essay on Philosophical Method*.

Metaphysics, as described both in *Speculum Mentis* and *An Essay on Metaphysics*, is guided by the a priori criterion of consistency. It is a peculiar kind of a priori, however, for, as we shall see, it is something which is itself subject to historical development: and, what is more, the philosopher becomes aware of it only in the course of his own activity as an historian. There are really two kinds of metaphysics, corresponding to the basic duality within philosophy itself, the difference between them being the difference between two types of consciousness. The first is primarily historical, having as its object past thought (whether that thought is first- or second-order is not important). The second is primarily systematic, having as its object the metaphysician's experience of himself. In practice, these activities are simultaneous and the distinction between them is logical, not temporal. The latter is the source, not only of one's own beliefs about the world's general nature, but also of the principles and presuppositions according to which the metaphysical analysis of both past and present beliefs is accomplished.

In *Speculum Mentis* Collingwood warns against treating the forms as co-ordinate species of a genus. Yet the description of philosophy as categorical universal and of history as categorical singular seems to do just that, for it implies that any proposition which is categorical must be one or the other, and that no proposition can be both at once. If this were Collingwood's view then he would himself be guilty of the very fallacy of false disjunction which he so skilfully exposed in the thinking of other philosophers.

But this is not Collingwood's view. The distinction is only tentative, like the distinction between philosophy and science discussed earlier (see above, ch. VII, s. 1). Being categorical singular is not necessarily exclusive of being categorical universal and vice versa; they are rather *coincidentia oppositorum*. A statement such as 'God exists' is therefore both at once. It is historical in the sense that it can be established that 'somebody believes it.' It is philosophical in the sense that the thought expressed by it is experienced, by someone who is self-conscious, as an intrinsic part of experience itself. The genuine historian (i.e., the historian whose activity is located somewhere near the top of the scale) is someone who not only establishes the fact that 'Aristotle presupposed that God did not create nature' (which is part of what Aristotle means by 'God exists'), but who criticizes this claim (as did the Patristic philosophers) in terms of his own experience, by demonstrating that Aristotle's presupposition is inconsistent with the presupposition of experience as lived through by the critic. In this way one set of presuppositions is replaced by another. But since the critic's experience is the dialectical product of Aristotle's experience there is a genuine continuity of overlap between the former and the latter, between the idea of God as unmoved mover and the idea of God as creator. I shall attempt in the remainder of this chapter to re-examine the *Essay* as well as parts of the *Idea of History* in the light of these considerations.

3 THE THEORY OF METAPHYSICS AS A SCIENCE OF PRESUPPOSITIONS

At the outset of the *Essay on Metaphysics* Collingwood distinguishes between metaphysics proper and ontology. The latter, which, according to Collingwood, is a mistake people have made about metaphysics, is derived from Aristotle's discussion of the science of being *qua* being. Thus conceived, metaphysics, or ontology, is a contradiction in terms. Collingwood's critique of the science of pure abstract being is essentially a criticism of the application of the abstract logic of classification and division to the whole of reality. It is basically the same argument with which he has all along criticized the theory of the abstract universal. To begin with, says Collingwood, the science of pure being would have a subject matter entirely devoid of peculiarities, a subject matter containing nothing to differentiate it from anything else, or from nothing at all:

> The universal of pure being represents the limiting case of the abstractive process. Now even if all science is abstractive, it does not follow that science will still be possible when abstraction has been pushed home to the limiting case. Abstraction means taking out. But science investigates not what is taken out but what is left in. To push abstraction to the limiting case is to take out everything; and when everything is taken out there is nothing for science to investigate. You may call this nothing by whatever name you like – pure being, or God, or anything else – but it remains nothing and contains no peculiarities for science to examine. (EM, 14)[8]

Thus Collingwood concludes that since the science of pure being has a subject matter which is not a something, but a nothing, a subject matter which has no special peculiarities and therefore gives rise to no special problems and no special methods, there can be no such science (EM, 15).

There is another definition of metaphysics which also originates with Aristotle. This is the definition of metaphysics as the science "which deals with the presuppositions underlying ordinary science" (EM, 11), where by science is meant "a body of systematic or orderly thinking about a determinate subject matter" (EM, 4). And Collingwood makes it quite clear that science, so defined, extends not only to natural science but to any organized body of knowledge. Indeed, he argues, the identity of science with natural science is a "slang sense of the word ... parallel to the slang use of the word 'hall' for a music hall or the word 'drink' for alcoholic drink" (EM, 4).

Thus conceived, metaphysics is essentially an historical science which seeks to establish what the people of any given time believed about the world's general nature (A, 66):

> All metaphysical questions are historical questions, and all metaphysical propositions are historical propositions. Every metaphysical question either is simply the question what absolute presuppositions were made on a certain occasion, or is capable of being resolved into a number of such questions together with a further question or further questions arising out of these (EM, 49) ... it will consider (for

example) whether absolute presuppositions are made singly or in groups, and if the latter, how the groups are organized; whether different absolute presuppositions are made by different individuals or races or nations or classes; or on occasions when different things are being thought about; or whether the same have been made *semper ubique ab omnibus*. And so on. (EM, 47)

In the *Autobiography*, written in 1938, a parallel account of metaphysical analysis is given. As we have already noted above, Collingwood claims in the *Autobiography* that the doctrine of metaphysics (which is treated there as a part of the more general "logic of question and answer") was originally conceived during the first world war and first written out in the unpublished and subsequently destroyed "Truth and Contradiction." At no time in the *Autobiography* does Collingwood suggest that he had abandoned the doctrine of "Truth and Contradiction" when he published *Speculum Mentis* in 1924, only to return to it again in 1938 and 1939. Yet, as I have already pointed out in chapter 1, this is what would follow if we accept both Collingwood's claim that the doctrine of 1938–39 was first expounded in 1917 and the Knox-Donagan interpretation that between 1924 and 1936 Collingwood held an entirely different doctrine.[9] That Collingwood could have held such a doctrine as early as 1917 is evidenced, as Donagan himself admits, by Collingwood's address at the Ruskin Centenary Conference in August of 1919. But, while recognizing the resemblance between the views of the essay on Ruskin and the doctrines of the *Essay on Metaphysics*, Donagan persists in his claim that the latter constitutes a radical break with the views of *Speculum Mentis* and *An Essay on Philosophical Method*. He therefore declares that between 1924 and 1936 Collingwood experimented with a different doctrine. But a close reading of the essay on Ruskin will, I believe, raise Donagan's conclusions into question.

"Ruskin's Philosophy" begins with a brief but carefully worded description of the presuppositions according to which Collingwood's examination of Ruskin is to be conducted. The mood of this section of the essay, like the mood of the *Autobiography*, is characterized by such confidence, precision, and clarity that the reader is immediately of the impression that it contains the mature views of a man who knows exactly what he is doing and what he wants to say. Taken together, these presuppositions bear a striking resemblance not only to the theory of metaphysics expounded in 1938–39 but also to the theory of dogmatic philosophy expounded in *Speculum Mentis*: a fact which further vindicates the claim that, contrary to the Knox-Donagan thesis, Collingwood's thought underwent a continuous development from 1916 to 1938.

The first and most fundamental presupposition according to which a philosopher may analyse the thought of another, writes Collingwood, is the recognition of the fact

> ... that there are certain central principles which a man takes as fundamental and incontrovertible, which he assumes as true in all his thinking and acting. These principles form, as it were, the nucleus of his whole mental life: they are the centre from which all his activities radiate. You may think of them as a kind of ring of solid thought – something infinitely tough and hard and resistant – to which everything the man does is attached. (RUP, 6)

In this notion of a "ring" of "principles" we have a clear reference to what Collingwood will later call a "constellation" of "absolute presuppositions." In the essay on Ruskin Collingwood further characterizes these principles as "convictions," a convention which tends to confirm my own characterization of them as 'existential commitments.' A ring of convictions, Collingwood continues, may be "hard and tough and resistant," "of exceedingly solid texture, capable of supporting great strains without damage" (RUP, 24), and "welded together by some force of mutual cohesion" (RUP, 6). Such language immediately suggests the doctrine of "consupponibility" which lies at the core of the *Essay on Metaphysics* (EM, 66, 331). On the other hand, the ring may be weak and unable to stand up to the heavy strain of criticism (RUP, 7). As in his later thought, so in 1919 Collingwood regarded a man's philosophy as a function of his character. He therefore declares that a man "... is a great man or a little, a valuable man or a worthless, largely according as this ring is strong or weak in structure, good or bad in material" (RUP, 7). And since all of the acts and decisions which shape a man's life are suspended from this ring (one thinks immediately of Aristotle's notion of *hexis*) we may, according to Collingwood, regard a man whose ring is weak as having an unworthy character, while a man whose ring is composed of "unsound" and "untrue" principles may be regarded as "bad" and "foolish." And while Collingwood does not expressly say so, it is implied by what he does say that, just as the character of an individual is bound up with the quality of his beliefs, so the character of an entire age is similarly to be regarded. This view clearly anticipates the attitude towards the dangers of first-level dogmatism in *Speculum Mentis*, the theory of the corrupt consciousness in the *Principles of Art*, and the critique of irrationalism in the *Essay*.

From this discussion of the existential role which a man's basic beliefs play in his thought and conduct Collingwood turns his attention to a more technical discussion of epistemological and methodological considerations. Of crucial importance here is the fact that we are often totally unaware of both the nature and existence of our ring of basic convictions; in the language of *Speculum Mentis* and the *Essay* they are "unconscious":

> The fact seems to be that a man's deepest convictions are precisely those which he never puts into words. Everything which he says and does is based upon his grasp of these convictions; but just because his grasp of them is so complete, so unquestioning, he never finds it necessary to express them at all. (RUP, 7)

Not only do our deepest convictions often go unexpressed, but when asked to state them, we are often mistaken as to what they are. For this reason Collingwood regards the attempt to discover what these convictions are as a fundamental form of self-knowledge essential to the healthy maintenance of life. This task Collingwood assigns to the philosopher:

> Now it is this attempt to discover what people's philosophy is that marks the philosopher. Much as everybody has a brain, but only the anatomist sets himself to discover what it looks like and how it works, so everybody has a philosophy, but only the philosopher makes it his business to probe into the mind and lay bare that recess in which the ultimate beliefs lie hidden. (RUP, 8)

The remaining sections of the essay (ss. 4 to 9) are ostensibly an application of this 'philosophical anatomy' to the analysis of Ruskin's unconscious philosophy. But the essay is as much a vehicle for the expression of Collingwood's thought as it is a critique of Ruskin. Not only is the essay an occasion for Collingwood to bring his own presuppositions to the surface; but the entire essay may be viewed as an application and re-statement of the theory of philosophy which Collingwood claims to have worked out in "Truth and Contradiction" a few years earlier.

The most outstanding feature of the philosophical process of revealing presuppositions is, according to Collingwood, its "historical" character. Collingwood characterizes the historicity of philosophy by means of a contrast between what he calls "logicism" and "historicism": a contrast which parallels the *Autobiography* account of the distinction between "realism" and "the logic of question and answer."

> The logical method of thinking proceeds on the assumption that every individual is an instance of some eternal and unchanging principle ... (RUP, 9) Where the logical mind looks for general laws, the historical mind looks for individual facts, and it explains these facts by appealing not to laws but to other facts. (RUP, 11)

Presupposed here is the distinction drawn in *Speculum Mentis* between the logic of the abstract universal and the logic of the concrete universal. In *Ruskin's Philosophy* logicism and historicism are each described as "habits of mind." From these habits are derived the specialized pursuits of science and history, which when properly pursued must be regarded as necessary and valid forms of human activity. But, as in *Speculum Mentis*, Collingwood warns against the elevation of a habit of mind to the rank of a general dogma concerning the whole of reality: "... the habit of mind which I call logicism consists in the application of this ideal [the logic of the abstract universal] to all forms of mental activity" (RUP, 13). In short, the "logicism" described in *Ruskin's Philosophy* is nothing less than a species of first-level dogmatism.

In section 5 of *Ruskin's Philosophy* Collingwood further characterizes the difference between logicism and historicism according to the criterion of their respective attitudes towards the notion of contradiction: a discussion which is particularly suggestive of the possible contents of "Truth and Contradiction." The logic of "logicism" is the abstract logic of classification and division, or the logic of genus and species. The new logic of "historicism," however (which Collingwood attributes mainly to the efforts of Hegel and nineteenth-century historical idealism [RUP, 21, 29]), is undoubtedly the basis of what Collingwood himself later describes as the dialectical logic of the overlap of classes (*An Essay on Philosophical Method*) and the logic of question and answer (*The Autobiography*). *Ruskin's Philosophy*, then, provides clear and unequivocal evidence that what in the *Autobiography* is called the logic of question and answer is in fact a development of the dialectical logic of Hegel: an admission which lends much support to my own claim that the logic of question and answer is a part of the wider dialectical logic of the scale of forms and the overlap of classes, sometimes referred to as the logic of the concrete universal.

The old logic, according to Collingwood, lays it down that of two contradictory propositions one must be false and the other true. To contradict yourself, on this view, is a sign of mental confusion. According to the new view, however, it is recognized that there are two sides to every question, and that there is right on both sides:

> ... from this, the inference is drawn that truth is many sided and that self-contradiction may easily be a mark not of weakness but of strength – not of confusion, but of a wide and comprehensive view which embraces much more truth than the one-sided consistency of the logicians. (RUP, 21)

This theory of truth, according to which truth is reached only through contradiction (or determinate negation), presupposes the logic of question and answer as expounded in the *Autobiography* as well as in *Speculum Mentis*. It is virtually the same position which is defended both in *An Essay on Philosophical Method* and the 1935 correspondence with Gilbert Ryle in which Collingwood argues that philosophical arguments must sometimes proceed by means of systematic fallacies (see below, ch. VIII, ss. 7 and 8). And I have already contended that all of these doctrines follow directly from the idealist doctrine of the concrete universal.

Consupponible with the presuppositions of the new logic, as expounded in sections 3 and 4 of *Ruskin's Philosophy*, are a further set of presuppositions concerning the theory of mind in terms of which the new logic is to be understood. This theory of mind bears a strong resemblance to the central doctrines of *Speculum Mentis*. In section 5 Collingwood describes it, in typically Crocian and Gentilian terms, as the principle of "the unity and indivisibility of the spirit" (RUP, 17), the principle, namely, that

... each form of human activity springs not from a special faculty – an organ of the mind, so to speak – but from the whole nature of the person concerned: So that art is not the product of a special part of the mind called the "aesthetic faculty", nor morality the product of a special "moral faculty", but each alike is an expression of the whole self. (RUP, 16–17)

This principle, which Collingwood ascribes to Ruskin, is represented as a consequence of any historically oriented philosophy (RUP, 17). Collingwood's argument is to the effect that while the logical habit of mind finds ultimate reality in abstract principles externally related one to another as the species of a genus, the historical mind regards each particular as sharing in the same concrete universal. The development of this universal is, of course, a dialectical succession of internally related actions. Thus in one passage, part of which is repeated almost verbatim in *Speculum Mentis* (page 289), Collingwood distinguishes the logicist from the historicist view of history as follows:

In the hands of a logically minded person, history becomes a mere succession of events, fact following fact with little or no internal cohesion. To a historically minded person, on the contrary, history is a drama, the unfolding of a plot in which each situation leads necessarily to the next. (RUP, 18)

From these presuppositions Collingwood draws certain conclusions concerning the nature of philosophical method and the goal which its application to particular problems seeks to achieve. In the first place, the new concept of philosophy is described as "... a conviction which necessarily issues in a synthetic habit of mind – a habit, I mean, of laying stress on the resemblances and connections between problems, instead of regarding every problem as intrinsically different from every other" (RUP, 31). Or, to use the language of the *Essay on Philosophical Method*, the new concept of philosophy regards all philosophical problems as existing on a scale of overlapping forms. In *Ruskin's Philosophy* Collingwood further characterizes this method in terms of what he calls the technique of "analogy" (RUP, 31), a technique which is regarded as the only appropriate one for studying the relations between the various activities of mind: "This analogical method of reasoning ... is a weapon of immense power, clearing the ground of unnecessary argument and accomplishing a vast amount of varied work with the least possible waste of energy ..." (RUP, 33).

Collingwood contrasts the method of analogy with two others, both of which he rejects: the belief on the one hand that the activities of mind are univocal – in which case you believe that there is no such thing as a distinction between faculties – and the contrary belief that the activities of mind are really a set of equivocals which proceed therefore from different "faculties" (RUP, 31). This tripartite division of method bears a close resemblance to the three ways of awarding the prize in *Speculum Mentis* (SM, 42–50), and further supports the thesis put forward in chapter III (s. 3) above concerning the three levels of philosophical analysis which underlies Collingwood's thought. The analogical method of reasoning referred to in *Ruskin's Philosophy* is a species of what I have been describing as third-level dogmatic philosophy: which means, of course, that it is an earlier version of the logic of the overlap of classes expounded in *An Essay on Philosophical Method*. I would further argue that it is precisely this analogical method which underlies Collingwood's attempt throughout the rest of his writings to establish a new basis for the unity of knowledge. Accordingly, in *Speculum Mentis* and other writings, he explicates the insights which in 1919 he credits to Ruskin, namely, that art (and the same can be said of morality, etc.) is not a thing in itself, which can thrive in a vacuum, cut off from the general interests of humanity: "The soil in which art grows is not art but life. Art is expression, and it cannot arise until men have something to express" (RUP, 34). Compare this criticism of the theory of art for art's sake with similar arguments in both *Speculum Mentis* and the *Principles*. Since all forms of experience, such as art and morality, are regarded as deriving not from separate faculties but from the nature of the whole man, it therefore follows that: "... if the self which you reveal in morality is bad how can the same self, when you reveal it in terms of art, be good?" (RUP, 35) And again:

> ... the art of a healthy nation is a direct expression of its spontaneous interest in life, while the art of an enfeebled and corrupt nation forgets its relation to reality and loses itself in technicalities and aestheticisms, in abstract canons and formal restrictions. (RUP, 36)

It is clear, then, that, so far as the rapprochement between theory and practice is concerned, there is a striking resemblance between the views of *Ruskin's Philosophy* and Collingwood's later analysis of the corrupt consciousness in the *Principles of Art* (PA, 284–5).

A second consequence of the historicist concept of philosophy is its implied theory of truth and judgment: a theory which Collingwood characterizes in 1919 as the principle of "tolerance": "the ability to live one's own life and yet to admire and love people who live by the systems which one rejects" (RUP, 20). Tolerance, says Collingwood, is the surest mark of the historical as opposed to the logical mind. The tolerant historian achieves, by "imaginative appreciation" of the past, admiration but not idolatrous worship, love of the past without the wish to destroy the present. Collingwood regards this attitude as depending on the principle "that every historical phase has its own individual character, ideals and virtues, and that every phase alike should be an object of admiration rather than of imitation" (RUP, 20–1). These conclusions should be compared with Collingwood's later views in the *Essay on Metaphysics*, the *Idea of History*, and the various papers on progress, in which he similarly argues for a new theory of truth which, rather than classifying and dividing all events into the mutually exclusive classes of right and wrong, good and bad, places them on a dialectically developing scale which is at once a series of errors as well as a series of "right" solutions (to specific problems). What distinguishes Collingwood's more mature thought is the growing recognition, referred to earlier (ch. v, s. 1), of a distinction between a "pathology of normalcy" (the basis of therapeutic dogmatism) and a "pathology of abnormalcy" (i.e., the pathology of the corrupt consciousness). This distinction respects (regarding the developing scale of healthy dogmatisms) the kind of "tolerance" advocated in 1919, and still valued in 1938–39, while encouraging from yet another standpoint (regarding the developing scale of abnormal or corrupt consciousness) the positive denunciation of those irrational and corrupt forms of dogmatism represented by Facism, Nazism, and Positivism.

It would seem, then, that *Ruskin's Philosophy* is in many ways a prolegomenon to Collingwood's own philosophical development. Indeed, his final tribute to Ruskin's philosophical position stands as an equally fitting description of the character of his own philosophy: a tribute which one can imagine being offered many years later by one of Collingwood's admirers:

It is the character of that philosophy that I wish to make clear to you: its historical and dialectical, as opposed to a mathematical and logical, character; its scorn of scholastic distinctions; its breadth and imaginativeness; above all, its intensely synthetic nature – its refusal to separate any one aspect of life from any other, and its resolute envisagement of the spirit as a single and indivisible whole. (RUP, 43)

A further resemblance between the two men is suggested by Collingwood's description of Ruskin's position in nineteenth-century England: a description which parallels in many of its details the account which Collingwood gives in the *Autobiography* of his own position at Oxford during the first part of the twentieth century. It is almost as though Collingwood's generation was a repetition of the cycle of events which characterized the age of Ruskin. As represented by Collingwood, Ruskin's contemporaries, like the "minute philosophers" of Collingwood's own day, were preoccupied with the logic of the eighteenth century: a logic which is characterized as "abstract," "formalistic," and "unhistorical." Ruskin, like the young Collingwood of the *Autobiography*, was apparently proceeding on the basis of a philosophy totally different from that of his contemporaries. Like Collingwood, Ruskin also derived inspiration from the philosophy of nineteenth-century "historical idealism." "Little wonder," writes Collingwood, "that Ruskin was no friend to philosophers, when he compared their philosophy with the philosophy of his own inmost consciousness" (RUP, 29). Collingwood's description of Ruskin's intellectual loneliness arises from a deep sympathy of understanding, an understanding which derived, no doubt, from his own experience at Oxford: "He was at cross-purposes with his age: all the fundamental assumptions which underlay his thought contradicted those which underlay his contemporaries'" (RUP, 29). In such a situation, Collingwood declares, there is no point in simply arguing with people, for you have no common ground on which to argue. "The only cure," he writes, "is to turn philosopher and drag your convictions and theirs into the daylight" (RUP, 30): which is precisely what Collingwood himself does, especially (as we shall see) in the *Essay on Metaphysics*.

"Ruskin's Philosophy" must therefore be regarded as representing an important stage in the development of Collingwood's thought. Not only does it appear to support Collingwood's own claim in the *Autobiography* to have arrived at the theory of presuppositions and the logic of question and answer early in his philosophical career but it is also probably the closest record we have of the actual views of "Truth and Contradiction." If this is so then my earlier contention that "Truth and Contradiction" may be regarded as an early statement of the doctrines of the *Essay on Metaphysics* is given further support. At the same time, as I have tried to show, just as the *Essay* may be regarded as fulfilling the requirements of *Speculum Mentis*, so the latter may be regarded as a systematic exposition of some of the main points of the essay on Ruskin. It therefore follows that, contrary to Donagan's interpretation, far from experimenting with a different doctrine, Collingwood's activity from 1924 to 1936, as he himself declared in the *Autobiography*, consisted primarily in applying the new "historicist logic" to the solution of various philosophical problems; thus the actual theory of metaphysics expounded in the *Essay* may be regarded as the formal exposition of a doctrine which had been consistently applied since 1924. "I did not really feel," wrote Collingwood concerning the youthful period of *Truth and Contradiction*, "any great desire to expound the philosophical ideas I have been setting forth in these chapters [he is referring of course to the doctrine of presuppositions] whether to my colleagues or to the public." Instead, he continues, "... I felt justified in turning to the more congenial task of applying them and thus testing them empirically" (A, 74). *Speculum Mentis* may therefore be regarded as an attempt to expound the presuppositions of consciousness in so far as the latter exists at the first ontological level. The *Idea of Nature*, the *Idea of History*, and the *Principles of Art* are attempts to expound the presuppositions of particular forms of experience, each of which has its own history and exists, as I have argued, on three distinct but related ontological levels. In practice, of course, Collingwood does more than merely describe these presuppositions; he criticizes them as well, by explaining how they arose in the first place, and in so doing 'vindicates' them from the absolute standpoint, which is precisely what the metaphysician of the *Essay on Metaphysics* is required to do. The metaphysician's business, he writes, is not only to identify several different constellations of presuppositions but also to find out on what occasions and by what historical processes one set has turned into another (EM, 73; A, 66). Presupposed by these claims are a special set of presuppositions which the metaphysician discovers when he reflects on his own experience as metaphysician – which is precisely what Collingwood himself is doing in the main body of *An Essay on Metaphysics*, the *Principles of Art*, and the 'Epilegomena' of the *Idea of History*.

To this extent, then, there is nothing in Collingwood's proposals of 1938–39 which had not already been both expounded and applied. If he had left the matter there and had gone on merely to expound systematically the theory which was already implicit in his earlier works, no serious breach of the unity of his thought would have been suspected. But in fact he did not leave the matter there, for when he went on to explain the nature of the presuppositions which it is the business of the metaphysician to disclose and expound, elements appeared in his thinking which could not be so easily traced to the doctrines of *Speculum Mentis* and *An Essay on Philosophical Method*. In particular, these 'foreign' elements derive from his description of the object of metaphysics not simply as presuppositions but as 'absolute' presuppositions.

4 METAPHYSICS AS THE SCIENCE OF ABSOLUTE PRESUPPOSITIONS

The theory of absolute presuppositions which is expounded in *An Essay on Metaphysics* begins with the proposition that every statement, whether affirmative or negative, is an answer to a question which is logically prior to that statement (prop. 1, EM, 23). Such a statement is either true or false and may be called a *proposition* while the stating of it may be called *propounding* it (def. 1, EM, 25).

In so far as the statement is an answer to a question it may be said to "arise" from that question. At the same time the question itself "arises" from an immediate "presupposition" which is "logically prior" to it. And since this immediate presupposition rests on other presuppositions, the original question indirectly presupposes these as well.

To say that a question "arises" immediately from a presupposition is to say that unless a certain presupposition were made, the question to which it is logically prior could not be logically asked. Collingwood cites the example of the famous question, Have you stopped beating your wife? which presupposes that the person to whom the question is addressed has been in the habit of doing this. If he is not supposed to have been in that habit, the question whether this practice will be dispensed with "does not arise." To say that a question "does not arise" is the ordinary English way of saying that it involves a presupposition which is not in fact being made (def. 2, EM, 26).

That which causes a given question to arise is the "logical efficacy" of its implied presupposition. This presupposition may take the form *either* of an affirmative statement (i.e., a proposition) *or* of a supposition (i.e., an assumption) (def. 3, EM, 27). For example, says Collingwood, suppose I am trying to decipher a worn and damaged inscription, using as evidence certain marks. Before answering the question, What does this particular mark mean? I must first assure myself that the mark in question is not an accidental but an essential part of the inscription. This may be done *either* by asserting as a proposition 'That mark means something' *or* by assuming (i.e., supposing) that it means something. Since (a) the logical efficacy of the supposition does not depend upon its truth (prop. 3, EM, 28) and (b) the logical efficacy of the *supposition* that the mark means something is identical with the logical efficacy of the *proposition* that it means something, then (c) the validity of the question-and-answer complex which we call the argument is in no way affected by the truth or falsity of the supposition.

All presuppositions are either relative or absolute (prop. 4, EM, 29). A relative presupposition is one which stands in relation to one question as its presupposition and in relation to another question as its answer (def. 5, EM, 29). For example, suppose I am engaged in a piece of surveying, in the course of which I ask myself questions like, "What is the distance between these two points?" (EM, 29) Each time I ask this question I presuppose that the answer as given by a reading on my measuring tape will be the right answer; I presuppose, in other words, that my tape is within a certain percentage of the length which it professes to be. But this is only a relative presupposition, for although a tape by a reputable maker is not likely to have been made grossly inaccurate in the first instance, it is quite likely to have stretched during its years of service, and a sensible man will check it from time to time against something not liable to that accident, for example, a surveyor's chain. Thus, so long as I am *using* it, that the tape is accurate is a *presupposition* of the questions I ask. But while I am *checking* it, it is one of the two possible answers (in this case the affirmative answer) to the question I ask (EM, 29).

The point is that certain presuppositions are "questionable" (and this is not disproved by the fact that the person who makes them fails to see that they are questionable). To question a presupposition is to demand that it should be "verified," that is, to demand that a question be asked to which the affirmative answer would be that presupposition itself. It is because verifying a presupposition such as "my measuring tape is accurate" involves asking a question which admits of the two alternative answers "the tape is accurate" and "the tape is not accurate" that such a presupposition must be spoken of as relative (EM, 30).

An absolute presupposition, on the other hand, "*is one which stands, relatively to all questions to which it is related, as a presupposition, never as an answer*" (def. 6, EM, 31): for example, the presupposition that everything that happens has a cause. Such absolute presuppositions are not verifiable. Indeed, the idea of verification is an idea which does not apply to them at all; for to speak of verifying a presupposition involves supposing that it is a relative presupposition. If anyone objects that presuppositions which are not verifiable are of no use to science, the answer is "that their use in science is simply their logical efficacy," and this, as we have already noted (prop. 3) does not depend on their being verifiable, because it does not depend on their being true: it depends only on their being supposed (EM, 32).

This leads us to the realization that absolute presuppositions are not propositions (prop. 5). This is "because they are never answers to questions (def. 6) whereas a proposition (def. 1) is that which is stated and whatever is stated (prop. 1) is stated in answer to a question" (EM, 32). Again, Collingwood affirms the thesis that the logical efficacy of an absolute presupposition is independent of its being true: which is to say that the distinction between truth and falsehood does not apply to absolute presuppositions at all but is peculiar to propositions alone.

Another way of putting this point is to say that absolute presuppositions are never "propounded" or asserted. The natural scientist, for example, presupposes the causal principle but it is not his business to propound it as true. Likewise, the metaphysician, once he has discovered what the presuppositions of a certain scientist are, does not propound these presuppositions as if they were propositions; what he does propound is the proposition that the presuppositions in question were in fact presupposed. "Hence," Collingwood concludes, "any question involving the presupposition that an absolute presupposition is a proposition, such as the question, 'Is it true?', 'What evidence is there for it?', 'How can it be demonstrated?', 'What right have we to presuppose it if it can't?', is a nonsense question" (EM, 33).

In his unpublished marginal comments to the *Essay* George Santayana raises the interesting possibility that what Collingwood really means to say is that while absolute presuppositions cannot be verified they can be either "optional" or "indispensable."[10] But, Santayana complains, "optional," is really just another name for "false": in which case, according to Santayana, Collingwood's so-called "reform of metaphysics" rests on nothing more than a "mere quibble." Santayana, however, has misunderstood Collingwood. The distinction between "false" and "optional" is more important than he realizes. The impression which Collingwood gives is that he is trying to dispense with the notion of truth altogether. This, however, is the misleading consequence of his obsession with the need to cure positivism of its anti-metaphysical tendencies. If dispensing with the notion of truth were Collingwood's chief goal then his characterization of absolute presuppositions could indeed be traced to a mere quibble. But the real point of Collingwood's discussion is to demonstrate that there are different ways of evaluating and justifying truth and falsity and that the ordinary method of verification together with its implied propositional logic is simply inappropriate to metaphysics: in the same sense, for example, that the methods of the natural sciences are inappropriate to history. Just a history is rooted in the activity of the a priori imagination so metaphysics is equally an activity of the a priori imagination. And the latter, as I will argue, is a critical activity which seeks to establish not only what is the case but also whether it is true. To show that a presupposition is indispensable is equivalent to showing that it is true only because its indispensability has survived the critique through which it has been elicited. The aim of such a critique is to show that it is consupponible with a variety of other presuppositions which together define the structure of a given form of life – in which case it would be better to speak of the "truthfulness" rather than truth of a presupposition. Truth is a property which belongs only to the whole, but a presupposition is "truthful" to the extent to which it contributes to the integrity of the whole – in the sense in which each form on a scale maintains the integrity of the whole scale to which it belongs. And since a scale may be internally consistent with itself and inconsistent with respect to other scales the very same presupposition may be "truthful" with respect to its place on the scale to which it most immediately belongs and false with respect to an entirely different scale. The purpose of metaphysics is therefore to expose both the implicit truthfulness (or falseness) of a presupposition with respect to its immediate form of life and its implicit falseness (or truthfulness) with respect to the world of knowledge as a whole.

The real point of the essay, then, is not simply to deny that absolute presuppositions are truth functional; its more important purpose is to outline the method whereby absolute presuppositions can be elicited and evaluated. The "reform of metaphysics" does not lie in banishing truth from the realm of presuppositions by means of a quibble; it lies rather in the development of a methodology which respects the notion of truth as a scale of forms. And this amounts virtually to an extension of the doctrines of *An Essay on Philosophical Method* to the problem of metaphysics.

In the *Essay on Metaphysics* the method of metaphysical enquiry is divided into two stages. The first he calls "disentangling," the second "arranging" (EM, 38). Take the question, "Have you left off beating your wife yet?" (EM, 38) Grammatically, this question has the form of a single question. But a skilled metaphysician would quickly disentangle this question into four:

1 Have you a wife?
2 Were you ever in the habit of beating her?
3 Do you intend to manage in the future without doing so?
4 Have you begun carrying out that intention?

But not only have these questions been disentangled, they have been arranged into a certain order. The question whether you ever beat your wife does not arise, according to Collingwood, until an affirmative answer has been given to the question whether you ever had one. And so on. Each question in the above list arises only when an affirmative answer has been given to the one before it. And these answers constitute the presuppositions of the questions.

Collingwood defines metaphysics as the attempt to discover what the people of any given time believe about the world's general nature, such beliefs being the presuppositions of all their physics, and the attempt to discover "the corresponding presuppositions of other peoples and other times, and to follow the historical process by which one set of presuppositions has turned into another" (A, 66; cf., EM, 47).

The question, what presuppositions underlie the physics or natural science of a certain people at a certain time is a purely historical question, to which the question whether these presuppositions are true or false is irrelevant. This is because the beliefs whose history the metaphysician has to study are not answers to questions but only presuppositions of questions, and therefore the distinction between what is true and what is false does not apply to them, but only the distinction between what is presupposed and what is not presupposed (A, 66).

But while the presuppositions underlying the natural science of a certain people at a certain time are not themselves either true or false, the statements made by metaphysicians certainly are, for they are answers to questions about the history of these presuppositions. Thus metaphysics becomes a science by approaching its subject matter historically, and by conceiving of its goal as the establishing of historical facts. The truth of metaphysical propositions is the truth of the historical fact (A, 67). To criticize absolute presuppositions according to the criteria applied to relative presuppositions (as positivism has recommended) leads to "pseudo-metaphysics." Pseudo-metaphysics will ask the very questions which metaphysics forbids: Is this proposition true? Upon what evidence is it accepted? How can it be demonstrated? What right have we to presuppose it if it cannot be demonstrated? But answers to questions like these are neither metaphysical truths nor metaphysical errors. They are nonsense: the kind of nonsense which comes of thinking that supposing is one of the attitudes we can take up towards a proposition, so that what is absolutely supposed must be either true or false (EM, 47–8). There are only two things you can do with absolute presuppositions. You can presuppose them, which is what the ordinary scientist does, or you can find out what they are, which is what the metaphysician does.

In seeking to uncover the presuppositions of thought, however, the metaphysician is confronted by the following perplexity concerning the form or logical status of sets of presuppositions. How are the presuppositions underlying the solution to one problem related to the presuppositions underlying the solution to another problem? Are they related by "implication" or "entailment," such that from the solution of one problem the solution of another can be deduced? (EM, 65) Collingwood's answer is an unequivocal "No," for he regards metaphysics as a dialectical rather than a deductive science. But, for reasons which are spelled out in more detail below (s. 6), instead of pointing out that the rules governing the relations among presuppositions are derived not from propositional but from dialectical logic, Collingwood attempts, in his effort to avoid using the language of dialectical logic, to communicate the meaning of dialectical logic by means of a neutral language. He therefore declares that presuppositions are not related as parts of a deductive system but instead constitute a "constellation." The latter however is simply a new way of characterizing what has hitherto been described as a dialectical system. Finally, he declares, the logical relation holding among presuppositions making up a constellation is one of *consupponibility*:

> The constellation, complex though it is, is still a single fact. The different presuppositions composing it are all made at once, in one and the same piece of thinking. They are not like a set of carpenter's tools, of which the carpenter uses one at a time; they are like a suit of clothes of which every part is worn simultaneously with all the rest. That is to say, since they are all presuppositions each must be consupponible with all the others; that is, it must be logically possible for a person who supposes any one of them to suppose concurrently all the rest. (EM, 66)

In the language of his earlier thought what Collingwood is trying to say here is that a constellation of presuppositions is really a single historical fact or concrete universal. The presuppositions comprising it may therefore be regarded as moments on a 'scale' of dialectically related forms, the structure of which has already been discussed in chapters VI and VII above. So regarded, presuppositions may be said to exhibit dialectical simultaneity: each, while it cannot be deduced from the other, is nevertheless implicit in it. It is my contention, therefore, that the doctrine of consupponibility (together with the whole theory of absolute presuppositions of which it is a part) is an unfortunate and misleading attempt to expound, in neutral language, the implications of dialectical logic as set forth in *Speculum Mentis* and *An Essay on Philosophical Method*. Indeed, it is only when interpreted according to the rules of this logic that the doctrine of the *Essay* becomes intelligible at all.

5 THE ALLEGED HISTORICISM OF THE SCIENCE OF ABSOLUTE PRESUPPOSITIONS

For most of Collingwood's critics this peculiar description of absolute presuppositions is plain evidence of Collingwood's conversion to Crocian radical historicism. Knox blames the rejection of eternal problems, the identification of the philosophical with the historical question, and the dogmatic claim that absolute presuppositions are neither true nor false for Collingwood's collapse into philosophical scepticism. As further evidence that Collingwood had undergone a radical conversion Knox cites the following passages from unpublished manuscripts. In a manuscript written in 1936, Collingwood declares, concerning the history of historiography:

St. Augustine looked at Roman history from the point of view of an early Christian; Tillemont, from that of a seventeenth-century Frenchman; Gibbon, from that of an eighteenth-century Englishman; Mommsen, from that of a nineteenth-century German. There is no point in asking which was the right point of view. Each was the only one possible for the man who adopted it. (IH, xii)

In 1939, according to Knox, Collingwood made an even greater concession to historicism when he wrote that "history is the only kind of knowledge" and proceeded to explain what he meant by adding that:

logic is an attempt to expound the principles of what in the logician's own day passed for valid thought; ethical theories differ, but none of them is therefore erroneous, because any ethical theory is an attempt to state the kind of life regarded as worth aiming at, and the question always arises, by whom? Natural science indeed is distinct from history and, unlike philosophy, cannot be absorbed into it, but this is because it starts from certain presuppositions and thinks out their consequences, and since these presuppositions are neither true nor false, thinking them together with their consequences is neither knowledge nor error. (IH, xii–xiii)

It was not really necesary, however, to quote from unpublished manuscripts. Similar passages can be found in works already published, for example, the following texts taken from the 1936 lecture on "Human Nature and Human History":

The *Republic* of Plato is an account, not of the unchanging ideal of political life, but of the Greek ideal as Plato received it and re-interpreted it. The *Ethics* of Aristotle describes not an eternal morality but the morality of the Greek gentleman. Hobbes's *Leviathan* expounds the political ideas of seventeenth-century absolutism in their English form. Kant's ethical theory expresses the moral convictions of German pietism; his *Critique of Pure Reason* analyses the conceptions and principles of Newtonian science, in their relation to the philosophical problems of the day ... All Kant could show was that eighteenth-century scientists did think in terms of that category; the question why they so thought can be answered by investigating the history of the idea of causation. If more than this is required; if a proof is needed that the idea is true, that people are right to think in that way; then a demand is being made which in the nature of things can never be satisfied. (IH, 229, 230)

Such texts are to be read, according to Knox, in connection with Collingwood's remark in *The Autobiography* that since only "correct" solutions to problems can be reconstructed, all history is therefore the history of 'correct' solutions or 'right' answers. Indeed, Collingwood declares that so far as the thought of any agent is concerned it is the same data which states his solution and serves as evidence of what the problem was. "The fact that we can identify his problem," he wrote, "is proof that he has solved it; for we can only know what the problem was by arguing back from the solution" (A, 70).

For Knox the most extreme implications of this position are contained in what Collingwood had to say in the *Autobiography* about the historian's reconstruction of the battle of Trafalgar. Concerning Nelson, Collingwood writes: "How can we discover what the tactical problem was that Nelson set himself at Trafalgar? Only by studying the tactics he pursued in the battle. We argue back from the solution to the problem." (A, 70) In Nelson's case, this is possible because he won the battle. But this is not the case with Villeneuve. Since Villeneuve did not succeed in carrying out his plan, no one, Collingwood argues, will ever know what it was. We can only guess, he says, and "guessing is not history" (A, 70).[11]

For Knox, such statements are an admission of the historicist principle that all standpoints, in so far as they can be known at all, are equidistant from God. Whatever can be known must be 'right.' Thus there is no point, after reconstructing the history of answers to such questions as, What is the state? in going on to ask, Which is the right (or true) answer? "If this analogy be pressed," writes Knox, "the inference would seem to be that we can understand a philosopher's problem only when he has won his battle, or solved his problem correctly, so that all philosophical writings are either true or unintelligible" (IH, xii).

But if these texts are to be taken as evidence of Collingwood's conversion to historicism, as a conclusive proof that Collingwood literally believed that all truth was historical and that valid criticism was therefore impossible, we must also take into account other texts from the same 1936 lecture in which Collingwood would appear to be contradicting this interpretation. Thus he declares, in a passage which contains an explicit and unequivocal repudiation of radical historicism,

> ... just as in the seventeenth and eighteenth centuries there were materialists, who argued from the success of physics in its own sphere that all reality was physical, so among ourselves the success of history has led some people to suggest that its methods are applicable to all the problems of knowledge, in other words, that all reality is historical.
> This I believe to be an error. I think that those who assert it are making a mistake of the same kind which the materialists made in the seventeenth century. (IH, 209)

Also repudiated is Knox's claim that for Collingwood history is a purely descriptive and non-critical attitude for which the question of truth and falsity does not arise:

> [Historical knowledge] is not a passive surrender to the spell of another's mind; it is a labour of active and therefore critical thinking. The historian not only re-enacts past thought, he re-enacts it in the context of his own knowledge and therefore, in re-enacting it, criticizes it, forms his own judgement of its value, corrects whatever errors he can discern in it. This criticism of the thought whose history he traces is not something secondary to tracing the history of it. It is an indispensable condition of the historical knowledge itself. Nothing could be a completer error concerning the history of thought than to suppose that the historian as such merely ascertains 'what so-and-so thought,' leaving it to some one else to decide 'whether it was true.' All thinking is critical thinking; the thought which re-enacts past thoughts, therefore, criticizes them in re-enacting them. (IH, 215–16)

And finally, Collingwood declares, regarding the charge of scepticism, that while it is important to recognize the historical character of all systems of thought,

> If these systems remain valuable to posterity, that is not in spite of their strictly historical character but because of it. To us, the ideas expressed in them are ideas belonging to the past; but it is not a dead past; by understanding it historically we incorporate it into our present thought, and enable ourselves by developing and criticizing it to use that heritage for our own advancement. (IH, 230)

These passages would seem not only to echo the conclusions of *Speculum Mentis* (316–71) and *An Essay on Philosophical Method* (IX, ss. 1, 2, 3) but to express as well the doctrine implicit throughout the *Essay on Metaphysics*, *The Principles of Art* and *The New Leviathan*.

Of course the very existence of apparently contradictory texts in the writings of 1936–39 can be interpreted in favour of the radical conversion hypothesis. For there is nothing to prevent anyone from drawing the conclusion that, although in the writings of 1936–39 Collingwood was ambivalent about the relationship between philosophy and history, by 1939 the tension was clearly resolved in favour of the historicist rather than anti-historicist tendencies of his earlier thought. It is my contention, however, both that the ambivalence is in fact rooted in a rapprochement in which both sides of the apparent tension exist as *coincidentia oppositorum*, and that the writings of 1936–39 give a misleading impression of resolving the tension in favour of historicism only because of the awkward way in which Collingwood expresses himself in these writings. The latter is primarily caused by the fact that the *Essay*, the chief evidence of Collingwood's conversion, was addressed to an audience of logical positivists, and, in an effort to express his views in a language which would be acceptable to that audience, Collingwood inadvertently contributed to a misunderstanding of his intentions.

6 THE ESSAY AS A RESPONSE TO LOGICAL POSITIVISM

In the *Autobiography* Collingwood declared that he did not feel any great desire to expound his theory of metaphysics conceived as the science of absolute presuppositions (A, 74). Within a year, however, his feelings must have changed, for in 1939 he produced the very thing which a year earlier he had apparently thought was unnecessary. The reason for this change in attitude was the sudden popularity and influence in 1938–39 of the anti-metaphysical doctrines of logical positivism.

In January of 1936 there was published in England a book which was destined to become one of the most influential of the first half of the twentieth century. The book was A. J. Ayer's *Language, Truth and Logic*. The doctrines which it expounded were derived from the early writings of Russell and Wittgenstein and represent the species of empiricism known as 'logical positivism.' The first chapter of Ayer's book is entitled "The Elimination of Metaphysics," and its thesis is that, since metaphysical statements are neither tautologies nor empirical hypotheses subject to empirical verification, they are meaningless.[12] It is to A. J. Ayer and his disciples that Collingwood specifically addresses *An Essay on Metaphysics*. These are the persons who, by denying the value of metaphysics, are running the risk of contributing toward the ruin of western civilization. Collingwood regarded logical positivism as an example of the kind of philosophical dogmatism which was criticized in *Speculum Mentis*. And since he believed that any dogmatism, by arresting the dialectic, brings the self-making process to an end, he felt it imperative that the philosophy of logical positivism be challenged immediately. Such a challenge, as *Speculum Mentis* makes clear, can only be produced *ab extra* from the absolute standpoint; for it is only from this standpoint that a genuine critique of either past or present thought is possible. Indeed, this dependence of historical criticism on the absolute or transhistorical standpoint confirms once again the ontological priority of philosophy over history.

As represented by Collingwood, positivism asserts the doctrine "that the only valid method of attaining knowledge is the method used in the natural sciences, and hence that no kind of knowledge is genuine unless it either is natural science or resembles natural science in method" (EM, 143). In other words, since the criterion of all meaning is empirical verification, any claim to knowledge which does not meet this criterion must be dismissed as meaningless. Since the propositions of traditional metaphysics cannot be verified by an appeal to observed facts, they must be treated as pseudo-propositions, in which case they are pure nonsense.

Now such an argument presupposes that metaphysical statements are verifiable "propositions" which are either true or false. Collingwood answers positivism by showing that, in fact, metaphysical statements are not propositions at all; on the contrary, they are "suppositions" which because they are *in principle* neither true nor false are *in principle* unverifiable. To treat suppositions as propositions is to mistake metaphysics for pseudo-metaphysics. The positivistic attack on metaphysics is consequently an attack only on pseudo-metaphysics (which, to repeat, is the result of the mistake of thinking that metaphysics is the attempt to justify by an appeal to observed facts the absolute presuppositions of our thought [EM, 162]). Collingwood goes on to argue that, in the case of natural science, the search for absolute presuppositions is an integral part of science itself, and to attack metaphysics is therefore to attack science. He concludes:

If by metaphysics is meant either (1) the absolute presuppositions of science, or (2) the attempt to find out what at any given time these presuppositions are, then clearly the positivistic attack on metaphysics, so far from aiding the cause of natural science, can only prove harmful to that cause in proportion to its own degree of success. (EM, 169)

Collingwood's quarrel with positivism resembles his earlier quarrel with Ryle concerning the possibility of categorical universal propositions;

but although the substance of his reply to the challenge of positivism is virtually the same as in his statement to Ryle, the form of it is remarkably different.

Like Ryle, the positivists regarded all propositions as either analytic or synthetic a posteriori; the validity of the latter depends entirely on their being verified. For Collingwood, of course, such claims are founded on a serious philosophical error, the error which in *Speculum Mentis* is described as the dogma of scientific philosophy. However, since he wants very much to strike a chord of common consent with the positivists – in order to increase the likelihood of having some therapeutic effect on them – he more or less concedes these conventions and, in effect, addresses himself to the task of showing that metaphysics is not concerned with propositions at all. He agrees, in other words, that absolute propositions are neither analytic nor empirically verifiable. But he argues that they were never intended to be verifiable in the first place. Indeed, he continues, if metaphysics were what the positivists mistake it for – an attempt to provide empirical justification for the presuppositions of science – it might actually prove detrimental to science itself: "... for when the discovery was made that no justification of this kind is to be had, the positivistic belief that it is nevertheless necessary might lead to the false conclusion that the whole fabric of scientific thought is rotten to the core" (EM, 169). Collingwood therefore regards the positivist as right, in a way, to fear metaphysics as he does. What the latter fears, however, is not metaphysics as it really is, but metaphysics as he misconceives it: an enterprise which in fact is neither required nor even possible (EM, 169).

Collingwood also argues that it does not follow that, because they cannot be so verified, both absolute presuppositions and the statements through which they are disclosed are therefore meaningless. Meaning is not equivalent to verification. It is at this point that Collingwood draws the line. He concedes that absolute presuppositions are neither true nor false but he denies that statements about them are therefore meaningless.

But having disposed of the objection that the object of metaphysics cannot be a proper object of thought, Collingwood must attempt a more positive account of the nature of metaphysical statements themselves. He thus points out that some of them at least are no more than statements of historical fact whose means of verification do fall within the limits of positivistic theory: they are verified by an appeal to the evidence. One does not ask of presuppositions per se whether they are true or false. But one can ask whether it is true that this is what so and so presupposed. And since this is a purely historical question, the answer will be a proposition of the synthetic a posteriori form.

The real dispute between Collingwood and positivism, however, has to do with the status of what was previously distinguished (ch. VIII, s. 2, above) as a second kind of metaphysical activity whose chief purpose is to subject absolute presuppositions to a process of critical evaluation. To do this is to treat them as categorical universal statements (which constitute a special class of the synthetic a priori).[18] Although in the *Essay* Collingwood avoided any direct discussion of this distinction, his implicit recognition of the need for this second type of activity may be represented by means of the following summary.

Positivism claims that metaphysical statements (such as 'God exists'), in order to be meaningful, must be either analytic or synthetic a posteriori; both kinds of statement must conform to the rules of propositional logic and the latter kind must be subject to the verification principle also. Because it can be shown that metaphysical statements cannot satisfy any of these conditions, positivism regards metaphysics as refuted. But in coming to this conclusion positivism is itself accepting presuppositions of the very sort which were claimed to be meaningless. The distinctions between analytic and synthetic, a posteriori and a priori, as well as the definition of truth as correspondence with facts, are all presuppositions which cannot themselves be employed without committing the fallacy of *petitio principii* and therefore presupposing themselves. *Speculum Mentis* has shown that in fact all of these distinctions and definitions rest on philosophical errors. But this does not mean that they are therefore meaningless. The dialectic of *Speculum Mentis* simply locates them in their proper place on a scale. Since this cannot be done according to the terms of propositional logic, it was necessary to develop an alternative logic, which Collingwood calls dialectical. Presuppositions, regardless of what standpoint they underlie, are neither a posteriori nor strictly a priori: dialectical logic actually cuts right across this distinction altogether. If they must be labelled at all, they may be regarded as a special type of synthetic a priori.

By synthetic a priori is meant not simply what Kant meant – although there are strong affinities. For Kant such statements derive from the categories of mind. Mind in turn is conceived of as a permanent and eternal substance, which is not subject to change. The principles which are derived from them have therefore the status of eternal truths. In Collingwood's philosophy, mind is an historical process, and the categories (or habits) are themselves the products of that process. They constitute a scale of forms which is such that as the scale develops, each form on the scale undergoes corresponding and significant changes. It is from such categories that synthetic a priori statements are derived; they are not eternal truths but must, like the categories they are derived from, be subject to historical change. They must therefore have special characteristics not shared by Kant's synthetic a priori propositions. Collingwood emphasizes these special characteristics by calling his synthetic a priori statements "absolute presuppositions," and with Kant he declares that they "are not 'derived from experience' but are catalytic agents which the mind must bring out of its own resources to the manipulation of what is called 'experience' and the conversion of it into science and civilization" (EM, 197). Their truth is, therefore, the truth of the moment of the concrete universal, whose development is essentially historical; for, in Collingwood's philosophy, truth is not a mere matter of correspondence with fact, but a dynamically developing scale which exemplifies the process of mind on its way to self-knowledge.

Now unless Collingwood was prepared to advance some such doctrine he would have had to count himself a disciple rather than a critic of positivism. Indeed the critical evaluation of absolute presuppositions is the only thing that would distinguish Collingwood's theory from the doctrines of positivism. For if Collingwood intended metaphysics to be a strictly descriptive historical science then he would be doing nothing more than elaborating on one of the key doctrines of *Language, Truth and Logic,* which declares, with respect to ethics, for example, that "There cannot be such a thing as ethical science, if by ethical science one means the elaboration of a 'true' system of morals ... All that one may legitimately enquire in this connection is, What are the moral habits of a given person or group of people, and what causes them to have precisely those habits and feelings? And this enquiry falls wholly within the scope of the existing social sciences."[14] But Collingwood did not write the *Essay* in order to demonstrate his agreement with this doctrine of positivism. He wrote it rather to emphasize the basis of his disagreement, which is that metaphysics, in addition to being a descriptive-historical science, is also an activity through which absolute presuppositions are critically evaluated according to the criteria of dialectical logic; in which case they are to be regarded as a special type of the class of synthetic a priori statements.

Of course Collingwood could not have expressed himself in this way because he knew he would not be understood. In particular he had an almost paranoid fear of being classified and labelled as some kind of old-fashioned idealist. He had not yet forgotten the review of *Speculum Mentis* in which his thought was referred to as "the usual idealistic nonsense" (A, 56). Nor had he forgotten Ryle's confessed failure to "make head or tail" out of the central doctrines of *An Essay on Philosophical Method.* He had no reason to suppose that the positivists would be capable of any greater insight, and having learnt his lesson from the past, he tried therefore to address them in their own language. Instead of trying to explain the real basis of his new dialectical logic, which would have meant representing some metaphysical statements as a special type of synthetic a priori, he chose to emphasize only those statements that report historical facts about what so-and-so absolutely presupposed. In short, he concentrated on the branch of metaphysics that could be reduced to some kind of empirically verifiable science and consisted solely of synthetic a posteriori statements. This meant creating what was really a false and abstract distinction between the statement, "so-and-so absolutely presupposed such and such," and the actual presupposition itself. The latter was removed from the realm of dispute altogether and the former was given respectability by being brought under the protection of history.

This is of course not the only place in the *Essay* in which Collingwood's attempt to translate his thought into what he regarded as a more acceptable language resulted in a distortion. There is, for example, the doctrine of consupponibility, already discussed (ch. VIII, s. 4 above). There is also his analysis of the idea of a metaphysical system in which he seems virtually to deny that metaphysics does in fact aim at building up a system (EM, 65). This contention might appear at first sight as a complete repudiation of the doctrines of *Speculum Mentis* and *An Essay on Philosophical Method*. In fact it is really only a further statement of the same doctrine, for what is rejected is not the 'open' and infinitely progressing dialectical system of *Speculum Mentis*, but the abstract, fixed, and closed system of deductive metaphysics (a notion which Collingwood rejected from the very outset of his career). As in his earlier thought, so in the *Essay on Metaphysics*, Collingwood regards the metaphysician's job as never finished:

... every historical subject, like the course of historical events itself, is open at the end, and however hard you work at it the end always remains open. People who are said to 'make history' solve the problems they find confronting them, but create others to be solved, if not by themselves, by their survivors ... every problem solved gives rise to a new problem. (EM, 65)

In other words, to cite once again the language of *Speculum Mentis*,

The life of the mind is not the rotation of a machine through a cycle of fixed phases but the flow of a torrent through its mountain-bed, scattering itself in spray as it plunges over a precipice and pausing in the deep transparency of a rock-pool to issue again in an ever-new series of adventures. (SM, 57)

It is clear, then, that if, as I have argued, Collingwood's plan in the *Essay* was to communicate his thought to an audience of positivists, we must pronounce his attempt to execute it a failure. Collingwood failed in this mission because in order really to have succeeded he would have had to accept a positivistic theory of history. For if the positivist is to be at all impressed with Collingwood's reduction of metaphysics to history it must be history as the positivist himself understands it. It cannot be the notion of history which in the *Idea of History* is put forward as an *alternative* to positivism; for this simply re-introduces everything which positivism is dedicated to repudiating. But, for Collingwood to accept a positivistic theory of history would be tantamount to committing philosophical suicide.

Nevertheless – and this is perhaps somewhat of a paradox – the reduction of metaphysics to a form of history (the true concept of which had already been worked out both in the published and as yet unpublished portions of what was eventually to become the *Idea of History*) provides the clue for a proper understanding of Collingwood's genuine theory of philosophy as a science of absolute presuppositions. For, if metaphysics is a special kind of history, then its character must derive from the principles which lie at the basis of *all* history. Chief among these principles is the requirement, stated in the previously cited passage from the *Idea of History*, that the historian in re-enacting past thought must criticize it as well. The passage is important enough to be repeated:

This re-enactment is only accomplished, in the case of Plato and Caesar respectively, so far as the historian brings to bear on the problem all the powers of his own mind and all his knowledge of philosophy and politics. It is not a passive surrender to the spell of another's mind; it is a labour of active and therefore critical thinking. The historian not only re-enacts past thought, he re-enacts it in the context of his own knowledge and therefore, in re-enacting it, criticizes it, forms his own judgement of its value, corrects whatever errors he can discern in it. This criticism of the thought whose history he traces is not something secondary to tracing the history of it. It is an indispensable condition of the historical knowledge itself. Nothing could be a completer error concerning the history of thought than to suppose that the historian as such merely ascertains 'what so-and-so thought', leaving it to some one else to decide 'whether it was true'. All thinking is critical thinking; the thought which re-enacts past thoughts, therefore, criticizes them in re-enacting them. (IH, 215–16)

This, together with the other principles of history, presupposes the rapprochement between philosophy and history implied by the conclusions of *Speculum Mentis* – a rapprochement which identifies philosophy with history without destroying its autonomy. For the autonomy of philosophy is an absolute presupposition of critical (as opposed to merely descriptive) history. This same rapprochement, while it is not explicitly expounded in the *Essay*, is nevertheless presupposed in various places. In particular, it is presupposed by the very examples with which Collingwood tries to illustrate his case, examples in which his reconstructions are as critical as they are descriptive. And this means, if I may sum up the theme of my argument, that the reduction of metaphysics to history is a vindication rather than a liquidation of philosophy.

7 METAPHYSICS AS A DIALECTICAL HISTORY OF ERRORS

The problems raised by the *Essay on Metaphysics* and the *Autobiography* have to do with the following claims: (i) that absolute presuppositions, the subject matter of metaphysics, since they are not propositions, are not therefore subject to the rules of propositional or truth-functional logic; (ii) that in spite of this they can nevertheless be criticized or justified, that is, while absolute propositions cannot be criticized or justified *de facto* within the framework of propositional logic, they can and must be criticized *de jure* within the framework of dialectical logic; and (c) that these considerations apply not only to absolute presuppositions but to all historical matters. All history is the history of thought. Propositional logic treats thought as though it were a mere species of nature, a spectacle to behold, an object with which we may be acquainted. And it assumes that historical thought is merely the succession of different answers to the same question. But thought is not this at all. It is a dialectically developing, self-making process which creates itself as it knows itself. It cannot therefore be understood within the framework of an acquaintance theory of knowledge.

I am suggesting, in other words, that the doctrine of absolute presuppositions, together with its implied rejection of eternal problems, is part of the wider doctrine which I have previously discussed under the heading of 'the concrete universal.' At the same time, I am suggesting that the rejection of the realist distinction between philosophy and history is a direct implication of the rapprochement of *Speculum Mentis*: thus committing myself to the further doctrine that so far as there is any implied identity of philosophy and history in the *Essay* it ought to be understood according to the terms of the same rapprochement. As we have seen, Collingwood himself declares in the *Autobiography* that the theory of presuppositions first expounded in *Truth and Contradiction* was part of a general attempt to develop an alternative logic to the propositional logic of realism. If, as I have already suggested, this alternative logic is the dialectical logic of *Speculum Mentis* and *An Essay on Philosophical Method*, then the identity of philosophy and history which is implied by the theory of presuppositions must be what follows from the rapprochement between philosophy and history which it is the purpose of dialectical logic to achieve.

If, furthermore, presuppositions are treated according to the terms of dialectical logic, then the following things can be said about them. Any presupposition (or set of presuppositions) is subject to two sorts of criterion: one having to do with meaning, the other with truth. These criteria are derived not from propositional but from dialectical logic.

According to the former, a statement has meaning if it signifies either of two conditions. Either it is the appropriate answer to a given question (as in the case of relative presuppositions) or it is logically presupposed as a *conditio sine qua non* of the intelligibility of the question-and-answer complex as a whole (as in the case of absolute presuppositions). In either case, the presupposition is meaningful if it satisfies the logical criteria of intelligibility. And Collingwood declares that the fact that we can even identify what a presupposition is, is proof that it has satisfied these criteria.

In addition to being 'intelligible,' every presupposition is part of a dialectical question-and-answer complex which occupies a place on a scale of overlapping forms. This is the basis for judging a presupposition according to the criteria of truthfulness. These criteria are derived, according to my interpretation of Collingwood, from a theory of truth which, as we have already noted, may be more accurately described as a dialectical history of errors. According to this theory, truth is the product of error: it must proceed and develop by means of contradiction, paradox, and ambiguity. The forms which make up the scale are, when treated singly, incompatible opposites; but when placed on the scale in proper relation one to another they are *coincidentia oppositorum*. As the scale progresses each form may be said to provide, in its own unique way, a more adequate embodiment of the implicit truth. Unless this were so there could be no progress. By progress, of course, we do not mean 'necessary' progress. We cannot predict the next stage until we have arrived at it. What is important about this progress is that it is made possible only through the critical reflection of each age on the presuppositions which lie at the basis of the question-and-answer complexes which characterize that age. And this of course means answering the question how these presuppositions came to be presupposed in the first place. The historian of his own age must become the historian of the past.

History, then, is not just the description of facts but an essential ingredient in the very constitution of the facts described. Collingwood calls that branch of history which specializes in the analysis of presuppositions 'metaphysics,' and it is clear that this science plays an important role in the perpetuation of culture and civilization; for if, as Collingwood himself declares in the *Essay*, absolute presuppositions are the catalytic agents by which the mind converts experience into science and civilization, then the institutions which perpetuate them (especially the questioning procedures of metaphysics) are sacred to the survival of that civilization (EM, 197). But what he did not make clear is the fact that such institutions are not merely descriptive and preservative but critical, therapeutic, and prophylactic as well.

A close examination of texts will demonstrate that this interpretation coincides with the theory implicit in the *Essay* and the *Autobiography* themselves. I shall deal with it under two heads, corresponding to the two sets of criteria mentioned above. My ultimate aim is to explain how not only absolute presuppositions but the entire question-and-answer complex of which they are part, can and must be judged by both sets of criteria at once. It would follow, on my interpretation and reconstruction of Collingwood's thought, that it is perfectly intelligible to say of any complex (or part thereof) that it is both 'right' (when judged by one set of criteria) and yet 'false' (when judged by the other set of criteria).

Let us examine again Collingwood's alternative to propositional logic. According to realism, knowledge lies in propositions, and truth is the correspondence of propositions to facts. Against this Collingwood advanced a doctrine according to which knowledge consists not simply of propositions but of these together with the questions they are meant to answer, such that (a) no two propositions can contradict one another unless they are answers to the same question, and (b) since the meaning of a proposition is relative to the question it answers, its 'truth' must be relative to the same thing: "Meaning, agreement and contradiction, truth and falsehood, none of these belonged to propositions in their own right, propositions by themselves; they belonged only to propositions as the answers to questions ..." (A, 33; see also A, 37). Although in these passages Collingwood is speaking only of questions and answers, the same considerations must apply to the presuppositions in terms of which these questions and answers are posed and without which an intelligible account of them cannot be given. The point is that the unit of knowledge, whether it be question or answer, an absolute or a relative presupposition, is never an independent entity but is always a necessary part of a larger whole or context. This seems to be the very point which Collingwood stresses in his 1935 correspondence with Ryle:

it seems to me that the individual "proposition" assented to on any given occasion is assented to only in context, never by itself; and this context is not a fortuitous context but a necessary one – the context is a logical context, consisting of other things which if we didn't think we couldn't think what hypotheses we are thinking. (CRG, I, 17)

Therefore, when Collingwood speaks of truth in the passage from the *Autobiography* cited above, he really means logical intelligibility – a concept which he chooses to explicate in the *Essay* in terms of the notion of consupponibility but which, as I have suggested above, can be more adequately explicated according to the rules of dialectical logic. More often, and more correctly, he refers to this quality as "rightness." On many occasions he speaks, not of the true and false points of view, or the true and false solution, but of the "right solution" and the "right point of view." The "right" question is the question which really has "arisen," while the right answer is the appropriate or relevant answer to the question, the answer which enables us to get ahead with the process of questioning and answering. If we distinguish between truth and falsity, on the one hand, and logical intelligibility or "rightness" on the other, then there will be no basic incompatibility between the rightness of a point of view and its truth or falsity. Collingwood himself says that the "logical efficacy" of a statement is independent of its truth or falsity. Indeed, it is perfectly conceivable that the same statement may be both right and false, as for example in a case where a thinker is following a false scent, either inadvertently or in order to construct a *reductio ad absurdum*:

Thus, when Socrates asks (Plato, *Republic,* 333B) whether as your partner in a game of draughts you would prefer to have a just man or a man who knows how to play draughts, the answer which Polemarchus gives – 'man who knows how to play draughts' – is the right answer. It is 'false' because it presupposes that justice and ability to play draughts are comparable, each of them being a 'craft', or specified form of skill. But it is 'right', because it constitutes a link, and a sound one, in the chain of questions and answers by which the falseness of that presupposition is made manifest. (A, 37–8)

Every question-and-answer complex includes absolute presuppositions and it is only in terms of these presuppositions that the "rightness" or "wrongness," "truth" or "falsity," of the answer can be judged. This very point is implicit in Collingwood's *Speculum Mentis* account of "knowledge as Question and Answer" (76–80). One of the vitally important things about questions, according to the *Speculum Mentis* account, is not that they look forward to answers, but that they arise out of a context of assertion (which may or may not be conscious) (SM, 77–9). Suppose some of these assertions have the status of absolute presuppositions; then, Collingwood's claim that no fact can be known until it has been sought by the imaginative act of questioning may be construed as meaning that not only answers but absolute presuppositions as well are revealed through the act of questioning. The process of knowledge, writes Collingwood, is not so much an alternation of question and answer as a perpetual restatement of the question with a perpetual revision of the answer (SM, 80).

If this is extended to include the perpetual discovery and revision of absolute presuppositions, then the *Speculum Mentis* account of the process of question and answer provides a clue to the meaning of the same doctrine in the *Autobiography* and the *Essay on Metaphysics*. According to the account given in *Speculum Mentis*, the question-and-answer process is a dialectical one which, over a period of time, assumes the shape of a scale of forms or concrete universal, an identity which contains all diversity within itself (SM, 80).

This is precisely what Collingwood had in mind when in the *Autobiography* he described the history of thought as a process whose "sameness is the sameness of an historical process, and the difference is the difference between one thing which in the course of that process has turned into something else, and the other thing into which it has turned" (A, 62). Thus, when Collingwood further argues in the *Autobiography* that the history of all thought, including metaphysics, can be approached through the logic of question and answer (A, 58, 65, 67), he is implicitly declaring that the question-and-answer complexes revealed by applying the logic of question and answer to the history of thought assume a dialectical scale of forms.

The relation between the logic of question and answer and the scale of forms may be illustrated by means of the following examples, adapted from Collingwood's own account, in the *Idea of Nature* and *An Essay on Metaphysics*, of the rise of natural science in Greece. Natural science, as practised by the Greeks, emerged from a context which was dominated by the attitude of magic. Suppose we were to compare the witch doctor's account of nature with that of the Ionian philosophers. A realist would no doubt regard each as a different answer to the same question, What is nature? What is more, he would declare that in answering this question the Greeks were right and the witch doctors wrong. According to the logic of question and answer, however, the Greeks and the witch doctors were not really competing for the same prize; if we take into account the fact that every question rests on certain presuppositions, we will become aware of hitherto unnoticed differences between the questions of magic and the questions of Ionian natural philosophy. Indeed, the logic of question and answer may be regarded as an effective antidote to the historical myopia of realism. For example, when the witch doctor asks, What is nature? (i.e., Why do things happen as they do?), he is presupposing absolutely 'that all things are full of Gods' (an attitude which for the sake of convenience I shall call 'polytheistic animism'). His answer therefore takes a mythopoeic form while his actions take the form of magic. Given his presuppositions, his answer is the 'right' one in the sense that it is the only appropriate response to the question he is asking.

At the same time, however, it is the 'wrong' answer because the presuppositions of the question-and-answer complex of which it is a part are false. They are false because people who are committed to them are limited in what they can explain and are limited in their freedom by being made dependent upon the supernatural powers of the witch doctor. But, according to the terms of dialectical logic, it was only by presupposing them in the first place and by correctly following out their existential implications that consciousness was able to re-experience nature in such a way that it was driven to adopt an entirely new attitude toward it: an attitude which supersedes the more primitive standpoint of magic.

This new attitude, which may be characterized as monotheistic religion, was in turn superseded by natural science. The latter, which owes its origins to the transition within religious consciousness from polytheism to monotheism, rests, according to Collingwood, on the following presuppositions:

1 That there are 'natural' things (IN, 29);
2 That 'natural' things constitute a single 'world of nature' (IN, 29);
3 That what is common to all 'natural' things is their being made of a single 'substance' or material (IN, 30).

All of this, according to *An Essay on Metaphysics*, is implicit in the purely religious belief, 'God exists.' Just as *An Essay on Philosophical Method* explores the structure of believing in the existence of God as a basis for a rapprochement between essence and existence, thought and being, so the *Essay on Metaphysics* examines the same proposition as a basis for the rapprochement between religion and science; science is here represented as the systematic rationalization of principles already implicit in the standpoint of monotheistic religion.

This is quite clearly a re-statement of the conclusions of *Speculum Mentis* which dealt with the phenomenological transition from religion to science; science as a universal and necessary habit of mind was shown to be the dialectical product of the habit or category of religion, which in turn was regarded as the dialectical presupposition of science.

Thus, *An Essay on Metaphysics* is a clear demonstration, in accordance with the claims of *Speculum Mentis*, that the "serial" or phenomenological development of mind, conceived as a system of necessary categories or habits, is exemplified in the actual history of the particular disciplines or activities to which these universal habits of mind give rise. In *Speculum Mentis* religion was shown to have its ground in the realization that the explicitly pluralistic monadology of art implicitly presupposes the monistic principle which lies at the basis of science. In the *Essay on Metaphysics* this phenomenological transition is exemplified in the historical transition from the aesthetic religion of polytheism to the more "religious" religion of monism, which by virtue of its monistic character contains within it the seeds of science. Thales' achievement is therefore represented as one of the implications of the transition from a polytheistic to a monotheistic religious consciousness. And, as in *Speculum Mentis*, this transition is regarded as a progress from error to truth.

In declaring that the scientific world view supersedes the religious world view (which in turn has superseded the aesthetic) we are recognizing that science at the same time implicitly sums up the truth of the more primitive standpoints. From the magical world view is retained the wondering attitude of supposal and questioning; from the religious world view is retained not only the notion of unity but the attitude of faith with which the *conditio sine qua non* of all science must ultimately be embraced. Magic, science, and religion, then, are not just different answers to different questions, they are, at the same time, internally related forms on an overlapping scale.

The same considerations may be seen to apply within the history of science itself. Take for example the history of science from Thales to Pythagoras. To a realist it might appear that each of the early Greek philosophers had given a different answer to the same question, What is nature? But by taking into account the presuppositions underlying their questions it will become clear that they were not in fact asking the same question at all. Thales and Anaximander were both interested in answering the question, What is the original unchanging substance which underlies all the changes of the natural world? And because they both presupposed absolutely 'That there is a universal primitive substance' and 'That from this substance we can deduce the world of nature,' their answers took the form they did; each tried to name this substance and to explain how it gives rise to the 'opposites' of the physical world. But the difference between Thales and Anaximander lay in the fact that, while each presupposed that there was a primitive substance, Thales assumed that it was itself of the same type as the ordinary things of nature, while Anaximander assumed that it was an 'undifferentiated' stuff which did not possess any of the qualities which are said to arise from it. In substituting the *apeiron* for Thales' 'water' Anaximander was at the same time taking issue with one of Thales' basic presuppositions.

This is, however, only a minor difference compared with the difference between the Thales-Anaximander school of thought and that of Anaximines. Anaximines could see that neither Thales nor Anaximander had adequately answered the question, Why if various kinds of natural substances are made of the same original stuff do they behave in different ways? Their answers had been to the effect that differences in nature were the result of different types of motion acting on the original substance. But motion alone could not account for the creation of opposites; how was it possible for contraries like hot and cold, dry and moist, to derive from the same substance? Anaximines became preoccupied, therefore, with the problem of supplying the middle term between motion and the opposites which would explain precisely how the two were connected. He had stopped asking questions about substance and, in effect, had begun asking questions about 'intervening variables.' His answer took the form of stating a new principle, the principle of condensation and rarefaction. And this was a revolutionary answer which, when analysed, could be shown to rest upon a new presupposition, namely, 'That the stuff out of which things are made, no matter what it is, undergoes different arrangements in space,' and that this is how the differences in nature can be accounted for. This is an entirely new solution to the problem of the one and the many. It is true that the new idea of nature retains the earlier notion that the unity of nature is *sui generis*. But this time, instead of grounding the unity of nature in 'substance' or 'matter,' the emphasis is placed on 'arrangement' or 'form.' It was left to the Pythagoreans to reap the harvest of Anaximines' achievement and to bring his thought to its logical conclusion. The fundamental principle of the Pythagorean philosophy of nature is that differences in the world of nature are the result of differences in geometrical arrangement; qualitative differences are the result of differences of quantity. From this standpoint the question for science ceases to be, What is substance? and becomes, What are the different quantitative arrangements which underlie the changes in the physical world? And this is a question which can only be answered by a mathematically based physics.

The transition from Thales to Pythagoras is a dialectical transition from one set of presuppositions to another: a transition which both exposes the absurdity of Thales' presuppositions and preserves their truth. It was, in other words, a rational (i.e., dialectical) transition in which a genuine progress through error can be detected. Indeed, it is only because the presuppositions underlying the question-and-answer complexes which make up the history of thought are so related that there can be historical progress at all.

But, although progress, according to Collingwood, implies "improvement," he does not mean by this what realists mean, namely a succession of better solutions to the same problem (THC, 444). If there is an improvement it is only in the sense that as the history of thought develops each new question-and-answer complex is less subject to internal stresses and strains. At the same time each new solution is an improvement in the sense that it explains everything which the previous one did as well as a variety of new phenomena which have hitherto gone unexplained. It is in this sense, according to Collingwood, that Darwin's theory of the origin of the species constitutes an improvement over the theory of special creation and that Einstein's theory of relativity is an improvement over the Newtonian theory of planetary motion (IH, 332).

Similarly, the development of political life may be regarded not as a progress from 'inferior' to 'better' things, but as a progress in the " ... creation of political systems more supple, more adaptable, more responsive to individual initiative from within, and to alterations of conditions without, than the systems of the past" (PP, 76). Thus the political systems of modern man may be regarded as an improvement over those of the past in the sense that the former are the only ones that suit *our* psychological structure and give scope to those things in us which *we* consider the most important (PP, 76). Such improvements, according to Collingwood, mark a progress not from 'bad' to 'good,' but from 'good' to 'better' (IH, 326) or from 'true' to 'truer.'

The model of progress which is implicit in Collingwood's various descriptions of the history of thought in the *Idea of History*, the *Idea of Nature*, and even *An Essay on Metaphysics* itself, is the scale of forms (exemplified in *Speculum Mentis* and systematically expounded in *An Essay on Philosophical Method*). According to the terms of this model each form on a scale, while it supersedes and is superseded by another, is in its own right neither strictly true nor strictly false (i.e., in the sense demanded by the propositional logic of realism); it is, on the contrary, a systematic moment in the total development of truth through error. The truth or falsity of any standpoint, in other words, is entirely relative to the place it occupies on the scale. In so far as a given standpoint constitutes a genuine and dialectical summation of whatever has gone before, it may be regarded as true; in so far as it is only a stage on the way to a higher dialectical synthesis it is 'false.' Yet *every* assertion, whether it looks backward or forward, is 'right,' by virtue of the very fact that it finds a place in the scale at all (i.e., arises in a systematic context). For, as we have already noted, it is only by presupposing certain errors in the first place that we can get on with the question-and-answer process through which error is eventually overcome; only through the labour of the notion – the gradual process of falling into and escaping from systematic error – does the mind work its way toward certainty and truth. Collingwood therefore declares, with regard to the history of thought in general, that each age solves its problems in the only way it knows how (THC, 444), each expounds the position reached by the human mind down to its own time (IH, 229), and each solution, therefore, "in so far as it succeeds, is absolutely the right solution for its own problem" (THC, 443). At the same time, however, in any genuine progress, the solution of each problem is itself the rise of the next (THC, 443). This is because every solution is inadequate when related to the needs of the total system of which it is a part and to which it implicitly gives rise. On these grounds every standpoint may therefore be regarded as both 'right,' according to the one set of criteria (to be examined in more detail below) and yet 'false,' when related to the needs of the scale as a whole.

There is one further criterion to which, according to Collingwood, every genuine progress must conform. A progress is not genuine if its changes occur either according to an abstract law of progress (which legislates a priori that every change is necessarily an improvement) or according to irrational prejudice. A real improvement can occur only if the impetus to change (whether this takes the form of a conscious or unconscious act) arises as a result of a genuine commitment to the standpoint, or way of life, in which this change occurs (or to which it implicitly leads). It is Collingwood's contention, however, that such a commitment is possible only to someone who knows both what he is rejecting and why – which means seeing the new life as the answer to a new question which the dialectic of history has confronted us with. And this of course, is the mark of historical knowledge. In short, writes Collingwood: "... the revolutionary can only regard his revolution as a progress in so far as he is also an historian, genuinely re-enacting in his own historical thought the life he nevertheless rejects" (IH, 326).

Such progress may be viewed, not only in terms of the logic of the overlap of classes, but also (as we have already seen) in terms of the metaphysical doctrine of historicity – that is, the doctrine that the onto-logical and epistemological condition of progress is that it can only be known to be progress by a mind which in knowing it at the same time creates it: "For progress is not a mere fact to be discovered by historical thinking: it is only through historical thinking that it comes to be at all"

(IH, 333). It is in this way that the continuity of history is established — that is, by the retention of the mind at one phase of what was achieved in the preceding phase. This doctrine provides a further basis for explaining the sense in which Einstein may be regarded as having made an advance on Newton. He does it, according to Collingwood:

> by knowing Newton's thought and retaining it within his own, in the sense that he knows what Newton's problems were, and how he solved them, and, disentangling the truth in those solutions from whatever errors prevented Newton from going further, embodying these solutions as thus disentangled in his own theory ... Thus Newton stands, in such a context, not for a man but for a theory, reigning during a certain period of scientific thought. It is only in so far as Einstein knows that theory, as a fact in the history of science, that he can make an advance upon it. Newton thus lives in Einstein in the way in which any past experience lives in the mind of the historian, as a past experience known as past — as the point from which the development with which he is concerned started — but reenacted here and now with a development of itself that is partly constructive or positive and partly critical and negative. (IH, 334)

In his preface to the *Phenomenology of Mind*, Hegel declares that the very survival of a culture depends upon how each generation relates to and relives its inheritance. That inheritance, even though it is already embodied in the culture of one's time, cannot simply be taken for granted. Its whole purpose lies in the force of its appeal to the generation to which it comes as a gift, and its very efficacy and power depends upon the style in which its incarnation into the here and now is finally consummated. That consummation rests on the ritual of labour through which the incarnated past comes to live once again in the present. Thus, Hegel writes,

> ... because the universal mind at work in the world, has had the patience to go through these forms in the long stretch of time's extent, and to take upon itself the prodigious labour of the world's history, where it bodies forth in each form the entire content of itself, as each is capable of presenting it; and because by nothing less could that all-pervading mind ever manage to become conscious of what itself is — for that reason, the individual mind, in the nature of the case, cannot expect by less toil to grasp what its own substance contains.[15]

Or, to cite Goethe's later formulation of the same insight, "What from your fathers you receive as heir, Acquire [i.e., earn] in order to possess it."[16] Like Hegel and Goethe, Collingwood stresses the fact that before the past can be either assimilated to or superseded by the present it must first be understood and lived through and this involves the laborious process of re-thinking it.

In the *Idea of History* (324 ff.) Collingwood further illustrates his notion of the progress with the example of a community of fish eaters who change their method of catching fish from a less to a more efficient way. Collingwood points out that the new, more efficient, way is not simply a better answer to the question, How do we get enough food to eat? which is no different from the question asked by the older generation and may be answered by finding new sources of food, like roots. In fact, Collingwood argues, the new form of behaviour is an answer to a new question, namely, How do we get enough food to eat and gain half a day's leisure at the same time? The real criterion of progress then is the emergence of the idea of leisure as an indispensable condition of the good life – an idea which constitutes an absolute presupposition of the new form of life. A generation which presupposes this will presumably commit itself to whatever is deemed necessary in order to create leisure – even if it means giving up the old way of life. Of course, to the older generation, for whom leisure is not yet an important reality, such changes will be regarded, not as progress, but as decadence.

As reconstructed here, Collingwood's theory of progress virtually ignores the possible contribution of pure fate, chance, and irrationality. "A truly historical view of human history," writes Collingwood, "sees everything in that history as having its own *raison d'être*" (IH, 77). What is more, he declares, "... in history as it actually happens there are no mere phenomena of decay: every decline is also a rise, and it is only the historian's personal failures of knowledge or sympathy – partly due to mere ignorance, partly to the preoccupations of his own practical life – that prevent him from seeing this double character, at once creative and destructive, of any historical process whatever" (IH, 164–5). In "The Subject Matter of History," he confines the subject of history to actions which are reflective and deliberate, that is, done on purpose (IH, 308–9). Included among such acts are political, economic, scientific, religious, moral, and aesthetic activities. In other places, as we have seen, he admits that the rationality of an action may be unconscious (SM, 85, 93–4), as is the case with absolute presuppositions (EM, 48). And early in part II of *The Idea of History*, he declares that "the recognition that what happens in history need not happen through anyone's deliberately wishing it to happen is an indispensable precondition of understanding any historical process" (IH, 48).

I would therefore contend that Collingwood's notion of rationality extends to both conscious and unconscious processes, so that the history of reflective acts "in which we know what it is that we are trying to do, so that when it is done we know that it is done by seeing that it has conformed to the standard or criterion which was our initial conception of it" (IH, 308) is in fact only one level at which history can be done, while the history of presuppositions, which are often unconscious, is another level at which it can be written. What characterizes both levels, however, is the fact that in each case the principle of rationality dominates: each level of activity yields to logical or dialectical analysis. At neither level is there any importance given to elements of chance and irrationality. That Collingwood was unable to find a role for the purely contingent element of chance points to one of the more important areas of weakness in this theory of history.

So far as the historian acts as the catalyst of historical progress he is necessarily committed to the rejection of some presuppositions together with the whole question-and-answer complexes of which they are a part. His reasons for doing so are twofold. In the first place, he will reject anything which has not been arrived at rationally and systematically, namely, dogmatisms and irrational prejudices. This is the basis upon which Collingwood himself rejected the political ideologies of Fascism and Nazism. Secondly, he is committed to rejecting as false those presuppositions which, while they may have played a systematic role in a previous standpoint, must now be rejected because they are no longer adequate to the present problems to which they have given rise. The falsity of these presuppositions derives not so much from the fact of their failure to conform to an abstract criterion of truth as from their historicity – the fact that they are necessary forms of error on a developing scale of truth.

It is in this sense that Collingwood criticizes and rejects many of the presuppositions of past philosophical systems: for example, his criticisms of Aristotle in *An Essay on Metaphysics*, which is a particularly good example of how Collingwood proceeds to evaluate the status of absolute presuppositions. Collingwood argues that Aristotle correctly conceived of his task as a search for the presuppositions of natural science, this being the science which he himself professed. He also, according to Collingwood, quite rightly recognized that it is the same science which studies God and studies his properties – thus providing a further exemplification of the intimate connection or rapprochement there must always be between the doctrines of religion and the foundations of natural science, between faith and reason. At the same time, however, Aristotle is criticized for falling into error on various points (such as the epistemological status of scientific presuppositions and the nature of motion) with the result that he provides a faulty or "incorrect" metaphysical analysis (EM, 219). And when Collingwood declares that these errors were corrected by the patristic philosophers he seems clearly to be placing the presuppositions of natural science on a progressing scale of forms which proceeds from error to truth. Precisely the same considerations apply to a variety of other examples within the *Essay* itself; in particular, the critique of psychology (pt. II, chs VIII–XII), the examination of the metaphysics of logical positivism (*ibid*, chs XIV–XVI), and the rather dramatic portrayal of the propaganda of irrationalism (*ibid*, ch. XIII).

Another place in which Collingwood seems to evaluate critically the status of absolute presuppositions is *The Principles of Art* in which, for example, he criticizes Plato's attack on contemporary art.[17] According to Collingwood, fundamental to Plato's theory of art are the beliefs "that amusement art arouses emotion which it does not direct to any outlet in practical life" and that amusement art signifies the coming of an artistic decadence and the imminent destruction of civilization itself (PA, 98). Collingwood declares that while Plato was right to hold the second he was wrong to hold the first. What is more, he continues, Plato's error was corrected by Aristotle.[18]

Further examples of the critical evaluation of presuppositions may of course be found in the *Idea of Nature* and the *Idea of History*. Knox himself cites the former as an application of the theory of the *Essay on Metaphysics* to the philosophy of nature (IN, v). But what he does not realize is that it, like the *Idea of History*, is an application, as well, of the theory of *An Essay on Philosophical Method*: a claim which seriously challenges Knox's thesis that the latter has been repudiated by the theory of *An Essay on Metaphysics*. For, not only do the *Idea of Nature* and the *Idea of History* disclose the presuppositions of science and history respectively and explain, within each discipline, the basis for the historical transition from one set to another; they also place the presuppositions which make up these histories on scales of overlapping forms. And, as we have already noted, the very fact that complexes of presuppositions can be placed on scales at all is proof not only that each is 'right' (i.e., fits into the system), but that taken together they exhibit a progress from error to truth – which is precisely what is meant in *Speculum Mentis* by the vindication of a standpoint from within.

Finally, there is the example from the *Autobiography* concerning the history of philosophy in general, and the history of political theory in particular (see above, ch. VI, s. 2). Collingwood himself declares that precisely the same considerations which led him to his theory of the history of philosophy led him also to his view of the nature of metaphysics. I have already argued that the former – which Collingwood explicitly regards as an application of the logic of question and answer (A, 58) – rests upon the doctrine of the concrete universal and constitutes, therefore, a dialectical history of errors. But if the logic of question and answer functions for metaphysics as it does for the history of philosophy, then my contention, based on the foregoing examples, that metaphysics is an application of the logic of question and answer to the organization of the history of absolute presuppositions into a scale of forms (or concrete universal), is given further support.

In actual practice, then, the theory of metaphysics rests upon the following presuppositions. *A parte subjecti*, metaphysics is an historical science in which the metaphysician (a) reconstructs in his own mind the absolute presuppositions of past thought, (b) exhibits the basis upon which one set of presuppositions gives way to another, and (c) criticizes them, that is, exposes their limitations and explains how these limitations have been overcome. These tasks can be accomplished, however, only if, *a parte objecti*, the absolute presuppositions which make up the subject matter of metaphysics satisfy at least two criteria. In the first place, they must satisfy the logical criterion of "rightness" – that is, they must be rational and intelligible – otherwise they could not even be reconstructed. In the second place, the metaphysician's activity must be guided by an a priori criterion of truth, derived not from propositional but from dialectical logic: not the truth which corresponds to a world of independently existing eternal forms, but the truth of spirit as outlined in *Speculum Mentis*. If this is a correct description of the metaphysician's actual behaviour, then the process of metaphysics is clearly in accordance with the main theme of the *Idea of History* in which, as we have already noted, Collingwood declares that "all thinking is critical thinking." To repeat:

> The historian not only re-enacts past thought, he re-enacts it in the context of his own knowledge and therefore, in re-enacting it, criticizes it, forms his own judgement of its value, corrects whatever errors he can discern in it. This criticism of thought whose history he traces is not something secondary to tracing the history of it. It is an indispensable condition of the historical knowledge itself. Nothing could be a completer error concerning the history of thought than to suppose that the historian as such merely ascertains 'what so-and-so thought', leaving it to some one else to decide 'whether it was true.' (IH, 215–16)

The criticism of past thought, which has for its goal the organization of that thought into a scale of forms, is the only genuine way in which the thought criticized can be vindicated as well – which is, after all, what, according to Collingwood, the ultimate aim of criticism ought to be (SM, 45).

Indeed, Collingwood clearly regards the historian's critical evaluation as a necessary ingredient in the very life of thought which is the object of criticism: without it there is virtually no object to be criticized (IH, 226; SM, 84, 250, 296); of everything that the mind does, it gives itself an account as it does it, and this account is inseparably bound up with the doing of the thing (SM, 84). When pursued by individual philosophers, metaphysics is neither a mere process of self-examination nor a mere process of criticism and condemnation directed against society and the thoughts of others. The metaphysician does not act in his private capacity. He is, on the contrary, the organ by which the corporate consciousness of a people examines and criticizes itself, and in so doing, makes itself. Each metaphysician, as he takes his place in the history of thought, criticizes the ideas of his contemporaries concerning what they are and what they are doing, in order thereby to criticize his own idea of what he is and what he is doing; and, in keeping with the requirements of his calling, he then re-fashions his own idea of himself in order to help re-fashion society's collective idea of itself.

Collingwood conceives of this task (as indeed he conceives of the whole of philosophy) as a 'divine' calling. Every philosopher, from Socrates on, is the organ of his own society's self-criticism, and as such is compelled to follow Socrates in the calling that led the first philosopher to condemnation and death:

That call came from Delphi; and the philosopher who makes his pilgrimage to Delphi sees there, not merely the place where long ago an event happened which was important in its time and may still interest the historian, but the place whence issued the call he still hears: a call which, to one who can hear it, is still being uttered among the fallen stones of the temple and is still echoing from the 'pathless peaks of the daughters of Parnassus.' (FML, 68)

Unless Collingwood so regarded metaphysics – in which case the latter could hardly be characterized as a purely descriptive and non-evaluative activity – he could not say, as he does, that the presuppositions according to which Plato met the crisis of his age were false (PA, 103); that the presuppositions of "irrationalism" are false and ought to be abandoned (EM, 113 ff.); that the presuppositions of positivism are false (EM, 143 ff.); that Aristotle's philosophy of science was false while that of the patristic philosophers was more correct (EM, 213 ff.). Nor could he declare that the histories of art, religion, science, and philosophy can be exhibited as dialectical histories of error in which there is nevertheless progress. And unless he so regarded metaphysics he would most certainly not have declared, as he does throughout the *Essay*, that upon its proper continuance (i.e., as an evaluative form of criticism) hangs the very future of civilization itself (EM, 46, 224).[19]

What applies to metaphysics applies, of course, to the whole of historical science. Historical knowledge, Collingwood argues in the *Idea of History*, is the medium through which humanity discovers its freedom.

The mind is what it does and the *discovery* of freedom is therefore synonymous with its activity or actuality (IH, 315, 318, 319–20). History does not presuppose mind; it is the life of mind itself, which is not mind except in so far as it both lives in historical process and knows itself as so living. Historical self-knowledge is therefore a form of historical self-making (IH, 226, 227).

Not only metaphysics but the whole of historical science is therefore regarded by Collingwood as no mere amusement "but a prime duty, whose discharge is essential to the maintenance not only of any particular form or type of reason, but of reason itself" (IH, 228). I would therefore suggest that if Collingwood appeared at times like a philosopher who was reluctant to judge, conceding to all standpoints the same degree of validity and truth, one need only read on to discover that not only did he judge, he asserted that, unless we judge, European civilization would be destroyed.

I have argued so far that metaphysics, as Collingwood conceives it, may be properly regarded as a dialectical history of errors, and as such, rests primarily on two related sets of concepts. In the first place there is the concept of 'logical efficacy,' indicating which presuppositions may be judged 'right' but not 'true.' In the second place, there is the concept of historical change, according to which (a) one set of presuppositions is replaced by another and (b) there is exhibited in this change a gradual progress towards truth. The first point, concerning the logical efficacy of presuppositions, will be considered more fully in section 8 below. The second point, concerning the conditions of historicity, will be dealt with in section 9 below.

8 THE THEORY OF ERROR AND THE CONDITIONS OF HISTORICITY

According to the implicit theory of the *Essay on Metaphysics*, metaphysics is a history of errors. These errors are neither deliberately made (this would be an act of the corrupt consciousness) nor absolute. They are 'systematic,' that is to say, necessary stages in the development of thought. History is a process in which thought creates itself by reflecting on its own presuppositions, thereby disclosing to itself the inconsistencies which exist between what it explicitly and implicitly presupposes. This process is exemplified in various ways: in the historical transition from one age to another, in the phenomenological development from one form of experience to another, in the historical development within a single form from one theory to another, and, finally, within the thought of a single thinker.

I have further argued that Collingwood's own philosophy is exemplary of this process, that the changes in his thinking are 'systematic' rather than radical. In such a case, where we find a man presupposing certain things which he later abandons, we should not immediately accuse him of inconsistency or of falling into fallacies. We should judge his work as a whole, for if it is a genuine philosophy it will of necessity involve systematic fallacies. It is only by becoming involved in the so-called fallacy in the first place that the philosopher gains the necessary insight which enables him finally to overthrow it, and in this way to progress up the scale towards a 'truer' self-knowledge. This means that the fallacies or errors which have been committed along the way are somehow 'necessary' and 'right.' In the language of *Ruskin's Philosophy*, the weakness which lies at the centre of a man's "ring of principles" and which is responsible for that ring breaking under the strain of criticism – which threatens, in other words, the alleged consupponibility of that ring – is, in a very important sense, a necessary ingredient for the healthy dialectic or progress which every ring of principles is required to undergo.

In both *An Essay on Philosophical Method* and his 1935 correspondence with Ryle, Collingwood cites the example of a philosopher who, in the course of expounding his ethics, commits (what his critics would call) the "fallacy of calculation" when *within* one of the three categories of pleasure, knowledge, and virtue, he compares particular manifestations of that category (e.g., different kinds of pleasures), but when he comes to the *relation* between the same categories *qua* categories, he drops this principle and follows a different method (EPM, 77–80; CRC, I, 15). Collingwood himself does precisely the same thing. In each of the metaphysical exercises on history, nature, philosophy, and art, where he is working *ab intra* within a single form, he makes certain distinctions (such as the distinction between nature and history, hypothetical and categorical thinking, etc.) which from the absolute standpoint are 'philosophical errors.' At the same time, they are recognized to be necessary, not only to the standpoint in question, but also to the dialectic of question and answer which places each standpoint in its proper place on the scale. To someone who has not yet recognized the dialectical nature of Collingwood's thought these distinctions will appear as examples of "the fallacy of false disjunction," while the alleged identity of philosophy and history in the *Essay on Metaphysics* will be taken as an example of the "fallacy of identified coincidents." Such a critic will accuse Collingwood of gross inconsistency. But Collingwood's reply (which was already implicit in *Speculum Mentis*) is neatly expressed in his first letter to Ryle:

You pillory me unfairly; on page x, it is true, I do fall into your fallacy; but on page y I correct it; you ought to take my work as a whole, and interpret x in the light of y; if you did so, you would see that the error was only a temporary slip at worst; and, at best, you might wonder whether it was not merely the exploration of a provisional point of view. (CRC, I, 15)

This theory of the 'rightness' of systematic errors may be further illustrated by various texts taken from the *New Leviathan* and the *Principles of Art*.

In the *New Leviathan* Collingwood offers the following definition of 'rightness':

The 'right' key for a given lock is any key, (not one key, but any one of a *set of right keys*) which in the case of that lock obeys the rules, which a locksmith has to know, governing the relations between lock-form and key-form. The 'right' drug for a disease is a drug which conforms with the rules, which physicians have to know, correlating diseases with drugs. The 'right' time is time kept by a timepiece whose movements conform with a rule correlating them with the movements of the standard clock at Greenwich Observatory. (NL, 112)

Suppose we adapt this criterion to the interpretation of history. Just as the 'right' action is an action that conforms to a rule, so the 'right' answer is the one that conforms to a rule. And just as there can be any number of 'right' actions which are not one's duty so there can be any number of 'right' answers which are not true. It follows, then, that any historian's interpretation of the past is the 'right' one so long as it proceeds according to the 'right rules,' that is, the rules which historians use in order to transform evidence into facts.

In the *Idea of History* Collingwood defines the process of historical reconstruction as a process of inference according to a complicated system of rules and assumptions (IH, 133). We have already (ch. v, s. 2) taken note of the 1928 essay in which Collingwood compares history to a game which is won not by the player who can reconstruct "what really happened," but by the one who can show that his view of what happened is the one which is supported by the evidence available to all players, even when criticized up to the hilt (LHK, 218; cf. IH, 246). Thus, for example, so long as Augustine, Tillemont, Gibbon, and Mommsen each followed the rules and concluded only what the evidence at their disposal indicated – in other words, so long as they were behaving like genuine historians – there is, as Collingwood correctly argues, no point in asking which was the 'right' point of view. Each was the only one possible for the man who adopted it (IH, xii). And when it is realized that not only does the available evidence change, but the principles by which this evidence is interpreted are also subject to change (IH, 248), then the existence of a variety of contrary but 'right' points of view is further accounted for.

This means, of course, that in history, as in all serious matters, no achievement is final. Collingwood is quick to point out, however, that this is not an argument for historical scepticism:

> It is only the discovery of a second dimension of historical thought, the history of history: the discovery that the historian himself, together with the here-and-now which forms the total body of evidence available to him, is part of the process he is studying, has his own place in that process, and can see it only from the point of view which at this moment he occupies within it. (IH, 248)

Indeed, Collingwood argues in "The Limits of Historical Knowledge" that scepticism is really "a self-contradictory position because it materially claims to possess the knowledge, which formally it denies; therefore whatever leads logically to scepticism leads to self-contradiction and is false" (LHK, 217).

The same considerations apply to the dialectic of standpoints in *Speculum Mentis*. Each standpoint is 'right' and yet 'false.' For it is only by committing the errors from which the differentiae of the separate standpoints derive, that the abstract construction of art, religion, science, and history come into existence at all. Thus Collingwood could easily have asserted, about the forms of experience in general, the sort of thing that (according to Knox) he wrote about the history of history (IH, xii): that art looks at reality from the point of view of the imagination; religion from the point of view of faith; science from the point of view of the abstract concept; history from the point of view of the concrete fact. There is no point in asking which is the 'right' point of view. Each is the only one possible for the person who adopts it.

Further evidence for this interpretation of the relation between the 'right' and the 'true' may be found in the theory of art as language, as expounded in the *Principles of Art*. There is a strong analogy between the expression of feelings in works of art (i.e., aesthetic language) and the expression of thought in both propositions and actions. The object of history is the reconstruction of past thought, using as evidence the expression of that thought in the present. In the same way, a work of art – for example, a piece of music – is not just a collection of noises, it is the tune

> in the composer's head: The noises made by the performers, and heard by the audience, are not the music at all; they are only the means by which the audience, if they listen intelligently (not otherwise), can reconstruct for themselves the imaginary tune that existed in the composer's head. (PA, 139)

Language then is not, itself, art or history but is the record of art or history, the means whereby the latter can be reconstructed.

The question now arises, Under what conditions can language be the occasion of the reconstruction of the aesthetic experience? The answer is implied in the following declaration:

> The definition of any given kind of thing is also the definition of a good thing of that kind: for a thing that is good in its kind is only a thing which possesses the attributes of that kind. To call things good and bad is to imply success and failure. (PA, 280)

In other words, a work of art is a conscious activity (the fact that there are also unconscious elements involved in no way affects our argument) in which the artist is trying to do something definite, and in that attempt he may succeed or he may fail. In so far as the artist has succeeded he has provided a basis for reconstructing the aesthetic experience which is the art object proper. In so far as he fails he has made it impossible to reconstruct the aesthetic experience because no such experience exists. The so-called 'bad' art, which is the name we give to this failure of expression is really a negative rather than a positive term; it is our way of indicating that in this case the 'language' or 'external expression' or 'evidence' is unable to lead us any further to the mind of the artist:

> What the artist is trying to do is to express a given emotion. To express it, and to express it well, are the same thing. To express it badly is not one way of expressing it ... it is failing to express it. A bad work of art is an activity in which the agent tries to express a given emotion, but fails. (PA, 282)

For these reasons we can speak of a history and theory of good art, but we cannot speak of a history and theory of bad art. We can only write the history and theory of something that exists. Bad art, however, is a 'failure' on the part of the artist to bring something into existence. One can only write the history and theory of a process which is rational, systematic, and guided by discernible criteria. And we can only know what these principles are when they become embodied in something actual. If the artist fails in this regard there is no way of knowing what his principles and intentions were. No artist can set out deliberately to 'fail.' Thus failing to produce a work of good art can never be construed as success in producing a work of bad art. Except in so far as the artist sets out consciously to produce a work of good art, he is not an artist proper but only one falsely so called. "In art falsely so-called there is no failure to express, because there is no attempt at expression; there is only an attempt (whether successful or not) to do something else" (PA, 282).

Suppose we treat the relation between the artist's intentionality and the work of art proper as an analogy from which to view the structure of expression in general. In the same sense that aesthetic consciousness cannot be reconstructed, except in so far as it has succeeded in expressing

itself, so thought in general cannot be reconstructed except in so far as
it has been properly expressed: it must be the 'right' answer to the question it was intended to answer, or the 'right' solution to the problem it
was intended to solve. In this sense 'rightness' is equivalent to good art.
If the agent has failed to express himself properly, then there is no object
for the historian to reconstruct, because just as in art, so in thought in
general, "expressing [a thought] ... is the same thing as becoming
conscious of it" (PA, 282). The act of consciousness is an act of selfknowledge, in which the agent makes himself as well as the world he is
coming to know (PA, 291), so that the object proper, whether it be art
or history, is the product of the agent's *successful* attempt to express
himself, answer his question, or solve his problem. The very existence of
the historian's object depends not just on the skill of the historian, but
on the agent's success in expressing himself.

This is presumably what is implied by the principle, cited in the *Idea
of History*: "After the historian has ascertained the facts, there is no
further process of inquiring into their causes. When he knows what
happened, he already knows why it happened." (IH, 214) This is just
another way of emphasizing that in order to establish what the answer to
a question is, we must first know both the question and the presuppositions which lie at the basis of the question-and-answer complex.[20] Unless
there is some rational or logical connection between question and answer
– which is all that we mean by 'right' – then no amount of skill could
establish anything more than an educated guess. And, as already noted,
guessing is not history (A, 70).

According to these terms, Collingwood's claim in the *Autobiography* that the historian's success in reconstructing an agent's views is
proof that the agent in question has successfully answered his question
begins to make sense. For indeed, if a person is so confused in his own
mind that he himself does not know what he is doing, we can hardly
expect his thought to become a proper object of history. Thus Collingwood writes about Leibniz:

> If Leibniz when he wrote this passage was so confused in his mind as to make a
> complete mess of the job of solving his problem, he was bound at the same time
> to mix up his own tracks so completely that no reader could see quite clearly what
> his problem had been. For one and the same passage states his solution and
> serves as evidence of what the problem was. The fact that we can identify his
> problem is proof that he has solved it; for we only know what the problem was by
> arguing back from the solution. (A, 69–70)

It may even be possible to explain Collingwood's strange remark about
Villeneuve. He says that we cannot reconstruct Villeneuve's plan be-

cause "he did not succeed in carrying it out" (A, 70). This is misleading if it means simply that in carrying out his plan he committed an 'error,' and because of this it is not possible to understand what he was trying to do. The reason why we cannot reconstruct his thought is not that he committed an 'error' – we have already seen that errors and systematic fallacies are necessary ingredients in every form of activity. It is because his behaviour is not systematic, that is to say, does not conform to the minima criteria for logical intelligibility. We cannot in history reconstruct 'irrational' behaviour. Thus Collingwood presupposes, as a cardinal principle of his own philosophy of history, Hegel's famous declaration, in the introduction to his lectures on the philosophy of history, that "The only thought which philosophy brings with it to the contemplation of history, is the simple conception of Reason; that Reason is the Sovereign of the World; that the history of the world, therefore, presents us with a rational process."[21]

9 TRUTH AND HISTORICITY: THE PRESUPPOSITIONS OF METAPHYSICS

According to Knox's interpretation of Collingwood's philosophy, metaphysics is a purely descriptive science that is unable to provide a rational account of changes from one set of presuppositions to another. For Knox this is evidence that Collingwood has abandoned the ideal that there can be a rational explanation of history; it is fate rather than reason which is the source and ground of historical change. The historian is therefore driven to refer the ground of the explanation of changes in presuppositions either to 'unconscious psychological processes' (IH, xiv) or to faith (IH, xvi). According to Knox, the latter alternative was adopted in the 1928 pamphlet *Faith and Reason*; the former is the position of the *Essay on Metaphysics*, as the following footnote from the *Essay* will testify:

I have hinted above (p. 45) and said explicitly below (pp. 49 seqq.) that absolute presuppositions change. A friend thinks readers may credit me with the opinion that such changes are merely 'changes of fashion', and asks me to explain what, otherwise, I believe them to be.

A 'change of fashion' is a superficial change, symptomatic perhaps of deeper and more important changes, but not itself deep or important. A man adopts it merely because other men do so, or because advertisers, salesmen, etc., suggest it to him. My friend's formula 'if we like to start new dodges, we may' describes very well the somewhat frivolous type of consciousness with which we adopt or originate these superficial changes. But an absolute presupposition is not a 'dodge', and people who 'start' a new one do not start it because they 'like' to start it. People are not ordinarily aware of their absolute presuppositions (p. 43), and are not, therefore, thus aware of changes in them; such a change, therefore, cannot be a matter of choice. Nor is there anything superficial or frivolous about it. It is the most radical change a man can undergo, and entails the abandonment of all his most firmly established habits and standards for thought and action.

Why, asks my friend, do such changes happen? Briefly, because the absolute presuppositions of any given society, at any given phase of its history, form a structure which is subject to 'strains' (pp. 74, 76) of greater or less intensity, which are 'taken up' (p. 74) in various ways, but never annihilated. If the strains are too great, the structure collapses and is replaced by another, which will be a modification of the old with the destructive strain removed; a modification not consciously devised but created by a process of unconscious thought. (EM, 48)

Knox is supported in his views by Donagan, who argues that Collingwood's claim that absolute presuppositions are neither true nor false leads to scepticism:

From Collingwood's theorem that absolute presuppositions are neither true nor false it follows inexorably that no good reason can be given for preferring one to another; and, if that is so, then changes in absolute presuppositions must be made either for bad reasons or for change's sake.

According to Donagan such a view not only leads to scepticism with regard to the possibility of providing a rational explanation of changes from one set of presuppositions to another, it leads also to scepticism regarding the possibility of criticizing (according to the criteria of truth and falsity) the answers to the questions to which absolute presuppositions give rise. This is equivalent to saying that, on Collingwood's view, the ground of changes in presuppositions is irrational. Donagan concludes that "Collingwood's projected reformation [of metaphysics] was therefore too riddled with confusions and contradictions to stay afloat; and no considerable part of its wreckage can be saved."[22]

The Knox-Donagan interpretation is not only inconsistent with the conclusions of my own interpretation, it is plainly inconsistent with what Collingwood himself says and does. The very definition of metaphysics as historical implies that it is necessarily committed to giving a rational account. Collingwood explicitly declares that the metaphysician must follow the historical process by which one set of presuppositions has turned into another (A, 66; EM, 73). The metaphysician, he writes, must explain why such and such a people at such and such a time make such and such absolute presuppositions (EM, 73). The answer to this question will take the form, "Because they or the predecessors from whom they inherited their civilization had previously made such and such a different set of absolute presuppositions, and because such and such a process of change converted the one set into another" (EM, 74). Thus, in order to account for one set of presuppositions the historian must relate it to a previous set. But in what way can one set of presuppositions enter into the explanation of another set? Collingwood's answer rests, in effect, on the claim that while the ideal of any given set of presuppositions is to be "consupponible," at no particular time is this ideal completely achieved. On the contrary, any given set of presuppositions is subject to a variety of stresses and strains. In becoming aware of its own basic presuppositions consciousness consequently becomes aware as well of the basic inconsistencies and inadequacies which characterize these presuppositions, with the result that the original presuppositions give way to new ones which are more consupponible than the previous ones, but still far from ideal.

Thus the strains which, according to Collingwood, lie at the basis of changes from one set of presuppositions to another, far from being irrational, are highly rational. Although Collingwood does not himself seem to have been aware of it, his own account of how these strains operate suggests that they are of two kinds, the first of which I will call logical, the second existential. By a logical strain I mean the sort represented, for example, by the contradiction (discussed earlier in ch. v, s. 2) within the standpoint of history between the presuppositions of the claim that the object of history is a fact which exists independently of the subject, and the presuppositions of the claim that historical perception is a form of mediation. Another example of this kind of strain is the contradiction within the standpoint of art, between (a) the claim of art to be sheer supposal and (b) the context of assertion in terms of which this claim is made (see above, ch. IV, s. 1).

By an existential strain I mean the kind which is exemplified by the situation in which a new standpoint arises as a result not merely of logical analysis, but of changes within the structure of experience itself. Thus, for example, within the history of art one might argue that the transition from the early symbolic representations of Egyptian and Babylonian art to the classical forms of Hellenic art occurs because, as a result of the very attempt to represent the object symbolically (by means of a temple, for example), the actual experience of the object was altered in such a way as to require a new form of representation, namely, the classical forms of Greek sculpture. Likewise, in *Speculum Mentis* the mind's representation of itself as art in general has existential implications which lead to the attempt at a new representation: religion. Consciousness, in other words, in becoming aware of the presuppositions which underlie any given standpoint, realizes as well that they are inconsistent with certain aspects of experience which are only brought into focus by the attempt to answer questions which arise from our original presuppositions. The result again is that the original presuppositions are replaced by new ones which are more adequate to the needs of experience. This is the existential dimension of the quest for consupponibility.

Both kinds of strains, the logical and the existential, can be accounted for in terms of the dialectical logic of the overlap of classes and the scale of forms as outlined in *Speculum Mentis* and *An Essay on Philosophical Method*. This claim may be supported by the following passages from the *Essay on Metaphysics*:

> The essential thing about historical 'phases' is that each of them gives place to another; not because one is violently destroyed by alien forces impinging on its fabric from without by war or from within by revolution, but because each of them while it lives is working at turning itself into the next ... The dynamics of history is not yet completely understood when it is grasped that each phase is converted into the next by a process of change. The relation between phase and process is more intimate than that. One phase changes into another because the first phase was in unstable equilibrium and had in itself the seeds of change, and indeed of that change. Its fabric was not at rest; it was always under strain. If the world of history is a world in which *tout passe, tout lasse, tout casse*, the analysis of the internal strains to which a given constellation of historical facts is subjected, and of the means by which it 'takes up' these strains, or prevents them from breaking it in places, is not the least part of an historian's work ... Where there is no strain there is no history. A civilization does not work out its own details by a kind of static logic in which every detail exemplifies in its own way one and the same formula. It works itself out by a dynamic logic in which different and at first sight incompatible formulae somehow contrive a precarious coexistence; one dominant here, another there; the recessive formula never ceasing to operate, but functioning as a kind of minority report which, though the superficial historian may ignore it, serves to a more acute eye as evidence of tendencies actually existing which may have been dominant in the past and may be dominant in the future. (EM, 73, 74, 75)

The main points of these passages, so far as the issue at hand is concerned, are the claims that the source of historical change is internal strains; that an analysis of these strains "is not the least part of the historian's work"; and that this analysis must be conducted according to a "dynamic logic." How else are we to interpret these concepts except in terms of the dialectical logic as expounded in *Speculum Mentis* and *An Essay on Philosophical Method*?

A further clue to the interpretation of these passages is provided in the

Essay itself, in a passage dealing with Hegel: "If Hegel's influence on nineteenth century historiography was on the whole an influence for the good, it was because historical study for him was first and foremost a study of internal strains" (EM, 75). Hegel's theory, which apparently lies at the basis of these remarks in the *Essay on Metaphysics*, is explained more fully in the *Idea of History*, in a passage which may be offered as a commentary on the above texts from the *Essay*:

> Now it is true that we do not need to use terms like opposition (let me call them *dialectical* terms) when we are talking only of the outward events of history; but when we are talking of the inward thoughts which underlie these events it seems to me that we cannot avoid them. For example, we can describe the mere outward events of the colonization of New England without using any dialectical language; but when we try to see these events as a deliberate attempt on the part of the Pilgrim Fathers to carry out in terms of practice a Protestant idea of life, we are talking about thoughts and we must describe them in dialectical terms; we must for example speak of the opposition between the congregational idea of religious institutions and the episcopal idea, and admit that the relation between the idea of a priesthood based on apostolic succession and the idea of one not so based is a dialectical relation. From this point of view Greek civilization is the realizing of the Greek idea of life, that is, the Greek conception of man; Roman civilization is the realizing of the Roman conception of man; and between these two conceptions the relation ... is a dialectical relation. (IH, 119)

If, as the above passages suggest, the transition from one set of presuppositions to another is a dialectical one, then it may be further argued (as indeed I have already done) that the presuppositions which undergo historical change, while they are certainly neither true nor false according to the terms of propositional logic, nevertheless exhibit a gradual progress: a progress which takes the form of a dialectical history of errors, a scale of forms, or a series of constellations of presuppositions which become more and more consuponible (i.e., come more and more to approximate the absolute standpoint).

The concept of metaphysics as a dialectical history of errors may be further explicated by examining it in the context of another doctrine which in the *Idea of History* is described as the doctrine of the "*a priori* imagination": a doctrine which underlies Collingwood's proposal for an a priori construction of history. This doctrine is explicitly expounded in parts III (ss. 5–7) and V (s. 2) of the *Idea of History*. It is true, of course, that these texts were composed in 1936 and 1935, respectively, which would probably invalidate them as suitable criteria for judging the doctrine of the *Essay* for anyone who has accepted Knox's interpretation that after 1936 Collingwood changed his mind radically. In answer to such objections I can only insist that, apart from such evidence as I have already cited for bringing this interpretation into question, I favour my own hypothesis because by assuming it the text is rendered that much more intelligible. I shall therefore continue to suppose what the evidence leads me to believe, namely, that the doctrine of the a priori imagination is a fundamental presupposition of *An Essay on Metaphysics*.

The doctrine in question may be summed up as follows. History is a kind of thinking in which the historian argues from evidence to facts according to a complicated set of rules and assumptions. The employment of these principles is guided by what Collingwood calls a "criterion of historical truth" (IH, 237). This criterion operates (a) in the historian's attempt to select from among the available or potential evidence that which is relevant; (b) in his reconstruction from this evidence of the events which he hopes to establish as a fact; and (c) in his attempt to criticize both the evidence and the facts which on the basis of this evidence he establishes. Such a criterion cannot be derived from history alone, for except in terms of it there can be no history. Nor can it be derived from the judgments of other historians for this would destroy the autonomy of our own judgments. It cannot even be derived from our own experience, as Bradley and Dilthey have suggested, for this presupposes that human nature, like nature proper, is permanent and unchanging and that whatever holds today must have held yesterday. What is required, then, is a criterion which arises from within the historian's own experience, yet is not purely subjective – which is objective and universal without threatening the autonomy of individual thought. This criterion, according to Collingwood, is the "*a priori* imagination" and the historian's picture of the past is therefore the product of the a priori imagination (IH, 245).

By imagination, of course, Collingwood does not mean the pure imagination of *Speculum Mentis*. Pure imagination, the source of arbitrary supposal and intuition, is the most primitive level of imagination and exists therefore at the bottom of the scale. The a priori imagination is imagination raised to its highest power, existing at the top of the scale, at what I have called the third level. It is here that the rapprochement between imagination and reason becomes fully manifest for the first time.

Within the a priori imagination itself a further scale may be distinguished, for there are different senses in which the a priori imagination functions. Thus in addition to its historical function there are at least two others from which the historical imagination should be distinguished.

In the first place, there is the imaginative reconstruction of the artist. A novelist, for example, composes a story where parts are played by various characters. But although the characters and incidents are all alike imaginary, the whole aim of the novelist is to show the characters acting and the incidents developing in a manner determined by a necessity internal to themselves: "The story, if it is a good story, cannot develop otherwise than as it does; the novelist in imagining it cannot imagine it developing except as it does develop" (IH, 242).[23]

Another familiar function, according to Collingwood, is the perceptual imagination:

> ... supplementing and consolidating the data of perception in the way so well analysed by Kant, by presenting to us objects of possible perception, which are not actually perceived: the under side of this table, the inside of an unopened egg, the back of the moon. Here again the imagination is *a priori*: we cannot but imagine what cannot but be there. (IH, 242)

This account of the perceptual imagination is fully consistent with Collingwood's claim in the early writings (SM, 204 ff.; ST, 74–5) that perception involves an element of mediation (see above, ch. V, s. 2, and below, ch. IX, ss. 1–2). This mediating factor is now seen to derive from the activity of the a priori imagination.

In history the a priori imagination functions in ways which are analogous to both aesthetic and perceptual imagination; or, to put it in terms of the logic of the overlap of classes, since the historical imagination occupies a place on the same scale as the perceptual and aesthetic imagination, traces of the latter two forms are present in the former. Indeed, as we have already noted above (ch. V, s. 2, p. 137), the only difference between what we ordinarily call perception and what we ordinarily call historical thinking is that the interpretive work which in the former is only implicit and only revealed by reflective analysis is in the latter explicit and impossible to overlook (NAPH, 168 ff.). Collingwood now characterizes the work of the historical imagination as "interpolation." The attempt to derive from statements borrowed from authorities (i.e., the evidence) other statements implied by them (IH, 240).[24] This definition may be compared with another description of historical thinking as a thoroughly inferential process proceeding according to a complicated system of rules and assumptions (IH, 133). This too may be seen as a function of the a priori imagination.

Although Collingwood himself does not so describe it, the process of interpolation may be seen to operate on at least three distinct levels. These levels may be illustrated by means of the following example, cited by Collingwood himself, concerning Caesar's alleged trip from Rome to Gaul. Concerning this event Collingwood writes: "Our authorities tell us that on one day Caesar was in Rome and on a later day in Gaul"

(IH, 240). Given this information, the historian's job is to "interpolate" what happened between the two fixed points which are Rome and Gaul. The first moment of interpolation rests on the a priori presupposition that if Caesar were in Rome and Gaul at successive times he must have travelled from one point to the other. This is perhaps the most general application of the a priori imagination and resembles Kant's schematization of the category of causality. In this respect the historical imagination resembles the ordinary act of perception, as illustrated by the example of a ship moving at sea:

If we look out over the sea and perceive a ship, and five minutes later look again and perceive it in a different place, we find ourselves obliged to imagine it as having occupied intermediate positions when we were not looking. That is already an example of historical thinking; and it is not otherwise that we find ourselves obliged to imagine Caesar as having travelled from Rome to Gaul when we are told that he was in these different places at these successive times. (IH, 241)

But while our authorities tell us that on one day Caesar was in Rome and on a later day in Gaul, they tell us nothing about the particular details concerning his journey from one place to another (IH, 240). This introduces the need for a second level of interpolation; a level which is governed by such criteria as consistency and coherence. In this respect history bears a strong resemblance to novel writing – the aim of which, like that of history, is to construct a picture that is coherent and consistent, that makes sense (IH, 245).[25] Nothing is admissible for either the historian or the novelist except what is necessary for the continuity and consistency of the whole; and the judge of this necessity is the a priori imagination.

But while history resembles novel writing with respect to such criteria as coherence and consistency, it differs from novel writing in so far as what history seeks is not just consistent but "true" (IH, 246). In other words, in history there is no necessary connection between the artistic merit of the account and its historical truth. In the case of art, however, "So far as the utterance is a good work of art, it is a true utterance; its artistic merit and its truth are the same thing" (PA, 287). The historian, argues Collingwood, must show that the picture that he provides is a picture of events "as they really happened" (IH, 246). There is a distinction, in other words, between a "legitimate historical construction" and the "arbitrary or merely fanciful" construction of art. This distinction, in keeping with the dialectic of *Speculum Mentis*, is between the standpoint of supposal which characterizes art and that of assertion which characterizes history. Thus Collingwood writes, concerning the example of Caesar's trip to Gaul, if we filled up the narrative of Caesar's doings with fanciful details such as the names of the persons he met on the way, and what he said to them, the construction would be arbitrary: it would be in fact the kind of construction which is done by an historical novelist. But if our construction involves nothing that is not necessitated by the evidence, it is a legitimate historical construction of a kind without which there can be no history at all. (IH, 240–1)

Compare this statement with a previous statement from part I of the *Idea of History* concerning the status of Thucydides as an historian. Collingwood characterizes Thucydides as "the man in whom the historical thought of Herodotus was overlaid and smothered beneath anti-historical motives" (IH, 30), primarily because Thucydides was interested not in what really happened but only in the general sense of what happened. He therefore reconstructed his speeches according to the criterion of what was roughly appropriate to the occasion.[26] Such a criterion, according to Collingwood, is highly subjective, and is derived in the last analysis merely from what Thucydides himself thought was appropriate (IH, 30). Collingwood therefore cites with approval Grote's famous charge that Thucydides' histories contain more imagination than history (IH, 30).[27]

There is a difference, then, between the necessity of the imagination and the necessity of history; and the basis of this difference is the fact that the historian, unlike the novelist, is tied down to the "evidence." In history, according to Collingwood, we admit nothing that is not necessitated by the evidence (EM, 56; IH, 246; A, 139; RB/ES, 259); indeed, it is precisely this relation of the historian's construction to the evidence upon which it is based which is the source of its truth. The true picture is the "right" picture which is arrived at by the person who can show that his view of what happened is the one which is supported by the evidence available to all historians, even when thoroughly criticized (LTK, 218). Thus Collingwood writes in the *Idea of History*:

The only way in which the historian or any one else can judge, even tentatively, of its truth is by considering this relation; and, in practice, what we mean by asking whether an historical statement is true is whether it can be justified by an appeal to the evidence; for a truth unable to be so justified is to the historian a thing of no interest. (IH, 246)[28]

Collingwood's characterization of this second level of interpolation as an attempt to establish the "truth" about what really happened, will no doubt lead some to charge him with inconsistency, on the grounds that this definition of history presupposes the very realist epistemology that he claims to have repudiated. Such a charge, however, begs the question by assuming a realist interpretation of 'what really happened.' For the realist, this is equivalent to 'whatever corresponds to the facts.' Realism presupposes the concept of the past as a separately existing body of facts conceived as things-in-themselves in order to distinguish the "objective" past from the concept of the past as a mere mode of present experience. But, as Collingwood himself points out, realism does not account for the possibility of historical knowledge. Realism in fact leads to scepticism, a conclusion which can be avoided only by replacing the concept of knowledge as that which conforms to the past as a thing-in-itself with the concept of knowledge as the outcome of a "game" which is won not by the player who can reconstruct "what really happened" but by the player "who can show that his view of what happened is the one which is supported by the evidence accessible to all players" (LHK, 218). In short, there is no way of knowing what view is "correct" except by finding out what the evidence proves when critically interpreted.

Thus the so-called rules which determine the validity of history, and which are subject to change, constitute both a permanent and a changing definition of what historical thinking is. The permanent definition is that historical thinking is nothing else than interpreting all the available evidence with the maximum degree of critical skill. The changing definition will depend upon what is meant at any given time by "critical skill." But, whatever is meant by this, the historian's picture of the past will always be a function of the historian's own critical activity rather than of the so-called real or independently existing past conceived as a thing-in-itself. There is therefore no longer any contrast between the historian's picture of the past and the real past. The historian's picture of the past, in so far as it is historical at all (i.e., conforms to the criteria of historical thinking), is the real past.

In the *Autobiography* Collingwood points out that this definition of historical thinking, of thinking about "what really happened," presupposes "that the past which an historian studies is not a dead past, but a past which in some sense is still living in the present" (A, 97), a notion which coincides with what Collingwood had always believed to be the very essence of knowledge itself: "the principle that in philosophical inquiry what we are trying to do is not to discover something of which until now we have been ignorant, but to know better something which in some sense we knew already" (EPM, 11). In the *New Leviathan* this principle is described as the distinguishing characteristic of the sciences of mind as opposed to the natural sciences: "whereas from a natural science a man often learns something utterly new to him, the sciences of mind teach him only *things of which he was already conscious*" (NL, 5–6). Hence Collingwood's lifelong concern for a new theory of knowledge "devoted to the special problems raised by historical thinking" (A, 77). It was clear that realism, with its emphasis on historical knowledge as correspondence with the past per se, was virtually an attempt to extend the methodology of the natural sciences to the field of history (A, 85). But, if history is to be possible at all, its possibility cannot be accounted for in the same way that natural science is accounted for. The theory of historical knowledge must be a theory about how the historian converts his present experience into knowledge of the past. And this is virtually a theory about the working of the a priori imagination. It is an act of imagination because it is an attempt to construct what, prior to the construction, is as yet "non-existent," but which nevertheless does exist as an implicit part of the historian's present experience. The imagination is that capacity of mind to render explicit what is already implicit.

For Collingwood then 'what really happened' refers not to an independently existing thing-in-itself, but to a past incapsulated in the present; it refers not to a dead but to a living past. The historical past is the product and activity of the historical imagination; it is 'transcendentally real' and not 'transcendentally ideal.' There are therefore no fixed points against which the historian can check his conclusions (IH, 245, 247). Not only the evidence but the rules according to which the evidence is interpolated are in a constant state of flux. Finding out "what really happened" is an ideal limit which is only gradually realized through the development of the historian's own historical consciousness. This is why the writing of history is a function of the growth of consciousness itself. "What really happened" is not a picture of the world as it is in itself, it is a statement about the world *quoad nos*. There is a difference, however, between how the world appears to be for us and what it really is for us. The latter is the necessary standpoint which mind in its present form of existence, subject to the limitations of its presently existing nature, is required to adopt. The criterion which the a priori imagination furnishes for determining the truth of history is a criterion, therefore, not for judging between experience and the thing-in-itself, but a criterion for distinguishing between two kinds of experience, two ways in which the mind experiences itself – for distinguishing, in other words, between the object as it appears to consciousness and the object as it is per se for consciousness. The dialectic of historical thinking is a dialectic within experience itself. Thus as consciousness itself develops towards truth and selfhood the past as an object of this consciousness must likewise be subject to a similar development.

The second level of interpolation, then, is characterized not only by the criterion of consistency but by the criterion of establishing truth on the basis of the evidence. But this does not yet make our construction fully historical. For what is imaginatively inferred in history is not simply an event (which is either immediately perceived or else established on the basis of authority alone) but a past event, which is, moreover, no mere event but an "action" having an inner thought side as well as an outer side (IH, 213). It is therefore not sufficient to establish merely the details concerning the external aspects of the event; it is necessary, at the same time, to interpret these details in terms of thought; for only when an event is so mediated can knowledge of it be genuinely historical.

At the epistemological level this ontological distinction between an event and an action gives rise to the distinction between perceiving and what Collingwood calls "rethinking": a distinction, incidentally, which must be understood according to the terms not of propositional but of dialectical logic, so that what Collingwood calls rethinking, rather than being radically distinct and separate from the act of perceiving, is, on the contrary, the becoming explicit of what is already implicit in perception. Perception and rethinking, in other words, do not mutually exclude one another, they overlap. This brings us to the third level of interpolation, the level which is characterized by the criterion of "rethinking." What makes an object historical, according to Collingwood, is not just the fact that it has been established according to the proper rules of inference, but also that it has been reconstructed (i.e., rethought) in the mind of the historian (IH, 282 ff.). The first two levels of interpolation are primarily methodological; the third is fundamentally "teleological" – it states the goal which the application of the method of history hopes to achieve.[29] Thus, to return to the example of Caesar's trip from Rome to Gaul, our knowledge of it is not historical until we include in our historical narrative what, in his actual discussion of the example, Collingwood himself fails to include, namely, a reconstruction of Caesar's thought. In so doing, we are only applying to this particular example a principle which is explicitly established by Collingwood himself when on another occasion he cites, as examples of historical events, Caesar's trip across the Rubicon at one date and the spilling of his blood on the floor of the senate house at another date. The former, he declares, can only be understood in terms of "Caesar's defiance of Republican law," the latter in terms of "the clash of constitutional policy between himself and his assassins" (IH, 213). In each case the historian's task is to reconstruct the intentionality of the event under consideration.

There are, of course, many difficulties arising from Collingwood's theory of historical knowledge. To deal with these in any detail would require a special study which is beyond the scope of this book. My main concern has been to disclose the considerations which led Collingwood to argue that the principles according to which the a priori imagination in history operates are not the same as the principles of aesthetic and perceptual imagination, because in history certain problems arise which do not arise either for art or for perception. This explains why we cannot simply borrow the principles of history from the principles of aesthetics or science but must arrive at them by means of a separate investigation, a philosophical critique of historical reason, having as its goal the discovery of those principles which constitute the necessary, that is, a priori, conditions of the possibility of achieving, not simply a perception, but an imaginative reconstruction or rethinking of the past. Such a critique would take the form of a transcendental analytic which, as Collingwood's critique of Kant is intended to show (EM, ch. 24), is really a form of metaphysics. For the transcendental analytic of historical reason is no other than the analysis of the absolute presuppositions of historical consciousness.

This transcendental analytic is itself a twofold process. On the one hand, there is the fundamentally historical metaphysics of past thought which issues in categorical singular propositions: propositions employing the metaphysical rubric, "On such-and-such an occasion so-and-so presupposed such-and-such." On the other hand, there is the more fundamental metaphysics of the historian's own historical consciousness, which issues in categorical universal propositions, to which the historian is committed, and which claim the synthetic a priori status of transhistorical truths. (The latter constitute what might be regarded as the presuppositions of the possibility of experience per se.) Whereas the former (the propositions of historical metaphysics) are justified merely by showing that they were (or are) in fact presupposed, the validity of the latter (the propositions of philosophical metaphysics) depends not only on the fact of their being presupposed but also on the success with which they are presupposed and on the logical fact that they are dialectically 'consupponible.' Finally, since the experience which these transhistorical principles purport to underlie is the product of a dialectical-historical development, to speak of the transhistorical presuppositions of experience per se is to speak of the transhistorical presuppositions of experience only in so far as it has thus far developed.

What then are the transhistorical presuppositions of historical thought as it presently exists on the scale of history, and to which every twentieth-century historian is committed in so far as he is an historian at all?

In every field of knowledge, according to Collingwood, there are certain fundamental principles or axioms which belong to the form or structure of that type of knowledge and are derived not from the empirical subject matter but from the point of view of the knower. In history, the general conditions of knowledge are derived from the fundamental principle that the knower is placed in the present, and from the point of view of the present is looking at the past. The first axiom of intuition for history (to adopt Kantian terminology) is that every historical event is situated somewhere in past time. This is not a generalization which is empirically discovered by the historian in the course of his enquiry, but is an a priori condition of historical knowledge, an absolute presupposition of the standpoint itself. The sequence of time is also derived from the point of view of the knower. The time relation of logical antecedent and logical consequent is a 'schematized' representation of the world of logical or conceptual relations (IH, 109). This gives rise to another absolute presupposition of historical thought, that:

... the necessary sequence by which one event leads to another in time is in some way identical in character with the necessary sequence by which one thing leads to another in a non-temporal logical series ... If this is denied, and if it is maintained that temporal sequence and logical implication have nothing to do with each other, historical knowledge becomes impossible, for it follows that we can never say about any event " this *must* have happened"; the past can never appear as the conclusion of a logical inference. If the temporal series is a mere aggregate of disconnected events, we can never argue back from the present to the past. But historical thinking consists precisely of arguing back in this way; and it is therefore based on the assumption (or, as Kant and Fichte would have said, on the *a priori* principle) that there is an internal or necessary connection between the events of a time-series such that one event leads necessarily to another and we can argue back from the second to the first. On this principle there is only one way in which the present state of things can have come into existence, and history is the analysis of the present in order to see what this process must have been. (IH, 110)

The historian's picture of the past must therefore conform to the structure of the historian's own mind; but this is itself a product of that past, and it is only because the past is incapsulated in the historian's present experience of reality that it can become an object of knowledge: "... the past which an historian studies is not a dead past but a past which in some sense is still living in the present" (A, 97). To say that all history is contemporary history, as Collingwood often does, is therefore the same as saying that the historian's picture of the past must conform to his experience, not of the present simply, nor of the past simply, but of the past in the present, or the past as it is per se for the historian's mind. "Historical knowledge is the re-enactment of a past thought incapsulated in a context of present thoughts which, by contradicting it, confine it to a plane different from theirs" (A, 114). And, finally, the historian must assume, as we have already noted above (ch. VIII, p. 8) that the process of history is a rational (i.e., intelligible) process, that unreason is a disguised form of reason (IH, 77, 81, 85), and that the rationale of history takes the form of a dialectical progress. Thus, in *An Essay on Philosophical Method* Collingwood declares that, by viewing the history of thought as a scale of forms (which means, in effect, according to the rules of dialectical logic), the prima facie irrationality which appears to characterize that thought will give way to the discovery that the history of this thought has a structure of its own and that "in its changes it is obeying the laws of that structure" (EPM, 224). The hypothesis that history is rational and intelligible is an absolute presupposition of history (conceived as a science) which historians *qua* historians must bring with them to the study of history as history. "If the scientist is obliged to assume that nature is rational, and that any failure to make sense of it is a failure to understand it, the corresponding assumption is obligatory for the historian, and this not least when he is the historian of thought" (EPM, 226).

These principles are the presuppositions of all history. They are therefore the presuppositions of metaphysics and, except in terms of them, the conditions which Collingwood lays down for metaphysics can never be met. As such, they are the result of the kind of metaphysics which I have all along referred to as the philosophical metaphysics of the metaphysician-historian's own experience. The conclusions of *this* science are not statements to whose truth or falsity the metaphysician can afford to be indifferent. In so far as they are the principles which are actually and logically implicit in the practice of history, historians are committed to their truth.

The nature of this commitment may be further explained by means of the paradigm case of the ontological argument, to which, as we noted above in chapter VII, Collingwood devotes a great deal of attention. The whole point of this argument, according to Collingwood, is to expose the belief in God as an absolute presupposition, which means that it has been removed from the arena of dispute and debate. What Anselm proved was not that God exists, but that we believe in God and that this belief is unavoidable. Anselm did not, as Kant charged, begin with our 'idea' of God and proceed thence to God's existence. It is not because our idea of God is an idea of *id quo maius cogitari nequit* that God therefore exists; it is because our idea of God is an idea of *id quo maius cogitari nequit* that we stand committed to a belief in God's existence (EM, 190). Collingwood therefore represents the ontological argument as establishing a truth not about an independently existing world of reality, the thing-in-itself, but about our experience of this world. Every experience is the result of thinking or acting according to presuppositions. Metaphysics is the act of thinking systematically about what presuppositions are actually in use (EM, 196–7), and faith is the activity of simply presupposing them in order to maintain the integrity of our experience.

One is therefore compelled to ask (as Collingwood has maintained with respect to the proposition, God exists, SM, 187) what difference it makes to the conduct of your enquiry whether you do or do not presuppose the principle in question. Collingwood's answer, which is implicit in his discussion of the ontological argument, may be reconstructed as follows. To the extent to which the 'essence' of the enquiry (i.e., its aims and purposes and general possibilities) presupposes such propositions, we are necessarily committed to believe in their truth, that is to say, to presuppose them. Failure to do so is a sign of the corrupt consciousness. At the same time, should we discover that what formerly we had taken to be absolute presuppositions are not in fact presupposed, but that we are really presupposing their contraries, then we are obliged by the same logic of commitment to withdraw our support from them. Failure to do so is also a sign of the corrupt consciousness. In both cases, where our behaviour is a result of the corrupt consciousness, we are no longer in a state of mere 'error' but have sunk to the level of 'lying'; the former is a bona fide mistake, the latter is a concealment of the truth.

Concealing the truth, however, is not always a case of deliberate lying. At the deepest level of experience, 'the lie in the soul' is unconscious. The unconscious lie in the soul is a form of behaviour which expresses itself in a variety of ways, and we must be careful, in attempting to explain this behaviour (which is characteristic of the single consciousness only), not to confuse it with what happens between one intellect and another. The corruption of consciousness has been described by psychologists in their own way: the disowning of experiences they call 'repression'; the ascription of these to other persons, 'projection'; their consolidation into a mass of experience, homogeneous in itself, 'dissociation'; and the building up of a Bowdlerized experience (i.e., one whose omissions are falsifications) which we will admit to be our own, 'fantasy building' (PA, 218–19). Finally, the condition of a corrupt consciousness which is exemplified in this behaviour is not only an example of untruth, it is an example of evil as well (PA, 220). This is reason enough for regarding metaphysics as a necessary ingredient in the health of culture, and the programme of anti-metaphysics as a disease leading to the death of culture.

Since the very fact that a given belief is an absolute presupposition of our experience means that we are obliged to believe in it, absolute presuppositions are not things which we can choose either to presuppose or not to presuppose any more than we can choose either to think or not to think in terms of the categories, to be free or not to be free, or for that matter, simply to be or not to be. This does not mean that we cannot behave in ways which are inconsistent with these presuppositions; it means only that if we should behave in this way our behaviour would be the product, not of a genuine free choice, but of the corrupt consciousness which is the antithesis of freedom.

10 METAPHYSICS AS TRANSCENDENTAL ANALYTICS

I have already made the point that Collingwood's theory of metaphysics is modelled on Kant's critical philosophy; metaphysics is a form of transcendental analytics. But there is, as we have also noted, an important difference between Collingwood and Kant. For Kant the behaviour of mind derives from a permanent and unchanging structure and the principles derived from this structure are eternal truths. For Collingwood, the a priori is itself a product of historical change. Transcendental analytics is therefore history. The presuppositions according to which we think and to which we are (under certain conditions) obliged to commit ourselves, are likewise subject to historical change. In other words, the very a priori criteria according to which the objectivity of historical metaphysics is guaranteed are themselves not only historically grounded but historically relative. But if this is so, how can we describe them as transcendental? And how is it possible for them to be both transcendental and relative at the same time? The answer is that if they are transcendental they are not so in the ordinary sense demanded by propositional logic. Their meaning and truth do not depend simply upon their correspondence with objectively existing facts. To apprehend the truth of such principles is not like apprehending the truth of the axioms and definitions of geometry. They are not analytic. Nor are they purely synthetic, being wholly derived from, and verifiable only by means of, experience. They are, as I have already suggested, a special kind of synthetic a priori. They derive from the categories of mind, and are entailed by the statement that mind exists. But, since the essence of mind is historicity, each category has its own history which takes the form not of a random sequence but of a progressive or serial scale of forms.

Thus the essential meaning of the statement, Mind exists, changes as the scale develops. The statement, "All thought is for the sake of action," for example, which is an absolute presupposition of experience in general, can only be understood in terms of a concrete universal whose meaning and truth value, although it changes from age to age, is nevertheless connected in a coherent system. For this reason, the history of past thought is never final. Each generation must reconstruct the past for itself, and in so doing, reveal to itself the a priori principles which lie at the basis of its experience. Becoming conscious of the principles which are implicit in experience leads in some cases to a recognition that there is a basic inconsistency between the implicit presuppositions of an experience and its explicit presuppositions. The result is that the latter are replaced by the former. Such changes are neither random nor irrational. They are, on the contrary, progressive, having the characteristics of a scale of forms. The idea of the past is therefore a scale of forms which takes shape in the course of the mind's own discovery of itself. It is an innate idea which is at once both the *source* of the activity of historical thinking and the *product of that activity*; for it is only by means of this activity itself that "we endeavour to provide this innate idea with detailed content. And this we do by using the present as evidence for its own past" (IH, 247).

> But neither the raw material of historical knowledge, the detail of the here-and-now as given him in perception, nor the various endowments that serve him as aids to interpreting this evidence, can give the historian his criterion of historical truth. That criterion is the idea of history itself; the idea of an imaginary picture of the past. That idea is, in Cartesian language, innate; in Kantian language, *a priori*. It is not a chance product of psychological causes: it is an idea which every man possesses as part of the furniture of his mind, and discovers himself to possess in so far as he becomes conscious of what it is to have a mind. Like other ideas of the same sort, it is one to which no fact of experience exactly corresponds. The historian, however long and faithfully he works, can never say that his work, even in crudest outline or in this or that smallest detail, is done once for all. He can never say that his picture of the past is at any point adequate to his idea of what it ought to be. But, however fragmentary and faulty the results of his work may be, the idea which governed its course is clear, rational, and universal. It is the idea of the historical imagination as a self-dependent, self-determining, and self-justifying form of thought. (IH, 248)

The presuppositions according to which we think and act are the product of this a priori imagination. We can never subject them to any special kind of proof, but the whole point of Collingwood's argument is to show that this is not necessary. Their meaningfulness, in other words, does not depend upon this kind of verification. The very fact that they are absolute presuppositions is proof that they are 'right.' As for their ultimate truth when judged from the absolute standpoint, there is no way of determining this except by continuing to use them until we are obliged to abandon them.

> How can we ever satisfy ourselves that the principles on which we think are true, except by going on thinking according to those principles, and seeing whether

unanswerable criticisms of them emerge as we work? To criticize the conceptions of science is the work of science itself as it proceeds; to demand that such criticism should be anticipated by the theory of knowledge is to demand that such a theory should anticipate the history of thought. (IH, 230)

The clue to the nature of the process in which presuppositions arise and fall is provided by *Speculum Mentis*. In my discussion of this book (ch. III) I suggested that the dialectic of experience proceeds on three levels, and that at the third level the ideal limit is the point at which the *ab intra* and the *ab extra* moments of criticism coincide. This is the point at which the absolute presuppositions of finite experience coincide with the absolute presuppositions of absolute experience. Such a progress can hardly be described as irrational – as Knox seems to suggest when discussing Collingwood's footnote cited above (pp. 270–1). I have argued that, contrary to Knox's interpretation, there is no incompatibility between the footnote in question and the avowed rationalism of the rest of Collingwood's philosophy.

In that footnote Collingwood declares that the basis of historical change is a process of unconscious thought. By unconscious, Collingwood does not mean irrational and therefore beyond the reach of explanation. He means no more than what he meant in *Speculum Mentis*: to say that something is 'unconscious' is equivalent to saying that it is an 'implicit' rather than an 'explicit' feature of experience (SM, 93). To be implicit moreover means to be necessarily bound up with the rational structure of experience. In *Speculum Mentis* the dialectic of experience is a dramatization of the contradiction between what consciousness explicitly (i.e., consciously) says, and what it implicitly (i.e., unconsciously) means. The implicit contradictions which lie at the basis of any given standpoint are not consciously recognized by the person adopting it. Only to the philosopher informed by the absolute standpoint is the truth of every other standpoint available. One might say in fact that the dialectical development of consciousness is the unconscious development of the criterion of truth, according to which consciousness *qua* philosopher judges itself. Neither the artist *qua* artist nor the scientist *qua* scientist, for example, are conscious of the fact that in asserting their standpoints as they do they have implicitly or unconsciously committed systematic fallacies. It is the philosopher *qua* metaphysician who confronts consciousness with evidence that these contradictions really do exist. When it is realized that the unconscious changes which characterize the history of presuppositions are to some extent perpetuated by the conscious attempt to reconstruct the history of these changes, the main reason for claiming that the changes are irrational seems to me to have been eliminated.

↔ IX ↔

HISTORY
and the Science of Human Nature

1 FROM FACTS TO THOUGHTS

The discovery on the part of the mind that history is implicit philosophy is the occasion upon which historical consciousness progresses to a higher level on its own scale of forms. This scale includes, as we have already noted above (ch. v, s. 3) an aesthetic history, a religious history, a scientific history, an 'historical' history, and, with the arrival of philosophy on the scene, a philosophical history. Thus, the arrival of philosophy means not the death of history but only its rebirth in a new form.

In order to consider in any further detail the basis for the transition from *Speculum Mentis* to *The Idea of History* we must consider once again the distinction introduced earlier (ch. IV, s. 2) between history as a habit of mind having as its object the 'facticity' of all things and the elevation of this habit to the rank of a dogma, a special science having as its object a certain class of facts themselves. The latter is a philosophical error, which, having been committed, immediately initiates a process of self-correction. This, as we have already noted, is precisely what happens in *Speculum Mentis*. Consciousness is continually transforming a permanent 'habit' of mind which is involved in any act of knowledge, into a special kind of knowledge, having the status of a separate science. And in similar fashion it transforms what is normally a permanent feature of the world into a special kind of object, the individual concrete fact. When this, which is really only an abstraction from a larger unity, is mistaken for a real object, history as a special science is born. And when this object is further identified with the whole of reality, first-level dogmatic historical philosophy is born.

In *Speculum Mentis* history was defined as the perception of the concrete fact, and this was distinguished from the perception of the abstract fact which is the mark of science. The world of abstract facts is a plurality of individual units held together by law so that any knowledge of the facts per se must be mediated by knowledge of the laws which hold them together. The world of concrete facts, however, is a single unified whole. The knowledge of single facts is mediated not by knowledge of abstract laws which exist independently of facts themselves, but by other facts, and ideally by the absolute whole. But, as we have already noted in chapter IV, consciousness falls into the error, the result of the continued influence on it of science, of treating the concrete whole as an object (or non-mind) distinct from the knowing subject. A contradiction arises therefore between two incompatible sets of presuppositions: between the presuppositions of the activity which seeks knowledge of facts and the presuppositions of the activity which seeks knowledge of mind *qua* concrete. As a result of this tension consciousness was represented in chapter III (s. 5) as having to choose either to replace its basic presuppositions or to revert to the scientific standpoint from which it was attempting to flee. The former alternative was recognized at the conclusion of chapter IV to be the basis of the transition from history to philosophy. We are now in a position to recognize that this same move is also the basis for a transition within history itself from a purely 'historical' to a 'philosophical' form of history. The object is no longer perceived as 'nature' in the form of the concrete fact but as mind, and the distinction between history and science is now seen to rest on the distinction between mind and nature. *A parte subjecti* this distinction expresses itself in the distinction between knowledge of mind and knowledge of nature.

But knowledge of mind is also the mark of philosophy (which on the scale of consciousness per se supersedes history). If history is to achieve its desired autonomy it must provide a basis upon which to distinguish itself from philosophy. The basis of this distinction is twofold. On the one hand, the object of history is defined as the 'past,' knowledge of which is achieved through the mediation of the present in which the past is incapsulated. What exists in the present is evidence, which is something perceptible. Instead of treating this evidence as a mere 'thing-in-itself,' as a 'fact' or finished product, history treats it as a problem to be solved, and the aim of history is to argue from this evidence to the thought which stands behind it. The historical object is therefore defined as embodied thought, having both an "inside" and an "outside." Historical thinking is the act of inferring from the "outside" to the "inside." The philosopher, on the other hand, is concerned not with "things thought about" but with "the act of thinking itself" (IH, 305). If for the sake of convenience we call the historian's activity of arguing from evidence to the facts 'first-order thinking,' then the philosopher's thought about the historian's thought is 'second-order thinking.'[1]

In history, mind makes itself by coming to know its own past. Since in history, as opposed to science, the subject and the object thought about are identical, knowing makes a difference to the object known. Both the historian's present experience and the past which is "incapsulated"[2] in it are affected by the historian's knowledge of it. What is more, the historian's own mind undergoes a corresponding change. History is not only self-knowledge, it is also self-making: history is that activity in which the mind makes itself by coming to know its own past. This is the characteristic mark of third-level historical consciousness. Philosophy is the reflective moment of this experience in which the self-making process itself is made an object of knowledge. If history is the mind's knowledge of the past incapsulated within its present experience, philosophy is the 'second-order' history of the mind's experience of knowing its own past.

The distinction between first- and second-order thinking is a formal distinction, which can be applied at various levels depending on the terms of reference. First-order thinking, the mind's knowledge of its past, constitutes what may be characterized as a 'horizontal' scale of forms which cuts across each moment of the 'vertical' scale (art, religion, etc.). The former represents all the possible subject matters of history, the various expressions of human thought. Corresponding to this is a scale of second-order activities. The relations among the various activities which constitute first- and second-order thinking are of course dynamic so that what for one purpose constitutes second-order thought becomes, for an entirely different purpose, first-order thought.

Thus, for example, the historical reconstruction of colonial expansion during the nineteenth century is first-order thought, as is the history of social revolutions. The historian's thought about these first-order activities is a second-order activity which may be called 'historiography.' The historiographer's thought, meanwhile, can itself be made the object of a further second-order historical study, and for that purpose assumes the status of a first-order activity. Thus arise such special studies as the history of the historiography of social history, and so on. The same considerations apply to science. There is scientific activity itself, which is a first-order activity. Then there is the second-order reflection on this activity, which is the philosophy of science. Finally, there is the second-order history of the philosophy of science, relative to which what formerly was a second-order activity becomes now a first-order activity.

Both sets of second-order activities described above possess the very characteristics which Collingwood assigns to metaphysics. Metaphysics is a scale of second-order activities ranging from an examination of the absolute presuppositions of practising historians and scientists to an analysis of the absolute presuppositions of historiographers and philosophers of science. Suppose we now make metaphysics itself the subject of a further study; this transforms it into a first-order activity, while the philosophy of metaphysics (transhistorical or meta-metaphysics) becomes a second-order activity – the second-order history of the mind's actual experience of coming to know the absolute presuppositions of past thought. This new knowledge, the philosophy of metaphysics, is expressed in statements. But, as the experience (of which these principles are constitutive) changes, the principles themselves suffer corresponding changes. Thus the purely philosophical 'meta-metaphysical' activity becomes itself absorbed into history and takes its place on the scale of the history of historiography, only to be made the subject of future meta-metaphysical critiques, which will produce new meta-metaphysical activities. This process, which exhibits a dialectical progress, will continue until the point is reached at which the presuppositions of human thought coincide with the presuppositions of the absolute standpoint (a phenomenon to be further discussed in chapter x). But, at this point history comes to an end and the very notion of presuppositions is dispensed with; there is no longer a distinction between thought as subject and thought as object, between thought and experience, or even between implicit and explicit consciousness and its presuppositions. At this 'eschatological' moment the ideal limit of philosophy is reached, the unhappy consciousness is redeemed, the alienation of the self with itself is overcome, and we have finally reached a standpoint without presuppositions.

2 THE STANDPOINT OF THE IDEA OF HISTORY

At the outset of the *Idea of History* Collingwood distinguishes between first- and second-order activities. History is described as a first-order activity, philosophy as a second-order one. On the basis of our conclusions in chapter III (s. 3), the *Idea of History*, which is offered as an example of the latter, may be viewed as an exercise in 'dogmatic' philosophy. And in view of the explicit declaration that the first-order activity which is being examined is an activity of self-knowledge, in which the distinction between subject and object has broken down, we are obliged to view it as a case of third-level dogmatic philosophy.

Third-level dogmatic philosophy is itself subject to various internal distinctions. In addition to the tension between the *ab extra* and the *ab intra* moments which, in the course of the history of third-level existence, is gradually healed, there is the fundamental ambiguity between the 'historical' (itself a first-order activity) and the 'philosophical' (which, relative to the 'historical' moment, is a second-order activity). The former assumes the shape of a history of past second-order reflective moments. The latter emerges as a critical examination of the historian's present experience, including a second-order history of the presuppositions according to which the former activity itself is being conducted. This is precisely how the *Idea of History* is organized. The first four parts are a history of the presuppositions of past thought: a metaphysics of historiography. Part v is a 'metaphysical Epilegomena,'[3] and constitutes the meta-metaphysics of the historian-philosopher's present experience. In keeping with the above distinctions, the second-order activity, which in parts I–IV examines the presuppositions of past thought, itself becomes, in the Epilegomena, the subject of a further second-order activity which I have called meta-metaphysics; or, to put it another way, the metaphysical rubric which in parts I–IV takes the form, 'I have concluded that so and so absolutely presupposed such and such,' becomes in the Epilegomena, 'In so far as such and such is an absolute presupposition of my own experience I am committed to believing in it as an absolute presupposition of experience itself.' Thus the 'particularist' who passes judgment throughout the first four parts becomes in the Epilegomena a 'universalist'; the judgments of metaphysics pass from the categorical singular judgments of history to the categorical universal judgments of philosophy; the philosopher who, *qua* historian, views the world *sub species singularis* ascends finally to a view of the world *sub species universalis.*

Dogmatic philosophy is the reasoned vindication of a standpoint from within. Third-level dogmatic philosophy is the reasoned vindication of a standpoint in which the breach between subject and object has been partially overcome. The distinction between 'mind' and 'non-mind' has given way to a distinction between mind as knower and mind as object. In the case of history, mind as object is (to use the language of the *Autobiography*) the past "incapsulated" in the present (A, 114). The task of dogmatic philosophy of history is to provide a *de jure* justification for the possibility of historical knowledge – to answer the question, in other words, how or under what conditions history as a science is possible. This is the *ab intra* task. There is also, as we have seen, an *ab extra* task, which involves criticizing the latter with special attention to the problem of the relation of history as a special form of knowledge to the *whole* of knowledge. Collingwood recognizes, in the *Idea of History*, the need for both aspects of the single activity of philosophy of history. But, as we have already noted, he emphasizes that the *Idea of History* is concerned solely with the first aspect:

> What I am attempting here is a philosophical inquiry into the nature of history regarded as a special type of form of knowledge with a special type of object, leaving aside, for the present, the further question how that inquiry will affect other departments of philosophical study. (IH, 7)

The *Idea of History* is therefore a philosophical inquiry into the science of history regarding itself as an autonomous form of knowledge, and conceiving of its object as belonging to it and it alone. Parts I–IV, as I have already indicated, provide a metaphysical analysis of the historical development of the *Idea of History*. Part V, on the other hand, is a metaphysical analysis of the *Idea of History* as it existed in Collingwood's own day. The first section, parts I–IV, consists of lectures written, according to Knox, during the first six months of 1936 and revised in 1940 (IH, v). Knox claims that it was Collingwood's intention to use these lectures as the basis of a book to be entitled "The Idea of History" which would eventually become a companion volume to the *Idea of Nature*. The Epilegomena (part V) is a collection of seven essays drawn from various sources. The first is the Inaugural Lecture which Collingwood delivered in October 1935 as Waynflete Professor of Metaphysical Philosophy, while the second is the British Academy Lecture which he gave in May 1936. Essays 4, 5, and 7 are drawn from the manuscript of 1936 from which the material for parts I–IV was also drawn. Finally, essays 3 and 6 are taken from the manuscript of "The Principles of History" which Collingwood apparently began in the spring of 1936, and which grew out of some of the lectures of 1936.

Unfortunately, Collingwood died before he had a chance to finish the "Principles of History." Knox, who as editor was responsible for the arrangement of the posthumous *Idea of History*, chose to publish only a small part of the existing manuscript. But the arrangement of the posthumous *Idea of History* does not, in my opinion do credit to Collingwood's philosophical genius. It lacks the order and coherence of his other published works, in particular *An Essay on Philosophical Method*. Since the manuscripts from which Knox drew his material are not available for study and examination, I shall attempt to show that when properly interpreted the material presented in the *Idea of History* provides sufficient evidence on the basis of which Collingwood's thought may be reconstructed into a reasonably systematic and coherent whole.

The first presentation of what eventually became the *Idea of History* proper was a 1930 paper entitled "The Philosophy of History." The structure and organization of this paper is almost identical with the structure and organization of the *Idea of History*. The paper is arranged into three parts. The first part corresponds to the introduction of the *Idea of History*, and is concerned primarily with the definition of 'philosophy of history.' History is defined as a universal and necessary human interest in a universal and necessary aspect of the world: the question is not, "Shall I be an historian or not?" but, "How good an historian shall I be?" (PH, 3) The philosophy of history is therefore a critical reflection on the conditions according to which human potentialities can best be realized. In this respect it may be said to translate the implicit fact of human nature into a reasoned fact; or, to put it another way, it transforms a universal element of human experience into a systematic science.

The second part corresponds roughly to parts I–IV of the *Idea of History*. The history of historiography is traced from the Greeks to the early twentieth century. In particular Collingwood applauds Croce's doctrine of the identity of the universal and the individual judgment as being the basis for the rise of history in the twentieth century – a point which was discussed earlier in chapter II (s. 5).

The third part, which corresponds to the Epilegomena, is entitled "Outline of a Philosophy of History." History is here described as a process of question and answer: "The beginning of historical research is ... not the collection or contemplation of crude facts as yet uninterpreted, but the asking of a question which sets one off looking for facts which may help one to answer it" (PH, 14). The question, moreover, must be asked with some reasonable expectation of one's being able to answer it by genuinely historical thinking. This may be expressed by saying that a question does or does not 'arise.' To say that a question 'arises' is to say that it has a logical connection with our previous thoughts, that we have a reason for asking it and are not moved by mere capricious curiosity (PH, 14). This is an obvious reference to the logic of question and answer which is later discussed in the *Autobiography*, and *An Essay on Metaphysics*.

The goal of history is to know the past. The past however is not an object of perception. It is a product of the activity of interpreting present evidence (PH, 13), and this process is guided by the questions that arise in the course of the study. History, then, while it is ostensibly knowledge of the past is actually knowledge of the present; it is basically an attempt to answer the question, How has the present come to be what it is? (PH, 16) This means, of course, that past facts as such do not exist until they have been established. The historical past is therefore very much dependent upon the present activities of historians (PH, 16). It follows that historical knowledge can never be final. The best it can do is state where our knowledge of the subject matter stands at the present time.

All history is thus an interim report on the progress made in the study of its subject down to the present; and hence all history is at the same time the history of history ... This is why every age must write history afresh. Everyone brings his own mind to the study of history, and approaches it from the point of view which is characteristic of himself and his generation. (PH, 15)

This conclusion is an implicit rejection of the concept of the past as a thing-in-itself, as well as of the dogma that the history of history is the history of different answers to the same question. The rejected theory is replaced by the concept of the past as the product of historical thinking, and the doctrine that the history of history is the history of different answers to different questions. Thus Collingwood declares, in 1930, that we do not ask which of the various points of view is right. Each is 'right' in its own way, being the appropriate answer under the circumstances (PH, 15). This does not, of course, reduce history to a series of arbitrary conclusions. It can still, regardless of this relativity, remain knowledge. Indeed, as we have already noted, on several occasions in the *Idea of History* and *An Essay on Philosophical Method* Collingwood declares that the objectivity of historical knowledge is not achieved in spite of this relativity, but because of it.

The Epilegomena of the *Idea of History*, in which the conclusions of part 3 of the 1930 essay are again taken up, may be represented as a systematic attempt to answer the following questions: (a) What is the object of history? (b) By what methods can this object be made an object of knowledge? (c) Under what conditions can this object be known? (d) For what purpose is this knowledge acquired? (e) What is the status of this knowledge? The answers to these questions fall under the following headings which describe the main topics of discussion in the *Idea of History*: (a) the subject matter of history, (b) the methodology of history, (c) historical knowledge, re-thinking, and the a priori imagination, (d) history as a form of self-knowledge, (e) the relativity of historical thought.

In the course of dealing with these problems various other problems also arise: the relation of history to science and psychology, the nature of facts, the use of generalizations in historical inference, the status of the historical past. Collingwood's answer to the questions posed by all of the above problems may be summed up as follows. The object of history is mind in the form of past thoughts incapsulated in the context of present thoughts. These thoughts are not, of course, objects of perception. But they are expressed or embodied in something which is perceptible, namely evidence. This evidence is something existing 'here and now.' As opposed to the scientist, however, who treats the 'here and now' as a collection of facts to be contemplated, the historian treats it as a problem to be solved, as the expression of something non-perceptible, namely thought. Collingwood characterizes the nature of this object by means of the distinction between the 'outer' and the 'inner':

> The historian, investigating any event in the past, makes a distinction between what may be called the outside and the inside of an event. By the outside of the event I mean everything belonging to it which can be described in terms of bodies and their movements: the passage of Caesar, accompanied by certain men across a river called the Rubicon at one date, or the spilling of his blood on the floor of the senate-house at another. By the inside of the event I mean that in it which can only be described in terms of thought: Caesar's defiance of Republican law, or the clash of constitutional policy between himself and his assassins. The historian is never concerned with either of these to the exclusion of the other. He is investigating not mere events (where by a mere event I mean one which has only an outside and no inside) but actions, and an action is the unity of the outside and inside of an event. He is interested in the crossing of the Rubicon only in its relation to Republican law, and in the spilling of Caesar's blood only in its relation to a constitutional conflict. His work may begin by discovering the outside of an event, but it can never end there; he must always remember that the event was an action, and that his main task is to think himself into this action, to discern the thought of its agent. (IH, 213)

One of the implications of Collingwood's 'inside-outside' theory is the exclusion from the field of history of everything other than what is an expression of rational thought. Collingwood lists among the possible objects of historical thought, politics, warfare, economic activity, morals, art, science, religion, philosophy, and history itself (IH, 309–15). Of everything other than thought there can be no history (IH, 304). In this class fall such things as biological functions, mere external behaviour, sensations, emotions, nature in general (IH, 212, 304), and such human actions as are determined by what may be called man's animal nature, his impulses and appetites, etc. (IH, 216).

We have already noted, in chapter IV above, that there is a discrepancy between the theory of history expounded in *Speculum Mentis* and that of the *Idea of History*. According to the former the object of historical thinking is the 'facticity' of all things; for the latter it is past thought only. I therefore raised a number of questions concerning the transition from the concept of history (in *Speculum Mentis*) as a knowledge of facts independent of mind, to the concept of history (in the *Idea of History*) as the knowledge of a part of mind itself. In order to answer this question I distinguished for Collingwood between history as a special habit of mind and history conceived as a special science (ch. IV, s. 2, above). As a general habit of mind its object is the world of fact as such, the facticity of all things. As a special science, however, it is the concrete universal *qua* past thought. In *Speculum Mentis* consciousness not only confuses these two activities but elevates the former to the rank of a dogma. Thus arises the realist theory of history which is repudiated in the *Idea of History*. But, as I have already argued, this repudiation is already implicit in *Speculum Mentis*, and the confusion upon which the realist theory of history rests is due not so much to an error on Collingwood's part as to the requirements of the dialectic itself.

This dialectical requirement is a result of the inherent contradiction which, as we have seen, pervades the whole of *Speculum Mentis*, between the presuppositions of realism (for which there is a distinction between subject and object) and the presuppositions of idealism (for which this distinction is overcome). When this conflict is dialectically resolved, consciousness elevates itself to the third ontological level of existence. Once having arrived at this level, history reconstitutes itself, this time under the influence of philosophy which is the final consummation of the rapprochement between subject and object. Thus arises the standpoint of the *Idea of History*, which is an analysis of third-level consciousness; the level at which the historian knows explicitly what in *Speculum Mentis* he knew only implicitly (or, to be more precise, what only the philosopher knows): that his own knowledge of facts is organic to the facts themselves; that his mind is these facts knowing themselves and these facts are his mind knowing itself. History is now defined as the science of mind *qua* past thought and as such is indeed perception raised to its highest power – a perception which has transcended the subject-object distinction and is now described as imaginative reconstruction.

So defined, the special problem of history is to reconstruct this past thought from "evidence" according to a complicated system of rules and assumptions. What makes any object a possible object of history is the fact that it can be rethought in this way. What makes it an actual object is the fact that it has been rethought. Collingwood's main question in the Epilegomena then is, Under what conditions is this rethinking possible? His answer constitutes what amounts to a transcendental deduction of the categories of historical thought, these giving rise to what I have previously called (ch. VIII, ss. 9–10) the a priori principles of history.

Of all the principles implied in the operation of the historical imagination, three may be singled out as the most important. The first is the principle that the historical past cannot be an object of knowledge unless it is 'incapsulated' within the context of the present experience of the historian. This means that in knowing the past I am also knowing the present. History is knowledge of past thought incapsulated within the context of present thought. History is therefore self-knowledge (A, ch. 10; IH, 217 ff.). The concept of history as self-knowledge leads to a second principle concerning the status of history as an object. In accordance with the conclusions of *Speculum Mentis*, the thought known by the historian of the *Idea of History* is his own thought and this means, if we interpret it according to the claims of *Speculum Mentis*, that the historian's knowledge makes a difference to the object known. Thus Collingwood declares, in the *Idea of History*, that the very object of history is itself created in the act through which it is known; history *a parte objecti* is the child of history *a parte subjecti* (IH, 226). Conceived as a mode of being, then, history is not only self-knowledge but self-making as well. As a science of human nature, it must therefore be regarded as an indispensable condition of the existence of that nature, as an essential ingredient in its very makeup (IH, 227). This leads to the third principle. Since history is a process in which its subject matter, mind, comes into being through the very act of knowing itself, not only mind, but the mind's knowledge of itself, is constantly changing. Historical knowledge, in other words, is never final (IH, 229, 248).

3 HISTORY AS SELF-KNOWLEDGE OF MIND

The concept of history as self-knowledge derives from the doctrine of the historicity of human nature according to which historical knowledge is a fundamental and necessary condition of historical being.

The doctrine of the historicity of mind has its origins in the early stages of Collingwood's thought. In *Religion and Philosophy*, for example, mind is defined as the pure act of thinking: "The mind seems to be not so much that which thinks as the thinking itself; it is not an active thing so much as an activity. Its *esse* is *cogitare*" (RP, 100). By this Collingwood means not that the mind is a pure abstract activity, but that it is an activity with a content: "... there is no thought in general but only particular thoughts about particular things. The *esse* of mind is not *cogitare* simply, but *de hac re cogitare*" (RP, 100).

The nature of the self which is the source of the unity of the mind as pure act is explained in *Religion and Philosophy*, according to the analogy of the concrete universal, as a case of identity in difference. The general principle through which the self is to be defined may be stated as follows: "The character or self of a thing, what it is, cannot be distinguished from its relations" (RP, 112). In the case of mind, these relations are simply attitudes of thought. The self is therefore determined by its 'acts of thought,' which, since these acts are in each case 'historical,' is the same as saying that the self is determined by its history.[4] In effect then, *Religion and Philosophy* would appear to contain within it the seeds of the later doctrine of *Speculum Mentis*.

Religion and Philosophy not only recognizes the historical character of the self, it explicitly affirms its transcendental character as well. This is evident in Collingwood's insistence that the divine act (i.e., God) is a necessary presupposition of the possibility of the finite act. In short, God is the unity of all finite minds (RP, 114), and the existence of God is therefore an absolute presupposition of the science of human nature. This, in the language of religion, is an affirmation of the doctrine which is later to appear in *Speculum Mentis*, that the absolute is the unity of all finite minds. In fact, in *Religion and Philosophy* the term "absolute" is used interchangeably with the term God, although Collingwood does not indicate, as he should have, that in switching from one term to the other, he was switching from the standpoint of religion to the standpoint of philosophy.

In *Religion and Philosophy* the "Absolute,"[5] in so far as it is defined at all, is no formless and empty abstract identity. "The formless and empty Absolute of this abstract metaphysics," Collingwood wrote, "perished long ago in the fire of Hegel's sarcasm" (RP, 116). "A real philosophy" he continues, "builds its Absolute ... out of the differences of the world as it finds them, dealing individually with all contradictions and preserving every detail that can lend character to the whole" (RP, 115). Thus began Collingwood's lifelong attack on abstract metaphysics and his substitution for this of a more concrete metaphysics (RP, 116).

Against the abstract metaphysics of being, Collingwood advanced, in *Religion and Philosophy*, a concrete metaphysics of being conceived as pure act. Collingwood referred to this as "the concrete identity of activity" (RP, 116). The abstract identity of mind is changeless, permanent, and eternal. The concrete identity of mind, however, explicitly presupposes change. Change, in fact, is an intrinsic property of this concrete self-identity (RP, 117).

The "Absolute" of *Religion and Philosophy*, like the "absolute mind" of *Speculum Mentis*, is infinite truth, free of all contradiction (RP, 116–17). This is, of course, the source of the later concept of 'transcendental philosophy' or *speculum speculi*. The finite mind, through the historical sciences, acquires of itself a *speculum mentis* which is, of course, constantly changing. But at the centre of the mind's constantly changing picture of itself lies the pure unity of transcendental knowledge or *speculum speculi*, which is what the mind achieves in its moment of self-transcendence when, viewing the world *sub species aeternitatis*, it becomes (through philosophy) identified with the absolute. And this identity is possible only because the absolute is with us from the start; God or the absolute (or however else you wish to describe the transcendental a priori ground of the possibility of all being and knowing) is immanent as well as transcendent. Thus the activity of finite mind consists (when it raises itself to the level of science) of an attempt to render explicit the implicit self-identity of absolute knowledge. This activity is precisely what Collingwood means by self-making.

The concept of self-making according to the immanent criterion of absolute knowledge is described in an essay, published after *Religion and Philosophy* but before *Speculum Mentis*, and entitled "The Devil" (1919). This essay forms an interesting bridge between the two works and concentrates chiefly on the dialectic of religion conceived as a form of self-making. Human nature (or the self), Collingwood argues here, is as yet unformed, incomplete, in process of being communicated to us (D, 474). As such, he continues, man is in need of a standard according to which his nature can complete itself. This standard is, of course, absolute truth, which to science appears as reality and to religion as God (D, 475); this implies that the standard of truth becomes explicit only through the actual practice of these forms of life.

More precisely, this standard becomes explicit only when the self brings it into existence by 'questioning' the grounds of its own being. Thus in "The Devil" Collingwood defines human action as not only becoming, but also "self-creation" (D, 475). Self-creation, moreover, is self-knowledge; not the self-knowledge of introspection, not the examination of the self that *is*, but an examination of the self that is *to be* – which is, of course, the very criterion according to which the self makes itself.

The phenomenology of *Speculum Mentis* is one example of this questioning; the *specimina philosophandi* of *An Essay on Metaphysics* are another. It will become clear in our examination of the *Idea of History* that since the questioning which is the mind's knowledge of itself, and through which the pure state of *speculum speculi* is achieved, is essentially an historical activity, history is therefore the true science of mind and the true medium of human self-making.

The *Idea of History* defines historical knowledge as the reconstruction of thought in the mind of the historian. The question therefore arises, What are the necessary presuppositions of the possibility of historical rethinking? Of central importance among these presuppositions is the same doctrine of historicity and self-making the details of which are described at some length in the Epilegomena. In several places there mind is defined as being equivalent to its acts and these acts are in turn described as historical. What makes them historical, Collingwood argues, is not the fact of their happening in time but simply the fact of their becoming known to us by "re-thinking the same thought which created the situation we are investigating, and thus coming to understand that situation" (IH, 218). In other words, historical existence, which is essentially a self-making process, is the active and conscious appropriation of the past. Only through such appropriation is self-making possible at all:

Since mind is what it does, and human nature, if it is a name for anything real, is only a name for human activities, this acquisition or ability to perform determinate operations is the acquisition of a determinate human nature. Thus the historical process is a process in which man creates for himself this or that kind of human nature by recreating in his own thought the past to which he is heir. (IH, 226; cf. IH, 169, 171)

Historical thinking is therefore not just the discovery of mind but its actualization as well. All thought exists for the sake of action and it is only through such action that the mind's nature is created at all (IH, 226). This is of course an expression of the very doctrine of mind developed in *Speculum Mentis*, the doctrine of mind as pure act. What is being denied here is the theory of mind as an abstract substance which exists independently of the process which knows it. If there is to be a transcendental knowledge of mind, it is not the abstract transcendental knowledge which Plato (in his theory of forms, for example) believed to be possible. The mind which in the *Idea of History* is the object of philosophical and historical science is the absolute mind of *Speculum Mentis*, described there as "an historical fact" (SM, 298), which "unites the differences of my mind and other peoples ... not as the abstract universal unites; but rather as the concrete universal of history unites" (SM, 299). This mind is described both in the *Idea of History* and in *Speculum Mentis* as a mind which makes its own laws, and which is immanent in the process of history itself. Thus Collingwood writes, in *Speculum Mentis*: "The absolute mind has nothing over against itself as a necessity by which it is bound: not even the laws of its own nature. These laws it creates by acting upon them ..." (SM, 300) and again in the *Idea of History*: "History does not presuppose mind; it is the life of mind itself, which is not mind except in so far as it both lives in historical processes and knows itself as so living" (IH, 227). Thought, in other words, is not the presupposition of historical knowledge. On the contrary: "It is only in the historical process, the process of thoughts, that thought exists at all; and it is only in so far as this process is known for a process of thoughts that it is one" (IH, 227). It follows that self-knowledge is not an accidental but an essential aspect of existence. Thus the *Idea of History* reaffirms the principle of the unity of thought and action, as well as the belief in the existential implications of historical science: "... historical knowledge is no luxury, no mere amusement of a mind at leisure from more pressing occupations but a prime duty whose discharge is essential to the maintenance, not only of any particular form or type of reason, but of reason itself" (IH, 288).

In the first essay of the Epilegomena, entitled "Human Nature and

Human History" (esp. pages 210–12), Collingwood carefully distinguishes between historicity on the one hand and time and change on the other. He does this by making self-comprehension a necessary condition of historicity. To be historical a process must not only change in time, it must comprehend this change in such a way that this comprehension is at the same time the cause of that change. Only a mind can change in this way; only a mind can, through its very attempt to know itself, bring itself into being; only a mind therefore can have a history. The general principle which is implied here concerning the distinction between nature and history and which runs throughout the whole of the *Idea of History* is that whereas nature is a mere phenomenon whose change can be known only by an intelligent observer who is totally detached from the process, history is a process whose change can be known to itself, in the sense that the knowing subject is both a part and a cause of the object known. Nature is a mere object of knowledge; history is self-knowledge:

Knowing yourself means knowing, first, what it is to be a man; secondly, knowing what it is to be the kind of man you are; and thirdly, knowing what it is to be the man *you* are and nobody else is. Knowing yourself means knowing what you can do; and since nobody knows what he can do until he tries, the only clue to what man can do is what man has done. The value of history then is that it teaches us what man has done and thus what man is. (IH, 10)

There are several ways in which history can lead to self-knowledge. There is first of all the 'phenomenological' history of mind as exemplified by *Speculum Mentis*. There is secondly the history which forms the basis of personal autobiography (IH, 219) and which, according to Collingwood, must be carefully distinguished from psychology (IH, 174). Collingwood provides an example of what he means by personal self-knowledge derived from autobiography in the course of his critique of Dilthey. Dilthey, Collingwood charges, "assumes that the self-knowledge of mind is identical with psychology" (IH, 174) because for him history means identifying yourself with your object until it becomes part of your immediate experience. The historian then makes this his object and analyses it in terms of the objective laws of psychology. But this is not, according to Collingwood, what really happens in the act of historical reconstruction. Suppose I now experience an immediate feeling of discomfort, and I ask myself why I have this feeling. I may answer by reflecting that this morning I received a letter criticizing my conduct in what seems to me a valid and unanswerable manner:

Here I am not making psychological generalizations; I am recognizing in its detail a certain individual event or series of events which are already present to my consciousness as a feeling of discomfort or dissatisfaction with myself. To understand that feeling is to recognize it as the outcome of a certain historical process. Here the self-understanding of my mind is nothing else than historical knowledge. (IH, 174)

If Collingwood had pushed this analysis further he could have pointed out that in order fully to understand why in my case the events thus described should produce a feeling of discomfort, I would have to become aware of certain presuppositions which make this connection between the two events a reasonable one. This means, of course, that I must in some sense employ certain principles borrowed from my knowledge of psychology, although their employment will no doubt differ from that of ordinary empirical psychology.

The very same considerations are implied by the historian's attempt to understand the thought of another (IH, 219). Suppose, writes Collingwood, I am trying to understand a certain experience of Julius Caesar:

... the way in which I incorporate Julius Caesar's experience in my own personality is not by confusing myself with him, but by distinguishing myself from him and at the same time making his experience my own. The living past of history lives in the present; but it lives not in the immediate experience of the present, but only in the self-knowledge of the present. (IH, 174)

In the language of *An Essay on Metaphysics,* I would distinguish myself from the agent whose thought I am studying by distinguishing clearly between the presuppositions of his thought and the presuppositions of my own thought. In this way, I will be doing metaphysics and not psychology. Similarly:

... The same historical method is the only one by which I can know the ... corporate mind ... of a community or an age. To study the mind of the Victorian age or the English political spirit is simply to study the history of Victorian thought or English political activity. (IH, 219–20)

The "same historical method" is of course the method of metaphysical analysis. It is only through the metaphysical analysis of the absolute presuppositions of a given age that the mind of that age can be properly (i.e., historically) understood.

The following example may serve to illustrate Collingwood's point. Suppose an historian of the next century is trying to understand the military policy of the Chinese communists during the 1960s. Suppose he asks himself how it was possible for the leaders of this nation openly to advocate a policy of war against the west, and what is more, be prepared to sacrifice seventy-five per cent of their population for this purpose. What is even more puzzling is how the population at large could support such a policy. It might be tempting to interpret this behaviour in terms of the objective laws of mass hysteria, which are common to both westerners and Chinese. But this would be psychology, not history. The correct way to interpret this behaviour, if we are to think historically, is to judge it in terms, not of the objective laws of behaviour common to all men at all times, but in terms of the set of absolute presuppositions which were held by the Chinese at that time and which were totally different from the presuppositions of the western nations. I am thinking in particular of those presuppositions concerning the status of individuality which seem to be implied by the behaviour of the Chinese communists. It is a good deal less difficult to understand why a nation which presupposed absolutely that there is nothing unique about individual human beings, that differences between persons are purely quantitative, and that therefore any given individual is easily replaceable, would be so willing to sacrifice its people. Such action, when viewed in terms of these presuppositions, seems quite rational.

The historian in reconstructing past thought does so, then, by distinguishing himself from this thought and by interpreting it in terms of its own presuppositions. This makes his knowledge historical. At the same time, however, the historian must make this experience his own (IH, 174). Because historical knowledge is not just the mind's knowledge of what it has done in the past, but is also the redoing of it, such knowledge is self-knowledge, revealing to the historian the processes of his own mind:

Since all he can know historically is thoughts that he can re-think for himself, the fact of his coming to know them shows that his mind is able (or by the very effort of studying them has become able) to think in these ways. And conversely, whenever he finds certain historical matters unintelligible, he has discovered a limitation of his own mind; he has discovered that there are certain ways in which he is not, or no longer, or not yet, able to think. Certain historians, sometimes whole generations of historians, find in certain periods of history nothing intelligible, and call them dark ages; but such phrases tell us nothing about those ages themselves, though they tell us a great deal about the persons who use them, namely that they are unable to re-think the thoughts which were fundamental to their life. (IH, 218–19)

A similar statement is contained in *The Autobiography*:

If what the historian knows is past thoughts, and if he knows them by re-thinking them himself, it follows that the knowledge he achieves by historical enquiry is not knowledge of his situation as opposed to knowledge of himself, it is a knowledge of his situation which is at the same time knowledge of himself. In re-thinking what somebody else thought he thinks it himself. In knowing that somebody else thought it, he knows that he himself is able to think it. And finding out what he is able to do is finding out what kind of a man he is. If he is to understand by re-thinking them, the thoughts of a great many different kinds of people, it follows that he must be a great many different kinds of man. He must be, in fact, a microcosm of all the history he can know. Thus his own self-knowledge is at the same time his knowledge of the world of human affairs. (A, 114–15)

History is self-knowledge in both a theoretical, and a practical sense. "The truth is," writes Collingwood, "that if the human mind comes to understand itself better, it thereby comes to operate in new and different ways" (IH, 85; cf. SM, 207, 250, and A, 114–15). While the historian cannot make scientific predictions concerning the future, he is nevertheless able to anticipate it, and his experience as an historian therefore enables him to cope more effectively with the crises of life.

The unity of thought and action is of course, a cardinal principle of Collingwood's philosophy. The past, in so far as it is appropriated into the present, is in that appropriation 'projected' into the future; a mind which has reconstructed its own past becomes a mind which is capable of behaving in new and unpredictable ways. Thus, again, the later philosophy of Collingwood links up with the conclusions of *Speculum Mentis*. The appropriated past passes "into the muscle and bone of the mind" and "becomes an element in the point of view from which the mind raises its next problem" (SM, 307).

4 HISTORICITY AND HISTORICAL RELATIVISM

The relativity of knowledge extends not just to the conclusions of historical science, but to philosophy as well. The historicity of philosophy is explicitly acknowledged in *An Essay on Philosophical Method*. It is here declared, however, that historical and philosophical thought is relative not simply to the age in which it is expressed but to the whole scale of forms which characterizes its development. And in so far as the development of this thought takes the form of a scale it is a logical and rational development:

So far as any man is a competent philosopher, his philosophy arises by objective necessity out of his situation in the history of thought and the problem with which he is confronted; but situation and problem are unique, and hence no philosopher's system can be acceptable to another without some modification. That each must reject the thoughts of others, regarded as self-contained philosophies, and at the same time reaffirm them as elements in his own philosophy, is due not to causes in taste and temperament but to the logical structure of philosophical thought. (EPM, 192)

The relativity of thought, therefore, far from being a basis for scepticism is, on the contrary, a necessary antidote to it. If the thought of the past is valuable, writes Collingwood, "... that is not in spite of [its] strictly historical character but because of it" (IH, 230). It is realism, with its belief in the abstract transhistoricity of truth, which leads to scepticism – particularly when it is realized that the ideal which it sets before itself can never be realized. Realism creates an absolute dualism between truth and error, permanence and change; this it does by declaring that knowledge of truth must be totally independent of error and that permanence and unity must be grasped in complete isolation from change.

It was Collingwood's aim to demonstrate that this distorted form of Platonism can only lead to a complete renunciation of the possibility of knowing anything at all. What is more, the sceptical implications of realism are the best way to encourage an epidemic of irrationalism culminating in the search for non-rational sources of knowledge. The paradox of western thought, as Collingwood represents it, is that the very aim of rational philosophy is implicitly repudiated by its underlying assumptions. It is only in a philosophy which overcomes the dualism between truth and error, permanence and change, being and becoming, that the possibility of knowledge can be guaranteed at all. Indeed, it is only in a philosophy which recognizes error as an essential ingredient in the growth of truth that the human mind, which is necessarily finite, can be rendered an effective instrument in the apprehension of truth. Thus philosophy often takes the form of a phenomenology of errors; and the history of philosophy takes the form of a history of errors. But this does not deny the value of either philosophy or the history of philosophy, for, as we have seen, it is only through error that truth can be realized at all. Collingwood therefore argues in several places throughout his philosophical writings that each system of thought, even though it must be reabsorbed into the process of history in which it was created, is a permanent and valuable contribution to posterity; and this, to repeat, is not simply in spite of its strictly historical character but because of it:

> To us, the ideas expressed in them are ideas belonging to the past; but it is not a dead past; by understanding it historically we incorporate it into our present thought, and enable ourselves by developing and criticising it to use that heritage for our own advancement. (IH, 230; cf. SM, 317)

The collapse of a system, Collingwood wrote in *Speculum Mentis*, is not equivalent to the cancellation of the process by which it came into being. For in constructing and subsequently destroying successive systems of thought – which is what the history of philosophy is all about – the mind has learnt a permanent lesson. It has triumphed over error and so discovered a truth (SM, 317).

Collingwood is therefore declaring not only that philosophy has a history – even realists would agree with this – but more importantly that the truth which philosophy seeks to apprehend in this history is itself the product of the attempt to apprehend it. This amounts to nothing less than an identification of the act of being with the knowledge of it. Yet this identification does not cancel the distinction between truth and falsehood. Not every claim to knowledge can be characterized by truthfulness. Only those claims which conform to the right rules are truthful. A claim conforms to the rules only when it can be shown to play a necessary role in the systematic development of a scale of forms.

The paradox of truth is that, on the one hand, it is identical with the knowledge of it and yet, at the same time, it transcends this knowledge in the sense of laying down the rules according to which such knowledge is possible. This paradox can only be explained by means of the model of the scale of forms and the logic of the overlap of classes which, when fully understood, will show why, at least for Collingwood, the identity of truth and knowledge, being and becoming, eternity and historicity, does not lead inevitably to scepticism or radical historicism. Scepticism results only from an abstract identity which treats any and every form of knowledge as a complete and total embodiment of the truth, which may be described as the truth from that point of view, or the truth of that perspective. Such a position is a retreat to the very logic of species and genus which also underlies the scientific philosophy or positivism which opposes historicism. Thus historicism and positivism are paradoxically derived from the same 'corruption,' which is the dogmatic assertion of the abstract universal.

The implication of radical historicism is that, while all philosophy is a form of human thought subject to change, there is no such thing as progress. The whole point of the logic of the overlap of classes, however, is to explain how, in spite of the fact that philosophy is a form of human thought subject to change and liable to error, it is nevertheless capable of progress (EPM, 180); more precisely, the logic of the overlap of classes seeks to show how progress is only possible because of philosophy. Genuine progress in philosophy means that the philosopher is not merely adding another item to an inventory, he must be shaping afresh in his own mind the idea of philosophy as a whole (EPM, 184). Thus, in

An Essay on Philosophical Method, philosophy is conceived of as a scale of philosophies – this is what it means for it to be a system

> ... each differing from the rest not only in kind, as dealing with a certain specific form of the one universal philosophical subject-matter by means of an appropriate and therefore specifically distinct method, but also in degree, as more or less adequately embodying the ideal of genuine philosophical method applied to genuinely philosophical subject-matter. (EPM, 190)

In such a scale each form sums up the whole scale to that point, in the sense that each form is itself a system which has appropriated the essential and valuable features of the subordinate forms. Thus, for example, the ethics of duty may be regarded as superseding utilitarian and regularian ethics, and philosophical idealism may be regarded as superseding the more primitive forms of empiricism and realism. Each contains traces of the superseded forms in its own makeup and each may therefore be regarded as summing them up. Such summations are dialectical: what is retained is only part of the original content which, conceived of as a self-contained and distinct form, is erroneous and incomplete. Indeed, it is only by being dialectically reabsorbed into a higher standpoint that the truth of an erroneous standpoint can be brought to the surface. When viewed as a self-contained and distinct philosophy, a given standpoint is simply an error to be avoided. As a form on the scale of a philosophical system, however, it exists not just as a form to be refuted, but as something essentially reabsorbed – as a truth: "... thus one side of the task of all systematic philosophizing is to show the truth of theories which, considered as self-contained and distinct philosophies, would have to be condemned as errors" (EPM, 190).

From this conception of philosophy as a system, Collingwood draws the following paradoxical conclusions. In the first place, a philosophical system claims finality yet, because of its historical character, this claim must always be false. To this paradox must be added the further one, which arises from the central doctrines of *Speculum Mentis*, that it is only by unequivocally making such a claim to absolute truth that the implicit error of such a declaration can be recognized. Collingwood resolves this paradox by appealing to principles derived from the same theory of philosophy as a system. To begin with, although every new philosopher, in assuming his place on a scale of forms, sums up the whole scale to that point, in reaching the point he does, he is already in sight of new problems, and for this reason his conclusions are never final, being relative to the incompleteness of his achievement. But they are relative also to the whole scale, including its as yet unactualized future progress; indeed, if this relativism is not admitted, no such progress is possible.

At the same time, however, every such summation can be done only once. It is in this sense that there is 'finality'; the problem which a philosophy must solve in order to be a distinct system is finally solved (EPM, 191).[6]

In the second place, writes Collingwood, "A philosophical system claims completeness; but in fact it can never be more than a contribution made by its author towards a wider synthesis" (EPM, 191). Here again the same principles, derived from the notion of philosophy as a scale of forms, dispel the paradox. As one single accomplishment claiming independence and autonomy, an individual philosophy or historical construction is one among many, a single moment in the history of thought, which future philosophers will have to treat as an error. But as a form on a dialectical scale, reinterpreting previous outlooks and reaffirming them as elements within itself, it sums up, as we have seen, the whole scale to that point and is thus universal as well as individual. In short, as an independent claim to truth it is a mere particular species of an abstract universal, competing with other species, to which it is externally related, for the prize; as a form on a scale it participates in the concrete universal (the moments of which are internally related) and thus achieves genuine individuality (see above, ch. II, s. 5, and ch. VI, s. 2).

Finally, a philosophical system claims objectivity, but in fact it can only express its author's private and personal views. Here again the logic of the scale of forms can resolve the apparent paradox. For, as we have already seen, if the development of philosophy is regarded as the deployment of such a scale, then each man's philosophy must arise by objective necessity out of the situation in the history of thought in which he finds himself (EPM, 192). It will be the purpose of the next and final chapter to explicate further – in terms, this time, of the metametaphysical doctrine of 'immanence-transcendence' – this notion of philosophy as historical (i.e., relative, incomplete, and subjective) and yet transhistorical (i.e., final, complete, and objective).

⌒ X ⌒

Philosophy as
SELF-KNOWLEDGE:
The Rapprochement between
Philosophy and History

I PHILOSOPHY AS IMMANENCE-TRANSCENDENCE

According to the terms of the rapprochement between philosophy and history, history is implicit philosophy while philosophy is itself historical. But philosophy is not only the reflective moment of each standpoint, and subject therefore to the conditions of historicity; it is also the standpoint, and the only standpoint, from which the other standpoints can be made intelligible. Philosophy, to coin a phrase, is not only *immanent* but *immanent-transcendent*. In its moment of immanence, philosophy is identical with historical self-knowledge; as transcendent it achieves the status of absolute knowledge, *speculum speculi*.

The meaning of the immanence-transcendence of philosophy is explained in *Speculum Mentis*. To begin with, philosophy is immanent because it is intrinsic to the very substance of the mind which it seeks knowledge of. For, as we have already noted:

In an immediate and direct way, the mind can never know itself: it can only know itself through the mediation of an external world, know that what it sees in the external world is its own reflection. Hence the construction of external worlds – works of art, religions, sciences, structures of historical fact, codes of law, systems of philosophy and so forth *ad infinitum* – is the only way by which the mind can come to that self-knowledge which is its end. (SM, 315)

But, if mind is the whole of reality, object as well as subject, does it not follow that the truth to which mind aspires, like the mind which aspires to it, is itself only a system of appearances? Collingwood's answer would appear to be, Yes. "The truth is not some perfect system of philosophy: it is simply the way in which all systems, however perfect, collapse into nothingness on the discovery that they are only systems, only external worlds over against the knowing mind and not that mind itself (SM, 316). He therefore argues that even the conclusions of philosophy, *philosophia quaedam perennis*, are "not a body of truth revealed once for all, but a living thought whose content, never discovered for the first time, is progressively determined and clarified by every genuine thinker" (SM, 13). In short, there is no such thing as a pure theory of mind, a body of permanent and unchanging truths, about a permanent and unchanging nature:

> It follows that the concrete life of philosophy is no mere haven of rest, but a ceaseless act of achieving this balance. The balance is achieved not by the static contemplation by mind of its own fixed given nature – mind has no fixed given nature – but by the self-creation of this nature in a perpetual discovery of fact which is at the same time the creation of fact: the creation of the fact of its discovery, which is only the indispensable subjective side of the fact itself. The life of absolute knowledge is thus the conscious self-creation of the mind, no mere discovery of what it is, but the making of itself what it is. (SM, 296)

There are two distinct propositions being asserted here. The first is that the mind's knowledge of itself is necessarily one of mediation. The second is that the knowledge which is achieved through mediation is progressively determined, and that no pure theory (in the sense defined above) is therefore possible. Prima facie there is no necessary connection between these two propositions. But, if we keep in mind the interpretation which Collingwood places on the concept of mediation, we see clearly that the second proposition does in fact follow from the first. For, since all mediations are necessarily and dialectically related, forming a system of errors progressively purifying themselves, then the knowledge which these mediations reveal must itself be progressively determined. From all this we are tempted to draw the conclusion that if by 'progressively determined' is meant 'subject to historical change' then philosophy is historical knowledge. And this is the ground of its immanence.

But if philosophy is historical knowledge in one sense, Collingwood argues that in another sense it is transhistorical. This is because the mind is not only intrinsic to the process of change but is able at the same time to know itself as such. And in so far as it *knows* itself as changing it is a triumph over change. "A mind which knows its own change," writes Collingwood, "is by that very knowledge lifted above change" (SM, 301). The act of self-knowledge is the act in which man, recognizing his finitude, thereby transcends it:

> Man recognizes himself as finite and knows that, if he really is finite, he is thereby debarred from that infinity to which he aspires. But just as a being really limited in time could not know of its own limitation – for it could have no conception

of a past and a future if it lived wholly in the present – so a being really finite could not know itself as finite. The self-knowledge of man as finite is already his assertion of himself as infinite. (SM, 302)

It is one thing, however, to argue that the mind's recognition of its finitude is an implicit affirmation of its infinity; it is another thing to argue that the mind *qua* infinite can be made an object of knowledge, in the sense that such knowledge can produce a criterion with which to conduct the systematic analysis of experience, as outlined in *Speculum Mentis*. But only if this is possible can the theoretical presuppositions of the possibility of a phenomenology of mind be justified. Such a criterion is involved, for example, in the transition from history to philosophy: in this case, the criterion of the 'concrete facts,' which rests on the claim that the knowledge of facts is intrinsic to the facts themselves. The necessity of such a criterion is explicitly affirmed at the very outset of *Speculum Mentis* when Collingwood discusses the qualifications which philosophy must have in order to be a judge of experience. It is not enough, he argues, that the judge of the forms of experience has in fact lived each of these forms. If he is to show that his choice of a form of experience is not capricious, but is a lead which other people ought to follow, he must vindicate the rationality of his choice. He must prove that the choice is inevitable, and that each of the other forms in turn has characteristics which drive him on to the one in which alone he claims to find satisfaction. "Now the characteristic mark by which a form of experience is shown to be satisfactory," Collingwood claims, "is simply that it is possible" (SM, 44). But what is this notion of possibility except an a priori criterion – like the a priori criterion mentioned in the *Idea of History*?[1]

The question therefore remains, How is it possible to reconcile the concept of an a priori criterion with the philosophical doctrine of historicity? How is it possible for the mind to be both in and out of change at the same time?

Collingwood's answer lies in his interpretation of absolute mind as 'pure act.' The mind as 'pure act' is a self-making activity whose very essence is to change by discovering the error of its past, and in so doing create its own future. As 'pure act,' philosophy, in its moment of transcendence, is the conscious insight into the 'phenomenality' of historical knowledge and this insight is the basis upon which the philosopher brings into existence, in his own person, that awareness of himself which he finds to be the fundamental characteristic of spirit or mind: "His knowledge is therefore explicitly action; he is creating himself by knowing himself, and so creating for himself an intelligible world, the world of spirit in general" (OPA, 94).

Collingwood likens the philosophic act to the process of aesthetic creation. Neither philosophy nor its object pre-exist the concrete process of experience itself which is historical. The pure idea or notion, in other words, while it transcends experience on the one hand, is nevertheless contingent upon it:

> Art as a whole, we saw, is the pure act of imagination, and this act has its life in a process of self-differentiation and self-concentration, diastole and systole, which generates the various forms and phases of aesthetic activity within the unity of imagination itself, and having generated them treats them as so much material by the mastery of which it vindicates this unity. The act does not find a material, given from without, to unify which is the problem of its life; it generates the material out of itself and thus sets itself the problem which it lives by solving. In the same way the life of the spirit differentiates itself into art, religion, and the rest in order that it may exhibit its own unity in this diversity; or rather, that it may through this diversity bring into existence a unity which is not the bare unity with which it began but a unity enriched by all the differentiations through which it has passed. (OPA, 94)

When Collingwood describes this process, which takes place in time, as 'eternal,' he is referring not to a static, unchanging eternity, but rather to a dynamic, self-making eternity:

> ... it is always beginning, it has always reached any given point, and it has always arrived at its conclusion, somewhat as – to revert to a previous simile – a river is always rising at its source, always flowing over each part of its course, and always discharging itself into the sea. (OPA, 94–5)

But because this process is a conscious one – the river should be aware of itself throughout its course – Collingwood denies that it merely travels through a fixed cycle of changes; rather, it finds itself at every stage altered in significance by the consciousness of what has gone before. The unity of the spiritual life is therefore characterized as "... the unity of an infinitely increasing spiral rather than the unity of a rotating circle" (OPA, 95). Finally, the "energy which causes the spiral to expand" (or, to put it another way for Collingwood, the fundamental presupposition of this life of the spirit so-defined) is simply the "pure activity which is the spirit" (OPA, 94): an act, which, as *Speculum Mentis* has made clear, must, in order to comprehend its own change, rise above and transcend that change.

It is in terms of the dual nature of philosophy as immanence-transcendence that its precise status as a form of knowledge must be determined. Has philosophy's exposition of the life of mind, as Collingwood has described it, justified its own right to be the ground of the mind's unity – that is, in the sense in which it is the organon and content of all other standpoints? More important still, how can philosophy reconcile its claim to genuine autonomy with the philosophical conclusion that the mind is an object which in knowing itself, even philosophically, is substantially changed (which implies the necessity for new philosophies ad infinitum)?

The answer to this question lies jointly with *Speculum Mentis* and *An Essay on Philosophical Method*. According to the former the mind achieves a transcendental insight into its own nature through the construction and destruction of external worlds. The important thing about this transcendental activity is that it is progressive. By progress Collingwood does not mean the mere accumulation of information; as we noted in chapters VIII and IX, he means dialectical progress in which the mind learns a permanent lesson and triumphs over error. If past errors were rejected *in toto*, then the mind would indeed be devoid of meaning. But the rejection of past errors is at the same time the creation of new standpoints. The mind *is* what it *does*. And what it does now turns out to depend on how it understands its own past. Indeed, it is only by knowing its own history that the mind comes to have a history at all. In recognizing the error of its standpoint the mind is, at the same time, learning the meaning of its past and, in so doing, the past, rather than being simply negated becomes an element in the point of view from which the mind raises its next problem:

For the life of the mind consists of raising and solving problems, problems in art, religion, science, commerce, politics, and so forth. The solution of these problems does not leave behind it a sediment of ascertained fact, which grows and solidifies as the mind's work goes on. Such a sediment is nothing but the externality of a half-solved problem: when the problem is fully solved the sediment of information disappears and the mind is left at liberty to go on. Philosophy, therefore, is not a prerogative kind of knowledge immune from this reabsorption into the mind's being: it is nothing but the recognition that this reabsorption is necessary and is indeed the end and crown of all knowledge, the self-recognition of the mind in its own mirror. (SM, 317)

2 THE THEORY OF THE MIND AS PURE ACT

The theory of the mind as pure act is explicitly discussed by Collingwood in an essay published one year before the appearance of *Speculum Mentis* and entitled "Can the New Idealism Dispense with Mysticism" (1923).[2] The ostensible purpose of this paper was to discuss the philosophy of Giovanni Gentile. It is clear, however, that the position outlined – referred to as "the common ground of all idealism" (CNI, 169) – resembles very closely the outlook of *Speculum Mentis*.

It is worth noting that Collingwood began his career as a translator. The first book he published was a translation of Croce's book on Vico (1913).[3] Then in 1921 he and A. H. Hannay published a translation of Guido de Ruggiero's *Modern Philosophy*,[4] part IV of which contained a lively exposition of nineteenth- and early twentieth-century Italian philosophy. Collingwood's translation was completed by 1920 and was no doubt preceded by a careful study not only of the book itself but also of the tradition in which it was written.[5] In particular, as we have already noted, the translators' preface suggests on their part a strong interest in and wide knowledge of Italian philosophy; and explicit reference is made to its historical character. "Idealism for these Italians," they wrote, "as it was for Hegel, is a philosophy deeply rooted in history, and claims to show its superiority to other philosophies in nothing more than its penetrating study and exposition of history" (MP, 6). According to the conclusions of this book, the concern for historicity, which is evident as early as Vico, reached its high point in the nineteenth century, in an attempt to re-express and develop the philosophy of Hegel by reinterpreting the absolute according to the category of historicity. The result was the gradual emergence of a doctrine culminating in the philosophy of Giovanni Gentile, which de Ruggiero calls the theory of "absolute immanence" (MP, 360). This theory is undoubtedly one of the main sources of the doctrine of immanence-transcendence which, according to my interpretation, lies at the basis of Collingwood's thought.

According to de Ruggiero, the doctrine of absolute immanence was implied for the first time in the philosophy of Vincenzo Gioberti. The significance of Gioberti's thought lies in his identification of thinking and creation: in particular in the claim that thought creates itself only in the process of reproducing itself for itself, that is, by rethinking itself (MP, 333). It is a short step from this doctrine to Gentile's theory that the mind makes itself through an act of reconstruction which is essentially historical. But, throughout the period of Italian philosophy which began with Gioberti and ended with Gentile, there was one problem which continually defied solution: the problem of accounting for the identity of thinking and being, in which the continuity and unity of being is not totally consumed by the activity of change. Or, to put the problem as I posed it for Collingwood in my earlier discussion, How is it possible to conceive of a mind which is a self-making activity but within which the transhistorical unity of the mind as pure act is preserved?

It is my contention that Collingwood's answer to this question was itself influenced by the various attempts on the part of Italian philosophers to answer it; in which case, de Ruggiero's account of the history of Italian philosophy may be considered an important factor in the development of Collingwood's thought. What is important about de

Ruggiero's book is not just the exposition of Italian thought which it offers, but the interpretation which the author places upon this development, or the point of view from which it is written. Indeed, it might even be argued that this book supplied Collingwood with a clear understanding of the issues and questions which arise in any attempt to effect a rapprochement between philosophy and history.

Take for example de Ruggiero's criticisms of the philosophy of Bertrando Spaventa. In the first place, Spaventa is criticized on the grounds that he implies the very standpoint from which he seeks to escape: namely, the affirmation of an abstract separation between the truth as it is *in itself* and the truth as it is *for itself* (MP, 337–8) – this being precisely the criticism which Collingwood himself levels against his idealist predecessors such as Bradley and Dilthey. Even more important is de Ruggiero's claim that Spaventa's failure was due to the fact that he entirely lacked "a phenomenology of error," with the result that he failed to give explicit recognition to the concept of truth as progress and development, and was left therefore with a concept of truth as a mere *in-itself*, as something created and already complete (MP, 338). It is interesting to place this criticism of Spaventa against Collingwood's attempt in *Speculum Mentis* to redefine the dialectical method as a phenomenology of error, and to overcome all abstract distinctions between that which changes and develops, on the one hand, and absolute truth on the other.

The parallel between Collingwood's thought and de Ruggiero's critique of Spaventa is further suggested by de Ruggiero's claim that implicit in Spaventa's thought is the notion that the dialectical development of thought is not a pure development of the Idea as such, but is an immanent activity of consciousness (in which case its development is not only logical and historical, but phenomenological as well). What is more, the act of thought is an eternal act in which past and present are one and in which reproduction is not distinct from production (MP, 335–8). De Ruggiero supports this claim by citing various passages in which Spaventa allegedly implies "the phenomenolization of reality in human thought" and "banishes all question of a dualism between thought in itself and thought for us, between a process of consciousness and a process of science" (MP, 340). In effect then, de Ruggiero is declaring that Spaventa has hit upon an early formulation of the doctrine of absolute immanence:

Here ... we have the new thought which concentrates all the vitality of Hegelianism. The concept of absolute relation ... [according to which] inasmuch as reality is neither the mere contingent nor the mere absolute, but the absolute process of the contingent, it is not merely a solution, nor a ready-made reality presented to our eyes in advance of any problem that may be raised, nor something that is always sought for and never attained, an eternal problem that is never a solution; but it is an eternal problem which is at the same time an eternal solution, an absolute possibility which is also absolute actuality. The development of this concept means the satisfaction of the thousand-years-old demand, first made by Aristotle, for the unification of actuality and potentiality; a satisfaction which can only be found in the absolute identity of each with the other. Pascal made the profound remark that we could not seek unless we had already found; to this we can now add Spaventa's equally profound saying that the spirit is an eternal problem which is an eternal solution, a saying that may well stand as the motto of our whole speculative life. (MP, 340)

It does not seem unreasonable to suggest that this motto applies equally to Collingwood's philosophy; he too attempted throughout the whole of his philosophical career to achieve a unification of actuality and potentiality. This was accomplished by positing absolute identity, to which difference is essential and organic, but which nevertheless strives to overcome these differences by reconciling them with one another. The need for such a reconciliation gives rise to the process of absolute thought. Collingwood describes this process as "the conscious self-creation of the mind, no mere discovery of what it is, but the making of itself what it is" (SM, 296). At the level of absolute mind regarded as a system of categories (i.e., universal and necessary habits of mind) this process is the subject of a phenomenology of error. At the level of absolute mind regarded as the concrete embodiment of itself in time, this process is the subject of history and metaphysics proper.

By far the most important sections in de Ruggiero's book, so far as the growth of Collingwood's thought is concerned, are those dealing with Croce and Gentile. De Ruggiero credits Croce with disposing of Hegel's errors and developing his truth, the most important of which, according to de Ruggiero, is the notion of the concrete concept as the synthesis of opposites (MP, 349). What is interesting about de Ruggiero's account is that Croce is represented as arguing a doctrine which is similar to the one argued by Collingwood himself in *Speculum Mentis*. Indeed, as one studies de Ruggiero's account of the development of Croce's philosophy the parallel between Collingwood and Croce becomes more and more pronounced. The fundamental preoccupation of each was to confront the realist conception of a permanent and unchanging truth underlying the world of phenomena and change with the concept of a dialectical development of truth which is at the same time a history of errors. This is particularly true of the explicit aims of *Speculum Mentis*.

When we come to Gentile an even more striking parallel obtains. The core of Gentile's philosophy, according to de Ruggiero, is an original thesis on the identity of philosophy with its own history. According to the terms of this rapprochement, philosophy emerges not as a static, motionless identity, but as development, in the sense that philosophy, in creating its own history, creates itself. Implied by this doctrine, according to de Ruggerio, is "an absolute immanence of philosophical truth in the historical process which is at the same time the phenomenological process of the spirit" (MP, 358). The latter is further characterized as an ideal history of error: "for error," according to de Ruggiero, "is nothing but the dialectical moment of the spirit, the necessary coefficient of development" (MP, 358).

De Ruggiero represents this doctrine of Gentile's as containing the spirit of modern philosophy, which he defines as "the negation of reality as object, as given, and its affirmation as subject, as creation, as history" (MP, 358). To assert the historical character of philosophy in this way means, according to de Ruggiero, asserting the identity of being or existence and the consciousness of being, of reality and of reflection upon reality. And this, de Ruggiero concludes, leads to a transformation of the concept of philosophy itself.

Compare this concept of the historicity of philosophy (which, according to de Ruggiero, forms the core of Gentile's philosophy of the spirit) with Collingwood's doctrine of the historicity of philosophy as expounded in *Speculum Mentis* and other places. Like Gentile, Collingwood explicitly declares the philosopher's knowledge to be a form of historical action: an act, to cite Collingwood's own words once again, in which "[the philosopher] is creating himself by knowing himself, and so creating for himself an intelligible world, the world of spirit in general" (OPA, 94).

The parallel between Collingwood and Gentile may be further explored by a direct appeal to Collingwood's own essay "Can the New Idealism Dispense with Mysticism." A careful reading of this essay will indicate that Collingwood is not simply expounding and defending the philosophy of Giovanni Gentile; he is at the same time outlining, in a brief but systematic way, the main themes of *Speculum Mentis* – by then virtually completed and soon to be published. In particular, we are exposed for the first time to the theory of absolute mind which lies at the basis of *Speculum Mentis*, the theory which I, for Collingwood, have called the doctrine of immanence-transcendence. The latter emerges in the course of a critical analysis of Gentile's theory of the mind as pure act. I would therefore argue that while the 1923 paper betrays the strong influence which Gentile had on Collingwood's thought, it reveals as well the main differences between the two thinkers. As portrayed by de Ruggiero, Gentile's concept of absolute-immanence seems (in its attempt to escape from the abstractionism which haunted earlier

Italian philosophy) to concentrate on immanence at the expense of transcendence.[6] As a result, it too easily gives the impression that in the end transcendence is totally consumed by immanence. This very point is the main theme of the 1923 essay, in which Collingwood tries to defend Gentile against the charge of radical historicism. While the basis of this defence was certainly implicit in Gentile's own thought, by rendering it explicit Collingwood is going beyond this thought: particularly in the sense, for example, that having affirmed the immanence of philosophy in the life of thought conceived as a system of dialectically related forms, he goes on to explain in some detail (not only in *Speculum Mentis* but in *An Essay on Philosophical Method*) the transcendence of philosophy as well. And in so doing Collingwood endows the doctrine of historicity, which is in danger of totally encompassing the whole of Gentile's thought, with a transcendental or transhistorical basis.[7]

The argument which, in "Can the New Idealism Dispense with Mysticism," Collingwood attributes to Gentile, may be summed up as follows. History is by definition something known. It is not merely a process but a known process. But a mind which knows a process can only do so by somehow detaching itself from, and rising above, this process. For if it were wholly immersed in process it could never make itself an object of knowledge; it could never know that it was changing. But unless change is known as a process it can never really *be* a genuine process. For a genuine process to exist at all it must occur against the background of a continuity without which change would be unintelligible. Implied by the notion of mind as pure change is the absurdity of a radical pluralism according to which one mind would perish at every instant and another would come into being; and this Collingwood declares, "is not change in a mind": "... change in a mind must be change for a mind; a change of which that mind is conscious; and to be conscious of it, the mind must somehow be raised above it" (CNI, 166). Collingwood thus holds that the mind, in order to make itself an object of knowledge, must somehow transcend its historicity – even though the latter is what fundamentally constitutes its essential nature. How is this apparent contradiction to be resolved? How is the mind to be at once in change and out of change? According to Collingwood Gentile's answer is:

Only if the mind *originates change in itself*. For then, as the source and ground of change, it will not be *subject* to change; while on the other hand, as undergoing change through its own free act, it will exhibit change. This double aspect of the mind as active and passive is the very heart of Gentile's philosophy. It is his favorite distinction of *act* and *fact*. The act is out of time in the sense that it creates time, just as it is supernatural in the sense that it creates nature; the fact is temporal, natural, subject to all those laws which constitute its finiteness. But between the act and the fact there is no division: the distinction is only an ideal distinction. In creating the fact, the act realizes itself, and does not live apart in a heaven of its own from which it issues mandates for the creation of facts; it lives in the facts which it creates, and can say to the fact, "Thou art my son, this day have I begotten thee." (CNI, 166–7)

Gentile is asserting, then, not only the transcendence of mind as a necessary condition of historicity, but also the characterization of transcendence as an act of creativity and the further identity of this transcendence with the products of its creation: this is the doctrine of the identity of act and fact which is central to the whole of Gentile's philosophy. In a passage worth quoting in full, Collingwood justifies this identity as follows:

This identity of act and fact ... is necessary for the following reason. If the active or creative mind were *merely* active and creative, if what it created were something other than itself, then this other, this created object, would be a mere flux of appearances without permanence, solidity, or substance. Only the permanent can change; and therefore the principle of permanence, the unchanging reality, must be immanent in the very process of change, or this process could not take place. If the changing were one thing and the unchanging another, if that which changed were not also permanent and that which is permanent were not also changing, then both the permanent and the changing would be illusory. If the permanent and changing principle is called God and the changing creation is called the World, we thus reach the formula that it is only the presence of God in the world that makes the world real, and only his self-expression in the act of creating the world that makes God actual. (CNI, 167)

The standpoint from which Collingwood discusses Gentile bears a striking resemblance to the theory of absolute mind which is expounded in *Speculum Mentis*. The notions of the "World" and "God," for example, with which Collingwood explicates Gentile's distinction between 'fact' and 'act' (or subject and object) have their origins in Collingwood's own system – the former in the dialectical scale of forms constituted by the partial and erroneous worlds of art, religion, science, history, and philosophy (and which in Collingwood's system replace the Gentilian triad of art, religion, and philosophy), the latter in the notion of absolute mind itself, which Collingwood defines as an activity of conscious creation, as both creative act (SM, 296) and historical fact (SM, 298). Following Gentile, Collingwood places the significance of the creative act in the fact that it is not only conscious but self-conscious – which, for Collingwood, is the ground of its permanence or transhistoricity. At the same time, because its creativity is an act of self-creation, it is also immanent, and as such expresses itself in the construction and destruction of external worlds or historical world views.

However, Collingwood departs from Gentile by conceiving of the notion of the pure act (or absolute mind) as the logic of the overlap of classes (EPM) which forms the basis for the new phenomenology of error (SM). So conceived, the concept of the pure act emerges as a paradigm for understanding the structure of each particular form of experience as well. Through works of art and acts of faith the mind brings itself into existence *qua* imagination; through scientific observation or perception it brings itself into existence *qua* abstract universal (or, as Collingwood sometimes calls it, understanding); through history and philosophy it brings itself into existence *qua* concrete universal (which Collingwood refers to as reason) (SM, 195 ff.).

As in the case of absolute mind so in each of the particular standpoints, it is only the presence of mind in the world that makes the world real and only its self-expression in the acts of creating works of art, acts of faith, scientific abstractions, historical facts, and philosophical truths, that makes mind actual – or, to cite once again Collingwood's doctrine of the historicity of human nature, which sums up implicitly the fundamental principles which lie at the basis of each level of absolute mind:

... the historical process is a process in which man creates for himself this or that kind of human nature by re-creating in his own thought the past to which he is heir ... By historical thinking, the mind whose self-knowledge is history not only discovers within itself those powers of which historical thought reveals the possession, but actually develops those powers from a latent to an actual state, brings them into effective existence. (IH, 226)

By making the proper substitutions, this passage may be adapted to give expression to the fundamental principle of Collingwood's theory of mind, which is that the processes of art, religion, science, history and philosophy, are processes in which mind creates for itself this or that kind of nature by creating through its own acts the objects by means of which it comes to know itself, such that through these acts the mind not only discovers within itself those powers of which art, religion, science and the rest, reveals the presence, but actually develops those powers from a latent to an actual state and thereby brings them into effective existence.[8]

3 THE PURE ACT AS THE TRANSCENDENTAL GROUND OF HISTORICITY

Collingwood's main interest in his 1923 essay on Gentile was to defend idealism against the charge of mysticism. The basis of this charge is fundamentally the same as the basis for the charge of radical historicism; in both cases, the possibility of accounting for a strictly rational body of philosophical knowledge is denied. Likewise, the grounds upon which the charges of mysticism and historicism are met are fundamentally the same. For this reason Collingwood's defence of Gentile is of some importance in determining the basis upon which Collingwood himself can answer the charge of historicism.

Gentile's theory of mind, as outlined (and apparently accepted) by Collingwood, seems to imply the following propositions: (a) reality is history, history is mind, therefore reality is mind; (b) mind knows its own history, and it is only by knowing its own history that it comes to have a history at all; (c) a mind which is able to comprehend its own history is in that very knowledge raised above its history. The first two propositions affirm the historicity of mind; the third affirms its transhistoricity. To employ a different distinction, the first two propositions point to the immanence of mind in historical change, the third points to the transcendence of mind. The mind as pure act, then, may be properly described under the category of immanence-transcendence.

To say simply that the mind as pure act transcends itself does not, of course, justify the possibility of a purely philosophical theory of it. Only if the mind as pure act – in its moment of transcendence – can be made an object of knowledge is this possible. In short, something like a Kantian transcendental analysis of mind as pure act is necessary. We must therefore ask the question, To what extent does the phenomenology of *Speculum Mentis* (and other relevant writings) prepare for this? In the first instance we must recognize that if philosophy is to articulate itself in language, then it is obvious that to some extent philosophical knowledge must be mediated by concepts. When it is recognized that all concepts are subject to historical change, the historicity of philosophical thought becomes apparent. At the same time it is also apparent that if philosophy is to justify its right to be the source of the unity of knowledge, then the conclusions of philosophy, *philosophia quaedam perennis,* must in some sense be truths, which are *semper ubique ab omnibus,* that is, eternal truths applying to mind as such, even though at the same time they constitute a progressively determined and changing body of knowledge.

This point is clearly established in the *New Leviathan* in which the theory of the mind as pure act is explicitly discussed. In this work Collingwood argues for an identity between the science of the pure act and Locke's plain historical method: indeed, the former is put forward as the theoretical presupposition of the possibility of history as a science of mind: "A study of mind on the historical method" he writes, "renounces with Locke 'all science of substance.' It does not ask what mind is; it asks only what mind does." Such a study is possible, he continues, "by holding that mind is 'pure act,' so that the question *what mind is* resolves itself without residue into the question *what mind does*" (NL, 61). But the same pure act is here made the basis not only of a purely historical knowledge of what mind is, which demonstrates that "what mind has done on a certain definite occasion is typical of what it always and everywhere does" (NL, 62). This claim must not be construed as a concession to positivism, as an admission that mind is governed by eternal and unchanging abstract laws. It would make more sense to interpret this passage according to the theory of *Speculum Mentis* which discriminates between a "serial" or phenomenological order of mind, and the historical presence of mind in the life both of the individual and of the race as a whole, the latter being in structure identical with the former. The phenomenological order may be regarded as the basis of "what [mind] always and everywhere does," while the historical order is the basis of "what mind has done on a certain definite [occasion]." Both, however, must be distinguished from the progress or development of mind according to law. In the case of mind there are no laws of development or progress (SM, 289–90, 300). This antipositivism with respect to mind is again defended in the *New Leviathan* (NL, 48) where mind is once more arranged "serially" (NL, 63), taking the form of what Collingwood calls an irregular series (NL, 63). So conceived, the logical development of mind is neither predictable nor synonymous with temporal development (NL, 64–5).

In short, the history of mind cannot be understood in terms of the laws of its temporal progress. On the contrary, the history of mind can be comprehended only in terms of the dialectic of its logical or serial development which is governed by what in the *New Leviathan* Collingwood calls the "LAW OF CONTINGENCY" (the earlier terms in a series of mental functions do not determine the later) and the "LAW OF PRIMITIVE SURVIVALS" (when A is modified into B there survives in any example of B, side by side with the function B which is the modified form of A, an element of A in its primitive or unmodified state) (NL, 65). These are the very principles which, as we have already seen, account for the phenomenological development of mind. It follows then that the model of the relation between what mind always does and what it does on a particular occasion is to be found not in the relation of particular temporal events to abstract universal laws but in the relation between the phenomenological and historical orders of mind. The former while immanent in the latter is also transcendental. The statement cited above may therefore be interpreted with reference to the relation of immanence-transcendence. For only if the transcendental structure of mind *qua* mind is in some sense immanent in the historical appearances of mind can the ordinary science of history (whether it be historical metaphysics, or the history of institutions: the science of what mind has done in the past) be converted into the science of what mind always and everywhere does. In this respect, the assumptions of the *New Leviathan* are the same as the conclusions of the *Idea of History* and *An Essay on Metaphysics*: philosophical statements about mind, although they are arrived at only in the course of historical study, are nevertheless categorical universal when they conform to the criteria specified in chapters VII and VIII above.[9]

The theory of the mind as pure act is intended to reconcile (at the highest ontological level) the doctrine of historicity with the possibility of a purely philosophical theory – the rapprochement towards which the whole of Collingwood's philosophy has been moving. Yet, in some respects at least, this possibility seems to be denied. In particular, the second proposition cited above seems to render the latter dubious. For the principle that only through historical self-knowledge does the mind come to have a history at all is, in its more abstract formulation, the principle of the identity of knowing and being in which being is assimilated to knowing. This seems to imply, at a more concrete level, the assimilation of philosophy to history. In short, by taking the second proposition to its logical conclusion, are we not led straight into radical historicism?

In support of this charge Collingwood's critics may be expected to advance the following arguments against my representation of Collingwood's theory of the mind as pure act. The theory, they will argue, rests entirely on a fundamental distinction (apparently derived from Gentile) between the mind as pure act and the mind as historical fact. As described by Collingwood, the mind as pure act is not something separate from, but is rather immanent in, the system of historical facts. It is represented as the source of the unity of history conceived as a concrete universal. Corresponding to this distinction, we might expect to find, on the side of the subject, two kinds of knowledge: knowledge of the historical fact which proceeds from the empirical (i.e., historical) ego, and knowledge of the pure act which proceeds from the transcendental ego. From the former would arise all the particular disciplines: art, religion, science, and history. From the latter would arise philosophy. But if we should examine this claim in the wider context of Collingwood's system, it becomes doubtful whether this distinction can be maintained. For, as Collingwood himself admits, all knowledge is necessarily mediate, not immediate. As such, it must arise out of fact, that is, from the world of history. But if, as he seems to be arguing, the categories of all knowledge are rooted in history – if they, like the facts they know, are subject to historical change – then, contrary to Collingwood's ostensible conclusions, philosophy arises entirely from the empirical and not the transcendental ego. Indeed, this interpretation would appear to be confirmed by Collingwood's own admission in *Speculum Mentis* that the mind can never know itself in an immediate and direct way, but only through the mediation of external worlds such as art, religion, science, structures of historical fact, codes of law, systems of philosophy, and so forth, *ad infinitum* (SM, 315).

What is more, the critic will continue, even if philosophy could arise from the transcendental ego, the very nature of this ego (or pure act) denies the possibility of philosophy. The pure act, as described by Collingwood, is totally undetermined, limited by nothing except its own limited spontaneity. It is, in short, a being whose existence is prior to essence. The nature of this being is revealed only in action, like the structure of a work of art. Collingwood describes such a being as a self-making activity from whom, in effect, *esse sequitur operationem*. The pure act, he says, is pure freedom which in creating *ex nihilo* passes itself *ex nihilo in aliquid*[10] – which is what is implied in Collingwood's various descriptions of absolute mind as being bound by no necessity, not even the laws of its own nature (SM, 300), and as having no fixed given nature, but as being rather the product of an act of self-creation (SM, 296). But if this is his conception of absolute being, it follows that there can be no *ratio* of it, no permanent body of knowledge concerning the essence of this being. On the contrary, since the pure act makes itself by mediating itself through historical forms, there can only be historical knowledge of it: which, since this knowledge is based on mediations, must be necessarily partial and erroneous. Indeed, this implicit scepticism, the critics will conclude, is nowhere more conclusively summed up than in Collingwood's own words, in the very last sentence of *Speculum Mentis* already cited:

> Philosophy, therefore, is not a prerogative kind of knowledge immune from this reabsorption into the mind's being: it is nothing but the recognition that this reabsorption is necessary and indeed the end and crown of all knowledge, the self-recognition of the mind in its own mirror. (SM, 317)

But, convincing as this argument may seem, it is based on a fundamental misunderstanding – anticipated by Collingwood himself – of the nature of the pure act. "This process of the creation and destruction of external worlds," writes Collingwood, "might appear to superficial criticism ... a declaration of the mind's inability to produce solid assets, and thus the bankruptcy of philosophy" (SM, 316). And although Collingwood does not himself explicitly point this out it may be argued, on his behalf, that such a "superficial criticism" presupposes, among other things, that in its moment of transcendence the mind as pure act ought to be totally distinct from, and even antithetical to, the mind as historical fact. It presupposes, in other words, a basic dualism between transcendence and immanence which it is the very purpose of the concept of immanence-transcendence to overcome. It commits a separation of worlds which, like the Platonic separation of idea and fact, can never again be reconciled. At the same time, by failing to recognize the purely philosophical character of transhistorical knowledge, Collingwood's critic is apparently viewing it as a mere extension of the knowledge which arises at the historical level. But the whole which is the unity of its parts is no mere extension of its parts; it is on the contrary something qualitatively different without being totally distinct. So the knowledge which lies at the basis of the particular sciences is no mere extension of these sciences, but a knowledge of a fundamentally different order; it is *scientia intuitiva* (or, as Collingwood himself prefers to call it, *speculum speculi*), a *theoria* in which the distinction between subject and object is overcome; it is the highest moment of self-mediation in which the mind has a vision of itself *sub species aeternitatis*. And from this vision derive the clear and distinct ideas which are the basic categories of philosophical analysis: categories which in spite of their transhistoricity must nevertheless, like the *logos*, clothe itself in the flesh of time, and in this descent from eternity to time speak the language of man which is historical, subject to change, progressively altered by each generation.

Speculum speculi is what is implicit in all historically grounded knowledge. But only through the latter can the former arise; only through time can eternity emerge. Thus there must be a history of *speculum speculi*; it takes time before the 'idea' manifests itself clearly and distinctly in consciousness. The history of philosophy – described by Collingwood as a dialectical history of errors – is the history of the gradual emergence of the transhistorical perception of truth which has all along been immanent in the process of error. This transhistorical perception is the a priori criterion of mediation.

Collingwood's position on this point may be compared with that of Hegel for whom a science of infinite mind was also possible. For Hegel, the mind is both finite and infinite. It is infinite mind which makes itself an object in the science of logic, and which discovers itself as mind *qua* mind at the conclusion of the dialectic of absolute mind. As finite, mind is historical, but there is, in spite of its historicity, the possibility of a complete transcendence *qua* infinite mind when the mind as such makes itself an object of knowledge, knows itself through the mediation of the 'notion.' This *scientia* was of course not equally possible at any time in history. It had to wait upon history before it could arise. According to Hegel all previous standpoints have been successive attempts to reach the standpoint of pure science. This accounts for the fact that the history of philosophy parallels the history of mind in general. Once the mind has reached a certain point in historical development the immanent possibility of pure science is rendered actual. There is, however, an important difference between Collingwood and Hegel. For Hegel, once the Truth has arrived on the scene it remains unmediated; Hegel seems therefore to have regarded his own philosophy as final, never to be superseded by another. In this respect, for Hegel, the final transcendence of mind is complete.[11] For Collingwood, however, this transcendence is never complete, never final, but always itself in the making. But even though the act of self-transcendence is itself subject to historical development it is nevertheless something permanent. Thus Collingwood declares, in his own defence, in a passage already cited in another context:

The collapse of a system of thought is therefore not equivalent to the cancellation of the process by which it came into being. It collapses, but it does not perish. In constructing and destroying it, the mind has learnt a permanent lesson: it has triumphed over an error and so discovered a truth. The destroyed system collapses not into bare nothingness but into immediacy, into a characteristic or attribute of the mind itself, passes as it were into the muscle and bone of the mind, becomes an element in the point of view from which the mind raises its next problem. (SM, 317)[12]

The theory of the mind as pure act, or, as I have preferred to describe it, the doctrine of immanence-transcendence, is the foundation of Collingwood's entire philosophy, and the basis upon which the rapprochement between philosophy and history is finally achieved. It is also the basis of the theory of absolute mind in *Speculum Mentis* and is regarded by Collingwood as "the solution of all those problems concerning finitude and infinity which have so vexed abstract thought" (SM, 302). Philosophy as absolute knowledge is the concrete life of mind. As such it is implicit in all other standpoints and is therefore the basis upon which each standpoint comes to self-consciousness. In this form philosophy is subject to its own historical development, a development which has its ground in the logical development of mind itself. At the same time philosophy is transcendental knowledge of the structure of mind as pure act – as it is revealed and only revealed in the history of thought. Philosophy discovers what it is doing by doing it, and in so doing creates its own laws.

Collingwood's defence against the charge of radical historicism may be further explicated by turning once again to his account of Gentile, from whom, as I have shown, his own doctrine of immanence-transcendence was derived. According to the account which is given in "Can the New Idealism Dispense with Mysticism," while Gentile regarded art as the essence of immanence, it was religion which he regarded as being the essential element of transcendence. These two elements, religion and art, are always found together in the synthesis which is philosophy. Philosophy therefore is, in effect, immanence-transcendence. What characterizes this synthesis, according to Collingwood, is the fact that while transcendence is always present, it is never the last word, it is not abstractly present to the exclusion of everything else; on the contrary, it is "dialectically present as one of two elements whose tension constitutes the life of the whole" (CNI, 168). The last word lies with the synthesis which is neither mere transcendence nor mere immanence, but the principle which de Ruggiero called absolute immanence:

The absolute ... is that which has reconciled its own opposite to itself, and therefore no longer stands in opposition to it ... Thus the metaphysic of absolute immanence is the philosophy whose primary principle, that of immanence, has overcome its abstractness by including in itself its own opposite, namely, the principle of transcendence ... That reconciliation of the opposing principles of immanence and transcendence which ... [is regarded by Gentile] as possible, necessary, and indeed actual ... [Gentile] calls ... philosophy. (CNI, 168)

Collingwood makes it quite clear that this conception of philosophy – a conception which is obviously at the centre of *Speculum Mentis* – does not reduce philosophy to a mere intuition or to mysticism, if by the latter is meant a non-cognitive, non-rational, non-discursive, apprehension of ultimate truths. On the contrary, according to Collingwood, the philosophical tradition in which the above conception of philosophy arose, namely the tradition of idealism, has always maintained "that ultimate truth is to be reached, if at all, only by hard thinking, by critical development of rational theory, and not by any kind of intellectual intuition" (CHI, 171). If it is true, Collingwood continues, that ultimate truths are to be reached by the path of intuition, and not by the labour of the notion, then certainly all scientific and historical thinking is futile, and modern philosophy is indeed bankrupt.[13] "It can only be a non-existent way of apprehending the non-existent" (CNI, 171); "... the only thing left for the person who wants to get at the truth is to return like Nebuchadnezzar to the level of the instinctive animals and *s'installer dans le mouvement*, instead of trying to raise himself above it in order to understand it" (CNI, 171).

The truth is, Collingwood asserts, that what often passes (under the name of mysticism) for supra-cognitive intuition, is in fact a mediation which while actually present is not wholly explicit. The mind reaches truths, but does not know how it has reached them. It is the business of scientific or philosophical thought "to lay bare this concealed process, to render explicit the mediation which in the mystical experience itself was only implicit" (CNI, 173). This is precisely the role of philosophy in *Speculum Mentis*. In the essay on Gentile, Collingwood cites Hegel's remark that "truth is not dependent for its first revelation upon philosophy" (CNI, 173–4). In the mystical experience (as indeed in every other experience) truth is actually attained, and it remains for philosophy to explain how it was attained. The necessity for the mystical experience, writes Collingwood,

lies in the principle that we discover new truths neither by the inference of the logic books nor by the intuition of Aristotle, but by an act of mind which reaches out beyond the given, grasps the new thought as it were in the dark, and only after that consolidates its new conquest by building up to it a bridge of reasoned proof. (CNI, 174)

But the building of this bridge, which is the task of reflection, is "nothing but the implicitness of thought in the mystical experience" (CNI, 174); "... the bringing out into visibility on the sensitive plate of what has already been recorded upon it, the rendering explicit of a mediation or proof which was already there implicitly" (CNI, 174).

This view of the rapprochement between philosophy and mysticism is, of course, an early formulation of the rapprochement between faith and reason. What is even more significant is the fact that Collingwood presents it in 1923 as the way "a modern idealistic philosophy" might achieve this rapprochement. It is tempting to suspect that the phrase "a modern idealistic philosophy" is a direct reference to Collingwood's own views in *Speculum Mentis*. Of course when we get to *Speculum Mentis* we find that Collingwood has departed from Gentile in certain respects. In the first place Collingwood replaces Gentile's absolute triad (art, religion, knowledge) with a quincunx. In the second place, it is clear that he regards philosophy (especially in its *ab extra* moment) rather than religion as the primary element of transcendence; indeed this view is already implicit in the 1923 essay. For how else could philosophy lay bare the concealed process of truth and render explicit "the mediation which in the mystical experience itself was only implicit"? It was for this reason that Collingwood was perhaps more successful than Gentile in developing a phenomenology of error. In recognizing that the transcendent, however you decide to characterize it, is immanently (i.e., concretely) rather than abstractly transcendent, Collingwood was remaining faithful to the tradition of Gentile. But in characterizing this immanence as philosophical and grounding it on the logic of the overlap of classes and the metaphysical doctrine of the scale of forms, Collingwood sought to avoid the historicism which threatens to engulf the thought of Gentile.[14]

4 SUMMARY AND RECAPITULATION

We may now sum up our conclusions concerning Collingwood's alleged reform of metaphysics. According to Collingwood, metaphysics possesses a twofold nature; it is the critic both of experiences other than itself and of its own critical activity. As the critic of experience in general, metaphysics may be said to have a twofold function: to describe the presuppositions of each particular standpoint on the one hand, and to show how they necessarily arise and fall on the other. But this is also the function of history (see above, ch. III, s. 2, and ch. VIII).

Not only is there a methodological overlap between history and metaphysics, but the same sort of overlap obtains even at the ontological level. For, according to Collingwood, the immediate experience which is the subject of philosophical analysis is an immediacy which is at the same time the active appropriation of past thought, and hence history (SM, 301–2, 316–17). Metaphysics and history are thus overlapping members of the same scale and constitute a dialectical identity in difference.

However, as the critic of its own thought, metaphysics is the transcendental articulation of the pure a priori idea which is the immanent unity of the variety of historical standpoints and the theoretical basis upon which these standpoints can arrive at self-understanding. The first stage in the life of philosophy is phenomenology as exemplified in *Speculum Mentis*. Phenomenology is the analysis of the most primitive presuppositions of the experience of consciousness per se as it proceeds through the various forms which make up the scale of conscious existence on the way to that absolute knowledge which is philosophy proper. The arrival of philosophy on the scene has the effect of transforming each standpoint into a new shape of experience and then reconstructing it into a systematic unity. At this level the philosophical (i.e., metaphysical) activity is exemplified in a series of writings, each of which is devoted to one particular form of experience. Thus, for example, the presuppositions of religion are set forth briefly in the pamphlet "Faith and Reason," of art in *The Principles of Art*, of science in *The Idea of Nature*, of history in *The Idea of History*, and of society and culture in *The New Leviathan* and parts of *An Essay on Metaphysics*. Since, as I have argued, the subject under discussion in each of these works has been reconstituted by philosophy, the results of the phenomenology of first-level experience, which is what we have throughout most of *Speculum Mentis*, will differ from the results of the more historical metaphysics of second- and third-level experiences: hence, for example, the treatment of art in *Speculum Mentis* differs from the treatment of art in the *Principles of Art*. The latter, of course, was already implicit in the former, but this could not be recognized until the arrival of philosophy on the scene. The purpose of the analysis of *Speculum Mentis* is to show how art defends its autonomy before philosophy has appeared, while the purpose of the *Principles of Art* is to describe the case for an aesthetic experience which, as a result of the influence of philosophy, has reconstituted itself but still considers itself to be autonomous. The phenomenological basis of these transformations within experience, and their reconstruction by philosophy into systematic philosophies, was discussed above in chapters III, IV, and V.

But metaphysics is not simply the critic of the other forms of experience; it is also one of the experiences criticized. As the critic of its own activity it has been characterized in this study as the philosophy of being *qua* being (see above, ch. I, s. 5) or, to use the term which formed the subject of discussion in this present chapter, the trancendental metaphysics of the mind as pure act. The latter is not, of course, a separate activity, abstracted from the rest, but is achieved only by means of the historically grounded philosophies of the separate standpoints – which Collingwood called metaphysics proper (see above, ch. I, s. 5 and ch. VI, s. 1).

In other words, the transcendental metaphysics of the pure act is possible only to a mind which is also engaged in the primarily historical metaphysics of the particular forms of experience. When mind reflects upon its own activity as metaphysician the result is the discovery of what Collingwood calls the idea of philosophy as a system; it is the discovery at the same time of the logic of the overlap of classes according to which this system is constructed. The statements which form the main body of philosophical systems, as well as the statements describing the logic according to which these systems are constructed, are characterized by Collingwood as categorical universal propositions. The latter, while they are historically grounded, are nevertheless transhistorical in their philosophical status; for they are, in effect, a part of the gradually developing concrete universal, mind (see above, ch. III, s. 4, ch. VIII, s. 8, ch. IX, ss. 4–5, and ch. X).

The exposition of the transhistorical concrete universal, which is both immanent and transcendent, is, according to Collingwood, the fundamental activity of absolute philosophy – or, as I have sometimes called it, the meta-metaphysics of the pure act. The principles of absolute philosophy, as expounded in *An Essay on Philosophical Method* (and also in *Speculum Mentis* and *An Essay on Metaphysics*) were systematically discussed in chapters VI and VII of this study, while the principles and problems connected with the pursuit of metaphysics proper (as expounded in the *Idea of History* and *An Essay on Metaphysics*) were discussed in chapters VIII and IX. Implied by Collingwood's theory of absolute philosophy is the claim that even absolute knowledge, which is the a priori criterion according to which both phenomenology and metaphysics proceed, is itself a progressively determined body of knowledge, and for this reason, as I have already pointed out, it is Collingwood's contention that each generation must analyse itself anew in order to give content to the a priori idea and in this way bring the concrete universal into existence. This is philosophy as history, the third-level metaphysics of past and present thought, which takes the form of a dynamic scale in which, as mind becomes the historian of its own philosophical experience (see above, ch. I, s. 5, and ch. VIII, s. 2), it brings into existence not only the present but the past as well. And although the question-and-answer process to which philosophy (in the course of this twofold metaphysical analysis) subjects mind is an ongoing and historical process, it nevertheless contains implicitly an a priori structure which the enquiring mind, through the experience of its historical appearances, apprehends transhistorically.

Thus even historical philosophy is implicitly transcendental; but only to a thought which is actually committed to and engaged in the historical reconstruction of itself do the theoretical presuppositions of the possibility of this reconstruction present themselves. What is revealed in this transhistorical perception is – to repeat – not the truth as truth, complete and unchanging, but rather the truth as a dialectically and progressively developing system.

Collingwood therefore characterizes each of his third-level adventures in metaphysics as attempts, not to expound the "eternal truth" about each of the various subject matters, but rather, to reach some understanding of the problems which artists, theologians, scientists, historians, and philosophers find themselves faced with at any given time (IH, 4; PA, vi); and, in similar terms, he characterizes absolute philosophy, or meta-metaphysics, as "not a body of truth revealed once for all, but a living thought whose content, never discovered for the first time, is progressively determined and clarified by every genuine thinker" (SM, 13).

5 THE DRAMA OF ABSOLUTE MIND

If Collingwood's rapprochement between metaphysics and history seems unnecessarily obscure it is only because he, like all great metaphysicians, is wrestling with a formidable God, a God whose only adequate means of communication may be a language charged with metaphor and imagery. To communicate, in the language of rational discourse, the results of its encounter with the absolute is perhaps the greatest challenge which finite mind can set itself. And at times, in its search for clarity, and in order to enrich its own rational insights, reason, which is after all only faith and imagination cultivating themselves, must return with proven humility to the language of metaphor and imagery, seeking more the mood than the logical anatomy of absolute truth. Collingwood, in keeping with his own convictions on this matter, resorts at times to such imagery. And in one particular passage, which sums up the essence of his philosophical achievement, he depicts the plight and drama of absolute mind in the language of religious imagery.[15] Religious imagery, he admits, cannot prove the truth of any philosophy because the interpretation put upon such imagery is already the work of philosophy. But, he continues, "it will illustrate, if it does not help to demonstrate, our conception of the absolute mind to point out the way in which one religion at least has expressed itself, when dealing with the ultimate questions which here concern us":

God is here conceived as the absolute spirit, alpha and omega, the beginning and the end. Behind him, beyond him, apart from him, there is nothing: neither matter nor law, neither earth nor heaven, neither space nor time. In the beginning, by an absolute act which was not itself subject to any determination of time or space, God created the heavens and the earth; the visible world, with all its order and furniture, even the very space in which it floats and the time in which it endures and changes, is the work of this absolute act. But this world is no mere toy shaped by God and thrown off from himself in contemptuous alienation. His spirit moves upon the face of the waters, even the waters of chaos, and this same breath becomes the soul of life in the man whom he creates in his own image. Man is one with God, no mere part of the whole but informed by the indwelling of the divine spirit. Now man by his misguided thirst for knowledge, partakes of that knowledge which is forbidden, namely error, or the human wisdom which negates God's wisdom. This error deforms his own true, that is divine, nature, and the deformation takes the shape of banishment from the presence of God into the wilderness of the visible world. Having thus lost even the sight of God, the knowledge of what he himself ought to be, he cannot recover his lost perfection until he comes to know himself as he actually is. But not knowing himself as he ought to be, he cannot know himself as he is. His error is implicit just because it is complete. It can only become explicit if God reveals himself afresh, if the true ideal breaks in upon the soul clouded by error. This, in the fulness of time, is granted. Human nature sunk in error is confronted by the confutation of its own error, and thus, through a fresh dialectical process, redeemed.

Now in this imagery there is one flaw, namely the transcendence of God; God standing aloof from the drama of human sin and redemption, a mere stage manager, is no true symbol of the absolute mind in its concreteness. But this is exactly where the truth of our religious imagery shines most brilliantly. It is God who accepts the burden of error, takes upon himself the moral responsibility for the fall, and so redeems not his creature but himself. (SM, 302-3)

For Collingwood, the absolute mind, which I have attempted to explicate in terms of the philosophical doctrine of immanence-transcendence, can never be more profoundly or impressively pictured than in this drama of the fall and redemption of man.

APPENDIXES

NOTES

BIBLIOGRAPHIES

INDEXES

Appendixes

APPENDIX I

POSITIVISM, HISTORICISM, AND THE IDEA OF A SCIENCE OF HUMAN NATURE*

I HISTORY AND BACKGROUND

The idea of history as an autonomous science of human nature, conceived of according to principles which are independent of the principles of natural science, is the product of a long historical development. In Greek philosophy, for example, human nature, like nature proper, was conceived of as a permanent and unchanging substance. Any knowledge which could be had of it was therefore a priori-deductive knowledge of essence rather than of existence. Collingwood claims that the same substantialistic metaphysic of human nature lay at the basis of thought in the enlightenment: "Just as the ancient historians conceived the Roman character, for example, as a thing that had never really come into existence but had always existed and had always been the same, so the eighteenth-century historians, who recognized that all true history is the history of mankind, assumed that human nature had existed ever since the creation of the world exactly as it existed among themselves. Human nature was conceived substantialistically as something static and permanent, an unvarying substratum underlying the course of historical changes and all human activities. History never repeated itself but human nature remained eternally unaltered" (IH, 82). Even Hume, who declared war on the concept of human nature as something solid and permanent, was nevertheless implicitly presupposing it. For in attacking the idea of spiritual substance he simply substituted the idea of constant tendencies to associate ideas in particular ways, and, writes

---

*Portions of this appendix were previously published in the introduction to my edition of Bradley's essay, The Presuppositions of Critical History (Toronto: J. M. Dent; Chicago: Quadrangle Books, 1968), and are reproduced here with the kind permission of the publishers.

Collingwood, "the laws of association are just as uniform and unchanging as any substance" (IH, 83).

As represented by Collingwood, the implication of Greek and Enlightenment philosophical thought concerning the relation between history and human nature was that if history was to be anything more than a mere description of phenomena, if it was to provide a genuine knowledge of human nature, then it must become a 'science.' But how was it to become a science? The answer, implicit in the thought of the eighteenth century, was, by adapting itself to the methods and principles of the established natural sciences. This programme was explicitly adopted, under the banner of positivism, throughout the latter part of the nineteenth century.

The history of this movement and of the open conflict which arose between it and the philosophy of historicism provides an important background against which the thought of Collingwood can be more easily understood. Positive philosophy developed eighteenth-century materialism into a world-view and proposed for the first time a complete programme for the creation of the human and social sciences by subsuming them all under the category of the material sciences. Typical of this approach was the attempt in 1857 by the English historian T. H. Buckle "to accomplish for the history of man something equivalent, or at all events analogous, to what had been effected by other inquiries for the different branches of the natural sciences" (*History of Civilization in England*, 2nd ed., New York: Appleton, 1858, 1, p. 5). If history is to be something more than trivial, if it is to acquire the status of a significant science, then, Buckle argues, the historian must presuppose that "when we perform an action, we perform it in consequence of some motive or motives; that those motives are the results of some antecedents; and that, therefore ... we are driven to the conclusion that the actions of men, being determined solely by their antecedents must have a character of uniformity, that is to say, must, under precisely the same circumstances, always issue in precisely the same results." And, Buckle continues, "as all consequences are either in the mind or out of it, we clearly see that all the variations in the results – in other words, all the changes of which history is full, all the vicissitudes of the human race, their progress or their decay, their happiness or their misery must be the fruit of a double action; an action of external phenomena upon the mind, and another action of the mind upon phenomena" (*ibid.*, 1, p. 13). This doctrine is not only the basis upon which past events may be explained; it is also, according to Buckle, the basis upon which future events may be predicted. It is therefore possible, Buckle concludes, assuming an intimate connection between human actions and physical laws (*ibid.*, 1, p. 25), the proof of which is derived from statistics (*ibid.*, 1, p. 24), given the whole of the antecedents together with all the laws of their movements, to predict with unerring certainty "the whole of their immediate results" (*ibid.*, 1, p. 13). The same doctrine was advanced some years later by the French philosopher and historian Hippolyte Taine (1828–93). "The modern method," wrote Taine, "which I seek to follow and which is beginning to be introduced in all the moral [i.e., cultural] sciences, consists in regarding human works ... as facts and products of which it is essential to mark the characteristics and seek the causes, and nothing more. Thus understood, science neither legislates nor pardons; it verifies and explains ... [the science of culture] proceeds as does botany, which studies the orange, the laurel, the pine, and the birch, with equal interest. It is itself a kind of botany, applied not to plants, but to the works of man. In this respect it follows the general movement of the day which assimilates the moral sciences to the natural sciences, and which, giving to the former the principles, safeguards and directions of the latter, thus gives to [the cultural sciences] the same stability, and assures them the same progress" ("The Philosophy of Art," in *Lectures on Art*, 2nd ed., trans. J. Durand, New York: Holt, 1875, 1, s. 2, pp. 37–9); cf. also, *The Philosophy of Art*; translated and revised by H. Taine [1865], pp. 20–1). There is no difference for Taine, in so far as our knowledge is concerned, between the facts of the physical world and the facts of the intellectual and moral world. In both cases our knowledge of particular facts is mediated by our knowledge of their causes. "No matter if the facts be physical or moral," writes Taine, "they all have their causes; there is a cause for ambition, for courage, for truth, as there is for digestion, for muscular movement, for animal heat. Vice and virtue are products, like vitriol and sugar; and every complex phenomenon arises from other more simple phenomena on which it hangs" (*History of English Literature*, trans. H. Van Laun, Edinburgh: Edmonston and Douglas, 1873, 1, s. 3, p. 6). "It therefore follows," Taine continues, that "every kind of human production ... literature, music, the fine arts, philosophy, science, the state, industries, and the rest ... has for its direct cause a moral disposition, or a combination of moral dispositions: the cause given, they appear; the cause withdrawn, they vanish: the weakness or intensity of the cause measures their weakness or intensity. They are bound up with their causes, as a physical phenomenon with its condition, as the dew with the fall of the variable temperature, as dilation with heat. There are similarly connected data in the moral as in the physical world, as rigorously bound together, and as universally extended in the one as in the other. Whatever in the one case produces, alters, or suppresses the first term, produces, alters, or suppresses the second as a necessary consequence. Whatever lowers the surrounding temperature, deposits the dew. Whatever develops credulity side by side with a poetical view of the world, engenders religion. Thus phenomena have been produced; thus they will be produced. As soon as we know the sufficient and necessary conditions of one of these vast occurrences, our understanding grasps the future as well as the past. We can say with confidence in what circumstances it will reappear, foretell without presumption many portions of its future history, and sketch cautiously some features of its ulterior development" (*ibid.*, I, s. vii, p. 18). Presupposed by this view is an explicit denial of any basic distinction between human nature and nature proper. Even man's apparent capacity for indeterminate action was regarded by positivists as explainable according to natural laws. Thus the nineteenth-century historian Guglielmo Ferrero declared, in support of what he called the "psychological and sociological interpretation of history" (*Les lois psychologiques du symbolisme*, Paris: Germin Baillière, 1895, p. vi) : "There is a very common belief that the further man is removed in time, the more he is held to be different from ourselves in his ideas and his feelings: that the psychology of mankind changes from century to century like fashions and literature. Likewise, no sooner do we find, in a somewhat ancient historical period, an institution, a custom, a law or a belief a little different from those which we see every day, than we proceed to seek all sorts of complicated explanations which most often may be reduced to phrases whose meaning is not very precise. But man does not change so quickly. His psychology remains at bottom the same. And if his culture varies greatly from one epoch to another that is not yet enough to change the functioning of his psyche. The basic laws of his psyche remain the same; at least for those short periods of history of which we have knowledge, and almost all phenomena, even the strangest ought to admit of an explanation according to these common laws of the psyche which we can verify in ourselves" (*ibid.*, p. vii).

Examples of what Ferrero called "the psychological and sociological interpretation of history" may be found within his own historical writings. In *Characters and Events of Roman History* (trans. Frances L. Ferrero, New York: Putnam, 1909), for example, Ferrero sets out to explain the corruption of the Roman world according to a "universal law of history" having to do with human motivation – namely, that each generation suffers an "automatic increase of ambitions and desires" which prevents the human world from crystallizing in one form or constrains it to continual changes in material make-up as well as in ideals and moral appearance (*ibid.*, pp. 21–2). Each new generation, he argues, in order to satisfy its own aspirations, must alter, in one way or another, the condition of the world it entered at birth. According to Ferrero, this phenomenon is governed by a "universal law of history – a law that can act with greater or less intensity, more or less rapidly, according to times and places, but that ceases to authenticate itself at no time and in no place" (*ibid.*, p. 22). This law is the source both of corruption and of progress. In *The Principles of Power* (trans. Theodore R. Saeckel, New York; Putnam, 1942), Ferrero similarly declares that the "fundamental essence of every human personality" lies in the tactics and strategy it employs in the struggle against death. All of our particular motivations, in other words, stem from the fundamental passion to live and avoid death (*ibid.*, p. 311). Thus, according to Ferrero, the permanent and unchanging essence of human nature is the instinct of self-preservation, the need of each individual to defend his life against death and time. This instinct, and the laws which govern it, explains not only the progress of society but its incurable imperfections as well. For it is a fact of human nature that, in spite of their desire to live together in peace and harmony, men must at the same time, of necessity, constantly mistrust one another (*ibid.*, p. 312). "The determination of each man to defend his own life as though it were a unique absolute, without relation to or bond with other lives is the mysterious force which explodes under the shock of life with intensity and in different and unforeseeable directions, at will or as it can" (*ibid.*, p. 312).

More contemporary expressions of the positivistic programme for a scientific history can be found in the writings of such philosophers as Carl Hempel and Patrick Gardiner. The main thesis of the neo-positivistic literature is that in historical as in scientific explanations general laws are both methodologically and logically required. They are methodologically required because the historian cannot arrive at his explanations without using them. And they are logically required because when the historian is challenged to defend his explanation the explanation will be shown to entail one or more such generalizations – in the sense that either (a) p entails q, if in order to defend p I must cite q, or (b) p entails q, if while I need not necessarily cite q in order to defend p, it would be unintelligible to assert the one and deny the other, or, finally, (c) p entails q if q has been deduced from p. The most explicit statement of orthodox neo-positivism is that by Carl Hempel who in his famous and influential paper "The Use of General Laws in History" (1942, reprinted in Patrick Gardiner, ed., *Theories of History*, Glencoe: Free Press, 1959) attempts to show "in some detail that general laws have quite analogous functions in history and the natural sciences, that they form an indispensable instrument of historical research, and that they even constitute the common basis of various procedures which are often considered as characteristic of the social in contradistinction to the natural sciences" (*ibid.*, 345). In keeping with this general thesis Hempel argues that the precise aim of historical explanation is to show "that the event in question was not a 'matter of chance', but was to be expected in view of certain antecedent or simultaneous conditions. The expectation referred to is not prophecy or divination, but rational scientific anticipation which rests on the assumption of general laws" (*ibid.*, p. 349). A position similar to Hempel's is summed up and discussed by Sidney Hook in *Theory and Practice in Historical Study: a Report of the Committee on Historiography* (New York: Social Science Research Council, Bulletin 54, 1946). Summing up the views of the positivistic approach to history Hook writes: "... historical understanding is a species of scientific understanding in general, and ... scientific understanding is theoretically equivalent to explanation. The criteria of adequate explanation are *formally* the same for all events and processes under investigation. An event or process is explained if it can be shown that it follows from a set of relevant antecedent events regarded as determining conditions ... Explanation is of varying degrees of generality but always involves the assumption of some general laws or statistical generalizations relating classes of phenomena, to one of which the event or process belongs." (*ibid.*, p. 127) A more moderate (and indeed considerably qualified) version of the covering law model has been given by Patrick Gardiner in *The Nature of Historical Explanation* (London: Oxford University Press, 1952). Gardiner affirms in principle the possibility of a full causal explanation of human action. But at the same time he tries to reconcile this claim with the concept of explaining human actions in terms of thoughts, desires and plans. For a discussion and criticism of both the Hempel and Gardiner version of the covering law model see W. H. Dray, *Laws and Explanation in History* (London: Oxford University Press, 1957).

For Collingwood no doubt some of the more serious implications of positivism lay in the area of morality, for as positivism spread in influence and popularity it became more and more the fashion to deny the existence of free-will and moral responsibility. Thus the sociologist Enrico Ferri declared, with regard to the application of positivism to the study of criminal behaviour: "How can you still believe in the existence of free-will when modern psychology armed with all the instruments of positive modern research, denies that there is any free-will and demonstrates that every act of a human being is the result of an interaction between the personality and the environment of man? And how is it possible to cling to that obsolete idea of moral guilt, according to which every individual is supposed to have the free choice to abandon virtues and give himself up to crime? The positive school of criminology maintains, on the contrary, that it is not the criminal who wills; in order to be a criminal it is rather necessary that the individual should find himself permanently or transitorily in such personal, physical and moral conditions ... which become for him a chain of cause and effect, externally and internally, that disposes him toward crime ... This illusion of a free-will has its source in our inner consciousness, and is due solely to the ignorance in which we find ourselves concerning the various motives and different external and internal conditions which press upon our mind at the moment of decision" (*The Positive School of Criminology*, trans. E. Untermann, Chicago: Charles H. Kerr, 1906, pp. 20, 21, 34). The presence of positivism in the twentieth century is perhaps most noticeable in the doctrines of psychological behaviourism. "The interest of the behaviourist," wrote John Watson, founder of the school of psychological behaviourism, "is more than the interest of the spectator – he wants to control man's reactions as physical scientists want to control and manipulate other natural phenomena. It is the business of behaviouristic psychology to be able to predict and to control human activity. To do this it must gather scientific data by experimental methods. Only then can the trained behaviourist predict, given the stimulus, what reaction will take place; or, given the reaction state what the situation or stimulus is that has caused the reaction" (*Behaviourism*, rev. ed., Chicago: University of Chicago Press, 1930, p. 11). But if Collingwood was disturbed by these proposals of Watson – as he no doubt was – he would have been even more alarmed by the proposals of Watson's disciples, such as B. F. Skinner. "If we are to use the methods of science," writes Skinner, "in the field of human affairs, we must assume that behaviour is lawful and determined. We must expect to discover that what a man does is the result of specifiable conditions and that once these conditions have been discovered, we can anticipate and to some extent determine his actions" (*Science and Human Behaviour*, New York: Macmillan, 1953, p. 6). In Skinner's world-view, values cease to be objects of choice and deliberation; rather, they are interpreted as necessary means of survival, as intervening variables to be determined by a functional analysis under the conditions characteristic of an experimental science (*ibid.*, p. 425). Through such an analysis the set of values which the individual appears to have chosen with respect to his own future is nothing more than "that condition which operates selectively in creating and perpetuating the behaviour which now seems to exemplify such a choice. An individual does not choose to live or die; he behaves in ways which work towards his survival or death. Behaviour usually leads to survival because the behaving individual has been selected by survival in the process of evolution" (*ibid.*, p. 433).

Against the dogma of positivism there arose in the nineteenth century, under the banner of historicism, various attempts to rescue the human and social sciences from the domination of the natural sciences. For most historicists their quarrel with positivism had serious existential implications concerning the foundations of culture itself. For they believed that the very survival of a culture depended upon its ability to resist the dehumanizing effects of positivism. Thus the German historian Johann Gustav Droysen declared, regarding the threat of positivism: "I am situated here amidst the most nefarious of all schools of thought, radical materialism, which endeavours to make for us, history, morality, philosophy and God Himself into a nasty and metabolistic business ... Woe to us if the polytechnical misery which since 1789 has fouled and dried up France spreads still more the Babylonian mixture of dissoluteness and calculation. It is that brute positivism which is now being cultivated in Berlin which acts as a hothouse for this revolution of the spiritual life of the mind ... God knows the universities have again a great and noble duty" (From a letter to Max Dunker, Jena, 17 July 1852; *Briefwechsel*, ed. Rudolf Hubner, Stuttgart and Berlin; Deutch Verlagsanstalt, 1929, II, p. 120). These sentiments have been echoed and re-echoed throughout the nineteenth and twentieth centuries; especially by such philosophers as Nietzsche: "It seems to me that ... historians cease to be instructive as soon as they begin to generalize (*The Use and Abuse of History*, trans. Adrian Collins, New York: Bobbs-Merrill, 1957, p. 46) ... Are we to continue to ... write history from the standpoint of the masses; to look for laws in it, to be deduced from the needs of the masses ... How could statistics prove that there are laws in history? Yes, they may prove how common and abominably uniform the masses are; and should we call the effects of leaden folly, imitation, love and hunger – laws? We may admit it, but we are sure of this too – that, so far as there are laws in history, the laws are of no value and the history is of no value either" (*ibid.*, p. 68); Croce: "If the formulas of ... positivism had been followed to the letter all light of thought would have been extinguished" (*History its Theory and Practice*, trans. Douglas Ainslie, New York: Russell, 1960, p. 309); and Ortega y Gasset: "We must shake ourselves free, radically free, from the physical, the natural approach to the human element ... The prodigious achievement of natural science in the direction of the knowledge of things contrasts brutally with the collapse of this same science when faced with the strictly human element ... the conviction of this incompetence is to-day a fact of the first magnitude on the European horizon" ("History as a

System" [1936], in *Philosophy and History*, R. Klibansky and H. J. Paton, eds., Oxford: Clarendon Press, 1936, pp. 293, 294, 295). Such remarks tend no doubt to confirm the observation of Ernst Cassirer, made in 1939, that "Instead of removing [the] cleft between natural science and the humanities, the development of philosophy in the Nineteenth century [and, he might just as well have added, in the early part of the Twentieth century] served only to widen it all the more ... choosing between science or the humanities, between naturalism or historicism, seems to be left to the feeling and subjective taste of the individual; more and more objective proof gives way to polemics" (*The Logic of the Humanities*, trans. Clarence Howe, New Haven: Yale University Press, 1961, p. 88). It was nevertheless in the spirit of the historicist assault on positivism that Collingwood himself, at various points in his career from 1919 to 1939, described positivism as a neurosis which, if it succeeds, will result in "the eradication of science and civilization" (EM, 46). And it was in the same spirit that he regarded history, properly conceived, as the only antidote to the spread of positivism and as, therefore, a "prime duty, whose discharge is essential to the maintenance ... of reason itself" (IH, 277–8).

Against the claim of positivism for a naturalistic theory of history, historicism argued for an autonomous science whose methods were appropriate to the true nature of its subject matter, *res humanae*. To distinguish the sciences of man from the sciences of nature proper the convention was adopted of referring to the latter as *Naturwissenschaften* and the former as *Geisteswissenschaften*. The term *Geisteswissenschaften* was first introduced by I. Schick, the German translator of J. S. Mill's *System of Logic*, who in 1849 rendered the title of book VI, "On the Logic of the Moral Sciences," as "Von der Logik der *Geisteswissenschaften oder Moralischen Wissenschaften*." As a result *Geisteswissenschaft* came gradually to designate the scientific study of all aspects of human affairs such as history, literature, art, politics, mythology, and so on. This use of the term became firmly established in 1883 when Dilthey in his *Einleitung in die Geisteswissenschaften* (*Gesammelte Schriften*, Leipzig and Berlin: Teubner, 1923 – [hereafter referred to as GS], I, pp. 1–39) defined it as the totality of the sciences which have historico-societal reality as their subject matter (cf. Hajo Holborn, "Wilhelm Dilthey and the Critique of Historical Reason," *Journal of the History of Ideas* [Jan. 1950]). In his later years, however, Dilthey came to the conclusion that it might be better to refer to these sciences as *Kulturwissenschaften*; although it is clear that he found none of these terms quite adequate as descriptions of the human sciences (GS, VII, 86; cf. also H. Rickert, *Kulturwissenschaft und Naturwissenschaft*, esp. ch. x

[6th and 7th revised edition], Tübingen, 1926, trans. G. Reisman, as *Science and History*, New York: Van Nostrand, 1962). Since in the eyes of historicists what basically distinguishes man from nature is the fact that man has a history, it followed that the methods of the *Geisteswissenschaften* must be historical. The history of historicism took the form, therefore, of successive attempts to construct what Dilthey called a "Kritik der historischen Vernunft" (see particularly GS, VII, pp. 191–204) which would do for the *Geisteswissenschaften* what Kant's *Critique of Pure Reason* had done for the *Naturwissenschaften*. As the latter had located and defined the a priori conditions of a science of nature so the former would locate and define the a priori conditions of a science of history and hence of human culture.

Dilthey's attempt at a critique of historical reason was begun in an atmosphere already stimulated by the work of others. Among the first to attempt a systematic critique of positivism and to argue the case for an autonomous science of history was Johann Gustav Droysen (1808–84). Droysen (whose influence and importance is vastly underrated) had an important influence not only on Dilthey, but, I suspect, on Collingwood as well: a claim which admittedly can only be supported by a direct comparison of Droysen's theory of historical understanding with that of Collingwood; for with the exception of one reference to Droysen's publications in the bibliography to Collingwood's 1930 essay on the philosophy of history and another very brief reference in *The Idea of History*, there are no other direct references to, and certainly no acknowledgements of, the possible influence of Droysen on Collingwood's thought. Indeed, in *The Idea of History*, Collingwood criticizes Droysen for merely presupposing the distinction between nature and history rather than trying to understand it (IH, 65–6). In spite of this, however, I would contend that there are many indirect and unacknowledged references to aspects of Droysen's thought with which Collingwood was in close agreement.

Droysen's views on the foundations of history were first presented in a lecture series given in 1852 in which he tried to develop a "methodology and encyclopaedia of the historical sciences" – the purpose of which was to argue the case for an autonomous science of history. These views were further developed in the second part of an essay published in 1854 and entitled "Zur Charakteristik der europäischen Krisis" (reprinted in J. G. Droysen, *Politische Schriften*, Felix Gilbert ed. [München and Berlin, 1933], see esp. pp. 324–6). In this essay Droysen made a clear distinction between the subject matter and methodology of the natural sciences and that of the human sciences. But the theoretical foundations of history in particular, conceived of as an autonomous science, were systematically described in what is generally regarded as Droysen's most important work, *Grundriss der Historik* (1858, 2nd ed., 1867, 3rd ed., 1881; in *Historik-Vorlesungen über Enzyklopädie und Methodologie der Geschichte*, ed. Rudolf Hübner, Darmstadt: Wissenschaftliche Buchgesellschaft, 3rd ed. 1958). The following discussion is based on E. B. Andrews' abridged English translation of the third edition, entitled *Outlines of the Principles of History* (Boston: Ginn & Co., 1893).

The general conclusion of this work, which is particularly suggestive of Collingwood, is the conception of history as the mind's self-knowledge of itself. "History," wrote Droysen, "is the 'self-knowledge' of humanity, its consciousness" (s. 74, p. 44, cf. also s. 86, p. 49). Historical action is defined as the sphere in which "humanity creates the cosmos of the moral world" (s. 48, p. 34) and thereby discovers its purpose by realizing it in action (s. 52, p. 35). Only a moral being is a human being (s. 73, p. 43) existing in a state of proper freedom (s. 75, p. 44) and only the historical man is the moral man (s. 52, p. 35). In short, the essence of human nature is historicity.

In 1862 Droysen launched an attack against positivism in a long and critical review of T. H. Buckle's *History of Civilization in England*. Buckle's work, as we have already noted, was a direct application of positive philosophy to the interpretation of history with the purpose of demonstrating that no events in the world of man (i.e., *res humanae*) were exempt from the rigid determination of the natural order, and that history conceived as a strict science can easily demonstrate that the alleged freedom of the human will is an illusion. This essay on Buckle is a further elaboration of the conception of history as self-knowledge. Historical knowledge is not only the source of our consciousness of the present, it is an act in which the existence of the "here and now" is extended: in which the mind, in other words, through knowing itself, is thereby enabled to develop itself. "The work of the centuries," writes Droysen, "is the entail of each new generation ... All past events, the whole of 'History', is ideally contained in the present and in that which the present possesses. And when we bring to our consciousness this ideal content of History; when we represent to ourselves in a kind of narrative form how that which is has come to pass, what else do we thus do but employ History in understanding that which is, the elements in which we move as thinking, volitional and active beings? This is the way, or at least one of the ways, immeasurably to extend, enrich and elevate the needy and lonesome Here and Now of our ephemeral existence ... History gives us the consciousness of what we are and have ("The Elevation of History to the Rank of a Science," in *Outlines of the Principles of History*, p. 74).

Not only is historical knowledge the extension of our present existence, it is, according to Droysen, a source of culture as well. Adapting a phrase of Goethe: "what thou hast inherited from thy ancestors, earn in order to possess it" (*ibid*, p. 74), Droysen defines culture as the product of historical thinking. Culture, he argues, is precisely what we have as a result of our having "lived and toiled through over again, as a continuation, that which has, in the history of times, peoples and humanity, been wrought out in men's spirit in the way of thought." "So long as we have not gained it through our own efforts," he writes, "and have not recognized it as that which is the result of incessant toil on the part of those who were before us, we hold it as if we had it not" (*ibid.*, pp. 74–5). From all this Droysen concludes that if history is a process of self-knowledge in which the object known is thereby brought into being, then Buckle's statistical approach is simply inappropriate (*ibid*, p. 79). To explain history in terms of general laws is like trying to reduce the beauty of a piece of sculpture to "the bronze out of which it is poured, the clay which formed the model of it, or the fire which melted the metal leaving aside entirely the creativity and intentionality of the artist" (*ibid*, p. 81).

The distinction between mind and nature, implicit throughout all of Droysen's work, is explicitly discussed in an appendix to the 1867 edition of the *Grundriss der Historik* entitled "Nature and History." For the most part this essay (which is reproduced in the English translation of 1893) is an expansion of what is already declared in the first two principles of the *Historik*. Nature is defined as a succession of forms which in essence repeat themselves. As an object of knowledge such a nature is characterized as a constant, "that which abides in the midst of change ... the rule, the law, the substance, that which fills space etc." (*ibid*, p. 98). In such a process the temporal element is reduced to accidental importance, so that the character of natural phenomena may therefore be regarded as being unaffected by time.

As distinct from nature, however, mind is a process whose very essence is to change and to give rise to new forms, each one of which is an individual, different from the others; "so different indeed," writes Droysen, "that each, as it assumes its place after its predecessor, is conditioned by it, grows out of it, ideally takes it up into itself, yet when grown out of it contains and maintains it ideally in itself" (*ibid*, p. 98). "Mind," Droysen continues, "is a continuity in which everything that precedes transplants itself into what is later, filling it out and extending it as 'a contribution to itself,' while the latter presents itself as a result, fulfilment and enlargement of the earlier" (*ibid*, p. 98). And in a passage which strongly resembles Collingwood's exposition of his own doctrine of the scale of forms, Droysen declares that this continuity is not that of a circle which simply returns into itself, nor of a period repeating itself; on the contrary, it is an endless succession in which each stage not only gives rise to a further one, but contains within it "the entire series of past forms" which it ideally sums up. "In this restless succession," he writes, "in this continuity advancing upon itself, the general notion of time wins its discrete content, which we designate by the expression 'History' " (*ibid*, p. 99). Thus Droysen reaffirms the principle, implicit in the *Historik*, that the essence of mind is historicity.

Droysen's account of the distinction between *res humanae* and *res naturae*, while certainly not deserving of Collingwood's censure in *The Idea of History*, was nevertheless primarily *de facto* (i.e., descriptive and impressionistic) whereas what was needed was a philosophical *de jure* justification of this distinction. It was not until Wilhelm Dilthey (1833–1911) attempted his monumental synthesis (which Dilthey had hoped would once and for all establish the autonomy of the *Geisteswissenschaften*) that the beginnings of the necessary *de jure* account appeared. Kant had asked, How is natural science possible? Dilthey asked, How is History possible? Kant wrote a critique of pure reason which located the a priori of nature; Dilthey proposed a critique of historical reason which would locate the a priori of history. This was required not just for the study of history, but, as Dilthey would hope to prove, for all science, including natural science. Hume had already singled out the science of human nature as the organon and foundation of all the other sciences (*Treatise*, ed. L. A. Selby-Bigge, Oxford: The Clarendon Press, 1951, p. xix). But Hume conceived this science as a strictly philosophical one. The difference between Dilthey and Hume lies in Dilthey's radical conception of this science as an exclusively historical one. "All knowledge," wrote Dilthey, "is empirical knowledge, but the original unity of all experiences and its resulting validity are conditioned by the factors which mould the consciousness within which it arises, i.e., by the whole of our nature. This standpoint, which consistently realizes the impossibility of going beyond these conditions ... I call the epistemological standpoint [*erkenntnisttheoretischen Standpunkt*]; modern knowledge can recognize no other" (GS, I, xvii; reprinted in H. A. Hodges, ed., *Wilhelm Dilthey, An Introduction* [including selections], London: Routledge and Kegan Paul, 1944, pp. 112–13).

For Dilthey, the conditions of consciousness were not simply, as they were for Kant, rigidly a priori categories of the intellect such as quantity, quality, relation, etc.; rather they included forms of will and feelings as well, all of which Dilthey calls "the integral nature of man" (*der ganzen Menschennatur*). The latter, rather than being permanent and eternal, is itself subject to the same "developmental history" (*Entwicklungsgeschichte*) to which it gives rise. "Against the background of the integral nature of man," he wrote, "as revealed by experience and by a study of language and history, I will present all elements of present day abstract and scientific thinking and seek their interconnection. It then appears that the most important elements of our image and our knowledge of the world [*Wirklichkeit*] as for instance, living unity of the person [*persönliche Lebenseinheit*], outer world [*Aussenwelt*], individuals outside ourselves, their living in time and their interaction can all be explained from this integral human nature of whose real living process, perception, will, and feeling form only different aspects. Not the assumption of our cognitive faculty being rigidly *a priori*, but only evolutionary history, which starts from the totality of our condition can answer the question we want to lay before philosophy" (GS, I, p. xviii; Hodges, *Wilhelm Dilthey, An Introduction*, pp. 113–14).

But having explicated the unique characteristics of human nature, Dilthey was still faced with the problem of defining the conditions under which so problematic a phenomenon as human nature can be made an object of scientific knowledge. How, in other words, is *Geisteswissenschaft* possible?

But Dilthey's answer, in terms of what he called "the epistemological standpoint," leads to a serious paradox. The goal of the *Geisteswissenschaften* is to arrive at an understanding of human nature by studying its expressions in human actions. To study human actions, however, requires interpreting these actions in terms of what we already know about the nature which they express. This latter knowledge concerning the integral nature of man is the a priori criterion of historical and cultural science. To the question, How is *this* knowledge to be arrived at? the answer must be (if the essence of human nature is historical) that it can only be arrived at through the study of history itself which must, therefore, already presuppose what it seeks to discover.

In short, the very criterion which constitutes the a priori basis of the science of history and which presumably would guarantee its objectivity, is itself historically relative. But, far from being embarrassed by this paradox, Dilthey argues instead that having revealed the historicity of human nature and the relativity of all criteria for the evaluation of this nature, historical science must recognize its own historicity. Even philosophy must be regarded as an expression of historically changing *Weltanschauungen*. "The theory of development," he writes, "is necessarily linked to the knowledge of the relativity proper to the historical life-form." Before the standpoint of "*Weltanschauungsphilosophie*," the absolute validity of any particular form of life-interpretation, of religion, and of philosophy, is made to disappear. Thus, he continues, "the cultivation of our historical consciousness destroys, more thoroughly than does surveying the disagreement of systems, the belief in the universal validity of any of the philosophies which have undertaken to express in a compelling manner the coherence of the world by an ensemble of concepts" (GS, VIII, p. 121).

Thus Dilthey not only recognizes the historicity of all thought; he proclaims its necessity and its virtue. Once we accept it, he argues, we become liberated from dogma, apologetics, and ideologies, and we are better able to understand the manifold reactions of humanity, the infinite adaptability of human life. "Man," he declares, "bound and determined by the reality of life is set free ... through the understanding of history [GS, VII, p. 216; Hodges, *Wilhelm Dilthey: An Introduction*, p. 124] ... The historical consciousness of the finitude of every historical phenomena, every human or social state, of the relativity of every sort of belief, is the last step towards the liberation of man. With it, man attains the sovereign power to wring from every experience its content, to surrender wholly to it, without prepossession ... Every beauty, every sanctity, every sacrifice, re-lived and experienced, opens up perspectives which disclose a reality ... And, in contrast with the relativity, the continuity of the creative force makes itself felt as the central historical fact" (GS, VII, pp. 290–1; Hodges, *Wilhelm Dilthey: An Introduction*, pp. 33–4; reproduced also in *Meaning in History*, trans. and ed. H. P. Rickman, London: Allen and Unwin, 1961, pp. 167–8).

Yet Dilthey was aware that to assert the historicity of all thought ran the risk of radical subjectivism and its corollary, scepticism. In order to avoid declaring the bankruptcy of historical knowledge to which such scepticism gives rise he found it necessary to explicate the concept of understanding in such a way that it would be seen to draw its validity from a thoroughly objective source. Dilthey found this objectivity in the analogy he drew between the historical problem of understanding others and the psychology of self-understanding through "autobiography" (*Selbstbiographie*) (GS, VII, pp. 199–201; Rickman, pp. 85–7).

All human action, he argued, involves three elements, cognition, affection, and conation. Man thinks, feels, and desires, all at the same time. The relations between these elements form what Dilthey called a structural system of lived experiences (*Erlebnis*) which can be perceived. Hence the key to the understanding of any action may be regarded as lying in the perception of this *Erlebnis*. But how is it possible for me to perceive the *Erlebnis* of others? Dilthey's answer seems to be that we understand other minds in precisely the same way that we understand our own. The historian, seeking to understand another's experience, appropriates that experience to himself; that is, he forms for himself and in his own consciousness a *Nachbild* of the experience which the agent's action expresses. In reliving (*nacherleben*) this *Nachbild* for himself the historian perceives its structural form (GS, VII, pp. 213–16; Hodges, p. 123). The perception of this structural form involves grasping the rationale of the act – seeing that it was done for this or that reason, motivated by this or that emotion, intended to accomplish this or that goal, and so on. He then projects this *Nachbild* into the other person, and thereby achieves understanding. Dilthey describes this projection as a transposition of self, the "rediscovery of the I in the thou" (*Wiederfinden das Ich im Du*) (GS, VII, p. 191; Hodges, p. 114; Rickman, pp. 67–8). But, as Collingwood rightly points out in his critique of Dilthey (IH, 171–6), the analogy between self-analysis and understanding others avoids the implications of radical subjectivism only by reintroducing the principles of positivism from which Dilthey was trying to escape. Defenders of Dilthey will, of course, point out that in the first stage of the process whereby the historian incorporates the experience of the past into his own present state of consciousness, Dilthey supersedes the methodology of positivism with the more open-ended techniques of imaginative re-living or *verstehen*. But even granted this point Collingwood's complaint still remains to be met. For when it comes to Dilthey's account of how it is possible for the re-lived experience to become an object of critical analysis – or, to put it another way, when it comes to the verification of whatever theses have been achieved by means of *verstehen* – we seem suddenly to be confronted by the presuppositions of positivism. If the historian's analysis of his present state of experience (which has been achieved by *verstehen*, the imaginative reconstruction of the past) is to be more than imaginative, if it is to be projected back into the past as "fact," then it is only because the historian's interpretation of his own experience rests upon the same psychological laws of human nature which operated in the historical past. In short, the analogy between past and present, between understanding others and self-understanding, presupposes the positivist principle of the uniformity of nature together with its metaphysics of naturalism. And this, as Collingwood himself clearly demonstrates, constitutes the very confusion between nature and history which historicism dedicated itself to repudiating.

But while Collingwood regarded Dilthey's 'epistemological solution' as a vain attempt to flee from the dogmas of naturalism, a younger contemporary of Dilthey, Edmund Husserl, focussed attention on Dilthey's inability to escape the implications of radical historicism (i.e., scepticism). Dilthey's failure, according to Husserl, lay in the fact that he was unable to account for the possibility of a transhistorical standpoint from which the truth of historicism could be validated. In response to Dilthey, Husserl recognizes the importance of history and the historical orientation of science. At the same time he stresses the necessity for a clear-cut distinction between philosophy and history: philosophy at least must be given a transhistorical basis if the historical dimensions of thought are to be given any kind of a rational basis at all. In asserting the autonomy of philosophy, however, we must not fall into the error of naturalism: philosophy is not to be regarded on the analogy of the natural sciences. On the contrary, says Husserl, the autonomy of philosophy conceived as a genuine transhistorical science can only be accomplished through the "phenomenological theory of essence": in which case, according to Husserl, the phenomenology of essences may be regarded as the only effective way of providing a foundation for the cultural sciences ("Philosophy as a Strict Science," translated by Quentin Lauer, *Cross Currents*, VI, 4 (1956), 331–5).

A more recent, but perhaps less successful, attempt at a phenomenological approach to the problem of the foundations of *Kulturwissenschaften* is the philosophy of Ernst Cassirer (e.g., in *The Logic of the Humanities*, New Haven: Yale University Press, 1962). Cassirer modifies Husserl's definition of phenomenology by regarding it as, not simply the science of pure essences, but the analysis of the forms of perception. In particular the foundations of the cultural sciences are to be located by means of a phenomenological analysis of the perception of the "person world" as opposed to the perception of the "thing-world": a distinction which Cassirer does not consider Husserl to have made. But, a case could be made to the effect that if Dilthey in his attempt to avoid scepticism was forced back into the position of naturalism from which he was also trying to escape, then Cassirer, in his attempt to avoid the ramifications of naturalism may be regarded as coming too close to the position of radical historicism. (For a fuller account of Cassirer's historicism see L. Rubinoff, "Historicism and the *A Priori* of History," *Dialogue: The Canadian Philosophical Review* [June 1964].)

It would seem, then, that while positivism can provide a basis for the sciences of human nature only by treating the latter as an object under the category of nature proper, historicism, precisely because it asserts the autonomy and uniqueness of human nature, would appear to deny the possibility of such a science altogether. It has therefore been the task of twentieth-century philosophy to reconcile the need for a science of human nature with the recognition of its essential historicity. This is the task to which Collingwood devoted his entire philosophy and his

IDEA OF A SCIENCE OF HUMAN NATURE 355

attempt at a rapprochement between philosophy and history – which in some respects bears a striking resemblance to Husserl's phenomenological approach – may therefore be regarded as the most recent attempt (and the only one in English) at a critique of historical reason.

Collingwood's attempt at a critique of historical reason draws its impetus not only from the tradition of German idealism but from the traditions of British and Italian idealism as well. Of special importance is the influence of the thought of F. H. Bradley. According to Collingwood, Bradley's main contribution to philosophy of history lay in his conception of historical science as the critical interpretation of evidence according to a criterion which is no other than the historian himself, his own experience of the world. It is this that tells the historian what is and is not possible. (See Bradley's own essay "The Presuppositions of Critical History" upon which Collingwood's account is based.) Thus Bradley declares, concerning the testimony of the past and the historian's own experience: "The experience of others has no meaning for us except so far as it becomes our own; the existence of others is no existence for us if it is not in our world that they live" (*The Presuppositions of Critical History*, ed. L. Rubinoff, Toronto: Dent, Chicago: Quadrangle, 1968, p. 94). Bradley, in other words, is correctly represented by Collingwood as declaring the personal experience of the historian as the long-sought-for a priori of historical interpretation. Only on the basis of his own personal experience can the critical historian judge whether the testimony of his witness is to be accepted or rejected (*ibid.*, pp. 104–5). But, as Collingwood rightly points out, this can only work if the historian and his witness are sufficiently alike in their characters and personalities (or, as Bradley himself puts it, history must be founded on the presupposition of "the universality of law, the assumption of the essential uniformity of nature and the course of events" [*ibid.*, pp. 96–9]). But this very requirement is simply inconsistent with Bradley's own admission that in fact "the historical witness is always the son of his time" (*ibid.*, p. 117), so that the mere progress of knowledge makes it virtually impossible that his point of view and standards of accuracy should be identical with those of the historian. It follows, therefore, that either the historian and his witness share the same fundamental experience (in which case the necessary analogy for historical judgment exists) or else, the historian is simply unable to judge the evidence at all (IH, 137–40).

Implicit in Bradley's solution are other difficulties to which Collingwood also draws attention. In designating the historian's own personal experience as the basis of historical judgment Bradley is, whether he is aware of it or not, making a serious concession to positivism. In effect

Bradley's criterion consists of a body of scientific knowledge concerning experience as such: knowledge which is regarded as ready made and complete before the work of historical reconstruction even begins, and which is conceived therefore "in the positivistic manner, as based on induction from observed facts on the principle that the future will resemble the past and the unknown the known" (IH, 139). Bradley was right, according to Collingwood, in holding that the historian is his own criterion, and in suggesting that to accept the testimony of his witness involves making the thought of the witness his own thought (IH, 138). His mistake, however, was in not realizing that the criterion which the historian brings with him to the study of history is the historian *qua* historian, and not the historian *qua* scientist. It is only by practising historical thought that the historian can learn to think historically (IH, 139–40). Collingwood suggests that Bradley's positivism is a direct consequence of his failure to retain the fundamental unity of thought and immediate experience. And because Bradley regarded thought, which he identified with objectivity, as fundamentally different from immediacy, which is regarded as subjectivity, he bequeathed to his successors the following dilemma: "Either reality is the immediate flow of subjective life, in which case it is subjective but not objective, it is enjoyed but cannot be known, or else it is that which we know, in which case it is objective but not subjective, it is a world of real things outside the subjective life of our mind and outside each other" (IH, 141). To accept either form of this dilemma is to rule out the possibility of a mind which both exists and knows itself, indeed, whose self-knowledge is the very ground of its existence. But if historical knowledge is to achieve a genuine autonomy – which is, after all, what Bradley is ultimately interested in – it can only be as the mind's self-knowledge of itself: which is precisely what Bradley's distinction between thought and immediacy implicitly denies. (For a critical discussion of Collingwood's evaluation of Bradley see my introduction to *The Presuppositions of Critical History*, pp. 45–52.)

In spite of these criticisms, however, Collingwood does credit Bradley with the discovery of the true nature of historical reality: a discovery which is implicit both in his logic and in his metaphysics. Collingwood points out that in the *Logic*, for example, Bradley dismisses both the abstract universal and the abstract particular as candidates for reality in favour of the concrete universal and the concrete particular – both of which are regarded as only different names for the same concrete *individual*. But the individual, although one and the same, is also a many, that is, it has internal differences. So far as it is one against other individuals it is *particular*. So far as it is the same throughout its diversity it is *universal*. By identifying reality with the *individual* which in turn is regarded as both concrete particular and concrete universal, Bradley is implicitly declaring, according to Collingwood, that "reality consists neither of isolated particulars nor of abstract universals but of individual facts or concrete universals whose being is historical" (IH, 141). When we turn to *Appearance and Reality* we find the same idea pushed a stage further. For the fundamental thesis here is that "reality is not something other than its appearances, but is these appearances themselves, forming a whole of which we can say that it forms a single system consisting of experience and that all our experiences form a part of it." A reality so defined "can only be the life of mind itself, that is, history" (IH, 141). What prevented Bradley from going any further was simply the error, already cited, of distinguishing, within experience itself, immediacy and thought, in such a way that reality (i.e., history) can never be regarded as knowing itself through the mediation of thought.

Collingwood considered that the separation between thought and immediate experience which marred the philosophy of Bradley was overcome in the philosophy of M. B. Oakeshott. In Oakeshott's philosophy, as represented by Collingwood, experience is defined as a concrete whole consisting of both subject and object and containing within itself both thought and mediation. As a result, reality is no longer divided into that which knows but cannot be known and that which is known but cannot know. In effect Bradley's dilemma is transcended and the mind's right to know itself is re-established (IH, 152). Collingwood goes on to argue that implicit in Oakeshott's philosophy of experience is the conception of the past as in some sense living (i.e., incapsulated) in the present and the conception of historical knowledge as the "re-enactment" in the historian's mind of the thought whose history he is studying (IH, 158). This conception of the past as living in the present is a consequence of the thesis that experience contains in itself an element of mediation or thought. For in so far as experience is thought, what thought experiences *as* real, is real. Thus, in so far as historical experience is thought, what it experiences or thinks as past, really is past (providing, as Oakeshott himself points out, that the historian's thought is supported by the evidence [see *Experience and its Modes* (Cambridge, 1933), p. 107]); and the fact that it is also present does not prevent it from being past. The historian thinks of his object as *there* or *then* (i.e., away from him in time) and, because history is knowledge and not mere immediate experience, the historian can experience it both as *then* and as *now*; *now* in so far as it is immediate, *then* in so far as it is mediate.

It is not likely, however, that Oakeshott did anything more than reinforce in Collingwood's mind doctrines with which the latter was already familiar; for Collingwood had already arrived at these conclusions some years before the appearance of *Experience and its Modes*. The principle of incapsulation is contained in *Speculum Mentis* (1924) and the concept of the past as a function of the historian's present thought which is nevertheless a genuine past is explicitly formulated in two essays on the philosophy of history written in 1928 and 1930, respectively. A more important and more direct influence on Collingwood's thought was the work of Benedetto Croce, the only philosopher, according to Collingwood, to have fully grasped the peculiarity of historical thought (IH, 191). "It was the clean cut which [Croce] made in 1893 between the idea of history and the idea of science that enabled him to develop the conception of history so much further than any philosopher of his generation" (IH, 193).

Collingwood regarded the principle of incapsulation, according to which nature and history may be distinguished, as part of the legacy of idealist thought and it was in terms of this principle that he was able to overcome the limitations of German historicism. Both Dilthey and Simmel, for example, correctly realized that history is an attempt to incorporate the past into the present; or, to use epistemological terms, to achieve some kind of identity between subject and object. Their problem, as Collingwood conceived of it, was not being able to give an adequate account of this identity; they could not explain how the same thing could be subjective and immediate on the one hand while still retaining its objectivity. They therefore found themselves faced with the following dilemma. Either historical knowledge is knowledge of the past and therefore not knowledge of the present or else it is knowledge of the present and not knowledge of the past. To accept the first horn of this dilemma leads straight to positivism, while to accept the second horn leads to scepticism. If, in the attempt to preserve the objectivity of knowledge the past is portrayed as the product of an inference mediated by an empirically verifiable body of scientific knowledge, then historical knowledge becomes a mere species of *naturwissenschaft*. If, on the other hand, the past is assimilated to the historian's own experience it runs the risk of becoming something private and personal, or at least, indistinguishable from what is idiosyncratic to that experience.

It has therefore been the task of twentieth-century philosophy of history to reconcile the need for an objective science of man with the conditions of subjectivity within which human knowledge necessarily arises. And it was precisely to this task that Collingwood devoted himself throughout his philosophical career, as he set out to show that historical knowledge is not "... either knowledge of the past and therefore not knowledge of the present, or else knowledge of the present and therefore not knowledge of the past; it is knowledge of the past in the present, and the self-knowledge of the historian's own mind as the present revival and reliving of past experience" (IH, 175).

2 THE CONCEPT OF RADICAL HISTORICISM

After Dilthey historicism developed in two distinct directions. By far the most common and most popular form is what has come to be known as radical historicism, the essence of which is contained in the writings of Croce (see chapter I, s. 4, pp. 8 above). The other direction is that leading to transcendental historicism. Radical historicism, as we have already noted, is the tendency to interpret the whole of reality in historical terms. According to the tradition of transcendental historicism, however, philosophic truth, while it is historically grounded, is nevertheless not entirely historical in character (i.e., although it is only through the historical process that truth brings itself into existence, and only through historical thinking that it reveals itself to thought, what is revealed at any given time in history is nevertheless absolute and transhistorical, a permanent aspect of the complete and infinite 'absolute' standpoint or concrete universal, whose final revelation, once achieved, would coincide with the end of all time and process). Included in the tradition of radical historicism (in addition to those already cited) are Nietzsche (whose historicism derives especially from the doctrine "Gott ist tot," *The Joyful Wisdom*, III, s. 125), Ortega y Gasset (e.g. *History as a System*, trans. Helene Weyl, New York: Norton, 1941, and *Man and People*, New York: Norton, 1957; see also *Reason and Life*, London: Hollis and Carter, 1956, by Ortega's disciple Julian Marias), the later Heidegger (see E. L. Fackenheim, *Metaphysics and Historicity*, Milwaukee: Marquette University Press, 1961, fn. 44, pp. 77–8), and Ernst Cassirer (*The Logic of the Humanities*); in the tradition of transcendental historicism are Hegel, Husserl (see e.g. *Phenomenology and the Crisis of Philosophy*, ed. and trans. Quentin Lauer, New York: Harper, 1965), H. Rickert (e.g. *Science and History*, Van Nostrand, 1962), the early Heidegger (e.g. *Sein und Zeit*, pt. I, division II, ch. v. esp. s. 77), some writings of Ernst Cassirer (e.g. *The Philosophy of Symbolic Forms*, 3 vols., New Haven: Yale University Press, 1957), and R. G. Collingwood. Other (albeit less satisfactory) examples of transcendental historicism can be found in the writings of Giovanni Gentile and Raymond Aron (see esp. *Introduction to the Philosophy of History*, trans. George J. Irwin, Boston: Beacon Press, 1961). For a more detailed discussion of Hegel and the tradition of transcendental historicism see E. L. Fackenheim, *Metaphysics and Historicity*. For more general information concerning the origins and difficulties of historicism, the following may be consulted: Carlo Antoni, *Lo Storicismo* (Rome: Edizioni Radio italiana, 1957), and *From History to Sociology* (trans. Hayden V. White, Detroit: Wayne State University Press, 1959); Ernst Cassirer, *The Logic of the Humanities* (esp. the introduction, pp. 3–38); Friedrich Engel-Janosi, *The Growth of German Historicism* (The Johns Hopkins University Studies in Historical and Political Science, series LXII, no. 2, Baltimore: The Johns Hopkins Press, 1944); Raffaello Franchini, *Esperienza dello Storicismo* (2nd rev. ed., Naples: Giannini, 1960); W. Hofer, *Geschichtsschreibung und Weltanschauung: Betrachtungen Zum Werk Friedrich Meineckes* (Munich: R. Oldenburg, 1950); Hajo Holborn, "Wilhelm Dilthey and the Critique of Historical Reason," *Journal of the History of Ideas*, XI (1950), 93–118; George G. Iggers, *The German Conception of History* (Middletown: Wesleyan University Press, 1968); Gerhard Krüger, *Grundfragen der Philosophie: Geschichte Warheit, Wissenschaft* (Frankfurt am Main: V. Klosterman, 1958); Helen P. Leibel, "Philosophical Idealism in the Historische Zeitschrift, 1859–1914," *History and Theory*, III (1964), 316–30; Maurice Mandelbaum, *The Problem of Historical Knowledge* (New York: Liverright, 1938); Friedrich Meinecke, *Die Entstehung des Historismus, Werke*, III, edited with an introduction by Carl Hinrichs (Munich: R. Oldenburg, 1959), *Zur Theorie und Philosophie der Geschichte, Werke*, IV, edited with an introduction by Eberhard Kessel (Stuttgart: K. P. Woehler, 1959), and "Historicism and its Problems," in Fritz Stern, ed. *The Varieties of History* (New York: Meridian, 1956); H. Rickert, *Die Probleme der Geschichtsphilosophie, Eine Einführung* (3rd rev. ed. Heidelberg: Carl Winters, 1924); Pietro Rossi, *Storia e Storicismo nella filosofia contemporanea* (Milan: Lerci, 1960); Lionel Rubinoff, "Historicism and the A Priori of History," *Dialogue: The Canadian Philosophical Review*, III (June 1964), pp. 81–8, and "Introduction" to *The Presuppositions of Critical History* by F. H. Bradley (Toronto: J. M. Dent; Chicago: Quadrangle, 1968); Alfred Stern, *Philosophy of History and the Problem of Value* (The Hague: Mouton & Co., 1962); Ernst Troeltsch, *Der Historismus und Seine Probleme*, Gesammelte Schriften, III (Tübingen: J. C. B. Mohr, 1922), "Die Krisis des Historismus," *Die Neue Rundschau*, XXXIII (1922).

3 A CRITIQUE OF RADICAL HISTORICISM

The main difficulty with the conception of radical historicism, as represented, for example, by Von Wartenburg, Croce, and Dilthey, is the extent to which it fosters scepticism and even nihilism. Historicism, on

IDEA OF A SCIENCE OF HUMAN NATURE 361

the one hand, implies that while history teaches us that there have been changing views, it cannot teach us whether the change was sound or whether the rejected view deserves to be rejected, without presupposing what it uses the evidence of history to deny – namely that there are eternal objective truths. At the same time, it cannot even assert as a truth about the history of human thought that since all human thought belongs to specific historical situations, all human thought is bound to perish with the situation to which it belongs and to be superseded by new unpredictable thoughts. Such an assertion cannot be made without a philosophical analysis which demonstrates a priori that all human thought depends ultimately on fickle and dark fate and not on self-evident principles accessible to man *qua* man. Such a philosophical analysis would amount to a critique of reason with the purpose, as Dilthey put it, of demonstrating the historicity of reason – that is, the denial of theoretical metaphysics and systematic philosophy in the classical sense. But such a critique, seeking to establish the historicity of all thought, would at least have to establish its own transhistorical autonomy and justify its conclusions. But how can this justification be rendered compatible with the claim that all standpoints are relative? In a forceful passage worth quoting in full, the American philosopher Leo Strauss describes well this self-contradictory character of historicism:

By asserting that all human thought, or at least all relevant human thought is historical, historicism admits that human thought is capable of acquiring a most important insight that is universally valid and that will in no way be affected by any future surprises. The historicist thesis is not an isolated assertion: it is inseparable from a view of the essential structure of human life. This view has the same transhistorical character or pretension as any natural right doctrine ... Historicism asserts that all human thoughts or beliefs are historical, and hence deservedly destined to perish; but historicism is itself a human thought; hence historicism can be of only temporary validity, or it cannot be simply true. To assert the historicist thesis means to doubt it and thus to transcend it ... historicism claims to have brought to light a truth which has come to stay, a truth valid for all thought, for all time; however much thought has changed and will change, it will always remain historical. As regards the decisive insight into the essential character of human thought and therewith into the essential character or limitation of humanity, history has reached its end. The historicist is not impressed by the prospect that historicism may be superseded in due time by the denial of historicism. He is certain that such a change would amount to a relapse of human thought into its most powerful delusion. Historicism thrives on the fact that it is inconsistently exempt itself from its own verdict about all human thought. The historicist thesis is self-contradictory or absurd. We cannot see the historical character of all thought – that is, of all thought with the exception of the historicist insight and its implications – without transcending history ... without grasping something transhistorical.

If we call all thought that is radically historical a 'comprehensible world view' or a part of such a view, we must say: historicism is not itself a comprehensive world view but an analysis of all comprehensive world views, an exposition of the essential character of all such views. Thought that recognizes the relativity of all comprehensive views has a different character from thought which is under the spell of or which adopts a comprehensive view. The former is absolute and neutral; the latter is relative and uncommitted. The former is theoretical insight that transcends history; the latter is the outcome of a fateful dispensation (*Natural Right and History*, Chicago: University of Chicago Press, 1953, pp. 24-5).

A more recent and somewhat different refutation has been given by E. L. Fackenheim in *Metaphysics and Historicity*, 1960:

Our refutation of historicism may seem to differ but slightly, if at all, from the standard refutation of relativism in general. But the difference is, nevertheless, important. Conceivably the standard refutation may be met by a doctrine which asserts that statements such as "all truth is relative" differ in logical type from statements such as "the statement 'all truth is relative' is true." But our ... refutation cannot be met by this doctrine ... For historicism asserts ... not only that all metaphysical assertions are historically relative; it adds that this is so because these assertions are part of an historically situated process of self-making. And it is then forced to concede that the assertion "historicism is true" is also part of this process of self-making. But the crux is that both statements, no matter how different in type, must be part of one and the same self-constituting process; and it is precisely this that historicism cannot account for without collapsing in self-contradiction." (p. 64, fn. 36)

Finally, for a further account of the self-contradictory and sceptical implications of radical historicism, see the writings of E. Husserl:

It is easy to see that historicism, if consistently carried through, carries over into extreme sceptical subjectivism. The ideas of truth, theory, science, would then, like all ideas, lose their absolute validity. That an idea has validity would mean that it is a factual construction of spirit, which is held as valid and which in its factual validity determines thought. There would be no unqualified validity, or validity 'in itself', which is what it is, even if no one has achieved it and though no historical humanity will ever achieve it. Thus too, there would then be no validity to the principle of contradiction nor for any logic, which latter, nevertheless, is still in full vigor in our time. The result perhaps will be that the logical principles of non-contradiction will be transformed into their opposites. And to go even further, all the propositions which we have just enunciated and even the possibilities that we have weighed and have claimed as constantly valid would in themselves have no validity, etc. ("Philosophy as a Strict Science," *Cross Currents*, VI [1956], 332–3)

Like Collingwood, Husserl recognized that a rational and scientific assessment of the historicity of thought presupposes criteria which are themselves non-historical. Such criteria cannot themselves be determined by a strictly empirical (i.e., historical) science without presupposing what this science seeks to prove. In other words, a strictly historical science cannot itself validate the criteria according to which it proceeds: neither can it refute the possibility of a strictly non-historical philosophy or science. Such refutations are only possible by presupposing what historicism seeks to deny – namely, the existence of "scientific philosophy." Indeed, it is clear that any kind of criticism "in so far as it is really to lay claim to validity, is philosophy, and in significance implies the ideal possibility of a systematic philosophy as a strict science" (*ibid.*, p. 334). Hence the need, as we have already noted, for a phenomenologically oriented theory of essence which alone can provide the basis for "a philosophy of the spirit" (*ibid.*, p. 335). In this respect Husserl's phenomenology plays a role similar to Collingwood's transcendental metaphysics of the pure act. The difference between Collingwood and Husserl, however, lies in their respective philosophies of mind: for there is nothing in Husserl to compare with Collingwood's theory of mind as immanence-transcendence. In fact, just as Gentile, who may be placed in the same tradition, seems to sacrifice transcendence to immanence, so Husserl may be accused of sacrificing immanence to transcendence. As a result, neither is able to achieve the necessary rapprochement between history and philosophy, which, as Collingwood has shown, is an absolute requirement of any attempt to provide a rational and scientific critique of the human condition.

APPENDIX II

TECHNICAL TERMS EMPLOYED IN THIS STUDY

EXPERIENCE is either PRIMARY or SECONDARY. Primary experience is IMMEDIATE, UNSYSTEMATIC, and UNMEDIATED. Secondary experience is MEDIATE and REFLECTIVE, constituting a SCALE OF FORMS (i.e., a developing hierarchy of philosophic activities). PHILOSOPHY may be either ABSOLUTE philosophy (i.e., THE PHILOSOPHY OF THE PURE ACT) or HISTORICAL philosophy. Absolute philosophy, at least in its highest mode, has no presuppositions; it rests on an absolute identity between subject and object and cannot be expressed in language; it is the pure unmediated activity of the mind knowing itself. It is therefore equivalent to ABSOLUTE KNOWLEDGE (SPECULUM SPECULI). Historical philosophy involves a distinction between subject and object which it seeks to overcome; it is necessary only because the ideal of philosophy, the absolute identity of subject and object, has not yet been reached. Historical philosophy may be either PHENOMENOLOGY or HISTORICAL PHILOSOPHY PROPER. As phenomenology it analyses the necessary CATEGORIES or HABITS of mind – IMAGINATION (aesthetic consciousness), FAITH (religious consciousness), UNDERSTANDING (scientific consciousness), and REASON (historical and philosophical consciousness). As historical philosophy proper it traces the historical development of the particular disciplines (art, religion, science, history, and philosophy) which derive therefrom. Since both the categories and their derivatives are subject to historical change, both phenomenology and historical philosophy proper must be redone each generation.

The historical philosophy of each particular standpoint is METAPHYSICS or DOGMATIC PHILOSOPHY. The aim of metaphysics (or dogmatic philosophy) is the vindication of experience: the discovery of *what* its absolute presuppositions are and the explanation of their origins and relations to other sets of presuppositions. As such, dogmatic philosophy or metaphysics must be distinguished into a narrow AB INTRA approach, which is purely *descriptive*, and a more critical AB EXTRA approach which is *normative*. Genuine dogmatic philosophy is the synthesis of both activities into a concrete and dynamic activity. The *ab intra* approach, taken by itself, which is sometimes mistaken for metaphysics proper, is only an abstraction from the complete activity and does not, therefore, give rise to any genuine dialectic or progress. Genuine metaphysics (i.e., as the dynamic synthesis of both *ab intra* and *ab extra*) is either of *past* or *contemporary* thought: the latter (i.e., the metaphysics of contemporary thought) is also defined as SYSTEMATIC METAPHYSICS.

Metaphysics vindicates experience on three ONTOLOGICAL LEVELS. At the FIRST it asserts the absolute priority of the standpoint examined; at the SECOND all standpoints are recognized as equally valid; at the THIRD each standpoint is placed on an OVERLAPPING SCALE OF FORMS, the higher SUPERSEDING yet summing up the lower. Within each single form the presuppositions are also placed on an overlapping scale. Such a scale is ordered by the LOGIC OF THE OVERLAP OF CLASSES which recognizes INTERNAL but not EXTERNAL relations. The ontological model of this logic is the CONCRETE UNIVERSAL, which is the synthesis of its particular expressions. The concrete universal is INDIVIDUAL in so far as it is a particular state of affairs, and judgments about it (HISTORY) are therefore CATEGORICAL SINGULAR (i.e., CATEGORICAL PARTICULAR). In so far as the concrete universal expresses itself in thought, i.e., through the mediation of universal concepts, it is UNIVERSAL, the object of CATEGORICAL UNIVERSAL judgments (PHILOSOPHY).

The history of thought is the history of different answers to different questions. All questions rest on ABSOLUTE PRESUPPOSITIONS, so that a change in the latter occasions the raising of new questions. Likewise, the raising of new questions may be the occasion for changes within a given set of presuppositions. The whole process of change is DIALECTICAL: each new set of presuppositions grows out of its predecessor as the resolution of tensions to which the raising of new questions gives rise. Since the process of question and answer is LOGICALLY and EXISTENTIALLY related to changes within sets of absolute presuppositions, the order of question and answer complexes parallels the order and arrangement of presuppositions. The basis of this order is the scale of forms, according to which the relation between forms, within both the general scale of habits or categories and any particular or single form, is not one of EXTENSION between classes (as, for example, is the case with the externally related co-ordinate species of a genus) but is an internal relation of INTENSION between concepts or categories.

The absolute presuppositions of any standpoint have CONSUPPONIBILITY as their ideal state. In fact they always exhibit a variety of stresses and strains of a logical and existential nature for which metaphysical analysis often acts as a catalyst. The drive towards changes of presuppositions is a sign of the HEALTHY CONSCIOUSNESS; refusal to advance is a sign of the CORRUPT CONSCIOUSNESS. Normal presuppositional development proceeds through error. Metaphysics and phenomenology may be regarded, therefore, as PATHOLOGIES OF NORMALCY; they exhibit the rationality of the concrete universal, MIND. The mind's progress through error is the act through which it endows itself with a nature as such: man's being is essentially *his own deed*. Since the discovery and correction of error is accomplished only through the mind's HISTORICAL and CRITICAL knowledge of itself, HISTORICAL SELF-KNOWLEDGE is equivalent to HISTORICAL SELF-MAKING. This is the source of a fundamental and systematic ambiguity in the meaning of the word history as both a science (subject) and a process (object) upon which so much of the argument turns.

APPENDIX III

THE CATEGORIES AND HABITS OF MIND		DISCIPLINES AND SEPARATE STANDPOINTS DERIVED FROM CATEGORIES
		absolute philosophy
REASON	(philosophical habit) philosophy	3rd level dogmatic philosophy 2nd level dogmatic philosophy 1st level dogmatic philosophy
	(historical habit) history	philosophical history and historiography philosophy of history historicism, realism
UNDERSTANDING	(scientific habit) science	philosophical science philosophy of science scientism, positivism
FAITH	(religious habit) religion	philosophical theology philosophy of religion theism
IMAGINATION	(aesthetic habit) – art	philosophical aesthetics philosophy of art aestheticism

APPENDIX IV

TYPES OF PHILOSOPHY

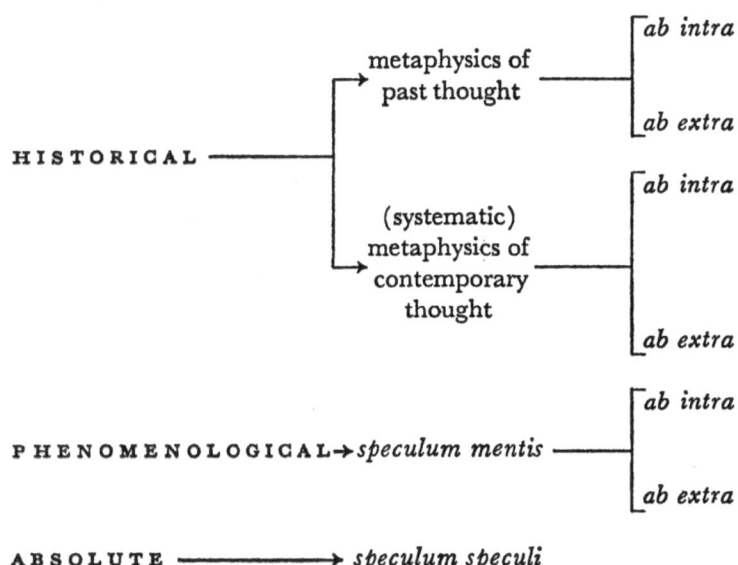

APPENDIX V

THE PRINCIPLES OF DOGMATIC PHILOSOPHY

FIRST ONTOLOGICAL LEVEL

Philosophy vindicates experience from its own point of view (i.e., *ab intra* only) (SM, 272). A person who is actually absorbed in any given form of experience is by this very absorption committed to the opinion that no other form is valid, that his form is the only one adequate to the comprehension of reality (SM, 43, 307). Thus, for example, from none of the particular points of view can the other forms of experience be regarded as co-existent and equally rational or defensible manifestations of thought; from the point of view of any single form, no other form exists (SM, 198–9); the particular conception of reality implied by any given standpoint is regarded as the whole of reality. This behaviour corresponds to what Collingwood calls the first way of awarding the prize (SM, 41). Finally, the forms are regarded as having fixed given natures, which are in no way affected by their being known, and are therefore conceived as self-identical types of events which by their recurrence in a fixed or changing order constitute human experience.

SECOND ONTOLOGICAL LEVEL

Philosophy (informed now by the dynamics of *ab extra* criticism) vindicates experience by regarding each form as one of a number of equally valid standpoints. This behaviour corresponds to what Collingwood describes as the second way of awarding the prize (SM, 42–4). The methodological criteria of analysis are derived from a logic of genus and species according to which the forms are treated as externally (i.e., extentionally) related *classes*. The epistemological attitude is characterized by the same abstract distinction between subject and object which obtains at the first level: with the result that there can be no genuine rapprochement between theory and practice; philosophy remains essentially a form of abstract thinking.

THIRD ONTOLOGICAL LEVEL

Philosophy vindicates a given form of experience by rendering *explicit* the *implicit* presuppositions of that experience and then organizing these presuppositions into a dialectical and historical scale of forms. The form per se is also itself regarded as one moment on an internally related dialectical scale of forms (alternatively regarded as a scale of errors) or concrete universal. At this level of analysis the methodological criteria are derived from a dialectical logic variously described as a phenomenology of error, a logic of the overlap of classes, and a logic of question and answer (SM, 288–91, 195–200; EPM, chs II–III; A, ch. V). In keeping with the transhistorical principles of absolute philosophy, which third-level analysis exemplifies (see appendix VI below), the behaviour of the latter exhibits a rapprochement between theory and practice, thought and action.

APPENDIX VI

THE TRANSHISTORICAL PRINCIPLES OF ABSOLUTE PHILOSOPHY

1 All thought exists for the sake of action; the philosophical analysis of any single form of life has existential consequences for the whole of life (SM, 15; EM, 45, 224; IH, 227–8). Of everything that the mind does it gives itself an account as it does it and this account is inseparably bound up with the doing of the thing (SM, 84, 256).

2 The forms of experience and their corresponding reflective moments form a system of overlapping forms. These forms have a serial or natural order of their own which expresses itself not only in the phenomenological structure of mind but in the actual history of the individual and of the race (SM, 51).

3 The forms are not (like the co-ordinate species of a genus) abstractly self-identical types (or classes) which by their recurrence in a fixed or changing order constitute human experience, but types whose recurrence perpetually modifies them so that they shade off into one another and give rise to new determinations at every turn (SM, 55–6; OPA, 94; see appendix I above).

4 The relations among the overlapping forms are dialectical – i.e., each form is implicit in its predecessor which it supersedes and is in turn superseded by a higher form to which it gives rise and which it implicitly contains (SM, 55, 164, 289–90; EPM, 48–50, 88–9). The overlap is therefore not a mere overlap of *extension* between classes, but an overlap of *intension* between concepts or categories, each in its degree or specification of its generic essence or concrete universality (EPM, 91).

5 Since the logical and phenomenological relations among the forms are exemplified in the actual course of historical events (SM, 51, 289), the historian is therefore committed to believe in the rationality of history (EPM, 226) : namely, that the relations among the events in history are dialectical, that there is an internal or necessary connexion between the events of a time series such that one event necessarily leads to the other (IH, 110) and, that such changes are stimulated by stresses and strains (EM, 73–5).

6 The life of absolute knowledge is the constant self-creation of mind; no mere discovery of what it is, but the making of itself what it is (SM, 296), through the mediation of the external worlds of art, religion, science, history, systems of philosophy, and so on (SM, 315); a process in which man creates for himself this or that kind of human nature by creating for himself works of art, theories of nature, objects of faith, and by recreating in his own thought the past to which he is heir (IH, 184; OPA, 91–5). Finally, in this way he achieves for himself a state of genuine freedom (SM, 222; IH, 315–20).

APPENDIX VII

THE SCALE OF THE FORMS OF EXPERIENCE AND THEIR CORRESPONDING MOMENTS OF PHILOSOPHICAL REFLECTION

THIRD LEVEL

Art
Aesthetic consciousness experiences itself as one moment on a dialectical scale of forms. Philosophical aesthetics vindicates this *ab intra* and *ab extra* according to the logic of the overlap of classes. Recognition of a rapprochement between imagination and reason and of a dialectical identity between subject and object.

Religion
Religious consciousness experiences itself as one moment on a scale of overlapping forms. Philosophical religion vindicates this according to the dialectical logic of the overlap of classes. Recognition of religion as a form of finite and absolute self-making. Transcendence of subject-object distinction.

Science
Scientific consciousness, now regarded as one moment on a scale of forms, is characterized by its experience of the historicity of nature and the scientific method. Philosophical science vindicates this in terms of a logic of overlap of classes. Scientific facts regarded as species of historical facts. Application of principle *esse est fieri*. Science is regarded as a form of self-making and nature is recognized as conforming to the structure of mind.

History
Historical consciousness experiences itself as one moment on a scale of forms. Philosophical historiography vindicates this by means of a logic of the overlap of classes. Recognition of rapprochement between philosophy and history. The object of history, the concrete fact, is now regarded as mind. As a form of knowledge, history is characterized as "rethinking." Recognition of dialectical identity between subject and object. History is not only self-knowledge but self-making.

SECOND LEVEL

Art
Aesthetic experience continues to experience itself as imagination but regards itself as only one among a number of equally valid standpoints. Philosophy of art vindicates this by means of a logic of genus and species. Formal recognition of distinction between creation and products – i.e., between mind and its object.

Religion
Religious consciousness experiences itself as one among a number of equally valid standpoints. Philosophy of religion vindicates this according to logic of genus and species. Language of religion recognized as symbolic only. Recognition of existence of non-religious truths. God experienced as object.

Science

Scientific consciousness regards itself as one among a number of equally valid standpoints. Philosophy of science vindicates this in terms of logic of genus and species. *A parte objecti*, the object of science is still regarded as the abstract universal. *A parte subjecti*, the analysis of science in epistemological terms is identical with the analysis of history and philosophy, and the distinction between them as separate kinds of knowledge is an illusion.

History

Historical consciousness experiences itself as one of a number of equally valid standpoints. Philosophy vindicates this in terms of a logic of genus and species. *A parte objecti*, history is the concrete fact whose existence is independent of the knowing subject. *A parte subjecti*, history is perception raised to its highest power. From the absolute standpoint history is therefore to be distinguished from philosophy for whom the distinction between subject and object has been overcome.

FIRST LEVEL

Art

Aesthetic consciousness experiences itself as pure imagination without assertion, i.e., as supposal. *A parte subjecti, esse est imaginaro; a parte objecti, esse est imaginari*. Aestheticism vindicates this by proclaiming the absolute priority of imagination's claim to Truth.

Religion

Religious consciousness experiences itself as pure faith. Theism (religious philosophy) vindicates this by asserting religion as the only mode of knowledge and being. Religion is thereby confused with theology and may be regarded as metaphor mistaking itself for literal assertion. At this level God is experienced as wholly other.

Science

Scientific consciousness experiences the world as pure symbol. Scientism asserts the absolute priority of the abstract universal arrived at by deduction and induction from appearances. Assertion of absolute separation between subject and object. Understanding (i.e., the faculty of subsuming particulars under universals) is regarded as the only mode of knowledge.

History

Historical consciousness experiences the world as pure fact. Historical philosophy vindicates this by asserting the absolute historicity (i.e., facticity) of all being and knowledge. Identification of history with perception.

APPENDIX VIII

CORRELATION OF COLLINGWOOD'S MAIN WRITINGS WITH THE THREE LEVELS OF PHILOSOPHIC ACTIVITY*

THIRD LEVEL

The New Leviathan (1940–2) – systematic metaphysics of culture.
The Idea of Nature (1933–42) – systematic metaphysics of scientific experience.
An Autobiography (1938)
An Essay on Metaphysics (1938–9) – primarily transhistorical philosophy of philosophy: some examples of historical metaphysics of past thought.
An Essay on Philosophical Method (1933) – systematic philosophy of philosophy (i.e., transhistorical philosophy)
The Principles of Art (1937) – primarily a systematic metaphysics of contemporary aesthetic experience.
The Idea of History (1936–1940) – Historical metaphysics of past (pts. I–IV and contemporary (pt. V) thought.
The Philosophy of History (1930) – Historical metaphysics of past and contemporary thought.
"A Philosophy of Progress" (1929)
"Political Action" (1928)
"Faith and Reason" (1928) } systematic metaphysics
"Reason is Faith Cultivating Itself" (1927)
"Economics as a Philosophical Science" (1925)
"Plato's Philosophy of Art" (1925) – historical metaphysics of past thought.
Speculum Mentis (1923) – chapters I, II, VII (1, 7–10), and VIII exemplify the transhistorical metaphysics of philosophy itself (absolute philosophy).
"What is the Problem of Evil" (1920) – systematic metaphysics of morality.
Ruskin's Philosophy (1919) – historical metaphysics of past and contemporary thought.

SECOND LEVEL

"Religion, Science and Philosophy" (1926)
"The Nature and Aims of a Philosophy of History" (1925)
"Outlines of a Philosophy of Art" (1925)
"Are History and Science Different Kinds of Knowledge" (1922)
Religion and Philosophy (1915)

Each may be regarded as an example of systematic metaphysics which is characterized by a lack of any genuine rapprochement between theory and practice, philosophy and history, subject and object.

FIRST LEVEL

Speculum Mentis (1923) – A phenomenological analysis of the basic categories of experience and of the first-level dogmatisms which derive therefrom.

*Dates given are dates of composition. For dates of publication see Bibliography.

Notes

CHAPTER ONE

1 See appendix 1 for a brief but more detailed account of the history of positivism and historicism. See also the Introduction to my edition of F. H. Bradley's essay, *The Presuppositions of Critical History* (Toronto: J. M. Dent, 1968) (Chicago: Quadrangle Books).
2 Although the term 'dialectic' has enjoyed a variety of different meanings throughout the history of philosophy, its employment here will conform strictly to its Collingwoodian usage, derived from Hegel, according to which experience, reality, or the life of mind is a creative synthesis in which one moment leads necessarily to the next through the instrument of 'determinate negation.' The latter operates on two distinct but related levels. The first is a strictly logical level in which the conscious attempt to vindicate a given standpoint gives rise to logical contradictions which can be resolved only if consciousness redefines its position and adopts a higher standpoint. Thus, for example, although consciousness *qua* art claims to be pure imagination, it soon discovers, when it attempts to explicate this claim that it is also a body of assertions. Indeed, it is only because it is assertion that it can claim not to be. Consciousness, in other words, in order to assert itself as art, must presuppose the very opposite of what it asserts. This contradiction is resolved, as we shall see, when consciousness adopts the standpoint of religion which explicitly asserts (rather than merely imagines) what it believes to be true. The second level of negation, implicit in the first, is the existential level in which consciousness is forced to adopt a different and higher standpoint as a result of its having come to re-experience the nature of its object and its own relation to it. For example, the very attempt to experience the whole of reality as a product of imagination generates within mind itself a series of new needs to which the conception of pure art is no longer adequate. Mind now realizes that, whatever its object is, it is more than art, the product of aesthetic creation; it must be, in addition, an object of faith as well as a work of reason. But it is a work of reason whose very being or existence is synonymous with the act of being rationally apprehended. Thus is initiated a process in which mind makes itself by continually revising its notion of what constitutes its proper object. The whole process begins with the assertion of an absolute and abstract separation between mind and its object and concludes with the recognition that the relation of mind to its object is really one of concrete self-identity. (More detailed accounts of the

nature of dialectic are given in ch. III, ss. 2–3, ch. VI, s. 4, ch. VIII, s. 9, and ch. X. The actual progress of the dialectic of experience, from art to philosophy, is illustrated in ch. IV.)

3 Cf. William James, "In a subject like philosophy it is really fatal to lose connexion with the open air of human nature, and to think in terms of shop-tradition only. Such are the rules of the professorial game – they think and write from each other and for each other and at each other exclusively. With this exclusion of the open air all true perspective gets lost, extremes and oddities count as much as sanities, and command the same attention; and if by chance anyone writes popularly and about results only, with his mind directly focussed on the subject, it is reckoned *oberflächliches zeug und ganz unwissenschaftlich.*" (*The Pluralistic Universe*, London: Longmans Green, 1909, pp. 17–18)

4 According to Collingwood, the more serious consequences of this kind of disruption, resulting from a breach of the unity of thought and action, was the effect of the latter on the teaching of moral philosophy during his own time at Oxford. The legacy of the Renaissance was at this time kept alive through the doctrines of philosophical realism. The great principle of realism, according to Collingwood, was that nothing is affected by its being known. This was thought to be as true of human action as anything else. Thus the new teachers of moral philosophy would say to their pupils, whether in words or not, "If Ethics interests you by all means study it; but don't think it will be of any use to you. Moral philosophy is only the study of moral action: it can't therefore make any difference to the practice of moral action" (A, 48). As a result of this attitude the impression was given that philosophy was a silly and trifling game and a serious breach was created between the philosopher and his audience. The school of Green had taught that philosophy was not a preserve for professional philosophers but every one's business; and the pupils of this school had gradually formed a block of opinion in the country whose members, though not professional philosophers, were interested in the subject, regarded it as important, and did not feel themselves debarred by their amateur status from expressing their own opinions about it. However, as these men died no one took their place. Thus by 1920 Collingwood found himself asking: "Why is it that nowadays no Oxford man, unless he is either 70 years old or else a teacher of philosophy at Oxford or elsewhere, regards philosophy as anything but a futile parlour game?" The answer, for Collingwood, was not difficult to find. It lay in the fact that the realists, unlike the school of Green, denied the doctrine of the unity of the sciences and, in true Renaissance fashion, thought philosophy a preserve for professional philosophers, and were loud in their contempt of philosophical utterances by historians, natural scientists, theologians, and other amateurs (A, 50).

5 *Briefwechsel zwischen Wilhelm Dilthey und dem Grafen Paul York Von Wartenburg: 1877–1897* (Halle: Max Niemeyer, 1923), p. 251.
6 *History as the Story of Liberty* (New York: Meridian Press, 1955), p. 33.
7 *Ibid.*, p. 63.
8 *Ibid.*, p. 33.
9 *Logic* (London: Macmillan, 1917), p. 324.
10 Carlo Antoni, *From History to Sociology* (Detroit: Wayne State University Press, 1959), p. xvii.
11 F. H. Heinemann, "Reply to Historicism," *Philosophy*, XXI (1946), 251–2.
12 *The Poverty of Historicism* (London: Routledge & Kegan, 1957), p. 3.
13 *The Open Society and its Enemies* (2nd ed., London: Routledge & Kegan Paul, 1952), II, p. 3.
14 *The Philosophy of Art History* (London: Routledge & Kegan Paul, 1959), pp. 119–20.
15 Thus, for example, he points out in the *Idea of History* that the assertion of

the historicity of all thought and reality is a mistake of the same kind which materialists made in the seventeenth century (IH, 209). Cf. also his somewhat ironical characterization of Croce's historicism as a victory for the very naturalism from which he (Croce) was trying to escape (CPH, 277).

16 Since the discussion of the doctrine of the overlap of classes is in the context of a general discussion and criticism of theories of logic, such as 'the logical doctrine of classification and division' (EPM, 28 ff.), we are justified in referring to the overlap of classes as a 'logic'; especially since it is by implication clearly referred to as a more genuine account of the logical structure of philosophical concepts (EPM, 31).

17 According to Knox, Collingwood's illness (which apparently took the form of tiny blood-vessels bursting in the brain) intensified in 1938 and had a definite and adverse effect on the philosophical output of his later years. "In these circumstances," Knox writes, "the wonder is not that his later books should lack serenity or be marred by febrility and overweening confidence, or contain matter which dismayed his friends; the wonder is that they were written at all, and still more that they should contain passages of outstanding worth" (IH, xxi). Concerning the probable effect of Collingwood's illness on his later thought (about which Collingwood himself declared: "I have never known any illness interfere with my power of thinking and writing, or with the quality of what I think and write" [A, 117]) the following remark by John Passmore is worth noting: "It is sometimes suggested by Idealist admirers of Collingwood that the brain disease from which he began to suffer in 1933 is reflected in his ultimate heterodoxies. When one contemplates the speculative freedom of these later works, one can only wish that his contemporaries could have been similarly afflicted" (*A Hundred Years of Philosophy* (London: Duckworth, 1957), 306, n1).

18 *The Later Philosophy of R. G. Collingwood* (Oxford: Clarendon Press, 1962), p. 12.

19 *Ibid.*, pp. 11–12.

20 *Ibid.*, p. 14.

21 See ch. VIII below for a further discussion of Donagan's views.

22 *The Later Philosophy of R. G. Collingwood*, pp. 2–22.

23 *Ibid.*, p. 16.

24 "Reply to Historicism," 252–3.

25 *Nature, Mind and Modern Science* (London: Allen and Unwin, 1954), pp. 35–8.

26 "Historicism and Philosophy: Reflections on R. G. Collingwood," *Revue internationale de Philosophie* (1957), 416–17.

27 On Collingwood's Philosophy of History, *Review of Metaphysics*, v (1952), 583 ff.

28 *Philosophical Quarterly* (1963), 371.

29 *Philosophical Books* (1963), 4.

30 *The Listener*, 27 June 1963, 1085.

31 *Australasian Journal of Philosophy* (1963), 413–15.

32 Introduction to Gentile's *Genesis and Structure of Society* (Urbana: University of Illinois Press, 1960), pp. 14–20.

33 *R. G. Collingwood* (Writers and their Works, no. 42, London: Longmans, 1953); "The Philosophy of R. G. Collingwood," *Ratio*, I (1958).

34 *Journal of Aesthetics and Art Criticism*, XXII (1963), pp. 84–5.

35 *R. G. Collingwood*, pp. 26–8.

36 "The Philosophy of R. G. Collingwood," 134. Tomlin bases this speculation on his own lecture notes of Collingwood's sketch of a cosmology which was originally intended as a conclusion to the *Idea of History* but which in fact has never been published.

37 Other interpretations which have appeared since the completion of this book

are *R. G. Collingwood: Philosophe et historien*, Albert Shalom (Paris, Presses universitaires de France, 1967); *R. G. Collingwood: The Formative Years*, W. M. Johnston (The Hague: Nihoff, 1968), and "Collingwood's Dialectic of History," Louis O. Mink, *History and Theory*, VII, 1 (1968), 3-37. Shalom's work lends support to the radical conversion hypothesis and is chiefly concerned with exposing the limitations and inadequacies of Collingwood's thought. As a result, Shalom's conclusions are somewhat disturbing to someone of my persuasion and I regret not having had a chance to deal with them in the main body of the text. But I suspect that what I do say with respect to other defenders of the radical conversion hypothesis will go some way towards meeting Shalom's general dissatisfaction with Collingwood's thought.

Johnston's book, on the other hand, is primarily an intellectual biography which concentrates heavily on the major influences on Collingwood's thought (especially John Ruskin). No real effort is made to deal with the various philosophical controversies to which Collingwood's work has given rise. Instead the author concentrates on providing a descriptive summary of Collingwood's system. But the impression is given that Collingwood's thought forms an organic system which grows from his earliest preoccupations. Johnston's book, then, would tend not to support the radical conversion hypothesis.

Finally, Louis Mink's article, which summarizes views more fully expounded in *Mind, History and Dialectic: The Philosophy of R. G. Collingwood* (Bloomington: Indiana University Press, 1969), argues vigorously in favour of viewing Collingwood's thought as a "dialectical system" (p. 5). As in my own study, Mink attempts an interpretation of Collingwood's entire thought in the light of his philosophy of mind, with the result that he reaches conclusions similar to my own. But these conclusions are reached by very different routes. Whereas I have attempted to develop Collingwood's theory of mind on the basis of a close reading of *Speculum Mentis*, Mink's sources lie chiefly in *The Principles of Art* and *The New Leviathan*. And I would contend that, valuable and incisive as Mink's study may be, it is limited by its lack of attention to the details of works like *Religion and Philosophy* and *Speculum Mentis*. Mink inadvertently conveys the impression, as do most Collingwood scholars, that everything before the publication of *An Essay on Philosophical Method* is juvenilia. A possible example of the effect of failure to attend carefully to the details of the early writings is a passage in Mink's article in which he stresses the Hegelian dimensions of Collingwood's thought and argues the necessity for viewing his system as an expression of "dialectical analysis," but then adds: "Collingwood does not himself use the word dialectical but it is clear that his theory of mind carries out in every relevant respect the program for the dialectical analysis of concepts which he had laid down in his *Essay on Philosophical Method*" (p. 9). Now, although Mink is quite right in what he says, his claim would be less open to question (on the grounds that it is purely speculative) if he had backed it up with an extensive analysis of the text of *Speculum Mentis* in which Collingwood not only uses the word dialectical but very carefully defines its meaning as well (pp. 206–8). What is more, had Mink given the attention to *Speculum Mentis* which it deserves he would have realized that the theory of mind elaborated there, while compatible with the doctrines of the *New Leviathan*, is nevertheless distinct in certain important respects. In Collingwood's own language, the development from *Speculum Mentis* to the *New Leviathan* is a development within an overlapping scale of forms from one level of analysis (dealing with one set of questions) to another level (dealing with an entirely distinct set of questions). And I would therefore raise into question the possibility of gaining an adequate understanding of the latter without having first exhausted the content of the former.

To support this claim naturally requires a great deal of argument and supplementation. However, since the manuscript for this book had virtually gone to press at the time Mink's work first appeared, I am unable to deal with it in the main body of the text. But I should make it clear that were I to have done so it would not be for the purpose of refuting his conclusions, they being in essence very similar to my own, it would be rather to demonstrate how his interpretation could be strengthened in the light of the kind of analysis which I have given and which has given rise to a somewhat different set of conceptual tools.

38 See L. Rubinoff, "Collingwood and the Radical Conversion Hypothesis," *Dialogue: Canadian Journal of Philosophy* (June 1966), and "Collingwood's Theory of the Relation between Philosophy and History: A New Interpretation," *Journal of the History of Philosophy* (Oct. 1968).
39 Milwaukee: Marquette University Press, 1960.
40 "Philosophy as a Strict Science," translated by Q. Lauer, *Cross Currents*, VI (1956), 332–3.
41 *Ibid.*, 334.
42 "Philosophy as a Strict Science," 335.
43 Readers of Mink will recall that he too argues that Collingwood represents the phenomenon of consciousness as "displaying a dialectically ordered series of levels of consciousness" (p. 8). But the fourfold analysis of consciousness which Mink elaborates takes the shape of a philosophical psychology and is based almost entirely on the text of the *New Leviathan* and the *Principles of Art*, whereas the tripartite analysis which I have developed is an ontological analysis derived primarily from *Speculum Mentis*. I am not suggesting that there is any basic incompatibility between the philosophical psychology of the *New Leviathan* and the ontology of *Speculum Mentis* but only that each is addressed to different kinds of problems. For a further discussion of the differences between my own and Mink's analyses see ch. III, n4, below.
44 Most of these topics have already been covered by Donagan.
45 I am indebted to Professor Gilbert Ryle for permission to quote from this correspondence which has recently been deposited in the Bodleian Library (ms. Eng. lett. d. 194).

CHAPTER TWO

1 *History: Its Theory and Practice*, translated by Douglas Ainslie in 1920 (New York: Sage and Russell, 1960), p. 151.
2 *Mind*, XXXI (1922).
3 See appendix 1 below for a discussion of Collingwood's reaction to Croce and Bradley.

CHAPTER THREE

1 For a discussion of this doctrine of Aristotle see chapter VII, sec. 2, pp. 188–91, below.
2 "The Exoteric Approach to Hegel's Phenomenology," *Mind*, XLIII (1934); "The Comedy of Immediacy in Hegel's Phenomenology," *Mind*, XLIV (1935).
3 Parts of this section have been previously published in the *Journal of the History of Philosophy*, VI, 4 (Oct. 1968), 363–80 and are here reprinted with permission of the editors.
4 I have already indicated (ch. I, n43, above) that the tripartite analysis of consciousness under discussion is not to be confused with the much different (although not unrelated) fourfold analysis employed by Louis Mink, and which is based almost exclusively on the text of the *New Leviathan*. To avoid

possible misunderstanding, however, it should again be stressed that the differences between the two theories of mind – the ontological analysis given in *Speculum Mentis* and the philosophical psychology elaborated in the *New Leviathan* – do not testify to any radical change of outlook on Collingwood's part (apart, that is, from any systematic changes which can be expected to occur in a dialectical system of thought). Collingwood's theory of mind is a comprehensive one which embraces both the philosophical psychology of the *New Leviathan* and the ontology of *Speculum Mentis*. Each represents a different level of analysis, and my only quarrel with Mink is to the effect that since questions to which the *New Leviathan* are addressed arise only when the questions to which *Speculum Mentis* are addressed have been answered, Mink's analysis would have been more effective had it included a more serious evaluation of *Speculum Mentis* (at least in so far as his article is concerned). And I would further argue that some of the problems which Mink attempts to solve by his analysis are more effectively solved by applying the threefold ontological analysis outlined above.

CHAPTER FOUR

1 Although this may appear to constitute an identity of subject and object, in fact it does not. As in the case of Berkeley's distinction between *esse est percepi* and *esse est percipere*, *imaginare* is an entirely separate being from *imaginari*.
2 Cf. Collingwood's criticisms of a slightly different version of the theory of art for art's sake in "The Place of Art in Education" (*Hibbert Journal* [1926], 437 ff.). According to the above theory all art is quite useless; its essence is to withdraw from the region of practical affairs "into the charmed circle of its own fairyland." On this view, the only justification for art is its beauty (*ibid.*, 436). Collingwood argues that by adopting such an attitude (which according to the terms of this thesis is a first-level one) art invites an interpretation which regards it not as a necessity to life but as an ornament, as a relaxation of the practical strain of life, as an escape. Just as *Speculum Mentis* explores the contradictions and flaws of the theory of art as pure imagination, so "The Place of Art in Education" explores the flaw in the theory of art as a useless grace. Thus Collingwood declares: "the aestheticism which revels in the luxurious conviction of the uselessness of art ... is based on ... a profoundly vicious philosophy of art. The error in question, like all errors, contains a grain of truth; and it is because the truth is important that error has vitality enough to be formidable. The truth is that beauty and utility are not the same thing, and that art as such is not practical life as such. The error is to suppose that, because art as such is not practical life as such, to say what it *is not* throws light on the question what it is: to suppose, in other words, that its own proper positive nature is determined by this bare negation, this bare statement of the fact that it is not something else" (*ibid.*, 437: cf. also RUP, 34 ff.).
3 Cf. "Ruskin's Philosophy." Collingwood writes: "The soil in which art grows is not art but life ... morality issues, not from a moral faculty, but from the nature of the whole man, and so with art; and if the self which you reveal in morality is bad, how can the same self, when you reveal it in terms of art, be good? ... the art of a healthy nation is a direct expression of its spontaneous interest in life, while the art of an enfeebled and corrupt nation forgets its relation to reality and loses itself in technicalities and aestheticisms, in abstract canons and formal restrictions" (*ibid.*, 34, 35, 36). Cf. also PAE, 340–2 and AE, esp. 240 ff.
4 In effect Collingwood recognizes two forms of corruption, which I have previously (see above, ch. III, s. 2) characterized as normal and abnormal (see also below, ch. V, s. 1). A corruption is normal if, upon its being disclosed to

consciousness, consciousness is prepared to adjust its behaviour in order to overcome it. It is abnormal if, instead of being consciously accepted, the implications of this disclosure are avoided by means of the various mechanisms which are available for such purposes, such as "repression" or "projection" or "dissociation," etc. (PA, 218–19). For mind, to arrest itself in this way at any particular stage of experience is tantamount to a relapse into an unhealthy form of dogmatism – described in *An Essay on Metaphysics* as the disease of irrationalism – from which it is difficult to escape.

5 See "The Place of Art in Education," for a similar third-level account of the theory of art as action: a theory which presupposes that art is a fundamental activity of mind through whose activities mind itself comes into being. "Art," writes Collingwood, is "not ornamental but structural" (*ibid.*, 439). It is, he continues, "one of these fundamental forms of mental activity which some philosophers call the categories of the spirit. Art is not a quality of objects (there are, strictly speaking, no *objets d'art*); it is a mode of acting; a necessary mode, in so far as every mind that is a mind at all acts in this way. Our ordinary name for this mode of acting is 'imagination'. To imagine is to be an artist; to imagine well is to be a good artist; to imagine superlatively well is to be a great artist. And there is no mind that exists without imagining; of that we can be tolerably certain, not only from introspection and observation, but from reflection on what it is to be a mind. To be an artist is to create for oneself a world of imaginary objects whose function is to express to oneself one's own mind" (*ibid.*, 339–40). In so far as the field of education is concerned it follows, according to Collingwood, that if "imagination is a fundamental mode of mind's activity" then "the right training of the imagination is therefore a fundamental part of education" (*ibid.*, 442). What is more, since art is the soil from which the other activities grow, the use of imagination may therefore be regarded as the first stage in the growth of mind and knowledge; in which case, aesthetic education ought to begin at an early age. And since the activity of all other activities depends on the purity of imagination, the whole possibility of success in education depends entirely upon the excellence of aesthetic education. The same point is forcefully made in "Aesthetic" (240 ff.).

6 Indeed, the contrast between the scale of the first-level activities of pure imagination and the scale of the third-level activities of imagination controlled by thought is explicitly discussed as early as 1926 in "The Place of Art in Education." The contrast is here presented in terms of a distinction between "poetry" and "prose": a distinction which is employed as a paradigm for the distinctions between art and science, education and life, and a variety of further distinctions within the life of art itself. Within the scale of forms characterizing the dialectical development of mind in general, poetry is synonymous with imagination, fantasy, and supposal, while prose is synonymous with science, philosophy, and thought in general. Thus Collingwood declares: "the life of mind is a constant movement from poetry to prose, from imagination to thought [*ibid.*, 447] ... The consciousness that first expresses itself in poetry, in fantasy and myth, afterwards clarifies out and sobers down into prose, into science and philosophy. The progress of thought is a perpetual passage from poetry to prose and a perpetual birth of new thought in the form of poetry" (*ibid.*, 442). Within the more particular dialectic of the scale of art conceived as a special and distinct form of life, poetry is synonymous with *pure* art or pure imagination (the "poetic poetry" of myth, fantasy, etc.) while prose is synonymous with the "prosaic poetry" of scientific and philosophical art (*ibid.*, 448). Collingwood defines the latter as imagination "working under the control of thought" (*ibid.*, 443). The same distinction is shown to cut across the development of each single art form as well: e.g., the art of bodily gesture (dance), literary activities (poetry, rhyme, novels, etc.), the use of the eye (drawing, painting, sculpting), the technique of

reading and speaking, music, and so on (*ibid.*, 444–7). Each of these single forms is characterized by the same rhythmic alternation between imagination and reason; each begins as "a poetry" whose function is to give way to "prose." From this scheme Collingwood draws certain practical implications concerning the nature of education. Since education may be regarded as the conscious and formalized control of the ideal development of mind, it too may be defined as "a poetry whose function is to pass over into prose" (*ibid.*, 443). This statement may be compared with another of Collingwood's slogans – "Reason is faith cultivating itself" – which might well have become the basis for a similar essay on the place of religion in education (see below, ch. iv, s. 1).

7 See also *Religion and Philosophy*, in which Collingwood first raised questions concerning the relation between religion and reason. "Is the distinction between religion and theology," he writes, "really that between poetry and prose, metaphor and literal assertion? And if so, which is the higher form and the most adequately expressive of the truth?" (*ibid.*, xvi). But then, Collingwood continues, "having raised the problem, I must ask the reader's pardon for failing to deal with it ... and can only add that I hope to make good the deficiency in a future volume" (*ibid.*).

8 *Hibbert Journal*, xxvi (1927).

9 A pamphlet in the Affirmations Series (London, 1928); reprinted in *God and the Modern World*, edited by A. A. David (New York: Dutton, 1929). Hereafter all references to *Faith and Reason* (FR) will be to both editions. The first reference will be to the 1928 pamphlet, the second to *God in the Modern World*. Thus (FR, 24; 222) means, p. 24 in the 1928 pamphlet and p. 222 in *God in the Modern World*.

10 For a further example of the application of the logic of the overlap of classes to the solution of a problem in religion, see "What is The Problem of Evil?" *Theology*, I (1920). For an analysis of this article see ch. vi, s. 3, pp. 172–4.

11 For a further discussion of Collingwood's philosophy of religion, see my edition of his writings in this area, *Faith and Reason* (Chicago: Quadrangle Books, 1968). For a criticism of my interpretation see reviews by Donagan (*Dialogue*, vii, 4 [1969], 678–81) and Mink (*Journal of the American Academy of Religion*, xxxviii [March 1970], 118–20).

12 This attempt to reconcile Collingwood's various claims concerning the relation between the idea of nature and the idea of history is an application of the same criterion with which I have in various places attempted to reconcile Collingwood's seemingly contradictory claims concerning the relation between history and perception (see below, ch. iv, s. 2 and ch. ix, s. 2).

13 Cf. Max Weber on the methodology of the historical and social sciences. Historical concepts, writes Weber, "attempt for their methodological purposes not to grasp historical reality in abstract general formulae, but in concrete genetic sets of relations which are inevitably of a specifically unique and individual character" (*The Protestant Ethic*, 48).

14 Elsewhere Collingwood writes: "the ... struggle between scientific dogmatism and the concept of self-knowledge is the way to all modern philosophy" (SM, 279); "The cry that philosophy must accept the results of science and adopt scientific methods ... is the prime obstacle to the healthy development of modern philosophy" (SM, 281); "The general problem bequeathed to posterity by the writers I have analysed in the first four parts of *The Idea of History* may be stated by saying that it concerns the distinction between history and natural science, or historical process and natural process" (IH, 175). Cf. Ernst Cassirer: "The inner crisis in science and philosophy in the last hundred years, since the deaths of Goethe and Hegel, stands out in no other feature so clearly, perhaps, as in the relation existing between natural science and the humanities" (*The Logic of the Humanities*, trans. Clarence Howe, New Haven: Yale University Press, 1961, 86). It is important to note

that what Collingwood means by science in the above cited passages is much closer to first-level science than to third-level science.
15 "From Facts to Thoughts," *Philosophy*, xxv (1960). See also "Historicism and Philosophy: Reflections on R. G. Collingwood," *Revue internationale de philosophie*, xi (1957); "History and Time: A Critical Examination of Collingwood's Doctrine," *Scripta Hierosolymitana* (Jerusalem, 1960).
16 "From Facts to Thoughts," p. 125.
17 *Ibid.*, p. 137.
18 In *The Later Philosophy of R. G. Collingwood*.
19 *Ibid.*, p. 218.
20 *Ibid.*, p. 219.
21 *The Phenomenology of Mind* (London: Allen & Unwin, 1949), p. 212.
22 The phrase "elevation of history to the rank of a dogma" was probably adapted from the title of Droysen's review of Buckle's *History of Civilization in England*, entitled "The Elevation of History to the Rank of a Science," *Historische Zeitschrift* (1862). For a more detailed discussion of Droysen's views, see Appendix 1.
23 For an ideal example of what Collingwood meant by this see Morton White, "Historical Explanation," *Mind* (1943), reprinted in revised form in *Theories of History*, edited by P. Gardiner (Glencoe: The Free Press, 1959).
24 *History of English Literature*, I, iii, p. 6. For a discussion of this maxim see Patrick Gardiner, *The Nature of Historical Explanation*, 70, and B. Croce, *History: Its Theory and Practice*, pp. 75–6.
25 *Phenomenology of Mind*, p. 142.
26 The view against which Collingwood is arguing may be summed up in the phrase (adapted from a familiar slogan of contemporary philosophy) that 'knowledge is not a predicate,' i.e., adds nothing to the essence of the object known which is not already contained in it prior to its being known. On this view knowledge is accordingly defined as a mere correspondence with the facts. Against this, Collingwood is arguing, in effect, that, at least in the case of history, knowledge is a predicate, i.e., it does make a difference to the very nature of the object known. This difference is not accounted for, however, by treating the predicate as a mere proper name denoting the existence of a new external relation (or property). On the contrary, the predicate is 'existential' and the real difference between the known and the unknown object lies therefore in the actual *behaviour* of both the knowing subject and the object known: indeed, it is this very discrepancy between the behaviour of the object and the behaviour of the subject that lies at the basis of progress in knowledge. At the same time, since the very essence of both subject and object are identified with their activities or behaviour, changes in behaviour are therefore *essential* rather than *accidental*, and knowledge, which is the catalyst of this change, is therefore *essentially* predicated of its subject. This is the basis for the claim that all historical knowledge is self-knowledge (cf. ch. III, n5, above).
27 Cf. John Laird's review of *Speculum Mentis*, in *Mind*, xxxiv (1925). Laird dismisses Collingwood's dialectical identity between *the* world and *my* world, between what things *are* and what they are *to me*, as "a really elementary piece of carelessness" (240).
28 With the arrival of philosophy on the scene, a more genuine basis for the unity of the sciences is provided. At the same time, the whole spirit of the age will be radically altered and the alienation which the division of the sciences has fostered will be finally overcome. This division, which, as we have seen, Collingwood traces to the consequences of the Renaissance, found its most extreme form of expression in a kind of "academic trade unionism," based essentially on the "error of conceiving philosophy as one specialized form of experience, instead of realizing that it is merely the self-consciousness of experience in general" (SM, 256).

CHAPTER FIVE

1 *Journal of Philosophical Studies*, III (1928).
2 *Proceedings of the Aristotelian Society*, XXVI, (1925–26).
3 Cf. Spinoza's distinction between *essentia actualis* and *essentia formalis*, ch. VI, s. 2.

CHAPTER SIX

1 *The Phenomenology of Mind*, translated by J. B. Baillie (London: Allen & Unwin, 1955), p. 136.
2 On this point, as indeed on several others, Collingwood's thought bears a remarkable resemblance to the much earlier views of John Dewey who as early as 1905 advocated the historicity not only of philosophy but of science as well. Dewey argues, for example, that in the field of morals (as indeed in every other field) it is only through historical understanding that genuine understanding is possible. Such knowledge, according to Dewey, is not only descriptive but theoretical and practical as well, giving us "insight into the operations and conditions which make for morality," and in this way, affording us "intellectual tools for attacking other moral facts" ("The Evolutionary Method as Applied to Morality," part I, *Philosophical Review*, XI [1902], 124). Like Collingwood, Dewey had to answer to the view which regarded the historical and the philosophical questions as absolutely separate – i.e., the view that history is purely descriptive, dealing with mere facts, while ethics (or philosophy) is primarily normative, dealing with the validity of values ("The Evolutionary Method as Applied to Morality," part II, *ibid.*, 354–5). Against this view Dewey contends that it is the same historical method that determines both *how* specific moral values came to be, and what their significance is (i.e., why they were held) (*ibid.*, 356). To separate completely the ethical from the historical is, according to Dewey, a result of failing to discriminate two meanings of validity. (Compare this with Collingwood's distinction in *An Essay on Metaphysics* between empirical and rational validity; see below, ch. VIII.) It assumes that because a genetic or historic account does not determine *ab initio* the moral point of view as such, it is therefore indifferent to the determination of questions of specific value – an obvious *mutatio conclusionis* (*ibid.*, 355). There are of course some important differences between Collingwood and Dewey, especially on the nature of the object of history. For Collingwood, this can only be thought, while for Dewey it would appear to include objects other than thought. But the similarities between the two philosophers are certainly close enough to warrant a comparative study of their views on the historical foundations of the sciences.
3 Again the resemblance to Dewey is striking. Dewey does not himself use the term concrete universal but the notion is clearly implicit in his thought. For Dewey, the aim of all the established sciences (including natural science) is "to discover the single process which, operating under different conditions, has manifested itself in these specifically different and outward forms." "Knowledge of difference," writes Dewey, "is just as important as that of the generic identity of the process" ("The Evolutionary Method as Applied to Morality," I, 122). Like Collingwood, Dewey contends that it is only through insight into diversification supplied by history that our knowledge of the object (now regarded as a process) becomes vital and concrete (*ibid.*).
4 *Proceedings of the Aristotelian Society*, XXIX (1928–29).
5 This conclusion follows when it is realized that according to the point of view in which substance and attributes are distinguished there can be no genuine science of attributes; the only proper object of science is substance. If, there-

fore, history is a mere knowledge of attributes then it cannot be a science (see IH, part I, s. 3, 20 ff.). The absurdity of this conclusion is regarded by Collingwood as betraying the weakness of the doctrine of the abstract universal when applied to history.

6 *The Principle of Individuality and Value* (London: Macmillan, 1912), pp. 37–8. The notion of the concrete universal was originally derived from Hegel. Hegel defines the concrete universal as a synthesis of pure universality and particularity (*Encyclopaedia Logic*, translated by W. Wallace (2nd ed., London: Oxford University Press, 1904), s. 163, p. 291) – i.e., a synthesis of pure self-identity with difference which yields the self-identity in difference called the concrete universal (*ibid.*, s. 164, p. 294). The differentia of self-identity in difference according to Hegel is *individuality*, "the reflection-into-self of the specific characters of universality and particularity; – which negative self-unity has complete and original i.e., unique determinateness, without any loss of its self-identity or universality" (*ibid.*, s. 163, p. 291). Hegel distinguishes the individual or concrete universal from the abstract universal which is simply that which is held in common "... arrived at by neglecting the particular features of things." As compared with this, the "universal of the notion i.e., concrete universal is not a mere sum of features common to several things, confronted by a particular which enjoys an existence of its own" (*ibid.*, s. 163, n2, p. 292). Cf. *Philosophy of Right*. Hegel writes: "In connexion with this word 'universality', what strikes representative thinking first is the idea of abstract and external universality; but in connexion with absolute universality – and the universal here in question is of this character – we have to think neither of the universality of reflection, i.e., 'all-ness' or the universal as a common characteristic, nor of the abstract universality which stands outside and over against the individual, the abstract identity of the Understanding ... It is the universality concrete in character and so explicitly universal which is the substance of self-consciousness, its immanent generic essence, or its immanent Idea. This ... is the universal which overlaps its object, penetrates its particular determination through and through and therein remains identical with itself (*Philosophy of Right*, translated by T. M. Knox (Oxford: The Clarendon Press, 1962), Introduction, s. 24, p. 31). For further discussions of the notion of the concrete universal see H. B. Acton, "The Concrete Universal," parts I and II, *Mind* (Oct. 1936, Jan. 1937), and A. J. M. Milne, *The Social Philosophy of English Idealism* (London: Allen & Unwin, 1962), pp. 15–55.

7 Another way of putting this is to characterize the relations between different periods of history as "internal" rather than "external." Thus Collingwood writes, concerning western civilization in general: "Western Civilization has formed itself by ... reconstructing within its own mind the mind of the Hellenic world and developing the wealth of that mind in new directions. Thus Western civilization is not related to Hellenic in any merely external way. The relation is an internal one" (IH, 163). (For the implications of this notion on the idea of historical progress see below, ch. VIII, s. 7).

8 This distinction, which is further explored in various places in the first four parts of the *Idea of History*, is explicated below in ch. IX (s. 3) in terms of the doctrine of self-making. For in the last analysis what constitutes the individuality of history is the fact that history is a process which knows itself, and this self-knowledge is the very essence of historicity per se. Cf., Droysen, "Nature and History," in *Principles of History*, translated by E. B. Andrews (Boston: Ginn & Co., 1893), pp. 90–105; Fackenheim, *Metaphysics and Historicity* (Milwaukee: Marquette University Press, 1961), and Cassirer, *The Logic of the Humanities*.

9 Collingwood's attitude towards dogmatic utilitarianism (i.e., the habit of judging *all* human activities according to the standards of utility), like his attitude towards realism and positivism, had many of the overtones of old

testament prophecy. Like all forms of irrationalism, dogmatic utilitarianism is a habit which we cannot afford to tolerate. Indeed, to allow this habit to invade and conquer the character of an age is an act of cultural suicide. Thus Collingwood declares: "The utilitarian trick of judging the worth of all human activities by assessing their utility is ... unworthy of any one who claims to be an educated and enlightened person; and it is morally disastrous, because it is the first step on the road to a moral bankruptcy brought about by some process in the moral life analogous to inflation in economic life. Inflation pushed to extremity means that real commodities, the things we really want to buy, cannot be bought; all we can handle is stuff that is called money; but nobody wants money, people want the things that money can buy, and if money cannot buy things it forfeits the very name of money. So the moral bankruptcy of which I speak is the experience of finding that life is not worth living, because everything one does is done in the hopes of purchasing by its means a satisfaction which never comes. The way to avoid this moral bankruptcy is to stop judging the value of actions in terms of utility, and to judge them in terms of intrinsic worth" (FML, 151).

10 For an interesting and helpful discussion of the concept of rational necessity in Collingwood's theory of history see W. H. Dray, "Historical Understanding and Re-thinking," *University of Toronto Quarterly*, XXVII (Jan. 1958). Dray distinguishes between the kind of necessity required of history by the positivists and the kind of necessity required by Collingwood. According to the positivists, an action cannot be necessitated except in terms of natural law, and only by means of such laws can historical understanding be achieved. For Collingwood, however, an historical action is necessitated "in the sense of its being rationally required." Dray explicates this notion as follows: "A set of antecedent conditions which explains a consequent event by virtue of a law of nature, shows the event to have been necessary in the sense of being 'the thing to have been expected, the laws of nature being what they are.' The thoughts or considerations which explain an action in Collingwood's context of discussion, show the action to have been necessary in the sense of being 'the thing to have done, the principles of reason being what they are.' We could put the point by saying that the necessity which is required for the explanation of action in history, according to Collingwood, is a *rational* rather than a *natural* necessity. If something happens in spite of natural necessity we call it a miracle. If an action is done in spite of rational necessity, we call it a stupidity, a mistake, an irrationality. It is Collingwood's claim that if, and only if, rational necessity can be shown, then we understand what the agent did. And he adds that such understanding does not require the further demonstration, by the methods of natural science, that what happened was a natural necessity as well" (*ibid.*, 209). In this study the notion of rational necessity is further explicated by viewing it as a form of dialectical necessity. Actions proceeding according to dialectical necessity are regarded as expressions of a normal and healthy consciousness, whereas actions done in spite of rational necessity (i.e., dialectical necessity) are regarded as expressions of an unhealthy or corrupt consciousness.

11 *Theology* I (1920).

12 For Hegel's definition of *aufheben* see, *Phenomenology of Mind*: "... to supersede [*aufheben*] is at once to negate and to preserve" (p. 164). Cf. also, *ibid.*, pp. 11–12. See also above, footnotes ch. I, n2.

13 The distinction between τὸ μηδαμῶς ὄν (ie., τό μή ὄν αὐτό καθ αὐτό) and τὸ μὴ ὄν εἶναι is employed by Plato in the *Sophist* to distinguish between *that which is not, absolutely*, and that which is not but nevertheless 'exists.' The distinction arises in the course of a refutation of Parmenides' dogma that there is no sense in which 'that-which-is-not can be' (*Sophist*, 256D–259D). As employed by Plato the distinction corresponds to Hegel's distinction between sheer nothingness (*Nichts*) and "a determinate nothing [*Ein bestimmtes*

Nichts] a nothing with a certain content [*ein Nichts von einem Inhalte*]" (*Phenomenology of Mind*, p. 163).

14 *Phenomenology of Mind*, p. 132.

CHAPTER SEVEN

1 Collingwood's characterization of science in *An Essay on Philosophical Method* has been criticized as naïve and unrepresentative of genuine scientific method. Thus Charles Hartshorne writes: "A criticism of the book might be that features of scientific method which the author holds not to apply to philosophy are, in some cases, of doubtful validity even in science" (review in the *International Journal of Ethics* [April 1934], 358). F. C. S. Schiller likewise criticizes "Mr. Collingwood's account of inductive science, which appears to have made no progress since Mill" (review in *Mind* [Jan. 1934], 118). Indeed Schiller contends that were Collingwood to have a more adequate grasp of contemporary science and mathematics he would see that "... there are not *three* methods of knowing but only one and the same, in philosophy and in *all* the sciences" (*ibid.*, 119). But, as in most other cases where Collingwood is required, for the purposes of the argument, to draw certain distinctions, the distinction which he draws between philosophy and science is intended not as a basis for providing a definitive account of science but rather as an account of a false way of doing philosophy. This is precisely the point which Collingwood himself made in a passage cited above (ch. III, s. 2) from the *Essay on Philosophical Method* (9–10). Hence there is no genuine inconsistency between the view of science with which philosophy is contrasted in the *Essay on Philosophical Method* (and with which history is contrasted in *The Idea of History*) and the more sophisticated views of *The Idea of Nature*.

2 The most significant thing about all of these non-hypothetical declarations is that they are indemonstrable (in the strictly scientific sense of the term). Since they are the product neither of deduction nor of induction, they cannot be said to be derived from the scientific process at all. This does not mean, of course, that they are not knowledge, but only that they are not scientific knowledge, and for this reason are not provable by scientific means, but must be justified by some other procedure such as, as we shall see in chapter VIII, metaphysics. Compare this argument of Collingwood with Plato's criticisms of science in *Republic* 510–11.

3 This doctrine, that the way to philosophy and science lies through history, that the hypotheses or abstractions of science rest on the knowledge of fact, is, according to Collingwood, the greatest discovery that thought has made since the time of Plato (SM, 199). It is the keynote of the Christian attitude towards the problem of knowledge – implicit from the beginning in the Christian gospel as a philosophy of history – and has been becoming progressively explicit ever since Descartes who, in his *cogito ergo sum*, laid it down that the historical fact was the absolute object of knowledge (*ibid.*). As represented by Collingwood, Descartes' position was that all science rests upon the indubitable certainty that I think therefore I am. "Now the thought and existence of which Descartes spoke were not abstractions – anything thinking anything or anything somehow getting itself thought about – as those wiseacres believe who offer to amend his formula to *cogitatur ergo est*, or *cogitare ergo esse* or the like. Descartes meant what he said; and what he said was that the concrete historical fact, the fact of my actual present awareness was the root of science. He was only going one step beyond Bacon, for whom the root of science was natural fact: Descartes, more profoundly, saw that before natural fact can be of any use to the scientist he must observe it, and that the fact of his observing it is the fact that really matters. Science presupposes history

and can never go behind history: that is the discovery of which Descartes' formula is the deepest and most fruitful expression" (SM, 202).

4 This interpretation of Spinoza, together with the foregoing discussion of Aristotle, is intended to demonstrate the continuity between the thought of Aristotle, Spinoza, and Collingwood, and to illustrate the possible influence of Aristotle and Spinoza on the development of Collingwood's thought. It is my contention that Collingwood regarded his own philosophy as an explicit solution to the problems raised by such philosophers as Aristotle and Spinoza. This distinguishes his work from that of his contemporaries, the Realists, who by and large were more concerned with the implications of Hume's philosophy.

5 *Lectures on the History of Philosophy*, translated by E. S. Haldane and Frances H. Simson (London: Routledge & Kegan Paul, 1955), I, p. 288.

6 Metaphysics is here being used as though it were equivalent to ontology, the theory of existence. Now while it is true that in the *Essay on Metaphysics* Collingwood dismisses ontology as nonsense, what he really dismisses, as we hope to show in ch. VIII, is the ontology of pure abstract being, i.e., the metaphysics of substance. But this does not eliminate the possibility of an ontology of concrete being. Each of the above concepts, *Deus sive natura*, τόὄν ἦ ὄν, and τό ἀγαθόν refers to a being whose essence involves existence, but it may do this as the object either of abstract or of concrete metaphysics. In so far as metaphysics regards its object as something actually existing there is no difference between Collingwood's metaphysics and classical metaphysics. The difference lies in the fact that, for Collingwood's predecessors, the metaphysician is committed only to the existence of a substance, an object, having a permanent and eternal nature. For Collingwood, the metaphysician is committed to the existence of being *qua* mind, which is an historical activity.

7 All references to what in this thesis is called "The Collingwood-Ryle Correspondence" (CRC) are to the original holographs which are now in the Bodleian library and from which the manuscript in my possession has been copied.

8 See for example, G. Ryle, "Mr. Collingwood and the Ontological Argument," *Mind* (April 1935); E. E. Harris, "Mr. Ryle and the Ontological Argument," *Mind* (Oct. 1936); and G. Ryle, "Back to the Ontological Argument," *Mind* (Jan. 1937). It is interesting to note that Collingwood himself refused to enter this controversy by publishing an answer to Ryle's article. Instead, he confined his remarks to private correspondence. But his behaviour on this particular occasion was simply typical of his general and apparently long-standing attitude towards the idea of defending oneself against criticism: an attitude which was clearly stated in the *Autobiography*: "Henceforth I shall spend all my available time in writing ... I take this opportunity, therefore, of saying that I will not be drawn into discussion of what I write. Some readers may wish to convince me that it is all nonsense ... Some may wish to show me that on this or that detail I am wrong. Perhaps I am; if they are in a position to prove it, let them write not about me but about the subject, showing that they can write about it better than I can; and I will read them gladly" (A, 118). No doubt Collingwood came to adopt this attitude as a result of his apparent failure at communicating with his contemporaries: a frustration to which he alluded on several occasions in the *Autobiography* (44, 51, 53–8) and which is dramatically illustrated in his 1935 correspondence with Ryle.

9 *The Later Philosophy of R. G. Collingwood*, p. 255. The following interpretation of Donagan's book is a revised version of an article which first appeared in "Collingwood and the Radical Conversion Hypothesis," *Dialogue: Canadian Philosophical Review*, v (1966), 71–83, and is reproduced here with permission of the editor.

10 *The Later Philosophy of R. G. Collingwood*, pp. 257–9.

11 In this example I will follow the form used by Donagan in his analysis of the statement 'Politicians exist' (*ibid.*, pp. 257–8).

12 *Ibid.*, pp. 258–9; cf., 15.
13 *Ibid.*, pp. 262–3.
14 "Mr. Collingwood and the Ontological Argument," *Mind*, XLIV (1935), 141.
15 *Logic and Language: First Series*, ed. A. Flew (Oxford: B. Blackwell, 1952) p. 18.
16 This doctrine is explicitly repudiated in Collingwood's first letter to Ryle (CRC, 26).
17 "Back to the Ontological Argument," *Mind*, XLV (1937), p. 53.
18 *Lectures on the History of Philosophy*, III, p. 230.
19 Cf. ch. VIII, ss. 8 and 10.
20 In *Appearance and Reality* (2nd ed. Oxford: The Clarendon Press, 1897), p. x.
21 *Proceedings of the Aristotelian Society*, XXVI (1925–6). For a discussion of this paper see above, ch. V, s. 2, pp. 143ff.

CHAPTER EIGHT

1 *A Hundred Years of Philosophy* (London: Duckworth, 1957), p. 306.
2 *The Later Philosophy of R. G. Collingwood*, p. 262. "Knox's demonstration," writes Donagan, "that between 1936 and 1938 Collingwood radically changed his mind about the relation of philosophy to history must be the foundation of any interpretation of his works" (*ibid.*, 12). But, as we have already noted (ch. 1, s. 4c) while Donagan agrees with Knox in regarding the *Autobiography* and the *Essay on Metaphysics* as historicist in outlook, he rejects Knox's inclusion of the *New Leviathan* in this group and he argues that it is more akin to the non-historicist and non-idealist writings which appeared after 1933, especially the *Principles of Art*. He also disagrees with Knox's further contention that the *Essay on Philosophical Method* was the high point of Collingwood's philosophical career and that everything written after that marked a decline in his thought. My interest here is chiefly with Donagan's acceptance of the claim that the *Autobiography* and the *Essay on Metaphysics* not only depart from the thought of the earlier works but are fundamentally historicist in outlook. In so far as Donagan accepts these conclusions he subscribes to what I have called 'the radical conversion hypothesis.'
3 *The Later Philosophy of R. G. Collingwood*, p. 263.
4 Hereafter *An Essay on Metaphysics* will be referred to as the *Essay*, except where confusion might result, in which case I will then revert to the full title.
5 Implied by this claim is a denial of the possibility of a psychological science of mind whose conclusions take the form of general hypotheticals. This does not mean that there is no such thing as psychology; it means only that whatever psychology is, it is not a science of mind. In the *Autobiography*, psychology is defined as "the science of sensation, appetite, and the emotions connected with them," on the one hand, and as "psychopathology and psychotherapy," on the other (A, 95).
6 At the political level this tendency expressed itself in the ideologies of Nazism and Fascism. In characterizing Fascism and Nazism as forms of irrationalism Collingwood is not thereby placing them beyond the limits of rational criticism. Irrationalism is founded on a variety of philosophical errors which are cunningly and dogmatically asserted as coherent truths. What is more, in spite of the inherent contradictions of such standpoints, consciousness surreptitiously ignores the call of reason and sinks therefore into an inescapable form of corruption. Such forms of corruption now become the object of a pathology (or metaphysic) of abnormalcy – a science which, although it has much in common with psychoanalysis, is plainly regarded by Collingwood as within the general province of the philosophic enterprise. Thus, just as in "Aesthetic,"

bad or corrupt art is made the object of the joint activity of philosophical aesthetics and psychopathology, so in "Fascism and Nazism" (1940), he insists that the most urgent facts of the time are the phenomena of Fascism and Nazism and that the philosopher can engage in no more urgent business than the attempt to understand these phenomena (FN, 176; cf. A, 157-9 and NL, 375 ff., in which Fascism and Nazism are again made objects of philosophic enquiry).

7 Collingwood's attack on psychology is, as we have already noted in the immediately preceding footnote, an attack on a pseudo-science of mind. It does not invalidate what Collingwood regarded as the proper concept of psychology – i.e., as the science of feeling, sensation, emotion, etc. Still less would it invalidate more contemporary views of psychology as an experimental science of behaviour. Collingwood's main reasons for rejecting psychology's claim to be the proper science of mind are set forth in the *Essay on Metaphysics* (chs IX-XII) and the *Idea of History* (221 ff.). For a lengthy and hostile discussion of Collingwood's views on psychology see L. S. Hearnshaw, "A Reply to Professor Collingwood's Attack on Psychology," *Mind* (1942).

8 Cf. Aristotle's own critique of the claim that Being is either the highest genus or an abstract universal (*Met.* 998B 20-7; 1006A-1008B; 1028B 1-7; 1042A 3-8).

9 Donagan, *The Later Philosophy of R. G. Collingwood*, p. 264.

10 I am indebted to the librarian of the Houghton library at Harvard for permission to quote from Santayana's notes.

11 For a critical discussion of this argument see J. W. N. Watkins "On Explaining Disaster," *B.B.C. Listener*, 10 January 1963, 69-70. See also Letters to the Editor, 24 January 1963, 170-1; 31 January 1963, 209-10; 7 February 1963, 251.

12 *Language, Truth and Logic* (London: Victor Gollancz, 1936), pp. 33-46.

13 At least two other writers who have seen the connection between absolute presuppositions and a priori concepts are Louis Mink and David Rynin.

14 *Ibid.*, p. 112.

15 *The Phenomenology of Mind*, pp. 90-1.

16 *Faust*, pt. I, ll. 682f.

17 "Plato's Philosophy of Art," *Mind*, XXIV (1925).

18 "Plato saw that amusement art arouses emotions which it does not direct to any outlet in practical life; and wrongly inferred that its excessive development would breed a society overcharged with purposive emotions. Aristotle saw that this did not follow, because the emotions generated by amusement art are discharged by the amusement itself" (A, 98).

19 Concerning the programme of anti-metaphysics Collingwood writes: "If this neurosis ever achieves its ostensible object, the eradication of metaphysics from the European mind, the eradication of science and civilization will be accomplished at the same time" (EM, 46). And, Collingwood contends, because science and civilization stand or fall together, an error in metaphysical analysis can be fatal to the civilization in which it occurs (EM, 224). On the relation of metaphysics, as Collingwood conceives it, to culture, cf. Margaret Mead: "In each age there is a series of pressing questions which must be asked and answered. On the correctness of the questions depends the survival of those who ask; on the quality of the answers depends the quality of the life those survivors will lead" (*New Lives For Old* [New York: Mentor, 1961], 17). In attacking the neurosis of anti-metaphysics as he does, Collingwood is following in the footsteps of Hegel. Hegel speaks of the "strange spectacle of a cultured people having no metaphysics." He likens this to a temple which is in all other respects richly ornamented yet lacks its Holy of Holies – theology (*Science of Logic*, I, 34). Indeed, Hegel declares: "If it is a remarkable thing when a nation finds that its Constitutional Theory, its customary ways

of thinking and feeling, its ethical habits and traditional virtues, have become inapplicable, it is certainly not less remarkable when a nation loses its Metaphysic, when the intellect occupying itself with its own pure essence, has no longer any real existence in the thought of the nation" (*ibid.*, 33).

20 On the subject of the logic of question and answer note the following remark by T. H. Green: "When we understand what the questions exactly were that a philosopher put to himself, and how he came to put them as he did, we are more than half-way towards understanding the answer ..." *Collected Works*, III, L. W. Nettleship (ed.), 2nd ed., London: Longmans Green, 1889, pp. 134–5.

21 *The Philosophy of History*, p. 9. To say that history is rational does not, of course, mean that every event in history must be *equally* rational (or equally right). The criteria laid down for rationality are, after all, ideal only. As I have tried to demonstrate in this book, Collingwood would have to admit that in fact, just as there is a scale of truth, so there are scales of 'rationality' or 'logical intelligibility,' degrees of success and failure with regard to the expression of thought.

22 *The Later Philosophy of R. G. Collingwood*, pp. 276, 279.

23 Brand Blanshard makes a similar point when he argues that "invention turns on a surrender to the working of a necessity in one's mind." He argues that Shakespeare, in writing the last act of *Othello*, wrote what he did: "for the same reason that we in reading or hearing it, find it satisfying, namely that with the given dramatic situation in mind 'he could do no other' ... What Shakespeare actually gives us is something completely organic with what has gone on before, a speech in which we feel in every syllable ... 'the formative pressure of the tone and structure of the entire work.' Given the character of Othello, his prevailing mood, his habits of speech, the situation in which he was placed, and given the need to round out the whole in accordance with the implicit demands of the aesthetic idea, there was only one course for the Moor to take, and that he did" (*The Nature of Thought*, II, p. 139).

24 Cf. Collingwood's notion of interpolation with W. H. Walsh's notion of "colligation." Colligation, writes Walsh, rests on the assumption that "different historical events can be regarded as going together to constitute a single process, a whole of which they are all parts and in which they belong together in a specially intimate way ... The first aim of the historian, when he is asked to explain some event or other, is to see it as a part of such a process, to locate it in its context by mentioning other events with which it is bound up" (*Introduction to Philosophy of History* [London: Hutchinson University Library, 1958], p. 23). Colligation, he continues, "is the process of explaining an event by tracing its intrinsic relations to other events and locating it in its historical context." Such a procedure involves "some sort of reference to general truths" (*ibid.*, p. 59) and "often proceeds in teleological terms" (*ibid.*, p. 60): i.e., the process of historical explanation may be regarded as an attempt to "colligate" individual events under "appropriate conceptions" by means of general truths or principles of a teleological or semi-teleological nature (i.e., having to do with the execution of a plan or policy).

25 For example, writes Collingwood, when Suetonius tells us that Nero at one time planned to evacuate Britain, we reject this statement, not because any authority flatly contradicts it, for of course none does; but because our reconstruction of Nero's policy based on Tacitus will not allow us to think that Suetonius is right. We choose Tacitus over Suetonius simply because we are able to incorporate what Tacitus tells us into a coherent and continuous picture of our own and cannot do this for Suetonius (IH, 244–5).

26 *The Peloponnesian War*, translated by Rex Warner (Penguin Books, 1954), I, ch. 1, pp. 24–5.

27 *History of Greece*, VII (London: J. M. Dent & Co. [New York: E. P. Dutton

& Co.] n.d.). Referring to the Melian dialogue, Croce writes: "There is indeed every reason for concluding that what we have read in Thucydides is in far larger proportion his own, and in smaller proportion authentic report, than any of the other speeches which he professes to set down" (p. 157).

28 It might be appropriate at this time to draw a distinction between 'methodological' and 'existential' truth. The former is the subject of discussion in the present context. A fact obtains if it can be supported by the evidence. There is, however, another sense of truth, to be discussed more thoroughly in chapters IX and X, which has to do with the development of freedom. This truth is the criterion of progress. Thus, while it may be methodologically true that a certain event occurred in the way in which it is described, it remains to be seen whether and to what extent this event has contributed to the progress of self-making or human freedom.

29 The distinction between what I call the methodological and the teleological moments of historical interpolation has important consequences for Collingwood's theory of historical knowledge. As we have seen, some critics, such as Walsh, have charged that in the last analysis historical understanding for Collingwood is intuitive and non-inferential. Some may even go so far as to charge that Collingwood's theory of method is virtually a theory of intuition and empathy. For example, Carl Hempel very likely had Collingwood in mind when in "The Function of General Laws in History" (in Patrick Gardiner ed., *Theories of History* [Glencoe: Free Press, 1959]) he referred to "the method of empathetic understanding." If the latter is Hempel's interpretation of re-thinking then he is very definitely confusing what Collingwood regarded as a conceptual or teleological analysis for a methodological one. I have already given some reasons for questioning the charge that Collingwood's theory of explanation emphasizes intuition to the exclusion of the more discursive procedures of inference. For further evidence in support of this general thesis see Donagan's very able and convincing reconstruction of Collingwood's theory of explanation in "The Verification of Historical Theses," *Philosophical Quarterly* (July 1956), and *The Later Philosophy of R. G. Collingwood*, pp. 215–16.

CHAPTER NINE

1 Collingwood himself uses the distinction "thought of the first degree" and "thought of the second degree" (IH, 1–3).
2 For further discussions of the principle of incapsulation, see above, ch. VIII, s. 9, and below, ch. IX, s. 2.
3 The term 'metaphysical Epilegomena' is cited in Knox's preface to *The Idea of History* (v) in such a way as to suggest that it was Collingwood's own.
4 Cf. F. W. J. Schelling: "... man's being is essentially *his own deed*" (*Of Human Freedom*, translated by James Gutmann (Chicago: Open Court, 1936), p. 63).
5 In *Speculum Mentis* the term 'absolute' is used in lower case; in *Religion and Philosophy*, however, it is often capitalized.
6 This does not mean, of course, that there is no reason for similar questions to be raised again by future generations (although, as we have seen, the sameness will be a sameness with a difference). Indeed, intrinsic to the solution of any problem is the creation of new questions demanding new answers. In any genuine progress, writes Collingwood, the solution of one problem "is itself the rise of the next" (TCH, 443). Thus if the original question is raised again, it will arise within a context of new presuppositions. For this reason, the solution of any historical problem has the character of a 'project.' The finality of any solution refers primarily to its 'synoptic' rather than to its 'definitive'

character; the orientation of finality is to the past rather than to the future.

CHAPTER TEN

1 The term 'possible' is here used in the same sense as 'rationally necessary' or 'rationally required.'
2 *Proceedings of the Aristotelian Society*, suppl. vol. III (1923).
3 B. Croce, *The Philosophy of Giambattista Vico* (London: Allen & Unwin). Other translations by Collingwood of Croce's works were *An Autobiography* (Oxford: Clarendon Press, 1927), and "Aesthetic," an article in *Encyclopaedia Britannica* (14th ed., 1929).
4 De Ruggiero's book was originally published in Italian in 1912 and could therefore have been read by Collingwood before he wrote *Religion and Philosophy*.
5 The period during which Collingwood translated this book was one in which Italian philosophy enjoyed a general popularity in the English-speaking world. Of the many books, articles, and translations having to do with Italian philosophy which appeared in English between 1919 and 1925, the following were of special importance in contributing to the intellectual climate under which Collingwood wrote: J. A. Smith, "The Philosophy of Giovanni Gentile," *Proceedings of the Aristotelian Society*, xx (1919–20); G. Gentile, *The Theory of the Mind as Pure Act*, translated with an introduction by H. Wildon Carr (London: Macmillan, 1922), and *The Reform of Education*, translated by Dino Bigongiare with an introduction by Croce (New York: Harcourt, 1922 [London: Ernest Benn] 1923); B. Bosanquet, *The Meeting of Extremes in Contemporary Philosophy* (London: Macmillan, 1921); reviews by Bosanquet of Gentile's *The Reform of the Hegelian Dialectic* and *The Summary of Educational Theory*, *Mind*, xxix (1920), *Lectures on Religion*, *Mind*, xxx (1921). For further discussions of the influence of Italian philosophy on British philosophy see G. R. Mure, "The Influence of Croce on Oxford," *Philosophical Quarterly*, IV (1954), and H. S. Harris, Introduction to Gentile's *Genesis and Structure of Society* (Urbana: University of Illinois Press, 1961), esp. pp. 7–24.
6 Indeed this kind of historicism is almost directly implied by the very phrase "absolute–immanence."
7 Hence the phrase 'immanence–transcendence' seems to me to convey more precisely the sense of Collingwood's version of this doctrine.
8 Cf. A. H. Hannay's description of what he calls "neo-idealism" in "Subject-Object Relation in Historical Judgement," *Proceedings of the Aristotelian Society*, xxv (1924–25).
9 Viewed as the science of mind, such a body of knowledge, according to the terms of what I have previously described as 'the logic of belief' (see above, ch. VIII, s. 2), is a source of commitment; and it is perhaps only to the extent to which I am prepared to honour these commitments that I may be said to be free at all.
10 I have derived the notions of *esse sequitur operationem* and *ex nihilo in aliquid* from Fackenheim (*Metaphysics and Historicity*, pp. 29–31) who originally derived them from what he calls the "meontological" tradition of Boehme, Schelling, and Berdyaev (*ibid.*, pp. 31–3).
11 There will of course be differences of opinion whether Hegel really believed this, especially in the face of such declarations by Hegel as: "To comprehend what is, this is the task of philosophy, because what is, is reason. Whatever happens, every individual is a child of his time; so philosophy too is its own time apprehended in thoughts. It is just as absurd to fancy that a philosophy can transcend its contemporary world as it is to fancy that an individual can overleap his own age, jump over Rhodes" (*Philosophy of Right*, p. 11).

But while it may be true that philosophy is only "its own time apprehended in thoughts," if an absolute character can be ascribed to a given time then the philosophy of that time will have achieved a transhistorical character never to be superseded. There is at least some evidence that Hegel regarded his own age as having achieved the necessary synthesis of absolute truths to make possible a philosophy of definitive proportions.

12 Cf. Karl Jaspers: " The picture we form of history, becomes a factor in our volition," *The Origin and Goal of History*, translated by Michael Bulloch (London: Routledge and Kegan Paul, 1953), p. 231.

13 Cf. Hegel on the 'scientific' character of philosophy. Philosophy, according to Hegel, can reach truth "only by the inherent life of the notion" (*Phenomenology*, p. 111). We must reject, he says, all interpretations of philosophy which place the emphasis on the feeling and intuition of truth, on unreflective and emotional knowledge. On such a view, philosophy is regarded as aiming not so much at insight as at edification (*nicht sowohol Einsicht als Erbauung gewähren*) (*ibid.*, p. 72). But, "philosophy must beware of wishing to be edifying" (*ibid.*, p. 74). The fact is, the search for truth can never escape from "the toil of science" (*ibid.*, p. 133) and the need for "measurable precision and definiteness" (*ibid.*, p. 74). Indeed, "Philosophic utterances about right, morality, and ethical life from those who would banish thought and have recourse instead to feeling, enthusiasm, the heart and the breast, are expressive of the utterly contemptible position into which thought and philosophic science have fallen, because what this amounts to is that even philosophic science itself, plunged in self-despair and extreme exhaustion, is taking as its principle barbarity and absence of thought, and would do its best to rob mankind of all truth, worth, and dignity." (*Philosophy of Right*, p. 30)

14 Cf. Hegel's attempt to resolve the tension between the historicity of finite thought and the transhistoricity of absolute thought: "In thinking I lift myself up to the absolute above all that is finite, and am infinite consciousness, while I am at the same time finite consciousness, and indeed am such in accordance with my whole empirical character. Both sides, as well as their relation, exist for me. Both sides seek each other, and both flee from each other ... I am the conflict ... I am not *one* of those taking part in the strife, but I am both the combatants, and am the strife itself" (*Lectures on the Philosophy of Religion*, translated by E. B. Spiers and J. B. Sanderson (London: Kegan Paul, Trench, Trübner, 1895), 1, pp. 63-4). Fackenheim cites this passage as "a key statement in modern metaphysics" (*Metaphysics and Historicity*, p. 68). Cf. also, F. W. J. Schelling who writes that man's being "is essentially *his own deed*." But, he continues, "The act which determines man's life in time does not itself belong in time but in eternity. Moreover it does not precede life in time but occurs throughout time ... as an act eternal by its own nature" (*Of Human Freedom*, pp. 63-4).

15 In addition to religious imagery there are other equally relevant images, derived from Collingwood's own writings. For example, by simply making the appropriate substitutions, Collingwood's description of imagination in *Speculum Mentis* (65) serves as a useful model for explicating the nature of the pure act. For, conceived on the analogy of the imagination, the significant thing about the *pure act* is that the knowing which is peculiar to it is at the same time an act of creation. The *absolute mind*, for example, which creates or *acts*, is itself created only in the act of *knowing itself. Esse est cogitare.* Neither the *known* object nor the *knowing* subject pre-exists the concrete process of knowing; for the very being of the subject is, here, to know, and of the object, to be known.

Bibliographies

BIBLIOGRAPHY I

THE WORKS OF R. G. COLLINGWOOD*

I   PHILOSOPHICAL BOOKS, ARTICLES, AND REVIEWS

1916 *Religion and Philosophy* London: Macmillan & Co.
      "The Devil," in B. H. Streeter and others, *Concerning Prayer*. London: Macmillan & Co.
1920 Review of *King's College Lectures on Immortality*
      W. R. Matthews, ed., *Theology*, vol. 1. November, pp. 299f.
1921 "Croce's Philosophy of History," *Hibbert Journal*, XIX
1922 "Are History and Science Different Kinds of Knowledge?" *Mind*, XXXI
      Ruskin's Philosophy an Address Delivered at the Ruskin Centenary Conference, Coniston, August 8th, 1919. Kendal: Titus Wilson & Son.
1920 "What is the Problem of Evil?" *Theology*, I
1923 "Sensation and Thought," *Proceedings of the Aristotelian Society*. XXIV, 1923–4
      "Can the New Idealism Dispense with Mysticism?" *Aristotelian Society, Supplementary Volume III*
1924 *Speculum Mentis* Oxford: The Clarendon Press

---

*Other bibliographies of Collingwood's philosophical works have been compiled by: T. M. Knox, *Proceedings of the British Academy*, XXIX (1943), pp. 474–5 (and further amplified by Knox in *The Idea of History*, p. vii); Alan Donagan, *The Later Philosophy of R. G. Collingwood*, pp. 308–10; W. Debbins in his edition of Collingwood's papers on the philosophy of history, pp. 141–8; W. M. Johnston, *The Formative Years of R. G. Collingwood*, pp. 156–65; Lionel Rubinoff, *Faith and Reason: Essays in the Philosophy of Religion by R. G. Collingwood*, pp. 304–11. Of these the ones by Debbins and Johnston have been the most complete. The Debbins volume contains an invaluable list of most of the reviews of Collingwood's philosophical books. A further comprehensive bibliography will be included in a volume of critical studies of Collingwood's thought, edited by Michael Krausz, to be published by the Clarendon Press, Oxford.

For a bibliography of Collingwood's writings in history and archaeology, see I. M. Richmond, *Proceedings of the British Academy*, XXIX (1943), pp. 481–5. Donagan has provided a valuable appendix in *The Later Philosophy*, pp. 311–13, which lists the dates on which Collingwood's philosophical books after *An Essay on Philosophical Method* were composed.

1925 *Outlines of a Philosophy of Art* London: Oxford University Press
"Plato's Philosophy of Art," *Mind*, xxxiv
Review of *A Theory of Monads* by H. Wildon Carr, *Hibbert Journal*, xxiii, 2, January, pp. 380–2
"The Nature and Aims of a Philosophy of History," *Proceedings of the Aristotelian Society*, xxv, 1924–5
"Economics as a Philosophical Science," *International Journal of Ethics*, xxxvi

1926 "Some Perplexities about Time: with an Attempted Solution," *Proceedings of the Aristotelian Society*, xxvi, 1925–6
"The Place of Art in Education," *Hibbert Journal*, xxiv
"Religion, Science and Philosophy," *Truth and Freedom*, ii, 7
Review of *Theory of History* by F. J. Teggart, *Journal of Philosophical Studies*, i, April, pp. 255–6

1927 "Aesthetic," in J. S. McDowall, ed., *The Mind*, London: Longmans
"Reason is Faith cultivating itself," *Hibbert Journal*, xxvi
"Oswald Spengler and the Theory of Historical Cycles," 2 parts, *Antiquity*, i
Review of *Plato: The Man and His Work* by A. E. Taylor, and *Etude sur le Parmenide de Platon* by Jean Wahl, *Monthly Criterion*, vi, pp. 65–8
Review of *Epicurus: The Extant Remains* by Cyril Bailey, ed., and *Epicurus: His Morals*, by Walton Charleton, ed., *Monthly Criterion*, vi, pp. 369–72
Review of *The Social and Economic History of the Roman Empire* by M. Rostovtzeff, *Antiquity*, i, pp. 367–8

1928 *Faith and Reason* a pamphlet in the Affirmation Series. London: Ernest Benn, reprinted in A. A. David, ed., *God and the Modern World*, New York: Dutton, 1929
"The Limits of Historical Knowledge," *Journal of Philosophical Studies*, iii
"Political Action," *Proceedings of the Aristotelian Society*, xxix, 1928–9
Review of *Art and Instinct* by Samuel Alexander, *Journal of Philosophical Studies*, iii, July, pp. 370–3
Review of *Hedonism and Art* by L. R. Farnell, *Journal of Philosophical Studies*, iii, October, pp. 547–8
Review of *Plato's Theory of Ethics* by R. K. Lodge, *Monthly Criterion*, viii, p. 159

1929 "Form and Content in Art," *Journal of Philosophical Studies*, iv
"A Philosophy of Progress," *The Realist*, i

1930 *The Philosophy of History* Historical Association Leaflet, No. 79. London: G. Bell & Sons
Review of *The Intelligible World* by W. M. Urban, and *The Idea of Value* by John Laird, *Monthly Criterion*, ix, 1929–30, pp. 320–7
Review of *The Meaning of Beauty: A Theory of Aesthetics* by W. T. Stace, *Journal of Philosophical Studies*, v, July, pp. 460–3 (see rejoinder by Stace in *Journal of Philosophical Studies*, v, pp. 653–4)

1931 Review of *The Philosophy of Art* by C. J. Ducasse, *Philosophy*, vi, July, pp. 383–6
Review of *Philosophy of the Good Life* by Bishop Gore, *Monthly Criterion*, x, April, pp. 560–2
Review of *Selected Essays of J. B. Bury* by Harold Temperley, ed., *English Historical Review*, xlvi, July, pp. 461–5

1932 Review of *A Study in Aesthetics* by L. A. Reid, *Philosophy*, vii, July, pp. 335–7
Review of *The Nature of Belief* by M. C. D'Arcy, *Monthly Criterion*, xi, 1931–2, pp. 334–6

1933 *An Essay on Philosophical Method* Oxford: The Clarendon Press
1934 "The Present Need of a Philosophy," *Philosophy*, IX, 1934, pp. 262–5 (reprinted in part in N. P. Stallknécht and R. L. Brumbaugh, eds., *The Spirit of Western Philosophy*, New York: Longmans, 1950, xliii–xx)
1935 *The Historical Imagination* an inaugural lecture. Oxford: The Clarendon Press
1936 "Human Nature and Human History," *Proceedings of the British Academy*, XXII; reprinted, London: Humphrey Milford
1937 Review of *The Issue in Literary Criticism* by Myron F. Brightfield, *Philosophy*, XII, January, pp. 114–16
1938 *The Principles of Art* Oxford: The Clarendon Press
"On the So-called Idea of Causation," *Proceedings of the Aristotelian Society*, XXXVIII, 1937–8
1940 *An Essay on Metaphysics* Oxford: The Clarendon Press
"Fascism and Nazism," *Philosophy*, XV
1941 *The Three Laws of Politics*. L. T. Hobhouse Memorial Trust Lectures, No. 11. London: Oxford University Press
1942 *The New Leviathan* Oxford: The Clarendon Press
1945 *The Idea of Nature* (T. M. Knox, ed.) Oxford: The Clarendon Press
1946 *The Idea of History* (T. M. Knox, ed.) Oxford: The Clarendon Press

II MEMOIRS

1939 *An Autobiography*, London: Oxford University Press. Reprinted by Penguin Books Ltd., 1944
1940 *The First Mate's Log*, London: Oxford University Press

III TRANSLATIONS

1913 B. Croce, *The Philosophy of Giambattista Vico*, London: Latimer. Reissued by Allen & Unwin in the Library of Philosophy Series
1921 With A. H. Hannay, G. de Ruggiero, *Modern Philosophy* London: Allen & Unwin
1927 B. Croce, *An Autobiography*, with a preface by A. J. Smith Oxford: The Clarendon Press
G. de Ruggiero, *The History of European Liberalism*, Oxford: The Clarendon Press
1928 B. Croce, "Aesthetic," in the *Encyclopaedia Britannica*, 14th edition

IV SELECTED BIBLIOGRAPHY OF HISTORICAL WRITINGS

1923 *Roman Britain*, London: Oxford University Press (Revised edition, Oxford: The Clarendon Press, 1934)
1930 *The Archaeology of Roman Britain*, London: Methuen & Co. Ltd.
1936 *Roman Britain and the English Settlements* (with J. N. L. Myres), Oxford: The Clarendon Press (2nd edition, 1937)
1937 "Roman Britain," in T. Frank, ed., *An Economic Survey of Ancient Rome*, Baltimore: John Hopkins Press (London: Oxford University Press), III, pp. 1–118
1947 *A Guide to the Roman Wall*, 4th edition revised by I. A. Richmond. Newcastle upon Tyne: A Reid, 1947
1965 *The Roman Inscriptions of Britain* (with R. P. Wright) Oxford: The Clarendon Press

V EDITIONS OF COLLINGWOOD'S WRITINGS

W. Debbins, ed., *Essays in the Philosophy of History by R. G. Collingwood*. Austin: University of Texas Press, 1965

A. Donagan, ed., *Essays in the Philosophy of Art by R. G. Collingwood*, Bloomington, Indiana University Press, 1964
M. L. Rubinoff, ed., *Faith and Reason: Essays in the Philosophy of Religion by R. G. Collingwood*, Chicago: Quadrangle, 1967
Domenico Pesce, ed. and trans., *Tre saggi di filosofia della storia* ("Human Nature and Human History," "Progress as Created by Historical Thinking" [from the *Idea of History*], "Croce's Philosophy of History"), with an introduction by Pesce. Padova: Liviana editrice, 1969

VI CORRESPONDENCE AND UNPUBLISHED MANUSCRIPTS

1935 Correspondence with Gilbert Ryle, 9 May and 6 June; deposited in the Bodleian library in 1964: MS Eng. lett. d. 194

In addition to the correspondence with Ryle, it is presumed that there exist a number of other manuscripts, in the possession of Collingwood's widow, which include, among other things, a series of lectures on ethics, and a copy of Collingwood's own Cosmology. The latter, according to T. M. Knox, was originally delivered as a set of lectures in 1934 and 1937 and was at one time intended as the concluding section of the *Idea of Nature*. In 1939, however, for reasons known only to himself, Collingwood replaced this section with another shorter piece. By the terms of Collingwood's will, none of the manuscripts in Mrs Collingwood's possession are available for examination and so are not included in the bibliography.

A copy of *Libellus de Generatione*, which Collingwood refers to in the *Autobiography*, exists among the papers of de Ruggiero to whom Collingwood admitted having sent a copy (A, 98–9). De Ruggiero's literary executor, Professor Renzo de Felice, of the Institute di storia moderna, Università di Roma, has explained that Collingwood gave explicit instructions to de Ruggiero not to show it to anyone. Professor Felice has indicated, in a letter addressed to Professor Michael Krausz and dated 9 October 1968, that Collingwood subtitled the manuscript, "An Essay in Absolute Empiricism." Collingwood claims to have burnt his own copy of the manuscript together with the manuscript of the unpublished "Truth and Contradiction," shortly after he wrote the *Autobiography*.

In the same letter Professor Felice also acknowledges possession of Collingwood's letters to de Ruggiero which are available for examination. In a letter to Professor Krausz, dated April 1969, Croce's daughter, Alda, acknowledges possession of Collingwood's correspondence with her father which cannot be released for publication until 1972.

Apart from those letters, the only other items of correspondence I know of are: a letter in Collingwood's handwriting to a Professor Rothenstein, dated 24 February 1929, which is deposited in the Houghton Library of Harvard University; a letter to Croce dated 29 January 1939, which is reprinted in Croce's article cited below ("In commemorazione ...," p. 399); some thirty letters from Collingwood to Macmillan of London which have recently been transferred from the Macmillan archives to the British Museum and are available for consultation; and five letters to Croce, written between 1929 and 1939, of which Croce himself published Italian translations, in *Nuove pagine sparse* (Naples 1949), I, pp. 28–33 (portions of the original English versions of these letters have been reproduced in Alan Donagan's *The Later Philosophy of R. G. Collingwood*, pp. 314–17).

BIBLIOGRAPHY II

CRITIQUES OF COLLINGWOOD'S THOUGHT

Anonymous   Review of *An Essay on Philosophical Method, Times Literary Supplement* (1 March 1934) 36
Anonymous   "Metaphysician's Faith" (review of *An Essay on Metaphysics*), *Times Literary Supplement* (18 May 1940) 240
H. B. Acton   Review of A. Donagan *The Later Philosophy of R. G. Collingwood, Listener* (27 June 1963) 1085

John A. Bailey   "A Reply to Mischel's 'Collingwood on Art as "Imaginative Expression"'" *Australasian Journal of Philosophy* XLI (December 1963) 372–8
B. M. Baldwin   Review of *An Essay on Metaphysics, Nature* CXLVIII 7 (January 1941)
Ernest Barker   "Man and Society" (a review of the *New Leviathan*), *Oxford Magazine* LXI, 11 (4 February 1943) 162–3
C. A. Beard   Review of the *Idea of History, American Historical Review* LII (July 1947) 704–8
C. H. L. Bouch   "In Memoriam (R. G. Collingwood)" *Transactions of the Cumberland and Westmoreland Antiquarian and Archaeological Society* XLIII (1943) 211–14
A. Boyce-Gibson   Review of A. Donagan *The Later Philosophy of R. G. Collingwood, Australasian Journal of Philosophy* XLI (December 1963) 412–17
S. G. F. Brandon   "Modern Interpretations of History and their Challenge" *Modern Churchman* XXXIX 3 (1949) 238–52
Merle Elliott Brown   *Neo-Idealistic Aesthetics: Croce-Gentile-Collingwood* Detroit: Wayne State University Press 1966
G. Buchdahl   "Logic and History: An Assessment of R. G. Collingwood's *Idea of History,*" *Australasian Journal of Philosophy* XXVI (September 1948) 94–113
——— "Has Collingwood been Unfortunate in his Critics?" *Australasian Journal of Philosophy* XXVI (August 1948) 95–108
R. Bultmann   *History and Eschatology* Edinburgh: Edinburgh University Press 1957 (ch. IX)
W. G. de Burgh   Review of "Human Nature and Human History" *Philosophy* XII (April 1937) 233–6
A. E. Burns   "Ascertainment, Probability, and Evidence in History" *Historical Studies: Australia and New Zealand* CI 4 (1951) 327–39

E. F. Carritt   Review of *The Principles of Art, Philosophy* XIII (October 1938) 492–6
J. V. L. Casserley   *The Christian in Philosophy* London: Faber and Faber 1949 pp. 200 ff.
George Catlin   Review of *The New Leviathan, Political Science Quarterly* LVIII 3, 435–6
Arthur N. Child   "History as Imitation" *Philosophical Quarterly* II (July 1952) 193–207
L. J. Cohen   "A Survey of Work in the Philosophy of History" *Philosophical Quarterly* XI (April 1952) 172–86
——— "Has Collingwood been Misrepresented?" *Philosophical Quarterly* VII (April 1957) 149–50

Benedetto Croce   Review of *Speculum Mentis, La Critica: Rivista di litteratura, storia, e filosofia* XXIII (1925) 55–9
——— "In commemorazione di un amico inglese, compagno di pensiero e di fede R. G. Collingwood" *Quademi della "Critica"* II 4 (1946) 60–73 (including text of letter to Croce dated 29 January 1939, p. 67)
R. H. S. Crossman   "When Lightning struck the Ivory Tower: R. G. Collingwood" *New Statesman and Nation* XVIII (1939) 222–3; reprinted in R. H. S. Crossman *The Charm of Politics and Other Essays in Political Criticism* London: Hamish Hamilton 1958 pp. 105–9

W. Debbins   Introduction to R. G. Collingwood *Essays in the Philosophy of History* Austin: University of Texas Press 1965 pp. ix–xxxiv
George E. Derfer   Review of A. Donagan *The Later Philosophy of R. G. Collingwood, Journal of the History of Philosophy* III (April 1965) 143–6
A. Donagan   "The Verification of Historical Theses" *Philosophical Quarterly* VI (July 1956) 193–208
——— "Explanation in History" *Mind* LXVI (April 1957) 145–64
——— "The Croce-Collingwood Theory of Art" *Philosophy* XXXIII (April 1958) 162–7
——— *The Later Philosophy of R. G. Collingwood* Oxford: The Clarendon Press 1962
——— Introduction to R. G. Collingwood *Essays in the Philosophy of Art* Bloomington: University of Indiana Press 1964 pp. ix-xx
——— "Does Knowing Make a Difference to what is Known? A Rejoinder to Mr. Post" *Philosophical Quarterly* XVI (1966) 352–5
——— Article on Collingwood in the *Encyclopedia of Philosophy*, Paul Edwards ed. New York: Macmillan & Co. and the Free Press 1967 pp. 140–4
——— Review of L. Rubinoff ed. *Faith and Reason: Essays in the Philosophy of Religion by R. G. Collingwood, Dialogue: Canadian Philosophical Review* VII 4 (March 1969) 678–81
——— Review of W. M. Johnston *The Formative Years of R. G. Collingwood, Journal of the History of Philosophy* VII (April 1969) 219–31
——— Review of Louis O. Mink *Mind, History, and Dialectic: The Philosophy of R. G. Collingwood, History and Theory* (forthcoming)
W. H. Dray   "R. G. Collingwood and the Acquaintance Theory of Knowledge" *Review internationale de philosophie* XI 42 (1957) 420–32
——— *Laws and Explanation in History* London: Oxford University Press 1957 (chs. IV, V)
——— "Historical Understanding as Re-Thinking" *University of Toronto Quarterly* XXVII (January 1958) 200–15
——— "R. G. Collingwood on Reflective Thought" *Journal of Philosophy* LVII (3 March 1960) 157–63
——— "Historical Causation and Human Free Will" *University of Toronto Quarterly* XXIX 3 (April 1960) 357–69
——— Review of A. Donagan *The Later Philosophy of R. G. Collingwood, Canadian Historical Review* XLV (1964) 130–2
J. Drummond   Review of *Concerning Prayer, Hibbert Journal* XV 2 (1917) 327–31
C. J. Ducase   "Mr. Collingwood on Philosophical Method" *Journal of Philosophy* XXXIII (13 February 1936) 95–106
Vergil H. Dykstra   "Philosophers and Presuppositions" *Mind* LXIX (January 1960) 63–8

T. S. Eliot   Review of *Religion and Philosophy, International Journal of Ethics* XXVII (July 1917) 543

W. J. Emblom   Review of A. Donagan *The Later Philosophy of R. G. Collingwood*, *Journal of Aesthetics and Art Criticism* XXII (Fall 1963) 84–5

Dorothy Emmet   Review of A. Donagan *The Later Philosophy of R. G. Collingwood*, *Philosophical Quarterly* XIII (October 1963) 371

Karl Dietrich Erdmann   "Das Problem der Historismus in des neueren englischen Geschichtswissenschaft" *Historische Zeitschrift* CLXX (1950) 73–88

R. Flenley   "Collingwood's Idea of History" *Canadian Historical Review* XXVII (1947) 68–72

P. Fruchon   "Signification de l'historie de la philosophie selon l'autobiographie de Collingwood" *Les Études philosophiques* XIII (1958) 143–60

Hans Georg Gadamer   *Wahrheit und Methode: Grundzüge einer philosophischen Hermeneutik* Tubingen: J.C.B. Mohr 1960 pp. 352 ff.

W. B. Gallie   *Philosophy and the Historical Understanding* London: Chatto & Windus 1964 pp. 56 ff, 213–25

G. Galloway   Review of *Religion and Philosophy*, *Mind* XXVIII (July 1919) 365–7

P. Gardiner   *The Objects of Historical Knowledge*, *Philosophy* XXVII (July 1952) 211–20

―――― *The Nature of Historical Explanation* Oxford: Clarendon Press 1952

Angelo A. de Gennaro   "Croce and Collingwood" *Personalist* XLVI (April 1965) 193–202

Morris Ginsberg   "The Character of an Historical Explanation" *Proceedings of the Aristotelian Society, Supplementary Volume* XXI (1947) 69–77

John Goheen   Review of *An Essay on Metaphysics*, *Journal of Philosophy* XXXVIII (January 1941) 48–50

L. J. Goldstein   "Collingwood's Theory of Historical Knowing" *History and Theory* IX 1 (1970) 3–36

C. K. Grant   "Collingwood's Theory of Historical Knowledge" *Renaissance and Modern Studies* I (1957) 65–90

―――― Review of A. Donagan *The Later Philosophy of R. G. Collingwood*, *Philosophical Books* IV (May 1963) 3–4

H. A. Hannay   Review of *An Autobiography*, *International Journal of Ethics* LI (April 1941) 369–70

E. E. Harris   "Mr. Ryle and the Ontological Argument" *Mind* XLV (October 1936) 474–80

―――― "Collingwood on Eternal Problems" *The Philosophical Quarterly* I (April 1951) 228–41

―――― *Nature, Mind and Modern Science* London: Allen & Unwin 1954 pp. 29–42

―――― "Objectivity and Reason" *Philosophy* XXXI (January 1956) 55–73

―――― "Collingwood's Theory of History" *Philosophical Quarterly* VII (January 1957) 35–49

―――― *The Foundations of Metaphysics in Science* London: Allen & Unwin, 1965

―――― *Hypothesis and Perception: The Roots of Scientific Method* London: Allen & Unwin 1970

H. S. Harris   Introduction to G. Gentile *Genesis and Structure of Society* (trans. H. S. Harris) Urbana: University of Illinois Press 1960 pp. 14–20

R. W. Harris   "Collingwood's *Idea of History*," *History* XXXVII (February 1952) 15–49

C. Hartshorne   Review of *An Essay on Philosophical Method*, *International Journal of Ethics* XLIV (April 1934) 357–8

Julian N. Hartt   "Metaphysics, History and Civilization: Collingwood's Account of their Relationships" *Journal of Religion* XXXIII 198–211

——— Review of L. Rubinoff ed. *Faith and Reason: Essays in the Philosophy of Religion* by R. G. Collingwood, *Journal of Religion* XLIX 3 (July 1969) 280–94
Van A. Harvey *The Historian and the Believer* New York: Macmillan 1966
L. S. Hearnshaw "A Reply to Professor Collingwood's Attack on Psychology" *Mind* LI (April 1942) 160–9
R. W. Hepburn "A Fresh Look at Collingwood" *British Journal of Aesthetics* III (July 1963) 259–61
H. A. Hodges *Philosophy of Wilhelm Dilthey* London: Routledge & Kegan Paul 1952
J. Hospers "The Croce-Collingwood Theory of Art" *Philosophy* XXXI (October 1956) 3–20
G. Dawes Hicks Review of *An Autobiography*, "Survey of Recent Philosophical Literature" in *Hibbert Journal* XXXVIII (October 1939) 128–31

Felipe Pardinas Illanes "Dilthey y Collingwood" *Filosofia y letras: Revista della facultad de filosofia y letras* (Mexico) XIX (February-March 1950) 87–105

W. M. Johnston *The Formative Years of R. G. Collingwood* The Hague: M. Nijhoff 1969
Peter Jones "Collingwood's Debt to his Father" *Mind* LXXVIII (July 1969) 437–9

Gordon Kaufman *Relativism, Knowledge and Faith* Chicago: University of Chicago Press 1960
G. S. Kirk "A Problem in Historical Technique: Collingwood and Ionian Physics" *Cambridge Journal* VI (June 1953) 515–33
T. M. Knox "Notes on Collingwood's Philosophical Work: An Appreciation with Bibliography" *Proceedings of the British Academy* XXIX (1943) 469–75
——— Editor's preface to R. G. Collingwood *The Idea of History* London: Oxford University Press 1946 pp. v-xxiv
——— "Professor R. G. Collingwood, F.B.A." *Nature* (6 February 1943) 163
——— "Collingwood, Robin George (1889–1943)" *Dictionary of National Biography 1941–1950* London 1959 (pp. 168–70)
——— "Collingwood, Robin George (1889–1943)" *Encyclopedia Britannica* 14th ed. VI p. 19
Michael Krausz ed. *Critical Essays on the Philosophy of R. G. Collingwood* (including contributions by A. Donagan, W. H. Dray, Leon J. Goldstein, Errol E. Harris, Peter Jones, Michael Krausz, W. Von Leyden, A. J. M. Milne, Louis O. Mink, Nathan Rotenstreich, Lionel Rubinoff, Stephen Toulmin, W. H. Walsh, and Richard Wolheim), Oxford: The Clarendon Press (forthcoming)

J. Laird Review of *Speculum Mentis*, *Mind* XXXIV (April 1925) 235–41
——— Review of *The New Leviathan*, *Philosophy* XVIII (1943) 75–80
Sterling P. Lamprecht Review of *An Autobiography*, *Journal of Philosophy* XXXVI (21 December 1939) 717–18
Susanne Langer *Feeling and Form* New York: Scribner's 1953 pp. 380–90
H. D. Lewis "On Poetic Truth" *Philosophy* XXI (1946) 147–66
Aline Lion Review of *An Essay on Metaphysics*, *Philosophy* XVI (January 1941) 74–8
J. Llewelyn "Collingwood's Doctrine of Absolute Presuppositions" *Philosophical Quarterly* XI (January 1961) 49–60

────── "Collingwood's Later Philosophy" *Philosophy* XXXIX (April 1964) 174–7
Margaret MacDonald "Art as Imagination" *Proceedings of the Aristotelian Society* LIII (1952–3) 205–26
A. M. MacIver "The Character of an Historical Explanation" *Proceedings of the Aristotelian Society, Supplementary Volume* XXI (1947) 33–50
R. M. MacIver Review of *The New Leviathan, Annals of the American Academy of Political and Social Science* CCXCIX 181–2
Donald S. Mackay "On Supposing and Presupposing" *Review of Metaphysics* II (September 1948) 1–20
D. M. Mackinnon Review of *The Idea of History, Journal of Theological Studies* XLVIII (1947) 249–53
John MacQuarrie *Twentieth-Century Religious Thought: The Frontiers of Philosophy and Theology 1900–1960* New York: Harper & Row 1963 esp. pp. 131 ff.
M. Mandelbaum Review of *The Idea of History, Journal of Philosophy* XLIV (27 March 1947) 184–91
R. B. McAllum "R. G. Collingwood: An Appreciation on his Death" *Proceedings of the British Academy* XXIX (1943) 463–85
────── "Obituary: R. G. Collingwood (1889–1942)" *Oxford Magazine* LXI (1942–3) 160–1
Jack Meiland *Scepticism and Historical Knowledge* New York: Random House 1965 esp. pp. 63–82
F. G. Marcham Review of *An Autobiography, Philosophical Review*, L (September 1941) 546
E. D. Meyers "A Note on Collingwood's Criticism of Toynbee" *Journal of Philosophy* XLIV (28 August 1947) 485–9
Louis O. Mink "Comment on Stephen Toulmin's 'Conceptual Revolutions in Science'" in R. S. Cohen and M. W. Wartofsky eds. *Boston Studies in the Philosophy of Science* III New York: Humanities Press 1963–4 pp. 348–55
────── "Collingwood's Dialectic of History" *History and Theory* VII 1 (1968) 3–37
────── *Mind, History and Dialectic: The Philosophy of R. G. Collingwood* Bloomington: University of Indiana Press 1969
────── Review of L. Rubinoff ed. *Faith and Reason: Essays in the Philosophy of Religion by R. G. Collingwood, Journal of the American Academy of Religion* XXXVIII (March 1970) 118–20
Theodore Mischel "Collingwood on Art as 'Imaginative Expression'" *Australasian Journal of Philosophy* XXXIX (1961) 241–50
────── "A Reply to Bailey's Defence of Collingwood" *Australasian Journal of Philosophy* XLII (1964) 391–3
J. Moffat "Survey of Recent Theological Literature" *Hibbert Journal* XV 4 (1917) 678
Fernando R. Molina "Collingwood on Philosophical Methodology" *Ideas y Valores* VI (1957) 1–15
Jose Ferrater Mora Article on Collingwood in *Dictionaris de Filosofia* 5th ed. Buenos Aires: Sudamericana 1958 p. 243
H. Morris-Jones "Art and Imagination" *Philosophy* XXXIV (July 1959) 204–16
J. H. Muirhead Review of *An Autobiography, Philosophy* XV (January 1940) 89–91
G. R. G. Mure "Benedeto Croce and Oxford" *Philosophical Quarterly* IV (October 1954) 327–31
A. E. Murphy Review of *The Idea of History, Philosophical Review* XLI (September 1947) 507–92

G. Norburn "The Philosophical Quest, II: Philosophy as Historicism" *Church Quarterly Review* CLI (October–December 1950) 51–62

J. B. Passmore   *A Hundred Years of Philosophy* London: Gerald Duckworth & Co. Ltd. 1957 pp. 304–9
——— "The Idea of a History of Philosophy" *History and Theory* v (1965) 1–32
H. J. Paton   "Fifty Years of Philosophy" in J. H. Muirhead ed. *Contemporary British Philosophy* third series, London: Allen & Unwin 1956 p. 345
Leslie Paul   *The English Philosophers* London: Faber and Faber 1953 pp. 351–2
Domenico Pesce   Introduction to *Tre saggi di filosofia della storia* Padua: Liviana editrice 1969 pp. 3–11
Michael Polanyi   *The Study of Man* London: Routledge & Kegan Paul 1959 pp. 100 ff.
Sir Karl Popper   "A Pluralist Approach to the Philosophy of History" in *Roads to Freedom: Essays in honour of F. A. von Hayek* edited by Eric Streissler, Gottfried Hebler, Friedrich Lutz, and Fritz Machlup, London: Routledge & Kegan Paul 1969 pp. 181–200
John F. Post   "Does Knowing Make a Difference to what is Known?" *Philosophical Quarterly* xv (1965) 220–8
——— "A Defense of Collingwood's Theory of Presuppositions" *Inquiry* vIII (1965) 332–54

Melvin Rader   "Art and History" *Journal of Aesthetics and Art Criticism* (winter 1967) 156–68
E. Gavin Reeve   "Does Fichte's View of History Really Appear so Silly?" *Philosophy* xL (January 1965) 57–9 (a reply to Collingwood's discussion of Fichte in *The Idea of History* pp. 106–11)
G. J. Renier   *History: Its Purpose and Method* London: Allen & Unwin 1950 esp. pp. 40–8
Nicholas Rescher   "On the Logic of Presuppositions" *Philosophy and Phenomenological Research* xxi (June 1961) 521–7
I. A. Richmond   "Appreciation of R. G. Collingwood as an Archaeologist, with Bibliography of writings in Archaeology and History" *Proceedings of the British Academy* xxix (1943) 476–85
——— "Obituary Notice: Robin George Collingwood: Born 1889, Died 9 January 1943" *Antiquaries Journal* xxx (1943) 84–5
——— "Robin George Collingwood" *Archaeologica Aeliana, or Miscellaneous Tracts Relating to Antiquity* xxi (1943) 254–5
A. D. Ritchie   "The Logic of Question and Answer" *Mind* LII (January 1943) 24–38
——— *British Philosophers* London/New York/Toronto: Published for the British Council by Longmans 1950 pp. 57–8
T. A. Roberts   *History and Christian Apologetic* London: SPCK 1960
Ronald Roblin   Review of L. Rubinoff ed. *Faith and Reason: Essays in the Philosophy of Religion* by R. G. Collingwood, *Philosophy and Phenomenological Research* (forthcoming)
C. F. Ronayne   Review of *An Essay on Philosophical Method*, *American Review* IV (March 1935) 627–33
Stanley H. Rosen   "Collingwood and Greek Aesthetics" *Phronesis* IV (1959) 135–48
N. Rotenstreich   "Historicism and Philosophy, Reflections on R. G. Collingwood" *Revue internationale de philosophie* xi 42 (1957) 401–19
——— "From Facts to Thoughts: Collingwood's Views on the Nature of History" *Philosophy* xxv (April 1960) 122–37
——— "History and Time: A Critical Examination of R. G. Collingwood's Doctrine" *Scripta Hierosolymitana* Jerusalem 1960

A. L. Rowse *The Use of History* London: Hodder & Stoughton 1946 pp. 147–9
——— Review of *An Autobiography, Spectator* CLXIII (August 1939) 262
Lionel Rubinoff Review of W. Debbins *Essays in the Philosophy of History by R. G. Collingwood, Dialogue: Canadian Philosophical Review* v (December 1966) 471–5
——— Review of A. Donagan *Essays in the Philosophy of Art by R. G. Collingwood, Dialogue: Canadian Philosophical Review* v (December 1966) 467–70
——— "Collingwood's Theory of the Relation between Philosophy and History: A New Interpretation" *Journal of the History of Philosophy* VI (October 1968) 363–80
——— Introduction and Commentary to *Faith and Reason: Essays in the Philosophy of Religion by R. G. Collingwood* Chicago: Quadrangle 1968
——— Introduction and Commentary to *The Presuppositions of Critical History by F. H. Bradley* Toronto: J. M. Dent / Chicago: Quadrangle 1968 pp. 1–74
——— Review of W. M. Johnston *The Formative Years of R. G. Collingwood, Dialogue: Canadian Philosophical Review* (forthcoming)
——— Review of L. O. Mink *History, Mind and Dialectic* and A. Shalom *R. G. Collingwood: Philosophe et historien, Journal of the History of Philosophy* (forthcoming)
Guido de Ruggiero *Storia della filosofia* x *Filosofia del Novecento* 3rd ed. Bari: Editori Laterza 1963 pp. 92–104
L. J. Russell Review of *An Essay on Philosophical Method, Philosophy* IX (July 1934) 350–2
Eric C. Rust *Towards a Theological Understanding of History* New York: Oxford University Press 1963
——— *Evolutionary Philosophies and Contemporary Theology* Philadelphia: Westminster Press 1969
G. Ryle "Mr. Collingwood and the Ontological Argument" *Mind* XLIV (April 1935) 137–51
——— "Back to the Ontological Argument" *Mind* XLVI (January 1937) 53–7
David Rynin "Donagan on Collingwood: Absolute Presuppositions, Truth, and Metaphysics" *Review of Metaphysics* XVIII (December 1964) 301–33
F. C. S. Schiller Review of *An Essay on Philosophical Method, Mind* XLIII (January 1934) 117–20
F. O. Schneider "Collingwood and the Idea of History" *University of Toronto Quarterly* XXII (1953) 172–83
Albert Shalon "R. G. Collingwood et la metaphysique" *Les Etudes philosophiques* x (1955) 693–711
——— *R. G. Collingwood: philosophe et historien* Paris: Presses universitaires de France 1967
Mumford Q. Sibley Review of *The New Leviathan, American Political Science Review* XXXVII (August 1943) 7245
L. S. Stebbing Review of *Speculum Mentis, Hibbert Journal* XXVIII 3 (1925) 566–9
——— Review of *An Essay on Metaphysics, Mind* L (April 1941) 184–90
H. F. Stewart Review of *Concerning Prayer, Journal of Theological Studies* XVIII (1917) 79–80
L. Strauss "On Collingwood's Philosophy of History" *Review of Metaphysics* v (June 1952) 559–86
N. Sykes "Some Current Conceptions of Historiography and Their Significance for Christian Apologetic" *Journal of Theological Studies* L (January-April 1949) 24–37
Judith Jarvis Thompson Review of A. Donagan *The Later Philosophy of R. G. Collingwood, Journal of Philosophy* LXI (24 December 1964) 784–6

Paul Tillich   "E. Troeltsch: Historismus und seine Probleme" *Journal for the Scientific Study of Religion* I (October 1961) 109 ff.
E. W. F. Tomlin   *R. G. Collingwood* writers and their works series no. 42, London: Published for the British Council by Longmans 1953
——— "The Philosophy of R. G. Collingwood" *Ratio* I (December 1958) 116–35
——— *The Western Philosophers* New York: Harper & Row, 1963 (pp. 336–7)
Stephen Toulmin   "Conceptual Revolutions in Science" in R. S. Cohen and M. W. Wartofsky eds. *Boston Studies in the Philosophy of Science* III New York: Humanities Press 1963–4 pp. 332–47
A. Toynbee   *A Study of History* IX London/New York/Toronto: Oxford University Press 1954 pp. 718–38
John Turner   "Diachronic Understanding" *Philosophy* XLIII (July 1968) 284–6

J. O. Urmson   Article on Collingwood *Encyclopedia of Western Philosophy* New York: Hawthorn Books 1960 pp. 81–2

Eric Voeglin   "The Oxford Political Philosophers" *Philosophical Quarterly* III (April 1953) 97–114

W. H. Walsh   "R. G. Collingwood's Philosophy of History" *Philosophy* XXII (July 1947) 153–60
——— "The Character of an Historical Explanation" *Proceedings of the Aristotelian Society, Supplementary Volume* XXI (1947) 51–68
——— *Metaphysics* London: Hutchinson University Library 1963 pp. 160–6
——— Review of A. Donagan *The Later Philosophy of R. G. Collingwood*, *Philosophical Review* LXXIV (January 1965) 119–22
——— *Introduction to the Philosophy of History* 3rd rev. ed. London: Hutchinson's University Press 1967
——— "Categories" in *Kant* edited by R. P. Wolff, New York: Doubleday Anchor Books 1967 pp. 54–70
H. R. Walpole   *R. G. Collingwood and the Idea of Language* Wichita: Kansas University Studies no. 55 1963
J. W. N. Watkins   "On Explaining Disaster" *Listener* (10 February 1963) 69–70. See also responses to this article in Letters to the Editor section, 24 January 1963, 171, 31 January 1963, 209, and 7 February 1963, 251
C. C. J. Webb   Review of *The Idea of History*, *Hibbert Journal* XLV (October 1946) 83–6
——— Review of *The Idea of Nature*, *Journal of Theological Studies* XLVI (1945) 248–51
Mortimer Wheeler   Review of *Roman Britain*, *Journal of Roman Studies* XXIX I (1939) 87–93
Hayden V. White   "Collingwood and Toynbee: Translations in English Historical Thought" *English Miscellany* IX (1957) 147–78
——— Review of A. Donagan, *The Later Philosophy of R. G. Collingwood*, *History and Theory* IV 2 (1965) 244–52
Edmund Whittaker   Review of *The Idea of Nature*, *Philosophy* XX (November 1945) 260–1
Burleigh Taylor Wilkins   "Collingwood Reconsidered" (Review of A. Donagan *The Later Philosophy of R. G. Collingwood*), *British Journal for the Philosophy of Science* XV (1964–65) 72–8
G. Wunberg   "Robin George Collingwood: *The Idea of History*," *Philosophischer Literatur Anzeiger* IX 4, 156–61

BIBLIOGRAPHY III

DOCTORAL DISSERTATIONS

Anthony W. Colver "Evidence and Point of View in the Writing of History" PH.D. dissertation, Harvard University 1957

Robert C. Cragg "Collingwood's Logic of Question and Answer; a Study of its Logical and Philosophical Implications, and its Bearing on Historical Method" PH.D. dissertation, University of Toronto 1949

Scott E. Crom "Collingwood and Metaphysics" PH.D. dissertation, Yale University 1952

William Debbins "The Philosophy of R. G. Collingwood" PH.D. dissertation, Syracuse University 1959

Howard DeLong "The Development of R. G. Collingwood's Theory of History" PH.D. dissertation, Princeton University 1960

W. J. Emblom "The Theory of Reality in the Philosophy of R. G. Collingwood" PH.D. dissertation, University of Illinois 1962

Francis-Thomas Ficarra "Collingwood's *New Leviathan*" PH.D. dissertation, University of Illinois 1961

Sister Thomas Marguerite Flanagan CSJ "Collingwood on the Nature of Metaphysics" PH.D. dissertation, St. Louis University 1964

G. K. Grant "Professor Collingwood's Conception of the Relations between Metaphysics and History, and its Consequences for the Theory of Truth" D.PHIL. thesis, University of Oxford 1950

Jasper S. Hopkins "Epistemological Foundations of R. G. Collingwood's Philosophy of History" PH.D. dissertation, Harvard University 1963

W. M. Johnston "The Formative Years of R. G. Collingwood" PH.D. dissertation, Harvard University 1965–66

Herbert Kamins "Aesthetic Claims: A Criticism of Collingwood's, Lewis's and Richard's Theories and an alternative Analysis of Critical Evaluations" PH.D. dissertation, Cornell University 1955

Gordon Kaufmann "The Problem of Relativism and the Possibility of Metaphysics: A Constructive Development of Certain Ideas in R. G. Collingwood, Wilhelm Dilthey and Paul Tillich" PH.D. dissertation, Yale University 1955

Michael Krausz "A Critique of R. G. Collingwood's Theory of Absolute Presuppositions" PH.D. dissertation, University of Toronto 1969

Rex Martin "Collingwood's Critique of the Concept of Human Nature" PH.D. dissertation, Columbia University 1967

D. M. Mathers "Historical Knowledge in the Philosophy of R. G. Collingwood" PH.D. dissertation, Columbia University 1954

Theodore Mischel "R. G. Collingwood's Philosophy of Art" PH.D. dissertation, Columbia University 1958

Ronald Roblin "R. G. Collingwood's Philosophy of History" PH.D. dissertation, University of North Carolina 1969

Lionel Rubinoff "The Relationship between Philosophy and History in the Thought of R. G. Collingwood" PH.D. dissertation, University of Toronto 1964

Edward M. Sayles "A Critical Evaluation of R. G. Collingwood's Views on Metaphysics" PH.D. dissertation, University of California at Los Angeles 1956

Hans Schneider "Die Geschichtsphilosophie R. G. Collingwood's" PH.D. University of Bonn 1950

Sherman M. Stanage "The Role of the 'Overlap' in Collingwood's Philosophy" PH.D. University of Colorado 1959

Nora Suranyi-Unger "Die Politische Philosophie von R. G. Collingwood" inaugural doctoral dissertation, University of Munich 1960

D. E. Williams "The Metaphysical and Political Theories of R. G. Collingwood" PH.D. dissertation, London School of Economics 1960

Robert P. Ziff "The Notion of a Work of Art with Special Reference to the Aesthetic Theory of R. G. Collingwood" PH.D. dissertation, Cornell University 1951

Indexes

INDEX I

PERSONS

Acton, H. B. 22
Anaximander 254
Anaximines 255
Anselm: and the ontological argument, 194, 208–9, 284
Aristotle 53, 56, 187, 188 ff., 190, 193, 195, 221, 222, 260, 263
Austin, J. L. 184
Ayer, A. J. 20, 33, 241

Blanshard, Brand 352 n23
Bosanquet, B. 156
Boyce-Gibson, A. 22
Bradley, F. H. 46, 47, 53, 144, 275, 317, 355–7
Buckle, T. H. 339–40

Cassirer, Ernst 24, 381 n14, 346, 354
Croce, B. 9, 37, 41, 42, 47, 48, 99, 106, 194, 295, 318, 365, 378; criticized by Collingwood, 11, 423

Descartes, R. 92, 205, 386 n3
Dewey, John 345 nn2,3
Dilthey, Wilhelm 9, 144, 211, 275, 303, 317, 346, 350–3
Donagan, Alan; interpretation of Collingwood 19 ff; 33, 108–9, 112, 197 ff., 214, 215, 223, 231, 271, 388 n2
Dray, W. H. 385 n10
Droysen, J. G. 345, 347–50

Emblom, W. J. 22
Emmet, Dorothy 22

Fackenheim, E. L. 24, 382
Ferrero, G. 341–2
Ferri, Enrico 343–4
Fichte, J. G. 283

Gentile, Giovanni 28, 34, 194, 315, 316, 318ff, 322, 323, 325, 329, 330
Gibson, A. Boyce 22
Gioberti, V. 316
Grant, C. K. 22
Green, T. H. 390 n20

Hannay, A. H. 3, 316
Harris, E. E. 21
Harris, H. S. 22
Hartshorne, Charles 386 n1
Hauser, Arnold 10
Hegel 24, 27, 53, 63, 105, 109, 119, 151, 156, 176, 187, 189, 193, 205, 211, 218, 219, 258, 270, 274, 316, 327, 328, 330, 384 n6, 385–6 nn12, 13, 389–90 n19, 392–3 n11, 393, nn13,14
Heidegger, M. 24
Heinemann, F. H. 21
Hempel, C. G. 391 n29, 342–3
Herodotus 278
Hobbes, T. 158, 238
Hook, Sidney 343
Hume, D. 6, 211, 338, 350
Husserl, E. 24–5, 55, 353–4, 362–3

Jaspers, Karl 393 n12
James, William 91, 375 n3
Johnston, W. M. 376 n37

Kant, I. 6, 85, 109, 173, 210, 211, 219, 238, 244, 245, 276, 282, 283, 284, 286
Knox, T. A.: interpretation of Collingwood, 16ff; 213, 214, 215, 223, 238–41, 270, 271, 274, 288, 294, 376 n17, 388 n2

Laird, John 382 n27
Loewenberg, Jacob 62

Mead, Margaret 389 n19
Mill, J. S. 48
Mink, Louis O. 23, 377 n37, 378 n43, 378-9 n4

Nietzsche, F. 365

Oakeshott, Michael 144, 357-8
Ortega y Gasset, Jose 345
Otto, Rudolph 91

Passmore, John 213, 376 n17
Plato 95, 158, 187, 195, 238, 385 n13
Popper, Sir Karl 10
Pythagoras 255

Rickert, H. 24
Rotenstreich, Nathan 21, 108

de Ruggiero, G. 316ff, 329
Ruskin, John: Collingwood's interpretation of, 223-30
Russell, B. 197, 202, 204, 216, 241
Ryle, G. 33, 196, 200ff, 205, 216, 242, 265

Santayana, George 234
Schelling, F. W. J. 391 n4, 393 n14
Schiller, F. C. S. 386 n1
Shalom, A. 377 n37
Skinner, B. F. 344-5
Spaventa, B. 317
Spinoza, B. 152, 188, 191ff, 195
Strauss, Leo 21, 361-2

Taine, H. 111, 340-1
Thales 254, 255
Thucydides 278
Tomlin, E. W. F. 22-3

Villeneuve, Admiral 239, 269-70

Walsh, W. H. 390 n24
Wartenburg, York von 9
Watson, John 344
Weber, Max 381 n13
Whitehead, A. N. 197, 202
Wittgenstein, L. 156, 241

INDEX II

GENERAL TOPICS

Absolute Mind 180, 300ff; as identity of subject and object 206; as pure act or absolute immanence 311ff; drama of, likened to the incarnation, 334–5

Absolute Presuppositions: defined 232; as distinguished from relative presuppositions 233; as catalytic agents 245; logical efficacy of, independent of truth-value 233–4; and consupponibility 237; constellation of 237; and verifiability 233; non-verifiability of, reconciled with claim that they are nevertheless meaningful 264ff, as subject to strains 272ff. See also *Presuppositions*

Absolute Standpoint 54, 61, 123, 151ff, 186; as ground of historical criticism 242

Anti-Metaphysics 220, 285, 389–90 n19

A Priori Imagination 274ff; in art 275–6; in historical interpolation 276–86; in perception 276

Art: phenomenology of aesthetic consciousness 76–87; as pure supposal (i.e. first-level dogmatism) 77–8; as second-level activity 79–81; as third-level rapprochement with thought 81–7; as action 342 n5; as philosophy 78; and aestheticism 129–30; and utility 341 n2; and psychoanalysis 78, 125ff

Behaviourism 4, 344–5

Being: as traditionally conceived 161; arguments against traditional concept of 161ff, 222ff, 300; as concrete activity 162; as pure act 300, 311ff. See also *Concrete Universal*

Categorical Thinking: as distinguished from hypothetical thinking 184–7; history of the idea of philosophy as categorical thinking 187–93; as an analysis of the presuppositions of experience 220–52; and the logic of belief 218–21; and the logic of modern realism 197–204; and metaphysics 204–8; and the ontological argument 194–7; and philosophy 184–212; and understanding the historical past 209–10; and rapprochement between faith and reason 208–9; and the problem of universals 213–18

Christianity 53; attitude towards the problem of knowledge 386 n3; and culture 90–1.

Collingwood, R. G.: and his critics 14ff; self-interpretation 14–16; Knox's interpretation 16–19; Donagan's interpretation 19–21; other interpretations 21ff; alleged illness of 376 n17.

Concrete Universal: definition of 156–8, 225ff; as categorical judgment 165; as being 152ff; and history 105ff, 116; and metaphysics 237, 248; illustrated by being applied to the history of political theory 154ff, 162; as underlying a dialectical history of errors 261; as reason or concrete thought 159ff

Consciousness: corruption of 62, 83ff, 124–5, 134, 220, 229, 285, 379 nn3,4
– three-fold ontological structure of natural consciousness 66ff; as providing a new conceptual framework for the interpretation of Collingwood's thought 72–5
– first-level consciousness 67–8; illustrated by means of dialectic of art 76–9, religion 87ff, science 94ff, philosophy of history 115, 133–4
– second-level consciousness 68; illustrated by means of dialectic of art 79ff, religion 91ff, science 98ff, philosophy of history 134–8
– third-level consciousness 69–9; illustrated by means of dialectic of art 81–7, religion 92–4, science 104ff, philosophy of history 138ff

Consupponibility 224, 237, 273

Dialectic: definition of 177–8, 336 n2; principle of development of 62; as iconoclastic comic method of revealing self-contradictions in situations 63; as criticism of error 65; dialectical necessity 153, 176ff. See also *Necessity*

Ethics 164; utilitarianism 167–9, 173ff, 384–5 n9; regularian 169; of duty 169–72

Evil: and punishment 64; analysed according to logic of overlap of classes 172ff

Experience: distinction between primary and reflective 55; relationship to philosophy 55–60; phenomenology of 76ff; dialectical development of within framework of tripartite ontological structure 66ff. See also *Consciousness*

Explicit and Implicit: principle of 51ff, 56

Facts: as actual and ideal 137; abstract vs concrete 290; history as assertion of concrete fact 105ff, 289ff

Faith: dialectic of 87ff; and categorical thinking 208–9; and reason 91, 92–4

Habit: of mind as the source of the various specialized disciplines 102ff, 113–14, 225–6; history as a habit of mind 103, 289, 297–8

Historicism: radical historicism defined 10, 308ff; transcendental historicism defined 24, 25; the problem of historicism defined 9–14; the history of the development of 345ff; a general critique of 360ff; refutation of by Collingwood 11ff, 329ff

Historicity: as distinguished from change and temporality 303; and human nature 299ff; and historical relativism 306ff; and the metaphysical history of errors 264–70; and progress 257; and truth 270; as grounded in the "Pure Act" 322ff

History: as concrete universal and categorical singular judgment 105ff, 111, 136, 209–10; as exhibition of dialectical drama 65–6; as an act of thought ranging from perception of facts to concrete reason and rethinking 107–15; as a form of inferential reasoning according to principles 266ff; subject matter of history expounded according to "inside-outside" theory 290, 297ff; and philosophical historiography 147–9; as mind 119–20; as science of human nature 5ff, 289ff; as self-knowledge and self-making 4, 34, 264, 291ff, 299–306, 303ff; as rethinking 144ff, 281ff, 301ff; as basis of ethics 171; practical wisdom, "insight" and "situational knowledge" 182–3; as distinguished from science 96; as the organon of science 98ff; and nature 159–60; and the a priori imagination 275ff; the negation of and transition to philosophy 117ff; transcendental presuppositions of 282ff; *The Idea of History* 292ff; dialectic of historical consciousness within the framework of tripartite ontological structure 113–114: first level 115–16, 133–4; second level 134–8; third level 116–17, 139ff

Identity: distinction between concrete and abstract identity of forms of experience 51

Imagination: as a source of action 342 n5; as a source of the corrupt consciousness 83, 124ff; as a source of philosophy 125ff; as a source of the historian's picture of the past 142ff, 295ff; and reason 85–7; the a priori imagination and history 275ff, 298ff; dialectic of 380–1 n6

Interpolation: in history: first level 276–8, second level 278–81, third level 281ff; and collegation 390 n24

Intersubjectivity 172

Irrationalism: as expressed in the antimetaphysical tendencies of positivism 220, 285, 389–90 n19; as expressed in political movements of fascism and nazism 229, 388 n6

Logic of Question and Answer 15; and the overlap of classes 175–6, 252ff; origins of doctrine in "Ruskins Philosophy" 225

Metaphysics: classical theory of rejected 6; historical as distinguished from systematic 220–1; as phenomenology 28; as analysis of past as well as of contemporary thought 28–9; as thinking systematically about presuppositions 65; as dogmatic

Stresses and Strains: as underlying the change from one set of presuppositions to another 272–4

Thinking: distinction between first and second order 291

Truth: correspondence theory of 154; as revealed through history of political theory 154ff; and absolute presuppositions 233ff; and contradiction 226; and historicity 270ff; as logical intelligibility 251ff

Unconscious: as source of corrupt consciousness 288; as source of changes of presuppositions 270–1, 285

Unity of Sciences 50ff

Universals: abstract 94ff, 162; as source of corruption of both positivism and historicism 308; concrete 29, 105, 153ff

Utilitarianism 167–9, 173ff, 384–5 n9

www.ingramcontent.com/pod-product-compliance
Lightning Source LLC
Chambersburg PA
CBHW020349080526
44584CB00014B/944